£5.95

CROSS-CULTURAL UNIVERSALS
OF AFFECTIVE MEANING

CROSS-CULTURAL UNIVERSALS OF AFFECTIVE MEANING

CHARLES E. OSGOOD

WILLIAM H. MAY

MURRAY S. MIRON

University of Illinois Press
URBANA CHICAGO LONDON

Library of Congress Cataloging in Publication Data

Osgood, Charles Egerton.
  Cross-cultural universals of affective meaning.

  Bibliography: p.
  1. Languages — Psychology.   2. Semantics, Compara-
tive. I. May, William H., 1933-   joint author.
II. Miron, Murray S., joint author. III. Title.
P106.08   401'.9   74-8498
ISBN 0-252-00426-4
ISBN 0-252-00550-3 pbk.

With the cooperation of the following colleagues:

AFGHANISTAN

Noor Ahmad Shaker, Pohantoon: Kabul University
Ahmad Jawid, Pohantoon: Kabul University
Mohammed Kabir Sarwari, Pohantoon: Kabul University

BELGIUM

Robert Hogenraad, Catholic University of Louvain
Hubert Rigaux, Free University of Brussels

COSTA RICA

Flora V. Rodríguez Zelaya (Brown), University of Illinois

FINLAND

Matti Haavio, University of Helsinki
Pertti Öunap, University of Helsinki

FRANCE

Abraham A. Moles, University of Strasbourg
Francoise Enel, University of Strasbourg

GERMANY

Suitbert Ertel, University of Göttingen

GREECE

Vasso Vassiliou, Athenian Institute of Anthropos

HONG KONG

Anita K. Li, Calgary, Canada
Brian M. Young, Hong Kong University

HUNGARY

Jeno Putnoky, Eötvös Loránd University

INDIA, CALCUTTA

Rhea Das, Wisconsin State University
Alokananda Mitter, Indian Statistical Institute

INDIA, DELHI

Krishna Gopal Rastogi, National Council of Educational Research
and Training
Raj Rani Rastogi
Ladli C. Singh, National Council of Educational Research and
Training

INDIA, MYSORE

B. Kuppuswamy, Institute for Social and Psychological Research
Ankalahali V. Shanmugam, United Nations Development Program,
Manila

IRAN

William Kay Archer, University of Illinois
Forough al-Zaman Minou-Archer, University of Illinois
Sharon Wolfe, Teheran Research Unit
Parvin B. Ziaee, Higher Teachers Training College

ITALY

Giovanni B. Flores d'Arcais, University of Leyden
Dora Capozza, University of Padua

JAPAN

The late Torao Obonai, Nihon University
Yasumasa Tanaka, Gakushuin University
Masaaki Asai, Nihon University
Yōko Iwamatsu, Gakushuin University

LEBANON

Lutfy Diab, American University of Beirut
Levon Melikian, American University of Beirut

MALAYSIA

Douglas Raybeck, Cornell University

MEXICO CITY

Rogelio Diaz-Guerrero, National Autonomous University of Mexico

MEXICO, CHIAPAS

Duane Metzger, University of California at Irvine

MEXICO, YUCATAN

Victor Castillo-Vales, University of Yucatan

NETHERLANDS

Mathilda J. Jansen, State Agriculture University
A. J. Smolenaars, University of Amsterdam

POLAND

Adam Sarapata, Polish National Academy

SWEDEN

Ulf Himmelstrand, University of Uppsala

THAILAND

Jantorn Buranabanpote-Rufener, Chulalongkorn University
Weerayudh Wichiarajote, College of Education

TURKEY

Beğlan B. Toğrol, Istanbul University
Doğan Cüceloğlu, Hacettepe University

YUGOSLAVIA

Djordje Kostić, Institute of Experimental Phonetics
Tomislav Tomeković, University of Belgrade

UNITED STATES OF AMERICA

Leon Jakobovits, University of Hawaii

Contents

Figures

Tables

Preface

THE CO-AUTHORS OF THIS BOOK, Professors William H. May and Murray S. Miron, feel that I should be the sole author of its preface — because I am most closely identified with the development of the semantic differential technique and its various applications, including its extension to cross-linguistic studies probing the affective dimension of subjective culture. So let me begin on a somewhat personal note.

When I was about ten years old, Miss Grace Osgood (Auntie Grae as I still call her) gave me a Roget's *Thesaurus* as a birthday present. I spent many hours exploring this guide to semantic space, and indeed my visual representation of the *Thesaurus* was a vivid image of word meanings as clusters of colorful star-like points in an immense space. But the notion of a potentially quantifiable semantic space lay dormant until I'd been at Dartmouth College (class of 1939) for a couple of years (filled with the popular illusion that I was going to earn my living as a newspaperman while I wrote the Great American Novel) and had met and worked with the man who was to have a marked influence on my life — the late Theodore Karwoski, Professor of Psychology. He was doing intriguing experiments on visual-auditory synesthesia ("color music"), and he had a notion of "parallel polarity" among the diverse dimensions of human perceptual-conceptual experience (e.g., visual *bright-dark,* auditory *loud-soft,* and verbal *strong-weak*). Later Ross Stagner was to bring to Dartmouth (and to me) his sophistication in attitude measurement and his intense concern with the issues of peace and war — with World War II just over the horizon.

This environment was ideally suited to a young man with visions of semantic sugarplums in his head. I had found the right balance between my need for creativity and my demand for rigor, and I completely forgot about writing the Great American Novel. Instead, in my apprenticeship with Karwoski, I did research on synesthetic and metaphorical "parallelisms" among sights, sounds, and words, both in the laboratory and (via firsthand ethnographies, being an anthropology minor) in the cross-cultural field; with Stagner I studied changes in the meanings of critical concepts (using the seven-step, bipolar adjectival scales that much later were to characterize the semantic differential technique) as the United States moved into World War II. Looking back, I can see that the basic framework of my scientific life was being set in those early years at Dartmouth.

Graduate work at Yale in the early 1940s was for me an immersion in experimental psychology generally and in Hullian learning theory particularly. But my thesis, entitled "Meaningful Similarity and Interference in Learning," reflected my continuing concern with things human (I've never pushed a rat) and things semantic. After a few years at Yale and then the University of Connecticut — where I taught and wrote furiously on what was to become my *Method and Theory in Experimental Psychology* (Oxford, 1953) — in 1949 came an invitation to the University of Illinois as an associate professor of psychology and (wonder of wonders!) *research* associate professor in communications.

The people who invited me (Hobart Mowrer, Wilbur Schramm, and Ross Stagner) wanted to know, obviously, what I planned to *do* with my research time. It was then that I dug my thesaurian vision of semantic space out from wherever one stores such things, coupled it with a mediational theory of meaning and a (then) new factor-analytic methodology (Illinois being then a hotbed of multivariate statistics), and went to work on what was to become the SD technique. Some faculty colleagues and many graduate students got entangled in this enterprise, but I must single out for mention in this preface George Suci (my first Ph.D. student) and Percy Tannenbaum (my second, I think), who were later to become colleagues in our Institute for Communications Research and co-authors with me of *The Measurement of Meaning* (University of Illinois Press, 1957). For reasons these authors never really understood, this little book caught the imaginations of others, and there was a minor explosion of applications of SD technique to a bewildering variety of problems (see the bibliography appended to Snider and Osgood, eds., *Semantic Differential Technique: A Sourcebook,* Aldine, 1969).

Let me quote from my own preface to this sourcebook (p. ix): "I must confess that sometimes I feel like the Geppetto of a wayward Pinocchio who has wandered off into the Big City, and Lord knows what mischief he is getting into. Some people think Pinocchio is a specific standardized test; he is not, of course, being subject to concept/scale interaction. Some think he is a measure of meaning-in-general; he is not, of course, reflecting primarily affective meaning by virtue of the metaphorical usage of his scales. And in recent years Pinocchio has been trotting around the world, introducing himself to people who speak different languages and enjoy different cultures;[1] but in these travels, Geppetto has at least been able to keep a hand on the puppet's strings."

[1] We wish to acknowledge gratefully the support, first, of the Human Ecology Fund (1960-63), and thereafter that of the National Institute of Mental Health

I should now like to say a few words about my co-authors — who are not in a position to speak for themselves and would never say what I am going to say in any case. Murray Miron was a graduate student at Illinois during the late 1950s, working first with the late Grant Fairbanks on experimental phonetics and later with me on psycholinguistics; his doctoral dissertation was appropriately enough entitled *A Cross-linguistic Investigation of Phonetic Symbolism* (1960, published 1961). As my research assistant, Murray was involved in the planning of the cross-cultural project reported in this book from the beginning — he taped the Allerton House conference (see Chapter 1 herein) at which the research plan took form. After earning his Ph.D., Miron became in effect a co-director of the project — he was "Mr. Inside" (responsible for the quantitative methodology and computer analyses); William K. Archer was "Mr. Outside" (responsible for the linguistic and ethnographic aspects of our work and serving as a sensitive culturological guide on our travels);[2] C.E.O. was obviously "Mr. Middleside." Murray left Illinois and the project in 1965, and Leon Jakobovits took over as co-director, a position which he held until 1970.

Bill May really came up through the ranks of our cross-cultural project. In 1961 he was a keypuncher while he studied computer processing technology and programming. Then he became Miron's right hand in processing the increasing masses of data as the number of communities involved in the project grew. When Miron left and Jakobovits took over, Bill May assumed primary responsibility for all of our quantitative work — and he also began assuming the role of informal adviser and confidant to graduate students serving us as research assistants. When Jakobovits left us, Bill became formally our co-director — a position which he richly deserved. If Bill May was Murray Miron's right hand in the early 1960s, I can truthfully say that he had become my whole right arm by the 1970s; it has been his service — as chief programmer, as business manager, and as "mediator" between me and our staff — that has made it possible for my role as director to be something less than fulltime.

During the late 1960s several of our foreign colleagues spent varying periods at our Center as visiting professors and contributed substantially to our research: Rhea Das from Calcutta (summer, 1966); Pim Levelt from the Netherlands (fall, 1966); Robert Hogenraad from Belgium (fall, 1966–

(MH07705, 1963–present) and the National Science Foundation (NSF GS 360 and 2012X, 1963–present). The Human Ecology Fund enabled us to get under way; and the continuing support of NIMH and NSF is a bit unusual, both in terms of its duration (now in its third five-year grant period) and its "jointness" (the two foundations supporting not different sub-projects but different aspects of the same total effort). We at the Center for Comparative Psycholinguistics and all of our colleagues around the world are indeed grateful for these sources of support.

[2] The authors wish to express their thanks to Bill Archer for his critical reading of early drafts of this book, particularly Chapter 1.

summer, 1967); Jorma Kuusinen from Finland (summer, 1967–spring, 1968); and Vid Pečjak from Yugoslavia (fall, 1968). Needless to say, we were delighted to have these colleagues with us and profited greatly from them; they participated fully as senior staff.

Over the past decade and a half, we have employed an average of about six graduate research assistants per year, most of whom were simultaneously working toward Ph.D.s in psycholinguistics. Nearly half of these junior staff members came to us from foreign countries, typically attracted to Illinois and our Center in the course of field work for the project — and most of them have returned to their homelands to teach and do research in this field, usually becoming senior colleagues in our on-going cross-cultural research. Here I can merely mention their names and the dates of their Ph.D. theses: Yasumasa Tanaka (1963), now our senior colleague in Japan; A. V. Shanmugam (1963), now working for the United Nations in the Philippines; Doğan Cüceloğlu (1967), now a senior colleague in Ankara, Turkey; Tulsi Saral (1969), now teaching at Governor's State University, Illinois, and a continuing research associate with the Center; Jantorn Buranabanpote-Rufener (1972), now a senior colleague in Thailand;[3] Oliver Tzeng (1972), now a research assistant professor on our Center staff; Gordana Opačić (1973), recently returned to her native Yugoslavia and continuing her close association with the project; Rumjahn Hoosain (1973), now doing collaborative research with us in Iran and hoping to relocate in Hong Kong, where he, too, will continue his close association with this research. Ladli Singh was on our staff for one year (1967-68), but obtained his Ph.D. (1969) from Delhi University.

Of course we have also had many U.S. citizens as research assistants, again usually working for Ph.D.s in psycholinguistics: John Limber (1968), now at the University of New Hampshire; James Martin (1968), now at Pennsylvania State University; Sara and William Smith (1971 and 1972), now at Long Beach and Fullerton Universities, respectively, in southern California; Ed Lakner (1970), now with the Survey Research Center at the University of Illinois; Meredith Richards (1974), now at the University of Virginia.[4] There were many other young people who served but did not pursue advanced degrees (or who were employed for relatively short periods), but we must mention the service-in-depth of Howard Bobren (our general business manager during the early 1960s) and Sharon Wolfe (computer specialist, who with Bill Archer in the mid-1960s helped to establish the Teheran Research Unit, a University of Illinois / University of Teheran

[3] Although not assistants on the project, Naunpen ("Penny") and Weerayudh ("Charlie") Wichiarajote both interacted with our staff on various tasks, received their Ph.D.s in educational psychology, and are now also senior colleagues in Thailand.

[4] One always has the gnawing, almost certain feeling of having missed people on such a roll; if that is the case here, I apologize for faulty memory and missing records.

cooperative venture). And there was Fran Adams, our first "librarian," but also an intellectual goad and co-author of a paper on color associations and symbolisms drawn from our *Atlas* data (Adams and Osgood, 1973). Although Kenneth Forster, now teaching at Monash University in Australia, was not an assistant on the Center staff, he was my Institute research assistant during the early 1960s and did his thesis research with me (1964); during the summer of 1969, Ken was a visiting professor in our Center.

If a single book could be dedicated to so many people, then this one should be dedicated to our senior colleagues and friends all over the world. Without them — their suggestions and critiques, their kindnesses and courtesies, their steady supports and efforts on often complex and difficult tasks — none of what is reported on these pages would have been possible. As at least a token of our deep gratitude, a second title page to this volume lists, along with their institutional affiliations, those who contributed to the designing and data collecting for the "tool-making" and *Atlas* "tool-using" phases of this research.[5] It might be noted in passing that we have encouraged all of our senior colleagues to publish articles in their own languages and in their own countries' journals — not only regarding the data for their own communities but also data for all communities — and many have done this.

The reader may think that this book represents a kind of culmination of my lifelong concern with the measurement of meaning — but of course this is not the case. Rather, this book catches us in mid-course. As we hope this first volume will demonstrate, we are now sitting on what we think will prove to be a potential gold mine of quantitative information about universals, subuniversals, and uniqueness in human semantic systems and subjective cultures more generally. Chapter 6 in this volume does illustrate this potential with the small Color category, but some fifty other conceptual categories remain to be mined, and this will be a time-consuming business — albeit a labor of love.

[5] Many others, usually including these senior colleagues, contributed to the interpretation of the *Atlas* data in our group meetings at seven locations (see Chapter 6 and Appendix H herein); appropriate acknowledgment of their help will be given in later volumes on *The Affective Dimension of Subjective Culture,* reporting specifically on the *Atlas* information.

C.E.O.

Urbana, June 9, 1974

CROSS-CULTURAL UNIVERSALS
OF AFFECTIVE MEANING

CHAPTER

1

On the Strategy of Cross-National Research into Subjective Culture

TECHNOLOGICAL DEVELOPMENTS of the twentieth century, particularly in the years since World War II, are producing a major revolution in the human way of life all across the world. They are also producing a revolution in the social and behavioral sciences. Transportation and communication technologies have shrunk the planet — politically, socially, and psychologically — and they are making it possible to do research on an international scale that would have been inconceivable only a few years ago. Automation and computer technologies are moving us toward a world of more leisure (or idleness) and more capacity to handle (or mishandle) ever larger masses of information — and they are making it possible for scientists to collect and analyze (if not always interpret) data in magnitudes undreamed of hitherto.

There are many hypotheses about human nature that demand cross-cultural and cross-linguistic designs, if we are to successfully disentangle what is common to the human species from what is specific to particular segments of it. Cross-national research in the social and behavioral sciences can be highly rewarding, both to the scientists and to the people studied. Indeed, such research is probably essential if we are to survive along with our technology. But, as has always been the case, new capabilities for re-

First draft prepared by Charles E. Osgood. Portions of this chapter, somewhat modified, appeared in a paper by the same title in *The social sciences: Problems and orientations* (The Hague: Mouton, and Paris: UNESCO, 1968), 6:5-37.

search bring along with them new problems and responsibilities as to
their use.

Comparisons across cultures are particularly difficult when what anthropologists term "nonmaterial traits" are involved. We shall use the term "subjective culture" for such traits. It is one thing to compare skull shapes, blood
types, or artifacts; it is quite another thing to compare peoples' values,
stereotypes, attitudes, feelings, or, most generally, meanings. In part, this is
an obvious consequence of the inherent nature of subjective as compared
with objective culture; but it is also due in part to the fact that subjective
culture traits are usually assessed through the medium of language, and
what is called "the language barrier" must somehow be circumvented. Many
years ago Edward Sapir and then Benjamin Lee Whorf phrased what would
now be called "The Hypothesis of Psycholinguistic Relativity." According to
this hypothesis, how we perceive, how we think, and even how we formulate
our implicit philosophies depend upon the structure of the language we
speak. If this were literally true and completely general, then cross-linguistic
comparisons in subjective culture would be impossible in principle.

Recent comparative studies in psycholinguistics are making it clear that
although languages do display superficial uniquenesses in phonology, grammar, and semantics which render them mutually unintelligible, at a deeper
level they display certain universals which render them mutually translatable.
Universals are found in the limited stock of phonetic features from which
each human language draws its phonemes, in the deep (cognitive) structure
of grammars from which all humans construct sentential propositions about
their world, and even in the sets of semantic features with which concept
meanings are differentiated. Thus the use of terms — the way the lexicon
carves up the world — appears entirely arbitrary until the ethnolinguist dis-
covers a framework of common semantic components. Thus in our own
studies of affective meaning we are discovering a common set of factors, a
reference frame within which the affective meanings of concepts are distributed, that seems constant across the human species. The essential thing
is this: to note differences within any phenomenal domain and to order
them in a rigorous fashion, one must have certain similarities in the dimensions of variation. Only to the extent that physical objects share such attributes as length, weight, and volume, and to the extent that these attributes
can be abstracted and quantified, can comparison among them be made on
anything other than an intuitive basis. The same holds true for subjective
culture.

Let us now say a few words about the strategy of this chapter. In a sense,
it is certainly presumptuous to pontificate about such a complex matter as
the strategy of cross-national research on the basis of the limited experience
of our own Center for Comparative Psycholinguistics. The only defense is
that we are uniquely familiar with our own experience. However, to give

somewhat broader perspective, we shall also draw evidence from two other cross-national studies of considerable scope — one by the late Hadley Cantril and his associates (reported in a book titled *The Pattern of Human Concerns,* 1965) and the other by Wallace Lambert and Otto Klineberg (reported in a book titled *Children's Views of Foreign People: A Cross-National Study,* 1967). Of course, it is also certainly presumptuous to use only U.S.-originated studies for this purpose, but it is a fact that up to the present time most large-scale cross-national studies in subjective culture have originated in the United States. This situation will surely change in the future.

Relying primarily, but not exclusively, on the procedures and findings of these three studies, we will take up certain general issues that we see as being involved in cross-national research in today's environment. One of these is the socio-political context within which cross-national research necessarily transpires; our "laboratory" is quite unlike that in which the experimental psychologist usually works, and there are no white coats or other badges of scientific purity. Another issue concerns the strategy of designing cross-national studies, where foreign colleagues are involved at almost all stages. Yet another issue is posed by the existence of "the language barrier" already referred to; from initial contacts, through preparation of materials and instructions, to final interpretation and communication of results, translation problems are ubiquitous. And then there are issues posed by the requirements of adequate sampling (of communities, of subjects within communities, of verbal materials) in cross-national research which seem to be unique to this field. Data collection and handling also raise some novel issues in cross-national research. Finally, an interpretation strategy is required to solve such vexing questions as the following: When is the same really the same? When is the same really different? When is the different really the same? When is the different really different? The translation bugaboo appears here with a vengeance. But before tackling these issues, a thumbnail sketch of each of the three studies is in order.

CANTRIL

In order to get at the patterns of concern of people in various countries, and render the data comparable, Cantril and his associates devised what they call "the self-anchoring striving scale." This is a ladder device having eleven steps. Each subject defines for himself, in his own terms, both the top step (what would constitute for him the best possible life) and the bottom step (what would constitute the worst possible life he can imagine). Then he indicates on the ladder where he thinks he stands at the present time, where he thinks he stood five years ago, and, finally, where he thinks he will stand five years from now. Then he does the same thing (hopes and fears; present, past, and future standing) for his country. Since the responses of subjects in defining the top (hopes) and the bottom (fears) for both self and country were recorded in their own words, the substance of their answers had to be categorized and coded before it could be quantified. The present, past, and future standings of self and country on the eleven-step ladder were directly quantified. Countries were compared with each other in terms of what the subjects mentioned in connection with hopes (e.g., health, decent standard of living, peace) and fears (e.g., health, children, war) for both self and nation and in terms of expressed progress (present vs. past) and expressed level of aspiration (future vs. present) on the ladder for both self and nation.

Lambert and Klineberg

This study on the origin and development of national stereotypes in the minds of children was the direct result of a suggestion made at a meeting at UNESCO in Paris about 15 years ago. Where do the stereotypes, favorable or unfavorable, of peoples in other lands come from? From adults to children, from one generation to another? Lambert and Klineberg went to six-, ten-, and fourteen-year-old children for their answers. These young subjects were asked: "What are you?" Then they were encouraged to name those people of other nationalities who were "like" and who were "not like" themselves. Next they considered seven standard reference peoples (Americans, Brazilians, Chinese, Germans, Indians from India,[1] Negroes from Africa, and Russians) and decided if these people were "like" or "not like" themselves. A series of standardized questions were asked — inquiring into what ways others were like or unlike themselves, what knowledge the children had about others, how much these others were liked or disliked and why, and who they would like (or not like) to be if they were not their own nationality — and the spontaneous responses were coded for statistical analysis.

Osgood *et al.*

The cross-national project which this book will report had both theoretical and practical motivation. It was designed to test the hypothesis-that, regardless of language or culture, human beings utilize the same qualifying (descriptive) framework in allocating the affective meanings of concepts; given verification of this hypothesis, efficient and comparable linguistic instruments could be devised in each language/culture community for measuring concept meanings — or, at least, their affective components. The primary hypothesis about affective semantic universality has been verified, cross-linguistic measuring instruments (semantic differentials) have been gen-

[1] Henceforth "Indians" will refer to Asians and "Amerindians" to American Indians.

erated, and a variety of cross-national comparative investigations have been undertaken, including the development of an *Atlas of Affective Meanings* for some 600 concepts. The design, execution, and interpretation of this study, along with the other two sample studies, will be given in relation to the strategy of cross-national research; this will also provide an introduction to the more detailed chapters which follow.

THE SOCIO-POLITICAL CONTEXT

Cross-national inquiries into subjective culture, as compared with objective culture, inevitably involve the investigator in matters of social structure and politics. He also must face up to the problem of cultural relativity. As Cantril puts it, "I have tried to minimize as much as possible any point of view brought to the people of a nation by an outside observer, especially a self-righteous or condescending observer. I have tried to understand people in their own terms" (p. 7). But cross-national research, by its very nature, must be entangled in the cultural and political matrix of the world at the time. This raises a number of significant issues.

EXPORTATION OF WESTERN CULTURE

Given the inequitable status quo between Western and non-Western technologies and economic well-being — including the technology and financial well-being of social science — there is likely to be some exportation of Western culture in every cross-nation experiment. On the one hand, this leads to invidious comparison and imbalance in cooperative researching; on the other, it leads to bias of interpretation, in the direction of "westernizing" the responses of non-Western subjects. Cantril is entirely correct in aspiration — to minimize the influence of his own Western mind upon interpretation of his findings — but he, we are sure, would have been the first to agree that this goal is extremely difficult to attain in practice. Ideally, in scientific endeavor the process of measurement should not influence the object of measurement, but this is most difficult to ensure in cross-national studies of subjective culture. The people we work with, our colleagues, are often themselves products of Western education, and the fact that we can communicate with them easily itself suggests a potential bias. The tendency of the human mind to project its own values and beliefs onto others is now clearly recognized in the area of culture conflict; it is not so clearly recognized in the area of cross-national social science research.

At a hearing of the Subcommittee on International Organizations and Movements of the House Foreign Affairs Committee on July 8, 1965 (Chairman Dante B. Facell presiding),[2] it was stated that "the role of the be-havioral sciences — what they can tell us about human attitudes and motiva-tions, and how this knowledge can be applied to governmental undertakings designed to carry out the foreign policy of the United States — has been of keen interest to our subcommittee." It is of equally keen interest to social and behavioral scientists, in other countries as well as the United States. The statement goes on: "There exists in every country a sensitivity to foreigners probing into delicate social and political matters. Also, the level of sensitivity varies according to who does the research and its subject matter." Social scientists face a dilemma here. They recognize the need for accurate infor-mation about other peoples — their motivations, their hopes, their fears, their aspirations, their conception of the world — but they also recognize the political sensitivity and the possible political misuse of such information. One committee member had this to say: "There is . . . an implicit attitude or relationship that this country bears to the rest of the world which, if I were not an American, I would find perhaps not highly offensive, but it sug-gests somehow we are the ones to find out the dynamics that are at work in these countries, in their societies, for the benefit of the Military Establish-ment. If I were a Latin American, I wouldn't find this a particularly happy arrangement. . . ."

None of the three projects discussed in this chapter has been in any way related to the "Military Establishment" or U.S. foreign policy, but such research inevitably becomes involved in the general issues. The stereotypes held by children of nations, including their own, the aspirations people have for themselves and their nation, and even the meanings they have for certain concepts (e.g., as being obtained in our own research) certainly have some political implications and bear upon international relations. Social scientists are, indeed, concerned about their image, about their continued access to colleagues and data in other countries, and about the political sensitivity of what they do. They are aware of the need for significant information about other countries, and they are aware of the danger of political entanglement in a world of competing nation states. Their problem is to maintain scien-tific objectivity in a situation which often works against it.

Being inevitable, what does the social scientist do about political entangle-ment? If scholars or scientists obtain support for a project — which, regardless of the source, is entirely under their own direction — then they should where possible deal with other scholars and scientists but not with governments. In other words, we believe that cross-national research into subjective culture ought to be conducted on a "professor-to-professor" basis. At the same time we are aware that this is not always possible. In our own study of semantic

    [2] Taken from "Testimony before House Subcommittee on International Organiza-tions and Movements of the Committee on Foreign Affairs," *American Psychologist*, 21 (1966): 455-470.

systems we have politely but studiously avoided "nation-to-nation" relations. The real issue is whether research can be objective from a scientific point of view, not whether its findings might have political repercussions. Indeed, the data from all objectively conceived and executed social science studies, including the three treated here, should be utilized by politicians and should, hopefully, have some repercussions.

EXPLOITATION VS. GENERATION

When one thinks about it, cross-national research faces many of the same problems as foreign aid. Given the onesidedness of available funds for research in social science, there is a strong tendency to *use* one's colleagues in other countries for one's own purposes rather than to collaborate with them. After all, *we* have the resources, the money, the computers, and all the rest that go with efficient research today, so why shouldn't we extract the data we want and then just say "good-bye"?

Let us indicate briefly how, in our own research, we have tried to avoid this pitfall. First, it has been our intent to deal with our senior colleagues in other countries as cooperating scientists rather than as hired hands. Typically we offer honoraria for time spent in actively planning research with us, but not salaries — on the assumption that they will do research indigenously, publish papers, and thereby receive the usual rewards of scientific endeavor in connection with our common undertaking. But, because we have funds and they often do not, we have usually paid the costs for research assistants, field workers, preparation of materials, and the like. Second, we have tried to shift gradually — between the "tool-making" and "tool-using" stages (see below) — from a radial organization, with the Center for Comparative Psycholinguistics at Illinois as the focus, to an interacting network organization, with ideas and control coming from anywhere within our group of some 25 countries. Third, we have encouraged and often supported purely indigenous studies in particular locations, particularly when they are implicitly comparative even if not explicitly so (e.g., studies of the concept of "work" in India).

We have also included the training of young social scientists from other countries in our program. Often they have originally been research assistants or field workers in the early phases of our research. So far we have provided assistantships and training, usually leading to advanced degrees, to young scholars from Japan, Thailand, India, West Germany, Finland, Turkey, Yugoslavia, Taiwan, Hong Kong, Italy, Costa Rica, and Iran. These people will for the most part be working on social science problems of their own devising in their own countries, but they will also, we hope, continue to be interested in cooperating on cross-national studies. In other words, it is our intent not to extract our bits of data and then depart, leaving little behind, but rather to contribute to the creation of a cooperating and knowledgeable group of colleagues in research, colleagues in many places who will pursue their own problems as well as common problems over the years to come.

CULTURAL INTANGIBLES

In any cross-national study what we may call "cultural intangibles" are involved, particularly in research into subjective culture. Given, for example, an implicit philosophy of monistic materialism on the part of a Western investigator, he may be shocked to have a senior colleague in India ask him seriously about the psychic implications of *advaita* dualism. Conversely, many students from foreign countries in our American universities suffer an unsuspected handicap in "making grades" simply because of the differences between their implicit metaphysics and ours — and this despite excellent command of ordinary English. For obvious reasons it is impossible for us to make explicit what we have felt to be effects upon our research from such cultural intangibles. Yet we know they are there.

If our American egalitarianism rubs against the Japanese or Thai sense of propriety, then surely their proprieties rub against our own sense of egalitarianism — as when they expect one of us to *lead* the group toward an unknown destination by an unknown path! With the best of scholarly intentions, one may express an opinion about race, sex, or even age and then somehow sense that, like an errant gust of wind, he has stirred the leaves of cultural incongruity in his colleagues. We had to re-do our sample of adjectival qualifiers — 100 young males asked to give the first "adjective" occurring to them when presented with 100 "nouns" — in both Japan and Hong Kong, and for opposite reasons. It appeared that the Japanese teen-agers implicitly assumed that "what most people would say" was expected of them, whereas the Hong Kong teen-agers assumed that "the most original word I can think of" was expected! It is through such a maze of cultural intangibles that cross-national research tries to wend its way.

Such intangibles also underlie readinesses to accept or reject collaboration with certain projects. Investigations into certain aspects of subjective culture are to different degrees tolerable in different societies. Cantril refers to this kind of problem: "I had to choose countries where it was possible to work, either from a technical or a political point of view. I tried to get official government permission in certain countries that must be left unmentioned, and which I wanted to include in the sample, but unfortunately certain cabinet ministers apparently felt that such inquiries might be a threat to them, even though, as already reported, I offered to transmit all tabulations at once to all people who had cooperated with me in the different countries" (p. 28). Lambert and Klineberg report similar experiences, and we could do the same. It is essential that cross-national projects allow for flexibility with respect to such matters. For example, in our own *Atlas* sample of some 600 concepts we have asked our colleagues in each country to use their own judgment and delete any concepts they feel might be sensitive or offensive in their own communities.

THE DESIGN OF CROSS-NATIONAL RESEARCH

Research design has many facets. It must have an original idea, an impetus, whether this comes from the outreaching of social science itself or from felt social need. It must have some rationale, which will determine its scope, its sample, and its execution. There are certain rules of procedure which scientists, social or otherwise, believe they must follow if their work is to warrant communication to others; these rules are designed to ensure objectivity, reliability, and fidelity of the "facts" they transmit to others in their society. However, in attempting to meet these ordinary criteria, cross-national research faces some rather unusual problems.

Who Are the Planners?

Ideally, cross-national research should be planned just as cooperatively as it is executed. This is not easy to do. The level of sophistication in social science varies markedly from country to country, as does its tradition or "flavor" — and, of course, each sees its own tradition as normative. Therefore, in our experience and in that of many others with whom we have discussed the matter, the original planning of such research is usually parochial. One man, or a few men, in one country conceive what they think is a significant problem, decide that they want to test it out against a cross-cultural matrix, and then design the project within their own tradition. This may not have been true of the Cantril and Lambert-Klineberg studies, but it was certainly true of the origins of our own research. This is not the way things ought to be, and we have been trying to change it. Although the "tool-making" stages of our project had to be standardized, by the very nature of the problem, the "tool-using" stages are relatively free. Given the measuring instruments, for both indigenous and cross-linguistic studies in subjective culture, we have encouraged our colleagues to design their own studies and to enlist the help of others around the world in carrying them out, including ourselves. We have found that some of our colleagues accept the burden of originality easily; others do not. This is more than a matter of individual differences; it is also a matter of cultural differences and of differences in training.

As a first step in getting our project under way, a conference was held in February, 1960, at the University of Illinois's Allerton House, to evaluate critically the proposed procedures. It was hoped that this might spare the investigators many of the blunders to which cross-linguistic and cross-cultural studies of this sort are liable. We also wanted advice on how to maximize the generality of our conclusions within the finite limits of our time and budget. The conference roster included anthropologists, linguists, psychologists, and others familiar with cross-cultural research and/or linguistics.[3] The project staff presented the proposed procedures, the problems, and their suggested solutions and received a great deal of constructive criticism. It is certain that the project would not have run as smoothly as it has without the guidance received in this pre-research conference.

Several criteria for the selection of countries within which to work were established at this conference. The samples should all represent "high cultures," that is, possessing a stabilized and normatively directed language and literature, a recorded and generally known history, and an educational system employing the indigenous language. In other words, it was decided to work first with literate subjects where group administration of tests in written form could be employed. Furthermore, it was agreed that the sample of sites should provide a maximum diversity of both language and culture, within the limit above, that they should have available institutions and competent social scientists from whom to enlist cooperation, and that they should be easily accessible. Accordingly, the following six sites were chosen for initiation of the project: Finland (Finno-Ugric); Japan (Japanese); Hong Kong (Sino-Tibetan); Mysore, India (Dravidian); Iran (Indo-European); and Lebanon (Semitic), with American English (Indo-European) as a common comparison base. It can be seen that this original sample represented six different language families linguistically and perhaps as reasonable a diversity in culture as "high cultures" would allow.

The original six countries were visited jointly by Archer and Osgood during the first spring and summer of the project. During initial visits adequate staff is arranged for, the overall nature of the research is discussed (and lectures to interested groups of students and staff are usually given), and the details of the initial phases are laid out; during subsequent visits corrections in procedure are made and subsequent phases prepared for. As would be expected, the degree of staff supervision from the Center varies considerably among the sites.

One solution to the problem of collaborative planning of research is the establishment of research centers — in locations other than the United States but with initial cooperation and support from American sources. We

---

[3] Conference participants were Raymond Bauer, John B. Carroll, Joseph B. Casagrande, Alfred G. Dietze, Clyde Kluckhohn, Hideya Kumata, Wallace Lambert, Howard Maclay, Wilbur Schramm, George Suci, Harry Triandis, and Leigh Triandis; representing the Human Ecology Fund, Samuel Lyerly and James Monroe; representing the project staff, William Kay Archer, Murray S. Miron, and Charles E. Osgood.

worked out one such arrangement with the University of Teheran, in Iran, under the supervision of Professor William K. Archer, originally of our own research staff.[4] Although this center was in part designed to facilitate our own project (by collection and analysis, via local computer facilities, of data from countries that were within reasonable distance), it was also intended to facilitate research by scholars in other fields, in both Iran and the United States. The setting up and support of such overseas research centers are in the long-term best interest of all countries involved.

THE VALUES OF PILOTING

Many cross-national researches have floundered because of insufficient pilot work. While it is reasonable to try to anticipate as many factors as possible — as we did, for example, in the three-day conference before initiating our project — anticipations are strictly limited by one's own culture and his experience therein. Lambert and Klineberg indicate that many of the decisions relating to their study of three age levels of children from 11 parts of the world, involving a total of 3,500 children, were based upon a pilot study. In the case of our own cross-cultural research the design followed in the "tool-making" stage was based upon nearly ten years of unicultural research in quantitative semantics, plus several studies of a crosslinguistic nature (but utilizing scales derived simply by translating English into language X). We knew what we wanted to do and, fairly well, how to do it. But nevertheless our first overseas study was a pilot study in a country where we had excellent social science support as well as a different language family and a somewhat different culture — Finland. In the "toolusing" phase of our project, we have encouraged our colleagues to similarly pretest their cross-national designs in their own countries before "exporting" them for comparative purposes.

HYPOTHESIS-TESTING VS. INFORMATION-GATHERING RESEARCH

Most cross-national research has been of the information-gathering sort. It derives from societal needs to know — what people in other countries feel and believe about this or that issue. Both the Cantril and the Lambert-Klineberg studies are primarily of this sort, but they are more than this by virtue of the treatment and interpretation of the data. Our own research into human meaning systems combined both motives explicitly. First, we wanted to test the general hypothesis that humans do, in fact, employ the

---

[4] The Teheran Research Unit (TRU), although originally established in connection with this project in 1966, has now broadened its scope to facilitation of research and other scholarly activities under agreement between the University of Illinois and the University of Teheran, on a university-wide basis.

same framework for differentiating the affective meanings of concepts. This was prerequisite to constructing comparable measuring instruments. Second, we wanted to use the instruments so devised to measure the affective loadings of significant concepts — in various areas of human activity — in comparable fashion. But any hypothesis-testing endeavor also yields information about the samenesses or differences among humans in different places on the planet. When Shirley Hill studies differences in mathematical concept learning (1964) or Roger Brown studies differences in the use of intimate or formal pronouns (Brown and Gilman, 1960), information about cultural similarities or differences is also being obtained.

STANDARDIZATION VS. NATURALNESS

Social as well as other scientists place a high value on standardization of procedures in research. They regard it, quite correctly, as one of the safeguards of scientific rigor. But standardization across diverse language/culture communities is quite a different matter than standardization within one language/culture community. The purpose of standardization is to render data from diverse samples comparable. In within-culture research this usually means identical instructions and procedures; in cross-culture research it may well mean deliberately *different* instructions and even procedures. One way of handling this problem is to make questions deliberately openended and rely upon categorization of the responses for comparability; this was done in the Lambert-Klineberg study. Cantril's awareness of this problem is evident in this statement: "The methodological problem faced in this study was essentially that of devising some means to get an overall picture of the reality worlds in which people lived, a picture expressed by individuals *in their own terms;* and to do this in such a way that without sacrificing authenticity or prescribing any boundaries or fixed categories it would still be possible to make meaningful comparisons between different individuals, groups of individuals, and societies" (p. 21). His answer was a self-anchoring scale. As he acknowledges, the substance of the "anchors" varies from culture to culture — from "having own house" in West Germany to "a happy family life" in the Kibbutzim communities in Israel — but presumably the steps on his ladder are relative to each man's best and worst possible worlds and hence are directly comparable.

In our own research on meaning systems we wished to guarantee naturalness and at the same time achieve standardization. We wished to expose native speakers in each language/culture community to the same task under the same kind of motivation, and yet leave their responses completely free of any Western influence. Specifically, we wanted to elicit in each community those ways of qualifying experience which are most frequent, productive (generalized), and independent of each other *for them in their own lan-*

guage. Then we wanted them to use the major dimensions of qualification thus derived in the judgment of concepts, so that we could determine if, in fact, a common framework (factor structure) existed. We discovered early in the game that modes of qualifying are not necessarily identical with adjectives in English, that the "same" instructions do not necessarily guarantee the same motivation or interpretation, and that what is quite different superficially may be quite similar basically.

CIRCUMVENTING THE LANGUAGE BARRIER

In conducting cross-cultural research where the communities involved speak different languages, translation problems arise at nearly every point. At the very beginning one must communicate the nature, purpose, and procedures to his foreign colleagues. Fortunately for American researchers — who are too rarely fluent in languages other than their own — many of the foreign scholars they deal with are reasonably fluent in English. And at the very end the results of research must be translated into the native language of the investigator if he is to be able to interpret and communicate them. Between these two end-points the degree of dependence upon translation will vary according to the nature of the task and the skill of the investigator. Of course, one might try to avoid translation problems entirely by using only bilinguals with respect to the investigator's native language as subjects. However, such samples would not only be highly selective, but they would, for English-speaking investigators, represent the most westernized people, and the sought-for cultural differences might disappear as a result.

Translation Strategies

Three basic strategies for trying to circumvent the language barrier can be distinguished.

(1) *Language-free instruments.* Cantril's ladder device illustrates this approach nicely. It is understood that the verbal definitions of the ends of the ladder will vary from country to country (and the expressed hopes and fears, it is true, must go through the translation gauntlet), but it is hoped that the subjects' placements of themselves and their countries along the ladder for the present, past, and future will be relatively language-free. This is why it has been termed a "self-anchoring" scale. In some of our research (Osgood, 1960b) we have employed semantic differentials in which the "scales" are defined by visual figures differing in only one respect, e.g., *large* vs. *small, white* vs. *black, jagged* vs. *smooth,* and so on. Incidentally, evidence for strong and cross-culturally consistent visual-verbal synesthesia was

obtained. More extensive research on this approach will be reported in Chapter 7. Such approaches attempt to solve the translation problem by minimizing the role of language in the testing instruments.

(2) *Language-invariant instruments.* This approach is illustrated by our own studies on human meaning systems. Here one searches for universals within language itself and uses them in constructing instruments which, although not translation equivalents of each other, can be shown to tap these universals. In our main project, begun in 1960, we have elicited modes of qualifying (adjectives in English) from monolinguals in each language/culture community and have determined by factor-analytic procedures that they do, indeed, utilize the same basic factors. It is then possible, within each language, to select those particular scales which best represent the common factors, even though the scales are usually not translation equivalents across the languages.[5]

(3) *Translation-equivalent instruments.* This is the most common procedure, but it has many pitfalls. If the translation from source to destination language is literal, then what are familiar idiomatic expressions in one are likely to seem strange in the other. If the translation is loose, then one must wonder if the same instructions, the same test, the same questions, are really being given to subjects in the different language/culture communities. The Lambert-Klineberg study illustrates what some of the problems are and how careful investigators attempt to surmount them. They say, with regard to the Brazilian testing, "The first translation was pre-tested on a small group so that the most appropriate idioms could be found, making the final versions a good translation and one readily understood by the children of both social classes at all three age levels" (p. 20).

The tactic of back-translation provides a rigorous method for checking translation equivalence. One group of balanced bilinguals translates the instructions or questionnaire from language A into language B, and then another group of bilinguals independently translates back from language B into language A. "The questionnaire was translated into Hebrew and then back into English by a different translator. The few discrepancies that turned up were resolved by the two bilinguals and the project director" (Lambert and Klineberg, p. 27).

There are some situations where back-translation cannot be used effectively, however. This is particularly the case where single words (e.g., as stimuli for word association) must be translated without context. This is obvious in the case of homonyms — if a word in language X is translated as *light* in English, back-translation into X may yield either the opposite of *heavy* or the opposite of *dark* — but it applies to the different senses of words as well.

---

[5] This phase of our research is detailed in Chapters 3 and 4.

TRANSLATION VS. ADAPTATION

The real purpose behind translation of instructions and materials is to guarantee that the conditions of data collection in various countries are as constant as possible. A perfect translation, as determined by back-translation, for example, may not be a perfect adaptation. Cantril reflects this concern when he says, "One of the methods often utilized in this translation process was to have someone who knew the native language, as a native, for example, an Arab, and who was completely fluent in English translate our questions into Arabic. Then someone whose native language was English but who had a perfect command of Arabic would translate the Arabic back into English so a comparison could be made with the original question and, through discussion and further comparisons, difficulties could be ironed out" (p. 26). The problems are often as much bicultural as they are bilingual, and bicultural informants (often one's senior colleagues) are needed to determine when a good translation is not a good adaptation into another culture. This is particularly obvious when one tries to translate questionnaire items into a language for whose speakers the cultural substance may be subtly different or even nonexistent. Imagine trying to use a literally translated statement like "I would not admit a Negro to my social club" with Bantus or a statement like "I go to church every Sunday" with Moslems or Buddhists!

THE INEVITABLE INADEQUACY OF TRANSLATION

In the last analysis, given the different ways the lexicons of different languages carve up the world, translation equivalence is a goal to be sought but never really achieved. The semantic spheres of translation-equivalent terms overlap to varying degrees but probably never coincide in perfection. Cantril found that "it was much better to have the coding done locally . . . by highly intelligent and highly trained people so that nuances of meaning in the native language would not be lost" (p. 27). Lambert and Klineberg found that since Hebrew has no general term for "child," sex automatically being indicated, it was impossible to separate two popular categories of response to the question "What are you?" — sex (*boy* vs. *girl*) and age level (*child*) — and Israel could not be compared with other communities in this respect. In an ethnocentrism questionnaire which Lambert and Klineberg adapted from a study by Else Frenkel-Brunswik, we find such items as "Do you think our country is a lot better off because of the foreign races that live here?," "Do you think that girls should only learn things that are useful around the house?," and "Do you think that you can protect yourself from bad luck by carrying a charm or good luck piece?" One wonders about the roles of translation (linguistically) and adaptation (culturally) in producing the finding that Bantu children appear the most ethnocentric and American children the least. The investigators advise caution in interpreting this aspect of their study on exactly these grounds.

THE PROBLEM OF SAMPLING

If the problems of adequate sampling are not different in kind for cross-national research than for within-national research, they are certainly different in complexity. In a within-country study of the information-gathering type (e.g., a public opinion survey), the criteria for guaranteeing representativeness of the sample are usually clear; in between-country studies of this type, the criteria vary from location to location. In a within-country study of the hypothesis-testing type (e.g., that the self-concepts of children vary in positiveness with their economic well-being), adequate control or comparison groups are those which are matched in all respects (age, intelligence, health, etc.) except the experimental variable; in between-country studies of this type, the "control" group often is the investigator's own community. This is a subtle form of projection in which one's own way of life is seen as normative.

Sampling of Language/Culture Communities

In principle, the sampling of countries for a cross-national study should depend upon the type of information or hypothesis under investigation; in practice, the sampling often depends upon contacts, accessibility, travel funds, time, and other such mundane matters. In our own case we wished to test the hypothesis that the major dimensions of affective meaning are independent of variations in both language and culture, so as our initial sample we selected six communities which we felt would maximize linguistic and cultural differences and yet provide literate speakers of "national" languages. As the project progressed, however, and proved efficient, more countries were added for a variety of reasons — colleagues who indicated strong interest, students returning to their own countries, and just simply places that seemed interesting to work in. One result is an overabundance of Indo-European languages in our total sample of now some 25 language/culture communities.

Cantril's concerns were different from ours, and this is reflected in his sample of 14 locations. He wanted "some that were highly advanced, some that were newly independent, some that were clearly underdeveloped, some that appeared to be in a state of political and economic crisis, some that had just gone through major revolutions..." (p. 28). He included four westernized locations (United States, West Germany, Yugoslavia, Poland), three underdeveloped giants (Brazil, Nigeria, India), three from the Middle East (Israel, Israel-Kibbutzim, Egypt), three Caribbean sites (Cuba, Dominican Republic, Panama), and finally the Philippines.

According to Lambert and Klineberg, "The idea was to choose as varied and representative a sample of nations of the world as possible within manageable time and financial limits. It became apparent that no generally accepted criteria for drawing a random sample of children of the world were yet available, and that if we were to limit our choice to about ten nations, we should only refer to it as 'a small, varied, and interesting sample' " (p. 15). Their 11 locations included the United States, the Bantu in South Africa, Brazil, English Canada, French Canada, France, Germany, Israel, Japan, Lebanon, and Turkey. It might be noted in passing that the presence of world-renowned social scientists in certain countries serves to attract cross-national projects the way flowers attract bees!

SAMPLING OF SUBJECTS WITHIN COMMUNITIES

Here the investigator comes face to face with a dilemma: does he want representativeness within each country or equivalence across countries? Maximizing representativeness within usually means minimizing equivalence between, and vice versa. A representative sample in India, for example, would involve proportionate numbers of many castes, many religions, and many languages, and it would include many illiterates and people in villages having minimal awareness of the outside world. Such a sample would hardly be comparable with one representative of the Netherlands, using its usual criteria. On the other hand, a sample of Indian college students obviously would be much more highly selected (less representative) than an "equivalent" sample of Dutch college students. What compromise between these poles is made in an investigator's sampling strategy depends primarily upon the purpose of the research.

Since Cantril's purpose was to compare the concerns of people in different countries *as a function of different economic, political, social, and education levels in these places,* he wished to maximize representativeness within each country. His Appendix B gives a breakdown of the sample in each country by education, economic level, age, and locus of dwelling (rural, urban); it is evident that the samples are by no means equivalent. For example, of approximately 2,700 respondents in both Brazil and the United States, only 35 Brazilians as compared with 527 Americans could be classified as "better educated" — but note that such sample differences are inherent to Cantril's comparisons. "No one knows better than I do," he says, "that some of the samples leave much to be desired. The Egyptian survey, for example, must clearly be regarded only as preliminary, since it was extremely difficult to get the proper number of rural interviews because of local suspicion of anyone except a government employee who went around asking questions" (p. 28). Awareness of such inequities of sampling makes all of us cautious about interpretations.

Since our purpose was to compare semantic systems *as a function of gross differences in both language and culture,* we wished to maximize equivalence of subjects (as representatives of their own languages and cultures), at least in the "tool-making" stages. At the preliminary Allerton conference we decided to use young (14-18) male students in average high schools in urban settings. We wanted young high school–level people because they have full command of their native language and are generally integrated with their native culture but are less likely than college students, for example, to have been exposed to other cultures and languages. We decided to use only males, on the ground that education of females is much more variable (selective) than for males across the world. We wanted to use students in classroom situations because of the efficiency and inexpensiveness of collecting data with pencil-and-paper tests. The use of urban settings (usually) was dictated simply by the fact that our foreign colleagues were typically associated with universities, and these in turn were typically in urban areas.

Now it is perfectly clear that a group of young, male, high school students in Lebanon, let us say, is not "representative" of the Lebanese population as a whole; it would not be at all satisfactory for Cantril's purposes. On the other hand, we had already demonstrated in numerous comparative studies in the United States that such variables as age, sex, political affiliation, or even schizophrenia (for testable patients, at least) produced no modifications in the basic factor structure for affective meaning. So, for the purpose of testing the hypothesis of generality of semantic factors, and building comparable semantic differentials on their basis, equivalent samples of young male students seemed satisfactory. However, when in our "tool-using" phase we come to measuring and comparing the meanings of specific concepts (e.g., FUTURE, MOTHER, POLICEMAN), it is obvious that our sample will not be representative of the total population in each country, and this fact will have to be kept in mind in interpreting these data.[6]

Lambert and Klineberg wanted to compare children's images of themselves and foreigners *as a function of their nationality and age.* Therefore, they wanted both equivalence, in the sense of age levels, sex ratios, intelligence, and the like, and representativeness, in the sense of socio-economic level and the like, so that differences could not be attributed to education of parents, for example. This required a compromise, which in their case appeared as a form of stratified sampling within otherwise equivalent groups.

---

[6] As a check on the nature of the distortion introduced by our homogeneous samples, representative samples (in terms of age, sex, and socio-economic levels) have been undertaken in Greece by Dr. Vasso Vassiliou and in the United States. These data will be reported in later publications.

Three age samples (100 six-year-olds, 100 ten-year-olds, and 100 fourteen-year-olds) were obtained in each country according to a standard scheme: "First, all children had to have at least normal intelligence as determined either by objective test results or by teachers' estimates. Second, an equal number of children from lower and middle socio-economic class levels, defined according to the standards of each nation, were to be included. Third, children from large urban centers only were considered, and, fourth, an equal number of boys and girls were to be included in each age and social class subgroup" (p. 16). Such a stratified sample clearly suits Lambert and Klineberg's purposes, whereas it would have been insufficient for Cantril's and unnecessary for ours.

SAMPLING OF VERBAL MATERIALS

In cross-cultural studies the "stimuli" may be questions, single words to be reacted to in some way, scaling devices of some sort, or even pictorial materials (e.g., T.A.T. or Rorschach cards). The "responses" may be completely free verbalizations, choices among presented alternatives, word associations, making check-marks on scales, or even simple pointings. The purposes of the investigator, again, will largely determine his sampling here — although it is also true that the same problem can usually be attacked by diverse methods. In some cases representativeness of the sample of stimuli is an issue; in other cases the nature of the stimuli is completely dictated by the purpose of the study (e.g., questions related to sex practices if this is the purpose). But in all cases, ideally, the stimuli should be equivalent for subjects of all nationalities, whether questions, words, or pictures, and this is usually difficult to guarantee. The degree of restraint put on the freedom of response usually varies with the need the investigator feels for naturalness vs. standardization, and the choice made here markedly influences the subsequent treatment of the data. With these points in mind, let us now look briefly at our three sample studies.

For Lambert and Klineberg, the stimuli were specified by the problem and highly structured ("What are you?" "What else are you?" "Anything else?" "Are there other people from other countries who are like you or similar to you?" "In what ways?" ... and so forth), but the responses were completely free. "Because we believed strongly that the procedure should be open-ended, particularly for the young children involved, the decision was made to use an interview which while structured would remain flexible enough to elicit whatever ideas, descriptions, and expressions of feeling children had about foreign peoples. . . . In addition, a maximum spontaneity of response was to be provided for, even though certain questions would be asked of all children in order that various cross-national comparisons could be made" (p. 12). But, given the spontaneity of the children's responses, making comparisons required that some coding system be developed. In a sense, subsequent coding is the equivalent of prior standardization — and each has its problems.

Cantril's study involved a tightly structured interview but a partially free and partially standardized response situation. The expressions of hopes and fears for self and nation were free, and the responses had to be subsequently coded, but the allocation of self and nation to the self-anchoring ladder device yielded standardized, quantified data which could be treated directly.

Our own research imposed standardization upon both verbal stimuli and responses in all phases. It also required representative sampling among both in its several stages. (1) *Qualifier elicitation:* A diverse sample of 100 culture-common, translation-equivalent substantives (nouns) was given as stimuli, with the subjects instructed to give the first qualifier (adjective) that occurred to them for each. (2) *Qualifier sampling:* The 10,000 responses obtained were analyzed so as to generate a set of qualifiers for each community, ordered according to three criteria — overall frequency of usage, diversity of usage across the 100 nouns, and independence of usage across the nouns (to avoid redundant dimensions). (3) *Opposites elicitation:* Small numbers of sophisticated subjects generated opposites for the ordered list of qualifiers (e.g., good-*bad,* strong-*weak,* etc.), items lacking agreed-upon opposites (e.g., red-??) being eliminated, until a set of 50 pairs was obtained. (4) *Concept-on-scale differentiation:* The 100 substantives of the original set were each rated against the entire set of 50 scales, now seven-step:

$$good\text{——}:\text{——}:\text{——}:\text{——}:\text{——}:\text{——}:\text{——}bad$$

by a new group of subjects. (5) *Scale sampling:* Utilizing factor-analytic procedures, the relations among the qualifying scales when used in judging concepts were determined and the major factors extracted. The first three factors proved to be qualitatively the same in nearly all cases.

Some of our colleagues in anthropology would object that the use of standardized, and often strange, eliciting procedures and the constraints placed upon the form of response tend to wipe out cultural differences, leaving only common human reactions. As a matter of fact, just such an objection was raised to our methods in a conference on Transnational Studies in Cognition (D'Andrade and Romney, 1964). One anthropologist said, ". . . it seems so artificial to force people to tell you whether 'Wednesday' is 'good' or 'bad.' And I don't understand what significance any consistency you may get in forced tasks such as this has for understanding a culture" (p. 238). Our reply, in essence, was that the arbitrariness of the elicitation procedure does not necessarily preclude the appearance of relevant cultural differences. For example, although we require subjects to give qualifiers to substantives as the first step, there is no restraint upon *what* qualifiers are given, with *what* frequencies and diversities. Similarly, although we force subjects to rate concepts on scales, there is no restraint upon *where* they rate and hence upon *what* the resulting factor structures and concept allocations within the space they define will be. Apart from the matter of constraint upon one's data, there is also a difference in purpose here: whether one is descriptively oriented toward providing a cameo of a particular culture as a unique gestalt (inherently incomparable) or is comparatively oriented toward the test of hypotheses concerning similarities and differences in restricted cultural domains (inherently incomplete descriptively).

DATA COLLECTION AND ANALYSIS

By the nature of things in cross-national research the data are usually collected from native speakers in their own local communities. This is not necessarily the case, of course; a considerable number of studies have utilized students from foreign countries studying in American universities, for example, or utilized visitors from abroad (e.g., at world's fairs). Furthermore, within countries where groups speaking different languages and still enjoying somewhat different cultures exist, essentially cross-cultural studies can be done intranationally. The locus of data analysis depends upon many factors — sophistication of personnel in each country, availability of data-processing equipment, nature of the raw data to be analyzed, and translation problems, to name only a few. In most cases (including the three studies being used as illustrations) the processing of data is shared on some basis dictated by factors such as those above. Only a few of these problems will be considered here.

Sharing on the Basis of Cost-Effectiveness

Transportation of raw data, which are often bulky, can be very expensive. There is also the real danger of loss or damage in the mails, and raw data cannot be replaced without new sampling. Therefore, it is usual to carry data analysis through to at least first-stage summarizations (means, frequencies, percentages, etc.) in the locus of collection; copies can then be made and shipped to another locus for further analysis. How much more than this is done in the locus of collection depends upon the competence of the personnel, the availability of equipment, and the relative costs for all concerned (often in terms of time vs. technology). In our own work, for example, factor analyses of the magnitude involved would be literally impossible without high-speed computers and sophisticated programming.

Translation problems also influence the division of effort in data analysis. Both the Cantril and the Lambert-Klineberg studies required translation and then coding of responses into categories, and in both it was decided that the coding should be done by social scientists in the country of collection.

The problem in this case, of course, is adequate communication among the cooperating scientists about the meaning of coding categories. In our case elicited qualifiers were transliterated into Roman script where necessary and tabulated alphabetically under each substantive; although translations were obtained for later interpretation, all computer analyses were done "blind" on the native-language materials. The concept-on-scale judgments are inherently quantified and were simply tabulated and then shipped to Illinois for factor analysis.

The degree of sharing in design and data processing varies with the type and duration of the research. In what might be termed, with no derogation implied, "one-shot" studies, the best balance will be sought in the beginning and followed. This was true for both the Cantril and the Lambert-Klineberg studies; a single collection of information was involved in each case. In a program of research such as our own, involving several stages of data collection in the "tool-making" phase and then varieties of designs and collections in the "tool-using" phase, the balance of sharing is likely to shift. In our "tool-making" phase, by virtue of the exigencies of standardization and complex analyses, as well as the need to minimize translation problems, a relatively heavy share of the burden in both design and analysis was centralized in the locus of origin of the project. As we move into the "tool-using" phase in more and more locations, this burden is shifting more onto our colleagues in other countries. Our local staff participate more as consultants in design and as aids in analysis, where our computer facilities can materially simplify the complexity and reduce the time of processing. In some locations research using semantic differential tools has become practically autonomous.

COMMUNICATION IN CROSS-NATIONAL RESEARCH

A word is in order concerning the problem of maintaining effective communication among the participants in cross-national research projects. We have found — and we are sure this experience is shared by those involved in the Cantril and the Lambert-Klineberg projects — that adequate communication presents one of the most serious problems in this type of research. This is so despite the remarkable developments in world communications technology. Needless to say, this problem increases (probably exponentially) with the number of cooperating countries. In our own case a local staff of three senior people and about ten graduate students and clerical people is interacting with approximately 50 people in other countries, and our foreign colleagues are interacting among themselves in steadily increasing amounts. Communications are amazingly diversified — designs and changes in design, shipping of raw data and return of their analyses, discussions of new ideas, matters of payments for services or honoraria, requests for reprints both ways, unexpected problems encountered, notification of travel plans, and so on ad infinitum.

Even by air mail (and we have found that everything important must be sent this way), one has to expect a lag of about two weeks between sending a message and receiving an answer — and this under the best conditions. But conditions are rarely optimal; people do have other obligations and must assign priorities, people do go on vacations and take other trips, people do have family problems, and so on. What is most disturbing on either side is a prolonged, absolute silence — particularly when data have been transmitted. To reduce such anxieties as much as possible, we introduced a card-return procedure, in which the sender encloses a self-addressed card indicating the material sent and a space to check "received" — figuring that a little increase in postage costs was more than repaid by a big decrease in tension. There is also a subtle psychological matter here: each sender in a communication situation, not knowing what the life activities of his receiver are in any detail, has the natural tendency to assume unconsciously that his message has top priority and, indeed, that the receiver has little else to do but await his messages and reply! Also, if the load is one-sided, as has been the case in our Phase I, there will be periods when data from several locations must queue up for computer analysis.

We also discovered that we had internal communication problems. In our local staff we had to delegate different responsibilities to different people — one person primarily responsible for budgetary matters, another for data processing, another for linguistic field problems, and so forth — but often the third hand didn't know what the second had done, the first what either the second or third had done. To help with this problem, we instituted a procedure whereby *all* senior staff get copies of *all* messages sent or received by anyone — figuring that replication of paper is less serious than communication failure. Similar communication failures between senior colleagues and field staff sometimes occurred in other locations.

But written communication at long distance, even under the best of conditions, is a pale substitute for face-to-face communication with a palpable colleague. A few days of conversation are worth more than a year of correspondence. So at least every other year one or more of our Illinois staff has visited each other country and spent about a week in consultation there. A noticeable uplift in level of activity across the entire project could be felt following these trips. But this does not provide for face-to-face interactions among our foreign colleagues themselves. We were able to support one ten-day conference of all senior personnel in Dubrovnik, Yugoslavia, about midway through the first phase of the project (1963, summer); we organized another in Teheran, Iran, at that point where the applied ("tool-using") phase was getting under way in most locations (1967, summer).

THE DUBROVNIK CONFERENCE

This conference convened on August 1, 1963, at the Hotel Neptune under the sponsorship of the Institute of Communications Research, University of Illinois, and in cooperation with the Federal Institute for Educational Research, Belgrade, Yugoslavia.[7] Inasmuch as this was to be a conference on work in progress, it was our aim that, as far as possible, all those who had participated in the research should attend. Thirty-six members of the project staff participated.[8]

The project had been in progress for nearly three years and at the time of the conference involved about 16 language/culture communities. In several locations we were already at the point of shift of emphasis from "tool-making" to "tool-using" activities (first, collection of data for the *Atlas of Affective Meanings*). It was felt that such a conference would not only serve to bring into focus what we believed we had accomplished thus far (establishing the cross-cultural generality of affective meaning systems and deriving psycholinguistic measures which would be comparable across cultures), but would also enable us to make systematic plans for future research activities. In this connection an essential difference between this and many other international gatherings should be stressed: our conferees had already been working "together" for several years, the agenda was clearly defined, and the participants were task-oriented.

The major purposes of the conference were thus the following: (a) a survey and review of general methods and results; (b) plans for local, regional, and international publications; (c) preparations of schedules, research designs, and responsibilities for "tool-using" research, with particular reference to pancultural and cross-cultural studies; (d) informal discussion of how our various researches could be integrated; (e) discussions of practical problems concerning research (e.g., uses of equipment, funding, exchanges of personnel); (f) communication problems; and (g) informal discussion of the desirability and possibility of an International Social Science Year, modeled upon the International Geophysical Year. The material presented at the conference under many of these topics will be discussed in

    [7] Funds for the conference were by grants from the Human Ecology Fund and the Wenner-Gren Foundation, whose assistance is gratefully acknowledged.
    [8] Locations represented and the participants were: *Afghanistan*, Mohammed K. Sarwari, Noor A. Shaker; *Finland*, Matti Haavio, Annika and Martti Takala; *France*, Abraham A. Moles; *Hong Kong*, Anita K. Li; *India*, B. Kuppuswamy, K. G. Rastogi, A. V. and Vijayakumari Shanmugam; *Iran*, Forough Minou-Archer, Shahpour Rassekh, Parvin B. Ziaee; *Japan*, Masaaki Asai, Torao Obonai, Yasumasa Tanaka; *Yugoslavia*, Djordje Kostić, Tomislav Tomeković, Smiljka Vasić, Spasenija Vladislavljević; *Lebanon*, Lutfy N. Diab, Edwin T. Prothro; *Netherlands*, Mathilda J. Jansen; *Sweden*, Ulf Himmelstrand; *Turkey*, Doğan Cüceloğlu, Beğlan B. Toğrol; *United States*, William K. Archer, Howard Bobren, William H. May, Helen K. and Murray S. Miron, Charles E. Osgood, Lawrence M. Stolurow, Harry C. Triandis, Sharon Wolfe.

later sections of this chapter and in those that follow. Many pertinent questions raised and discussed contributed to the analyses to be made of the large mass of data at hand. For example, methodological questions were raised which suggested that adequate samples had not been obtained for certain purposes; new questions were put to the existing data (e.g., analysis of opposites collected in the scale-on-scale tasks).

In an effort to use more fully the wide diversity of talents available and to combine efforts where common interests existed, several sessions were held in which the participants presented their own interests and enlisted the criticism and cooperation of others. At these sessions the emphasis was on research projects to which the Illinois staff might be able to offer facilities, such as computer processing, and act as a clearinghouse for the total group. A breakdown of the major areas of expressed interest showed the following: One group of participants was particularly interested in questions of personality and national self-images. Another area of major interest was in questions concerning the effects of industrialization and urbanization. The role of women in the developing nations was yet another area of shared concern. More traditional psycholinguistic areas, such as language learning (especially as represented in multilingual nations like India and Yugoslavia) and symbolism (visual-verbal synesthesia, color, and phonetic symbolism), were also presented as general interests. Among topics of more specific interest to particular investigators were the following: investigation of culture-specific semantic factors in the already existing data from the concept-on-scale task (an intracultural study); study of problems associated with the teaching of the national languages in the multilingual Indian subcontinent (an intranational problem, but multilingual and thus of cross-cultural interest); studies of political stereotypes and the possibility of measuring political creativity; studies of facial expressions cross-culturally; studies of elites, to be compared with our high school–student samples.

THE TEHERAN CONFERENCE

The second conference which brought together all the colleagues associated with our cross-cultural project was held in Teheran, Iran, in August, 1967. It was attended by 43 persons,[9] most of whom stayed for ten days.

[9] K. G. Agrawal, William Archer, G. B. Flores d'Arcais, Masaaki Asai, Jantorn Buranabanpote, Bhupen Das, Rhea Das, Lutfy Diab, Rogelio Diaz-Guerrero, Suitbert Ertel, Ulf Himmelstrand, Albert Imohiosen, Leon Jakobovits, Mathilda Jansen, Djordje Kostić, B. Kuppuswamy, Jorma Kuusinen, Wilhelm Levelt, John Limber, William Mackey, William May, Forough Minou-Archer, Helen and Murray Miron, Abraham Moles, L. R. Nair, Morteza Nassefat, Torao Obonai, Charles Osgood, Pertti Öunap, K. G. Rastogi, Hubert Rigaux, Adam Sarapata, A. V. Shanmugam, L. C. Singh, A. J. Smolenaars, Martti Takala, Yasumasa Tanaka, Tomislav Tomeković, Harry Triandis, Miss Vahanian, Vasso and George Vassiliou, Sharon Wolfe.

The discussions were kept informal, and because the group was fairly large, smaller groups were formed on the basis of more specialized interests within the overall project. A listing of the discussion topics will give an indication of the diversity of interests that may exist even within such a specialized group: naming and interpretation of the affective factors; the psychological reality of the E-P-A system; the problem of concept-scale interaction; individual differences in factor structure; some problems in the administration of the SD; the *Atlas,* its measures and interpretation; social problems; symbolism and aesthetics; language development; multilingualism; and policy questions of the Center for Comparative Psycholinguistics.

The last-mentioned topic brought together various questions that were raised by our colleagues concerning administrative policy matters of the Center having to do with funding, publication, and interaction within the cross-cultural network. As our colleagues began to take increasing initiative in the formulation and execution of projects, a problem arose concerning the criteria the Illinois staff used to make decisions about their support. Since our funds were limited, it was not always possible to give support to every proposal that our colleagues submitted to us. Apart from the financial issue, a further restriction was imposed on content: only those projects could be supported which were outlined in the proposal for which the Center received its support from the granting agencies. Because many of the projects in that proposal were stated in sufficiently broad terms, our colleagues had the opportunity of making significant contributions to the overall project by working out the details of their implementation from the vantage point of their own culture. A premature commitment to such details in the original proposal would thus have been detrimental to the overall project.

THE MATTERS OF INFORMED CONSENT AND CONFIDENTIALITY

Collection of data relating to subjective culture always involves potential misuse as well as potential invasion of the privacy of the individual. In recent years this has become a public issue in the United States, with a subcommittee of the House of Representatives holding hearings on the use of psychological and other tests. The hearings have raised two salient issues: first, the degree of informed consent that the tested individual should exercise; second, the degree of confidentiality that should be maintained in the use of the collected information. Although the members of the House Subcommittee on Invasion of Privacy were concerned primarily with the rights of individuals, the same ethical issues face cross-national researchers, and perhaps in intensified form.

There are several dilemmas here. Most generally, to what extent does the potential long-term gain to society from scientific knowledge balance out the potential loss of privacy or confidentiality for individuals? Privacy is always a matter of degree, and serious invasion of such privacy probably comes down to possible personal injury. On the other hand, confidentiality of information in the broad sense is anathema to science. For many, if not most, scientific questions, confidentiality of information *about any particular individual* is not even at issue — the individual subject's anonymity can be preserved without in any way hampering the collection and communication of data. This is true of the three studies under consideration.

However, one may raise the issues of privacy and confidentiality of information *with regard to nations* as well as to individuals, and in this form they are very much the concern of people doing cross-national research. Since by the nature of things national privacy and confidentiality of information are incompatible with communication of research results, either formal or informal acceptance of the research activity must be obtained. We have relied on informal acceptance, through mediation of the judgment of our scientific colleagues. In the same spirit we have encouraged them to delete any items or procedures which, in their judgment, would be in any way "sensitive" in terms of moral, political, or other criteria.

The matter of informed consent poses another dilemma: how can one inform subjects of the international nature of the research without biasing their responses? The solution adopted in all three of the studies under consideration was to completely inform the senior colleagues in each country with whom the research was to be conducted but not the individual subjects. The senior colleague, in turn, was primarily responsible for informing and obtaining consent from appropriate persons. In our own case we have no absolute guarantee, of course, that the teen-age subjects were always unaware of the international nature of the research.

PROBLEMS OF INTERPRETATION

It is in the interpretation of the results of cross-national studies that problems of translation come back with a vengeance. Are the differences one finds due to language, due to culture, or simply due to inadequate translation? In our own project we face translation problems in both the "tool-making" and "tool-using" phases, but they are more obvious in the latter, as will be seen in later chapters. Suppose that a particular scale for a particular language/culture community displays a divergence in usage which is surprising (to Westerners, at least). For example, the Kannada scale which translates as *fatty-slim* is simultaneously negative on Evaluation and positive on Potency and Activity — *fatty* thus being full of Malevolent Dynamism for

Indian subjects in Mysore.[10] This, of course, is quite the reverse of feeling-tones about *fatty* for American teen-agers as far as Dynamism is concerned. Does this really indicate a cultural fact about Mysorean culture? Or a linguistic fact about the Kannada language (*fatty* having metaphorical connotations of Badness, Strength, and Activity)? Or do we have here nothing more than a too literal translation of a multi-sense term (analogous perhaps to *square* in American English)? Of course, as is probably the case in this example, *both* cultural and linguistic propositions could be valid; traditionally, the taxes due some maharajas were determined by their weight (literally), and the term *fatty* thereby acquired Malevolent Dynamism, which readily generalized metaphorically. But, again, how are we to be sure in most cases?

There is no easy solution to these problems of interpretation. As Cantril notes, "... no matter how close the correspondence may be between all the factors involved in giving one person an awareness of another person's experience under certain circumstances, he still has to interpret their experience in terms of his own experience" (p. 6). No matter how much Hadley Cantril, Wallace Lambert, Otto Klineberg, or people at our Center for Comparative Psycholinguistics may try to immerse themselves in other cultures, they cannot fully share the experiences, and hence meanings, of natives of those cultures. Investigators into subjective culture cross-nationally are therefore peculiarly prone to *projection* of their own cultural norms, values, and expectations when attempting to interpret their data.

Are there any ways of at least reducing the tendencies toward projection, as far as interpretation of data is concerned? For one thing the investigator should accept the frailties of translation — being persistently suspicious about the "fit" of word-in-A to word-in-B. What looks like cultural ambivalence of Thai subjects toward their brothers may simply reflect the fact that in Thai there is no word for "brother," only "older brother" *or* "younger brother." For another thing, the investigator can continually check his own "natural" interpretations against those of his bilingual *and bicultural* colleagues. Deviations in the affective meaning of "red" (color) for Serbo-Croatian speakers in Yugoslavia may have historical cultural origins, being used by Slavs as a symbol of "love." The investigator can also try to design his research so as to minimize his own linguistic and cultural biases — by reducing dependence upon translation as much as possible, by presenting data in objective forms that can be readily interpreted by others than him-

---

[10] So that interested readers can evaluate the adequacy of translations against their own knowledge of the language in question, in what appear to be critical cases we will give, in footnotes, the translation to the original language or, in the case of non-Roman scripts, the transliteration. The latter can be checked in the *Atlas* for the language, where the rules for transliteration are given. In the present example the scale translated as *fatty-slim* was transliterated from the Kannada script as *kobbidda-badavaadda*.

self, and by ensuring the existence of internal checks and balances, across languages, across cultures, and across contrastive concept sets. None of these things is easy, of course, nor are all of them really sufficient.

WHEN IS THE SAME REALLY THE SAME?

For the social scientist interested in human universals, the most important thing is the demonstration of sameness. Given the surface variations in language and culture, this becomes a very difficult business. Why? Because what is really the same may be expressed quite differently. Of the three projects being used as examples, only our own is primarily concerned with demonstrating universals, so let us see how this has been done. The standard 100 concepts were rated against 50 scales derived indigenously; the pattern of ratings was analyzed factorially to yield the most pervasive dimensions of judgment. In order to interpret these indigenous factors, we had to rely upon translation — but the translations, thankfully, were not of single terms but of entire sets of qualifiers. As translated (usually by our senior colleagues), the first three factors in nearly every language/culture community were identifiable as Evaluation, Potency, and Activity.

Can we avoid the problem of subjective judgment based on translation? To put *n* factorizations in the same space, mathematically, at least one source of variance must be constant — in our case, subjects, concepts, or scales. Subjects are not the same (being from different language/culture communities), and scales are obviously not the same (we get *fatty-slim* from one group, *bloody–not bloody* from another, and so on); but the 100 culture-common concepts are at least closely translation-equivalent.[11] So, in a rather mammoth computer exercise, we relate every scale (regardless of culture origin) to every other scale across the 100 common concepts and determine the common factors. They turn out to be our old friends Evaluation, Potency, and Activity, and in this analysis they are even more sharply defined than before. But what if, as must actually be the case to some degree, the 100 concepts are *not* really translation-equivalent? All this could do is introduce "noise" in our correlations, lower them, and decrease the likelihood of common factors.[12] We interpret this as evidence that the same really *is* the same across human groups as far as the structure of the affective meaning space is concerned.

[11] See p. 70 in Chapter 3 for a discussion of our procedures with respect to translation of these concepts.

[12] In fact, just such a situation did occur quite by accident in an early analysis of some of our cross-linguistic data. Owing to an error in matching, the translation-equivalent nouns in one analysis were all displaced by one item so that each noun was inappropriately matched with another noun of all other languages. The correlation structure which resulted was easily detected as being in error, the preponderance of correlations being near zero.

By virtue of the stratification by age, the Lambert-Klineberg study also makes possible tests of certain hypotheses concerning national stereotypes in children. They report, for example, that "the less diversified the *evaluative* features of a group's description are, the *more* friendly that group is likely to be toward foreign peoples" (p. 173). This tendency increases with age, but not evenly. "There is strong cross-national evidence from our study that children are most inquisitive and friendly toward foreign peoples and most prone to see others as similar at the 10-year age level than at either the 6- or 14-year levels" (p. 225). The Cantril study could only reveal human universals in terms of expressed hopes and fears about self or country. However, as coded, the data of this study reveal *differences* in both hopes and fears primarily as a function of economic status but also as a function of recent political changes.

WHEN IS THE SAME REALLY DIFFERENT?

There are many reasons why what appears to be the same may actually be quite different. The uninterpretable bias of translation may tend to magnify apparent similarities, and so may the rigid standardization of eliciting procedures. We have evidence of this in the fine grain of the common factors in our pancultural factor analysis: Evaluation is defined, in part, by American English-speakers in terms of sensory experiences (e.g., *sweet-sour*), by Lebanese Arabic-speakers in terms of *merciful-cruel*, by Finnish as *light-gloomy*, by Indian Hindi-speakers as *ambrosial-poisonous*, by Japanese as *comfortable-uncomfortable*, by Mexican Spanish-speakers as *friendly-repelling*, and so on.[13] It would appear that the *metaphors* of "good-bad" vary with the cultures under consideration. This in itself is an intriguing research problem — what determines which modes of qualifying will be generally evaluative in different cultures? The level of economic, technological development? The cultural tradition, as revealed in music and poetry? It may be that subtle cultural differences will be revealed in the secondary factors for each community. We already know, for example, that the Japanese have an interesting fourth factor, apparently an aesthetic factor, with high loadings on such scales as *beautiful-ugly, graceful-awkward,* and *delicate-rough.*

We plan to do oblique rotations of the data from each language/culture community in order to determine more clearly the possible uniquenesses of cultural semantic systems. For example, is it true that people in militant societies (over a prolonged period of time) tend to fuse Evaluation, Potency, and Activity factors into a single "benevolent dynamism" vs. "malevolent

---

[13] *Merciful-cruel: rahim-zalim; light-gloomy: valoisa-synkkä; ambrosial-poisonous: rritmay-hahriilaa; comfortable-uncomfortable: kokoroyoi-fukaina; friendly-repelling: simpático-antipático.*

listlessness" factor? Do different cultures abstract from their common Evaluation factor different aspects for stress — aesthetic goodness, social goodness, moral goodness? And do these semantic characteristics relate in any way to the characteristics of national behavior? Moving to the meanings of particular concepts, the entire purpose of our *Atlas of Affective Meanings* (the first "tool-using" study) is to delineate differences in the affective meanings of concepts which are translation-equivalent for different culture groups. The American politician who uses the concept FUTURE with his own Good, Strong, Active affect might fail to communicate this intention when he talks to an audience in Finland, where FUTURE is Good and Strong, but Passive.

Cantril was well aware that often in his study what appears to be the same may be quite different. "It should also be made clear that no claims are made that the Self-Anchoring Striving Scale gets at 'everything' it is important to know about an individual . . . individuals do not mention aspects of life they take for granted — thus, for example, American college students tend not to mention a high standard of living, which they assume they will have, but on the other hand will talk about the place in society they want to attain or how they measure up to their own standards" (p. 25). In other words, the implications and behavioral correlates of "good" and of "bad" for self and country vary markedly with what one "has" (or "has not") at the moment. For Cantril's purposes this was largely irrelevant, but the differences in frame of reference remain as culturally significant facts despite the (measured) indication of sameness.

WHEN IS DIFFERENT REALLY THE SAME?

When the investigator has woven his way through the intricacies of translation — both in input instructions and in output data — he has usually become acutely aware of the possibility that what appear as differences may actually be samenesses. The various metaphors of *good-bad* in our own research, as described above, illustrate the point. Although such scales as *sweet-sour, merciful-cruel, light-gloomy, ambrosial-poisonous,* and *friendly-repelling* are denotatively quite distinct, they are used affectively in the same way and represent a common "evaluative" factor. Nevertheless, the fact that the scales *do* have different denotation despite their common affective components means that they may be used literally with certain relevant concepts, producing what we call "concept-scale interaction." Thus for a few concepts (e.g., LEMON, COCA-COLA, SUGAR) the English "evaluative" scale *sweet-sour* will be used denotatively; such possibilities must be checked in making interpretations.

The Cantril self-anchoring scale is a case where differences (in the hopes and fears which provide the anchoring) are explicitly presumed to yield samenesses (in where one locates himself and his country on the ladder).

Thus it is assumed that a shift from present to future locations by Cubans of nearly 2.0 steps as compared with a shift of only 1.0 for Americans does mean a higher level of aspiration for the Cubans, even though much of *what* they aspire for may already be taken for granted by Americans. Lambert and Klineberg report that Turkish, American, English Canadian, German, Israeli, and Bantu children make relatively frequent use of the response "a person" to the "What are you?" question, whereas Japanese, French Canadian, French, Lebanese, and Brazilian children give this response relatively rarely. Does this represent "cultural variations in the privileges and rights granted children" as the authors speculate (p. 95), or are linguistic factors at play? Is the Japanese translation equivalent for "person," for example, a homonym for the term for nationality, and hence does it get coded in the latter category (the Japanese do happen to have the highest usage of the latter category)? Is the semantic sphere for the French translation equivalent of "person" restricted to legally mature individuals? We take it for granted that Lambert and Klineberg, being sophisticated in matters linguistic, have considered these possibilities and eliminated them, but such questions illuminate the problems of interpretation.

Where scaled data are available, as in our case, the question always arises as to whether the investigator should use actual or standardized scores. The first alternative assumes that by virtue of standardized procedures, carefully adapted instructions, and selection of factorially equivalent dimensions, any constant biases that appear are faithful reflections of real cultural differences and should not be masked by any data transformation. The second alternative assumes that such constant biases are errors of measurement owing to any of the many pitfalls we have treated here and, if not removed, will create illusory cultural differences which in fact do not exist. One feature of our semantic *Atlas* data will serve to illustrate this dilemma. For each of some 600 concepts from each community we compute E (Evaluation), P (Potency), and A (Activity) composite scores, based upon the four highest-loading scales for that community in the global pancultural factor analysis. It turns out that for Hindi speakers the Activity scores are markedly biased toward the negative — that is, most concepts are judged Passive to some degree. Is this a valid reflection of the Hindi "world view," or is it perhaps due to the fact that among the Hindi Activity scales there is a *gay-sober* scale,[14] and most concepts would be viewed as somewhat more sober (serious?) than gay by any language/culture community? The only solution we can see to this problem is to include *both* types of data in the *Atlas:* actual scores to permit interpretation of possible cultural constants and standardized scores (about the mean of the composite factor scores, defined as neutrality) to permit interpretation of *relative* degrees of favorableness, potency, and activity of concepts across cultures.

[14] Transliteration from Hindi script: *cancal-gambhiir.*

WHEN IS DIFFERENT REALLY DIFFERENT?

This is the question to which most cross-national researchers have addressed themselves. The immediate answer — "when they are not really the same" — may be obvious, but it is not very helpful. A somewhat more adequate answer is that differences which remain after procedural, sampling, and translation equivalences have been assured can be attributed to differences in semantics and/or culture with reasonable confidence. But one can go a bit further than this. First, he may look for *congruent patterns of differences* within his own data. Isolated deviations, even though of considerable magnitude, are usually uninterpretable. Second, he may look for *correlations with other studies,* indicating consistency of the differences noted with the larger body of cross-cultural information. Third, he may check the differences observed against *knowledge of the culture in question.* This last procedure obviously involves the help of sensitive and sophisticated people who are both bilingual and bicultural — again, often one's senior colleagues in cross-national research.

If, for example, one finds that evaluation regularly favors the feminine members of minimal pairs (e.g., HUSBAND-WIFE, MALE-FEMALE, BOY-GIRL, BROTHER-SISTER, etc.) in one group but regularly favors the masculine members in another, then the inference for a real cultural difference is strengthened. Occasionally an isolated fact can be interpreted by a bicultural colleague. An example of this occurred when we reported at an international conference that, for no reason we could fathom, the concept WEDNESDAY was neutral for most communities but highly favorable in Holland and Belgium. Professor Duijker of the University of Amsterdam, chairman of the symposium, pointed out that Wednesday happened to be the one weekday when school children had the afternoon off in Holland and Belgium! Similarly, the relatively high evaluation of cow in India is no surprise. The use of correlation with data outside one's own research is neatly illustrated in the Lambert-Klineberg study. They observed great variation across countries in the frequency of "student" as a response to the question "What are you?" Since 9 of the 11 countries had also been included in McClelland's (1961) study of need for achievement, a correlation could be run; the correlation between frequency of identifying oneself as "student" and McClelland's need-for-achievement rating proved to be .60, significant at the 5% level.

How *much* of a difference makes a difference? This is more than a question of statistics. If the data from a cross-national study are quantitative and lend themselves to statistical manipulation, then the investigator should ask himself formally whether the differences observed are reasonably beyond chance. But statistical significance in itself provides no safeguard against the hazards of biases in sampling, translation, and the like. Nor is it true that all differences which are statistically significant are psychologically or culturally significant. For example, in our *Atlas* data we can show that concepts like LOVE, MOTHER, PLEASURE, FRIEND, FREEDOM, and PEACE are universally favorable and significantly different in evaluation from concepts like PAIN, DANGER, CRIME, SNAKE, POISON, and WAR — but this is hardly exciting. Similarly, Cantril finds that Americans are more concerned with their personal health or illness than most other people, and Lambert and Klineberg find that Bantu children see themselves as less similar to all other groups tested, most of whom were non-Negro, and most often mention their race in answer to the question "What are you?" — clearly significant differences, but hardly surprising. Of course, the fact that a datum is readily interpretable (and in that sense noninformative or scientifically trivial) does not eliminate it from the realm of cultural facts.

In the last analysis, differences which are most likely to make a difference in cross-national social science are those which test hypotheses. These may be derived from general theories about the bases of human universals and human uniquenesses. They may also be derived from culturological theories (social psychological, sociological, economic, political). The data of each of the projects discussed in this chapter can be entered, categorized, and analyzed so as to test a wide variety of hypotheses. For example, in the Cantril data the differences in past, present, and future "ladder" ratings could be analyzed to test hypotheses about the independence or dependence of satisfaction and aspiration upon economic well-being. The Lambert-Klineberg data could be analyzed to test hypotheses about the relation of child-rearing practices to other-directed hostility or affection. Our *Atlas* data could be categorized and analyzed to test hypotheses about differences in the world views of "have," "transitional," and "have-not" peoples.[15]

In this chapter we have tried to put our own cross-cultural project on human meaning systems into perspective — by comparing it with two other large-scale cross-cultural investigations of subjective culture and by using all three to illuminate some of the problems faced in all cross-national research. This exploration of cross-national research problems in general has also served, we hope, to orient the reader to our own research and introduce him to the rationale, procedures, analyses, and applications which will be treated in greater detail in the chapters which follow.

[15] Professor Rogelio Diaz-Guerrero, our senior colleague in Mexico, is designing just such a study.

CHAPTER

2

Rationale and Background of the Research

THE SYSTEMATIC CROSS-CULTURAL and cross-linguistic investigation described in this book was based upon a decade of research — 1950 through 1960 — on the nature and measurement of meaning. This work was done primarily in the United States, utilizing as subjects American English-speakers who were participants in the American version of Western culture. For the most part these subjects were the usual "college sophomore," but this nonrepresentativeness did not concern us because most of the work during this decade dealt with methodological problems. *The Measurement of Meaning* (Osgood, Suci, and Tannenbaum, 1957) summarizes this research up to the date of its publication. A paper titled "Studies on the Generality of Affective Meaning Systems" (Osgood, 1962) brings the picture more nearly up to date and introduces the cross-cultural work.

In social science, where measurement techniques are added and discarded from the armamentorium with amazing alacrity and where fashion often rules the paths of inquiry, it is gratifying that the semantic differential (SD) technique has so far outlived its initial rush of acceptance as a fad. Actually, it labored under a double handicap. First, it could be construed as simply another opinion-scaling device, coupled only remotely to a theoretical rationale. Second, it required reference to and some understanding of multivariate, factorial models. The latter handicap alone might well have been sufficient

First draft prepared by Murray S. Miron and Charles E. Osgood. Portions of this chapter appeared, in modified form, as Ch. 27 of Raymond Cattell, ed., *Handbook of multivariate psychology* (Chicago: Rand McNally, 1966), pp. 790-819.

to ensure stillbirth, since experimental psychologists have traditionally viewed with distrust the multivariate methods in general and the factor-analytic models in particular. They have viewed with equal distrust mentalistic notions like "meaning." Nevertheless, the technique seems to be gaining a reasonably secure place in the growing nomological network of psycholinguistic theory.[1]

The goal of this chapter is to review the theory and methodology of the SD technique, qua technique, before the cross-cultural and cross-linguistic studies which constitute the heart of this book are reported. No attempt will be made to survey all of the research employing the SD; instead, only those investigations which appear to shed light on the logic and validity of the method as a means of defining the dimensionality of semantic qualification will be treated in any detail.

A HYPOTHETICAL SEMANTIC SPACE

Try to imagine a space of some unknown number of dimensions. (We realize this is impossible for organisms inhabiting a three-dimensional universe!) This will be our hypothetical semantic space, and we can explore it by drawing an analogy with the more familiar color space. Like all respectable mathematical spaces, this one is assumed to have an origin, which we define as complete "meaninglessness" (analogous to the neutral grey center of the color space). The meaning of a sign can be conceived as some point in this n-dimensional space and can thus be represented by a vector from the origin to that point: the length of this vector would index the "degree of meaningfulness" of this sign (like saturation in the color space), and its direction would index the "semantic quality" of this sign (analogous to both hue and brightness in the color space).

To talk about "direction" in any space requires that we have some reference coordinates. Again the analogy with the color space will serve. Just as complementary colors are defined as points equidistant and in opposite directions from the origin in the color space, which when mixed together in equal proportions cancel each other to neutral grey, so may we conceive of verbal opposites as defining straight lines through the origin of the semantic space. Lexicographers assure us that true verbal opposites do cancel each other semantically, component for component, when "mixed." Imagine now a whole set of different straight-line "cuts" through the semantic space, each passing through the origin and each defined by a pair of opposites. In order to discover the location of concept X in this space, we might play a game of "Twenty Questions" with our subject: it is *beautiful,* not *ugly* (cut no. 1) ;

---

[1] A recent book of readings includes 52 papers and a bibliography of nearly 1,500 references relevant to the technique: J. G. Snider and C. E. Osgood, eds., *Semantic differential technique: A sourcebook* (Chicago: Aldine, 1969).

it is *soft,* not *hard* (cut no. 2) ; it is *quick,* not *slow* (cut no. 3) ; and so forth. If these "cuts" were at right angles to each other, and hence independent, then each such binary decision would reduce uncertainty about the location of *x* by half. Or, if each straight-line "cut" were scaled into seven discriminable steps, as we have done in our work, then each decision would reduce uncertainty of location by six-sevenths, and only three "cuts" would yield a space of 343 discrete regions.

But the assumption of independence (orthogonality) of dimensions demands justification, of course, and we still have the problem of reference coordinates. Is the up-down, north-south, and east-west of the semantic space to be completely arbitrary, or is there some "natural" organizing principle of this space analogous to the gravitational and magnetic determinants of geophysical space? The logical tool for answering such a question about semantic spaces is some variant of factor analysis. We need to take a large and representative sample of qualitative dimensions defined by verbal opposites, determine their intercorrelations when used by subjects in differentiating the meanings of a representative sample of concepts, and then see if in fact they do fall into "natural" clusters which can serve to direct the location of reference coordinates.

Those sensitive to the subtle nuances of qualification that languages provide for their speakers may not be very sanguine about the prospects for discovering such structure in natural languages. The hope is that certain gross and universal features of meaning can be isolated in this fashion, even though many fine distinctions may be obscured. Again, the color system provides an ideal case. Although, as we know, colors come in a bewildering variety of shades, it happens to be the case that all of these shades can be exactly characterized by reference to only three physical attributes — hue, saturation, and brightness. Assuming only 50 degrees of discriminable variation along each of these three dimensions, their combinations would still yield in excess of 100,000 discriminably different shades.

In at least some respects the adjectives of English do seem to behave like colors. For example, combination of an adjective with its opposite typically has the effect of canceling the imports of the terms taken separately, just as the additive mixture of complementary hues yields neutral grey. As will be evident in our data, native speakers of diverse languages appear to have little difficulty in agreeing upon what the opposites of familiar adjectives are. Linguistically, we can identify adjectival opposites by the fact that they are mutually substitutable in most utterances. For every statement that contains one of a pair of adjectives there is at least a theoretically opposite utterance containing its opposite. For every *strong* man, building, drink, or point, a *weak* counterpart is available. Not so with pairs like *good* and *lazy,* as can readily be seen by the semantic anomalies which result when these two terms are substituted for *strong* and *weak* in the above sets.

Although colors exist in continuously variable gradations, color adjectives are quite small in number, and even descriptive phrases like *pea green* and *brownish orange* provide a very restricted set of distinctions. This restriction is probably due to the limitations of human memory for distinctive coding; it is certainly not due to the visual apparatus per se. This is true for qualification generally. The adjectives in even a very large lexicon provide only a sketchy coverage of the total domain of possible discriminations. But, of course, even this sketchy coverage involves a very large absolute number of semantic distinctions. Nonetheless, it still may be the case, as with colors, that a *relatively* small number of basic dimensional attributes (or semantic features) of the adjectives will serve to characterize their multitudinous diversity.

Therefore, let us pursue a bit further the analogy of an *n*-dimensional meaning space with the more familiar three-dimensional color space. Each adjective of the language specifies some particular locus of the possible variations in meaning encompassed by the entire space, just as each color specifies a particular variation of the chromatic visual stimulus. The closer two adjectives lie within this space, the more nearly similar their meanings. Just as red and orange would be expected to lie closer in the color space than red and blue, so we should expect that *good* and *nice* would be in closer proximity than *good* and *heavy*. But how are we to systematize our intuitions about such meaningful similarities? The answer is deceptively simple. We inquire of the speakers of the language whether or not they would judge a large set of concepts to be appropriately qualified by the same set of adjective terms. If many speakers agree that MOTHERS may appropriately be said to be *good, nice,* and *gentle* and that FOOTBALL PLAYERS (by some, e.g., high school co-eds) are said to be *good, nice,* and *rough,* we are well on the way to a specification of the fact that the language exhibits more similarity between *good* and *nice* than between each of these terms and *gentle.* If we extend this approach to a large list of noun concepts and adjectives and allow gradations of degree of qualification, such as *extremely good* and *slightly nice,* we have what has been called the semantic differential technique. The degree to which subjects choose and rate the same adjective terms as appropriate to the list of concepts establishes the degree of intercorrelation between those terms in the language the subject employs.

A MEASUREMENT MODEL

Now let us look at one possible measurement model — not the only one, by any means. In the semantic differential task a subject judges a series of concepts (e.g., MY MOTHER, THE CHINESE, MODERN ART) against a series of bipolar seven-step scales defined by verbal opposites (e.g., *good-bad, strong-weak, fast-slow, fair-unfair,* etc.). Concepts may be rotated against scales in a continuous form, or more usually (and more satisfying to subjects, apparently), a single concept may be placed at the top of a page and judged successively against a series of scales:

MY FATHER

*good*___:___:___:___:___:___:___*bad*
*weak*___:___:___:___:___:___:___*strong*

etc.

On the basis of early research, seven steps seem to be an optimum degree of discrimination for rapid yet reasonably reliable judging. We assume that subjects perform a very quick succession of two types of decision. (1) Is the concept (noun, substantive) characterized by the properties of one as opposed to the other of a pair of adjectives or not characterized distinctively by either of them; e.g., is a BABY *large* or *small* for the class of human organisms or neutral in this respect? (2) If not neutral, to what degree is it characterized by the properties of the adjective in question; e.g., is a BABY *slightly small, quite small,* or *extremely small* for the class of human organisms? These particular quantifiers have been shown by Norman Cliff (1959) to yield approximately equal increments in intensity, with *quite* having a unitary multiplier effect (i.e., equal to an unquantified adjective). Combining a point of neutrality, or nondifferentiation, with two qualifiers (directions) and three quantifiers (degrees) thus yields the seven-step scale, e.g., *extremely large* ($+3$), *quite large* ($+2$), *slightly large* ($+1$), *neutral with respect to relative size* (0), *slightly small* (-1), *quite small* (-2), and *extremely small* (-3).[2]

It might be noted in passing that the SD technique shares with nearly all other approaches used by linguists (e.g., Zellig Harris, 1954) and philosophers (e.g., Zeno Vendler, 1967) dependence on rules of usage, or distribution, in determining similarity and difference in meaning. Each item as checked by a subject on an SD form is, in effect, a little sentence he has produced — "Babies are quite small," "The color red is extremely active," "Tornados are extremely unfair" — given the available lexical material in the item. All such "sentences" have the same implicit structure — "N be Q A." Two

[2] The usual instructions with the SD technique define the midpoint of scales as "equally X and Y" (MOST PEOPLE, *tall-short*), "either X or Y" (SPONGE, *wet-dry*), or "neither X nor Y, or irrelevant" (BOULDER, *happy-sad*), since these are all logical possibilities. However, in the cross-cultural studies described in this book we emphasized only the neutrality notion of "equally X and Y" so as to encourage the use of metaphorical judgments by our teen-age subjects in different cultures. We were afraid that otherwise they might only use other than midpoint (0) judgments for denotatively relevant items like FIRE, *hot-cold* (but not DEFEAT, *hot-cold*), and JUDGE, *fair-unfair* (but not TORNADO, *fair-unfair*).

adjectives will be similar in meaning to the extent that they display the same patterns of usage across the set of nouns; two nouns will be similar in meaning to the extent that their usage with respect to adjectives and quantifiers is the same; and we can even speak of two subjects as having similar semantic systems to the extent that their patterns of "sentences" are the same.

It should also be noted, however, that SD instructions require subjects to rate *all* items, i.e., to produce "sentences" for all combinations of substantives with qualifiers. This means that in a large proportion of cases our native speakers are encouraged to create "sentences" that — literally speaking, in their own ordinary languages — would be semantically anomalous and therefore unlikely to actually appear in any corpus. Literally speaking, a TORNADO cannot be either *fair* or *unfair* (only humans can have these attributes), and subjects ought to judge the item as irrelevant by checking the zero position on the scale. The fact of the matter is that nearly all native English-speakers, *working under SD conditions,* judge TORNADO to be *extremely unfair.* This characteristic of the SD technique — the way it forces the use of metaphors — turns out to be highly significant both for its power to reveal affective universals and for its limitation in revealing other types of semantic features. We will return to this matter in a final, theoretical chapter.

The details of SD procedures and typical instructions, as well as procedural experiments comparing alternative methods, are available in *The Measurement of Meaning* and will not be repeated here. However, as emphasized in this earlier book and worth re-emphasizing here, there is nothing sacred about any particular set of concepts or scales (except for specialized purposes, of course). That is why there is, contrary to some people's expectations, no such thing as "*the* Semantic Differential" as a particular test but, rather, only a "Semantic Differential Technique." As will become clear in our cross-cultural work, essentially the same kind of (affective) information about concepts can be obtained from sets of scales that are not even translation equivalents of each other.

When a group of people judge a set of concepts against a set of adjectival scales, a cube of data is generated. Such a cube is illustrated in Figure 2:1. The rows of this cube are defined by the scales, the columns by the concepts being judged, and the "slices" from front to back by the subjects doing the judging. Each cell represents with a single value how a particular subject rates a particular concept against a particular scale. In analyzing such data, we are usually — but not necessarily — interested in the correlations among the scales. We may correlate them across subjects or across concepts or both; we may collapse the subject dimension of the cube when we are interested in "cultural meanings"; we may run separate analyses for single subjects, single concepts, or classes of either, correlating across concepts to get at subject semantic spaces and across subjects to get at concept semantic spaces. In

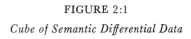

FIGURE 2:1

Cube of Semantic Differential Data

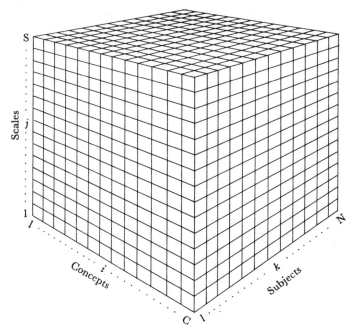

other words, there are many ways one can slice this semantic cake, each appropriate for answering a different kind of question.

Data cubes produced by SD technique contain a great deal of information. How can such information be most economically described? Fortunately, factor analysis is available as a statistical technique for discovering the dimensional structure of a content domain for which the structure is unknown on *a priori* grounds. From the patterns of the intercorrelations among a finite but large number of characteristics of the domain of interest, we infer the existence of a basic set of dimensions whose combinations could give rise to all of the observed variations. For example, on intuitive grounds alone, it is easy to see that if two characteristics of the items of a context domain always yield the same quantity, as would be the case for the measurement of characteristics A and B of Figure 2:2, we may safely discard one of the characteristics as redundant in the unique specification of the domain.[3] If,

[3] The technique does not give us any clue as to which characteristic should be discarded. Much of the misunderstanding about factor analysis stems from the belief that we will retain the "true" characteristic, that we would somehow maintain A of the diagram rather than B. The hope is unwarranted. Both are merely representatives of a more abstract property of the domain in question.

FIGURE 2:2

Model of a Three-Mode Data Sample

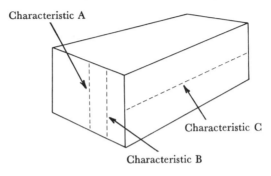

Characteristic A

Characteristic C

Characteristic B

however, we were to observe a characteristic which never gave us any knowledge of any other characteristic, if the characteristic never systematically varied with any other characteristic, as C in the figure theoretically behaves with respect to A or B, it should be equally clear that such a characteristic supplies us with valuable new information about the objects being measured.

Since our research depends heavily on the technique of factor analysis, a word may be in order at this point about the conditions under which factor analysis may be employed as a hypothesis-testing device. Factor analysis is usually viewed as a quantitative exploratory device with which one can reproduce the interrelationships among a relatively large number of variables in terms of a relatively small number of constructs, or factors, and hence arrive at a more efficient description. This, in part, is the problem we have here — we want to reduce the apparent multiplicity of dimensions in terms of affective meanings to a relatively small number of basic dimensions in terms of which we can then construct an efficient measuring device. It has been argued that factor analysis is not a hypothesis-testing technique because the factors one derives are essentially arbitrary, depending on the methods of factoring and rotating and on the particular sample of subjects and variables. This is certainly true of any single factor analysis. But one can test the hypothesis of generality or stability of a particular factorial description of a domain by replication, *provided that the replicated samples of subjects and variables are independent of the original sampling* (although necessarily within the same domain). This is the kind of hypothesis testing that we have done with replicated factor analyses, using different subjects, different sets of concepts, and different samples of scales. It has also been said that all one gets out of a factor analysis is what he puts in. This is true of any method. Just as one can select subjects so as to make any hypothesis seem to come out in univariate experiments, so can one select nearly synonymous variables in terms of some *a priori* hypothesis in factor analysis so as to make the same structure appear. The safeguard in both cases lies in adhering to rigorously defined sampling procedures which are independent of the results that have been obtained in the past or are expected to be obtained in the future.

EARLY EXPLORATORY STUDIES

Three primary studies served as the earliest basis for the conclusion that a stable and low-rank structure could be attributed to the qualifier domain of American English. These analyses, originally reported in *The Measurement of Meaning,* had as their basic goal the sampling of the adjectives of English and the discovery of a structure, if such existed.

ANALYSIS I

In the first of these analyses, qualifier terms were elicited from a large group of subjects as responses to a small number of stimuli selected from the Kent-Rosanoff word list in a restricted word-association task. The domain of generality in this analysis was restricted to those qualifiers found to have highest frequency of occurrence as responses to the aggregate stimulus set. The 50 highest-frequency qualifiers were chosen and opposites selected for each in order to construct contrastive attribute dimensions. Since the sampling was therefore nonrandom, it is necessary to justify the reasons for so restricting the sample to high-frequency qualifiers. Although no justification was given in this early analysis, the rationale is certainly both clear and sound. Other investigators have gathered evidence which indicates that the frequency of emission of a lexical unit will be isomorphic with the frequency of experience with that unit (see Underwood and Schultz, 1960). This means simply that the responses of a group of subjects will tend to reflect the general frequency of usage of items in a language. Granting this rather reasonable assumption, at least one possible strategy is to limit the domain of generality of a factorial structure to those items which have high frequency of usage and thus presumptively to those items which are the most productive in the linguistic sense. (Other possible choices in sampling strategies for qualifiers will be discussed later in this chapter.)

Since the purpose of these early analyses was to determine the existence and nature of a structure in the adjective domain, the concept sample was arbitrarily selected and assumed to be fixed. It remained for later analyses to determine whether the structure would be invariant under changing concept and subject samples. The results of this first analysis indicated that the first three centroid-qualifier factors following orthogonal rotation accounted for approximately 50% of the total subject × concept variance.[4]

---

[4] In all of the analyses of this section unities are used in lieu of communality estimates, and each subject-concept combination is treated as a separate observation.

These factors were interpretatively labeled Evaluation, Potency, and Activity. The remaining factors had small variance contributions and were arbitrarily discarded.

ANALYSIS II

Since it could be argued that the factor structure obtained in Analysis I was limited to the universe of qualifiers applicable to only those concepts chosen, it follows as a next logical step that the investigators should vary the concept sample, holding the qualifier and subject samples constant. If the structure could be replicated, the subject sample could then be varied in order to determine the influence of this further source of variation. Instead, the investigators chose to vary both subject and concept variables simultaneously. This strategy could lead to equivocal interpretations if the structures were not replicated, but it would be efficient if the same structure were in fact obtained. However, it should be pointed out that the subject samples were highly similar and presumably equivalent even if not identical (college sophomores).

The "concepts" in this second analysis were qualifier terms themselves. Each of the 50 attribute scales was judged against all remaining scales in a dichotomous rating task. The subjects were required to select that one term of the contrastive scale qualifiers which was judged to "go best with" the arbitrarily picked first term of the "concept" qualifiers. It was assumed that all qualifier scales were in perfect opposition and that accordingly the judgment of one term determined the judgment of the second without need for testing.[5] The matrix of percentage judgments was factored by applying the diagonal method directly to the raw scores. Since the raw scores already reflected the degree of interrelatedness of the scale items, the method yields results which reflect the degree of similarity in the patterns of interrelatedness. A number of criteria indicated that the results of the first and second analyses were sufficiently alike to accept the structures as being equivalent. As before, the dimensions of Evaluation, Potency, and Activity, in that order, were identified and found to account for roughly similar percentages of the total variance.

ANALYSIS III

The third analysis attempted to increase the generality of the previous findings by more adequately sampling the range of possible qualification modes in the language. It is a truism that the structures obtained in a factor analysis cannot adequately summarize the domain of application if the full diversity of the domain is not at least potentially represented. Accordingly, if the di-

[5] This may not have been a fully justifiable assumption; see Green and Goldfried (1965).

mensions isolated are to be interpreted as those salient for the entire domain, all potential dimensions should have equal or proportionate chance of representation in the samples chosen. Roget's *Thesaurus* represents a unique attempt on the part of one lexicographer to stratify analytically the domain of the meanings of words in English, and it was to this source that the investigators turned for their sample of qualifiers. Because of computer limitations at that time, of the 289 contrastive adjective pairs selected from the categories in *Thesaurus,* 76 pairs were finally retained after a series of subject and investigator judgmental procedures. The primary basis for scale selection in this case was representativeness within the semantic domain (as defined by Roget) ; within the sample of categories thus determined, a secondary criterion for selecting particular qualifiers was, again, frequency of usage or familiarity. Thus this analysis, like those preceding, can be said conservatively to apply only to the domain of high-frequency modes of qualification. Nonetheless, as indicated earlier, the logic of generalization to high-frequency qualification is sound and reasonable as a first approach to characterizing the structure of qualification in a language. However, as was pointed out at the time, the sensitivity to fine semantic distinctions of the accomplished speaker of English is, of course, hopelessly lost in the lowest common denominator of a structure discoverable for words any ten-year-old can understand.

In this analysis the ratings of 100 college students for each of 20 heterogeneous concepts, different from those of the previous analyses, were intercorrelated for all scale pairs. Each of the subject-by-concept ratings was considered a unique judgment. Two factoring procedures were employed in this analysis: (a) centroid and (b) diagonal with forced pivots. Only the latter analysis is reported in detail in *The Measurement of Meaning,* and it leaves much to be desired. The pivots chosen by the investigators on the grounds of maximum independence were the scales *good-bad, hard-soft,* and *active-passive,* qualifiers also maximally identified with factors discovered in the previous analyses. Although the factor coefficients reported for these scales indicated that it was possible to establish an orthogonal coordinate system of three dimensions when the structure was forced to conform to these pivots, the percentage of variance accounted for by these forced dimensions is not sufficiently high to establish unequivocal confidence in a conclusion that the same dimensions as in the previous analyses were being identified. (A re-analysis of these data is presented later.)

Table 2:1 displays the percentages of variance for each of these analyses extracted by the first three dimensions. It will be seen that the forced-pivot analysis (Analysis III) accounted for only about three-fifths of the total variance extracted by the same factors of the other two analyses. Thus, insofar as the sampling procedure tended to represent more of the potential dimensions of the adjective domain, the percentage of variance accounted for by the previously discovered high-frequency dimensions is not accounted for

TABLE 2:1

Percentage of Total Variance Extracted by the Identified Factors of Each Analysis

FACTOR NUMBER	FACTOR IDENTIFICATION	ANALYSIS NUMBER		
		I	II	III
1	Evaluation	34%	29%	16%
2	Potency	8	10	7
3	Activity	6	5	5
	Total	48%	44%	28%

in this third analysis. On the other hand, the variance duplicated in this analysis indicates that the earlier dimensions are present, even if having less importance when the entire domain, rather than only the high-frequency subdomain, is under consideration. Of course, it should be observed that the culling procedures employed in this analysis, in which adjectives of lower familiarity in a Roget classification already represented were deliberately discarded, would tend to reduce the weights of all specific factors.

A study by Ware (1958) is relevant here. If the structure discovered in these three analyses is linguistically primitive, in the sense of being organismically basic,[6] then it should be the case that this structure would not differentiate among the nonprimitive aspects of linguistic behavior. Ware addressed himself to this problem by inquiring whether the semantic structures of the highly intelligent could be distinguished from those of lesser intelligence. Separate factor analyses were performed for individual subjects judging the same concepts against the same scales. None of six measures of the diversity of the structures of the semantic spaces was found to relate to intelligence, even though all six were highly reliable and differentiated among individuals. For example, the average cumulative percentage of total variance accounted for by the first three centroid factors of 15 individuals with IQ scores 120 or above was 48.3; for 18 individuals with IQ scores 93 or below, the average percentage was 49.8. An average of 5.9 factors was required to account for 70% of the total variance for the high IQ subjects and an average of 5.8 factors for the low IQ subjects. Clearly, then, whatever else the semantic structure is reflecting, it does not seem to be a correlate of variables associated with intelligence.

In a very real sense, however, it is precisely this lack of sensitivity to intellectual variables — the basic and primitive nature of the dominant factors revealed in SD measurement — which leads to the hope that this semantic structure may be generalizable beyond a single culture or linguistic community. These early factorial studies, then, lead to the conclusion that a reasonably stable structure of qualification will be found whenever qualifiers are sampled which are applicable to, and frequently used with, heterogeneous

[6] Further discussion of this matter will be found in Chapter 7, pp. 394-396.

concept terms. These findings led us to begin probing the limits of the generality of this structure across both subject and concept domains — but before tracing this course we must take up some statistical matters.

FACTOR ANALYSIS OF SD DATA

The SD technique generates a three-dimensional data cube containing observations on each of N subjects rating each of C concepts on each of S scales. Analyzed in terms of Abelson's (1960) formulation, concepts are the objects of discrimination, the scale items are the modes of discrimination, and the subjects are the agents of discrimination. The conventional factor-analytic models can only be applied to two-way classification data matrices. Consequently, the investigator was forced to somehow collapse the three-classification SD data into two modes. A number of statistical strategies for reduction of the classifications are available.

Two-Mode Solutions

Stringing out. The first of these, and the one consistently employed by Osgood, Suci, and Tannenbaum in the three analyses just reported, is to string out the observations on each subject-by-concept combination as unique observations. By opting for this procedure, the investigators were placed in the position of being unable to disentangle the subject variance from the concept variance supposedly being explained by the scale structure. Accordingly, the qualifier dimensions discovered in these analyses can be interpreted as describing either or both the concept and subject variances, depending upon the contributions to the total variance made by each. If the subject variance, as is implicitly assumed, is small or zero, the structures are then, and only then, attributable to an underlying organization of qualifiers as applied to concept terms.

Summation. The second procedure employs some variant of a summation strategy. The investigator chooses the one classification mode which is of least interest and collapses the data cube into two dimensions by taking sums across the unimportant dimension. Since subjects are usually considered to be the instruments for assessing concept differences on scale items, and thus to contribute only to instrument errors, typically the investigator sums over the individual subject replications. As in the first procedure, the subject $\times$ concept variance is unassessed and must be assumed to be negligible in order to assign the resulting structure to the action of the scale agent in concept discrimination.

Average correlation. A third procedure, although a variant of the summation procedure, is sufficiently different in computation to warrant separate discussion. In this procedure scale correlation matrices are obtained for each of the concept replications on each subject and then averaged over the N subjects. Thus the mode reduction is obtained by calculating a series of N-scale intercorrelation matrices which are averaged to obtain a single two-dimensional scale matrix. If the correlation matrices entering into this average vary greatly from individual to individual, the same difficulties in interpretation of the final structure accrue to this method as to the others.

Thus in all instances it is necessary to assess the amount of variance contributing to the total observed score which is attributable to each of the classification modes if one is to make unequivocal statements about the structure of any single mode. Several empirical studies provide evidence about the magnitude of the subject variation in the semantic differential task.

In 1963 in the first of these studies Ware utilized 40 personality concepts as rated by 20 subjects (10 married couples) on 40 personality-relevant semantic scales. The data were analyzed by separately computing the correlations between each scale pair for each subject as in the average correlation procedure discussed above. However, instead of averaging these intercorrelations, the cross-products of the corresponding cells of each pair of the 40 × 40 scale matrices were computed. These cross-products formed a new matrix of order 20 summarizing the degree of similarity in the patterns of scale intercorrelations used by each of the 20 subjects. If all subjects had identical patterns of intercorrelations among the 40 scales, the sum of these cross-products would be maximal and a factor analysis of the cross-products matrix would reveal a single subject factor. The results of a factor analysis of these cross-products, in fact, revealed a first dimension which accounted for 63% of the total variance and a second factor which accounted for only 5% of the remaining total variance, with subsequent factors diminishing as expected. Thus, at least for these data, we may conclude that the subject mode has an essentially unifactorial composition and, therefore, that the strategies for collapsing that dimension are justified.

Still another way to assess the contribution of subject variance to the structure of qualification is to compare the results of factor analyses of the data matrices collapsed by means of the summation and stringing-out procedures. If the comparison is made using the same data matrix for both procedures, whatever change in structure is observed can be attributed to the subject variation. Table 2:2 A and B summarizes the structures obtained by these two procedures. The data are taken from Analysis III of the previous section. The factor coefficients for A and B are those obtained from unrotated principal-component solutions with unities replacing communality estimates. Table 2:2 C summarizes the factor structure obtained for these data when communality estimates are used. The communalities were entered into the principal diagonal of the correlation matrix calculated from the summed individual scores. The estimates were calculated by means of an approach suggested by Tucker (see Levin, 1963), utilizing what Harmon (1960, pp. 88ff.) has called a "complete approximation," i.e., one which utilizes all observed correlations. The communality estimates are given by the expression

$$h_j^2 = |r_{jk}| \cdot \frac{\sum_{k'} |r_{jk'}|}{\sum_{k'} |r_{kk'}|}$$

where r_{jk} is the largest correlation for variable j and $j \neq k' \neq k$.

Inspection of Table 2:2 indicates that the structures are qualitatively very similar under all three procedures. There is ample evidence that communality estimates for correlation matrices exceeding 20 variables do not appreciably change the factor patterns (see Harmon, 1960), but it is reassuring to find that the consistent use of unities in the analyses reported has not altered the interpretations given those analyses. This observed similarity in structure for the communality and component analysis solutions (unities in the principal diagonal) can be interpreted as reflecting the relatively small unique variance of the scale items. The similarity between the structures obtained when the subject variance is manipulated indicates that subject variation does not appreciably influence the obtained structure and independently confirms the results of the Ware analysis.

A THREE-MODE SOLUTION

Obviously the analyses of the previous section are at best only indirect tests of the interactions between the modes of classification of semantic differential data. What is clearly needed is a factorial solution which does not require collapsing of any of the modes. Until recently only these indirect approaches were possible, but with the development of a three-mode solution for the factor problem by Tucker (1963a, 1963b), it is now possible to explore each mode separately and in combination with each of the other modes. As its name implies, three-mode factor analysis is an extension of the classical factor solution to matrices of three-way classification. In brief, the method treats a triple array scores matrix $_iX_{jk}$ according to the elementary defining formula

$$x_{ijk} = \sum_m \sum_p \sum_q a_{im}\, b_{jp}\, c_{kq}\, g_{mpq}$$

where the $_iA_m$, $_jB_p$, and $_kC_q$ matrices are the factor-loading matrices for the I, J, and K classifications, and the $_mG_{pq}$ cube matrix is the simultaneous interrelation of factor scores of the I, J, and K variable factors. For the semantic differential the I, J, and K variables would correspond to scales, concepts, and subjects. The solution is comparable to that which is obtained for the scale factors when the concept-by-subject observations are treated by

TABLE 2:2

Salient Principal-Component Scales for (A) Stringing Out, (B) Summation, and (C) Summation with Communality Estimate Methods

A.

Factor I (16.6%)		Factor II (6.6%)		Factor III (5.5%)		Factor IV (3.6%)	
good-bad	.77	hard-soft	.70	excitable-calm	.53	constricted-spacious	.44
kind-cruel	.69	masculine-feminine	.56	colorful-colorless	.50	awkward-graceful	.42
harmonious-dissonant	.69	strong-weak	.55	ornate-plain	.47	sensitive-insensitive	.38
beautiful-ugly	.69	severe-lenient	.50	heretical-orthodox	.45	hot-cold	.36
wise-foolish	.68	heavy-light	.49	active-passive	.44	excitable-calm	.36
reputable-disreputable	.67	tenacious-yielding	.49	changeable-stable	.44	weary-refreshed	.35
successful-unsuccessful	.66	fast-slow	.47	complex-simple	.42	small-large	.32
grateful-ungrateful	.66	angular-round	.40	rash-cautious	.40	constrained-free	.30
true-false	.63	mature-youthful	.40	fast-slow	.38	grateful-ungrateful	.28
sane-insane	.61	serious-humorous	.38	heterogeneous-homogeneous	.37	cooperative-competitive	.27

B.

Factor I (30.2%)		Factor II (15.4%)		Factor III (12.1%)		Factor IV (8.7%)	
believing-skeptical	.92	objective-subjective	.78	active-passive	.77	private-public	.76
good-bad	.91	tenacious-yielding	.76	complex-simple	.74	constricted-spacious	.67
true-false	.90	colorless-colorful	.76	pungent-bland	.72	weary-refreshed	.64
positive-negative	.88	hard-soft	.72	proud-humble	.71	awkward-graceful	.59
optimistic-pessimistic	.87	plain-ornate	.71	heterogeneous-homogeneous	.70	small-large	.54
harmonious-dissonant	.86	constrained-free	.70	hot-cold	.68	humble-proud	.53
kind-cruel	.86	stable-changeable	.70	intentional-unintentional	.63	constrained-free	.48
reputable-disreputable	.86	strong-weak	.68	excitable-calm	.60	sane-insane	.47
grateful-ungrateful	.85	mature-youthful	.63	sophisticated-naive	.56	excitable-calm	.44
sober-drunk	.82	opaque-transparent	.57	fast-slow	.56	erratic-periodic	.43

TABLE 2.2 (Continued)

C.

Factor I (41.1%)		Factor II (20.5%)		Factor III (16.0%)		Factor IV (11.5%)	
good-bad	.92	objective-subjective	.77	active-passive	.75	private-public	.74
believing-skeptical	.91	colorless-colorful	.75	pungent-bland	.74	constricted-spacious	.65
true-false	.90	tenacious-yielding	.74	complex-simple	.73	weary-refreshed	.63
positive-negative	.88	hard-soft	.73	proud-humble	.68	awkward-graceful	.60
optimistic-pessimistic	.87	plain-ornate	.71	heterogeneous-homogeneous	.68	humble-proud	.52
kind-cruel	.86	constrained-free	.70	hot-cold	.67	small-large	.52
reputable-disreputable	.86	stable-changeable	.69	intentional-unintentional	.62	constrained-free	.48
harmonious-dissonant	.86	strong-weak	.66	excitable-calm	.60	sane-insane	.47
grateful-ungrateful	.85	mature-youthful	.62	savory-tasteless	.55	sensitive-insensitive	.43
sober-drunk	.82	opaque-transparent	.55	sophisticated-naive	.54	excitable-calm	.42

Note: Factor percentages are proportions of total variance.

the stringing-out method, but it extends the analysis to the concept, subject, and triple-interaction factor matrices.

Levin (1963) has employed the three-mode factor solution in a re-analysis of data collected by Ware (1958). Ware had collected data from 60 high school students rating 31 concepts on 20 qualifier scales. The scales were chosen to represent 10 factors previously isolated in other studies. The concepts were chosen to sample equally the range of concept locations in the coordinate space defined by the three major dimensions of Evaluation, Potency, and Activity. Thus both the concepts and the scales were relatively heterogeneous in content. The raw rating scores were expressed as scale values varying between $+3$ and -3, with zero assumed to be the true scale midpoint. It was also decided to retain the differences in scale dispersion (i.e., size of scale unit differences), and thus the raw scores were considered to be both centered and standardized. Accordingly, cross-products rather than correlations were employed throughout.

Inspection of the latent roots for the subject, concept, and scale factor matrices indicated that one subject factor, four concept factors, and four scale factors could be identified in the data. The criterion used was based upon a comparison of the ratios of the successive latent roots. At that point for which the ratios of the ordered roots, R_n/R_{n+1}, can be judged to be constant, it is argued that all factors beyond this point are unique. A constant ratio of roots would be expected if the data under analysis had been drawn from a table of random numbers. A convenient method for determining this point is to plot the logarithm of each root as a function of the rank order of the root, since equal ratios will plot as a straight line after logarithmic transformation. Figure 2:3 displays the latent roots of the factors extracted from each mode of the Levin analysis. As can be observed, there is a precipitous drop in the latent roots of the subject mode after the first value, and accordingly we may conclude that there is a single "idealized" subject type for these data. The interaction between subjects and scales as well as that between subjects and concepts is minimal for this relatively homogeneous subject population. This finding confirms the conclusion drawn from the Ware analysis of an entirely independent sample of subjects using different scales and concepts. The concept and scale latent roots appear to become asymptotic after the fourth value, although more clearly so for the concept roots.

Tables 2:3 and 2:4 present the most salient scale and concept items of the factor matrices for their respective modes, as determined by Levin. Factor I of the scale analysis is readily identifiable as the Evaluation factor extracted in all the previous analyses reported. Factor II apparently represents a coalescence of the Potency and Activity dimensions previously isolated. This coalescence has been observed before (Triandis and Osgood, 1958) and appears to occur whenever the Activity dimension is not well represented in the scale items chosen. When this fused dimension has appeared, it has

FIGURE 2:3

Latent Roots of Levin Three-Mode Factor Analysis

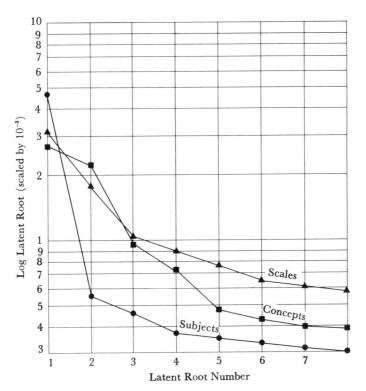

TABLE 2:3

Summary of Highest Coefficients of the Rotated Scale Factors

FACTOR I Evaluation		FACTOR II Dynamism		FACTOR III Stability		FACTOR IV Warmth	
usual-unusual	.66	strong-weak	.66	even-uneven	.67	warm-cool	.54
good-bad	.61	fast-slow	.58	predictable-unpredictable	.61	hot-cold	.52
fair-unfair	.60	powerful-powerless	.55	good-bad	.46	emotional-unemotional	.38
true-false	.56	hard-soft	.46	sociable-unsociable	.43		
kind-cruel	.56			unemotional-emotional	.32		
moral-immoral	.52			straight-twisted	.28		

TABLE 2:4

Summary of Highest Coefficients of the Rotated Concept Factors

FACTOR I Human		FACTOR II Agitation		FACTOR III Slickness		FACTOR IV Toughness	
MOTHER	.64	SIN	.55	BUTTER	.44	ARMY	.45
BABY	.52	ANGER	.54	JELLY	.43	STATUE	.39
SEX	.50	FEAR	.53	SNOW	.43	COP	.36
ME	.45	SICKNESS	.50	SNAIL	.39	STREET	.35
SLEEP	.40	INSANE MAN	.50	DIRT	.36	LAMP	.33
FOOD	.38	PAIN	.49	SILK	.30		
DREAM	.34	GRIEF	.43				

TABLE 2:5

Core Matrix of Concept and Scale Factor Combinations

CONCEPT FACTORS	SCALE FACTORS			
	Evaluation I	Dynamism II	Stability III	Warmth IV
Human I	18	03	−01	18
Agitation II	−03	10	−19	03
Slickness III	12	−13	−06	−15
Toughness IV	03	21	09	−14

been labeled a Dynamism factor. The third factor appears to be the Stability factor also observed in the past (Nunnally, 1961; Osgood, Suci, and Tannenbaum, 1957, Analysis III). The fourth factor was identified as a Warmth factor by Levin. The concept factors were labeled Human, Agitation, Slickness, and Toughness factors in the Levin analysis. No other published factorings of the concept mode are available with which these can be compared,[7] but they are obviously a function of the particular sample when it is small, as is the case here.

The core matrix expressing the factor loadings of the combinations of these factors directly specifies the amount of interaction between each of the modes of the SD data. Table 2:5 displays these factor loadings for the Varimax rotations of the concept and scale factors. As can be seen, the Evaluation and Warmth scales are most salient in the ratings of Human concepts. Agitation concepts are best characterized by Stability scales, Slickness concepts by Warmth scales, and Toughness concepts by Dynamism scales. These results indicate that had the concepts been drawn from any single one of the domains summarized by these four concept factors, at the very least

[7] Since the writing of this chapter, other concept factorings (utilizing the three-mode method) have appeared. See Chapter 7, pp. 344-345.

an entirely different order of scale factor importance would have emerged. Stated in other terms, there is good evidence for a large concept-by-scale interaction which is masked in the ordinary two-mode analysis of SD data. The Evaluation-Potency-Activity structure apparently can be expected to obtain when a large and heterogeneous concept sample is employed, but not when the concept sample is homogeneous. A re-analysis of the data of Analysis I, done by Shaw (1955), for example, found significant shifts in the scale intercorrelations when the concept terms were varied. Although this indicates that the investigator must be cautious when trying to generalize the scale structure to particular content domains, it is nonetheless the case that the structure of qualification when these interactions are averaged is of considerable interest in itself. This structure represents the most general aspects of the implicit dimensionality of attribute qualification for the widest class of concept terms.

GENERALITY OF THE E-P-A STRUCTURE

The SD technique attempts to provide a method for distinguishing individuals and/or concepts on the basis of an efficiently small number of natural language dimensions of contrastive attributes. The extent to which such discrimination is possible depends entirely upon demonstration of the existence and replicability of a low-rank structure of the ways in which natural languages organize the domain of attribute terms. The domain of attribute terms, for the purposes of this technique, is made coextensive with the domain of qualifiers in a natural language. Although it is theoretically possible to enumerate the members of the set of qualifiers in any natural language and accordingly to avoid the necessity of estimating sampling error, in practice the set is too large to make such enumeration practicable. If we further assume that the dimensionality of this set changes with the different classes of concepts to which the attributes may be applied, then although the set of attributes for each class decreases in size, the order of the dimensionality increases.

Thus both the attribute and concept spaces require strategies for sampling — as does, of course, the subject domain. Given equivalence of sampling strategies, if the structure of at least the qualifier domain can be shown to be relatively invariant over many such samples, while the remaining sources of sampling error are fixed, it can be inferred that there exists a potentially discriminating structure for the fixed values of the other domains. In order to demonstrate generality of such discrimination, however, it is necessary to show that this qualifier structure remains relatively invariant under varying concept and subject samples.

GENERALITY ACROSS SAMPLES OF SCALES

We shall use the term "E-P-A structure" to refer to the first three factors regularly found in the original factor analyses (Analyses I, II, and III above) — Evaluation, Potency, and Activity. This structure obviously depends upon a representative sampling of qualifier dimensions. By selecting subsets of quasi-synonymous scales (e.g., *sharp–dull, angular–rounded, pointed–blunt,* etc.), one could generate any set of factors he desired. The test of generality of the E-P-A structure, as part of the "natural" organization of the semantic space, therefore requires repeated sampling from the qualifier domain, with each sampling independent of the factorial results of prior samplings. Analyses I and II (scales determined by frequency of usage) vs. Analysis III (scales determined by categories in Roget's *Thesaurus*) provided the first test of generality across independent samplings of the qualifier domain. The cross-cultural studies to be described in this volume provide further evidence; although the same *rules* for sampling the qualifier domain in each country were applied, the contents of the 25 or so samples varied.

GENERALITY ACROSS SAMPLES OF SUBJECTS

The two-mode analyses (Analyses I, II, and III) were based on data collected from normal, adult, college-educated, English-speaking members of the American version of Western culture. The question naturally arises whether the E-P-A structure repeatedly obtained is limited to groups of humans having these particular characteristics. Research conducted under our own auspices, as well as research elsewhere, clearly indicates that this structure is not so limited.

As a function of age. The E-P-A structure was found to hold for adults. What about children from the same linguistic and cultural population? Is the child's increasing facility with his linguistic code reflected in the structure of qualification which he employs?

Small (1958) had a total of 275 third-, sixth-, and ninth-graders rate each of 24 heterogeneous concepts on a 23-scale form of SD. Sixteen of the scale items were chosen to represent the E-P-A structure, and seven additional scales were chosen (e.g., *real–make believe*) because of their theoretical interest. As was the case when intelligence was varied in the Ware (1958) study, there was little or no change in the total percentage of variance accounted for by the first five centroid factors when age or sex was varied. The evaluative first factor in particular showed no appreciable change as a function of age. Small had predicted that if there was to be any change in the structures of the age groups, it would appear in the relative dominance of the Evaluation factor. Younger children, it seemed reasonable to predict, should utilize evaluation relatively more than older children. This, of course, was essentially the same hypothesis Ware felt worthy of study, and, as in that study, the hypothesis again fails to be confirmed. In all age groups of the Small study the first centroid factor after Quartimax rotations was characterized by the scale items *good-bad, clean-dirty, happy-sad,* and *important-unimportant* — clearly identifiable as the Evaluation factor. The second rotated factor, also similar for all age groups, had highest loadings on the scale items *strong-weak, large-small,* and *fast-slow* — appearing again to be a coalescence of Potency and Activity into a Dynamism dimension. The third factor of the Small data was characterized by the scale items *hot-cold* and *sharp-flat.* All groups evidenced a similar fourth factor characterized by *real-make believe* and *true-pretend.* The first three factors in all age groups accounted for 75-85% of the common variance of the first five factors and 56-66% of the total variance. Small concluded that "the similarity of the factors obtained in our children's groups as compared with adult groups suggests that the cultural use of the polar terms of the dominant semantic dimensions is adequately learned by the third grade level" (p. 67), a conclusion which appears to be inescapable. Of course, it could be argued that the structure was at least in part forced by the choice of scales. The scales, after all, were chosen to represent the factors eventually isolated by Small — scales which were representative of the structure found for adults, not necessarily children.

An extensive study by DiVesta (1964a, b, 1965, 1966a, b, c) has attempted to rectify this fault. DiVesta initially had 100 school children in each of grades two, three, four, five, and six supply qualifiers in a restricted word-association test.[8] A single adjective was elicited as a response to each of 100 noun stimuli. The qualifiers obtained in this manner thus represent the qualification modes actually employed by the children and provided the pool of items from which appropriate semantic scales could be drawn. In essence, the selection procedure is designed to choose those qualifier terms which are (a) high in overall frequency of usage, (b) diverse in context of usage, and (c) independent in context of usage. Of the 264, 288, 306, 422, and 554 qualifier types obtained in the five increasing grade groups, 25 qualifiers maximizing the above criteria were selected for each grade level. Opposites were determined for each of these selected modifiers and semantic scales constructed. The concepts rated on these scales were the noun stimuli of the elicitation step and are identical to those used in the cross-linguistic investigations to be described in subsequent chapters.

The factor results of these analyses essentially duplicate the findings of Small. In fact, the most interesting aspect of this research is that the quali-

---

[8] DiVesta's procedures with children were actually modeled on the design of our cross-cultural studies, reported in this book, the essential difference being that age level rather than language and culture was varied.

fiers elicited from each of the grade levels are extremely similar. When the elicited qualifiers are ordered by frequency of occurrence, the correlations among the first 50 most frequently employed adjectives form a simplex ordered by age. That is, the qualifiers found at each grade level correlate highest with the qualifiers found at the nearest grade and least with those found at the furthest removed grade. Despite this orderly progression in the magnitude of the correlation coefficients as grade level is increased, the average intercorrelation between each pair of grade levels for the 50 most frequent responses is .93. Although this high degree of correlation in availability of qualifiers across age groups does not require that the same factor structures appear in their usage, it certainly enhances that possibility. DiVesta's results indicate that the same E-P-A factor structure does hold for all age groups, even for second-graders. We are thus again led to the conclusion that, whatever linguistic regularities these dimensions reflect, Evaluation, Potency, and Activity are already dominant in the qualification structure of the seven-year-old.

The reasonable hypothesis — that a gross, undifferentiated E-P-A (simultaneously Good, Strong, and Active vs. Bad, Weak, and Passive) will gradually "unfold" like the petals of a flower into more and more independently used E, P, and A as age increases — is not necessarily refuted by the Small and DiVesta data. It may well be that this "unfolding" does in fact occur, but at a much earlier age. The problem here is methodological — how is one to get at the semantic factor structures of preschool children in a sufficiently sensitive way? This problem is not unsolvable, we suspect; for example, one might forgo the niceties of scaling and simply ask children either-or questions. Is MOMMY *hard* or *soft?* Is THE KITTY *hard* or *soft?* Is DADDY *big* or *small?* Ervin and Foster (1960), in fact, have demonstrated such development in children's use of descriptive terms, but using generalization of usage (e.g., *big* used coextensively with *good*) rather than factorial methods.

For the sake of completeness, it is of interest to examine developmental changes in concept meanings for children in their demonstratedly equivalent scale system. Donahoe (1961), using groups of first-, third-, sixth-, and college-grade students rating concepts on three scales representing each of the major dimensions, found that profiles for concepts with respect to E and P attributes stabilized to the adult's level at ages 9 and 12 respectively, while the profiles for the A attribute did not vary across age levels for these concepts. Whether this means that Activity stabilizes before Evaluation and Potency (which seems unlikely) or that the particular set of concepts provided insufficient variation on this factor (which seems more likely) is not clear from this study. In any case, study of semantic development in children, with the same intensity that is now being invested in study of grammatical development, is a high-priority research area.

As a function of sex. Although it seems an obvious question — whether males and females differ in their semantic factor structure — it has seldom been asked directly. It has occasionally been raised indirectly in studies aimed at other problems: for example, by Hallworth and Waite (1963) on the value judgments of adolescent girls, by Lazowick (1955) in a study on the nature of identification, and by Small (1958) in the study referred to above. In a study primarily concerned with the relation between intelligence and semantic structure, Ware (1958) also compared the factor structures of male and female subjects. In none of these cases was there significant variation *in factor structure* between males and females; there are, of course, differences based on sex in the meanings of particular concepts.

As a function of political orientation. A semantic analysis of voters in the 1952 presidential election by George Suci is reported in detail in *The Measurement of Meaning.* His sample included Eisenhower Republicans (those who preferred Eisenhower and voted for him), Taft Republicans (those who preferred Taft but voted for Eisenhower), and Stevenson Democrats (those who preferred Stevenson and voted for him). Although these groups differed markedly in their meanings of specific concepts (e.g., of HARRY TRUMAN), and in ways that would be expected, the factor structures they used were practically identical (see *The Measurement of Meaning,* Table 14, p. 120). This structure was *not* the familiar E-P-A, but one apparently characteristic of political concepts (see below under Concept Sampling). In other words, presented with a particular class of concepts, these three classes of subjects used essentially identical judgmental frames of reference.

As a function of normality. The earliest study of which we are aware using the SD technique on this problem was by Joan Bopp (1955). She compared the factor structures of normals and schizophrenics, splitting each group into randomly assigned halves. The indices of factorial similarity (cf. *The Measurement of Meaning,* pp. 223-226) were as high across groups (schizo/normal) as within (normal/normal and schizo/schizo). Although not, strictly speaking, a matter of normality, another early comparison of High vs. Low Ethnocentrics by Suci (1952) is relevant here. The only apparent difference in factor structure was a tendency for the High Ethnocentrics to fuse P and A into a single Dynamism factor (see *The Measurement of Meaning,* pp. 222-223, for details). In the last decade a large number of studies applying the SD technique to various clinical populations have been reported. These studies have all assumed similarity of factor structure in order to make the semantic comparisons involved, and a few have tested this matter. In no case have significant differences in factor structure appeared. The type of clinical population where one might expect to find differences, perhaps, would be that in which language disturbances are involved, e.g., aphasics. As far

as we are aware, no studies of semantic factor structure using such populations have been made.[9]

All of these comparisons across subject samples — differing in age, in sex,
in intelligence, in political orientation, in normality, and so forth — have been
made within a single language/culture community. It seemed possible that
even this affective semantic structure might vary with language, culture, or
both, and the research which this book reports was aimed at this question.

The suggestion that all human beings share a common affective semantic
framework — uncontraverted by the evidence presented so far — in no way
implies that they also share the same meanings for the concepts differentiated
within this framework. We have already noted, for example, that people
differing in their political orientations differ in predictable ways in their meanings of politically relevant concepts, despite their use of a common semantic
reference frame. The concept HARRY TRUMAN, for example, was *unfair* and
weak but *quite active* for Taft Republicans, *less unfair* and *less weak* but
equally *quite active* for Eisenhower Republicans, but decidedly *fair, strong,*
and *active* for Stevenson Democrats. It is precisely this distinction — between
similarity in qualifying framework and difference in allocation of concepts
within it — that gives potential to the SD technique as a tool in applied
social science research.

We expect individuals drawn from the same language/culture community
to differ in their affective meanings of certain concepts. We may call such
concepts *attitude objects*. Concepts on the meanings of which participants in
the same language/culture community must agree in order to communicate
with one another we shall call *common-meaning terms*. In the assertion
"Ex-senator McCarthy of Wisconsin was a fair and just man," for example,
the word-forms in the phrase "Ex-senator McCarthy of Wisconsin" constitute
an attitude object — contemporary American English-speakers will differ in
their affective meanings for this concept and yet understand what is being
asserted. The affective meanings of the word-forms *fair* and *just* must be
agreed upon within the language/culture community, or else there will be
communication failure — listener B may think that speaker A also disapproves
of the tactics of the late senator! In the sense of this distinction, a semantic
differential is an attempt to use common-meaning terms in a systematic way
to measure differences in the meanings of attitude objects. Since the term
"attitude" usually refers only to the evaluative dimension of affect, perhaps a
better label would be "objects of affect."

---

[9] Informal tests with two aphasic patients, using a visual form of SD in which
simple pointing to, e.g., *white* circle vs. *black* circle (see Osgood, 1960b), in response
to repeated verbal stimuli, suggested normality of affective E-P-A (Osgood and
Miron, 1963, pp. 133-135). In her doctoral dissertation Sylvia Sheinkopf (1970) has
made an extensive test of aphasics with the same visual SD form, obtaining similar
results. Our colleague Dr. Kostić, director of the Institute of Experimental Phonetics
in Belgrade, plans to replicate this study with Serbo-Croatian-speaking aphasics.

Even within a single individual the same "objects of affect" may differ in type of affect from time to time and from situation to situation. A rather dramatic instance of this was the case of triple personality described by Thigpen and Cleckley (1954). Osgood and Luria (1954) made a blind analysis of this case, based solely upon the ratings of a set of relevant concepts (MYSELF, MY MOTHER, HATRED, etc.) against a standard SD representing the three affective factors when the woman was "in" the personalities of Eve White, Eve Black, and Jane. The affective meanings of these concepts were shown to shift markedly with the shift from personality to personality, and the nature of the changes in meaning permitted a "blind" interpretation which the therapists considered surprisingly accurate.[10]

There is much evidence for differences in concept meanings for different classes of individuals within the same language/culture community. Mogar (1960), for example, has reported that high F-scale scorers tend to be more extreme in their SD ratings (i.e., concepts tend to be more emotionally polarized). Mitsos (1961) has shown that the ratings of subjects allowed to choose their own scales also gave more extreme ratings. Luria (1959) and Endler (1961) both have shown significant and predictive shifts in the meaning of the self-concept during psychotherapy. Korman (1960) was able to discriminate among psychologists, social workers, and psychiatrists on the basis of their ratings of diagnostic and therapeutic terms. Cook (1959) reported significant improvement in predicting academic achievement when the meanings of concepts like MYSELF AS AN IDEAL STUDENT were added to standard predictors. Katz (1959) was able to discriminate between troubled and untroubled married partners on the basis of their ratings of certain concepts. *The Measurement of Meaning,* in which the last study is reported, contains many other applications of the SD technique to concept differentiation.

AcROSS SAMPLES OF CONCEPTS

We have seen evidence that scale factor structure is relatively impervious to variation in subject populations, even, as we shall show, populations differing in both language and culture. We have also seen evidence for great variations in the meanings of concepts within this common qualifier affective meaning space. A final question we must ask is this: Will the factor structure of modes of qualifying prove impervious to variations in concept populations? Even on the basis of what data we have to this point, e.g., the Levin analysis (pp. 54-57), the answer to this question seems to be clearly negative. This conclusion was foreshadowed in *The Measurement of Meaning* by the quite

---

[10] Osgood, Luria, and Smith have recently made a blind analysis of another case of multiple personality treated by Dr. Robert F. Jeans of Chicago. This analysis, along with Dr. Jeans's case description and evaluation of the blind analysis, is planned for publication as a monograph in the *Journal of Abnormal Psychology.*

different structures yielded by factoring single concepts from the *Thesaurus* analysis and by Suci's findings that the usual three-factor space collapsed into two (Benevolence and Dynamism) for political concepts.

In a more recent study Osgood, Ware, and Morris (1961) had American college students rate Morris's "Ways to Live" against a form of SD; for this class of concepts — all "values" — the usual three basic factors collapsed into one, termed Successfulness (i.e., a combination of Good, Strong, and Active). Kilby (1963) collected the same kind of data from Hindi-speaking students in India.[11] Alexander and Husek (1962) have demonstrated a unique structure for qualification when concepts tapping situational anxiety are studied.

In the study by Ware previously mentioned (p. 50), where 40 personality concepts were judged against 40 scales by 40 mature male and female subjects, the actual factors apparently shared across subjects are worth reporting. As given in Table 2:6, they were Morality (variant of Evaluation), Rationality, Uniqueness, Excitability (variant of Activity), Sociability, Toughness (variant of Potency), Urbanity, and Tangibility. It should be noted that the proportions of variance accounted for are much more evenly distributed than in the usual E-P-A results for heterogeneous concepts.

TABLE 2:6

Varimax Rotation of Eight Factors of a Personality Differential

Factor I (7.9%) Morality		Factor V (6.5%) Sociability	
moral-immoral	78	gregarious–self-contained	76
reputable-disreputable	78	sociable-solitary	72
wholesome-unwholesome	73	extroverted-introverted	66
Factor II (7.1%) Rationality		Factor VI (6.0%) Toughness	
logical-intuitive	66	tough-tender	78
objective-subjective	66	insensitive-sensitive	71
rational-irrational	60	rugged-delicate	63
Factor III (6.7%) Uniqueness		Factor VII (5.2%) Urbanity	
unique-typical	77	proud-humble	65
unusual-usual	74	sophisticated-naive	58
individualistic-regular	70	deliberate-casual	53
Factor IV (6.6%) Excitability		Factor VIII (4.0%) Tangibility	
excitable-calm	81	formed-amorphous	72
tense-relaxed	77	predictable-unpredictable	56
emotional-unemotional	52	tangible-intangible	42

[11] Both of these studies indicate the flexibility of the "concepts" that can be measured in SD research; here they were approximately 100-word statements of each "Way to Live," which the subjects were easily able to read and react to globally.

A study by Capell and Wohl (1959) of the structure of frequently used dimensions of clinical judgment comes surprisingly close to the E-P-A structure, provided one is allowed a fair degree of leeway in the interpretation of what the clinical terms really mean. Capell and Wohl found that when the first factor dimension was forced through the evaluative qualifier scales *pleasant-unpleasant, kind-cruel,* and *honest-dishonest,* the first factor had highest coefficients for such clinical terms as "distorted reality testing" and "orally demanding." The second unforced dimension was characterized by such terms as "dependent," "hostile," "narcissistic," and "inadequate," which might have as nonclinical synonyms the adjectives *weak, soft,* and *impotent.* Peterson (1965), in fact, concludes that the personality factors typically discovered are probably topical variants of the more general ways of attributing meaning to objects, and they accordingly should display a qualifier structure comparable to that for concepts in general. In the Ware study we note analogues of E, P, and A but with additional, more finely discriminative factors as well. This may well be the pattern to expect for classes of concepts having affective variability but denotative distinctions as well. More recent cross-cultural studies of the personality domain will be reported in Chapter 7.

ORIGINS OF THIS CROSS-CULTURAL PROJECT

It was out of this research background that the authors began, in late 1959, to plan a cross-cultural and cross-linguistic research program, designed to test rigorously the limits of the generality of the E-P-A system. As has been seen, despite deliberate and independent variations in the sampling of scales, of subjects, and of concepts (as long as they were diversified in nature), the same Evaluation, Potency, and Activity factors have kept reappearing. This suggests that there are at least three "directions" of the total semantic space which are regions of relatively high density, in the sense that they are represented in the language by many closely related modes of qualifying. Furthermore, these "directions" appear to be orthogonal to each other, in the sense of being independently variable ways of making semantic discriminations. However, most of the studies done up to this time had been both monocultural and monolinguistic; they utilized English-speaking participants in American culture, and to that extent the findings were limited in generality.

However, during this period a few cross-linguistic and cross-cultural investigations with the SD technique were undertaken. The first was a study by Kumata and Schramm (1956) using Japanese and Korean subjects who were bilingual with respect to English; monolingual American English-speakers served as controls. The striking finding in this study was that indices of factorial similarity for the bilinguals taking the SD test first in one language and then later in the other (direction counterbalanced) were as high as those for the American controls taking the same test twice in the same language over the same time intervals. In other words, shifting from one language form to another translation-equivalent language form had no noticeable influence on affective semantic structure. Kumata (1957) compared the semantic systems of American and Japanese (in Japan) monolinguals, using translation-equivalent SD forms; again no differences in factor structure were apparent. Triandis and Osgood (1958) compared the semantic systems of American and Greek college students — again using translation-equivalent SD forms — and the same basic factor structure appeared. Suci (1960), working on the Southwest Project on Comparative Psycholinguistics sponsored by the Social Science Research Council, was able to get (admittedly somewhat rough) translations of typical English SD scales from informants in several Southwest Indian cultures (Hopi, Navajo, Hopi-Tewa). The factor structures resulting from subsequent judgments by these Indian subjects of various concepts against the scales thus derived were not as clearly defined as with literate groups, but nevertheless the nature of the factors seemed quite similar to the familiar E-P-A system.

Even though the details of the methods varied, as did the selection of semantic scales and concepts judged — and essentially the same factor system kept appearing — one very dubious aspect of methodology ran through all of these early cross-cultural studies: the samples of scales used were selected either partly or wholly on the basis of factorial results obtained in the prior American English investigations. The scales used were often simply translated into the languages of the other groups under study. Despite the care with which these translations were made (see Kumata, 1957), the fact that translation served as the vehicle for demonstrating cross-linguistic and cross-cultural similarities in factor structure seemed to be the most likely source of bias, if indeed the similarities were artifactual. It could well be that we were literally forcing people in other cultures, speaking different languages, to operate within a semantic framework determined by American English-speakers, and when thus forced to use scales characteristic of the affective system for this language/culture community, these other people displayed the same structure. Given an opportunity to determine their own qualifying framework, non-American and non-English-speaking peoples might display quite different semantic systems.

To avoid the potential bias of translation, and the resultant ethnocentric bias, the procedures for selecting qualifiers that would eventually serve as the dimensions of judgment in SD tasks had to be entirely intracultural; each language/culture group must determine its own descriptive scales. However, the overall methodology of these intraculturally independent samplings had to be standardized in order to make possible the intercultural comparisons required for testing the primary hypothesis of structural equivalence. Additionally, it was clear that testing the limits of generality demanded as heterogeneous a sample of both languages and cultures as could be practically obtained. If under these conditions sufficient similarities in factor structure could be demonstrated, then the shared factors could provide the basis for constructing semantically comparable instruments for measuring various aspects of "subjective culture," e.g., values, attitudes, stereotypes, and concept meanings generally.

3

Modes of Qualifying Human Experience

DATA COLLECTION and analysis in the "tool-making" part of this project fall rather naturally into two phases. Phase I involves the collection of a large and representative sample of modes of qualifying experience in each language/culture community. By analyzing the distribution-of-usage characteristics of each sample by standardized methods, it is possible to select from this large sample of qualifiers a subset which maximizes certain criteria: salience, diversity, and independence in usage. This subset can then be the basis for constructing bipolar scales for use in subsequent SD analyses. As a first step in further reducing complexity and increasing economy of description, this subset of scales for each language/culture community can be factor-analyzed, with scale terms serving as "concepts" to be judged against the other scale terms. This sequence of procedures is elaborated in this chapter.

QUALIFIER ELICITATION

In psychological research, as in other social and biological fields, sampling from a population according to certain rules is a familiar procedure. When the "population" is something other than organisms (human or otherwise), and its characteristic parameters are not well known, special problems arise. This is certainly the case in sampling from the domain of qualifier modes. Our early research first used frequency and then representativeness (via

First draft prepared by Murray S. Miron.

Roget's *Thesaurus,* as described in Chapter 2) as sampling criteria. Although these criteria proved convenient and yielded very similar factor structures, they are not readily applicable in cross-national research. For most languages there are neither frequency-of-usage tables (like Thorndike-Lorge) nor *thesauri* available, and the labor involved in constructing such sampling sources would be prohibitive as an adjunct to our primary concerns.

Another critical consideration for us was to avoid the potential linguicentric bias of merely translating English scales into the languages of the other groups we wished to study. As noted in the preceding chapters, simple translation might not allow dimensions of high salience for other groups to appear at all and thereby influence their apparent semantic structure. But, on the other hand, if comparisons of structures were to be made, then the procedures for sampling modes of qualification had to be standardized. Following recommendations made and evaluated at the preliminary Allerton House conference, it was decided to use a modified word-association procedure to elicit qualifiers in each site — a procedure in which subjects give the first qualifier (adjective, in English) that occurs to them when presented with each substantive (noun, in English). We wanted to maximize comparability and simplicity of eliciting conditions while minimizing translation bias and constraint upon content of response.

CULTURE-COMMON SUBSTANTIVES AS ELICITORS

An initial choice was whether to employ a standard list of verbal stimuli as elicitors or to allow elicitors to be determined freely within each language/culture community. The former alternative would require translation from English into each of the other languages, with all the problems this involves; the latter would permit wide variations in stimulus sets, with all the problems *this* involves. We decided on the former course, for two primary reasons. First, if a set of substantives common and familiar to all groups could be found, translation at this point, before any collection of data from subjects, should have minimal influence upon the variables we were interested in. Second, the danger of influencing qualifier sampling as a function of differences in the stimuli used seemed too serious. (In a subsequent section it will be shown that we probably overemphasized this danger.)

A second choice concerned the source of substantives to be used as stimuli in the word-association elicitation procedure. One immediately thinks of the Kent-Rosanoff stimulus words as being a ready-made standardized list. But on second thought (and inspection of this list of 100 terms), it becomes obvious that it is decidedly a product of Western culture. Participants in the Allerton conference pointed out that items used in glottochronological investigations (see Swadesh, 1950; Lees, 1953) — in studying rates of language change — were deliberately designed to be culture-common. Starting with these lists as a basis, and adding items from the Kent-Rosanoff list and from the category headings in the Human Relations Area Files Index, a pool of 200 nouns in English was assembled which, it was hoped, would prove to be culture-common. We use this term rather than "culture-free" because the latter refers to something inherently unachievable — and untestable even if it might be achievable. Reduction of this pool of possible stimuli was accomplished by eliminating items which failed to meet either of two criteria, translation fidelity and productivity.

To estimate *translation fidelity,* all substantives were translated into Arabic, Cantonese, Finnish, Hindi, Japanese, Kannada, and Farsi by panels of approximately ten fluent English/mother-tongue bilinguals. Forms prepared for this task required these translators, responding independently, to list a first and a second translation for each item, to indicate the presence or absence of homonyms, and to rate the difficulty of translation on a four-point scale. Translators were informed that the translations were to be submitted to high school–aged subjects in their countries for use in subsequent testings and that, accordingly, they should give preference to frequent and simple equivalents. Translators were also instructed not to use dictionaries. Each of the 200 substantives was inspected in translation for a clear majority agreement on either the first or second translation across all the pilot languages, and informal checks on back-translation were made. Items showing no clear agreement and/or rated as above average in difficulty of translation in one or more of the languages were submitted for re-examination to the translators of the language or languages evidencing difficulty. *If, after discussion with these translators, the lack of an adequate equivalent was confirmed for any one of these languages, the item was dropped from all languages.* If discussion revealed the existence of a compromise translation judged to be moderately accurate in rendering the sense of the English term, the item was retained.

To estimate *productivity,* the 200 substantives were administered as stimuli for qualifier association in Finland and the United States to a sample of 100 high school–aged males in each location. Stimulus items found to elicit the fewest different qualifier types for both Finnish and English were eliminated *from all languages.* Thus, for example, the stimulus item BLOOD was found to elicit predominantly the single response *red* in both languages and was accordingly deleted from the stimulus pool. This second criterion was instituted in order to assure that the largest possible number of qualifier types would be obtained in the elicitation procedure. The final stimuli selected were, accordingly, those with maximum fidelity and ease of translation for seven language/culture groups and highest productivity in terms of qualifier diversification for two groups.

Inspection of the verbal stimuli remaining after applying these criteria suggested that obviously culture-bound, diffuse, or ambiguous terms had been eliminated. After these procedures 108 items remained. Primarily for aesthetic reasons, but also to more nearly equalize concrete and abstract nouns, an additional eight concrete items were eliminated. The final 100-item substantive stimulus list is given in Table 3:1. This list, as translated, has been used in all subsequent qualifier elicitation, and it contains a rough (60/40) balance of concrete and abstract nouns. Oblique evidence for the success of the initial pruning — and for the culture-commonness of the remaining items — is the fact that, of this set of 100 substantives selected by pretesting in only seven languages, only two or three words have proven difficult to translate in each of the nearly 20 additional languages that have been added subsequently. It also should be emphasized that this initial step is the only point in the entire data-collection and analysis process at which translation could influence the results. All subsequent analyses were handled within each native language, translations being used only for interpreting results.

ELICITATION PROCEDURE

A model procedure for eliciting qualifier-restricted associations to the 100 substantive stimuli was devised, and appropriate English instructions were written. The procedure and instructions were kept as simple as possible. However, for a variety of reasons (see Chapter 1) it is not possible simply to translate English instructions into other languages and expect to get comparable results. The essence of the instructions was that the subjects were to place each of the 100 stimulus words in an appropriate linguistic frame and then complete the frame by supplying a single qualifier which, in their judgment, would fit the frame and the given noun. These instructions were modified to suit the grammatical requirements of each language.[1] The particular test frames thus varied from language to language as the syntactical requirements for qualifier distribution varied. In American English the test frames were given as "The BUTTERFLY is _____" and "The _____ BUTTERFLY," with subjects instructed to supply an appropriate adjective in the blank. Both frames define words of Fries's (1952) Class 3. In each language a competent native-speaking resident field worker, with the aid of our staff, devised appropriate frame patterns following the American English examples. It was also necessary to adapt the instructions somewhat to each culture, in order that their intent and effect be as constant as possible.

Thus in all instances, although the specific form of the frame varied, the Fries conception of grammatical class was uniformly followed. The criteria of acceptability for any qualifier are therefore relative to the language in

---

[1] William K. Archer, the ethnolinguist on our project staff, was primarily responsible for making these modifications in each location — in collaboration with our research colleagues there, of course.

TABLE 3:1

The 100 Substantive Stimuli as Used in Qualifier Elicitation

1. HOUSE	26. RAIN	51. HORSE	76. SUN
2. GIRL	27. TREE	52. MARRIAGE	77. DOG
3. PICTURE	28. STONE	53. GAME	78. MONEY
4. MEAT	29. TOOTH	54. COLOR	79. SMOKE
5. TRUST	30. EAR	55. HEART	80. FISH
6. PAIN	31. RESPECT	56. FRIEND	81. MAN
7. DEFEAT	32. LAUGHTER	57. DEATH	82. WEDNESDAY
8. BOOK	33. MOON	58. KNOWLEDGE	83. CHAIR
9. LAKE	34. WIND	59. FREEDOM	84. GUILT
10. STAR	35. WORK	60. BELIEF	85. LUCK
11. BATTLE	36. STORY	61. SUCCESS	86. PEACE
12. DANGER	37. PUNISHMENT	62. ROPE	87. HAIR
13. SYMPATHY	38. WEALTH	63. HAND	88. FOOD
14. PROGRESS	39. WOMAN	64. MOTHER	89. SEED
15. CUP	40. CLOUD	65. KNOT	90. POLICEMAN
16. COURAGE	41. CAT	66. LIFE	91. FATHER
17. THIEF	42. POISON	67. HEAD	92. FEAR
18. BREAD	43. CRIME	68. THUNDER	93. PLEASURE
19. LOVE	44. HUNGER	69. TRUTH	94. PURPOSE
20. FRUIT	45. CHOICE	70. AUTHOR	95. FIRE
21. BIRD	46. NOISE	71. MUSIC	96. DOCTOR
22. SNAKE	47. NEED	72. SLEEP	97. POWER
23. HEAT	48. HOPE	73. FUTURE	98. WINDOW
24. MAP	49. ANGER	74. EGG	99. RIVER
25. HUSBAND	50. TONGUE	75. ROOT	100. WATER

question, not to any arbitrary grammatical scheme. The field workers were instructed to use these criteria in collating their qualifier data, using the same frames in testing dubious responses. In addition, the field workers were instructed to regularize the possible grammatical variants where such features were irrelevant to the lexical meaning of the response. To facilitate machine data analysis, orthographic schemes were devised in languages whose alphabetization practices made this necessary; all orthographic variants of a form were also regularized in the field. When received at Illinois, the qualifier data were thus in transliterated form, ready for direct transfer to punched cards without any translation or further modification. Wide latitude was practiced in judging the acceptability of qualifier responses; slang, neologisms, and even multiword responses which formed lexical units were accepted if they had been judged appropriate for the linguistic frames provided by the field staff and our own ethnolinguist. Our assumption was that nonconforming responses, as well as rare ones, would tend to be eliminated by the automatic selection procedures to be described in the next major section of this chapter.

Testing was carried out in regular school classrooms, subjects being run in groups comprising their normal classes.[2] Each language/culture group contributed 100 subjects to this task. Reports indicate that the task is easily completed within a single class period. Subjects were instructed to supply a response to each of the 100 stimulus items, but in some cases (varying from site to site) they did not, or perhaps could not, comply. For most of the countries in the earlier samples involved, one or two of the local project staff were actually present either during or just prior to this initial qualifier sampling, since we tried to get this phase under way during our first visit. The 100 responses (counting failures and errors as unique events) to each stimulus word were collated, transliterated according to the given rules, where necessary, in the field, and then shipped to Illinois for analysis. These qualifier lists (e.g., in English, TREE: *green* (28), *tall* (17), *big* (12), *good* (9), *shady* (8), etc.), then, constitute the raw data with which this research begins.

TESTS OF THE "SPEW HYPOTHESIS"

There are good reasons to expect that the frequency of emission of any lexical unit of a language will be isomorphic with the frequency of experience with that unit via all modes of decoding and encoding. Underwood and Schultz (1960), for example, adduce considerable experimental evidence for this relationship and have called it the "spew hypothesis." For a word-association task this is equivalent to saying that the more frequently a word is used (as indexed, e.g., in the Thorndike-Lorge tables), the more likely it is to occur as an emitted associate. However, this hypothesis assumes that responses elicited in the word-association task are independent of the words used as stimuli. In the extreme case, of course, this cannot be true — as is evidenced by the differences in hierarchies of associates to different single stimulus words. The real issue, then, comes down to whether samples of qualifier associates are relatively independent of the *samples* of stimulus words, when these samples are varied.

In order to gather evidence on this matter, the following pilot study was carried out. Thirty-three undergraduate students at the University of Illinois gave a single adjective response appropriate to each of five sets of 30 stimuli. The five classes of stimulus items, in their order of presentation to the subjects, were:

(1) NS — no stimuli offered, subjects being required in this condition to respond to each of 30 blank spaces.

(2) PO — black-and-white pictures of common objects (e.g., a chair, a hammer, etc.).

---

[2] The only exception is Tzeltal for the communities reported here. Tzeltal data were collected on a single-informant basis by Dr. Duane Metzger in 1963.

(3) GF — simple geometric forms and abstract connected line drawings (e.g., a triangle, a nonsense form).

(4) RS — substantives (nouns in English, e.g., house, danger, etc.) selected at random from the original pool of 200 noun items.

(5) HS — substantives displaying highest uncertainty (H) values also selected from the pool of 200 pretested noun items.

Conditions 4 and 5 were administered at the same time. These subjects responded to the same 200 nouns which had been used in the earlier and independent pretestings employing different subjects. The items for testing conditions 4 and 5 were drawn from the total list of 200 items administered to the subjects of this experiment. The remaining items were not analyzed. In none of the conditions was there duplication of stimulus items, except in conditions 4 and 5, where 6 of the 30 stimuli were present in both conditions. In all conditions subjects were instructed to restrict their responses to qualifiers or "adjectives" in English, the form class of items intended as the basis for scale construction in the major investigation.

It is reasonable to assume that the no-stimuli condition represents the minimum case of bias attributable to the action of specific stimuli in word association. Presumably, the subjects in this condition were selecting adjectives on the basis of an undetermined but nonspecific set of internal stimuli. Consequently, the analysis of the data utilized the no-stimulus condition as the base with which all the other conditions were compared. We shall accordingly restrict ourselves to questions of how much overlap of responses was obtained for the various conditions when compared to the no-stimulus condition. Table 3:2 summarizes these overlaps in the various conditions.

The overlap values of Table 3:2 were obtained in the following manner. After ordering the adjective types obtained in the no-stimulus condition from highest frequency of occurrence to lowest, the first 50 and the first 100 most frequent response *types*[3] were identified. These high-frequency responses were then searched for in each of the remaining conditions. The overlap of types is defined as the occurrence of an identical response in any of the comparison conditions regardless of the frequency of that response in the comparison condition. Overlap of response tokens (i.e., considering the multiple occurrences of a single adjective type as separate responses) is indicated in the table column headed "Tokens." For example, the first 50 most frequent no-stimulus condition adjective types accounted for a total of 401 responses, while the 43 overlapping adjective types also found in the pictured-object condition accounted for 349 responses. An examination of the type overlap values for the various conditions indicates that the greatest

[3] A single word *type* is defined as a unique form, regardless of how often it may occur; a *token* is any word occurrence. Thus in the sentence "Types are classes of responses, whereas tokens are simply responses," there are eight word types but ten word tokens (types *are* and *responses,* each occurring twice).

TABLE 3:2

*Summary of Response Frequencies Obtained in Each of the Experimental
Conditions*

| | TOTALS | | | OVERLAP WITH NS | | | | | |
| | | | | First 50 | | | First 100 | | |
CONDITION	Types	Tokens	T/T[a]	Types	Tokens	T/T	Types	Tokens	T/T
No Stimuli (NS)	474	990	.48	50	401	.12	100	468	.21
Pictured Objects (PO)	362	990	.37	43	349	.12	65	556	.12
Geometric Forms (GF)	451	990	.46	33	147	.22	55	226	.24
Nouns (RS)	410	990	.41	46	458	.10	82	566	.14
High *H* Nouns (HS)	425	990	.43	43	322	.13	78	466	.17

[a] T/T symbolizes type/token ratio.

communality of response types occurred in the random substantive condition. Of the 100 most frequent no-stimulus adjectives, 82 of these adjectives were also found in the random substantive condition. These 82 shared responses, in fact, account for a higher number of token responses than were accounted for by the 100 most frequent no-stimulus types.

It will be noted that the no-stimulus condition produced the highest number of total types and a correspondingly high type/token ratio, while the pictured-object condition produced the least. This particular ordering of conditions appears to be entirely reasonable; pictured objects provide the most concrete and restrictive stimuli for a subject while the no-stimulus condition represents the least concrete or restrictive. The geometric-form condition produced the next highest number of total types, a fact which might be interpreted to mean that the abstract line drawings of that condition were sufficiently ambiguous to elicit nearly as many responses as the no-stimulus condition. If we examine the correlations obtained between the no-stimulus and geometric-form conditions, to be discussed in detail in a moment, it is clear, however, that the overall character of the high-frequency responses obtained in the two conditions is quite different. The first 50 most frequent responses in the no-stimulus condition correlated −.01 in relative frequency with the overlapping responses of the geometric-form condition. The divergence in responding for these two conditions can also be seen in the low number of overlapping responses for the no-stimulus condition first 50 and first 100 most frequent responses, summarized in Table 3:2.

Table 3:3 presents the correlations obtained between each of the conditions for the first 50 and first 100 most frequent no-stimulus condition responses. Since these correlations are based on only those responses shared with the no-stimulus condition by each of the remaining conditions, the correlations other than those of the first row represent the amount of correlation through the mediation of the no-stimulus condition. That is to say, all

TABLE 3:3

A. Intercorrelations among the Five Experimental Conditions Using the First 50 Most Frequent No-Stimulus (NS) Responses as Base

	NS	PO	GF	RS	HS	AVERAGE MUTUAL OVERLAP
NS	1.00	.53	−.01	.57	.36	.41
PO		1.00	.25	.41	.16	.36
GF			1.00	.05	−.07	.10
RS				1.00	.53	.46
HS					1.00	.30

B. Intercorrelations among the Five Experimental Conditions Using the First 100 Most Frequent No-Stimulus (NS) Responses as Base

	NS	PO	GF	RS	HS	AVERAGE MUTUAL OVERLAP
NS	1.00	.50	.10	.62	.43	.43
PO		1.00	.41	.39	.25	.41
GF			1.00	.07	.02	.14
RS				1.00	.53	.45
HS					1.00	.33

correlations involving any condition except the no-stimulus condition express the degree of co-variance between these other tests only with respect to the amount of common co-variation they each have separately with the no-stimulus condition. Thus the correlations among conditions 2, 3, 4, and 5 represent a kind of partial correlation involving only the overlapping variance of each with condition 1. Using this interpretation of the correlations, it is possible to estimate the condition having maximum mutual overlap with all other conditions.

Summing the Z transformations of the correlations of each condition with all other conditions, we find that the random substantive condition has the highest such mutual overlap. Thus the elicitation condition most like that used in the total research produced a distribution of responses which was more nearly equivalent across all stimulus conditions than the no-stimulus base condition itself. The most unique qualifiers were obtained in the geometric-form condition, as indicated both by the low number of shared qualifiers and by the low average intercorrelation value for that condition. It seems reasonable, then, to conclude that the random substantive condition produces qualifier responses of high diversity and of highest communality with the qualifiers produced by the other means of stimulation employed.

There are several advantages that accrue to the use of noun stimuli in addition to the empirical evidence just presented. It is possible to increase the diversity of qualifier types obtained with these stimuli by judicious selection of the noun items. The fifth condition of this study employed noun stimuli which had been selected on the basis of pretesting as having had the highest uncertainty (H) values in a group of 200 noun stimuli administered in a word-association task employing 100 subjects. The uncertainty value is computed using Shannon's conditional entropy measure $H_i(j)$, and it indexes the shape of the probability distribution of responses obtained for each of the stimuli. It will be noted that these 30 high H stimuli produced a somewhat larger number of total types than did the randomly selected noun stimulus items. But it is also of interest to note that the average mutual overlap value, displayed in Table 3:3, for these high H nouns is not as great as that for the randomly selected nouns. Inspection of the responses for these two conditions indicates that the low average correlation is produced by the fact that more rare and infrequent responses are being generated by the high H stimuli. The response distribution for these stimuli is more nearly rectangular in shape than for any other condition. Nonetheless, the high H stimuli did produce a very nearly equal number of the same response types as did randomly chosen noun stimuli.

What may we conclude from these tests of the "spew hypothesis"? In the first place, observing the divergence of associates to the geometric stimuli from those to the no-stimulus condition, it is evident that a restricted class of stimuli will produce a biased sample of qualifiers. On the other hand, comparison of the random substantives drawn from our set of culture-common elicitors with the no-stimulus condition indicates that the former yield as many qualifier types and ones that overlap with those elicited in the no-stimulus condition. Should we conclude that in the major cross-cultural project we might have used a no-stimulus condition in each language/culture community and thereby avoided translation entirely? This may be the case. However, a number of other concerns were involved in the choice of the elicitation procedure. First, it is relatively difficult for subjects to comprehend a task in which they are required to produce a response from a specific word class in the absence of any stimulus. In fact, in some languages, e.g., Thai, such a task would be nearly impossible. Second, without a common stimulus basis, at least initially, we would not have had available any ordering criterion for comparing the different linguistic responses. Our later analyses do not require this comparability in terms of common stimulus items, but initially it was crucial in the "boot-strapping" procedure we contemplated. (See Chapter 4 for further exposition of these procedures.) Third, without an initial stimulus identification the procedures for selecting qualifiers relatively independent in usage would not have been possible. However, these tests justify our using a translation-equivalent set of culture-common substantives (nouns) by demonstrating that such stimuli do produce samples of qualifiers which are much like those produced simply by "spewing."

DISTRIBUTION CHARACTERISTICS OF QUALIFIER USAGE

In the first steps of this research we are interested in obtaining from each language/culture community a set of qualifiers which is representative of how language is used in that community, and this independently of American English influences via translation. Since the factor-analytic methods to be used in later stages to describe the structure of the domain of qualification cannot create dimensions that are not represented in the modes of qualifying included in the sampling of that domain, it is critical that the sample include as many productive modes as possible. No intuitive method could be free of the linguistic and cultural biases of the investigators.

With 100 subjects in each community being employed in the qualifier-elicitation task, each subject giving one qualifier in response to each of 100 substantives (nouns), we obtain a "basketful" of 10,000 qualifier tokens in each location — potentially.[4] After key-punching all responses according to the eliciting nouns (transliterated into Roman script where required), completely computerized procedures are applied. The procedures were designed to order qualifier types in terms of three criteria: *salience* (total frequency of usage across all substantives), *diversity* (number of different substantives with which used), and *independence* (lack of correlation with other qualifiers across substantives). The first two criteria, salience and diversity, can be combined into a single index, the information-theory measure H — which we may term *productivity,* in much the same sense that linguists use this term. In other words, working "blindly" with standardized computer procedures, we wish to derive uniquely for each language/culture community a set of terms that comprise its most characteristic and productive modes of qualifying experience and that, by excluding highly redundant modes, maximize the opportunity for as many independent dimensions of qualification as possible to emerge in subsequent factor analyses.

Overall Frequency Distributions of Qualifier Types[5]

A first question we may put to the qualifier data is this: do they display lawful regularities of distribution? Many alternative theoretical laws of word-frequency distribution have been advanced. An early one was proposed by G. Kingsley Zipf (1935) — that log-frequency is an inverse function of log-

---

[4] We say "potentially" because there are always some subjects who either fail to respond at all to certain nouns or who produce responses which, even according to our liberal criteria, are judged to be nonqualifiers by our ethnolinguist and our colleagues in that location. All such nonqualifiers are treated as tokens of one type, just as all nonresponses are treated as tokens of one type; i.e., ten nonresponses are considered as ten occurrences of the single type "blank."

[5] Based on data from 12 communities available in 1963. Adapted from Miron and Wolfe (1964). Since the details have been published, only a brief summary is given here.

rank (in frequency). Herdan (1956) more recently has brought together a series of analyses, the import of which is to establish a lognormal function for frequency against rank frequency. Still more recently Howes and Geschwind (1964) have used lognormal transformations of word frequencies with success in characterizing the *ad libidum* speech of aphasic patients. These laws are all mathematical variations on the same theme and are similar in principle to the Hullian (1943) notions of habit-family hierarchies and their momentary modifications by an oscillation mechanism.

Method of analysis. Each qualifier type in our data has an associated frequency of occurrence representing the total number of tokens of the type across all subjects and all stimulus nouns. These types can be classified by occurrence frequency: category i contains all n_i types which share occurrence frequency f_i. It was hypothesized that the distribution of the random variable F, which takes on values f_i, is lognormal; i.e., if the variable $X = \log F$ is introduced, the distribution of X is normal. These empirical estimates of the probabilities were used to obtain least-squares estimates for μ and σ, the parameters (mean and variance) of the normal distribution. The least-squares estimates for μ and σ for the token distributions were calculated by the same method as for types.

A further test of the lognormality of the distributions for both types and tokens can be made. It can be shown (see Herdan, 1956) that the distribution about the jth moment of a lognormal variate with parameters μ_0 and σ^2 is also a lognormal variate with parameters $\mu_j = \mu_0 + j \cdot \sigma^2$, where logarithms are taken with respect to the base e. For this study, with $X = \log F$, the mean of the jth moment becomes $\mu_j = \mu_0 + \log_e 10 \cdot j \cdot \sigma^2$. Thus the variance for the tokens distribution should equal that for the types distribution, and the means should show the relationship expressed above; since $j = 1$ in this case, the equation becomes $\mu_{\text{tokens}} = \mu_{\text{types}} + \log_e 10 \cdot \sigma^2_{\text{types}}$.

Results. Figure 3:1 displays the primary results of the foregoing analysis for each of 12 language samples. The distributions for qualifier types are displayed as the upper lines and those for qualifier tokens as the lower lines in each subfigure. If lognormality holds and if the f_i are plotted against cumulative proportions on lognormal paper, a straight-line graph should result. Although none of the extant significance tests commonly employed for estimating goodness of fit is entirely appropriate for functions of this kind, inspection of the figures clearly indicates sensible linearity for a major proportion of the transformed empirical points. Correlation coefficients computed between predicted and obtained Z scores ranged between .990 and .999 for the type distributions and between .990 and .998 for the token distributions. Since the squared correlation coefficient gives the proportion of variance of the obtained distribution accounted for by the predicted distribution, the fit would seem to be remarkably good.

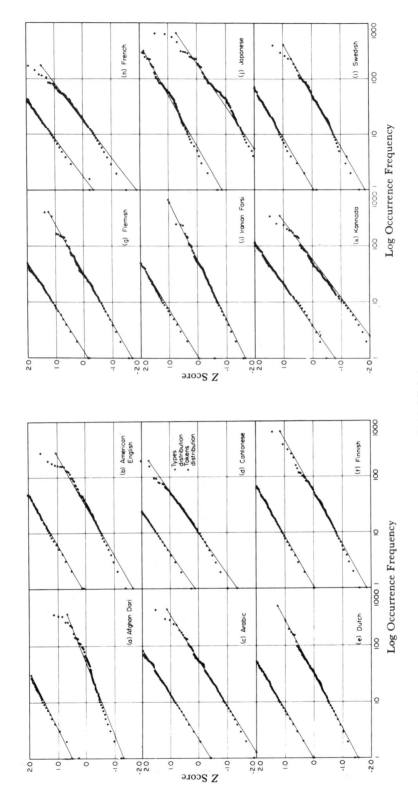

FIGURE 3:1

Distributions of Qualifier Types (upper line) and Tokens (lower line)

Nevertheless, there are differences among the 12 samples, as can be seen by inspection of Table 3:4. Of all the languages, Afghan Dari exhibited the flattest slope (highest variance, σ) for both type and token distributions, indicating that for this group of subjects responses tended to be evenly distributed across occurrence categories. The French data, on the other hand, tended to have greater variation in numbers of responses in the different frequency-of-occurrence categories; i.e., the French distributions displayed lowest variance and steepest slope. This difference is apparently attributable, at least in part, to the greater number of single-occurrence responses in the French data.

The preferential emission of either low- or high-frequency qualifiers could have its basis in either linguistic or cultural characteristics of the speech community, or both. Samples with high mean occurrence frequencies (μ) reflect a preference for using qualifiers elicited from most of the other respondents and by most of the noun stimuli (high stereotypy), while samples with low means reflect predominant usage of qualifiers idiosyncratic to the individual or to particular nouns (low stereotypy). Since stereotypy seems to be a function of both parameters, a working definition for this concept is given by the ratio μ/σ as given in Table 3:4. These ratios indicate that the *type* distributions for Afghan Dari have the lowest stereotypy, and then English, Cantonese, and Dutch in that order; Japanese displays the greatest stereotypy, and then Kannada, Arabic, and French in that order. For the *token* distributions the samples with least stereotypy in decreasing order were: Afghan Dari, Cantonese, Dutch, and Iranian Farsi; those with greatest stereotypy in decreasing order were: Japanese, Kannada, Arabic,. and Finnish.

Since the token distribution should conform to the distribution about the first moment of the distribution for types, the two lines for a given language in Figure 3:1 should be parallel (i.e., have equal variances),[6] and they should be separated by a distance of $\log_e 10 \cdot \sigma^2$. The μ value for tokens and that computed from the relationship of the moments of the lognormal distribution, specified by the equality $\mu_1 = \mu_0 + \log_e 10 \cdot \sigma^2$, ranged between .76 and .05. The value for σ^2 used in these computations was obtained by averaging the variances of the type and token distributions for each language. Owing to the absolutely small magnitude of the standard error, all of these differences are significant beyond the 1% level, for the individual languages as well as for all languages in aggregate, when tested by t. Thus, although the magnitude of the separation between the means closely approximates that predicted by theory, significance tests indicate that these departures from predicted values are significant.

---

[6] As is evident from Table 3:4 (values of σ) and from visual inspection of Figure 3:1, type and token distributions are least parallel, interestingly enough, for Afghan Dari and Iranian Farsi, essentially variants of the same language.

TABLE 3:4

Estimated Lognormal Parameters, Transformation Constants, and Number of Determinations on Which Based[a]

LANGUAGE	TYPES							TOKENS					
	N	n	m	k	μ	σ	μ/σ	N	m	k	μ	σ	μ/σ
Arabic	708	71	1.23	−.40	.33	.81	.41	8,749	1.22	−2.12	1.74	.82	2.12
Cantonese	2,509	65	1.38	.10	−.07	.73	−.10	9,730	1.35	−1.36	1.01	.74	1.36
Dutch	1,442	68	1.20	.04	−.03	.83	−.04	9,557	1.04	−1.55	1.49	.96	1.55
English	1,138	62	1.12	.13	−.12	.90	−.13	7,349	1.11	−1.66	1.49	.90	1.66
A-Dari	1,681	36	1.00	.50	−.50	1.00	−.50	9,582	.79	−1.33	1.68	1.26	1.33
I-Farsi	1,117	43	1.19	−.04	.03	.84	.04	9,612	.93	−1.65	1.77	1.07	1.65
Finnish	1,072	73	1.12	−.03	.03	.90	.03	9,768	1.08	−1.87	1.73	.93	1.86
Flemish	1,260	66	1.25	−.13	.10	.80	.13	9,572	1.13	−1.69	1.50	.89	1.69
French	1,566	67	1.45	−.34	.23	.69	.33	9,813	1.50	−1.86	1.24	.67	1.85
Japanese	290	81	1.13	−.85	.75	.89	.84	9,997	1.33	−2.97	2.22	.75	2.96
Kannada	612	75	1.34	−.78	.58	.74	.78	9,600	1.39	−2.42	1.74	.72	2.42
Swedish	903	68	1.13	−.04	.03	.88	.03	7,881	1.09	−1.84	1.68	.92	1.83

[a] N = Number of word types or tokens obtained, n = number of occurrence categories, and m and k are constants in the linear equation $y = mX + k$.

Interpretation. Previous successful applications of the lognormal transformation to word-frequency distributions have been made on nouns, function words, and all word occurrences in running texts (see Herdan, 1956). Apparently we may now add qualifiers as obtained from a restricted word-association procedure to the growing list of such successful applications.

No compelling linguistic explanation appears to exist for the obtained ordering of the groups in terms of their joint parameter variations. Although three of the lowest stereotypy languages are of Indo-European origin, the presence of a Sino-Tibetan language (Cantonese) in this group makes it unlikely that language-family differences alone will suffice. The four highest stereotypy samples comprise four different language families: Japanese, Kannada (Dravidian), Arabic (Semitic), and Finnish (Finno-Ugric). It seems necessary to invoke some cultural explanation, but what that might be is by no means obvious. It is possible that these variations might be due to the nature of student-teacher interactions. Variation in the formality of secondary school education would be expected to influence the amount of innovation the students perceive as being permitted. It is of interest to note in this regard that the Japanese sample, for which a high degree of formality in secondary education is a well-attested fact, exhibits the highest stereotypy values.

QUALIFIER ANALYSIS

QUALIFIER PRODUCTIVITY

The first step in the treatment of the qualifier data was to arrange the adjectival associates into an ordered list. Investigators seeking an ordering of responses to a stimulus or an aggregate of stimuli have typically utilized the relative frequency of a given response as an indicant of its position in a hierarchy of alternatives. Hull's (1943) notion of the habit-family hierarchy, for example, assumes varying degrees of habit strength for such alternative responses, as indexed by some frequency, intensity, or latency measure. Strictly speaking, such measures of response strength apply to individual organisms and are indexed by observations over an extended period; in practice, they are often estimated from frequencies of responding over a set of individuals, on the assumption of a linear relation between probability of occurrence among equivalent individuals and habit strength within an individual. In Figure 3:2 we display several hypothetical associative hierarchies. The strengths of the various Noun(N)–Qualifier(Q) associations in this figure are indexed by the frequencies of responding (hypothetically), f, across a set of 50 subjects and are also expressed as probabilities of occurrence, p, within the set.

These hierarchies illustrate various degrees of stereotypy, B the most and C the least; they also illustrate the fact that the same qualifiers may be

FIGURE 3:2

Hypothetical Hierarchies in a Word-Association Task

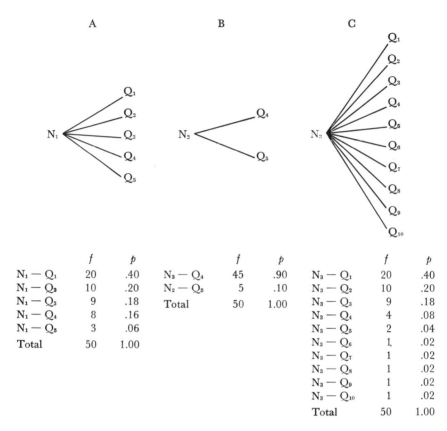

	f	p		f	p		f	p
$N_1 - Q_1$	20	.40	$N_2 - Q_4$	45	.90	$N_3 - Q_1$	20	.40
$N_1 - Q_2$	10	.20	$N_2 - Q_5$	5	.10	$N_3 - Q_2$	10	.20
$N_1 - Q_3$	9	.18	Total	50	1.00	$N_3 - Q_3$	9	.18
$N_1 - Q_4$	8	.16				$N_3 - Q_4$	4	.08
$N_1 - Q_5$	3	.06				$N_3 - Q_5$	2	.04
Total	50	1.00				$N_3 - Q_6$	1	.02
						$N_3 - Q_7$	1	.02
						$N_3 - Q_8$	1	.02
						$N_3 - Q_9$	1	.02
						$N_3 - Q_{10}$	1	.02
						Total	50	1.00

given to different noun stimuli, but with widely different frequencies. But illustration is a far cry from quantification. We need some way of representing mathematically how hierarchy C differs from hierarchy A despite the fact that the first five qualifiers in each are identical, how B differs from both A and C despite including no additional responses, and so on. Furthermore, such hierarchies provide no information about the probabilities of the nouns which give rise to them. A given qualifier, e.g., *red* as Q_4 in hierarchy B, may have a high probability of occurrence to a particular and perhaps rare noun, e.g., BLOOD, and yet its probability in response to the aggregate set of nouns may be quite small. One obvious way to index the differences apparent in A, B, and C would be simply to count the number of different response types in each; another might be to compute the ratio of the dominant response type to all others; and yet another might be to compute the frequencies of Q_1 vs. Q_2 vs. Q_3 etc. across all hierarchies. Yet none of these reflects adequately the relative frequencies and diversities of modes of qualification.

The H index. Fortunately there is a powerful model already available for this kind of problem. The model is that for information transmission proposed by Shannon (Shannon and Weaver, 1949), which, although devised for an entirely different purpose, appears to fit the word-association situation quite well. Shannon has proposed that the degree of coupling of two communication systems may be indexed by the entropy (equivocation or uncertainty) formula:

$$H_i(j) = - \sum_i \sum_j p(ij) \log p_i(j)$$

where i and j are the systems in question, $p(ij)$ is the probability of the joint occurrence of states i and j, and $p_i(j)$ is the probability of state j given state i. The degree to which states of system j are unpredictable from knowledge of the states of system i, or vice versa, is known as the equivocation of the coupled systems. If the states of neither i nor j are predictable from each other, then the systems can be said to be independent and display maximum equivocation. States of system j contingent upon states of system i can be displayed in exactly the same manner as the hierarchies of Figure 3:2. In this instance we identify the i system as the set of noun states and the j system as the set of qualifiers. We wish to determine whether system j can be considered independent of system i and to what degree.

Another way to view this situation is to imagine that the noun stimuli of the word-association task represent a system of transmitted messages from some source, and the adjectival responses we observe represent the reception of these messages. The degree of "noise" present in the transmission channel is indexed by the degree of unpredictability of the reception given the transmission. The "noise" in our system is the variability of human subjects reacting to the nouns and producing qualifiers. Mathematically, the equation can be said to index the average shape of the probability distribution of qualifiers to each noun. If we choose to consider each of the j consequent states separately, we can derive an equation which specifies the partial equivocation given each of the i antecedent states. The sum of these partial values yields the equivocation of the entire system.

Table 3:5 presents some hypothetical data and the calculation of these values. We assume, for purposes of this example, that 5 qualifiers exhaust the possible responses of 16 subjects. Each subject of the sample matrix has responded with a single qualifier to each of 4 stimuli, yielding a total of 64 observations. Since Shannon's entropy measure includes both overall frequency information and diversity (across the stimulus states) information, we shall now shift to using the term *productivity*, in keeping with the preceding rationale for our cross-cultural qualifier sampling. Considering first the relative productivities of the noun stimuli in our example, i.e., the

TABLE 3:5

Sample Calculation for Equivocation Values

		$j =$ good	big	happy	nice	strong	$\sum_i$
Frequency Matrix	$i =$ HOUSE	0	4	0	8	4	16
	MAN	4	4	4	2	2	16
	STAR	8	8	0	0	0	16
	HOPE	16	0	0	0	0	16
	$\sum_i$	28	16	4	10	6	

		good	big	happy	nice	strong	p_i
$p(i, j)$ Matrix	HOUSE	0	1/16	0	1/8	1/16	1/4
	MAN	1/16	1/16	1/16	1/32	1/32	1/4
	STAR	1/8	1/8	0	0	0	1/4
	HOPE	1/4	0	0	0	0	1/4
	p_j	14/32	8/32	2/32	5/32	3/32	

$p_i(j)$ $[p_j(i)]$ Matrices		good	big	happy	nice	strong
	HOUSE	0 [0]	1/4[1/4]	0 [0]	1/2[4/5]	1/4[2/3]
	MAN	1/4[1/7]	1/4[1/4]	1/4[1]	1/8[1/5]	1/8[1/3]
	STAR	1/2[2/7]	1/2[1/2]	0 [0]	0 [0]	0 [0]
	HOPE	1 [4/7]	0 [0]	0 [0]	0 [0]	0 [0]

$$H_i(j) = - \sum_i p_{ij} \log_2 p_i(j) \qquad \text{index}H_j = - \sum_i p_{ij} \log_2 p_j(i)$$

$$H_i(j) \text{ rel} = H_i(j)/H_j$$

$$H_j(i) = - \sum_i p_{ij} \log_2 p_j(i) \qquad \text{index}H_{good} = .603$$

$$\text{index}H_i = - \sum_i p_{ij} \log_2 p_i(j) \qquad \text{index}H_{big} = .375$$

$$\text{index}H_{happy} = .0$$

$$\text{index}H_{\text{HOUSE}} = .375 \qquad \text{index}H_{nice} = .113$$

$$\text{index}H_{\text{MAN}} = .563 \qquad \text{index}H_{strong} = .086$$

$$\text{index}H_{\text{STAR}} = .25$$

$$\text{index}H_{\text{HOPE}} = .0 \qquad H_j(i) = 1.18$$

$$H_j(i) \text{ rel} = 1.18/2.00 = .59$$

$$H_i(j) = 1.19 \qquad H_j(i) \text{ rel} = H_j(i)/H_i$$

$$H_i(j) \text{ rel} = 1.19/32 = .51$$

equivocation values of the qualifier responses made to them, we see that MAN produced the greatest diversity of qualifiers with the most nearly rectangular distribution of probabilities and accordingly has the greatest productivity. In contrast, HOPE is the least productive noun, since only a single qualifier type is recorded for this stimulus (in our hypothetical example, of course). Turning to the adjectival responses, we see that *good* has the greatest productivity and *happy* the least.

In the actual cross-cultural research approximately 1,000 qualifier types exhaust the responses typically obtained from 100 subjects reacting to 100 substantives, making the net yield of the procedure something like one new qualifier for every ten observations. However, it is true for both the example and the actual data that the sum of all responses to any given stimulus yields the number of subjects, and this is a constant for every stimulus, as long as failures to respond and nonqualifier responses are included (as tokens of the two types). The two numerical indices, overall frequency of occurrence (salience) and number of substantive categories for occurrence (diversity), were obtained for each unique qualifier type, based on the orthographic identities in the punched-card raw data.[7] In theory, the frequency score can vary from zero (the qualifier never occurs) to 10,000 (all subjects give the same qualifier to all stimuli), and the diversity score can vary from zero (the qualifier never occurs) to 100 (the qualifier is given by at least one subject to each of the 100 stimulus words).

Both of these characteristics are combined conveniently in the productivity index (H) for each qualifier type. The absolute value of H increases either with increase in the total frequency of tokens for a qualifier type or with increase in the number of stimulus categories in which it appears. A value of $H = 0$ is obtained whenever a qualifier occurs to only a single substantive, i.e., when it has a diversity score equal to 1, regardless of its total frequency. The theoretical maximum value of H would be obtained only if all subjects gave exactly the same response, e.g., *good,* to all stimuli.

Although the stimulus and response systems in our hypothetical example both have approximately the same equivocation values $(H_i(j) = 1.19$ and $H_j(i) = 1.18)$, the relative equivocation values $(H_i(j)_{rel} = .51$ and $H_j(i)_{rel} = .59)$ of the two systems indicates that prediction of the response set given knowledge of the stimulus set is, on the average, less accurate than prediction of the stimulus set given knowledge of the response set.[8] This is the state of affairs actually obtained in our data. Invariably, the stimulus set has higher average equivocation values than the response set in all of the data we have collected. This datum serves as further justification of the word-association procedure as a means of obtaining lexical items in a language. With relatively little input to the human organism we always observe a gain in output alternatives. Although $H_S(R)$ is invariably greater than $H_R(S)$ (where S and R refer to the stimulus and response sets respectively), it is not the case that the inequality is a constant for all languages. To the

[7] The latter index represents an all-or-nothing scoring, in that a single occurrence of a type in a category is treated as equivalent to N such occurrences.

[8] This circumstance defines a situation to be expected in any few-to-many mapping.

contrary, the degree of inequality appears to be a sensitive measure of linguistic usage. For example, the inequality between the equivocations of the stimulus and response systems of Japanese is far smaller than for American English; the majority of languages classified as Indo-European are about equal in this respect. It cannot be stated that we have isolated any or all of the determinants of this inequality, but we feel that this index may lead to some insights into the interaction between cultures and languages.

Ordering of qualifiers by relative productivity. Applying the H index, as described, to the qualifier types within each language sample yields an ordered list, from the most productive to the least productive modes, i.e., from those modes of qualifying which are most frequent and diverse in usage to those which are least. Tables 2 of the *Atlas of Affective Meanings* give such ordered lists for the first 200 qualifiers within the section for each language/culture community. Table 3:6 here gives only the top ten most productive qualifiers for each of the communities available at the time of this writing.

Certain universals of human qualifying are apparent in Table 3:6. The basic qualifiers for either Evaluation or Potency, *good* or *big* (or close synonyms), have the highest productivity in all but 3 of these 25 language/culture communities; the exceptions are *many* for Iranian Farsi (synonym of *big?*), *tall* for French (the translation of *grand*), and *beautiful* for Tzeltal in Chiapas. The opposites of these "positive" qualifiers, *bad* and *little* (or their close synonyms), also appear among the top ten in productivity for most of the groups. The qualifiers *beautiful* or *pleasant* (or close synonyms) appear among the top ten everywhere except in American English, Afghan Dari, Kannada, and Polish. There are also uniquenesses: *awful, profuse,* and *extreme* for Bengali; *lovable* for Cantonese; *ruined* for Afghan Dari; *kind* for Iranian Farsi; *firm, spoilt,* and *difficult* for Finnish; *intense* for Flemish; *fine* and *soft* for French; *clean* for Greek; *more* and *sharp* for Hindi; *reliable, glad,* and *splendid* for Japanese; *slight, dark,* and *fair* for Kannada; *curious* for Polish; *hard* and *necessary* for Serbo-Croatian; *amusing* for Swedish; *die* for Thai; *wicked* for Turkish; *not beautiful* for Tzeltal.[9]

It is also evident that color qualifiers often appear among the top ten in productivity, but unevenly with respect to language/culture communities. Since this seems of sufficient interest for separate analysis, Table 3:7 presents the H ranks for color terms appearing among the top 40 H ranks for each group. *Black* and *white* and the single hue *red* are clearly the most productive for our sample of human communities, appearing among the top 40 H ranks everywhere except Japan and possibly Mysore (Kannada) — if we do

---

[9] Although these uniquenesses in modes of qualifying undoubtedly merit cultural interpretation in many cases, we will not attempt it here. For one thing, we are dealing with rough and perhaps misleading translations in particular instances (e.g., Afghan Dari *xaraab*, transliteration, to English *ruined*).

not accept *dark* and *fair* for *black* and *white* respectively. The term translating as *yellow* appears in 11 places and *blue* in 9, but if we add the Tzeltal *blue-green* there are 10 "blues." *Red* and *yellow* are discriminated by separate high-productivity terms in 11 locations; blue and green are discriminated in only 3 locations. Other color terms that occur among the top 40 *H* ranks

TABLE 3:6

Ten Highest H-Ranked Qualifiers (Q) for 25 Language/Culture Communities[a]

AMERICAN ENGLISH		LEBANESE ARABIC		BENGALI		CANTONESE		AFGHAN DARI	
Q	H	Q	H	Q	H	Q	H	Q	H
good	228	large	324	good	327	big	092	good	710
big	140	beautiful	241	beautiful	321	great	086	large	172
great	091	great	168	big	169	beautiful	071	many	166
small	082	severe	122	*awful*[b]	143	frightening	062	bad	162
large	076	small	121	*profuse*	140	very big	037	much	137
bad	072	long	104	bad	118	small	037	*ruined*	121
little	067	strong	088	black	095	*lovable*	034	black	089
long	063	plentiful	085	little	087	huge	031	white	083
hard	053	white	065	*extreme*	062	long	026	big	076
strong	043	red	058	tall	060	good	025	little	071

DUTCH		IRANIAN FARSI		FINNISH		FLEMISH		FRENCH	
Q	H	Q	H	Q	H	Q	H	Q	H
large	519	many	464	good	393	big	425	tall	132
good	255	good	421	big	374	good	203	good	083
beautiful	137	big, great	349	*firm*	185	beautiful	166	deep	048
small	093	bad	141	small	158	little	078	white	045
much	084	small	130	beautiful	119	hard	066	hard	044
hard	063	little	128	long	097	long	061	black	037
heavy	059	beautiful	113	bad	087	strong	060	*fine*	036
long	041	pretty	101	pleasant	067	thick	058	violent	031
bad	040	black	056	*spoilt*	060	*intense*	058	pleasant	031
thick	033	*kind*	039	*difficult*	043	bad	053	*soft*	030

GREEK		HINDI		ITALIAN		JAPANESE		KANNADA	
Q	H	Q	H	Q	H	Q	H	Q	H
big	561	good	737	big	433	big	349	good	336
good	233	beautiful	467	beautiful	179	pretty	323	big	172
beautiful	206	many	235	good	140	beautiful	311	*slight*	115
small	132	big, great	228	strong	098	*reliable*	250	much	093
much	059	*more*	221	long	094	fearful	190	*dark*	083
strong	053	bad	200	small	081	small	141	*fair*	074
bad	050	black	191	immense	047	*glad*	131	severe	072
beautiful	049	long	124	hard	044	strong	123	bad	068
deep	046	*sharp*, swift	107	much	043	*splendid*	116	dreadful	067
clean	044	small, little	098	big, thick	040	good	110	small	067

[a] A number of items in the table are not qualifiers. This is a result of difficulty in translation of the original item into English.
[b] Unique (within top ten) are italicized.

TABLE 3:6 (Continued)

MALAY		PASHTU		POLISH		SERBO-CROATIAN		MEXICAN SPANISH	
Q	H	Q	H	Q	H	Q	H	Q	H
big	315	good, pleasant	1.020	big	240	big	421	big	392
small	107	much, many	553	great	215	little	179	good	226
pretty	101	big	294	small	193	nice	164	strong	119
good	094	bad	226	good	141	good	141	bad	105
strong	084	white	138	long	056	strong, violent	088	pretty	093
long	082	black	103	heavy	055	*hard*	082	small	079
tall	058	large	096	terrible	054	terrible	063	pleasant	064
white	050	severe, heavy	079	enormous	051	*necessary*	056	beautiful	061
black	050	red	072	black	041	beautiful	051	hard	058
red	040	sweet	070	*curious*	039	fast, quick	046	white	052

SWEDISH		THAI		TURKISH		TZELTAL		YORUBA	
Q	H	Q	H	Q	H	Q	H	Q	H
big	381	good	367	good	397	beautiful	924	big	592
good-1	165	much	305	big	389	good	526	good	286
good-2	150	big	208	beautiful	341	white	519	bad	233
small	123	pretty	145	much	199	big	463	small	229
hard	096	little	102	*wicked*	160	*not beautiful*	445	many	216
beautiful	085	small	096	bad	135	red	216	black	184
long	071	not good	059	long	113	blue green	182	large	132
strong	069	*die*	057	small	109	black	178	red	121
bad	059	black	049	sweet	081	strong	110	nice	114
amusing	044	long	043	yellow	076	yellow	095	hard	109

are *blue-green, reddish,* and *whitish* (Tzeltal), *grey* (Swedish), *brown* (English, Swedish), and *gold(en)* (Greek).[10]

The comparative productivities of color terms are also interesting: *black* is more productive (i.e., lower H ranks) than *white* for 15 of these 25 communities; *white* and *black* are also more productive than any hue for 16 of the 25 groups (the exceptions usually being *red*); comparing the high wavelength (*red, yellow*) and low (*blue, green*) ends of the spectrum, we find that in every case the red-end term is more productive than the blue-end term; with two exceptions (Swedish and Turkish), *red* is always more productive than *yellow; blue* is more productive than *green* in all cases but three, and they are interesting — Arabic, Afghan Dari, and Iranian Farsi. These data seem consistent with a theory of cultural evolution in color terminologies (see Berlin and Kay, 1969), as will be shown in Chapter 6. However, our productivity data provide no support for a synchronic parallel

[10] This productivity of Brightness terms and the red end of the Hue dimension is consistent with what we later find are universal trends in the affects of colors (see Chapter 6, pp. 293-299).

TABLE 3:7

H Ranks for Color Terms Occurring among Top 40 in Rank

	American English	Arabic	Bengali	Cantonese	Dari	Dutch	Farsi	Finnish	Flemish	French	Greek	Hindi	Italian	Japanese	Kannada	Malay	Pashtu	Polish	Serbo-Croatian	Mexican Spanish	Swedish	Thai	Turkish	Tzeltal	Yoruba	
black	11	11	7	14	7	14	9	23	19	6	12	7	14	…	5 (dark)	9	6	9	12	13	21	9	14	8	6	black
white	15	9	12	18	8	34	14	37	13	4	24	14	16	…	6 (fair)	8	5	16	13	10	13	13	11	3	11	white
red	12	10	14	35	12	15	24	21	16	11	25	16	17	…	14	10	9	19	22	18	17	20	15	6	8	red
yellow	36	34	…	…	30	…	39	33	…	…	…	31	…	…	…	33	…	…	…	27	14	…	10	10	…	yellow
blue	21	…	…	…	…	…	36	38	…	31	…	…	…	…	36	…	18	…	…	23	33	…	20	…	…	blue
blue-green	…	…	…	…	…	…	…	…	…	…	…	…	…	…	…	…	…	…	…	…	…	…	…	7	…	blue-green
green	40	32	…	…	31	…	35	…	…	…	…	…	…	…	…	…	…	…	…	35	…	…	…	…	…	green
grey	…	…	…	…	…	…	…	…	…	…	…	…	…	…	…	…	…	…	…	…	24	…	…	…	…	grey
brown	25	…	…	…	…	…	…	…	…	…	30	…	…	…	…	…	…	…	…	…	36	…	…	…	…	brown
gold(en)	…	…	…	…	…	…	…	…	…	…	…	…	…	…	…	…	…	…	…	…	…	…	…	…	…	gold(en)
reddish	…	…	…	…	…	…	…	…	…	…	…	…	…	…	…	…	…	…	…	…	…	…	…	33	…	reddish
whitish	…	…	…	…	…	…	…	…	…	…	…	…	…	…	…	…	…	…	…	…	…	…	…	40	…	whitish

between such evolution and what might be termed "cultural complexity" — Tzeltal has as rich and productive a color terminology as American English, Swedish, or Iranian Farsi; Dutch, Flemish, and Italian color terms are as unproductive as those in Thai and Yoruba. The apparent lack of productive color terms in Japanese is actually an artifact; our total data indicate that Japanese color terms are so finely differentiated that none of them have high enough overall frequencies to be among the top 40 H-ranked.

CORRESPONDENCE ACROSS LANGUAGE/CULTURE COMMUNITIES IN MODES OF QUALIFYING

Inspection of even only the top qualifier modes for various sites as given in Table 3:6 suggests that considerable similarity exists. It was decided to check the overall similarities in H ranking of qualifiers for all communities against American English as a base, using the 200 highest ranking in each place. Since the burden of the comparison must be carried by translation of each language into English, it was felt that some procedure approximating objectivity in translation was required.[11] The semantic range of a term in one language rarely covers an identical range in a second language, except perhaps in trivial instances. Translation can be viewed as the mapping of one semantic area onto another. Using this conception of the translation process, the following procedure was adopted.

The first 200 highest-ranking modifiers, as determined by the H statistic, were selected from each of the 15 languages displayed in Table 3:8. The 200 qualifiers so selected in all languages other than American English were considered the *range* of alternatives onto which the similarly selected number of American English qualifiers, the *domain,* were to be mapped. The mapping was arbitrarily restricted to single-value translations; i.e., one and only one transformation of a given item in the domain was allowed. Accordingly, the frequencies and diversities of the multiple meanings in the foreign range language of an English homonym were summed (separately) to yield single entries and treated as if the two items represented a comparable range homonym.

An example of this case is provided in Figure 3:3 by the entry for *tall.* Single-word entries in the range language identified as O-T (other-tongue) homonyms having more than one counterpart in the English domain were split into equal parts and arbitrarily assigned as transformations of the differing terms in the domain. Thus the 257 occurrences of French *grand* were divided into equal thirds and assigned to the three English qualifiers *great, large,* and *tall,* representing the three major senses of the French term.

---

[11] The translation procedure proved to be quite complicated — it is a difficult and disjunctive process at best — so only the first 15 languages available at the time of this analysis were studied.

FIGURE 3:3

Schematic Representation of Translation Procedures

CORRELATION FREQUENCY ENTRY	ENGLISH DOMAIN	FRENCH RANGE
177	good (436)[a]	*bon* (177)
47	big (264)	*gros* (47)
257/3	great (195)	*grand* (257)
257/3	large (153)	
257/3 + 19/3	tall (45)	
0 + 19/3	high (27)	*haut* (19)
0 + 19/3	loud (172)	
56	small (156)	*petit* (56)
64	bad (150)	*mechant* (64)
0	bright (127)	*lumineux* (0)

[a] Token frequencies, if within top 200 *H*-ranked qualifiers, given in parentheses.

Similarly, the 19 occurrences of French *haut* were fractionated into three equal parts and assigned to the English terms *tall, high,* and *loud.* Both procedures, i.e., fractionating and summing, jointly satisfy the formal requirements of a mapping with unique inverse. Such an inverse, however, can only be approximated, owing to the absence of bi-directional equivalence in the translations provided by the particular dictionary editor or lexicographer. If bi-directional equivalence between English and each of the other languages were established, it would be possible to establish the bi-directional equivalence of each of the O-T pairs through the mediation of English. Such, however, is not the case, although the procedures tend to approximate such a condition.

Several other arbitrary criteria were observed in the translation process. The direction of translation was always from English to O-T. The first listed translation entry for an English item was selected unless the lexicographer indicated it was a literary or otherwise uncommon form. Homonym translations followed the same rule, the first listed O-T term for the alternate meaning being selected. If a given English item yielded a translation which was not among the first 200 *H*-ranked other-language items, the English word was considered to have no transformation into that particular language and was accordingly entered. This case is exemplified in Figure 3:3 by the entry for English *bright.* The French equivalent, *lumineux,* occupied an *H* rank of 298, having occurred with a frequency of 6 and a diversity of 3. However, since its rank precluded its admission, an entry of 0 was recorded for it. All translations were deliberately made by individuals unacquainted with the *H* ordering of the O-T terms. Although many, if not most, of the translations are almost certain to be inadequate by rigorous standards, the procedures emphasized errors in the direction of destroying rather than magnifying similarities across languages.

The results of this translation-correlation analysis are displayed in Table 3:8. Separate correlation values are reported for the two components of *H*, frequency and diversity. Because of the bi-directional equivalence problem discussed above, only those coefficients in the top rows of the two matrices can be fully supported by our procedures. The remaining coefficients may be viewed, however, as conservative lower-bound estimates of the correlations to be expected. In view of the stringent conditions imposed upon this analysis, these correlations are of respectable magnitude, all being well in excess of chance levels. These findings imply that the relative importance (in terms of frequency and diversity of usage) of various modes of qualifying experience are generally shared by humans regardless of their language or their culture. It is also important to note that this sharing of modes of qualifying does not seem to depend on any obvious cultural or linguistic similarities. English is more closely related to both Finnish and Kannada than to the other Indo-European groups in this analysis.

QUALIFIER INDEPENDENCE

As already indicated, it was our intention to obtain a relatively small number of qualifier modes in each language/culture community which would be representative of the most productive and independent dimensions of qualification and which could be factored to reveal what these dimensions were. The smallest number of qualifier types obtained was 290 (Japanese data), and the largest number was 2,509 (Cantonese data); the average of all samples was approximately 1,000. Obviously, even the languages with the smallest number of obtained qualifier types provided much too large a number to be used in a semantic differential task. A culling procedure was therefore used which would maximize the number of *different* dimensions of qualification. What was required was a "blind" (for computer use on untranslated data) procedure which would reduce semantic redundancy among the retained, most productive, modes of qualifying and yet be independent of any prior assumptions about semantic factor structure.

Fortunately, a procedure which might accomplish this purpose was available in psycholinguistic theory. If we define the meaning of a term much as Harris (1954) theoretically and Deese (1962) empirically have done, the initial selection and final semantic differentiation procedures can be kept separate. Harris postulates that the meaning of a term is completely specified by the unique total set of syntactical environments within which it appears in the language. Deese defines associative similarity of words by the amount to which the distributions of their associations overlap. Although Deese cautiously restricts his definition to associative meaning, it is clear that the method rests on the assumption made by Harris, an assumption providing both a convenient measurement approach and reasonable face

TABLE 3:8

Correlations in Qualifier Usage across Languages

FREQUENCY

	French	Flemish	Dutch	Swedish	Finnish	Spanish	Italian	Polish	Serbo-Croatian	Turkish	Arabic	Hindi	Bengali	Kannada	Japanese
English	*58*	65	66	81	78	72	55	64	62	73	52	71	70	76	43
French		*55*	53	57	61	52	46	48	46	43	33	60	50	45	34
Flemish			*95*	64	71	56	49	43	74	49	32	60	42	56	34
Dutch				*64*	73	52	49	43	75	47	28	63	43	59	29
Swedish					*80*	70	51	52	62	59	44	61	56	62	47
Finnish						*67*	45	46	67	56	35	72	57	66	39
Spanish							*50*	61	47	63	51	60	58	54	42
Italian								*53*	45	33	44	36	28	34	28
Polish									*39*	45	53	51	58	51	30
Serbo-Croatian										*29*	30	41	34	47	35
Turkish											*50*	69	74	68	38
Arabic												*29*	38	32	38
Hindi													74	78	22
Bengali														69	30
Kannada															32
Japanese															

DIVERSITY

	French	Flemish	Dutch	Swedish	Finnish	Spanish	Italian	Polish	Serbo-Croatian	Turkish	Arabic	Hindi	Bengali	Kannada	Japanese
English	*53*	56	56	75	68	57	58	54	58	64	64	57	69	70	60
French		*42*	41	56	63	47	50	54	46	41	49	52	46	46	48
Flemish			*89*	49	54	49	43	40	49	50	39	64	44	52	37
Dutch				*48*	49	42	48	37	47	48	37	59	42	48	33
Swedish					*72*	63	51	47	55	59	51	54	60	58	48
Finnish						*60*	48	51	57	51	58	57	55	53	56
Spanish							*47*	43	40	45	50	59	53	53	38
Italian								*42*		45	52	47	39	45	53
Polish									*38*	50		49	53	48	30
Serbo-Croatian										*30*	35	40	33	51	44
Turkish											*49*	56	70	57	35
Arabic												*48*	50	49	44
Hindi													57	58	36
Bengali														57	37
Kannada															39
Japanese															

validity. Insofar as our sample of 100 substantives can be considered a representative sample of the possible environments of the qualifiers in a language, this approach is defensible.

An index of distributional quasi synonymy. Let us assume that the total[12] set of utterances containing any lexical item of a language exactly specifies the meaning of that item, in the sense of distinguishing it from other items. This is not an unreasonable initial assumption. Experimental investigation has shown that a nonsense form can be "given" meaning by embedding it in a series of utterances: "*Krubbing* relatives can be a nuisance," "*Krubbing* is one way of getting out of having ideas," etc. (see Werner and Kaplan, 1950; Dodge, 1955). Let us also assume that a sample of the members of the set of total utterances can be drawn at random — so that we can invoke the central-limit theorem — and further that this sample is in some way representative of the whole. A set of 100 nouns in a language, when presented as stimuli in a restricted word-association task, constitutes such a sample of the utterance environments of qualifiers. Note that we require that subjects be instructed to choose qualifiers in the association task by reference to a set of frames, e.g., in American English "The BUTTERFLY is _____" and "The _____ BUTTERFLY."

We desire an index of qualifier usage which will enable us to determine when two items are similar enough in meaning to justify eliminating one of them as redundant. Two lexical items could be said to be synonymous if their distributions of usage within the sample of utterances were identical. However, this definition is far too restrictive; in fact, it is doubtful if any two words in a language could be found that would meet this criterion. It is apparent that we must relax our criterion and rely on some statistical approximation. What we are really concerned with is what might be called *quasi synonymy* among qualifiers — items which have highly similar, even if not identical, distributions of usage (e.g., *good* and *nice*).[13]

The specific measure we have selected to index quasi synonymy among qualifiers is the *phi* statistic. We have chosen a rejection level for quasi synonymy at a high criterion in order to guard against Type I errors — that is, assuming sameness when difference is in fact the case. A significance level of .005 was arbitrarily set for rejection of the less productive qualifier.

The *phi* statistic is a fourfold index of the degree of correlation between two dichotomous variables. The variables are the qualifier terms obtained in the word-association task, ordered according to the H index. Each quali-

---

[12] Since the utterances in a language are potentially infinite, what is really meant here by "total" is a very large sample.

[13] It should be noted that qualifier opposites will very often satisfy the requirements of this definition of quasi synonymy. This is not only reasonable, since opposite qualifiers would be expected to fit into many of the same linguistic frames, but it also serves in most cases to eliminate from the final ordered list of qualifiers those items which would yield each other in the subsequent opposite-elicitation task.

fier is scored either as having occurred at least once in the same stimulus-noun category as another comparison qualifier or as having not occurred in that category. Figure 3:4 illustrates this analysis, showing both productivity (H) and independence (phi) measurements for two words, *andda* and *ssunddara* (both translated as English *beautiful*), drawn from the data for the Kannada language collected in Mysore, India. The *phi* coefficient

FIGURE 3:4

H *and* Phi *Calculations for Kannada Qualifiers* Andda *and* Ssunddara

		andda freq	ssunddara freq
1	HOUSE	13	
2	GIRL		20
3	PICTURE		21
8	BOOK	9	
10	STAR		17
15	CUP	14	
20	FRUIT	1	
21	BIRD		22
22	SNAKE	1	
24	MAP	9	
25	HUSBAND		13
27	TREE	4	
28	STONE	1	
29	TOOTH	15	
30	EAR		16
36	STORY		1
39	WOMAN		14
40	CLOUD	1	
41	CAT	6	
50	TONGUE	3	
51	HORSE	8	
54	COLOR	9	
63	HAND		25
64	MOTHER		4
67	HEAD	4	
70	AUTHOR		1
76	SUN	10	
77	DOG	6	
80	FISH	10	
81	MAN		2
87	HAIR	9	
96	DOCTOR		1
98	WINDOW	12	
99	RIVER		1
	f	145	158
	Diversity	20	14

$$H = 1/N_T \left[\sum_i (f_{ij} \log_2 f_{ij}) - f_j \log_2 f_j \right]^*$$

Calculation for *andda:*

$$H = \frac{1}{10,000} (459.36 - 145 \log_2 145) = .058$$

Calculation for *ssunddara:*

$$H = \frac{1}{10,000} (637.79 - 158 \log_2 158) = .052$$

$$phi = \frac{ab - bc}{\sqrt{(a+b)(c+d)(a+c)(b+d)}}$$

where:

+	−	
a	b	$a+b$
c	d	$c+d$
$a+c$	$b+d$	$\lceil N$

with + and − headers on top and +/− on left side.

Calculation for *andda* with *ssunddara:*

$$phi = \frac{(0)(66) - (14)(20)}{\sqrt{(14)(86)(20)(80)}}$$

where:

andda

	+	−	
+	0	14	14
−	20	66	86
	20	80	100

(left axis labeled *ssunddara*)

$$phi = \frac{-280}{\sqrt{1,926,400}}$$

$$= \frac{-280}{1,388}$$

$$= -.20$$

* This partial H is the index H_j from Table 3:5; index $H_j = - \sum_i p(ji) \log p_j(i)$; where $p(ji) = f_{ij}/N_T$, and $p_j(i) = f_{ij}/N_j$.

is negative, reflecting complementary distribution of usage for these two qualifiers in Kannada. *Andda* occurred with a total of 20 noun stimuli and *ssunddara* with 14, but they never occurred with the same nouns. This suggests the operation of a strong selection rule (see Chomsky, 1965). It is apparent in Figure 3:4, for example, that *ssunddara* is appropriate for modifying humans (GIRL, HUSBAND, WOMAN) and, apparently, distinctively human parts (EAR, HAND), but that *andda* is not.[14]

Application of the distributional quasi-synonomy index. The *phi* measure was made for each qualifier against every other qualifier having a lower *H* value in the productivity-ordered lists for each language/culture community. By way of illustration, Table 3:9 presents results for the 25 highest-ranking qualifiers for Kannada and Swedish respectively. In these tables the 25 highest-ranking qualifiers in productivity are listed in order in the first column, the numbers assigned representing the *H* ranks. For convenience in interpretation, approximate English translations are also given (all analyses are independent of translation, however). Any qualifier marked by an entry in the third column, labeled "Selected," is selected as an independent qualifier, not sufficiently similar in distribution of usage (*phi* below the .005 significance level, i.e., ≤ .295) to any item higher in the retained list. An entry in the next column, labeled "Rejected," indicates that the qualifier in question was found to have significant distributional similarity to some other higher-ranking qualifier already selected; such qualifiers are eliminated from the final list. The higher-ranking item responsible for rejection of a lower-ranking qualifier is given in the column labeled "By." Thus, for example, in the Kannada data the item *bahalla* (*much*) is rejected because it was found to correlate significantly with the third-ranking item *ssvalpa* (*slight*).

It will be noted that most of the rejections in these illustrative tables make intuitive sense. They are often quasi synonymous (e.g., the two forms translating as *good* in the Swedish data, *god* and *bra*) or opposed (e.g., *liten* and *stor,* translating as *small* and *big*). Often the similarity between selected and rejected terms is more metaphorical than literal — for example, *vit* (*white*) with *vacker* (*beautiful*), *farlig* (*dangerous*) with *hemsk* (*ghastly*), and *varm* (*warm*) with *röd* (*red*) in the Swedish data. Occasionally, even with our strict criterion, a significant correlation is found in the usage of two qualifiers which is surprising and counter-intuitive; Swedish *grå* (*grey*) with *snabb* (*swift*) is one example, and Kannadese *ddodxda* (*big*) with *billi* (*fair*) is another.[15] These occasional cases indicate that the

---

[14] Our Kannada-speaking colleague, Dr. A. V. Shanmugam, admitted that he was not aware of this distinction, but when presented with the data for this figure, he remarked that he indeed used the terms in just that way.

[15] Curious spellings like these are the result of the arbitrary transliterations made to transform non-Roman scripts into an alphabet the computers can handle.

TABLE 3:9

A. Phi *Selection Procedure as Applied to First 25 H-Ranked Kannada Qualifiers*

	QUALIFIER	TRANSLATION	SELECTED	REJECTED	BY
1.	olllleya	good	X		
2.	ddodxda	big	X		
3.	ssvalpa	slight	X		
4.	bahalla	much		X	3
5.	kappu	dark	X		
6.	billi	fair		X	2
7.	heccu	severe	X		
8.	ketxta	bad		X	1
9.	bhayankara	dreadful	X		
10.	cikka	small		X	2
11.	andda	beautiful		X	2
12.	ssunddara	beautiful	X		
13.	atti	exceeding		X	3
14.	kempu	red	X		
15.	upayuktta	useful	X		
16.	attyaddhika	great		X	3
17.	kadime	less		X	7
18.	udddda	long	X		
19.	gundu	round		X	2
20.	gatxti	strong		X	18
21.	ssannnna	small		X	2
22.	addbhutta	wonderful	X		
23.	prakaasa	bright		X	14
24.	vipariitta	exceeding		X	3
25.	bhaari	huge	X		

B. Phi *Selection Procedure as Applied to First 25 H-Ranked Swedish Qualifiers*

1.	stor	big	X		
2.	god	good	X		
3.	bra	good		X	2
4.	liten	small		X	1
5.	hård	hard	X		
6.	vacker	beautiful	X		
7.	lång	long	X		
8.	stark	strong	X		
9.	dålig	bad	X		
10.	rolig	amusing	X		
11.	svår	grave	X		
12.	hemsk	ghastly	X		
13.	vit	white		X	6
14.	gul	yellow		X	6
15.	snäll	kind	X		
16.	farlig	dangerous		X	12
17.	röd	red	X		
18.	snabb	swift	X		
19.	tråkig	tedious		X	10

TABLE 3:9 (Continued)

	Qualifier	Translation	Selected	Rejected	By
20.	*rund*	round	X		
21.	*svart*	black	X		
22.	*fin*	fine	X		
23.	*varm*	warm		X	17
24.	*grà*	gray		X	18
25.	*hög*	high	X		

method is not merely demonstrating the obvious and, indeed, they provide material for special study. They may also reflect either poor translations or limitations of our sample of 100 eliciting substantives.

H-ranked qualifier data of this sort lend themselves to a variety of special studies, some of which we intend to follow up systematically. Cross-culturally, one may ask how particular modes of qualifying rank comparatively; for example, the qualifier *beautiful* (as translated) ranks 2 in productivity for Lebanese Arabic, 3 for Netherlands Dutch, Belgian Flemish, and Japanese, 5 for Finnish, 7 for French, 11 for Kannadese, and 18 for American English. Do such differences in the productivity of certain modes of qualifying have cultural significance? Across age levels, one may ask how various modes of qualifying develop in children. DiVesta's data (1965, 1966a) lend themselves nicely to this problem. For example, one can trace the rise and fall in productivity of various color terms with increasing age, or one can trace which members of common opposites first become productive (casual inspection of his data suggests that evaluatively favorable members of opposite pairs appear earlier and retain higher rank).[16]

SCALE SELECTION

Following the procedures just described, a final list of 60 to 70 qualifiers, ranked according to *H* (productivity) and pruned according to *phi* correlations (independence, lack of semantic redundancy), is returned to the local staff at each site. This list of qualifiers is now to be used in constructing a set of 50 bipolar scales, data from the use of which will serve as the basis for factor analyses. The field staffs first obtain opposites for these qualifiers, eliminating those for which no agreed-upon opposites exist. Then they reduce the list to 50 (or increase it to this number if necessary by going further down the *H* rankings) and finally construct test forms in which the opposite pairs define the ends of seven-step scales.

Opposite-elicitation procedure. The full list of 60-70 selected qualifiers is

[16] A recent study by Boucher and Osgood (1969) checks this both cross-culturally (data from this project) and cross-developmentally (DiVesta data).

first screened by the field staff for what may be inappropriate qualifiers. Some of the words may be only marginally qualifiers (e.g., they may be used mainly as substantives, adverbs, and the like). This criterion for elimination is *not* "good usage" or "correct" or "proper" language. The lists of selected qualifiers are then submitted to approximately ten independent informants who are judged to be sophisticated in their own language. These informants are instructed to respond with the best opposite word for each qualifier on the list. If there are two or more synonymous opposites available (such as both *unhappy* and *sad* for *happy*), the informant gives first the one considered more frequent in usage. If a qualifier has two meanings in one form (that is, if it is a homonym, such as English *light* = *not heavy, light* = *not dark*), the informant is asked to give two opposites in an order indicating which meaning he recognized first. When two opposites occur with near-equal frequencies among the informants (and they are not reflections of homonymy), they are re-presented as a forced-choice task (e.g., *powerful: weak* or *powerless?*); if informants still are not nearly unanimous, the item is dropped.

All qualifiers which have received a unanimous opposite are automatically taken as scale items. The remaining opposite pairs are ordered from high to low *H* value, and scales are retained or discarded according to whether there was a clear majority for the opposite and according to whether either of the polar terms had been retained as a scale item to this point. When 50 scales have been chosen in this fashion, the opposite-elicitation process has been completed. It is perhaps interesting to note in passing that we have never encountered any difficulty in explaining the opposite-elicitation task or in the elicitation process. It would appear that semantic opposition, and its recognition by native speakers, are psycholinguistic universals.

Pruning of evaluative scales. The high-ranking qualifiers typically contain a large number of diverse ways of evaluating (e.g., *good, sweet, nice, pleasant, beautiful, kind, honest,* etc.). In one sense this simply reflects the well-attested fact that evaluation is the dominant mode of human qualifying. On the other hand, this overweighing of evaluators among the high-ranking qualifiers reduces the chances of sampling other, nonevaluative modes. Therefore, in our present procedures[17] the field staff is asked to add 10 scales which they think are important in their own community yet failed to survive the automatic data processing. This makes a list of 60 scales used for concept-on-scale judgments. The list will be pruned to 50 scales after initial factorization, and a final set of 50 scales is retained. The final 50 scales obtained for each language/culture community are included in Tables 3 and 9 in the *Atlas.*

---

[17] Earlier procedures, utilizing scale-on-scale factorizations (see next section), used the results of this initial factor analysis as a basis for pruning evaluative scales.

SCALE-ON-SCALE ANALYSES

In the original design of our research Phase I concluded with a scale-on-scale (S/S) data collection and factor analysis. In this task the terms defining each scale are rated as concepts against every other scale, e.g.,

STRONG   *hard*——:——:——:——:——:——:——*soft.*

This proved to be — by all odds — the most complicated, difficult, expensive, and time-consuming of all the tasks in the project. By the end of the second year of our operation, with data from ten countries on which to compare the results of scale-on-scale vs. concept-on-scale factorizations, it was apparent that essentially the same information derived from both procedures. Therefore, the more cumbersome scale-on-scale task was omitted. However, this task did provide certain information about the reliability of semantic judgments and about the reciprocity of scale terms, along with information about the nature of factors, which could not have been obtained otherwise. This information will be briefly summarized in this section.

DESIGN OF TASKS I AND II

Preliminary explorations on the design of the scale-on-scale task were carried out in the United States and Finland. The preliminary form, which we shall refer to as Task I, employed all possible combinations of pairs of the 50 sets of polar terms. All possible orderings of scales within each pair were utilized. This form, displayed in the upper portion of Figure 3:5, contained 5,000 judgments obtained from a total of 200 subjects in each of the two countries. The reversal of scale items as concepts is represented in Figure 3:5 by a comparison of the A vs. C and B vs. D matrices. Reversal of the roles of the scales (as either rated or rating scales) is represented in the figure by comparison of matrices A vs. B and C vs. D.

The condition intercorrelations and reliabilities for Task I are presented in Table 3:10 for data corrected for test length and attenuation. The correlations between conditions are presented as the off-diagonal values, and the reliabilities (based on split halves) are presented in the principal diagonal. The corrected correlations between the conditions where the rated and rating pairs are reversed (GOOD on *big-little* vs. BIG on *good-bad* and BAD on *big-little* vs. LITTLE on *good-bad*) were high ($r_{A,B} = .94$ and $r_{C,D} = .91$). The reliabilities for all variations in ordering of the constituent pair items also can be seen to be uniform and reasonably high, ranging between $r = .73$ to $r = .80$ (the principal diagonal of Table 3:10).

Although the correlations between conditions in these data are all generally high, it was felt that the correlations for one set of conditions were sufficiently low to warrant experimental control. The conditions where the rated terms are opposites (GOOD on *big-little* vs. BAD on *big-little*) have

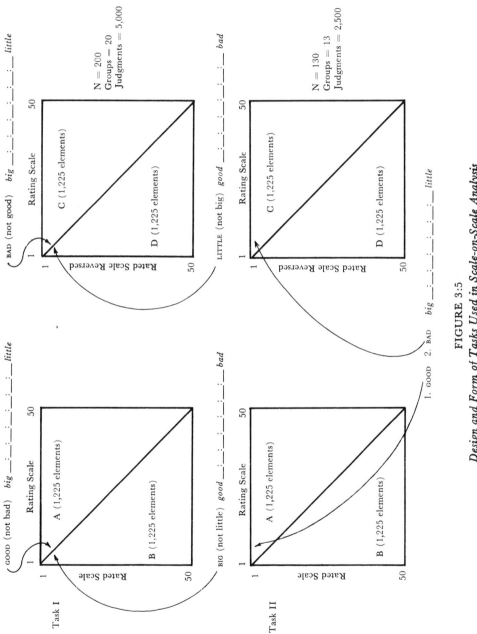

FIGURE 3:5

Design and Form of Tasks Used in Scale-on-Scale Analysis

TABLE 3:10

*Reliabilities and Condition Correlations for S/S Task I, Corrected
for Shortened Test Length and Attenuation*

	CONDITION			
	A	B	C	D
A	.80	.94	−.89	**
B		.75	**	−.84
C			.80	.91
D				.73

** Values not computed.

corrected correlations $r_{A,C} = -.89$ and $r_{B,D} = -.84$. Controlling for this one variable and discarding control of the reversal of rating scale roles resulted in the decision to reduce the total judgment task to 2,500 items. This new task, indicated as Task II, is displayed in the lower portion of Figure 3:5 and was adopted for all subsequent testings.

In detail, Task II was designed so that small subgroups of the total 130 subjects could conveniently complete a small segment of the total number of judgments required. Each of 12 groups of 10 subjects each was given 94 scale pairs and a 13th group of 10 subjects given 97 scale pairs. Each scale pair required the separate judgment of the two terms of the rated scale on the rating scale as depicted by the example (Figure 3:5):

1. GOOD 2. BAD   *big*———:———:———:———:———:———:———*little.*
In other words, conditions A and C were modified and run jointly, and conditions B and D were eliminated. Subjects were instructed to rate the first capitalized item on the scale using its identification number and then to rate the second item on the scale using the second identification number. No attempt was made to force reciprocity in these judgments of the opposites; on the contrary, subjects were told they should feel free to place the terms at any position relative to each other, including identical ratings, that they felt was indicative of the relationship of each to the scale provided. The order of the scale pairs given to the subjects within a subgroup was haphazardly arranged. Care was taken not to present repeated terms close to one another in the task.

COMPARISON OF TASKS I AND II

In order to substantiate the comparability of these two versions of the scale-on-scale task, as well as to gather data on the reliabilities of the factorial dimensions of these data, both versions of the task were administered to subjects in the United States. Table 3:11 displays the highest-loading scales

TABLE 3:11

Salient Scales after Principal-Component Factoring of Scale-on-Scale Tasks for American English

Task I		Task II	
Factor I (54.3%)		Factor I (47.2%)	
good-bad	.95	fine-coarse	.90
clean-dirty	.94	clean-dirty	.90
nice-awful	.93	good-bad	.89
fresh-stale	.92	straight-crooked	.88
beautiful-ugly	.92	shiny-dull	.88
shiny-dull	.91	happy-sad	.88
Factor II (12.8%)		Factor II (13.9%)	
strong-weak	.83	big-little	.84
big-little	.82	powerful-powerless	.77
powerful-powerless	.68	strong-weak	.74
hard-soft	.64	long-short	.72
loud-soft	.63	high-low	.62
long-short	.62	many-few	.61
Factor III (7.7%)		Factor III (7.1%)	
noisy-quiet	.66	burning-freezing	.78
burning-freezing	.58	hot-cold	.64
momentary-everlasting	.56	fast-slow	.55
hot-cold	.54	funny-serious	.55
young-old	.53	shallow-deep	.48
fast-slow	.43	young-old	.41

in each of the first three factors from the two tasks, and the close correspondence is evident from inspection; rank-order correlations across scales for Factors I, II, and III were .96, .93, and .82 respectively. Given this result, it was decided that all other samples of scale-on-scale data would utilize the Task II design.

ANALYSIS OF SCALE RECIPROCITY

Since the SD form utilizes scales defined by adjectival opposites, the degree to which the adjectives comprising each of the scales are actually used by subjects as opposites is a matter of interest. The degree of oppositeness or reciprocity of the polar terms of an SD scale may be defined by the degree to which the ratings of each of the terms considered separately is found to be equally displaced or polarized on opposite sides of the center position of a scale. Since judgments of each of the polar terms defining each scale were obtained separately in the Task II design of the scale-on-scale task, it is possible to obtain measurements of reciprocity of the opposites from these data, in terms of the subject means for each adjective as it was rated on each of the 49 other scales.

An illustrative example of these calculations is displayed in Table 3:12 for the data obtained from the American English subjects responding to the terms *hellish* and *heavenly*. For purposes of these calculations, the seven positions of a scale are assigned values from −3 to +3, the left-hand member of a scale pair always being coded as −3 and the right-hand member as +3. Next, we calculate the algebraic sum of the ratings of the ten subjects responding to each of the terms as rated on a single scale. For the term *hellish* as rated on the scale *everlasting-momentary* this sum equals 1 (mean = .1), while the term *heavenly* as rated on the same scale yielded a sum of −15 (mean = −1.5). For the *hellish-heavenly* example, the obtained

TABLE 3:12

Analysis of A (Normal) and C (Reversed) Concept Ratings of Task II, Exemplified by the Scale Differences Obtained for hellish-heavenly

Exemplary Calculation: Each term of *hellish-heavenly* summed on *everlasting-momentary*

$$d_{(A-C)} = \sum_{Ss} hellish + \sum_{Ss} heavenly = 1 - 15 = -14$$

Rating Scale	$d_{(A-C)}$	Rating Scale	$d_{(A-C)}$
fresh-stale	−1	everlasting-momentary	−14
empty-full	1	freezing-burning	10
poor-rich	2	light-heavy	−5
noisy-quiet	0	shallow-deep	2
awful-nice	−1	many-few	−4
sour-sweet	1	tender-tough	0
strong-weak	0	hard-soft	0
powerful-powerless	0	slow-fast	1
fine-coarse	0	needed-unneeded	−4
dull-shiny	−3	safe-dangerous	0
useless-useful	4	dry-wet	−7
square-round	−2	sane-mad	−3
dark-light	−2	happy-sad	−3
young-old	−1	dishonest-honest	−3
sharp-dull	−4	helpful-unhelpful	3
mild-harsh	0	clean-dirty	−2
big-little	−2	rough-smooth	−1
short-long	−3	unbroken-broken	−2
high-low	0	good-bad	1
hot-cold	−8	alive-dead	10
false-true	−1	beautiful-ugly	−1
dumb-smart	1	white-black	3
crooked-straight	3	faithful-unfaithful	0
known-unknown	−4	soft-loud	0
funny-serious	3	$\Sigma |d_{(A-C)}| = 126$	

sums indicate that neither term was rated as being *momentary* — which is certainly reasonable! These sums are next algebraically added to yield a signed sum reflecting the degree of reciprocity in the departure of the two terms from the zero point of the scale ($d_{(A-C)}$). Accordingly, if the opposites were equally polarized around the zero scale position, this algebraic sum would equal zero. The degree to which the terms are not equally polarized around the midpoint will be reflected by the absolute magnitude of the summed polarities. The entries in Table 3:12 indicate the degree of oppositeness obtained for the two terms on all other 49 scales. The sum of absolute values of these 49 individual reciprocity scores is used to index the overall reciprocity in polarization of the opposite pair as rated on the scales. In the example of Table 3:12 the sum of the 49 scale values is 126, indicating a mean absolute deviation from perfect reciprocity of .26 scale unit for the pair *hellish-heavenly* over all scales.

Considered overall, the mean absolute deviation of all scales in the American task was found to be .24 scale unit, which is not significantly deviant from chance expectations (standard error of the mean $s_{\bar{x}} = .28$, $t = .82$). Reliability for this new task based on correlations between split halves of the subjects was $r = .65$ (uncorrected). The correlation between conditions A and C in this task was $r = .97$ (see Table 3:10).

The ranked absolute sums of each of the opposite pairs were uniformly inspected in each language. Items found to have the highest lack of reciprocity in a given language were considered for deletion in the concept-on-scale task to be described in Chapter 4. The median reciprocity values for five communities in which scale-on-scale data were collected (English, .24; Cantonese, .44; French, .47; Lebanese Arabic, .32; Swedish, .20) are all less than .50 scale unit.

These results are consistent with an earlier study by Taylor and Kumata,[18] who had four concepts judged against ten scales, either unipolarly (four steps, 0 to 3) or in the usual bipolar fashion (seven steps, $+3$ to -3). If the scales approximated linearity and bipolarity, one would expect an algebraic summation of the unipolar judgments (i.e., *good* being $+$ and *bad* being $-$ in the appropriate degrees indicated) to replicate the distribution of bipolar judgments. Only 4 of the 40 concept-scale items yielded significant differences between unipolar and bipolar distributions. The present data expand the scale sample considerably and use what we believe to be a more defensible method, one which eliminates single-qualifier ambiguity. When, to take an extreme case, *light* defines a unipolar scale, some concepts (e.g., COLOR) will select its sense as opposed to *dark* and others (e.g., TRUCK) its sense as opposed to *heavy*. Each qualifier in a bipolar scale serves to "anchor" the sense of the other, e.g., *light-dark* vs. *light-heavy*.

[18] Unpublished research cited in Osgood, Suci, and Tannenbaum (1957, p. 153).

FACTORIZATION OF SCALE-ON-SCALE DATA

The Task II scale-on-scale data, with conditions A and C (see Figure 3:5) averaged after reversing the C means, for the ten communities listed in Table 3:13 were factor-analyzed, using the principal-components solution. The means for each scale, as rated on each of the other 49 scales, were correlated with the means obtained from every other scale as similarly rated. This set of intercorrelations of every scale with every other scale forms the matrix which is factored. After factorization the solutions were inspected for "meaningful" configurations of the factors. Since our goals require using the factor-analytic approach as a hypothesis-testing device, we are interested in determining whether the solutions can be found to confirm and replicate the factors found in previous work. Accordingly, we usually attempt some rotation of the obtained factors in an effort either to confirm or reject the replication hypothesis. We have usually employed the Varimax method of rotation, which yields an orthogonal solution.[19] In some instances, however, inspection of the rotated solutions indicates structures without any obvious "psychological meaning," and in such cases the "raw" unrotated principal-components factors are simply retained (this being one of an infinite number of possible rotations). Choice of the number of factors to be rotated remains a rule-of-thumb procedure, and in this instance the problem is confounded by the necessity of finding a defensible analytic procedure that could be applied uniformly to all language/culture groups. The procedure chosen involves determination of the point where the ratios between successive characteristic roots appear to be converging (see Chapter 2, p. 54, for the rationale).

Table 3:13 displays the results of the scale-on-scale factorial analyses. The six highest-loading scales for each of the identifiable factors are presented in this table. Factor names are obviously heuristic, and the arrangement in the columns labeled "Evaluation," "Potency," and "Activity," based on the investigators' judgment, should be checked by the reader himself. Whereas the assignments to "Evaluation" and "Potency" seem clearly justified by the scale correspondences, this is not so obviously the case for the "Activity" column (usually the third factor in order of extraction and the least in relative magnitude). Quantitative analyses of factorial similarities are deferred to the results of the concept-on-scale analyses in Chapter 4. However, even at this stage it is apparent that for all language/culture groups approximately the same proportions of variance are extracted — roughly 40%, 15%, and 10% respectively — for Evaluation, Potency, and what we are calling Activity.

The concept-on-scale effectively replicates the determination here of the

[19] Oblique rotations have occasionally been used to test certain hypotheses; see Chapter 5, pp. 213-216.

TABLE 3:13

*Scale-on-Scale Analysis: Salient Scales after Orthogonal Rotation
of Principal-Component Factors*[a]

	EVALUATION		POTENCY		ACTIVITY	
ENGLISH	FACTOR I (44%)		FACTOR II (15%)		FACTOR III (9%)	
	nice-awful	.92	big-little	.86	burning-freezing	.81
	fine-coarse	.92	powerful-powerless	.81	hot-cold	.76
	heavenly-hellish	.91	strong-weak	.77	fast-slow	.66
	smooth-rough	.91	long-short	.75	sharp-dull	.53
	mild-harsh	.88	full-empty	.67	light-dark	.50
	clean-dirty	.87	many-few	.65	young-old	.49
DUTCH	FACTOR I (42%)		FACTOR II (15%)		FACTOR III (10%)	
	beautiful-ugly	.93	impressive-insignificant	.84	thin-thick	.73
	pleasant-unpleasant	.93	loud-soft	.75	yellow-blue	.70
	good-bad	.92	big-little	.73	loose-firm	.61
	pretty–not pretty	.92	strong-weak	.72	fast-slow	.55
	happy-unhappy	.91	wild-tame	.67	unexpected-expected	.49
	tasty-dirty	.91	much-few	.67	new-old	.49
FINNISH	FACTOR I (47%)		FACTOR II (11%)		FACTOR IV (7%)	
	right-wrong	.95	large-small	.77	young-old	.74
	honorable-despicable	.94	deep-shallow	.76	growing-diminishing	.69
	good-bad	.94	heavy-light	.73	strong-weak	.53
	valuable-worthless	.93	difficult-easy	.64	courageous-timid	.50
	useful-useless	.93	black-white	.63	fast-slow	.45
	clever-stupid	.92	dark-light	.63	glad-sad	.44
FLEMISH	FACTOR I (42%)		FACTOR II (11%)		FACTOR III (10%)	
	agreeable-disagreeable	.94	deep-shallow	.78	violent-calm	.81
	good-bad	.94	serious-frivolous	.73	impetuous-quiet	.77
	magnificent-horrible	.91	big-small	.71	quick-slow	.57
	beautiful-ugly	.91	difficult-easy	.66	strong-weak	.57
	pleasant-boring	.90	long-short	.63	young-old	.57
	clean-dirty	.90	heavy-light	.62	frequent-seldom	.57
JAPANESE	FACTOR I (45%)		FACTOR II (16%)		FACTOR III (7%)	
	pleasant-unpleasant	.94	deep-shallow	.86	cheerful-lonely	.75
	good-bad	.93	thick-thin	.81	noisy-quiet	.67
	happy-sad	.93	complex-simple	.68	near-far	.62
	skillful-unskillful	.90	strong-weak	.68	hot-cold	.53
	thankful-troublesome	.90	sturdy-fragile	.67	intense-calm	.49
	agreeable-unagreeable	.90	heavy-light	.67	early-late	.41
KANNADA	FACTOR I (49%)		FACTOR III (7%)		FACTOR II (8%)	
	best-mean	.94	big-small	.73	fast-slow	.83
	clear-unclear	.92	wide-narrow	.65	wonderful-ordinary	.66
	soft-rough	.91	huge-small	.58	many-few	.57
	pure-impure	.90	great-little	.55	red-black	.54
	beautiful-ugly	.89	plenty-few	.54	public-secret	.49
	delicate-rough	.88	many-few	.53	fatty-slim	.45

[a] Except for Dutch, Japanese, and Swedish, where loadings are for unrotated principal-axes solutions.

TABLE 3:13 (Continued)

	EVALUATION		POTENCY		ACTIVITY	
SWEDISH	FACTOR I (27%)		FACTOR II (12%)		FACTOR III (7%)	
	nice-nasty	.80	solid-hollow	.70	lean-thick	.53
	amusing-tedious	.80	strong-weak	.70	young-old	.50
	kind-cruel	.80	raw-boiled	.62	hungry-satisfied	.47
	kind-evil	.79	hard-soft	.62	lively-apathetic	.45
	wise-stupid	.79	tough-tender	.61	swift-slow	.3
	friendly-angry	.77	firm-frail	.59	strong-weak	.38
ARABIC	FACTOR I (44%)		FACTOR II (12%)		FACTOR III (6%)	
	soft-coarse	.90	strong-weak	.72	plentiful-rare	.82
	merciful-cruel	.90	real-imaginary	.70	general-particular	.77
	calm-tumultuous	.89	rational-emotional	.69	apparent-hidden	.49
	enlivening-fatal	.88	solid-infirm	.62	open-closed	.48
	sympathetic-cruel	.88	important-trivial	.57	large-small	.44
	pleasant-bitter	.87	great-contemptible	.56	simple-difficult	.43
CANTONESE	FACTOR I (34%)		FACTOR II (15%)		FACTOR III (12%)	
	clean-filthy	.86	strong-weak (light)	.79	alert–slow-motioned	.78
	kindly-cruel	.86	big-small	.77	speedy-slow	.73
	good-bad	.85	important-unimportant	.74	fresh–old, shabby	.73
	good–bad, poor	.83	red-green	.72	human-animal	.61
	respectable-lowly	.82	powerful-powerless	.72	strange-ordinary	.58
	free–restrained, tied	.82	coarse, big–tiny	.67	pretty-ugly	.57
FRENCH	FACTOR I (39%)		FACTOR II (13%)		FACTOR III (11%)	
	likable-repugnant	.90	strong-mild	.77	keen-sedate	.80
	pleasant-unpleasant	.89	hard-soft	.73	superficial-deep	.74
	gay-sad	.89	dangerous-safe	.73	tiny-huge	.55
	pure-impure	.89	severe-indulgent	.72	active-dull	.53
	healthy-unhealthy	.88	red-verdant	.70	fair-dark	.51
	superb-hideous	.87	strong-weak	.68	thin-fat	.51

scale interrelatedness but utilizes an entirely different task and another, independent sample of subjects.

It is worth noting at the conclusion of this report on the first stage of the "tool-making" phase that the overall plan of the project emphasizes comparisons at as many points as possible. So far we have presented data indicating similarities (a) in the frequency/diversity orders of usage of modes of qualifying when obtained in a standard elicitation procedure, (b) in the common lawfulness of the frequency distributions of these qualifiers from a strictly statistical point of view, and (c) in the factorial descriptions of the dimensions of these qualifiers when made into semantic differential scales. Chapter 4 continues our report on the "tool-making" phase of this research.

CHAPTER

4

Cross-Cultural Generality of Affective Meaning Systems

In Chapter 2 we traced some unicultural tests of the generality of the E-P-A (Evaluation, Potency, and Activity) factor structure underlying affective meaning systems. Comparisons of samples of people drawn from within the English-speaking American culture — children vs. adults, males vs. females, high IQs vs. relatively low IQs, Republicans vs. Democrats, and even schizophrenics vs. normals — yielded no significant deviations from the E-P-A pattern of primary affective factors. Several tests of cross-cultural generality were also reported in Chapter 2, but they were all based on translation into other languages of descriptive scales usually representing the E-P-A structure obtained for Americans and hence were liable to cultural bias. In Chapter 3 factorizations of scale-on-scale data were reported for ten communities, and again the E-P-A structure was quite clear. In this chapter we report the results of factor analyses based on qualifying dimensions determined indigenously for more than 20 language/culture communities.

In Chapter 3 the process whereby dimensions of qualification were obtained in each site was detailed. There was only one point at which translation from English into other languages was involved. This was translation of the list of 100 substantives, considered to be culture-common, to be used as stimuli in the elicitation of modes of qualifying. It should be noted that this one instance of translation was prior to any data collection, that the final list of 100 substantives has proved to be familiar to people of all cultures, and that our young male subjects were free to produce any qualifiers

First draft prepared by William H. May.

that happened to occur to them. The qualifier types obtained in each location — transliterated in some cases, but untranslated — were analyzed "blindly" by computer so as to generate a list simultaneously ordered according to (a) overall frequency of usage, (b) diversity of usage across the 100 substantive frames, and (c) independence of usage with respect to other, higher-ordered qualifiers. This ordered list of qualifiers was used to elicit opposites, and those for which familiar opposites existed were made into seven-step bipolar scales.

In the second stage of the "tool-making" phase of this research, the original 100 substantives (nouns in English; see Table 3:1) are judged against these scales by 200 new subjects, also young high school–level males, in each language/culture community. The usages of scales are correlated and factor-analyzed, and the factor structures for different groups are compared. These analyses have two purposes, one theoretical and the other practical. The theoretical purpose is to determine if the E-P-A system found for English-speaking Americans is linguistically and culturally universal for the human species. The practical purpose is to be able to construct, within each language, a short, efficient semantic differential which is demonstrably comparable with similar instruments for other languages, by virtue of including scales which represent corresponding affective factors. Obviously, the practical purpose can only be met if the theoretical purpose is satisfied.

SOME PRELIMINARIES

In preparing for the standardization of data collection and analysis at this stage, several preliminary checks were made. For one thing, we wished to further refine our scale sample from each country, particularly to reduce the influence of the first (Evaluation) factor and increase the likelihood of other factors appearing; it was necessary to check the effects of this "pruning" upon the factor structure obtained. For another thing, the magnitude of the concept-on-scale rating task (100 concepts judged against 50 or 60 scales) required that subgroups of subjects work with subsets of concepts, these subgroups further divided into two different orderings of concepts for rating; we wished to check on the effects of ordering, if any existed. We were also interested in the comparability of scale-on-scale and concept-on-scale factorizations; for reasons that will be given, only the American English data lent themselves to a direct comparison of these two methods of data collection.

Scale Refinement and Its Effects

The automatic criteria used in choosing qualifiers (Chapter 3) operate to select scales roughly in proportion to the relative salience of factors. Thus there are characteristically twice as many E qualifiers as there are P and usually more P qualifiers than A. This is appropriate when one wishes to determine the relative importance of semantic factors. However, when one wishes to identify and clarify subordinate factors, and only 50 scales are used, the dominance of the E factor (accounting typically for 45% of the total variance in the scale-on-scale analyses; see Table 3:13) functions in a fashion analogous to noise in hearing, serving to obscure the nature of less prominent factors. It has been our experience that the scale-on-scale task tends even further to exaggerate the influence of the already dominant Evaluation factor. This is possibly because subjects will react in terms of evaluation in rating one scale against another, if they can detect *any* evaluative relationship whatsoever. In making concept-on-scale judgments, on the other hand, the meaning of the concept can influence the qualifier properties noted.

For the early language/culture communities, where the full scale-on-scale task had been completed, the following criteria were used in "pruning" scales for the concept-on-scale task. (1) Factorially impure scales which were dominantly evaluative (e.g., *smooth-rough* in English) were eliminated, while the purely evaluative scales (e.g., *good-bad* in English) were retained. This typically reduced the scale set by another ten scales. (2) Scales found to be definitely not bipolar (linear) by the scale-on-scale test described in Chapter 3 (pp. 105-107) were also eliminated — typically only two or three. (3) Scales clearly representative of factors found in other groups — only one or two for a factor — were added, provided that they were judged to be easily translated and salient in the language in question. For example, where the scale-on-scale factor analysis had yielded an Activity factor that was difficult to interpret, the scale *fast-slow* was added in order to aid interpretation in subsequent concept-on-scale analyses. (4) To bring the full complement back to 50, the field staff in each location added scales which they felt were salient in their own culture but which had not survived the "blind" qualifier-analysis procedures.

As already noted in Chapter 3, in the later sites where the scale-on-scale task was deleted, 10 scales were *added* by the field staff to the 50 generated by the automatic methods to bring the full complement to 60. In making these additions, the field staffs were asked to avoid redundant evaluative scales and seek scales they deemed to represent important dimensions of judgment in their communities which had not appeared in the automatic selection procedures.[1]

---

[1] Following is the procedural guide for the selection of scales: "The scales you add should be chosen to represent two general types [of qualifiers]. The first type are scales which you feel are frequent and important in your particular country. For example, you may feel that the honorifics of your country, if such exist, are important and if no scale is included in your set which expresses this kind of qualification you

For six of the communities which completed the full scale-on-scale procedure, two independent factorizations of the concept-on-scale task were made: one for the refined set of 50 scales (termed "full complement") and one for only those scales generated by the automatic procedures, hence eliminating the added scales (termed "reduced complement"). The purpose of this double analysis was to make it possible to specify the impact (and possible bias) of the scales added on a largely judgmental basis. Correlations between all pairs of scales of either the reduced or the full complements are taken across the means of the 100 concepts. The resulting intercorrelation matrices are then factored, using the principal-components method.

Table 4:1 presents the results of the factorizations of the full- and reduced-scale complements of these six languages. Comparison of reduced- and full-complement analyses provides an appropriate check on whether the added scales are in truth culturally meaningful for each of the language groups. If substantially similar factors are extracted from both full and reduced analyses, it is possible to assert that the addition of scales did not force the resultant structure where no such structure in truth existed. That such forcing was minimal is evident from the close similarities of the obtained factors in the two analyses. With only two exceptions — the reduced-scale analyses for Kannada and for Japanese — the three major factors isolated in both types of analysis for all communities are readily identifiable as E, P, and A. At the same time, however, it should be pointed out that some of the added scale items were chosen in an attempt to clarify the structures obtained in the scale-on-scale analyses. It was reasoned that if an independent factorial entity existed in a given language group, but was observed to be only vaguely defined in the earlier analysis, the addition of one or two scale items potentially representing this factor should aid in its identification — if such a factor were actually present in the language.

This particular circumstance is well represented by the factorial representations of the Kannada data displayed in Table 4:1. Reference to the reduced-scale analysis shows no clear distinction between the second and third factors for the Kannada group. However, the small two-scale cluster of Factor III (*big-small* and *huge-small*) suggests a Potency dimension. The single highest-loading scale of Factor II, *frightful-calm* (*ohayankara-*

---

might consider adding it. It is difficult to guess what may be important in your language or culture, hence the decisions concerning these additions will have to be yours.

"The second type are scales that will increase the number of scales contributing to the dimensions which do not seem to be as well represented as they might. For example, if you note that there seems to be a shortage of activity scales (in the original list of fifty) you should try to add scales like *active-passive, wild-tame, hot-cold,* etc. Typically we find that it is the Activity dimension which is not well represented."

Principal-Component Factors of Full-Scale and Reduced-Scale Instruments as Used in Concept-Scale Task[a]

AMERICAN ENGLISH

	Factor I		Factor II		Factor III	
Full	(45.5%)		(12.0%)		(5.6%)	
	nice-awful	.96	big-little	.81	fast-slow	.64
	sweet-sour	.94	powerful-powerless	.75	noisy-quiet	.56
	heavenly-hellish	.93	deep-shallow	.69	young-old	.55
	good-bad	.93	strong-weak	.68	alive-dead	.55
	mild-harsh	.92	high-low	.64	known-unknown	.48
	happy-sad	.91	long-short	.64	burning-freezing	.36
Reduced	(37.2%)		(14.7%)		(7.0%)	
	nice-awful	.95	big-little	.81	fast-slow	.65
	mild-harsh	.93	powerful-powerless	.77	noisy-quiet	.56
	heavenly-hellish	.93	deep-shallow	.69	young-old	.56
	clean-dirty	.89	strong-weak	.68	alive-dead	.54
	fine-coarse	.89	high-low	.68	known-unknown	.45
	useful-useless	.87	long-short	.65	burning-freezing	.40

DUTCH

	Factor I		Factor II		Factor III	
Full	(27.8%)		(17.8%)		(5.9%)	
	pleasant-unpleasant	.95	fascinating-dull	.81	big-little	.70
	cozy-cheerless[b]	.93	changeable-constant[b]	.74	long-short	.66
	nice-not nice	.93	active-passive[c]	.72	heavy-light	.63
	happy-unhappy	.92	wild-tame	.71	thick-thin	.57
	good-bad	.91	impressive-trivial	.70	strong-weak	.56
	beautiful-ugly	.88	changing-steady	.69	hard-soft	.41
Reduced	(28.9%)		(14.6%)		(6.9%)	
	pleasant-unpleasant	.95	fascinating-dull	.79	big-little	.61
	nice-not nice	.93	impressive-trivial	.74	thick-thin	.61
	happy-unhappy	.93	wild-tame	.68	heavy-light	.61
	good-bad	.91	special-common	.64	long-short	.61
	beautiful-ugly	.89	fast-slow	.62	strong-weak	.53
	fine-coarse	.79	deep-shallow	.61	coarse-fine	.37

[a] Excluding Flemish; factor coefficients reported for that language were obtained by Varimax rotation.
[b] Scale added in field.
[c] Scale added at Institute of Communications Research.

TABLE 4:1 (Continued)

	Factor I		Factor II		Factor III	
FINNISH						
Full	(30.8%)		(9.2%)		(7.8%)	
	nice-not nice	.88	agile-clumsy[b]	.68	long-short	.56
	light-gloomy	.88	delicate-sturdy[b]	.63	sharp-dull	.52
	pleasant-unpleasant	.85	capricious-steady[b]	.60	energetic-unenergetic[b]	.50
	sweet-sour	.82	light-heavy	.56	large-small	.49
	good-bad	.80	flexible-rigid[b]	.56	strong-weak	.48
	happy-unhappy	.80	fast-slow	.53	sturdy-delicate[b]	.48
Reduced	(32.4%)		(8.4%)		(6.6%)	
	light-gloomy	.89	large-small	.68	sharp-dull	.62
	nice-not nice	.88	heavy-light	.65	fast-slow	.61
	pleasant-unpleasant	.87	thick-thin	.62	multicolored-unicolored	.52
	good-bad	.83	long-short	.56	dangerous-safe	.42
	sweet-sour	.81	high-low	.54	voluntary-compulsory	.41
	happy-unhappy	.81	strong-weak	.54	red-blue	.38
FLEMISH						
Full	(27.2%)		(8.0%)		(7.8%)	
	agreeable-unagreeable	.90	sanguine-phlegmatic	.69	long-short	.78
	cozy-cheerless	.89	shrewd-naive	.69	big-small	.77
	pleasant-boring	.89	quick-slow	.68	strong-weak	.64
	magnificent-horrible	.89	sharp-blunt[b]	.64	deep-shallow	.60
	beautiful-ugly	.88	active-passive[c]	.64	old-new	.54
	good-bad	.84	violent-calm	.44	old-young	.51
Reduced	(27.2%)		(11.5%)		(9.8%)	
	pleasant-boring	.87	impetuous-quiet	.80	big-small	.84
	magnificent-horrible	.87	violent-calm	.71	long-short	.81
	beautiful-ugly	.87	quick-slow	.70	deep-shallow	.73
	agreeable-unagreeable	.87	frivolous-serious	.57	strong-weak	.59
	light-dark	.86	accidental-necessary	.53	heavy-light	.57
	soft-hard	.82	winding-straight	.49	high-low	.52

[b] Scale added in field.
[c] Scale added at Institute of Communications Research.

JAPANESE

	FACTOR I		FACTOR II		FACTOR III	
Full	(41.0%)		(13.0%)		(8.5%)	
	comfortable-uncomfortable	.96	heavy-light	.76	cheerful-lonely	.76
	pleasant-unpleasant	.95	difficult-easy	.71	vivid-subdued[b]	.68
	good-bad	.94	strong-weak	.65	noisy-quiet	.68
	happy-sad	.93	brave-cowardly	.63	active-inactive[b]	.61
	troublesome-thankful	.93	solid-fragile	.62	fast-slow[c]	.60
	decent-indecent	.92	thick-thin	.60	early-late	.58
Reduced	(41.1%)		(15.9%)		(7.3%)	
	comfortable-uncomfortable	.95	heavy-light	.77	cheerful-lonely	.76
	pleasant-unpleasant	.94	difficult-easy	.72	noisy-quiet	.70
	good-bad	.94	strong-weak	.63	near-far	.60
	happy-sad	.93	trying-easy	.61	hot-cold	.52
	thankful-troublesome	.92	brave-cowardly	.61	early-late	.52
	great-unimportant	.90	thick-thin	.60	shallow-deep	.40
	fine-trifling					

KANNADA

	FACTOR I		FACTOR II		FACTOR III	
Full	(30.8%)		(7.2%)		(4.8%)	
	merciful-cruel	.89	many-few	.68	fast-slow	.53
	good-bad	.86	big-small	.68	active-dull	.45
	calm-frightful	.84	huge-small	.68	fatty-slim	.42
	beautiful-ugly	.83	great-little	.54	unstable-stable	.42
	delicate-rough	.82	plenty-little	.54	noisy-quiet[c]	.36
	soft-rough	.79	strong-weak[c]	.44	hasty-considered[b]	.34
Reduced	(28.0%)		(12.5%)		(7.2%)	
	merciful-cruel	.90	frightful-calm	.90	big-small	.61
	good-bad	.86	poisonous–not poisonous	.86	huge-small	.55
	beautiful	.85	hard-soft	.85	not poisonous–poisonous	.51
	delicate-rough	.83	many-few	.83	uncommon-common	.50
	soft-rough	.80	plenty-little	.80	many-few	.50
	useful-useless	.76	clear-unclear	.76	black-red	.47

[b] Scale added in field.

[c] Scale added at Institute of Communications Research.

sswmya), may suggest an Activity dimension, albeit poorly determined. When the scale items *noisy-quiet* (*gaddddala-nisyabddha*) and *hasty-considered* (*aatturadda-ssvaavaddhanavulla*) are added, however, a well-defined third factor emerges in the full-complement analysis, and it is easily identifiable as Activity. Similarly, the addition of the scale item *strong-weak* (*balishtha-durbala*) contributed to a clarified cluster of scale items defining Factor II of the full-complement analysis, which is identifiable as a Potency factor. The added scales did not themselves define the full-complement factors in Table 4:1, since in all cases indigenous scales are higher in loading. A similar, though less extreme, effect can be seen for Finnish.

A CHECK ON CONCEPT-ORDERING EFFECTS

In the procedure finally adopted for the concept-on-scale task, half of the subjects in each subgroup (N = 20) were given the concepts in one order and the other half were given them in the reverse order. Since a total of 500 judgments was required from each subject (10 concepts × 50 scales), it seemed at least possible that some constant fatigue effects might be operating, producing either an increase or a decrease in polarization (extremeness of judgment). This possibility was checked with the American data. Figure 4:1 presents the mean scale ratings for the two orderings of concepts averaged over all ten groups for concepts presented in the ten

FIGURE 4:1

Order Effect Analysis for Concept-on-Scale Task, American English Data

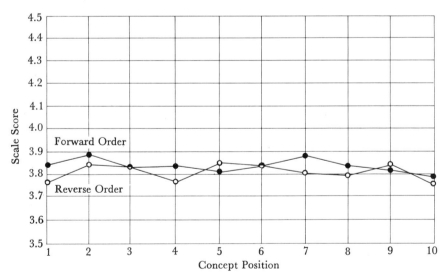

positions within a group. No systematic order effects are discernible. There is no shift in mean rating for either order from the first concept rated to the tenth, and the differences between positions for the two orderings are well within chance levels. The slight constant bias away from the midpoint of the scales (4.0) is presumably due to the fact that the 100 concepts are not distributed evenly through the three-factor space (see Chapter 5, p. 227).

COMPARISON OF SCALE-ON-SCALE AND CONCEPT-ON-SCALE FACTORIZATIONS

The highest-loading scales for each factor for each of the six communities given in Table 4:1 (concept-on-scale) can be compared with the highest-loading scales for the same communities given in Table 3:13 (scale-on-scale). In the majority of cases there has been a reduction in percentage variance of the first factor from the scale-on-scale task to the concept-on-scale task. This, it will be recalled, was the purpose of the scale-sample refinement procedures already described, and it appears that these procedures were successful.

It is equally clear from comparison on Table 3:13 with Table 4:1 that the semantic content of the three major factors is not changed by the type of task given the subject. E, P, and A characterize the structures obtained in both scale-on-scale and concept-on-scale tasks. It was on the basis of this finding that we decided to drop the complicated scale-on-scale judgment task after the second year of the project. The information yielded was redundant as far as the determination of factor structure and construction of comparable semantic differentials were concerned.

Actually, with the exception of American English, direct comparison of the two methods is not possible. This is because, as a result of the scale-refinement procedures applied at the beginning of the concept-on-scale stage, the samples of scales entering the two methods were not identical. The American group had exactly the same set of 50 scales in both scale-on-scale and concept-on-scale tasks (scales being deleted for comparison with other countries only after the data had been collected). Table 4:2 places the three most prominent factors obtained in one task alongside the three most prominent obtained in the other task, as represented by the six highest-loading scales for each factor. Although the scales representing corresponding factors are not identical, the overlap in semantic content seems clear and there are some common "marker" scales in each case.[2] This comparison provides further justification for deleting the scale-on-scale task from our standard sequence of procedures.

[2] It can also be noted that there is *not* a drop in the percentage of total variance extracted by the E factor between scale-scale and concept-scale analyses for American English as compared with most other samples.

TABLE 4:2

American English Factors for Scale-Scale Task and Concept-Scale Task

SCALE-SCALE

FACTOR I (44.2%)		FACTOR II (15.0%)		FACTOR III (8.7%)	
nice-awful	.92	big-little	.86	burning-freezing	.81
fine-coarse	.92	powerful-powerless	.81	hot-cold	.76
heavenly-hellish	.91	strong-weak	.77	fast-slow	.66
smooth-rough	.91	long-short	.75	sharp-dull	.53
mild-harsh	.88	full-empty	.67	light-dark	.50
clean-dirty	.87	many-few	.65	young-old	.49

CONCEPT-SCALE

FACTOR I (45.5%)		FACTOR II (12.0%)		FACTOR III (5.6%)	
nice-awful	.96	big-little	.81	fast-slow	.64
sweet-sour	.94	powerful-powerless	.75	noisy-quiet	.56
heavenly-hellish	.93	deep-shallow	.69	young-old	.55
good-bad	.93	strong-weak	.68	alive-dead	.55
mild-harsh	.92	high-low	.64	known-unknown	.48
happy-sad	.91	long-short	.64	burning-freezing	.36

INDIGENOUS FACTOR ANALYSES

There are many research problems of interest to investigators within a given language/culture community that are unilingual and unicultural in nature. For example, a Japanese colleague may wish to compare the images of nations held by college-educated people with those held by non-college-educated people in Japan itself.[3] The most appropriate SD for this purpose will be one whose scales best represent the factors obtained in the concept-on-scale task as conducted in Japan itself, without any regard to cross-linguistic comparability. The results of the factor analyses to be reported in this section have been made available to our colleagues in each community, of course. In several places the procedures and results of the "tool-making" phase, concluding with a recommended short form of SD for indigenous use, have already been published in local journals by our colleagues, and the instruments are being used by them and other social scientists in their countries.

PROCEDURE

It will be recalled that, according to our present procedures (with the scale-on-scale task omitted), the qualifier-selection stage terminates with a set of 50 modes of qualifying which have survived our selection procedures

---

[3] And Professor Yasumasa Tanaka has done this sort of study with national and other political concepts.

and which produced familiar, agreed-upon opposites. To this set the field staff adds 10 additional scales which they believe are important but which failed to be generated by the automatic procedures. The original 100 "culture-common" substantives, as translated and used as stimuli for eliciting the qualifiers, are now to be used as concepts, each being judged against the entire set of 60 scales.

Since the total task, involving 100 × 60 or 6,000 judgments, would be prohibitively time-consuming and exhausting for any single subject, the concept list was divided into 10 subsets of 10 concepts each. Assignment of concepts to these subsets was random, but then adjustments were made to avoid co-occurrence of obviously related words (e.g., both FATHER and MOTHER in the same set). The order of concepts within each subset was also determined randomly, but again with adjustments made to avoid obvious sequential effects (e.g., GIRL following MARRIAGE). Twenty subjects rated the 10 concepts successively against the entire set of 60 scales, half doing this in the concept order determined as above and the other half in the reverse order. Figure 4:2 presents a sample page from the Kannada concept-on-scale form; the concept being rated appears at the top of each page. The order and the left-to-right orientation (*good-bad* or *bad-good*) of the scales is determined once by randomization procedures (but again with an eye toward avoiding sequences of scales having similar meaning) and then kept constant for all concepts and subjects.

This concept-on-scale task thus generates a 60 (scale) × 100 (concept) × 20 (subject) cube of data from each site. The total data for this phase of the project can be envisioned as a series of some 25 such cubes, one for each language/culture community. Although 200 subjects are involved in the task in each community, the design is such that only 20 subjects contribute to each datum (concept-scale pairing); we have found that the means for groups of this size are reasonably stable (cf. Osgood, Suci, and Tannenbaum, 1957, Ch. 4). In the process of analysis, each data cube is collapsed along the subject dimension, yielding a 100 × 60 matrix of means. This process loses information about individual subjects, of course, but at this point we are primarily interested in the relations among the various modes of qualifying as a *cultural* phenomenon.

The first step in analysis is generation of a 60 × 60 (or 50 × 50 in some locations) matrix of the correlations of each scale with every other scale across the 100 concepts. This matrix is then factored by the principal-components method. If the unrotated solution is clear and interpretable, as is often the case, then this is considered a terminal analysis. If the unrotated solution is semantically obscure, a Varimax rotation is applied.[4] These pro-

---

[4] The criterion for deciding how many factors to rotate is described in Chapter 2 (p. 54). In terms of this criterion, the rotations are not entirely arbitrary or automatic.

FIGURE 4:2

Kannada Concept-on-Scale Judgment Form

ಪಕ್ಷಿ

ನಿಗೂಢ ——:——:——:——:——:——:——:——	ಪ್ರಕಟ
ಅಪಾಯಕರ ——:——:——:——:——:——:——:——	ಅಪಾಯರಹಿತ
ಚುಚ್ಚದ ——:——:——:——:——:——:——:——	ಚುಚ್ಚುವ
ಒಳ್ಳೆಯ ——:——:——:——:——:——:——:——	ಕೆಟ್ಟ
ಸಾಲದಷ್ಟು ——:——:——:——:——:——:——:——	ಬೇಕಾದಷ್ಟು
ಸಡಿಲ ——:——:——:——:——:——:——:——	ಬಿಗಿ
ನಿರ್ದಯ ——:——:——:——:——:——:——:——	ಕರುಣಾಮಯ
ಅಲ್ಪ ——:——:——:——:——:——:——:——	ಮಹಾ
ವಿಷಪೂರಿತ ——:——:——:——:——:——:——:——	ವಿಷರಹಿತ
ಚಿಕ್ಕ ——:——:——:——:——:——:——:——	ದೊಡ್ಡ
ಕೆಂಪು ——:——:——:——:——:——:——:——	ಕಪ್ಪು
ಸಾಧಾರಣ ——:——:——:——:——:——:——:——	ಅಸಾಧಾರಣ
ಕಿರಿದು ——:——:——:——:——:——:——:——	ಅಗಲ
ಕಠಿಣ ——:——:——:——:——:——:——:——	ಮೃದು
ಸೌಮ್ಯ ——:——:——:——:——:——:——:——	ಭಯಂಕರ
ಬಣ್ಣಬಣ್ಣದ ——:——:——:——:——:——:——:——	ಸಾದಾ
ನಿರ್ದಿಷ್ಟ ——:——:——:——:——:——:——:——	ಅನಿರ್ದಿಷ್ಟ
ಬಲಿಷ್ಠ ——:——:——:——:——:——:——:——	ದುರ್ಬಲ
ಗದ್ದಲ ——:——:——:——:——:——:——:——	ನಿಶ್ಶಬ್ದ
ಆಕ್ರಮಣಶೀಲ ——:——:——:——:——:——:——:——	ರಕ್ಷಣಾತ್ಮಕ
ಸ್ವಾರ್ಥ ——:——:——:——:——:——:——:——	ನಿಃಸ್ವಾರ್ಥ
ತಾತ್ಕಾಲಿಕ ——:——:——:——:——:——:——:——	ಶಾಶ್ವತ
ಆತುರದ ——:——:——:——:——:——:——:——	ಸಾವಧಾನವುಳ್ಳ
ವಿರಕ್ತಿ ——:——:——:——:——:——:——:——	ಮಮತೆ
ರಚನಾತ್ಮಕ ——:——:——:——:——:——:——:——	ವಿನಾಶಕ

cedures yield a unique factorization for each language/culture community and reveal the dimensionality of the affective meaning space for its particular set of qualifiers.

RESULTS

Table 4:3 gives the six highest-loading scales for each of the first three factors for the 22 language/culture communities which had completed data collection and analysis through this stage at the time of this writing. Complete factor loadings for all scales are available as Tables 3 in the *Atlas of Affective Meanings;* these tables also include Varimax and Oblimax (oblique) rotations — the latter will be discussed in Chapter 5. For the locations marked by an asterisk, the unrotated principal-axis factorization served as a terminal solution; for those unmarked in this manner, a Varimax rotation (usually of the first four or five factors) was made.

The first thing we note is that the first factor in magnitude of variance accounted for is, in every case, clearly identifiable as Evaluation. A factor identifiable as Potency is usually (17 out of 22 communities) the second factor in order of magnitude, and if not second is always third. A factor less clearly identifiable as Activity is occasionally second in magnitude, usually third in magnitude, but fourth in order of extraction in some cases. Scales suggestive of P and A are quite often fused in the same factor, suggesting what we have in earlier studies referred to as a Dynamism factor; this is particularly notable for the Greek indigenous analysis. It should be kept in mind, however, that these intuitive judgments are based upon translations of the scale terms.

Is there any evidence in these indigenous factorizations suggestive of "types" based on language, culture, or geography? The groups were categorized (dichotomously) in terms of several possible characteristics. (1) *High vs. low proportions of total variance accounted for by the E factor:* six groups were coded as High (American English, Mexican Spanish, Lebanese Arabic, Thai, Hong Kong Cantonese, and Japanese) and the remainder as Low. (2) *P > A vs. A > P on percentage variance:* only six groups had A > P, and they were Belgian Flemish, Netherlands Dutch, Finnish, Greek, Calcutta Bengali, and Afghan Dari. (3) *Activity being either second or third vs. fourth:* only Lebanese Arabic, Afghan Pashtu, and Hong Kong Cantonese fail to include Activity among the first three factors in variance accounted for. (4) *Evidence for fusion of P and A into a Dynamism factor:* Finnish and Greek display this tendency pretty clearly, and possibly Italian, but no others. Characteristic 1 is present in groups representing several language families, quite different cultures, and widely different geographical areas. Characteristic 2 holds for the Dutch and Flemish speakers but also for Finns, Greeks, and Afghans. The Lebanese, Afghans, and Hong Kong

TABLE 4:3

Factor Analysis of Full-Scale Instrument as Used in Concept-Scale Task

AMERICA, ENGLISH *

FACTOR I (45.5%)		FACTOR II (12.0%)		FACTOR III (5.6%)	
nice-awful	.96	big-little	.81	fast-slow	.64
sweet-sour	.94	powerful-powerless	.75	noisy-quiet	.56
heavenly-hellish	.93	deep-shallow	.69	young-old	.55
good-bad	.93	strong-weak	.68	alive-dead	.55
mild-harsh	.92	high-low	.64	known-unknown	.48
happy-sad	.91	long-short	.64	burning-freezing	.36

AFGHANISTAN, DARI

FACTOR I (22.0%)		FACTOR II (18.6%)		FACTOR III (10.7%)		FACTOR IV (10.5%)	
good-bad	.81	humane-inhumane	.86	nimble-lazy	.83	limitless-limited	.72
safe-dangerous	.79	religious-irreligious	.81	fast-slow	.82	long-short	.67
necessary-unnecessary	.78	learned-ignorant	.79	sharp-dull	.80	great-small	.67
fresh-fetid	.77	moslem-heathen	.78	fat-thin	.62	exaggerated-sparse	.65
correct-wrong	.76	courageous-timid	.76	powerful-powerless	.58	excessive-sufficient	.62
whole-broken	.76	unadulterated-adulterated	.72	active-inactive	.56	huge-tiny	.62

AFGHANISTAN, PASHTU

FACTOR I (21.1%)		FACTOR II (10.3%)		FACTOR III (8.3%)		FACTOR IV (7.1%)	
good-bad	.92	pashtoon-coward	.70	high-low	.79	wet-dry	.83
attractive-unattractive	.91	alive-dead	.66	light-dark	.67	liquid-solid	.61
tasty-tasteless	.91	elder-younger	.65	upon-under	.66	soft-hard	.56
lucky-unlucky	.90	domestic, internal-foreign	.65	big-small	.66	natural-artificial	.53
loving-hating	.89	brave-cowardly	.63	overt-covert	.59	long-short	.50
excellent-not excellent	.88	learned-ignorant	.59	wide-narrow	.56	fast-slow	.45

* Factor analyses for these languages are unrotated principal-components solutions; all others involve Varimax rotation.

TABLE 4:3 (Continued)

BELGIUM, FLEMISH

Factor I (27.2%)		Factor II (8.0%)		Factor III (7.8%)	
agreeable-disagreeable	.90	sanguine-phlegmatic	.69	long-short	.78
cozy-cheerless	.89	shrewd-naive	.69	big-small	.77
pleasant-boring	.89	quick-slow	.68	strong-weak	.64
magnificent-horrible	.89	sharp-blunt	.64	deep-shallow	.60
beautiful-ugly	.88	active-passive	.64	old-new	.54
good-bad	.84	violent-calm	.44	old-young	.51

CALCUTTA, BENGALI

Factor I (30.6%)		Factor II (10.2%)		Factor III (9.8%)	
beautiful-ugly	.94	hot-cold	.75	huge-minute	.74
lovely-repulsive	.94	intense-mild	.64	deep-shallow	.66
superior-inferior	.93	powerful-powerless	.60	tall-short	.66
good-bad	.93	unruly-quiet	.59	big-little	.65
pleasing-saddening	.93	sharp-blunt	.59	open-shut	.63
good-evil	.93	fast-slow	.56	powerful-powerless	.61

DELHI, HINDI

Factor I (30.9%)		Factor II (7.0%)		Factor III (6.3%)	
sanguine-desperate	.90	hard, rigid-soft, flexible	.75	fast-slow	.61
helpful-harmful	.90	thick-thin, slim	.68	difficult-easy	.59
constructive-destructive	.89	heavy-light	.59	disingenuous-ingenuous	.48
good-bad	.88	strong-weak (of its kind)	.54	brave-cowardly	.45
superior-inferior	.88	strong-weak	.50	black-white	.42
glad-not glad	.88	sober-gay	.44	pointed-round	.41

TABLE 4:3 (Continued)

FINLAND, FINNISH*

FACTOR I (30.8%)		FACTOR II (9.2%)		FACTOR III (7.8%)	
nice–not nice	.88	agile–clumsy	.68	long–short	.56
light–gloomy	.88	delicate–sturdy	.63	sharp–dull	.52
pleasant–unpleasant	.85	capricious–steady	.60	energetic–unenergetic	.50
sweet–sour	.82	flexible–rigid	.58	large–small	.49
good–bad	.80	light–heavy	.56	strong–weak	.48
happy–unhappy	.80	fast–slow	.53	sturdy–delicate	.48

FRANCE, FRENCH*

FACTOR I (35.7%)		FACTOR II (11.6%)		FACTOR III (6.7%)	
likable–unlikable	.95	huge–tiny	.80	lively–languid	.75
pleasant–unpleasant	.94	big–little	.80	fast–slow	.74
good–bad	.93	strong–weak	.77	living–dead	.48
marvelous–awful	.93	powerful–not powerful	.62	young–old	.45
nice–wicked	.92	heavy–light	.60	hot–cold	.43
gay–sad	.91	solid–fragile	.55	red–green	.42

GREECE, GREEK

FACTOR I (35.2%)		FACTOR II (7.3%)		FACTOR III (6.2%)	
worthy–unworthy	.90	strong–weak	.65	big–small	.81
honest–dishonest	.88	quick–slow	.64	long–short	.61
polite–impolite	.88	active–passive	.52	many–few	.57
filotimos–afilotimos	.88	difficult–easy	.52	rich–poor	.46
good–bad	.88	curious–indifferent	.47	tall–short	.43
friendly–hostile	.87	young–old	.46	slow–quick	.34

* Factor analyses for these languages are unrotated principal-components solutions; all others involve Varimax rotation.

TABLE 4:3 (Continued)

Hong Kong, Cantonese

Factor I (43.9%)		Factor II (13.0%)		Factor III (6.3%)		Factor IV (6.0%)	
good-bad	.96	tall, big-short, small	.87	extreme-balanced (the golden mean)	.76	fast-slow	.78
good-poor	.96	big-little	.85	difficult-easy	.59	agile-clumsy	.78
respectable-despicable	.95	thick, big-thin, small	.79	wonderful-ordinary	.51	alive-dead	.59
lovable-hateful	.95	long-short	.75	deep-shallow	.49	powerful-powerless	.46
beneficial-harmful	.93	strong-weak	.69	deep-superficial	.48	red-green	.39
kind-cruel	.93	deep-shallow	.67	red-green	.45	strong-willed-weak-willed	.36

Iran, Farsi

Factor I (35.1%)		Factor II (14.4%)		Factor III (9.4%)	
good-bad	.91	big-little	.77	exciting-spiritless	.76
safe-dangerous	.91	thick-thin	.74	active-inactive	.74
harmless-harmful	.90	heavy-light	.70	fast, sharp-slow, dull	.70
life-giving-killing	.90	stout-slim	.68	burning-frozen	.68
just-tyrannical	.89	large-tiny	.68	influential-uninfluential	.66
best-worst	.89	broad-narrow	.65	unique-commonplace	.58

Italy, Italian

Factor I (34.2%)		Factor II (11.0%)		Factor III (9.4%)	
sweet-bitter	.93	strong-weak	.79	unexpected-expected	.69
good-bad	.93	big-small	.73	unstable-stable	.68
beautiful-ugly	.91	active-passive	.64	liquid-solid	.65
gentle-cruel	.91	deep-superficial	.62	vague-precise	.57
affectionate-ill-tempered	.90	sturdy-fragile	.61	fast-slow	.55
nice-awful	.90	absolute-relative	.55	unlimited-limited	.54

TABLE 4:3 (Continued)

JAPAN, JAPANESE*

Factor I (41.0%)		Factor II (13.0%)		Factor III (8.5%)	
comfortable-uncomfortable	.96	heavy-light	.76	cheerful-lonely	.76
pleasant-unpleasant	.95	difficult-easy	.71	vivid-subdued	.68
good-bad	.94	strong-weak	.65	noisy-quiet	.68
happy-sad	.93	brave-cowardly	.63	active-inactive	.61
thankful-troublesome	.93	solid-fragile	.62	fast-slow	.60
decent-indecent	.92	thick-thin	.60	early-late	.58

LEBANON, ARABIC*

Factor I (53.7%)		Factor II (7.9%)		Factor III (5.5%)	
great-contemptible	.96	large-small	.59	rare-plentiful	.63
good-bad	.95	strong-weak	.56	little-much	.62
loyal-treacherous	.95	logical-emotional	.53	particular-general	.53
merciful-cruel	.94	heavy-light	.52	hidden-apparent	.48
honest-dishonest	.93	fast-slow	.48	thin-thick	.48
safe-dangerous	.93	sturdy–not sturdy	.46	light-heavy	.36

MYSORE, KANNADA*

Factor I (30.8%)		Factor II (7.2%)		Factor III (4.8%)		Factor IV (3.5%)	
merciful-cruel	.89	many-few	.68	fast-slow	.53	fast-slow	.61
good-bad	.86	big-small	.68	active-dull	.45	short-long	.44
calm-frightful	.84	huge-small	.68	fatty-slim	.42	active-passive	.40
beautiful-ugly	.83	great-little	.54	unstable-stable	.42	closed-open	.34
delicate-rough	.82	plenty-little	.54	noisy-quiet	.36	narrow-wide	.34
soft-rough	.79	strong-weak	.44	hasty-considered	.34	hot-cold	.33

* Factor analyses for these languages are unrotated principal-components solutions; all others involve Varimax rotation.

Malaysia, Malay

Factor I (39.0%)		Factor II (10.0%)		Factor III (9.4%)	
affectionate-hating	.95	big-little	.81	quick-slow	.84
fitting, proper-not fitting	.95	high, tall-low, short	.77	sharp-dull	.78
good-bad	.94	broad-narrow	.72	brave-afraid	.70
good-evil	.94	long-short	.66	fast-slow	.67
noble-mean, humble	.94	round-oval	.64	energetic-weak, enervated	.63
clean-dirty	.93	thick-thin	.60	strong-weak	.59

Mexico, Spanish*

Factor I (50.2%)		Factor II (8.8%)		Factor III (6.1%)	
good-bad	.95	giant-dwarf	.80	active-passive	.74
loving-hateful	.95	major-minor	.78	rapid-slow	.56
admirable-despicable	.95	big-small	.76	young-old	.45
friendly-repelling	.95	immense-tiny	.71	much-little	.39
marvelous-frightful	.94	strong-weak	.65	industrious-lazy	.39
beautiful-horrible	.94	long-short	.63	hot-cold	.38

Netherlands, Dutch*

Factor I (27.8%)		Factor II (17.8%)		Factor III (5.9%)	
pleasant-unpleasant	.95	fascinating-dull	.81	big-little	.70
cozy-cheerless	.93	changeable-constant	.74	long-short	.66
nice-not nice	.93	active-passive	.72	heavy-light	.63
happy-unhappy	.92	wild-tame	.71	thick-thin	.57
good-bad	.91	impressive-trivial	.70	strong-weak	.56
beautiful-ugly	.88	changing-steady	.69	hard-soft	.41

* Factor analyses for these languages are unrotated principal-components solutions; all others involve Varimax rotation.

TABLE 4:3 (Continued)

SWEDEN, SWEDISH

FACTOR I (28.7%)		FACTOR II (9.7%)		FACTOR III (7.5%)	
good-bad	.94	strong-weak	.77	lively-lazy	.81
nice-nasty	.94	firm-frail	.69	quick-slow	.77
kind-evil	.90	big-small	.66	active-passive	.76
friendly-angry	.90	high-low	.60	sanguine-not sanguine	.53
kind-cruel	.90	long-short	.58	warm-cold	.47
amusing-boring	.88	insensitive-sensitive	.52	sensitive-insensitive	.43

THAILAND, THAI*

FACTOR I (47.3%)		FACTOR II (8.5%)		FACTOR III (4.6%)	
right-wrong	.95	heavy-light	.67	quick-inert	.86
comfortable-uncomfortable	.95	old-young	.67	fast-slow	.76
happy-suffering	.94	big-little	.61	loud-soft	.48
good-bad	.94	hard-soft	.60	little-much	.28
pleasing-hurting	.94	thick-thin	.60	thin-thick	.28
useful-harmful	.94	deep-shallow	.56	naughty-well behaved	.25

TURKEY, TURKISH*

FACTOR I (31.0%)		FACTOR II (10.3%)		FACTOR III (6.3%)	
beautiful-ugly	.94	big-little	.64	young-old	.55
sweet-bitter	.92	terrific-ordinary	.61	fast-slow	.51
pleasant-unpleasant	.92	high-low	.57	intense-mild	.47
good-bad	.92	large-small	.54	small-large	.44
tasteful-tasteless (aesthetic)	.91	heavy-light	.54	alive-not alive	.43
comfortable-uncomfortable	.90	deep-shallow	.53	fresh-stale	.43

* Factor analyses for these languages are unrotated principal-components solutions; all others involve Varimax rotation.

TABLE 4:3 (Continued)

YUGOSLAVIA, SERBO-CROATIAN

FACTOR I (36.7%)		FACTOR II (13.1%)		FACTOR III (7.0%)	
pleasant-unpleasant	.94	big-little	.84	alive-dead	.75
good-bad	.93	bulky-tiny	.81	fast-slow	.71
gentle-rough	.92	wide-narrow	.77	sharp-blunt	.68
lovable-disgusting	.91	strong-weak	.72	clever-stupid	.50
beautiful-ugly	.91	high, tall–low, short	.68	elongated-round	.43
bearable-unbearable	.90	deep-shallow	.58	political-apolitical	.40

Chinese, deviating on characteristic 3, could only be said to be continentally akin, and in this as far removed as possible. The Finns and Greeks representing the Dynamism characteristic 4 are of different language families, quite different geographies, and not very similar cultures. We must conclude that whatever the determinants of these differences in indigenous factor structures may be, they are in no obvious ways related to language, culture, or geography.

There is evidence for factors beyond E, P, and A, although they are generally more obscure and are represented by fewer scales. The fourth factor for American English appears to be a Thermal-Dermal factor (*burning-freezing*, .65; *hot-cold*, .63; and *dry-wet*, .52). The third factor for Lebanese Arabic might be termed something like Uniqueness (*rare-plentiful*, .63; *little-much*, .62; *particular-general*, .53; *hidden-apparent*, .48). The second factor in magnitude for Afghan Dari has definite Ethical tones (*humane-inhumane*, .86; *religious-irreligious*, .81; *learned-ignorant*, .79; *moslem-heathen*, .78; *courageous-timid*, .76; *unadulterated-adulterated*, .72). A fourth factor for Finnish, interestingly enough, might be called a Daylight factor (*high-low*, .52; *light-dark*, .47; *red-blue*, .33; *white-black*, .33) — perhaps not too surprising when one considers the significance of daylight in this Land of the Midnight Sun. The fourth factor for Hindi might be called Bountifulness (*many-few*, .60; *open-closed*, .58; *dense-scattered*, .53; *big-little*, .49; *current–not current*, .48; *sufficient-insufficient*, .45; *fresh-stale*, .40). Cultural differences of this sort will be explored in greater depth in Chapters 5 and 7, when we shall observe the effects of oblique rotations of these indigenous factor analyses and of factor analysis of partial correlations.

INDEPENDENT INDIGENOUS STUDIES

One of the best protections against an investigator's unconscious bias in favor of his pet hypotheses is confirmation (or lack thereof) by entirely independent investigators. One instance of this is a study done by H. Akuto and his associates in the Marketing Center Company, Tokyo, Japan.[5] Some 100 monolingual Japanese subjects rated 90 concepts (subsets of concepts being rated by subgroups of subjects) against 50 indigenously selected scales in Japanese. Table 4:4 gives the loading for the five highest scales (estimated) on each of the first three factors obtained in an unrotated centroid solution. Although the scales representing E, P, and A in this study are not, for the most part, the same as those given in Table 4:3 for our own Japanese data — which would not be expected — the semantic flavor of the three factors seems to be identical. The proportions of variance extracted by the three factors also are consistent (although smaller) with what we find. It is worth noting that a fourth factor was identifiable as a kind of

[5] Subsequently published as a paper by Sagara *et al.* (1961).

TABLE 4:4

Marketing Center Company of Tokyo Study: Unrotated Centroid Factor Loadings for Five Highest-Loading Scales on First Three Factors

	I	II	III	
comfortable	85	−20	09	uncomfortable
pleasant	83	−24	−07	unpleasant
bright	81	−20	−19	dark
good	76	−18	19	bad
beautiful	76	−25	21	ugly
strong	45	57	05	weak
masculine	11	53	−06	feminine
active	45	51	−20	passive
intense	−16	49	−37	mild
large	33	48	16	small
lively	−39	−07	49	lonely
noisy	26	−20	48	quiet
young	−44	08	47	old
shallow	24	23	44	deep
fast	−33	−28	40	slow
Percentage of Total Variance	30	09	06	

Aesthetic Evaluation, characterized by scales like *pleasurable-painful, cheerful-gloomy,* and *beautiful-ugly.*

CROSS-CULTURAL FACTOR ANALYSES

The indigenous factor analyses provide one test of the generality of the E-P-A affective meaning system, but it is necessarily indirect — subjective and intuitive. It further admits to the interpretation process some unknown degree of possible bias in translation. In making the translations of their scale terms into English, our colleagues in other lands may have erred in the direction of forcing them toward the English scale terms with which they were already familiar, or they may have "leaned over backward" to avoid this bias and in effect decreased apparent similarities. All we can do in comparing the indigenous structures is to point to what we consider the rather remarkable similarities in semantic tone among the scales presumed to represent corresponding E, P, and A factors, and then ask the reader to use his own intuitions about the meanings of words — all on the assumption that the translations were adequate.

The second purpose of this stage in the research was to make it possible to construct SD instruments for measuring aspects of subjective culture *comparably* across different cultures using different languages — i.e., to find a way of circumventing the language barrier in at least the area of affective meaning. We could, of course, simply take the three or four highest-loading scales for the corresponding factors in each indigenous analysis and let them constitute an SD presumed to be comparable with others. However, if the bundle of scales representing a given factor for a given language goes off in a somewhat different direction within the hypothetical semantic space, despite its general similarity and overlap, then the most characteristic scales indigenously would not necessarily be the most comparable cross-culturally.

Logic of Mathematically Direct Factorial Comparison

Since comparing factors across independently computed analyses is necessarily an intuitive affair, guided entirely by the semantic flavors of only roughly translated terms, we would like to have a more direct approach. To make such comparisons rigorously in a mathematical sense, it is necessary to place the variables being compared within the same mathematical space. In the usual two-mode problem (people × tests), this means that either the people must be the same (having taken two different batteries of tests) or the tests must be the same (having been taken by two different sets of people). In our three-mode problem (people × concepts × scales), this would mean that at least one of these sources of variance would have to be constant across our indigenous samples. In a strict sense this condition cannot be met in our research: subjects obviously and deliberately are from different language/culture communities; scales at best are merely translation-equivalent and at worst are incommensurate (e.g., *filotimos-afilotimos* for Greek or *nectarful-poisonous* (*rritmay-hahriilaa*) for Hindi); and our 100 "culture-common" concepts are translation-equivalent but not necessarily identical in meaning to the people in our different samples.

However, there are two approximations to "the same factor space" that can be made. (1) *We can use balanced, coordinate bilinguals.* These would be people who had learned language A in the context of culture A and language B in the context of culture B, and to about equal degrees of fluency. They would rate a set of translation-equivalent concepts, once against their native-language indigenous scales and once against American English indigenous scales. Since the same subjects do the judging, the scales from the different languages become merely different "tests" that can be directly correlated and thereby compared in the same space. In this case, however, imbalance in bilingualism (e.g., subjects translating regularly into their dominant language) and compoundness of bilingualism (e.g., having learned English in schools in their own country via their native language as a mediator) would both work toward increasing factorial similarities — i.e., a potential bias *in favor of* our hypothesis. (2) *We can assume that the original 100 concepts are constant in meaning across language/culture com-*

munities. We could then correlate scale X for group A with scale Y for group B directly, using the means for A on X and B on Y paired across the translation-equivalent concepts, and thereby throw X and Y into the same mathematical space. This assumption is obviously contrary to fact in its extreme form, but, as will be shown, its failure to be met can only lower the resulting correlations — i.e., a potential bias *against* our hypothesis.

The logic of using the 100 translation-equivalent concepts as a basis for pairing scale means and correlating them across different samples can perhaps be clarified by using a more familiar analogue. If we wish to determine the correlation in intelligence of identical twins, we pair the IQ scores for individuals according to their genetic relatedness — i.e., Jones twin A with Jones twin B, Smith twin A with Smith twin B, and so on down the line — and run the correlation across the paired scores (the correlation in this case is usually about .90, as high as the reliabilities of the IQ tests allow, incidentally). This is analogous to our pairing scores on English scale X with Japanese scale Y according to the translation-equivalent concepts. Now suppose that, in the identical-twin analogue, we were to make a list of the scores for one member in each set of twins (Jones A, Smith A, Johnson A, and so forth) but then pair them *at random* with the remaining members (e.g., Johnson B with Jones A, Jenkins B with Smith A, and so forth) — what would the correlation be? It would, on the average, approximate zero. In our case, to the extent that the meanings of translation-equivalent concepts are *not* the same across groups, we must approach the condition of random pairing of scores and hence approach zero correlations. In other words, we use translation equivalence of concepts as a basis for nonrandom pairing of scale scores across language samples, just as we did for pairing scale scores within language samples; to the extent that our assumption of semantic constancy of concepts is *not* met, "noise" is introduced, correlations are lowered, and the possibility of demonstrating meaningful pancultural factors is reduced.

Assuming that there is sufficient similarity of meaning across groups in the meanings of translation-equivalent concepts to yield interpretable structures, just what relationship might we expect between indigenously determined and panculturally determined factors? We may represent one pole of an indigenous factor, with its included cluster of high-loading scales, as a cone originating at the origin of the hypothetical semantic space. For example, if scales called evaluative in all communities tend to be used similarly in the judgment of translation-equivalent concepts, then the result described visually in Figure 4:3 should be obtained in the pancultural factor analysis. The cones representing the E clusters for the various communities should be oriented toward the same region of the common space and should overlap, as shown in the figure. In this case all communities would contribute more or less equally to the characterization of the factor, as evi-

FIGURE 4:3

Overlapping Cones for Corresponding Factors for
Different Language/Culture Samples in Semantic Space

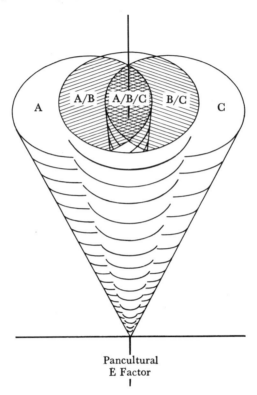

Pancultural
E Factor

denced by equally high loadings of their E scales on the common pancultural factor.

Another possible relationship is illustrated by Figure 4:4. Here we assume
that the historically related Western Indo-European language/culture communities, of which we have a considerable number of representatives (e.g.,
American English, Mexican Spanish, French, Italian, Dutch, Flemish,
Swedish, Serbo-Croatian), form a tightly overlapping core that defines the
pancultural E factor, but our other samples representing quite different
languages and cultures fall in distinctly different, nonoverlapping regions
of the space. In this case the indigenous E scales for the Western Indo-
European groups would have equal and high loadings on the pancultural
factor, but the indigenous E scales for other communities would be relatively
low in loading on this common factor, and uniformly so. If the loadings of
representative scales for a corresponding factor are about as high in the

FIGURE 4:4

*Nonoverlapping Cones for Corresponding Factors for
Different Language/Culture Samples in Semantic Space*

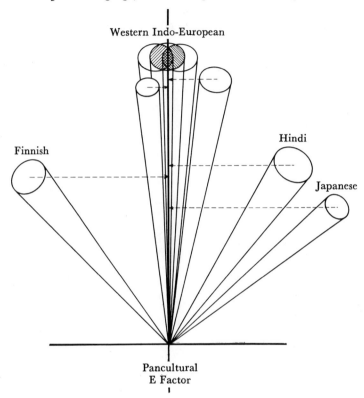

pancultural factor analysis as in the indigenous analyses, then the first (overlapping) situation holds; if they are significantly and consistently lower in
the pancultural as compared with the indigenous analyses, then the second
(nonoverlapping) situation holds.

BILINGUAL FACTOR ANALYSES

We undertook bilingual tests of factorial similarity in only two carefully
selected locations where sufficient numbers of balanced, coordinate bilinguals
could be obtained during the early stages of the project. These were Finland
and Mysore. The reasons for not continuing this type of test of cross-cultural
generality of the factors were (a) it was difficult to find sufficient numbers
of bilinguals in many locations who met both of the necessary conditions —
balance in fluency and evidence for coordinateness of type — and (b) any

bias owing to failure to meet these conditions would favor the confirmation of our hypothesis.

Comparison with previous studies. However, the bilingual checks do provide one type of information that other methods do not provide as clearly — evidence that particular linguistic codes do not dictate the structure of the meaning space utilized by a subject when he switches from one code to another. It will be recalled from Chapter 2 that Kumata and Schramm (1956) had made such a bilingual test for both Japanese and Korean subjects who were bilingual with respect to English. There was no evidence for any change in semantic factor structure as a function of linguistic code switching, and the fact that translation served as the basis for generating the scales in both Japanese and Korean does not invalidate this demonstration. The analyses to be reported for Finnish/English and Kannada/English in this section further support the conclusion from the Kumata-Schramm study.

However, there is one salient difference in method that must be noted. Whereas the Japanese and Korean subjects in the Kumata-Schramm experiment rated translation-equivalent concepts against scales that were also translation-equivalent in their two languages, *in our cases the bilingual subjects rate translation-equivalent concepts against scales which are not, for the most part, translation-equivalent.* The scales in each of the languages were uniquely and indigenously generated by the procedures of our project already described in Chapter 3.

Procedure. The first problem was to select bilingual subjects meeting our criteria. Exploration of the literature at that time revealed no standard means for determining balance in fluency (however, see Lambert, 1955), so we devised a method which we thought would serve this purpose. Our "fluency" test required potential subjects to give opposites to sets of high-frequency qualifiers (as selected in our elicitation procedures) in each of their languages; bilinguals displaying large differences in speed of responding in the two languages were to be discarded. This fluency test assumes that for the native speaker of any language the production of opposites is a highly automatic, overlearned, and essentially nonsemantic task; for example, in word-association tests opposite responses are typically given with shorter latencies than other types of responses (see Osgood, 1953). We reason that if a bilingual is not both fluent and coordinate with respect to his non-native language, he will necessarily translate into his native tongue, think of the opposite, and then translate back into the other language — all of which should take much more time than the automatic productions of the fluent native speaker.

Forms were prepared for the concept-on-scale test in both languages. A random subset of 20 of the total 100 concepts was employed, the same concepts being used in both languages. A total of 20 Finnish/English and of

20 Kannada/English bilinguals were used. Two forms of standard SD booklets were prepared. One form was in the native tongue, both scales and concepts. The second form contained the English scales and concepts. Half of the subjects took the English form at the initial session and the native-tongue form at a second session, and the other half of the subjects took the tests in the reverse order. Principal-component factor analyses were made, first for each language separately (analogous to our indigenous factorial comparisons), and second for the two languages in a single analysis (analogous to the pancultural factorial analyses to be detailed later).

Results. Table 4:5 presents the highest-loading scales for the first five unrotated principal-component factors for each of the two languages in the Finnish study. Table 4:6 presents equivalent data for the Kannada study. Factors clearly identifiable as E and P appear in both languages for both bilingual comparisons. E is Factor I in order of magnitude in all cases; P appears as Factor II for Finnish/English, III for Finnish/Finnish, II and III (ambiguously) for Kannada/English, and II for Kannada/Kannada. Evidence for A is a little less clear, but it appears as Factor III (and V) for Finnish/English, II for Finnish/Finnish, IV for Kannada/English, and III and IV (vaguely) for Kannada/Kannada. Note that these orderings of factors reflect quite well the orderings of the indigenous monolingual factor analyses given in Table 4:3.

The fact that a particular factor — for example, Potency in the Finnish study — can be second in magnitude among the scales generated for one language (English) but third among the scales generated for another (Finnish), *and this within the nervous systems of identical bilingual individuals,* has some interesting implications. It suggests first that language/culture communities do differ somewhat in the relative salience of certain modes of qualifying, and that with only 50 or so dimensions "blindly" selected, we are liable to represent inadequately certain modes in certain places. Second, it suggests that such inadequately sampled modes of qualifying in a given community may be reacted to as a productive factor by people from that community when appropriate scales are made available to them. This implies that novel factors clearly isolated in one location should be sought in other locations where they may exist and be used, but be less salient. The remarkable consistency in proportions of variance accounted for by the ordered factors *within each group of bilingual subjects and regardless of the factorial composition of the factors, but not across the two groups of subjects,* is also a bit of information to conjure with. We have no ready explanation for this phenomenon, if it is indeed more than coincidental.

Table 4:7 gives the results of a combined factor analysis of the Finnish bilingual data, all scales in both languages being correlated with each other across the translation-equivalent concepts. Table 4:8 provides similar results for the Kannada bilingual study. These tables are equivalent to the bicul-

TABLE 4:5

Principal-Component Factors: Finnish Bilingual Concept-on-Scale Task

English Scales		Finnish Scales	
Factor I (43.7%)		Factor I (38.3%)	
nice-awful	.98	light-gloomy	.96
good-bad	.97	pleasant-unpleasant	.93
heavenly-hellish	.94	good-bad	.93
sweet-sour	.94	nice–not nice	.93
happy-sad	.93	happy-unhappy	.91
fine-coarse	.93	sweet-sour	.89
beautiful-ugly	.91	valuable-worthless	.85
Factor II (14.2%)		Factor II (14.6%)	
strong-weak	.71	capricious-steady	.74
sharp-dull	.70	flexible-rigid	.69
powerful-powerless	.67	agile-clumsy	.67
high-low	.66	fast-slow	.67
smart-dumb	.57	multicolored-unicolored	.65
noisy-quiet	.57	delicate-sturdy	.64
hot-cold	.57	wrong-right	.60
Factor III (12.4%)		Factor III (13.1%)	
momentary-everlasting	.82	small-large	.69
short-long	.72	smooth-rough	.68
shallow-deep	.70	easy-difficult	.64
young-old	.65	boring-interesting	.63
fast-slow	.63	short-long	.56
noisy-quiet	.58	rounded-angular	.55
funny-serious	.55	thin-thick	.54
Factor IV (6.0%)		Factor IV (6.2%)	
soft-hard	.61	shallow-deep	.53
few-many	.56	red-blue	.50
burning-freezing	.48	hard-soft	.48
high-low	.47	short-long	.46
long-short	.44	unicolored-multicolored	.46
dull-sharp	.43	strong-weak	.44
Factor V (4.6%)		Factor V (6.1%)	
slow-fast	.55	fat-thin	.71
unfaithful-faithful	.42	abundant-scanty	.61
dishonest-honest	.42	thick-thin	.47
quiet-noisy	.40	getting smaller–getting bigger	.46
false-true	.39	sturdy-delicate	.43
light-dark	.34	rich-poor	.37

tural factor analyses to be reported in the next section — with the added basis for common factorization being that the same subjects are involved.

The first thing to note is that for all factors and for both bilingual groups the loadings for English and other-language scales fully overlap; in other

TABLE 4:6

Principal-Component Factors: Kannada Bilingual Concept-on-Scale Task

ENGLISH SCALES		KANNADA SCALES	
FACTOR I (52.7%)		FACTOR I (47.9%)	
sweet-sour	.98	good-bad	.98
nice-awful	.98	beautiful-ugly	.96
happy-sad	.98	attractive-repulsive	.95
fine-coarse	.98	merciful-cruel	.95
good-bad	.97	pure-impure	.95
beautiful-ugly	.97	constructive-destructive	.95
FACTOR II (9.2%)		FACTOR II (10.4%)	
big-little	.84	strong-weak	.74
high-low	.68	wonderful-ordinary	.66
burning-freezing	.65	uncommon-common	.66
long-short	.64	huge-small	.64
strong-weak	.61	big-small	.62
powerful-powerless	.56	fatty-slim	.57
FACTOR III (7.1%)		FACTOR III (7.0%)	
strong-weak	.64	humble-pretentious	.83
powerful-powerless	.58	stable-unstable	.62
round-square	.54	permanent-temporary	.57
many-few	.50	short-long	.57
rich-poor	.48	black-red	.52
hard-soft	.48	tight-loose	.41
FACTOR IV (6.2%)		FACTOR IV (6.6%)	
fast-slow	.63	noisy-quiet	.54
noisy-quiet	.57	fatty-slim	.51
burning-freezing	.56	plenty-insufficient	.50
momentary-everlasting	.54	many-few	.45
hot-cold	.53	small-huge	.44
poor-rich	.53	temporary-permanent	.39
FACTOR V (4.4%)		FACTOR V (4.9%)	
dry-wet	.54	red-black	.72
shallow-deep	.53	secret-public	.60
known-unknown	.48	strong-weak	.38
quiet-noisy	.47		
unbroken-broken	.41		
sharp-dull	.32		

words, the factors are common to both languages. For both Finnish and Kannada bilinguals the E factor is clearly defined in both languages. The second factor in magnitude is definitely Potency for the Kannada bilinguals (in both languages), but for the Finns the second factor is definitely Activity. For the Finns, the third factor is P (particularly in their own language), but for the Kannada speakers the third factor is A (but with a considerable tendency toward fusion with P, or Dynamism). Comparing the separate

TABLE 4:7

*Principal-Component Factorization of Combined English and
Finnish Concept-on-Scale, with Bilingual Subjects*

Factor I (39.7%)		Factor II (13.7)%		Factor III (13.2%)	
ENGLISH SCALES					
nice-awful	.97	noisy-quiet	.78	deep-shallow	.79
good-bad	.96	hot-cold	.71	long-short	.75
happy-sad	.95	loud-soft	.66	everlasting-momentary	.72
sweet-sour	.95	fast-slow	.65	strong-weak	.61
heavenly-hellish	.94	burning-freezing	.63	big-little	.60
fine-coarse	.92	sharp-dull	.63	heavy-light	.58
beautiful-ugly	.89	high-low	.53	serious-funny	.54
FINNISH SCALES					
light-gloomy	.96	lively-subdued	.71	strong-weak	.73
pleasant-unpleasant	.94	energetic-unenergetic	.66	large-small	.71
good-bad	.94	interesting-boring	.64	sturdy-delicate	.69
happy-unhappy	.91	flexible-rigid	.63	deep-shallow	.67
nice-not nice	.91	sharp-dull	.62	heavy-light	.62
sweet-sour	.88	hot-cold	.61	steady-capricious	.58
valuable-worthless	.88	fast-slow	.61	long-short	.58

TABLE 4:8

*Principal-Component Factorization of Combined English and
Kannada Concept-on-Scale, with Bilingual Subjects*

Factor I (49.6%)		Factor II (9.2%)		Factor III (6.5%)	
ENGLISH SCALES					
sweet-sour	.97	strong-weak	.76	many-few	.62
beautiful-ugly	.97	big-little	.74	shallow-deep	.56
white-black	.97	powerful-powerless	.69	round-square	.52
happy-sad	.97	high-low	.61	fast-slow	.47
nice-awful	.97	short-long	.48	little-big	.45
good-bad	.96	serious-funny	.48	strong-weak	.44
fine-coarse	.96	loud-soft	.47	noisy-quiet	.43
KANNADA SCALES					
good-bad	.98	strong-weak	.71	noisy-quiet	.57
beautiful-ugly	.97	big-small	.68	fatty-slim	.53
constructive-destructive	.96	huge-small	.66	plenty-insufficient	.49
attractive-repulsive	.96	wonderful-ordinary	.63	small-huge	.47
bearable-unbearable	.94	uncommon-common	.62	short-long	.45
clear-unclear	.93	wide-narrow	.58	strong-weak	.45
pure-impure	.93	fatty-slim	.50	hasty-considered	.39

(Tables 4:5 and 4:6) with the combined (Tables 4:7 and 4:8) factorizations, it can be seen that whereas the scales having highest loadings on E are nearly identical in both types of analyses, this is not the case for A in either group and holds for P only for Kannada. It is perhaps significant that the ordering of factors by percentage variance in the combined factorizations is closer to the native languages than to English, the second language.

BICULTURAL FACTOR ANALYSES

When in 1962 we first conceived the idea of doing pancultural factor analyses — by correlating scales from different language/culture communities with each other across the translation-equivalent concepts — our computer capacities placed limits on the number of communities we could simultaneously analyze in this manner. As a matter of fact, at that time we did not expect it would ever be possible to analyze simultaneously a 20+ (country) × 50 (scale) × 100 (concept) cube of data containing 100,000 or more measures (item means). Now — thanks to much larger-capacity computers and some breakthroughs in programming — we would be able to include as many as 30 language/culture communities in one monstrous factorization.

Because of this limit on feasibility, as we saw it then, we decided to run bicultural factor analyses first of all possible pairs of communities in our sample, then of all possible triplets, and so on until the ceiling of our capacity was reached. It soon became obvious that this would be wasted effort, since any particular combination of communities (for any particular cross-cultural research project) could be analyzed "on demand." If one were planning to use the SD technique for a research project involving a given pair, triplet, etc. of locations included in our sample, then the most appropriate short-form instrument for each location would be that whose scales best represented the affective factors common to the particular set of countries. The Iranian Farsi SD most appropriate for a study involving Iran, India, and Lebanon may be slightly different in composition from the one most appropriate for a study involving just Iran and India or Iran and Turkey.

Tables 5 in the *Atlas of Affective Meanings* give complete bicultural factorizations for all communities vs. English — because English happens to be the common medium of translation. By way of illustrating the effects of various bicultural pairings with one community held constant, Table 4:9 presents the results of the AE/X bicultural factorizations with ten of our communities (at least one from each of the regional groupings, Western European (ND), Scandinavian (FF), Latin American (MS), Mediterranean (TK), West Asian (IF), Indian (MK), and East Asian (TH), and

TABLE 4:9

Illustration of Data from Atlas Tables 5: Bicultural Factorizations of AE/X, for Ten Representative Communities[a]

AMERICAN ENGLISH AND DUTCH

	FACTOR I (32.8%)		FACTOR II (10.1%)		FACTOR III (8.0%)	
AE	nice-awful	.94	noisy-quiet	.58	big-little	.81
	sweet-sour	.93	fast-slow	.51	strong-weak	.71
	heavenly-hellish	.93	sharp-dull	.40	powerful-powerless	.68
	happy-sad	.91	alive-dead	.38	heavy-light	.63
	beautiful-ugly	.90	dangerous-safe	.30	long-short	.63
ND	happy-unhappy	.89	fast-slow	.78	heavy-light	.67
	good-bad	.85	active-passive	.77	big-little	.62
	nice-not nice	.85	wild-tame	.76	strong-weak	.61
	pleasant-unpleasant	.85	fascinating-dull	.75	hard-soft	.59
	beautiful-ugly	.82	excitable-calm	.74	thick-thin	.46

AMERICAN ENGLISH AND FINNISH

	FACTOR I (36.5%)		FACTOR II (9.1%)		FACTOR III (6.7%)	
AE	nice-awful	.94	big-little	.83	fast-slow	.65
	sweet-sour	.93	powerful-powerless	.70	noisy-quiet	.51
	heavenly-hellish	.91	deep-shallow	.67	alive-dead	.48
	happy-sad	.91	strong-weak	.66	burning-freezing	.36
	good-bad	.91	high-low	.64	young-old	.34
FF	nice-not nice	.89	sturdy-delicate	.71	agile-clumsy	.70
	light-gloomy	.87	large-small	.65	flexible-rigid	.68
	pleasant-unpleasant	.87	heavy-light	.54	fast-slow	.67
	good-bad	.84	strong-weak	.52	lively-subdued	.56
	reassuring-frightening	.79	thick-thin	.46	lively-tired	.49

[a] All results presented are for the principal components except those for Dutch and Farsi, which are for Varimax rotations of five and four principal-components factors.

TABLE 4:9 (Continued)

AMERICAN ENGLISH AND MEXICAN SPANISH

	FACTOR I (45.7%)		FACTOR II (9.2%)		FACTOR III (4.8%)	
AE	nice-awful	.96	big-little	.80	fast-slow	.68
	good-bad	.93	powerful-powerless	.68	alive-dead	.53
	sweet-sour	.92	deep-shallow	.66	known-unknown	.47
	heavenly-hellish	.91	strong-weak	.64	noisy-quiet	.44
	helpful-unhelpful	.90	long-short	.62	young-old	.39
MS	agreeable-disagreeable	.94	giant-dwarf	.74	active-passive	.63
	good-bad	.93	big-small	.69	fast-slow	.52
	beautiful-horrible	.93	strong-weak	.67	young-old	.50
	admirable-despicable	.93	major-minor	.66	hot-cold	.46
	comforting-painful	.93	tiny-immense	.61	little-much	.38

AMERICAN ENGLISH AND TURKISH

	FACTOR I (36.4%)		FACTOR II (9.7%)		FACTOR III (5.2%)	
AE	nice-awful	.96	big-little	.74	fast-slow	.60
	sweet-sour	.93	powerful-powerless	.68	noisy-quiet	.58
	good-bad	.93	deep-shallow	.67	young-old	.54
	happy-sad	.91	high-low	.61	alive-dead	.52
	helpful-unhelpful	.90	long-short	.59	little-big	.32
TK	beautiful-ugly	.92	big-little	.70	fast-slow	.64
	pleasant-unpleasant	.91	high-low	.57	young-old	.61
	good-bad	.91	large-small	.57	alive-not alive	.54
	sweet-bitter	.91	heavy-light	.57	intense-mild	.46
	tasteful-tasteless (aesthetic)	.91	deep-shallow	.47	rough-calm	.40

TABLE 4:9 (Continued)

AMERICAN ENGLISH AND FARSI

	Factor I (31.2%)		Factor II (14.7%)		Factor III (8.2%)		Factor IV (6.2%)	
AE	nice-awful	.91	nice-awful	.33	big-little	.80	fast-slow	.63
	sweet-sour	.90	needed-unneeded	.33	deep-shallow	.72	alive-dead	.57
	good-bad	.90	heavenly-hellish	.31	high-low	.66	hot-cold	.53
	happy-sad	.89	good-bad	.31	long-short	.64	burning-freezing	.50
	heavenly-hellish	.89	safe-dangerous	.30	heavy-light	.61	sharp-dull	.48
IF	good-bad	.76	whole-torn	.71	heavy-light	.70	exciting-spiritless	.69
	worthwhile-worthless	.72	clean-dirty	.71	thick-thin	.61	active-inactive	.67
	harmless-harmful	.71	broad-narrow	.70	severe-gentle, mild	.49	fast, sharp-slow, dull	.65
	safe-dangerous	.69	badly colored-well colored	.69	big-little	.47	burning-frozen	.61
	auspicious-ominous	.68	light-dark	.67	difficult-easy	.45	warm-cold	.57

AMERICAN ENGLISH AND MYSORE KANNADA

	Factor I (34.7%)		Factor II (7.5%)		Factor III (4.7%)		Factor IV (4.0%)	
AE	nice-awful	.95	big-little	.80	hot-cold	.48	fast-slow	.65
	good-bad	.92	powerful-powerless	.74	burning-freezing	.43	noisy-quiet	.64
	sweet-sour	.92	strong-weak	.69	sharp-dull	.40	alive-dead	.55
	heavenly-hellish	.90	deep-shallow	.64	rich-poor	.32	young-old	.49
	mild-harsh	.90	long-short	.61	high-low	.31	known-unknown	.40
MK	merciful-cruel	.84	big-small	.58	little-great	.39	active-dull	.41
	delicate-rough	.81	huge-small	.53	dangerous-safe	.38	noisy-quiet	.41
	calm-frightful	.80	great-little	.49	impure-pure	.37	fast-slow	.39
	good-bad	.80	wonderful-ordinary	.45	indefinite-definite	.36	little-plenty	.34
	soft-rough	.78	many-few	.37	temporary-permanent	.35	strong-weak	.32

TABLE 4:9 (Continued)

AMERICAN ENGLISH AND THAI

	FACTOR I (43.1%)		FACTOR II (9.0%)		FACTOR III (4.5%)	
AE	nice-awful	.95	big-little	.81	fast-slow	.72
	sweet-sour	.93	powerful-powerless	.64	noisy-quiet	.64
	good-bad	.92	heavy-light	.64	alive-dead	.48
	happy-sad	.91	deep-shallow	.63	young-old	.45
	heavenly-hellish	.91	strong-weak	.60	known-unknown	.40
TH	happy-suffering	.93	heavy-light	.55	quick-inert	.70
	pleasing-hurting	.93	big-little	.54	fast-slow	.56
	comfortable-uncomfortable	.93	hard-soft	.51	loud-soft	.44
	right-wrong	.92	deep-shallow	.51	near-far	.42
	useful-harmful	.91	old-young	.50	alive-dead	.34

AMERICAN ENGLISH AND GREEK

	FACTOR I (37.4%)		FACTOR II (9.0%)		FACTOR III (6.5%)		FACTOR IV (3.8%)	
AE	good-bad	.93	powerful-powerless	.93	big-little	.56	fast-slow	.44
	nice-awful	.93	strong-weak	.93	old-young	.53	sharp-dull	.40
	faithful-unfaithful	.91	big-little	.91	long-short	.50	fresh-stale.	.39
	helpful-unhelpful	.91	heavy-light	.91	high-low	.48	noisy-quiet	.37
	useful-useless	.90	rough-smooth	.90	deep-shallow	.46	alive-dead	.33
GK	good-bad	.93	strong-weak	.66	old-young	.59	cunning–simple-minded	.43
	superb-awful	.92	brave-cowardly	.57	eternal-temporary	.55	unstable-stable	.33
	friendly-hostile	.90	big-small	.47	slow-quick	.54	uneasy-easy	.34
	tame-savage	.87	sincere-insincere	.43	big-small	.54	young-old	.31
	useful-useless	.85	honest-dishonest	.41	fat-thin	.46	wrong-right	.30

AMERICAN ENGLISH AND ARABIC

	FACTOR I (45.7%)		FACTOR II (8.8%)		FACTOR III (5.1%)		FACTOR IV (3.8%)	
AE	nice-awful	.94	big-little	.66	sharp-dull	.59	fast-slow	.64
	good-bad	.92	deep-shallow	.62	high-low	.47	alive-dead	.52
	helpful-unhelpful	.90	powerful-powerless	.62	hot-cold	.46	known-unknown	.45
	sweet-sour	.90	heavy-light	.60	burning-freezing	.42	noisy-quiet	.44
	needed-unneeded	.89	hard-soft	.58	shiny-dull	.39	young-old	.40
LA	safe-dangerous	.93	large-small	.64	little-much	.41	fast-slow	.55
	merciful-cruel	.93	strong-weak	.55	not sturdy-sturdy	.38	hot-cold	.43
	great-contemptible	.93	logical-emotional	.49	empty-full	.38	active-passive	.40
	good-bad	.93	long-short	.48	emotional-logical	.37	near-far	.34
	vivifying-fatal	.93	sturdy-not sturdy	.46	temporary-permanent	.34	alive-dead	.33

AMERICAN ENGLISH AND AFGHAN DARI

	FACTOR I (37.8%)		FACTOR II (9.0%)		FACTOR III (5.9%)		FACTOR IV (5.0%)	
AE	nice-awful	.91	rough-smooth	.58	big-little	.70	hot-cold	.45
	good-bad	.90	heavy-light	.58	long-short	.61	burning-freezing	.44
	faithful-unfaithful	.88	hard-soft	.58	high-low	.56	fast-slow	.35
	helpful-unhelpful	.88	powerful-powerless	.56	deep-shallow	.50	powerful-powerless	.34
	sweet-sour	.88	loud-soft	.54	old-young	.47	noisy-quiet	.31
AD	good-bad	.90	great-small	.56	big-little	.54	tiny-huge	.56
	auspicious-inauspicious	.90	military-civilian	.51	religious-irreligious	.43	sufficient-excessive	.48
	perfect-imperfect	.87	absolute–not absolute	.49	courageous-timid	.41	narrow-wide	.45
	safe-dangerous	.86	not bloody–bloody	.44	moslem-heathen	.39	limited-limitless	.45
	lovely-ugly	.85	learned-ignorant	.44	humane-inhumane	.37	warm-cold	.43

three which are among the most deviant (GK, LA, and AD)), but only
the five highest-loading scales on each factor are given here. Looking first
at the seven representatives from various regions, we may note that on bicultural E the AE and X loadings are always high and there is usually overlap in the ranges of the loadings, but with AE always dominating. There is
more variation on P and the loadings are somewhat lower generally; AE
dominates in all cases, but there is no overlap for MK and TH. On bicultural A the loadings are still lower and even more variable — with ND, FF,
TK, and IF dominating AE (but there is overlap in all cases except ND) —
and in the factorization with MK and IF the A factor is displaced to fourth
in order by a unique one: for MK the third factor is dominated by *hot-cold*
and *burning-freezing* in AE but has *little, dangerous, impure, indefinite,* and
temporary for MK; for IF the second factor is dominated by IF with scales
whole, clean, and *broad,* AE having no overlapping scales.

Looking now at the three "problem" AE/X bicultural factorizations (GK,
LA, and AD), we may first note that there is no problem at all with E — the
loadings are all in the high .80s or .90s and there is complete overlap with
AE. The Potency factors correspond well with GK and LA (with slight AE
dominance) but not with AD, where the bicultural analysis yields *two* AE
"P" factors, the first a Strength factor (with *rough, heavy, hard, powerful,*
and *loud* for AE but *great, military, absolute, not bloody,* and *learned* for
AD, yet with overlapping loadings) and the second a Magnitude factor
(with *big, long, high, deep,* and *old* for AE but *nimble, religious, courageous,
moslem,* and *humane* for AD, and with little overlap). It appears as though
two quite different AD factors (perhaps Social Power vs. In-group–Moral)
are acting to differentiate the usual AE Potency into Strength (going with
Social Power) and Magnitude (going with, and even dominating, AD's
In-group–Moral — and suggesting that the latter does have functional "magnitude" tones).

In the bicultural analysis with GK, interestingly enough, it is a *third* factor which extracts a combined Age-Magnitude factor for both (*big, old, long,
high,* and *deep* for AE and *old, eternal, slow, big,* and *fat* for GK) and thus
pushes Activity to fourth in order of magnitude. In the analysis with LA,
on the other hand, it is some kind of Liveliness-Emotional factor (really
impossible to intuit in translation) which displaces Activity to fourth in
magnitude (*sharp, high, hot, burning,* and *shiny* for AE and *little, not sturdy,
empty, emotional,* and *temporary* for LA). Activity is clear, however, and
overlaps for AE with both GK and LA (as the fourth factor), but even
here the GK "flavor" is unique (*cunning, unstable, uneasy, young,* and
wrong). Although the (displaced) fourth factor for AE in the bicultural
analysis with AD is clearly Activity (*hot, burning, fast, powerful,* and *noisy*),
it is actually dominated by AD scales which have little to do in any obvious
way with A (*tiny, sufficient, narrow, limited,* and *warm*); this apparently

means that scales which happened to be translated thus are in fact used functionally much as AE use certain of their Activity scales.

We should also note that, in general, the same scales for American English tend to keep reappearing as the highest loading, despite the shifts in pairing with other languages. This is not always the case, of course, as can be seen by inspection. If this were to hold up across the board, it would mean that the best general scales for a given country's SD would, on the average, be those determined in the all-sample, pancultural analysis to be presented later in this chapter.

Bicultural factorizations for pairings other than English-based are illustrated in Tables 4:10 through 4:12. Table 4:10 combines Flemish and Dutch, the two most closely related language/culture communities in our sample. The close similarity in the scales isolated for the factors is apparent, even through the fourth, Modernity. Table 4:11 combines Cantonese and Japanese — two different language families but, with Chinese being sampled in Hong Kong, presumably somewhat similar cultures. The first, Evaluation factor, is similar and shared, and so is the third, Activity factor, but the flavor of the second, Potency factor, seems different — more size for the Cantonese and more intensity for the Japanese; the fourth factor in this comparison is not readily interpretable. Table 4:12 combines a Western Indo-European community (Flemish) with an Eastern non-Indo-European community (Japanese), and the compromise factors are very interesting: Evaluation is similar and shared; Potency is dominated by the Japanese system (note that P was the second factor indigenously for Japan but the third for Belgium); Activity is shared; the fourth factor is also shared, and it appears to be some sort of "magnitude" dimension. It is interesting to note that the fourth factor in the Flemish/Dutch combination is a Modernity dimension, whereas the fourth in the Flemish/Japanese takes on this different "magnitude" flavor.

The relative weights of factor loadings is evidence for "dominance" in the combined factorizations — one community "dominates" when the factor vector goes more nearly through its scales (high loadings) and less close to the other community's scales (lower loadings). This is presumably due to the number of scales representing the factor in the "dominant" community and their degree of correlation. Evaluation is shared in all three combinations of Tables 4:10 through 4:12, both communities having equally high-loading scales. Potency is shared by the Dutch and Flemish and by the Japanese and Cantonese (albeit differently), but it is dominated by Japanese in the Flemish/Japanese combination. Activity appears to be dominated by Dutch in the Dutch/Flemish combination (despite the linguistic and cultural similarity), is somewhat dominated by Japanese in the Japanese/Cantonese combination, yet is clearly shared in the Flemish/Japanese combination. This slight evidence from a few bicultural combinations suggests that

TABLE 4:10

Principal-Component Factorization of Combined Flemish and Dutch Concept-on-Scale

Factor I (28.0%)		Factor II (13.0%)		Factor III (6.5%)		Factor IV (5.4%)	
Flemish							
good-bad	.93	active-passive	.67	serious-frivolous	.60	short-long	.53
agreeable-unagreeable	.92	sharp-blunt	.59	heavy-light	.59	expensive-cheap	.49
beautiful-ugly	.92	free-bound	.55	big-small	.58	modern–old-fashioned	.46
cozy-cheerless	.91	quick-slow	.54	high-low	.58	new-old	.46
magnificent-horrible	.91	violent-calm	.54	thick-thin	.50	young-old	.45
Dutch							
pleasant-unpleasant	.94	fascinating-dull	.79	heavy-light	.58	little-big	.51
good-bad	.90	changeable-constant	.71	thick-thin	.52	new-old	.49
happy-unhappy	.90	active-passive	.70	big-little	.46	short-long	.44
cozy, snug–cheerless	.90	wild-tame	.68	hard-soft	.42	modern–old-fashioned	.40
nice–not nice	.90	impressive-trivial	.68	strong-weak	.40	special-common	.39

TABLE 4:11

Principal-Component Factorization of Combined Cantonese and Japanese Concept-on-Scale

Factor I (41.5%)		Factor II (12.2%)		Factor III (5.8%)		Factor IV (4.2%)	
CANTONESE							
good–poor	.94	strong–weak	.80	agile–clumsy	.61	wonderful–ordinary	.46
respectable–despicable	.94	deep–shallow	.74	fast–slow	.52	thin, small–thick	.42
good–bad	.94	significant–insignificant	.70	red–green	.50	agile–clumsy	.31
lovable–hateful	.93	big–small	.68	alive–dead	.38	new–old	.31
happy–sad	.92	tall, big–short, small	.66	new–old	.32	round–square	.29
JAPANESE							
good–bad	.93	difficult–easy	.74	cheerful–lonely	.64	weak–strong	.52
fine, great–trifling, unimportant	.91	trying–easy	.67	vivid–subdued	.61	few–many	.49
comfortable–uncomfortable	.91	intense–calm	.64	fast–slow	.57	fragile–sturdy	.48
pleasant–unpleasant	.90	heavy–light	.64	noisy–quiet	.57	rare–common	.37
thankful–troublesome	.90	tight–loose	.63	early–late	.56	little–big	.36

TABLE 4:12

Principal-Component Factorization of Combined Flemish and Japanese Concept-on-Scale

	Factor I (33.9%)		Factor II (9.8%)		Factor III (7.1%)		Factor IV (4.8%)	
Flemish								
	good-bad	.93	big-small	.58	quick-slow	.69	short-long	.50
	magnificent-horrible	.92	heavy-light	.57	impetuous-quiet	.58	sanguine-phlegmatic	.48
	beautiful-ugly	.92	deep-shallow	.56	violent-calm	.57	expensive-cheap	.46
	agreeable-unagreeable	.91	strong-weak	.54	active-passive	.57	green-red	.45
	cozy-cheerless	.90	difficult-easy	.53	changeable-unchangeable	.49	small-big	.45
Japanese								
	comfortable-uncomfortable	.94	heavy-light	.72	vivid-subdued	.70	short-long	.54
	pleasant-unpleasant	.94	big-little	.66	cheerful-lonely	.62	narrow-wide	.48
	good-bad	.93	brave-cowardly	.65	active-inactive	.60	little-big	.43
	happy-sad	.92	difficult-easy	.63	noisy-quiet	.56	few-many	.40
	thankful-troublesome	.91	strong-weak	.62	fast-slow	.50	complex-simple	.34

the salience of factors is a function neither of language nor of culture. It will be recalled that the same conclusion was reached when we observed the correlations across communities in the productivity of modes of qualifying (Chapter 3, Table 3:8) and when we looked for "types" among the indigenous factorizations (this chapter, pp. 123-132).

A final question we may ask of these data is, how does the "flavor" of semantic factors vary as a function of bicultural combination in factorization? Both Flemish and Japanese appear in two combinations. The Flemish E factor remains essentially constant, with Dutch and with Japanese; the Flemish P factor, however, has a "seriousness" quality when combined with Dutch but a "magnitude" quality when combined with Japanese; the Flemish A factor has more "freedom" and "sharpness" when combined with Dutch but more "impetuousness" when combined with Japanese. Japanese E is reasonably constant, whether with Cantonese or Flemish; Japanese P, however, is related to "difficulty" with Cantonese but more to "magnitude" with Flemish; Japanese A remains constant regardless of combination. If the reader will go back to Figure 4:3, he will see that — in theory — the scales within overlapping indigenous factors selected in bicultural analyses will necessarily be a function of the semantic similarities in usage (across the 100 concepts). Since the regions of maximum overlap vary from combination to combination, the "flavor" of the factors will also vary. By tracing the shifts in factor quality from combination to combination, one should be able to zero in on the particular semantic quality of a given community's E, P, or A factors.

A Trilingual Factor Analysis of Bengali, Hindi, and Kannada

Our project includes three language groups in India. It therefore seemed eminently reasonable to do pan-Indian factorization, both because of its theoretical interest and to provide the subcontinent with SD instruments for at least three of its major languages to be used in various indigenous studies. Bengali and Hindi are both Indian variants of Indo-European, whereas Kannada is a Dravidian language. The responsible investigators were Dr. Rhea Das (Bengali, Calcutta), Professor B. Kuppuswamy (Hindi, Delhi), and Dr. A. V. Shanmugam (Kannada, Mysore); the factor analysis was done at the Center for Comparative Psycholinguistics in Illinois.

Table 4:13 presents the highest-loading scales for a Varimax rotation of the first five factors in a principal-axes solution for the combined scales of Bengali, Hindi, and Kannada. Again, scale correlations were taken across the 100 translation-equivalent (via English) concepts. The first thing to note is that, with the exception of Factor II, Bengali clearly "dominates" this pan-Indian factorization; this is because the Bengali data include tighter clusters of more highly intercorrelated scales representing the termi-

TABLE 4:13

*Highest-Loading Scales for Varimax Rotation (Five Factors) of Principal-
Components Solution of Trilingual Pan-Indian Factorization*

FACTOR I (27.2%)

BENGALI		HINDI		KANNADA	
beautiful-ugly	.93	useful-harmful	.85	*good-bad*	.83
superior-inferior	.92	constructive-destructive	.85	merciful-cruel	.82
lovely-repulsive	.92	*good-bad*	.84	beautiful-ugly	.79
good-bad	.92	sanguine-desperate	.83	calm-frightful	.78
pleasing-saddening	.91	glad–not glad	.82	delicate-rough	.78
good-evil	.90	ambrosial-poisonous	.81	useful-useless	.77
kind-cruel	.89	superior-inferior	.81	best-mean	.75
famous-obscure	.88			safe-dangerous	.72
best-worst	.87			soft-rough	.71
elevated-depressed	.86				

FACTOR II (5.6%)

difficult-easy	.68	*rigid-flexible*	.72	tight-loose	.62
hard-soft	.66	thick, fat–thin, slim	.59	*hard-soft*	.47
unyielding-yielding	.61	heavy-light	.56	rough-soft	.42
viscous-nonviscous	.57	tight-loose	.50		
heavy-light	.55	strong-weak	.48		
thick-thin	.54	strong–weak (of its kind)	.42		

FACTOR III (5.3%)

sharp-blunt	.78	*fast–slow, mild*	.61	wonderful-ordinary	.47
powerful-powerless	.71	difficult-easy	.42	active-dull	.47
fast-slow	.61	brave-cowardly	.41	*fast-slow*	.43
industrious-lazy	.61	ingenuous-disingenuous	.40	bright-dim	.30
intense-mild	.57				
strong-weak	.54				
alive-dead	.50				

FACTOR IV (5.3%)

huge-minute	.61	*big-little*	.58	long-short	.47
long-short	.59	dense-scattered	.56	*big-small*	.37
big-little	.58	much, many–little, few	.40	many-few	.34
deep-shallow	.54	high-low	.39	huge-small	.32
open-shut	.40	strong-weak	.39		

FACTOR V (4.0%)

numerous-scarce	.85	with somebody–alone	.41	public-secret	.44
many-few	.85	*much*, many–*little*, few	.37	*plenty-little*	.36
many-one	.83	heart-felt–pretentious	.36	colorful-plain	.31
much-little	.80	sober-gay	.30	many-few	.29
		false-true	.28	long-short	.26
		ordinary-extraordinary	.28	plenty-sufficient	.26

nal factors. This in turn may be due either to greater reliability of the Bengali as compared with the Hindi and Kannada data or to a less diffuse affective semantic system for Bengali as compared with the other two languages. However, it can also be seen that the semantic flavors of the factors, even out to the fifth, are remarkably similar for all three languages.

The first factor, as we would now expect with great confidence, is Evaluation. A scale which translates into English *good-bad* appears for each of the languages, but, whereas the tone of the Bengali E factor seems to be a combination of aesthetic and social evaluation, the tone of the Hindi and Kannada E factors is more utilitarian and emotional. Two types of Potency factors are delineated in this pan-Indian structure: Factor II might be termed a Toughness factor, terms translating as *hard-soft* (*rigid-flexible*) appearing in all three groups; the "flavors" are much the same (*rigid, heavy, tight*), but with Bengali adding viscosity, Hindi adding strength, and Kannada adding roughness. Factor III is more a fusion of P and A into Dynamism than a pure Activity factor. It is characterized by *fast-slow* in all languages but adds sharpness and power for Bengali, difficulty, bravery, and cunning for Hindi, and wonderfulness and brightness for Kannada. Factor IV might be called a Physical Size factor, with terms translating as *big-small* appearing in all groups; Bengali adds length and depth, Hindi adds density and altitude, and Kannada adds length and numerousness. Factor V isolates clearly for the first time a dimension of meaning we have seen only vaguely in minor factors elsewhere[6] — what may be termed a Bountifulness factor. It is characterized in all three groups by *much, plenty–little, less,* including numerousness for Bengali, gregariousness and heartiness for Hindi, and publicness and colorfulness for Kannada.

The appearance of five quite sharply differentiated factors — two types of Evaluation (Goodness and Bountifulness), two types of Potency (Toughness and Bigness), and one type of Activity (Dynamism) — in this three-language but one-culture[7] analysis is theoretically very significant when compared with the pancultural analyses involving 20 groups varying in both language and culture, to be reported in the next section. In the latter case three massive affective factors (E-P-A) appear, but subsequent factors are of relatively very small magnitude, even though interpretable in most cases. It would seem that homogeneity of culture, like homogeneity of concept categories (e.g., personality concepts; see Chapter 2, p. 64; Chapter 7, pp. 375-380), makes it possible for more denotative, less metaphorically based dimensions to be isolated.

---

[6] However, this type of factor does appear often in the factorizations with E-P-A partialed out (see Chapter 5, pp. 216-227).

[7] We are aware, of course, that Bengali-, Hindi-, and Kannada-speaking cultures are not identical, but they are certainly much more similar than would be, say, American, Lebanese, and Thai.

A Bilingual and Bicultural Tri-Community Factor Analysis
of Iranian Farsi, Afghan Dari, and Afghan Pashtu

These three geographically (northwest Asian) and religiously (Moslem) similar communities provide another interesting group. Iranian Farsi and Afghan Dari are both variants of Persian, whereas Afghan Pashtu is no more related to the Persian language than it is to Urdu as spoken in Pakistan and parts of India. On the other hand, the two Afghan groups presumably share a more similar culture as against the clearly transitional culture of the rapidly modernizing city of Teheran in Iran. Table 4:14 presents the results of a tri-community factorization.

Factor I in the tri-community analysis is clearly Evaluation, and it is somewhat dominated by IF (.90-.85 loadings on *good* through *worthwhile* as compared with .80-.72 for AP on *good* through *auspicious* and .82-.76 for AP on *attractive* through *loving*). Factor II is entirely dominated by AD (.85-.72 on *humane* through *unadulterated*), with AP following closely (.67-.50 on *pashtoon* through *expensive*) and IF not really displaying the factor at all (.33-.29 on *colorful* through *lawful*); this factor is clearly identifiable as an In-group–Moslem–Intimacy dimension (*learned, moslem/pashtoon, religious/faithful,* etc.). Factor III is again dominated by IF (.74-.62 on *broad* through *stout*), is less prominent for AD (.60-.46 on *great* through *exaggerated*), and is only lightly represented in AP (.44-.30 on *wide* through *long*); but the semantic flavor is clearly Potency (*big/huge, heavy/great/full,* etc.), and it is most interesting that *short* (not *tall, long*) is Potent in Iran. Factor IV is definitely Activity-Dynamism and it is fairly well represented in all three communities (IF .64-.26 on *active* through *smooth-tender,* AD .66-.43 on *sharp* through *powerful,* and AP .77-.51 on *fast* through *brave*), and one should note that in both IF and AD it is *stout* and *fat* respectively that are on the Dynamic side.

Factor V is difficult to characterize; it is dominated by AP (.66-.50 on *hard* through *overt*), followed by AD (.44-.34 on *colorful* through *untimely*), and only remotely reflected in IF (.37-.24 on *uninfluential* through *old*).— perhaps, judging from AP, a kind of Toughness factor? Finally, Factor VI appears to be a Thermal-Dermal dimension (see pp. 184-186 in this chapter and p. 226 in Chapter 5), quite evenly represented in all three communities (IF .69-.27 from *burning* to *unique,* AD .64-.27 from *warm* to *sufficient,* and AP .72-.30 from *hot* to *high*). However, the top two or three scales are what indicate the semantic tone (*burning* and *warm* for IF, *warm* and *burning* for AD, and *hot, dry,* and *cooked* for AP).

Evaluation, Potency, and Activity (Dynamism) are clearly represented in this tri-community analysis (with IF dominating on E and P and AP dominating on A), but AD and AP together insert the In-group–Moslem factor (*not* represented in IF) as the second in magnitude. AP and also AD to

TABLE 4:14

Highest-Loading Scales for Varimax Rotation (Six Factors) of
Principal-Components Solution of Tri-Community Factorization:
Iran (Farsi), Afghanistan (Dari), Afghanistan (Pashtu)

FACTOR I (35.9%)

FARSI		DARI		PASHTU	
good-bad	.92	good-bad	.80	attractive-unattractive	.82
best-worst	.92	safe-dangerous	.74	useful-useless	.81
harmless-harmful	.88	lovely-ugly	.74	good-bad	.81
life-giving–killing	.88	necessary-unnecessary	.73	tasty-tasteless	.80
auspicious-ominous	.87	fresh-fetid	.72	excellent–not excellent	.77
worthwhile-worthless	.85	auspicious-inauspicious	.72	loving-hating	.76

FACTOR II (17.0%)

colorful-colorless	.33	humane-inhumane	.85	pashtoon-coward	.67
just-tyrannical	.31	learned-ignorant	.84	learned-ignorant	.66
kind-unkind	.31	courageous-timid	.82	acquainted-stranger	.57
detailed-brief	.30	religious-unreligious	.82	faithful-unfaithful	.54
influential-uninfluential	.29	moslem-heathen	.80	domestic, internal–foreign	.52
lawful-unlawful	.29	unadulterated-adulterated	.72	expensive-cheap	.50

FACTOR III (12.1%)

broad-narrow	.74	great-small	.60	wide-narrow	.44
big-little	.73	long-short	.57	light-dark	.38
thick-thin	.72	limitless-limited	.53	big-small	.36
heavy-light	.71	many-few	.48	high-low	.36
short–tall, long	.64	huge-tiny	.48	full-empty	.30
stout-slim	.62	exaggerated-sparse	.46	long-short	.30

FACTOR IV (8.5%)

active-inactive	.64	sharp-dull	.66	fast-slowly	.77
fast, sharp–slow, dull	.51	fast-slow	.63	alive-dead	.61
exciting-spiritless	.48	nimble-lazy	.61	natural-artificial	.57
stout-slim	.31	active-inactive	.45	awake-asleep	.56
well colored–badly colored	.27	fat-thin	.43	fast-slow	.55
smooth, tender–rough	.26	powerful-powerless	.43	brave-cowardly	.51

FACTOR V (6.9%)

uninfluential-influential	.37	colorful-colorless	.44	hard-soft	.66
spiritless-exciting	.34	hard-soft	.44	complete-incomplete	.52
colorful-colorless	.33	wide-narrow	.39	high-low	.52
round-long	.30	huge-tiny	.37	unbroken-broken	.50
inactive-active	.28	magnificent-paltry	.36	solid-liquid	.50
old-fresh	.24	untimely-timely	.34	overt-covert	.50

FACTOR VI (5.1%)

burning-frozen	.69	warm-cold	.64	hot-cold	.72
warm-cold	.55	burning-frozen	.59	dry-wet	.51
round-long	.37	short-long	.33	cooked-uncooked	.41
fast, sharp–slow, dull	.29	yellow-green	.32	empty-full	.37
exciting-spiritless	.28	timely-untimely	.27	short-long	.34
unique-commonplace	.27	sufficient-excessive	.27	high-low	.30

some degree define some kind of Toughness factor (which is also unidentifiable for IF), and the last factor is shared by all, a kind of Thermal-Dermal dimension — which seems appropriate for a northern arid region which experiences great extremes in climate. It is noteworthy that on both factors which have grossly unequal weights across these three communities (II Ingroupness and V Toughness) the culturally similar AD and AP are closer to each other than the linguistically similar IF and AD.

PANCULTURAL FACTOR ANALYSIS

Given our present computer capabilities, we are able, in principle, to generate a complete pancultural factor analysis as each new community submits its concept-on-scale data. However, for the purposes of this book, we are reporting on only the 21 communities that had completed the "toolmaking" phase by June, 1970.[8] In these pancultural factor analyses all of the scale means from all communities for the 100 original substantives make up the data matrix. From this monstrous "table" we can extract any bicultural, tricultural, etc. combination which is of interest.[9] A number of our "tool-using" projects are potentially pancultural in nature, and the 620-concept *Atlas of Affective Meanings* is extended to all of our present communities. Such projects require in each community the most comparable scales for each affective factor as determined from factor analyses which include all data from all communities.

There is obviously a near-infinite expansion possible here: our project includes some 25 language/culture communities, but this is a rather small sample of the world's linguistic and cultural entities. In the coming years we hope to extend this sample gradually, while conducting various "tool-using" projects in those communities where comparable SD instruments already exist. Judging from the results so far obtained, the scales representing the pancultural affective factors for each community will change less and less as each new data cube is added to our total sample. This simply reflects the generality of the affective meaning system across human societies.

Table 4:15 gives, for each community, the five highest-loading scales on the first three factors from the pancultural principal-components factor analysis. For convenience in inspection, the communities are ordered, very roughly, from the most "Western" (American English) to the most "Eastern" (Japanese). But as scanning the set will show, the data suggest a more

[8] At the time of this writing the "tool-making" phase is nearly completed for Hungarian Magyar and Black English.

[9] This large data matrix is factored utilizing the Eckart-Young (1936) theorem for approximating the rank of one matrix by a matrix of lower rank. We find the characteristic roots and vectors of the 100×100 substantive cross-product matrix centered about the scale means and use these roots and vectors to solve for the 2,000 (scale) $\times$ 10 (factor) matrix of scale factor loadings.

TABLE 4:15

Highest-Loading Scales for First 3 Factors
in 21-Community Pancultural Factor Analysis

Factor I (31.4%)		Factor II (6.9%)		Factor III (4.8%)	
English					
nice-awful	.94	powerful-powerless	.68	fast-slow	.61
good-bad	.92	big-little	.68	alive-dead	.55
sweet-sour	.90	strong-weak	.57	young-old	.45
helpful-unhelpful	.89	deep-shallow	.57	noisy-quiet	.40
needed-unneeded	.89	heavy-light	.55	soft-hard	.36
French					
pleasant-unpleasant	.90	big-little	.68	lively-languid	.61
good-bad	.89	strong-weak	.59	fast-slow	.57
nice-wicked	.88	huge-tiny	.57	living-dead	.56
marvelous-awful	.86	heavy-light	.52	young-old	.42
healthy-unhealthy	.85	powerful-powerless	.48	hot-cold	.35
Flemish					
good-bad	.91	strong-weak	.58	quick-slow	.69
magnificent-horrible	.89	big-small	.57	active-passive	.65
agreeable-unagreeable	.88	heavy-light	.54	sanguine-phlegmatic	.42
beautiful-ugly	.88	deep-shallow	.50	impetuous-quiet	.40
useful-useless	.86	difficult-easy	.46	shrewd-naive	.40
Dutch					
pleasant-unpleasant	.91	big-little	.57	active-passive	.72
happy-unhappy	.91	heavy-light	.55	fast-slow	.71
good-bad	.90	strong-weak	.54	fascinating-dull	.49
pretty–not pretty	.87	special-common	.48	excitable-calm	.46
beautiful-ugly	.83	impressive-trivial	.47	warm-cold	.45
Swedish					
good-bad	.86	difficult-easy	.51	sauguine–not sanguine	.66
nice-nasty	.84	high-low	.50	quick-slow	.63
kind-evil	.82	strong-weak	.47	lively-lazy	.62
right-wrong	.82	long-short	.45	sensitive-insensitive	.55
kind-cruel	.81	big-small	.45	active-passive	.54
Finnish					
nice–not nice	.88	large-small	.60	fast-slow	.67
pleasant-unpleasant	.87	sturdy-delicate	.59	flexible-rigid	.67
good-bad	.86	heavy-light	.51	agile-clumsy	.64
light-gloomy	.81	rough-smooth	.41	soft-hard	.53
reassuring-frightening	.79	strong-weak	.39	lively-subdued	.52
Spanish (Mexican)					
admirable-despicable	.93	giant-dwarf	.60	active-passive	.56
agreeable-disagreeable	.93	big-small	.58	young-old	.46
good-bad	.92	major-minor	.55	fast-slow	.44
friendly-repelling	.92	strong-weak	.54	soft-hard	.37
bearable-unbearable	.91	long-short	.44	hot-cold	.31

TABLE 4:15 (Continued)

FACTOR I (31.4%)		FACTOR II (6.9%)		FACTOR III (4.8%)	
ITALIAN					
valuable-worthless	.93	big-small	.66	fast-slow	.66
beautiful-ugly	.92	strong-weak	.55	mortal-immortal	.48
desirable-undesirable	.92	wide-narrow	.54	young-old	.48
good-bad	.92	high, tall–short	.49	sensitive-insensitive	.41
just-unjust	.89	heavy-light	.47	tender-hard	.40
SERBO-CROATIAN					
pleasant-unpleasant	.93	big-little	.72	alive-dead	.63
good-bad	.92	bulky-tiny	.67	fast-slow	.54
lovable-disgusting	.91	strong-weak	.67	young-old	.45
beautiful-ugly	.89	high, tall–low, short	.55	soft-hard	.41
bearable-unbearable	.88	wide-narrow	.53	new-old	.31
GREEK					
superb-awful	.93	big-small	.60	quick-slow	.55
good-bad	.91	strong-weak	.60	young-old	.52
friendly-hostile	.88	brave-cowardly	.46	active-passive	.39
useful-useless	.85	difficult-easy	.39	thin-fat	.39
tame-savage	.83	sincere-insincere	.37	curious-indifferent	.35
TURKISH					
beautiful-ugly	.91	big-little	.67	fast-slow	.50
good-bad	.90	heavy-light	.58	alive–not alive	.49
tasteful-tasteless	.90	large-small	.53	soft-hard	.44
pleasant-unpleasant	.90	high-low	.51	young-old	.43
sweet-bitter	.88	strong-weak	.43	thin-thick	.39
ARABIC					
safe-dangerous	.90	large-small	.51	light-heavy	.36
good-bad	.90	strong-weak	.42	fast-slow	.35
beautiful-ugly	.90	long-short	.40	short-long	.33
vivifying-fatal	.89	heavy-light	.38	not sturdy–sturdy	.31
beneficial-injurious	.89	high-low	.36	thin-thick	.30
FARSI (IRANIAN)					
good-bad	.92	heavy-light	.60	active-inactive	.53
worthwhile-worthless	.89	severe–gentle, mild	.50	exciting-spiritless	.52
best-worst	.88	thick-thin	.47	fast, sharp–slow, dull	.41
auspicious-ominous	.88	stout-slim	.43	thin-thick	.32
harmless-harmful	.87	broad-narrow	.42	warm-cold	.29
DARI (AFGHAN)					
good-bad	.88	great-small	.55	nimble-lazy	.52
auspicious-inauspicious	.86	military-civil	.45	sharp-dull	.41
safe-dangerous	.84	absolute–not absolute	.40	soft-hard	.41
lovely-ugly	.83	high-low	.37	courageous-timid	.39
perfect-imperfect	.80	learned-ignorant	.33	narrow-wide	.36

TABLE 4:15 (Continued)

Factor I (31.4%)		Factor II (6.9%)		Factor III (4.8%)	
Pashtu (Afghan)					
attractive-unattractive	.88	big-small	.54	alive-dead	.61
good-bad	.88	brave-cowardly	.47	fast-slow	.48
lucky-unlucky	.86	high-low	.42	soft-hard	.46
loving-hating	.86	light-dark	.39	awake-asleep	.44
useful-useless	.86	awake-asleep	.38	fast-slow	.30
Hindi					
glad–not glad	.83	fast-slow	.48	gay-sober	.47
good-bad	.83	brave-cowardly	.47	thin, slim–thick, fat	.36
ambrosial-poisonous	.81	heavy-light	.46	soft, flexible–hard, rigid	.36
superior-inferior	.80	difficult-easy	.44	fast-slow	.31
auspicious-inauspicious	.80	big-little	.42	loquacious-taciturn	.30
Bengali					
beautiful-ugly	.93	huge-minute	.62	sharp-blunt	.49
lovely-repulsive	.93	powerful-powerless	.60	alive-dead	.48
kind-cruel	.91	strong-weak	.55	industrious-lazy	.43
superior-inferior	.91	big-little	.54	fast-slow	.42
good-evil	.90	sharp-blunt	.52	light-heavy	.39
Kannada					
merciful-cruel	.78	wonderful-ordinary	.45	active-dull	.50
good-bad	.76	huge-small	.41	loose-tight	.36
delicate-rough	.75	big-small	.41	unstable-stable	.34
calm-frightful	.74	great-little	.34	fast-slow	.33
best-mean	.73	active-dull	.26	few-many	.28
Thai					
useful-harmful	.88	heavy-light	.50	quick-inert	.56
right-wrong	.87	deep-shallow	.49	fast-slow	.44
loving-hating	.87	old-young	.43	thin-thick	.40
comfortable-uncomfortable	.86	loud-soft	.43	soft-hard	.35
pure-impure	.86	hard-soft	.42	new-old	.30
Cantonese					
lovable-hateable	.92	tall, big–short, small	.76	agile-clumsy	.68
good-bad	.92	big-little	.75	fast-slow	.54
good-poor	.91	strong-weak	.72	alive-dead	.50
respectable-despicable	.90	significant-insignificant	.68	red-green	.43
kind-cruel	.89	thick, big–thin, small	.62	free-restrained	.32
Japanese					
good-bad	.93	heavy-light	.66	noisy-quiet	.48
comfortable-uncomfortable	.92	big-little	.63	pliable-rigid	.45
pleasant-unpleasant	.91	difficult-easy	.59	active-inactive	.44
happy-sad	.91	brave-cowardly	.56	fast-slow	.42
thankful-troublesome	.91	strong-weak	.52	vivid-subdued	.42

circular pattern, at least with respect to similarity to English factor structure. The semantic character of the first three factors is now very clear: I is Evaluation, II is Potency (strength-magnitude), and III is Activity, but this last factor is only weakly represented for Lebanese Arabic.

However, there are some rather differing metaphors of these basic affective factors. As modes of evaluation, we note the *sweet-sour* of English, the *marvelous-awful* (*superbe-affreux*) of French, the *light-gloomy* (*valoisa-synkka*) of Finnish, the *friendly-repelling* (*simpático-antipático*) of Mexican Spanish, the *bearable-unbearable* (*podnosljiv-nepodnosljiv*) of Serbo-Croatian, and the *delicate-rough* (*naajuuku-oratu*) of Kannada. As expressions of potency, we note the *impressive-trivial* (*indrukwekkend-onbeduidend*) of Dutch, the *stout-slim* (*tanumand-laaghar*) of Iranian Farsi, the *military-civil* (*askari-molki*) and *learned-ignorant* (*daana-naadan*) of Afghan Dari, the *wonderful-ordinary* (*addbhutta-ssaddhaaranna*) of Kannada, and the *old-young* (*gaiel-orornl*) of Thai. Ways of expressing activity include the *shrewd-naive* (*sluw-naief*) and *sanguine-phlegmatic* (*onbloedig-bloedig*) of Flemish, the *fascinating-dull* (*boeiend-saai*) of Dutch, the *sanguine–not sanguine* and *sensitive-insensitive* (*kanslig-okanslig*) of Swedish, the *flexible-rigid* (*joustava-jaykka*) of Finnish, the *mortal-immortal* of Italian, the *curious-indifferent* (*periergos-adiaforos*) of Greek, the *gay-sober* (*cancal-gambhiir*) of Hindi, and the *vivid-subdued* (*hadena-jimina*) of Japanese.[10] Some of these metaphors, of course, may be more apparent than real, being due to inadequacies of translation into English.

Do all communities contribute more or less equally to the definition of these three affective factors? Figures 4:3 and 4:4, it will be recalled, contrasted two alternative hypothetical relationships between indigenous and pancultural factors — the former being a rather tight relationship, with a region of common overlap, the latter being a rather loose relationship, with little overlap but similar orientation within the semantic space. If the former condition holds (Figure 4:3, a truly pancultural factor), then the magnitudes of loadings of scales representing a given factor for different communities should overlap in the pancultural analysis. If the latter condition holds (Figure 4:4, a quasi-common factor), then loadings from the various communities should all be positive and of reasonable magnitude, but some should be very high (the set of communities defining the pancultural factor) and others relatively low. We may now look at each of the three factors with these alternatives in mind.

The highest single loading on pancultural E is that for American English

---

[10] The scales which translate into English as *hard-soft* show an interesting and very stable pattern: when they appear within Potency factors, *hard* is Potent and *soft* is Impotent, but when they appear within Activity factors, *soft* is Active and *hard* Passive. Evidently the *hard-soft* dimension runs at roughly a 45° angle with respect to affective Factors II and III, *hard* being $^+$P, $^-$A and *soft* being $^-$P, $^+$A.

nice-awful (.94), so this most closely "defines" this factor; the fifth-loading English scale given is .89. French, Flemish, Dutch, Mexican Spanish, and Italian among the Western Indo-European groups have fully overlapping loadings for their E scales. Among the non-Western communities, Arabic, Bengali, Cantonese, and Japanese have overlapping values and help define the E factor. With the exceptions of Hindi and Kannada, which fall clearly outside this region of overlap (the loadings of their E scales are in the .80s (Hindi) and .70s (Kannada)), all the remaining communities fall nearly in the same range. From this evidence, we seem justified in concluding that the E factor approximates the condition of Figure 4:3 — a truly pancultural Evaluation factor.

The highest single loading on pancultural P is that for Cantonese *tall, big–short, small* (.76),[11] so we shall take this scale as most closely "defining" this factor; the fifth-loading Cantonese P scale has a value of .62. English, French, Italian, Serbo-Croatian, Turkish, and Japanese nearly overlap with Cantonese in defining this P factor; Flemish, Dutch, Finnish, Mexican Spanish, Greek, Iranian Farsi, and Bengali fall nearly in the middle range of loading; Swedish, Arabic, Afghan Dari and Pashtu, Hindi, Kannada, and Thai have loadings from the low .50s down to the .30s on this factor and hence must be considered somewhat obliquely related. This picture seems to approximate that given in Figure 4:4 — a quasi-common factor — except that the defining core of communities clearly is not Western Indo-European.

Dutch *active-passive* is the highest-loading scale (.72) on pancultural A and best defines it; the fifth-loading Dutch scale has a value of .45 — which is a considerable range, testifying to the looser clustering of this factor. All communities with the exception of Arabic fall within this range, but Afghan Dari, Hindi, Kannada, and Japanese just barely reach the range with a single scale. It is interesting to note in passing that the communities which contribute most to the definition of this pancultural A factor — Flemish, Dutch, Swedish, and Finnish — are all northern European. If this is something other than happenstance, it cannot be linguistically determined, since Finnish is included but English is not. Is it conceivable that a cold climate operates pervasively to generate a more distinct Activity factor? In any case, despite its generally lower loadings, pancultural A seems to fall between the situations observed for E and P — more overlapping than P (in part owing to the looser indigenous factors) yet much less tightly integrated than E.

Which communities are most "deviant" from the total sample on these pancultural factors? Hindi and Kannada have relatively low loadings on all three factors, E, P, and A; Lebanese Arabic and Afghan Dari deviate on P and A; Thai is low only on P; and Bengali, Turkish, and Japanese

---

[11] The Barnett (1950) transcription for this scale is *ghow drai–qaai sio.*

deviate only on A. It is notable that all of these groups are non-Western cultures and many of them are non-Indo-European. This may be indicative of "real" differences in affective meaning systems as a function of culture, language, or both, but it could also indicate increasing difficulties in maintaining comparability of instructions, translations, motivations, and other conditions of data collection as communities deviate more and more from American culture and the English language.

There is another possible reason for differences in magnitudes of factor loadings that must be considered — comparative reliability of data. Just as the correlation of one variable with another cannot be any higher than their reliabilities, so the loading of a scale on a factor cannot exceed its reliability. Thus the orientation of an indigenous factor might coincide perfectly with a pancultural factor, yet its projections onto (loadings on) the factor might be relatively low because of low reliability of the data. Since only 20 subjects contributed to each concept-scale mean, and no test-retest reliability checks were run (our interest in the concept-on-scale task lay in correlations across means rather than individuals), direct estimates of scale reliability cannot be made.[12] However, there is an indirect way to determine if unreliability may have influenced the pancultural factor analyses. If a scale has a reasonably high loading on its indigenous factor but a considerably lower loading on its pancultural factor, then the low pancultural value cannot be attributed to low scale reliability. Only if the indigenous scale loading is low, relative to other communities, *and the pancultural loading is as low,* can the latter be attributed to unreliability. In other words, a scale cannot be less reliable in one factor analysis than another when exactly the same data enter into both.

Table 4:16 compares factor loadings for identical scales in the indigenous and pancultural analyses. It was generated in the following manner. The median (second) of the three highest-loading scales for each community on each factor in the pancultural analysis was selected (e.g., *good-bad,* .92, for the E factor in English) and its loading entered under "Pan." in the table; then the loading of the same scale in the corresponding indigenous analysis was entered under "Ind." in the table (e.g., *good-bad* in American English had a loading of .93 in its indigenous analysis). The highest value in each pair indicates the minimum reliability of the scale in question. It would be expected that loadings on indigenous factors would usually be higher than on pancultural factors, and this is the case. The occasional exceptions (in italics in the table), such as *active-passive* for Flemish, represent cases where the scale in question happened to be well within the region of overlap and actually lies closer to the pancultural factor than the centroid of its own

[12] Reliability checks on the *Atlas* data — where 40 subjects contribute to each mean — are being made.

TABLE 4:16

Factor Scores for Indigenous vs. Pancultural Analyses, Based on Median (second)
of Three Highest-Loading Scales in the Pancultural Analysis

	E		P		A	
	IND.	PAN.	IND.	PAN.	IND.	PAN.
English (American)	.93	.92	.81	.68	.55	.55
French	.93	.89	.77	.59	.74	.57
Flemish	.89	.89	.77	.57	*.64*	*.65*ª
Dutch	.92	.91	.70	.55	*.67*	*.71*
Swedish	.94	.84	.60	.50	.77	.63
Finnish	*.85*	*.87*	*.47*	*.59*	*.58*	*.67*
Spanish (Mexican)	.95	.93	.76	.58	*.45*	*.46**
Italian	.91	.92	.79	.55	.68	.48
Serbo-Croatian	.93	.92	.81	.67	.71	.54
Greek	*.88*	*.91*	.65	.60	*.46*	*.52**
Turkish	.92	.90	*.54*	*.58*	*.43*	*.49**
Arabic	.95	.90	.54	.42*	.61	.35
Farsi	*.87*	*.89*	*.32*	*.50**	.76	.52
Dari	*.73*	*.86*	*.16*	*.45**	.80	.41
Pashtu	.91	.88	.67	.47	.61	.48
Hindi	.88	.83	*.15*	*.47**	*.00*	*.36**
Bengali	.93	.93	.60	.60	*.22*	*.48**
Kannada	.86	.76	.68	.41	*.18*	*.36*
Thai	.95	.87	.56	.49*	.76	.44
Cantonese	.96	.92	.85	.75	.78	.54
Japanese	.96	.92	*.58*	*.63*	.61	.45

ª Italics indicate cases where indigenous loadings are lower than pancultural.
* Cases of relatively low pancultural as well as indigenous factor loadings, and hence evidence for possible low reliability.

indigenous factor. Finnish provides an interesting case where the representative scale for all three factors has higher loading on pancultural than indigenous factors.

Returning to the matter of unreliability as a reason for low pancultural loadings, we look for cases where both indigenous and pancultural loadings are relatively low and nearly equal. These are marked by asterisks in Table 4:16. The Finnish case, already referred to, does not count because the pancultural loadings are relatively high for all factors. Mexican Spanish A (*young-old*), Greek A (*young-old*), Turkish (*alive–not alive*), most obviously Hindi A (*thin-thick*), Kannada A (*loose-tight*), and Bengali A (*alive-dead*) may reflect unreliability, as may Arabic P (*strong-weak*), Farsi P (*severe-gentle*), Dari P (*military-civil*), Hindi P (*brave-cowardly*), and Thai P (*deep-shallow*) as well. However, even in some of these cases there is still a considerable drop in loading between indigenous and pancultural loadings, indicating obliqueness as well as possible low reliability. The fact that many translation-equivalent scales appear for communities having both relatively high and relatively low pancultural loadings (e.g., *big-small, huge-small, great-little* on the Kannada P factor are translation-equivalent with scales on many other P factors) would be consistent with the obliqueness hypothesis; within their indigenous clusters such scales would be expected to be closer to those defining the pancultural factor. Most significantly, with the possible exception of Kannada, there is no evidence of this sort for unreliability of the E scales, and it is difficult to conceive of unreliability owing to instructions, translations, motivations, and the like affecting some factors and not others. In sum, unreliability does not seem to be a sufficient explanation for the relatively low pancultural P and A loadings for some communities.

Although there is no compelling evidence that either American English specifically (witness its A factor) or Western Indo-European languages generally (witness Cantonese on the P factor) determined the results of the pancultural factorization, there was an overrepresentation of this group (7 of 21). Therefore it was decided to run another pancultural factorization with only two, quite different, representatives of this group included. French, Flemish, Dutch, Swedish, and Italian were eliminated and Mexican Spanish and American English were retained — the latter because it is the translation medium.[13] Table 4:17 presents pancultural factor loadings for this reduced set of 13 communities, and it is directly comparable with Table 4:15. The 13-community pancultural factor analysis has about the same magnitude of loadings on the first two dimensions, but the loadings on the third dimension have been raised, except for Hindi, Kannada, and Finnish, which fall, and Iranian Farsi, which remain the same.

The E factor is now represented equally by English *nice-awful,* Mexican Spanish *admirable-despicable,* Greek *superb-awful,* and Japanese *good-bad* (all .93). The fifth-loading scale for Greek is .82 and its fourth-loading scale is .85, extending the range of overlap from the full pancultural analysis of Table 4:15. Serbo-Croatian, Arabic, Iranian Farsi, and Cantonese all overlap with the four defining languages. Finnish, Afghan Dari, Hindi, and Thai fall nearly in the same range. Only Kannada falls clearly out of this region of overlap, but it has about the same loadings and scales as in the full analysis.

The highest single loading P factor scale is again Cantonese *tall, big–short, small* (.72) ; the fifth-loading Cantonese P scale has a value of .63. English, Serbo-Croatian, and Japanese overlap with Cantonese as before; Finnish, Spanish, Greek, and Iranian Farsi fall somewhat below this range; and Arabic, Afghan Dari, Hindi, and Kannada fall far below the Cantonese range. Here the picture again approximates that given in Figure 4:4 — non-overlapping but co-directional. For the pancultural A factor, Cantonese

---

[13] This was a 13-community (rather than 16) analysis because at the time it was done, data for Bengali, Pashtu, and Turkish were not available.

TABLE 4:17

Highest-Loading Scales for First 3 Factors in a 13-Community
(5 Western Indo-European Deleted) Pancultural Factor Analysis

E (34.7%)		P (6.7%)		A (4.4%)	
ENGLISH					
nice-awful	.93	powerful-powerless	.65	fast-slow	.63
good-bad	.92	big-little	.64	alive-dead	.59
sweet-sour	.89	strong-weak	.58	noisy-quiet	.44
helpful-unhelpful	.89	heavy-light	.58	young-old	.42
needed-unneeded	.89	deep-shallow	.55	smart-dumb *	.31
FINNISH					
nice–not nice	.87	sturdy-delicate	.61	agile-clumsy	.60
pleasant-unpleasant	.86	large-small	.58	fast-slow	.58
good-bad	.85	heavy-light	.54	flexible-rigid	.57
light-gloomy	.79	rough-smooth	.46	lively-subdued	.46
valuable-worthless	.79	strong-weak	.41	young-old *	.43
SPANISH					
admirable-despicable	.93	giant-dwarf	.56	active-passive	.58
agreeable-disagreeable	.92	strong-weak	.54	young-old	.50
good-bad	.92	big-small	.54	fast-slow	.46
friendly-repelling	.91	major-minor	.49	hot-cold	.35
excellent-lousy *	.91	scarce-abundant *	.45	relaxed-tensed *	.31
SERBO-CROATIAN					
good-bad	.92	big-little	.69	alive-dead	.64
pleasant-unpleasant	.92	strong-weak	.67	fast-slow	.56
lovable-disgusting	.91	bulky-tiny	.66	young-old	.41
beautiful-ugly	.89	high, tall–low, short	.55	clever-stupid *	.33
bearable-unbearable	.88	heavy, difficult–light, easy *	.55	sharp-blunt *	.30
GREEK					
superb-awful	.93	strong-weak	.58	quick-slow	.57
good-bad	.91	big-small	.56	young-old	.55
friendly-hostile	.87	brave-cowardly	.46	active-passive	.47
useful-useless	.85	difficult-easy	.41	brave-cowardly *	.41
safe-dangerous *	.82	sincere-insincere	.36	unfaithful-faithful *	.40
ARABIC					
good-bad	.90	large-small	.52	fast-slow	.43
safe-dangerous	.90	strong-weak	.44	hot-cold	.37
great-contemptible *	.90	long-short	.42	short-long	.34
vivifying-fatal	.90	heavy-light	.41	light-heavy	.31
beautiful-ugly	.89	logical-emotional *	.38	active-passive *	.30
FARSI (IRANIAN)					
good-bad	.91	heavy-light	.60	active-inactive	.50
worthwhile-worthless	.90	severe–gentle, mild	.51	exciting-spiritless	.46
auspicious-ominous	.87	thick-thin	.48	fast, sharp–slow, dull	.41
harmless-harmful	.87	strong-weak *	.44	thin-thick	.33
best-worst	.87	stout-slim	.43	narrow-broad *	.33

* Scale does not appear in Table 4:15.

TABLE 4:17 (Continued)

E (34.7%)		P (6.7%)		A (4.4%)	
DARI (AFGHAN)					
good-bad	.88	great-small	.55	nimble-lazy	.60
auspicious-inauspicious	.86	military-civil	.47	courageous-timid	.50
safe-dangerous	.84	absolute–not absolute	.40	sharp-dull	.45
lovely-ugly	.82	high-low	.39	active-inactive*	.42
perfect-imperfect	.81	mounted (rider)–wayfarer (pedestrian)*	.33	able-unable*	.40
HINDI					
good-bad	.84	heavy-light	.48	gay-sober	.37
glad–not glad	.84	difficult-easy	.45	fast-slow	.33
superior-inferior	.81	brave-cowardly	.45	narrow-wide	.33
auspicious-inauspicious	.81	fast-slow	.43	big-little*	.31
sanguine-desperate*	.81	big-little	.42	loquacious-taciturn	.31
KANNADA					
merciful-cruel	.78	huge-small	.44	active-dull	.53
good-bad	.77	wonderful-ordinary	.41	fast-slow	.31
delicate-rough	.74	big-small	.40	loose-tight	.27
best-mean	.74	great-little	.33	few-many	.27
calm-frightful	.73	hard-soft*	.32	little-plenty*	.25
THAI					
useful-harmful	.88	heavy-light	.52	quick-inert	.59
pure-impure	.87	hard-soft	.51	fast-slow	.47
right-wrong	.87	old-young	.49	thin-thick	.38
comfortable-uncomfortable	.87	deep-shallow	.47	little-much*	.33
loving-hating	.86	loud-soft	.41	little-big*	.32
CANTONESE					
lovable-hateable	.92	tall, big–short, small	.72	agile-clumsy	.68
good-poor	.91	strong-weak	.70	fast-slow	.56
good-bad	.91	big-little	.70	red-green	.51
respectable-despicable	.90	significant-insignificant	.67	alive-dead	.49
kindly-cruel	.89	thick, big–thin, small	.63	scorching hot-cold*	.35
JAPANESE					
good-bad	.93	heavy-light	.69	noisy-quiet	.55
comfortable-uncomfortable	.91	difficult-easy	.63	active-inactive	.46
pleasant-unpleasant	.90	big-little	.58	fast-slow	.42
happy-sad	.90	brave-cowardly	.55	early-late*	.41
thankful-troublesome	.90	trying-easy*	.55	cheerful-lonely*	.41

* Scale does not appear in Table 4:15.

agile-clumsy (.68) is the best defining scale, and there is an even wider range to the fifth-loading scale (.35) or even fourth-loading scale (.49). Arabic, Hindi, and Kannada fall outside this range, but Mexican Spanish, Serbo-Croatian, Iranian Farsi, and Thai have moderate overlap. The remaining six communities display nearly complete overlap; hence there is again a picture like Figure 4:3, but looser than the E factor. The conclusion seems to be that elimination of five of the seven Western Indo-European groups does not in any notable way change the pancultural structure.

Comparison of the scales contributing to Tables 4:15 and 4:17 also provides evidence for the stability of the particular sample of dimensions for each language/culture community, despite variations in the nature and number of included groups. We may ask how many specific scales appearing in the 21-community pancultural analysis for each community fail to appear in the 13-community pancultural analysis as being among the 5 with highest loadings. Out of the total of 65 scales for each factor, only 4 changed on the E factor and they represented differences in loadings in the range of only .01 to .03. Seven scales are different for the P factor. However, omission of *long-short* (Spanish), *wide-narrow* (Serbo-Croatian), *high-low* (Arabic), *broad-narrow* (Farsi), *learned-ignorant* (Dari), *active-dull* (Kannada), and *strong-weak* (Japanese) does not suggest that any specific Western influence is being removed.

On the other hand, the 20 scales that disappear for the A factor do suggest that a specific Western influence is being removed. Elimination of *soft-hard* (English, Finnish, Spanish, Serbo-Croatian, Dari, Hindi, and Thai), *pliable-rigid* (Japanese), *thin-thick* and *not sturdy–sturdy* (Arabic), *thin-thick, fat* (Greek and Hindi), *warm-cold* (Farsi), and *unstable-stable* (Kannada) suggests that Softness, at least as an aspect of Activity, was somehow drawn in by the Western Indo-European communities. But since the eliminated Western communities (see French, Dutch, Flemish, Swedish, and Italian data in Table 4:15) do *not* include *soft-hard* among their five highest-loading A scales, this must mean that most of the *other* languages (in the 13-group analysis) use the terms which translate as *soft-hard* in ways similar to the Western version of Activity.

Selection of Scales for Most Comparable Pancultural Short-Form SDs

The practical purpose of the pancultural factor analysis is to make it possible to construct for each language/culture community a short, efficient SD with factors made up of scales having maximal comparability with those of all other communities. Even in the case where indigenous factors display some degree of obliqueness with respect to the centroid defined by the majority of communities, as was the case with the Potency factor, those scales having the greatest similarity in usage (often translation equivalents) still will be selected in the pancultural factorization.

For practical measurement purposes we usually represent each affective factor with three or four scales. This is a somewhat arbitrary compromise among several purposes. If a single scale were used to represent a factor

(e.g., *hot-cold* to represent A), for certain concepts it would be literally relevant (e.g., STOVE), would be used denotatively, and would thereby fail to
reflect affective meaning. When several scales are used to represent a factor
(e.g., *hot-cold, quick-slow, lively-dull*), the likelihood of them all being
simultaneously relevant denotatively to a given concept is reduced (e.g.,
STOVE may be denotatively *hot,* but it is also metaphorically *slow* and *dull*).
A closer approximation to the affective feeling-tone is thereby made. More
than four scales can be — and often are — used to represent each factor,
but redundancy increases and factorial purity decreases as the number of
scales increases.

In recommending the four scales to be used to represent each factor for
each community, the following criteria have been used. (1) The loading of
the scale on the pancultural factor should be as *high* as possible; it should
also have its highest loading on that factor (a condition which is met in
almost all cases). (2) The scale should represent its factor as *purely* as possible; in other words, its loadings on other factors should be as low as possible.
(3) Among scales which meet the first two conditions about equally, those
which are also *translation-equivalent* with scales for many other communities
should have priority; this increases the likelihood that denotative concept-
scale interaction will have similar effects in cross-cultural studies. Thus an
ideal scale for the P factor would have .00, 1.00, .00 loadings on the three
pancultural factors and would translate as *strong-weak*. Needless to say, this
ideal is never reached. It is approached with the E factor, however.

Table 4:18 shows the results of applying these criteria to the pancultural
data, partly represented in Table 4:15. In this case we give the loadings on
all three factors so that the degree of purity of factor representation can be
determined by the reader. Signs have been omitted from these loadings,
since our interest here is simply in magnitudes.[14] The four scales selected by
our criteria are usually from among the highest-loading five given in Table
4:15, but not always. The reason for this is that in some cases a high-loading
scale on the given factor may also have considerable, or even higher, loading
on another factor. For example, the scale *hard-soft* appears as the fourth
scale for the Dutch P factor rather than *special-common* or *impressive-trivial*
— because the latter two higher-loading scales were even less purely Potency
than *hard-soft* (which itself is not as good a representative as one would
wish). Scales not drawn from among the highest loading, as given in Table
4:15, are indicated by asterisks (there are 22 instances); scales for which the
represented factor does not have the highest loading are indicated by italics
(there are 13 of these).

[14] However, they are always positive with respect to the order of the scale terms on
the factor represented. The complete pancultural factorization results for each community are given in the *Atlas of Affective Meanings* as Tables 6.

TABLE 4:18

Recommended Pancultural Scales for Short-Form Semantic Differential with Loadings from Pancultural Analysis (Absolute Values)

	Factor I				Factor II				Factor III		
	E	P	A		E	P	A		E	P	A
ENGLISH											
nice-awful	.94	.15	.08	powerful-powerless	.22	.68	.08	fast-slow	.14	.20	.61
good-bad	.92	.09	.12	strong-weak	.11	.57	.13	young-old	.32	.39	.45
sweet-sour	.90	.14	.00	deep-shallow	.09	.57	.11	noisy-quiet	.30	.34	.40
helpful-unhelpful	.89	.09	.09	big-little	.01	.68	.29	alive-dead	.52	.12	.55
FRENCH											
pleasant-unpleasant	.90	.13	.01	strong-weak	.08	.59	.00	lively-languid	.20	.24	.61
good-bad	.89	.05	.04	huge-tiny	.01	.57	.13	fast-slow	.17	.23	.57
nice-wicked	.88	.06	.09	low-pitched–high-pitched*	.11	.43	.04	living-dead	.48	.06	.56
marvelous-awful	.86	.02	.00	big-little	.23	.68	.14	*young-old*	.55	.17	.42[a]
FLEMISH											
good-bad	.91	.10	.08	strong-weak	.20	.58	.15	quick-slow	.16	.16	.69
magnificent-horrible	.89	.08	.04	big-small	.01	.57	.20	active-passive	.24	.34	.65
beautiful-ugly	.88	.09	.02	long-short*	.09	.42	.12	sanguine-phlegmatic	.27	.12	.42
agreeable-unagreeable	.88	.13	.00	deep-shallow	.02	.50	.05	shrewd-naive	.33	.27	.40
DUTCH											
happy-unhappy	.91	.06	.16	big-little	.02	.57	.15	fast-slow	.10	.28	.71
pleasant-unpleasant	.91	.12	.10	heavy-light	.31	.55	.30	active-passive	.04	.35	.72
good-bad	.90	.09	.01	strong-weak	.10	.54	.00	excitable-calm	.32	.29	.45
pretty-not pretty	.87	.08	.16	hard-soft*	.35	.46	.31	fascinating-dull	.29	.35	.49
SWEDISH											
good-bad	.86	.10	.02	high-low	.01	.50	.25	sanguine-not sanguine	.19	.10	.66
nice-nasty	.84	.17	.04	strong-weak	.03	.47	.17	quick-slow	.14	.16	.63
right-wrong	.82	.04	.13	long-short	.02	.45	.26	lively-lazy	.20	.14	.62
kind-evil	.82	.13	.13	difficult-easy	.30	.51	.01	active-passive	.11	.22	.54

* Scale not drawn from five highest-loading scales in Table 4:15.

[a] Italics indicate that the scale does not have its highest loading on the factor it represents.

TABLE 4:18 (Continued)

	FACTOR I				FACTOR II				FACTOR III		
	E	P	A		E	P	A		E	P	A
FINNISH											
nice–not nice	.88	.12	.08	large–small	.09	.60	.26	fast–slow	.02	.11	.67
pleasant–unpleasant	.87	.12	.04	sturdy–delicate	.19	.59	.38	flexible–rigid	.22	.03	.67
good–bad	.86	.10	.13	strong–weak	.10	.39	.14	agile–clumsy	.01	.13	.64
light–gloomy	.81	.08	.19	heavy–light	.19	.51	.33	lively–subdued	.40	.08	.53
SPANISH (MEXICAN)											
admirable–despicable	.93	.02	.08	strong–weak	.06	.54	.10	active–passive	.01	.23	.56
friendly–repelling	.92	.01	.07	big–small	.23	.58	.23	fast–slow	.21	.09	.44
agreeable–disagreeable	.93	.13	.11	giant–dwarf	.29	.60	.18	young–old	.40	.22	.46
good–bad	.92	.10	.09	major–minor	.24	.55	.04	soft–hard	.34	.30	.37
ITALIAN											
valuable–worthless	.93	.04	.05	big–small	.09	.66	.19	fast–slow	.14	.15	.66
beautiful–ugly	.92	.10	.04	strong–weak	.12	.55	.02	mortal–immortal	.09	.08	.48
good–bad	.92	.14	.01	wide–narrow	.28	.54	.20	young–old	.31	.11	.48
desirable–undesirable	.92	.12	.08	high, tall–short	.27	.49	.06	*hot–cold**	.51	.02	.39
SERBO-CROATIAN											
pleasant–unpleasant	.93	.01	.04	big–little	.25	.72	.08	alive–dead	.37	.23	.63
good–bad	.92	.01	.02	bulky–tiny	.12	.67	.21	fast–slow	.07	.34	.54
lovable–disgusting	.91	.00	.02	strong–weak	.09	.67	.06	*young–old*	.48	.17	.45
bearable–unbearable	.88	.01	.05	unlimited–limited*	.07	.42	.16	soft–hard	.30	.35	.41
GREEK											
superb–awful	.93	.03	.07	big–small	.08	.60	.25	quick–slow	.14	.11	.55
good–bad	.91	.04	.02	strong–weak	.18	.60	.19	young–old	.23	.04	.52
friendly–hostile	.88	.01	.06	difficult–easy	.04	.39	.04	curious–indifferent	.06	.06	.35
useful–useless	.85	.07	.15	brave–cowardly	.36	.46	.25	active–passive	.33	.20	.39

* Scale not drawn from five highest-loading scales in Table 4:15.

TABLE 4:18 (Continued)

	FACTOR I				FACTOR II				FACTOR III		
	E	P	A		E	P	A		E	P	A
TURKISH											
beautiful-ugly	.91	.11	.02	big-little	.11	.67	.13	fast-slow	.02	.32	.50
good-bad	.90	.12	.13	heavy-light	.24	.58	.26	alive-not alive	.41	.01	.49
tasteful-tasteless	.90	.15	.02	strong-weak	.19	.43	.10	young-old	.36	.20	.48
pleasant-unpleasant	.90	.16	.04	deep-shallow*	.00	.42	.01	rough-calm*	.29	.18	.37
ARABIC											
beautiful-ugly	.90	.06	.13	large-small	.37	.51	.29	fast-slow	.05	.27	.35
good-bad	.90	.04	.17	long-short	.19	.40	.33	hot-cold*	.21	.28	.31
safe-dangerous	.90	.09	.15	strong-weak	.43	.42	.14	emotional-logical	.12	.30	.28
vivifying-fatal	.89	.00	.12	open-closed*	.31	.33	.03	thin-thick	.49	.15	.30
FARSI (IRANIAN)											
good-bad	.92	.09	.09	heavy-light	.17	.60	.20	active-inactive	.31	.34	.53
worthwhile-worthless	.89	.05	.08	thick-thin	.02	.47	.31	fast, sharp-slow, dull	.08	.38	.41
auspicious-ominous	.88	.00	.06	stout-slim	.19	.43	.12	exciting-spiritless	.47	.30	.52
best-worst	.88	.05	.13	strong-weak*	.31	.42	.02	warm-cold	.53	.17	.29
DARI (AFGHAN)											
good-bad	.88	.06	.06	military-civil	.27	.45	.11	nimble-lazy	.33	.17	.52
auspicious-inauspicious	.86	.09	.08	great-small	.49	.55	.14	sharp-dull	.31	.19	.41
safe-dangerous	.84	.00	.03	long-short*	.24	.30	.11	soft-hard	.30	.26	.41
lovely-ugly	.83	.13	.01	exaggerated-sparse*	.26	.28	.05	fast-slow*	.24	.15	.33
PASHTU (AFGHAN)											
loving-hating	.86	.01	.07	big-small	.21	.54	.17	alive-dead	.19	.30	.61
attractive-unattractive	.88	.05	.10	brave-cowardly	.16	.47	.16	fast-slowly	.08	.25	.48
tasty-tasteless*	.83	.00	.01	strong-weak*	.14	.35	.09	soft-hard	.04	.14	.46
good-bad	.88	.02	.19	high-low	.32	.42	.16	awake-asleep	.14	.38	.44

* Scale not drawn from five highest-loading scales in Table 4:15.

TABLE 4:18 (Continued)

Factor I	E	P	A	Factor II	E	P	A	Factor III	E	P	A
HINDI											
glad–not glad	.83	.03	.04	difficult-easy	.01	.44	.05	gay-sober	.08	.14	.47
good-bad	.83	.01	.14	heavy-light	.09	.46	.25	narrow-wide*	.04	.02	.29
ambrosial-poisonous	.81	.01	.09	*brave-cowardly*	.54	.47	.12	loquacious-taciturn	.04	.11	.30
superior-inferior	.80	.02	.19	fast-slow	.05	.47	.32	thin-thick	.02	.12	.36
BENGALI											
beautiful-ugly	.93	.06	.03	huge-minute	.28	.62	.20	fast-slow	.40	.27	.43
lovely-repulsive	.93	.04	.06	powerful-powerless	.09	.60	.11	*industrious-lazy*	.24	.44	.43
kind-cruel	.91	.02	.03	big-little	.28	.54	.23	*alive-dead*	.50	.27	.48
superior-inferior	.91	.01	.12	strong-weak	.16	.55	.00	thin-thick*	.06	.08	.30
KANNADA											
merciful-cruel	.78	.10	.01	big-small	.04	.41	.14	active-dull	.36	.24	.50
good-bad	.76	.04	.09	wonderful-ordinary	.18	.45	.15	loose-tight	.14	.07	.36
calm-frightful	.74	.19	.01	great-little	.01	.34	.18	fast-slow	.22	.15	.33
delicate-rough	.75	.16	.04	huge-small	.28	.41	.23	*unstable-stable*	.35	.07	.34
THAI											
useful-harmful	.88	.04	.09	heavy-light	.08	.50	.18	quick-inert	.02	.24	.56
pure-impure	.86	.03	.03	deep-shallow	.18	.49	.11	fast-slow	.25	.14	.44
fragrant-foul*	.86	.01	.03	loud-soft	.11	.43	.20	thin-thick	.06	.36	.40
comfortable-uncomfortable	.86	.09	.09	hard-soft	.18	.42	.34	little-much*	.23	.14	.25
CANTONESE											
lovable-hateable	.92	.09	.05	big-little	.18	.75	.01	agile-clumsy	.33	.17	.68
good-poor	.91	.01	.08	tall, big–short, small	.12	.76	.19	fast-slow	.18	.18	.54
good-bad	.92	.07	.13	strong-weak	.02	.72	.18	red-green	.08	.24	.43
respectable-despicable	.90	.03	.07	deep-shallow*	.02	.63	.05	*alive-dead*	.53	.16	.49

* Scale not drawn from five highest-loading scales in Table 4:15.

JAPANESE	FACTOR I			FACTOR II			FACTOR III		
	E	P	A		E	P	A		E	P	A
good-bad	.93	.01	.18	heavy-light	.17	.66	.29	fast-slow	.05	.13	.42
comfortable-uncomfortable	.92	.04	.12	big-little	.25	.63	.21	vivid-subdued	.05	.06	.42
happy-sad	.91	.05	.02	difficult-easy	.25	.59	.02	noisy-quiet	.45	.20	.48
pleasant-unpleasant	.91	.07	.16	rare-common*	.07	.50	.02	cheerful-lonely*	.39	.03	.37

* Scale not drawn from five highest-loading scales in Table 4:15.

Inspecting Table 4:18, it can be seen that the E factor is uniformly represented by high-loading and relatively pure scales. The most impurity we find is a .19 loading on A for Finnish *light-gloomy,* Pashtu *good-bad,* and Hindi *superior-inferior,* and this is insignificant. There is also considerable translation equivalence: a scale translating as *good-bad* appears for all communities except two (Thai and Bengali); *nice-awful* (or *nice-nasty* or *nice–not nice,* etc.) appears in four communities; *pleasant-unpleasant* occurs six times, *beautiful-ugly* (or *pretty* or *lovely*) seven times, and *happy-unhappy* three times.

The P factor is not represented by scales having such high loadings on it, but the translation equivalence is even greater than for E (which is probably due to the greater diversity in modes of evaluating). A scale translating as *strong-weak* occurs in the P sets for 16 of the 21 communities (interestingly enough, from Afghan Dari eastward, with the exception of Pashtu, Cantonese, and Bengali, it disappears); *large, big–small, little* (or a very close synonym) occurs in 17 of the 21 groups; *heavy-light* appears seven times, *long-short* four times, *difficult-easy* four times, and *deep-shallow* four times. But the purity of the P scales is much less than for E, as can be seen. However, in all but two instances (Arabic *strong-weak* and Hindi *brave-cowardly*), the scales do have their highest loading on the P factor.

The A factor is represented by scales having lower loadings on the assigned factor and less purity than either E or P. There are several cases where scales do not have their highest loadings on A (French *young-old,* Italian *hot-cold,* Serbo-Croatian *young-old,* Arabic *emotional-logical* and *thin-thick,* Iranian Farsi *warm-cold,* Bengali *industrious-lazy* and *alive-dead,* Kannada *unstable-stable,* Cantonese *alive-dead,* and Japanese *cheerful-lonely*) and many where this is nearly true. Nevertheless, there is considerable translation equivalence: scales translating as *fast-slow* or some very close synonym (*quick, swift, speedy* vs. *slow*) occur in 20 of the 21 communities; *active* appears in seven communities; *live* or *lively* vs. *dead* or *inert* and the like occur ten times, *young-old* seven times, *hot, warm–cold* three times, *thin, slim–thick* four times, and *noisy-quiet* three.

The overall similarities in the semantic flavors of these sets of scales is intuitively apparent. Although there are some scales having very special denotations (e.g., the *military-civil* of Afghan Dari, the *mortal-immortal* of Italian, the *loquacious-taciturn* of Hindi, and the *red-green* of Cantonese), they are likely to be used metaphorically with most concepts and, where denotatively relevant, will be compensated for by the other scales in the set. If one *were* to select just one scale to represent each factor in each community, it is clear that it should be the translation equivalents of *good-bad* for E (19 of 21 communities), *strong-weak* for P (16 of 21), and *fast-slow* for A (20 of 21).

EVIDENCE FOR ADDITIONAL PANCULTURAL FACTORS

The principal-components factorization of the total data for the 21 communities available at the time of this writing was carried through 10 orthogonal factors. The first three were clearly E, P, and A and have been discussed at length in the preceding sections. Together they account for 43% of the total variance. With the variance attributable to these gross, affective factors extracted, the computer continues searching for further regions of the semantic space still having relatively dense clusters of scale-vectors. Such remaining clusters could represent large and unique indigenous factors for single communities; in this case only a single community would have very large loadings on the factor and all others would have few if any scales with significant loadings. The remaining clusters could also represent modes of qualifying uniquely characteristic of some linguistic, cultural, or even geographic subset of our communities. In this case an identifiable subset of communities would have relatively high-loading scales on the factor and the remainder low-loading scales. Or the remaining clusters could be pancultural in nature; in this case all or nearly all communities would have some scales loading significantly on the factor, and these scales would share some semantic character.

The problem here, of course, is to be able to identify and give some name to the "shared semantic character" of these more subtle factors — if, indeed, they are something more than "noise." A name doesn't influence the existence or nonexistence of a "real" factor, or its nature if it does exist, but it certainly is an aid to understanding, to say nothing of communicating. The E, P, and A factors practically name themselves, by virtue of the consistency of the meanings of the scale terms which comprise them. We cannot expect such consistency for less prominent factors, but there are several aids to interpretation. (1) We can scan the terms on one side or the other of the bipolar scales across the language/culture groups and try to induce the common semantic "flavor." Needless to say, the pitfall of translation bias is ever present in such an intuitive operation. (2) We can pay particular attention to the highest-loading scales across all communities and see if they have something in common. (3) We can make a frequency list of the qualifiers having either positive or negative loadings on a factor and then try to condense it meaningfully. (4) We can take note of the substantives (concepts) which have the highest positive and negative factor scores on the factors. That this last guide to inference might have been helpful in interpreting E, P, and A — had we needed help — is evident from the first three columns of Table 4:20. This table gives some of the highest-scoring concepts on each of the ten factors.

Table 4:19 presents the five highest-loading scales for each community on each of Factors IV through X. Communities are ordered as they were in Table 4:15, roughly "from West to East." Perhaps before reading the para-

TABLE 4:19

*Highest-Loading Scales for 21 Communities on Factors IV
through X in Pancultural Factorization*

Factor IV (3.5%)		Factor V (2.8%)		Factor VI (2.6%)		Factor VII (2.0%)	
ENGLISH							
short-long	.33	slow-fast	.38	freezing-burning	.69	noisy-quiet	.44
low-high	.33	few-many	.37	cold-hot	.65	square-round	.39
little-big	.32	square-round	.33	wet-dry	.54	loud-soft	.32
poor-rich	.29	weak-strong	.24	low-high	.31	known-unknown	.32
FRENCH							
mortal-immortal	.55	low-pitched– high-pitched	.43	cold-hot	.54	artificial-natural	.28
hard-soft	.45	languid-lively	.38	green-red	.46	solid-fragile	.27
tiny-huge	.36	pale-colorful	.32	pale-colorful	.35	hard-soft	.23
solid-fragile	.27	rare-abundant	.32	raw-cooked	.27	strong-weak	.21
FLEMISH							
unchangeable- changeable	.50	serious-frivolous	.42	green-red	.47	temporal-eternal	.31
bound-free	.46	deep-shallow	.32	cold-warm	.44	strong-weak	.27
tough-tender	.44	weak-strong	.31	blue-yellow	.40	modern–old- fashioned	.26
steady-changing	.43	colorless-colorful	.31	juicy-dry	.30	changeable- unchangeable	.24
DUTCH							
firm-loose	.54	blue-yellow	.34	wet-dry	.63	loud-soft	.32
constant- changeable	.50	special-common	.31	cold-warm	.49	trivial-impressive	.29
little-big	.43	slow-fast	.30	green-red	.48	common-special	.29
steady-changing	.41	weak-strong	.29	blue-yellow	.46	angular-round	.29
SWEDISH							
stable-unstable	.49	empty-full	.44	blue-red	.58	angular-rounded	.36
shallow-deep	.44	weak-strong	.39	cold-warm	.54	empty-full	.35
tough-tender	.44	slow-quick	.34	green-red	.51	shallow-deep	.35
reliable-unreliable	.44	indistinct-distinct	.33	dark-light	.34	smoky-clear	.34
FINNISH							
scanty-abundant	.38	weak-strong	.38	blue-red	.54	energetic- unenergetic	.49
steady-capricious	.36	slow-fast	.31	cold-hot	.45	voluntary- compulsory	.32
poor-rich	.34	thin-thick	.29	dark-light	.35	near-distant	.31
hard-soft	.28	clumsy-agile	.26	low-high	.29	multicolored- unicolored	.31
MEXICAN SPANISH							
tiny-immense	.50	weak-strong	.39	wet-dry	.63	artificial-natural	.28
minor-major	.36	slow-fast	.36	cold-hot	.51	hot-cold	.18
hard-soft	.36	artificial-natural	.33	fresh-suffocating	.34	hard-soft	.18
little-much	.34	broken-whole	.28	natural-artificial	.26	insignificant- grand	.16

TABLE 4:19 (Continued)

Factor IV (3.5%)		Factor V (2.8%)		Factor VI (2.6%)		Factor VII (2.0%)	
ITALIAN							
solid-liquid	.61	unicolored-multicolored	.47	cold-hot	.50	artificial-natural	.34
precise-vague	.47	deep-superficial	.37	long-short	.32	strong-weak	.33
stable-unstable	.47	slow-fast	.33	natural-artificial	.28	near-far	.31
mortal-immortal	.46	broken-unbroken	.30	uncolored-colored	.28	sturdy-fragile	.29
SERBO-CROATIAN							
hard-soft	.51	unlimited-limited	.38	elongated-round	.49	different-same	.21
opaque-transparent	.47	human-inhuman	.37	cold-warm	.47	ramified-constricted	.21
same-different	.32	political-unpolitical	.36	dark-bright	.25	empty-full	.20
calm-agitated	.29	deep-shallow	.34	alive-dead	.24	big-little	.19
GREEK							
stable-unstable	.46	slow-quick	.41	cold-hot	.63	empty-full	.35
few-many	.43	scarce-abundant	.32	quick-slow	.32	brunette-blonde	.34
scarce-abundant	.42	weak-strong	.29	brunette-blonde	.32	temporary-eternal	.30
short-long	.41	brunette-blonde	.29	dark-brilliant	.27	false-true	.29
TURKISH							
careful-careless	.31	thin-thick	.34	wet-dry	.58	dry-wet	.34
calm-rough	.30	slow-fast	.32	cold-hot	.33	ordinary-terrific	.28
hard-soft	.30	colorless-colorful	.29	alive-not alive	.27	empty-full	.27
wise-stupid	.27	straight-round	.26	unemotional-emotional	.25	young-old	.27
ARABIC							
fast-slow	.37	little-much	.42	cold-hot	.56	full-empty	.33
sturdy-not sturdy	.37	learned-ignorant	.41	male-female	.21	matte-bright, brilliant	.26
hot-cold	.30	hidden-apparent	.36	much-little	.19	indolent-industrious	.25
near-far	.30	rare-plentiful	.33	full-empty	.19	much-little	.24
IRANIAN FARSI							
narrow-broad	.31	colorless-colorful	.45	frozen-burning	.53	long-round	.34
tall, long-short	.23	well colored-badly colored	.42	cold-warm	.49	terminable-interminable	.32
strong-weak	.21	slim-stout	.34	long-round	.43	uncertain-certain	.29
less-more	.20	tiny-large	.29	colorless-colorful	.25	unreal-real	.27
AFGHAN DARI							
firm-loose	.50	humane-inhumane	.45	frozen-burning	.56	slow-fast	.37
nimble-lazy	.37	colorless-colorful	.41	cold-warm	.54	limited-limitless	.30
powerful-powerless	.34	brotherly-unbrotherly	.36	colorless-colorful	.34	timely-untimely	.27
learned-ignorant	.32	learned-ignorant	.34	nimble-lazy	.24	dull-sharp	.21

TABLE 4:19 (Continued)

Factor IV (3.5%)		Factor V (2.8%)		Factor VI (2.6%)		Factor VII (2.0%)	
Afghan Pashtu							
solid-liquid	.55	slowly-fast	.46	cold-hot	.72	artificial-natural	.41
hard-soft	.45	weak-strong	.44	wet-dry	.63	black-white	.38
domestic, internal–foreign	.43	lean-fat	.39	short-long	.44	low-high	.36
unbroken-broken	.41	slow-fast	.38	uncooked-cooked	.32	dry-wet	.33
Hindi							
hard-soft	.42	thin-thick	.39	cold-hot	.54	two-folded–unfolded	.49
scattered-dense	.39	light-heavy	.38	wet-dry	.45	with somebody–alone	.47
little, few–much, many	.38	sober-gay	.38	pointed-rounded	.36	dry-wet	.33
dry-wet	.33	cold-hot	.27	skilled-unskilled	.27	strong-weak	.30
Bengali							
shallow-deep	.44	pale, faded–colored	.45	cold-hot	.56	many-one	.36
shut-open	.40	blue-red	.42	tall-short	.40	ordinary-extraordinary	.35
minute-huge	.40	weak-strong	.38	low-high	.40	many-few	.30
fettered-free	.34	thin-thick	.37	blue-red	.34	numerous-scarce	.27
Kannada							
tight-loose	.34	slim-fatty	.28	long-short	.28	noisy-quiet	.30
common-uncommon	.31	not piercing–piercing	.25	useful-useless	.21	strong-weak	.27
strong-weak	.25	slow-fast	.24	good-bad	.21	many-few	.26
short-long	.25	insufficient-plenty	.22	plenty-insufficient	.20	big-small	.23
Thai							
hard-soft	.43	human-animal	.46	wet-dry	.53	much-little	.38
costly-inexpensive	.34	slow-fast	.33	cold-hot	.37	near-far	.35
short-long	.34	inert-quick	.25	animal-human	.17	father-mother	.35
narrow-wide	.32	mine, ours–his, hers, theirs	.20	alive-dead	.16	new-old	.32
Cantonese							
limited-infinite	.57	human-bestial	.54	cool–scorching hot	.52	square-round	.37
solid-hollow	.44	yielding-"pushy"	.36	green-red	.49	open-secret	.33
restrained-free	.36	deep-shallow	.32	alive-dead	.27	ordinary-wonderful	.26
short, small–tall, big	.30	democratic-feudal	.31	solid-hollow	.23	balanced-extreme	.25
Japanese							
narrow-wide	.45	slow-fast	.52	blue-red	.52	cheerful-lonely	.47
short-long	.37	late-early	.50	cold-hot	.48	near-far	.45
rigid-pliable	.37	modest-arrogant	.33	subdued-vivid	.38	many-few	.39
subdued-vivid	.31	few-many	.31	lonely-cheerful	.26	noisy-quiet	.34

TABLE 4:19 (Continued)

Factor VIII (2.0%)		Factor IX (1.7%)		Factor X (1.5%)	
ENGLISH					
round-square	.25	shallow-deep	.27	old-young	.27
few-many	.22	known-unknown	.24	light-dark	.23
old-young	.21	powerful-powerless	.23	cold-hot	.23
poor-rich	.18	short-long	.22	shiny-dull	.21
FRENCH					
easy-difficult	.36	indispensable-superfluous	.27	superficial-deep	.28
natural-artificial	.31	abundant-rare	.25	artificial-natural	.28
deep-superficial	.28	blind–clear-sighted	.25	insignificant-important	.25
solid-fragile	.21	useful-useless	.24	pale-colorful	.23
FLEMISH					
old-new	.36	realistic-romantic	.38	little-much	.29
old-fashioned–modern	.34	cheap-expensive	.35	old-young	.29
low-high	.31	short-long	.30	thin-thick	.25
steady-changing	.29	old-young	.28	quick-slow	.22
DUTCH					
old-new	.43	light-heavy	.25	distasteful-tasty	.27
steady-changing	.35	short-long	.24	loud-soft	.27
predictable-unpredictable	.35	old-fashioned–modern	.24	little-much	.23
round-angular	.34	yellow-blue	.19	empty-full	.23
SWEDISH					
round-angular	.32	active-passive	.26	old-young	.29
dull-shiny	.27	tender-tough	.26	clear-smoky	.25
old-young	.24	difficult-easy	.23	shiny-dull	.23
warm-cold	.22	crooked-straight	.23	sour-sweet	.21
FINNISH					
rounded-angular	.39	short-long	.31	getting smaller–getting bigger	.29
soft-hard	.27	boring-interesting	.30	blue-red	.25
unicolored-multicolored	.26	unfaithful-faithful	.24	lively-tired	.24
safe-dangerous	.25	dull-sharp	.23	subdued-lively	.24
MEXICAN SPANISH					
profound-superficial	.27	short-long	.33	old-young	.28
soft-hard	.23	dwarf-giant	.23	fast-slow	.28
natural-artificial	.22	known-unknown	.21	artificial-natural	.22
red-blue	.22	small-big	.21	cold-hot	.20
ITALIAN					
natural-artificial	.32	short–high, tall	.31	sparse-dense	.38
poor-rich	.27	small-big	.27	short-long	.25
difficult-easy	.27	short-long	.25	artificial-natural	.24
complicated-simple	.26	impetuous-calm	.24	scarce-abundant	.23

TABLE 4:19 (Continued)

FACTOR VIII (2.0%)		FACTOR IX (1.7%)		FACTOR X (1.5%)	
SERBO-CROATIAN					
same-different	.26	low, short–high, tall	.24	thin-fat	.27
constricted-ramified	.24	strong-weak	.23	white-black	.25
empty-full	.24	general-specified	.20	constricted-ramified	.25
thin-fat	.23	guileless-cunning	.18	transparent-opaque	.20
GREEK					
easy-difficult	.33	short-tall	.31	unripe-ripe	.35
old-young	.30	simple-minded–cunning	.26	short-long	.27
simple-complicated	.27	small-big	.24	cold-hot	.26
hot-cold	.22	indifferent-curious	.23	inhospitable-hospitable	.23
TURKISH					
old-new	.44	strong-weak	.27	open-closed	.29
easy-difficult	.43	cheap-expensive	.27	not alive–alive	.26
cheap-expensive	.34	angry-calm	.19	straight-round	.24
unemotional-emotional	.32	double-single	.19	calm-rough	.22
ARABIC					
old-young	.39	closed-open	.29	little-much	.25
poor-rich	.33	lazy-industrious	.26	short-long	.24
brilliant-matte	.27	tumultuous-calm	.26	logical-emotional	.20
full-empty	.21	cruel-compassionate	.26	brilliant-matte	.19
IRANIAN FARSI					
old-fresh	.36	strong-weak	.40	tall-short	.32
little-much	.29	fresh-old	.35	uninfluential-influential	.27
less-more	.27	influential-uninfluential	.32	governmental-national	.25
black-white	.22	burning-frozen	.25	old-fresh	.25
AFGHAN DARI					
yellow-green	.35	exaggerated-sparse	.28	fetid-fresh	.34
old-new	.33	timely-untimely	.25	thin-fat	.26
paltry-magnificent	.33	tiny-large	.23	short-long	.23
little–very much	.32	necessary-unnecessary	.22	powerless-powerful	.21
AFGHAN PASHTU					
elder-younger	.35	unlimited-limited	.25	fast-slowly	.26
natural-artificial	.29	strong-weak	.25	light-dark	.25
hot-cold	.29	small-big	.24	white-black	.23
empty-full	.27	covert-overt	.23	high-low	.23
HINDI					
old-new	.27	fresh-stale	.38	loose-tight	.30
easy-difficult	.26	sufficient-insufficient	.35	open-closed	.27
alone–with somebody	.23	dense-scattered	.33	cold-hot	.24
inexpensive-expensive	.20	strong-weak	.32	inexpensive-expensive	.20

TABLE 4:19 (Continued)

FACTOR VIII (2.0%)		FACTOR IX (1.7%)		FACTOR X (1.5%)	
BENGALI					
one-many	.46	strong-weak	.29	straight-curly	.30
few-many	.36	industrious-lazy	.23	open-shut	.29
little-much	.35	deep-shallow	.21	short-tall	.28
scarce-numerous	.32	few-many	.20	light-heavy	.27
KANNADA					
loose-tight	.32	hasty-considered	.32	considered-hasty	.25
not poisonous–poisonous	.26	plain-colorful	.27	protecting-encroaching	.20
piteous-pitiless	.24	encroaching-protecting	.23	loose-tight	.19
soft-hard	.21	narrow-wide	.22	selfish-unselfish	.19
THAI					
old-new	.43	near-far	.31	fast-slow	.30
easy-difficult	.36	light-heavy	.27	transparent-opaque	.26
little-much	.30	inexpensive-costly	.23	bright-dark	.25
inexpensive-costly	.30	mine, ours–his, hers, theirs	.22	shallow-deep	.23
CANTONESE					
yielding-pushy	.41	omnipotent-powerless	.34	agile-clumsy	.31
easy-difficult	.37	powerful-powerless	.30	fast-slow	.30
round-square	.34	strong-willed–weak-willed	.25	open-secretive	.25
balanced-extreme	.30	useful-useless	.23	talented-untalented	.22
JAPANESE					
subdued-vivid	.32	new-old	.35	thin-thick	.32
old-new	.31	violent-calm	.28	fast-slow	.25
easy-difficult	.29	tense-relaxed	.22	early-late	.25
pliable-rigid	.26	trying-easy	.19	short-long	.24

graphs which follow — reporting our own attempt to find meaning, if any, in these additional pancultural factors — the reader will want to scan this table himself, assigning names to factors where he thinks he can, and then check our intuitions against his own. As noted above, Table 4:20 shows which concepts had extreme allocations along these factors, including E, P, and A, and this may be of some use in the inference process. Rather than taking up the factors in order of magnitude, we shall consider them in order of semantic clarity — as we see it.

Factor VI seems to be readily identifiable despite the low proportion of variance it accounts for. Running one's eyes down the column, the feel of "cool, green wetness" is quite compelling. Indeed, *cold, freezing, frozen* occurred 23 times, *blue* or *green* 10 times, and *wet* 8 times. The highest-loading scales, few in number but of respectable magnitude, are almost always either *cold-hot* (or close synonyms), *wet-dry*, or *blue, green–red*. The concepts most extremely differentiated on this factor (Table 4:20) are things like WATER, RIVER, RAIN vs. SUN, FIRE, HEAT. The fusion of semantic qual-

Concepts Having High Positive or Negative Factor Scores on Pancultural Factors

Factor I +	Factor I −	Factor II +	Factor II −	Factor III +	Factor III −	Factor IV +	Factor IV −	Factor V +	Factor V −
MOTHER	CRIME	SUN	EGG	CAT	STONE	POLICEMAN	CLOUD	RESPECT	SUN
LOVE	THIEF	BATTLE	CUP	BIRD	TREE	TOOTH	WATER	DEATH	FIRE
FATHER	POISON	COURAGE	BREAD	WOMAN	HOUSE	HEAD	WIND	DEFEAT	HORSE
FREEDOM	GUILT	SUCCESS	SEED	DOG	CHAIR	EAR	RIVER	PEACE	DOG
MARRIAGE	DANGER	THUNDER	BIRD	GIRL	ROPE	HAND	LAUGHTER	AUTHOR	TREE
PROGRESS		PROGRESS	CAT			KNOT	LAKE	HUNGER	CAT
			HAIR			FATHER	PLEASURE	CHOICE	FISH
						HUSBAND		TRUTH	THUNDER

Factor VI +	Factor VI −	Factor VII +	Factor VII −	Factor VIII +	Factor VIII −	Factor IX +	Factor IX −	Factor X +	Factor X −
WATER	SUN	LAUGHTER	LAKE	SUN	HOUSE	SEED	LAKE	MOON	TREE
RIVER	FIRE	NOISE	STAR	MOON	BOOK	EGG	HORSE	WINDOW	ROOT
RAIN	HEAT	GAME	FISH	DEATH	GAME	BREAD	HOUSE	WIND	LOVE
ROOT	STAR	CHAIR	EGG	MOTHER	PROGRESS	HAND	GIRL	TOOTH	MEAT
WIND	PICTURE	SMOKE	LIFE	TONGUE	WEALTH	KNOT	STAR	MAP	BREAD
TREE	SMOKE	ROPE	SUCCESS	HEART	TOOTH	WATER	WOMAN	STAR	FRUIT
HORSE		FRIEND	WATER	EAR	SUCCESS	WIND	PICTURE	EAR	GIRL
SNAKE				FATHER	PICTURE	FOOD	MARRIAGE		
				HORSE	MONEY	FIRE	FRIEND		
				SLEEP	FUTURE	TOOTH	TRUST		
						MONEY			

ities seems clear enough, but English seems to contain no single term for it. We shall call it a Climatic factor. Since all communities with one exception (Kannada in Mysore) have appropriate scales loading on this factor, it appears to be pancultural. The reason Kannada does not contribute to this factor also is probably simply that, in the automatic process of qualifier selection, no thermal scale, no wetness scale, and only one color scale (*red-black*) entered into the final 50 scales used in Phase II. It should also be pointed out that a few Activity scales go with the Cold side of Factor VI, *alive, nimble,* and *quick,* and none of their opposites ever occurs on the Cold side. What is interesting about this is that on the Activity factor itself, *hot* and *red* regularly appear as metaphors of Activity. Does the fusion of Activity with Coldness on Factor VI reflect the invigorating nature of temperate climates or seasons?

The central semantic theme of Factor VIII can also be identified with some certainty. In running down the column in Table 4:19, one is particularly struck by the feeling of "age and quietness." *Old-new* occurs three times among the six scales with loadings of .40 or more. A term for *old* (vs. either *new, young,* or *fresh*) occurs with reasonable loadings for 13 of our 21 communities. Inspection of the most frequent qualifiers reveals two contrastive clusters of correlated properties, one apparently related to old age in the human sense and the other to what might be called traditional values: on the one hand, *little, poor, piteous, empty, dull, lonely,* and a few others of similar flavor occur 26 times; on the other hand, *easy, round, natural, simple, profound, predictable, deep,* and a few other types occur 25 times. Inspection of the concepts discriminated most by this factor shows the parental figures FATHER and MOTHER, along with SUN, MOON, DEATH, and SLEEP (but also TONGUE, EAR, HORSE, and HEART) on the positive side and concepts like SUCCESS, PROGRESS, MONEY, WEALTH, GAME, and FUTURE on the other; these are consistent with the scale analysis. It seems reasonable to dub VIII as an Age factor, with the understanding that more than human age is involved. Since all communities except Bengali seem to express this same factor in some way, and with scale loadings of about the same magnitude, we may also accept this as a pancultural factor.

The fourth factor in order of magnitude should be easier to interpret than any further factors down the line, but it is not. Scanning the left-hand members of the polar terms in column IV of Table 4:19 gives one the vague feeling of "the serious side of life"; however, scanning the right-hand members gives one more of a feeling of expansiveness and excitement. The highest-loading scales are *mortal-immortal* (French), *unchangeable-changeable* (Flemish), *firm-loose* (Dutch), *tiny-immense* (Mexican Spanish), *solid-liquid* (Italian), *hard-soft* (Serbo-Croatian), *firm-loose* (Afghan Dari), *solid-liquid* (Afghan Pashtu), and *limited-infinite* (Cantonese) — which seems to confirm the first impression. Left-hand terms such as *hard, solid, firm,* and *sturdy* occur 23 times; *shallow, narrow, short,* and the like occur 23 times; yet terms like *calm, stable,* and *steady* also occur with a frequency of 12. In Table 4:20 the positive concepts look like rather serious things for the young males who make up our samples (POLICEMAN, FATHER, HUSBAND, and KNOT along with some body parts), whereas the negative concepts seem almost like a shorthand description of a vacation (CLOUD, WIND, WATER, LAKE, PLEASURE, and LAUGHTER). We suggest Work-and-Play as a possible name for Factor IV, but it might also be called Realism-Idealism and in many places it carries a "stable-unstable" flavor.[15] In any case, it seems to relate to the two poles of the human estate, pain and pleasure. Again we seem to be dealing with a pancultural factor, the loadings being spread across most groups in about equal magnitudes and with the same semantic flavor. Only Afghan Dari (*firm, nimble, powerful, learned*) fails to display this flavor in its top-loading scales.

Factor V provides an illustration of how the sets of concepts discriminated by a factor can shed some light on an otherwise rather obscure semantic situation. But let us look first at the scales. The highest-loading scales on V are *weak-strong* (four times), *colorless-colored* (four), *thin-thick* (four), *slow-fast* (eight), and *human-animal* (four) — not a very readily interpretable set. Looking at qualifier frequencies, human-related terms like *human, humane, learned, political, democratic,* and *brotherly* occur 11 times; terms like *weak, thin, pale,* and *colorless* occur 23 times; *serious, deep, sober, square,* and the like occur 7 times; terms like *empty, few, insufficient, rare, special,* and *late* have a frequency of 10. All of these qualifiers are drawn from left-hand members, of course. Just what the common semantic property here may be is still hard to discern. But Table 4:20 reveals a most interesting breakdown between concepts having high positive factor scores on V (left-hand members) and concepts having high negative factor scores: every positive concept is *abstract* and *human-oriented;* every negative concept, with the possible exception of THUNDER, is *concrete* (either animate or inanimate). Looking back now at the qualifiers, it becomes apparent why the left-hand members should be simultaneously *colorless* and *empty,* yet *serious* and *deep* (properties of abstractions), while at the same time being associated with humanness as opposed to animalness and thingness (most of the abstractions in our set of 100 concepts related to human mental, emotional, and motivational states). We shall call this an Abstractness factor, keeping in mind that abstractness is the primary distinction between human and nonhuman here. Since all communities contribute to this factor with scales of roughly equal magnitudes, it also appears to be panhuman. Interestingly, this is the first time a factor familiar to linguists and lexicographers, Abstract-Concrete, appears in our data.

---

[15] A Stability factor appeared as fourth in the early *Thesaurus* factor analysis of American English (see Chapter 2, p. 47).

Scanning the left-hand terms for Factor VII gives us the impression of ordinariness — "the humdrum of everyday, familiar, public life." There are very few high-loading scales on it, the highest (in the .40s) being *energetic-unenergetic* for Finnish and *two-folded–unfolded* for Hindi, *cheerful-lonely* and *near-far* for Japanese, *noisy-quiet* for American English, and *artificial-natural* for Afghan Pashtu. Nevertheless, there is considerable concentration in the meanings of qualifiers having relatively high loadings on this factor, as indicated by a frequency analysis: *noisy, loud, cheerful, two-folded, with somebody,* and *many* account for 13 terms; *near, known, ordinary, open,* and *common* account for 12; *temporary, timely, terminable,* and *limited* account for 5; *shallow, empty, artificial, square,* and the like account for 16. The positive concepts for Factor VII in Table 4:20 appear reasonably consistent with these clusters of left-hand terms, including as they do LAUGHTER, NOISE, GAME, CHAIR, SMOKE, ROPE, and FRIEND — surely rather familiar everyday affairs. We feel justified in calling VII an Immediacy factor. Note that the high negative concepts include some rather remote notions, e.g., STAR, LIFE, and SUCCESS.

As might be expected, Factor X has very low loadings. The highest is .38 (*sparse-dense* for Italian), and there are only a few other loadings above .30 — *unripe-ripe* for Greek, *tall-short* for Iranian Farsi, *fetid-fresh* for Afghan Dari, *loose-tight* for Hindi, *straight-curly* for Bengali, *fast-slow* for Thai, and *agile-clumsy* for Cantonese. There is certainly no common semantic character among these highest-loading scales, except possibly "openness," and it is therefore surprising to discover any consistency in the most frequently appearing scales. Terms referring in one way or another to brightness (*light, transparent, bright, shiny, white, brilliant, pale,* and *clear*) occur 14 times and always on the left-hand side; activity terms (*quick, fast, lively,* and *agile*) occur 9 times and always on the left-hand side; but terms referring to small magnitudes also occur 15 times on the left-hand side (*little, short, thin, sparse,* and *shallow*). The concept differentiations in Table 4:20 are of some help; MOON had an extremely high positive factor score here, and we also find "visuals" like WINDOW, MAP, and STAR. If we identify Factor X as a Brightness factor, then we have to admit (a) that the highest-loading scales on it have nothing directly to do with brightness, and (b) that it is not shared panculturally. American English, Swedish, Serbo-Croatian, Pashtu, and Thai seem to have such a factor, but not the others. For French Factor X is a Superficiality factor and for Cantonese it is a Dynamism factor. In any case, given such small and ambiguous loadings, nothing much should be made of it.

Factor IX defies interpretation as far as we are concerned. The semantic flavor keeps shifting from community to community. Among the scales with loadings of .35 or higher, *fresh* (vs. *stale* and *old*) appears twice and *new* once, but *realistic, cheap, sufficient,* and *strong* also appear. There are several loose clusters of scales in the frequency analysis, but they do not hang together in any obvious way: *strong, powerful, omnipotent,* and *strong-willed* occur 12 times; *short, small,* and the like occur 15 times; *tumultuous, exaggerated, abundant, dense, sufficient,* and *encroaching* occur 6 times, each once; *near, timely, realistic, indispensable,* and *useful* occur 7 times; and *shallow, closed, boring, dull, plain* (once each), and *known* and *cheap* occur 9 times. These are all left-hand terms. The concepts differentiated by this factor most clearly seem best described by the Flemish high-loading scale *realistic-romantic,* with "realistic" things like BREAD, HAND, WATER, MONEY, and FOOD on the left-hand, positive side and "romantic" things like LAKE, GIRL, PICTURE, HORSE, STAR, MARRIAGE, and FRIEND on the right-hand, negative side. Apparently the necessities of life are simultaneously potent, abundant, realistic, and boring! There may be the faint outlines of a meaningful factor here, but it would be pan-cultural only by virtue of the fact that all loadings are low and hence overlap.

CONCLUSIONS ON THE SIMILARITY OF HUMAN MEANING SYSTEMS

The last two chapters, on modes of qualifying experience and on the factorial structure of these modes as they are used in judging concepts, have been primarily concerned with *semantic similarities* across human cultures and languages. We have found evidence for similarities at all levels or stages in this "tool-making" phase of our research. The statistical distributions of qualifier usage are similar. The two most common modes of qualifying right across the world are *good* and *big* (or some close synonym). When we rank the qualifiers obtained in each community in terms of both frequency and diversity of usage (i.e., productivity) and then correlate rankings in terms of translation equivalents, we find sizable and significant relationships. Human beings, no matter where they live or what language they speak, apparently abstract about the same properties of things for making comparisons, and they order these different modes of qualifying in roughly the same way in importance.

In the present chapter we have used factor-analytic techniques to determine similarities in the organization or structure of these modes of qualifying as they are actually used in the differentiation of 100 diversified concepts. Perhaps the clearest evidence for shared semantic factors has come from the pancultural factorization. The first three factors were Evaluation, Potency, and Activity in that order. E was fully shared, as evidenced by high-loading scales of similar semantic flavor contributing to the factor from all communities; P was somewhat less shared, as evidenced by the scales of some communities having relatively low values on the common factor; A was more shared than P, even though its average loadings were lower. In the cases of both P and A, however, the same semantic flavor was apparent in all locations, many scales being translation-equivalent across communities as well.

We feel that the theoretical purpose of this research has been achieved. We have been able to demonstrate conclusively that the three affective factors of meaning are truly pancultural — at least to the extent that our sample of some 21 language/culture communities is representative of all human societies. The practical purpose of our research is to use this demonstrated similarity in semantic framework as a basis for investigating differences in what we call subjective culture — by constructing efficient semantic differentials within each language which optimally represent the pancultural affective factors. In this chapter we have suggested scales for each factor for each community which approximate this ideal as closely as our data permit. In the two chapters which follow we shift our emphasis to *semantic differences* across the human cultures and languages included in our sample.

5

An Atlas of Affective Meanings

THE FIRST HALF of this book has dealt primarily, although not exclusively, with underlying similarities or universals across language/culture communities. What appear to be human universals have been found in the modes of qualifying experience, their salience and factorial structure. This demonstration is essential for the construction of cross-linguistically comparable instruments for measuring subjective culture — common "yardsticks." At this point we shift our attention primarily, although not exclusively, to cultural differences or uniquenesses. We shall find many cultural differences, particularly in the meanings of concepts, and yet evidence for universals as well. In this chapter the organization, tabular contents, and potential uses of an *Atlas of Affective Meanings* will be described. In the next chapter ways of extracting, analyzing, and applying the *Atlas* information as probes into subjective culture will be illustrated.

Differences between cultures derivable from the data we are collecting can be classified into three general categories. First, there are differences that fall out more or less automatically from the "tool-making" procedures described in previous chapters. The standardization of procedures enhances the significance of such differences. Second, the short-form, pancultural differentials, reported at the end of Chapter 4, are being used for the compilation of the *Atlas of Affective Meanings*, which will include, along with the basic tables generated in the "tool-making" operations, semantic profiles and other measures on 620 concepts, selected to sample as widely as possible

First draft prepared by William H. May.

human activities, relationships, and concerns. Third, a number of special data collections and treatments have been made which also shed light on cultural differences. Comparative information of this sort about languages should have a wide variety of uses. Linguists, psycholinguists, anthropologists, and others can make lexical and semantic analyses of such data — for example, on the comparability of "semantic fields" of the translation-equivalent substantives, as determined by overlap in the qualifiers they produce. There is a present trend of interest among linguists in "language universals," and these data can contribute to the study of universals in the lexico-semantic aspects of language. The *Atlas* can also serve as a source of verbal materials having known affective properties for use in many types of cross-cultural psycholinguistic experiments — experiments on human cognition, perception, learning, and so forth.

The *Atlas of Affective Meanings* will be organized as sets of tables for each language. The sequence of tables in the *Atlas* will be as given in Table 5:1.

The various steps of the project also provide a great deal of quantitative psycholinguistic information obtained in standardized fashion from subjects in various language/culture groups. For example, we obtain lognormal functions characterizing the overall distributions of modes of qualifying; entropy indices, reflecting both frequency and diversity of usage, for both qualifiers

TABLE 5:1

Index of Atlas of Affective Meanings

Tables 1. Qualifier Responses with Frequency Greater than One as Given to Each of the 100 Substantives in the Qualifier-Elicitation Task.

Tables 2. *H* Indices, *H* Ranks, and Total Frequency and Diversity Scores for the 200 Highest *H*-Ranked Qualifiers in the Qualifier-Elicitation Task.

Tables 3. Scale Loadings in the Factor Space Based on Indigenous Factorizations, Derived from the Concept-on-Scale Task.

Tables 4. Factor Scores from Indigenous Scale Factors on the Standard List of 100 Substantives (Concepts).

Tables 5. Scale Loadings in the Space Based on Bicultural Factorizations; Each Language Combined with English.

Tables 6. Scale Loadings in the Space Defined by the Pancultural Factorization.

Tables 7. The Generalized Semantic Differential (12 Scales) Used for *Atlas* Concept Rating, Based on Pancultural Factorizations.

Tables 8. Allocations (Composite Factor Scores and Standardized Composite Factor Scores), Familiarity Ratings, Polarizations (Distances from the Origin), and Cultural Instabilities of the 620 *Atlas* Concepts, Obtained with the Short-Form Pancultural Differentials.

Tables 9. Transliteration Rules (Where Necessary), Translated and Transliterated 50 Scales as Used in the Concept-on-Scale Task, and Translated and Transliterated Forms of the *Atlas* Concepts from Tables 8.

---

and substantives; factors and resultant vectors for all scales utilized; and so forth. Such data derive automatically from the necessary operations of the "tool-making" phases.

In the organization of this chapter we shall follow the sequence of *Atlas* tables, which is also the sequence of "tool-making" steps and *Atlas* "tool-using" steps. All quantitative information is tabled in the *Atlas,* and the reader is referred to that source for complete sets of data.[1] However, examples will be drawn from the *Atlases* to illustrate the contents of the various tables, and other analyses based on these data will also be presented. The "tool-using" to be reported here will be restricted to the 620-concept *Atlas* data collected with the short-form, pancultural SDs. Description of the special analytic methods devised for evaluation of these *Atlas* data per se, and interpretation of some samples of these data, will be reserved for Chapter 6. In order to facilitate interpretation of similarities and differences, both here and in Chapter 6, Table 5:2 gives the site of collection, language family, and geographical region of each of our communities. The communities are identified by both location and language since there might be confusion (e.g., American English vs. British English, Australian English, etc.). The two-letter symbols (e.g., AE for American English) will often be used in tables and text to save space; where both location and language need to be specified, the first letter refers to location and the second to language (e.g., AD or Afghan Dari vs. AP or Afghan Pashtu); in cases where confusion is unlikely, or where application of the above rule would duplicate symbols, a location/language symbol is used (e.g., FF for Finnish but FR for French, and YC for Yucatan (Mayan) Spanish since YS already refers to Yugoslavian Serbo-Croatian).

ATLAS TABLES 1[2]

In Chapter 3 the procedures for eliciting qualifier responses to the basic list of 100 substantives were described, and evidence for the overall similarity of modes of qualifying experience across cultures was also given, e.g., correlations across languages based on the top 200 *H*-ranked qualifiers (Table 3:8) and distributions of qualifier types and tokens as lognormal functions (Figure 3:1). *Atlas* Tables 1 and 2 will give the data underlying such analyses.

---

[1] Although *Atlas* tables are available for the 23 communities which have reached this stage at the time of this writing, publication of the *Atlases* will be delayed until all communities now underway (a total of about 26) have reached this stage.

[2] The use of the plural, "Tables," indicates that there is one such table for each community in our sample, except GG, CS, and YC, where only Tables 7, 8, and 9 are available. For these three communities the tool-making stages were bypassed. YC and CS went directly to *Atlas* testing using the Mexican Spanish short-form SD; and GG used scales inferred from the surrounding communities BF, ND, and SW.

TABLE 5:2

General Indices and Two-Letter Key for 29 Language/Culture Communities

KEY	LOCATION, LANGUAGE	SITE OF COLLECTION	LANGUAGE FAMILY	GEOGRAPHIC REGION
AD	Afghanistan, Dari	Kabul	Indo-European (Iranic)	West Asian
AE	United States, American English	Illinois State	Indo-European (Germanic)	North American
AP	Afghanistan, Pashtu	Kabul, Kandahar	Indo-European (Iranic)	West Asian
BE	United States, Black English	Trenton, Chicago	Indo-European (Germanic)	North American
BF	Belgium, Flemish	Brussels	Indo-European (Germanic)	West European
CB	Calcutta (India), Bengali	Calcutta	Indo-European (Indic)	South Asian
CS	Costa Rica, Spanish	San Jose, Liberia, C. Quesada	Indo-European (Romance)	Central American
DH	Delhi (India), Hindi	Delhi	Indo-European (Indic)	South Asian
FF	Finland, Finnish	Helsinki	Finno-Ugric	North European
FR	France, French	Paris, Strasbourg	Indo-European (Romance)	West European
GG	Germany (West), German	Münster	Indo-European (Germanic)	West European
GK	Greece, Greek	Athens	Indo-European (Greek)	Mediterranean
HC	Hong Kong, Cantonese	Hong Kong	Sino-Tibetan	East Asian
HM	Hungary, Magyar	Budapest	Finno-Ugric	Central European
IF	Iran, Farsi	Teheran	Indo-European (Iranic)	West Asian
IT	Italy, Italian	Padua	Indo-European (Romance)	Mediterranean
JP	Japan, Japanese	Tokyo	Japanese	East Asian
LA	Lebanon, Arabic	Beirut	Afro-Asiatic (Semitic)	Mediterranean–West Asian
MK	Mysore (India), Kannada	Mysore City, Bangalore	Dravidian	South Asian
MM	Malaysia, Bahasa Kebangsaan	Kelantan State	Malayo-Polynesian	Southeast Asian
MS	Mexico, Spanish	Mexico City	Indo-European (Romance)	North American
ND	Netherlands, Dutch	Amsterdam, Haarlem	Indo-European (Germanic)	West European
PO	Poland, Polish	Warsaw	Indo-European (Slavic)	East European
SW	Sweden, Swedish	Uppsala	Indo-European (Germanic)	North European
TH	Thailand, Thai	Bangkok	Kadai	Southeast Asian
TK	Turkey, Turkish	Istanbul	Altaic	Mediterranean–West Asian
TZ	Chiapas (Mexico), Tzeltal	San Cristobal las Casas	Mayan	North American
YC	Yucatan (Mexico), Spanish (Mayan)	Ticul, Chablekal, Kom Chiem	Indo-European (Romance)	North American
YS	Yugoslavia, Serbo-Croatian	Belgrade	Indo-European (Slavic)	Mediterranean–East European

MODES OF QUALIFYING

These tables of qualifier usage for each language/culture community are
the data with which the "tool-making" process begins. The 100 translation-
equivalent substantives (nouns in English) used as stimuli in eliciting these
qualifiers have already been listed (Table 3:1). *Atlas* Tables 1 summarize,
for each of the 100 substantives, the qualifier response types and the percentage of subjects responding with each type (since N of subjects equals
100, percentage occurrence of a qualifier type is the same as its frequency).
Blanks (omitted responses) were coded as XX and appear in the tables;
responses clearly not qualifiers (adjectives in English) were coded as the
single type NA and appear as such in the tables.[3] Unique types (response
types with a subject frequency of 1) are not tabled. Small samples of Tables
1 of the *Atlas* are given as Appendix A, drawn from American English (AE)
and Calcutta Bengali (CB) respectively. The symbol "DIV" stands for the
diversity of types for the substantives, i.e., the number of *different* qualifiers
given to each stimulus; since single-occurrence types have been omitted, DIV
will in all cases be larger than the number of types appearing in the tables.
The *H* indices for substantives are computed from the frequency tables,
including the single-occurring types; they appear in the *Atlas* Tables 1
under the symbol "*H*."

INFORMATION INDICES FOR SUBSTANTIVES

As already shown in Chapter 3, extensive similarities in the rankings of
H-ordered *qualifiers* exist across all samples analyzed to date; in other words,
language/culture communities tend to agree in the relative salience of various modes of qualifying experience. But what about the things qualified?
Do human groups agree or disagree on the degree of stereotyping of the
nominal *substantives*? Here we anticipate disagreement — MOTHER may
well be stereotyped in one place and quite amorphous in another. Agreement on modes of qualifying coupled with disagreement on the meanings
of what is being qualified does not involve any logical contradiction. On the
contrary, if differences between cultures in the meanings of concepts did
not exist, no useful purpose would be served by having a common measuring
instrument for their assessment.

At this stage of the analysis we accordingly inquired into the comparative
entropies of the 100 substantives for the various language/culture groups.
Although entropy differences do not directly reflect differences in the meanings of these concepts, as do the factorial indices to be discussed at a later
point, differences in the diversity of qualifiers elicited by the substantives

---

[3] Since all cases of "non-adjective" (NA) — not usable for determining most productive qualifiers — were combined, this "type" often has relatively high frequencies.

cross-culturally do reflect an attribute found to correlate with meaning as defined by the semantic differential (see Staats and Staats, 1958).

The H statistic can be used to order the eliciting substantives in terms of the number and distribution of frequencies of the qualifiers they elicit. This ranking was carried out separately for each language. Calculation of the H index for the substantives was described in Chapter 3 (pp. 85-88) and illustrated in Table 3:5. It will be recalled that the H index represents the average shape of the probability distribution of the responses to each stimulus (concept). The data in Tables 1 of the *Atlas,* illustrated here by Appendix A, are thus the frequency distributions being indexed.

INTRACULTURAL STEREOTYPY

A substantive to which many subjects gave the same response (e.g., STAR-*bright*) would have a low H-index value and could be called a *culturally stereotyped concept,* whereas one to which subjects tended to give many idiosyncratic responses would have a high H-index value and could be called a *culturally amorphous concept.* Table 5:3 extracts entries from *Atlas* Tables 1 for the concepts GIRL and POLICEMAN from all the language/culture communities available at this time. GIRL is the concept which most often receives a low H-index value while POLICEMAN most often receives a high H-index value. The mean diversity of GIRL across cultures is 22.4 and of POLICEMAN is 45.1; POLICEMAN elicits an average of 22 more response types than GIRL. Only for Kannada is the relationship equal — 20 response types for each. The predominant responses for GIRL (either first, second, or third in order for each site) are *beautiful* (19 groups), *pretty* (10 groups), *good* and *nice* (6 and 5 groups each), *small* (4 groups), and *lovely* (3 groups). For POLICEMAN the dominant responses are more diverse: *good* (12 groups), *severe* (6), *strong* (4), *bad* (4), and *brave* (3 groups each), with 28 response types appearing only twice or once.

Although the more frequent responses tend to be similar across cultures, some unique types appear in various communities. For GIRL we note the hair colors of French and Turkish and the peculiar translation *sweet-hot* in Dutch (in Dutch it was not a regular form — *liefheet*). In Bengali GIRL elicited *brisk* for some reason. POLICEMAN, with its higher amorphousness, elicits more unique response types. Some appear to reflect current conditions — for example, *female* in Dutch, *four* in Bengali, and *water* in Thai. But also unique are French *illogical,* Greek *well-shaped,* Turkish *truncheoned* (or club-carrying), and Serbo-Croatian *blonde.*[4] Of the seven Western Euro-

[4] We are, of course, aware of the pitfalls of translation bias here, particularly of the possible homonyms in the destination languages of translation. Although the qualifiers used subsequently as the defining terms of scales have been carefully checked for adequacy of translation, this could not be done for all qualifiers (particularly the many unique types).

TABLE 5:3

Entries from Atlas *Tables 1 for* (A) GIRL *and* (B) POLICEMAN

A. GIRL

	H	DIV	
America (AE) English	.036	31	pretty (40), beautiful (11), small (7), NA (6), big (3), cute (3), fat (2), nice (2), shapely (2), sharp (2), ugly (2)
Afghanistan (AD) Dari	.034	24	beautiful (27), lovely (22), good (14), small (8), pretty (5), young (3), charming (2), moral (2), virgin (2)
Belgum (BF) Flemish	.031	22	lovely (33), pretty (29), little (5), young (5), charming (4), good-looking (4), slim (3), friendly (2), sympathetic (2)
Calcutta (CB) Bengali	.033	22	beautiful (28), good (20), brisk (16), little (8), naughty (5), calm (5), shy (2), well-known (2)
Delhi (DH) Hindi	.024	15	beautiful-1 (54), good (14), fickle (10), black (6), beautiful-2 (3), dirty (2), innocent (2), little (2)
Finland (FF) Finnish	.025	20	beautiful (56), small (17), gay (3), good-natured (3), pretty (3), pleasant (2), stupid (2), young (2)
France (FR) French	.043	36	nice (24), young (10), handsome (8), blonde-haired (7), small (7), fine (5), black-haired (3), engaging (3), intelligent (3), charming (2), pleasant (2), tall (2)
Greece (GK) Greek	.043	40	beautiful-1 (23), beautiful-2 (16), good (7), sweet (5), young (5), clever (4), polite (3), cute (2), loved (2), moral (2), provocative (2)
Hong Kong (HC) Cantonese	.037	24	lively (19), beautiful (18), pretty (12), lovable (10), innocent (7), clever (6), naughty (5), small (4), girlish (2), plump (2), XX (2)
Hungary (HM) Magyar	.024	23	beautiful (59), nice (12), golden (3), XX (3), charming (2), young (2), kind (2), fair (2)
Iran (IF) Farsi	.032	18	beautiful (22), pretty (19), good (16), charming (14), small (8), big (4), ugly (3), chaste (3), polite (2)
Italy (IT) Italian	.034	22	beautiful (32), pleasant (16), nice (15), attractive (5), good (4), blonde (3), charming (3), intelligent (3), kind (3), handsome (2), pretty (2), ugly (2)
Japan (JP) Japanese	.022	9	beautiful-1 (36), dear (29), beautiful-2 (22), lovely (5), gentle (2), rare (2), small (2)
Lebanon (LA) Arabic	.030	20	beautiful (36), polite (24), small (9), kind (7), large (4), brown (3), clean (3), industrious (2)
Mysore (MK) Kannada	.037	20	beautiful (20), good (13), bad (10), sweet (9), delicate (8), talkative (7), attractive (6), smart (4), brave (3), fair (3), mischievous (3), stubborn (3), active (2), intelligent (2), young (2)
Malaysia (MM) Bahasa Kebangsaam	.028	24	pretty (57), clever (5), pretty (5), small (4), fat (3), NA (3), tall (2), skillful (2), dumb (2), weak (2)
Mexico (MS) Spanish	.030	19	lovely (38), beautiful (18), pretty (13), handsome (6), attractive (3), intelligent (3), pleasant (3), ugly (3), good (2), young (2)

TABLE 5:3 (Continued)

	H	DIV	GIRL
Netherlands (ND) Dutch	.034	21	sweet (18), jolly (17), nice (16), smart (16), beautiful (10), small (4), young (3), charming (2), sweet-hot (2)
Poland (PO) Polish	.034	29	pretty (44), beautiful (11), nice (5), smart (4), young (4), lovely (3), maidenly (3), charming (2), extra-terrific (2), good-looking (2), wise (2)
Sweden (SW) Swedish	.015	14	beautiful (37), pretty (27), tidy (18), small (4), XX (4), fair (2)
Thailand (TH) Thai	.029	20	pretty (44), lovely (20), small (7), fat (5), good (3), naughty (3), proper (3), short stature (2), tall (2)
Turkey (TK) Turkish	.033	29	beautiful (47), blonde (7), yellow (7), brunette (4), small (4), bad (2), big (2), genial (2), long (2), ugly (2), wicked (2), NA (2)
Chiapas (TZ) Tzeltal	.017	14	fair (16), beautiful (10), big (7), a little short (4), short (3), tall (3), small (2), thin (2)
Yugoslavia (YS) Serbo-Croatian	.028	21	pretty (50), nice (14), slim (6), ugly (5), beautiful (4), young (3), blonde (2), dear (2), small (2)

B. POLICEMAN

	H	DIV	
AE	.045	41	NA (24), big (9), kind (5), tall (5), bad (4), helpful (4), nice (4), XX (4), honest (3), ugly (3), friendly (2), large (2), mean (2), stern (2)
AD	.054	56	quick (13), good (5), guarding (5), brave-1 (3), gendarme (3), large (3), much (3), trained (3), traffic (3), working (3), active (2), brave-2 (2), cruel (2), honest (2), learned (2), many (2), understanding (2), un-uniformed (2), wise (2), young (2)
BF	.045	51	severe (35), courageous (3), gruff (3), judicial (3), angry (2), audacious (2), black (2), furious (2), good-hearted (2), smart (2), strong (2), tall (2), thick (2), XX (2)
CB	.051	52	corrupted (14), NA (9), brave (7), good (6), angry (5), bad (5), naughty (3), well-known (3), countless (2), four (2), pitiless (2), spirited (2)
DH	.046	44	good (25), much-1 (9), bad (6), mighty (4), C.I.D. (3), cowardly (3), horrible (3), strict (3), able (2), black (2), clever (2), danger-ous (2), much-2 (2), nasty (2), terrible (2), much-3 (2)
FF	.041	33	severe (18), good (5), necessary (4), overzealous (4), quick (4), strong-1 (4), good-natured (3), put on airs (3), strong-2 (3), NA (3), angry (2), big (2), fat (2), helping (2), kind (2), little (2), long (2), nasty (2), polite (2), precise (2), slow (2), systematic (2)
FR	.055	61	severe (12), wicked (8), kind (5), serious (4), blue (3), illogical (3), nice (3), bearded (2), good (2), nervous (2), redoubtable (2), stupid (2), tall (2), with arms (2), NA (2)

TABLE 5:3 (Continued)

POLICEMAN

	H	DIV	
GK	.052	55	good (12), strict (10), bad (5), conscientious (5), beautiful (3), high (3), honest (3), just (3), faithful (2), grim (2), hard (2), loyal (2), obliged (2), prudent (2), quick (2), stupid (2), well-shaped (2)
HC	.055	59	brave (8), fair (7), good (6), dutiful (5), responsible-1 (5), responsible-2 (5), keeping order (4), corrupt (2), faithful (2), Hong Kong's (2), polite (2), proper (2), righteous (2), self-important (2), upright (2)
HM	.054	56	stupid (7), transport (6), severe (6), imbecile (5), polar (5), NA (5), clever (3), rustic (3), brave (2), angry (2), uniformed (2), just (2), unjust (2), blue (2), quarrelsome (2), illiterate (2), bad (2), grey (2)
IF	.050	47	good (19), self-sacrificing (9), kind (5), expert (5), XX (4), conscientious (4), traffic (4), strong (4), experienced (4), doing (3), excellent (3), smart (2), clever (2), proficient (2), courageous (2), school (2)
IT	.053	52	severe (8), cunning (7), clever (6), courageous (6), honest (6), attentive (5), bad (3), just (3), NA (3), bold (2), daring (2), ignorant (2), intelligent (2), obtuse (2), pleasant (2), private (2), shrewd (2), tenacious (2), vigilant (2)
JP	.038	31	fearful-1 (36), kind (7), strong (7), disagreeable (4), fearful-2 (4), gentle (4), reliable (4), annoying (3), hateful-1 (3), necessary (3), good (2), hateful-2 (2), interesting (2), right (2)
LA	.037	27	NA (30), secret (16), brave (8), military (6), strong (5), energetic (4), polite (4), expert (3), intelligent (3), awake (2), dangerous (2), just (2)
MK	.038	20	good (16), bad (15), strong (10), cruel (10), dishonest (7), honest (7), corrupt (6), kind (5), dark (4), NA (4), fat (3), understanding (3), efficient (2), stubborn (2)
MM	.047	45	dark (23), cruel (6), NA (6), brave (4), good (4), guarding (4), fierce (4), energetic (3), tall (2), many (2), clear (2), round (2), industrious (2), numerous (2), smart appearance (2), awakened (2), XX (2)
MS	.052	49	efficient (8), good (8), audacious (7), blue (5), XX (5), auxiliary (4), uniformed (4), NA (4), astute (3), federal (3), fretful (3), honorable (3), energetic (2), low (2), nimble (2), polite (2), reliable (2), vigilant (2)
ND	.046	47	XX (26), large (8), female (5), good (5), friendly (3), gruff (3), harsh (3), nice (3), attentive (2), corruptible (2), enormous (2), fat (2), honest (2)
PO	.055	61	bad (8), severe (7), kind (6), stupid (6), tall (6), dark blue (4), ill-mannered (3), blue (2), fierce (2), malicious (2), nice (2), old (2), tired (2)

TABLE 5:3 (Continued)

	H	DIV	POLICEMAN
SW	.046	39	NA (12), XX (11), severe (10), strong-1 (10), good (7), stupid (5), helpful (3), kind (3), strong-2 (3), angry (2), bad (2), clinging (2), hard (2), just (2), useful (2)
TH	.050	46	catch (12), skilled (10), good (8), courageous (6), inspect (4), strong (4), traffic (4), conscientious (3), thai (3), water (3), bad (2), big (2), die (2), polite (2), short stature (2), tall (2), to work (2)
TK	.048	46	NA (17), good (11), strong (7), civilian (6), bad (4), big (3), courageous (3), long (3), wicked (3), cunning (2), fearful (2), much (2), ready (2), truncheoned (2), weak (2)
TZ	.019	17	big (11), fair (9), tall (8), beautiful (4), dark (4), good (4), bad (2), not beautiful (2)
YS	.047	48	stupid (24), strict (8), blonde (6), brave (6), clever (3), dangerous (3), fair (3), bad (2), conceited (2), hard-working (2), high (2), mean (2), rough (2)

pean communities, only in Netherlands Dutch does POLICEMAN not elicit *severe.*

For the concept POLICEMAN there is a continuum in the ratio of positive to negative response types (as simply judged) listed in Table 5:3. We can arbitrarily group the communities according to four divisions in terms of this ratio: *very high* (> 6.0 — at least six positive responses to each negative response type), *high* (5.9 to 3.0), *middle* (2.9 to 1.6), and *low* (< 1.6). This might be taken as an "anti-authoritarian" index. The higher the ratio, the fewer negative terms elicited in proportion to positive. Lebanon, Iran, Afghanistan, Thailand, Malaysia, and Hong Kong are in the very high group; Italy, Mexico City, Turkey, and Yucatan in the high; Greece, the United States, Finland, France, the Netherlands, and Mysore (India) in the middle group; and Belgium, Japan, Calcutta, Sweden, Delhi (India), Poland, Yugoslavia, and Hungary in the low group. The order within each group is from high to low, thus forming a continuum.

CROSS-CULTURAL STEREOTYPY

A concept whose *H* index, either high (amorphous) or low (stereotyped), tends to remain relatively constant across cultures can be called a *cross-culturally homogeneous concept,* whereas one whose *H* index varies markedly across cultures can be called a *cross-culturally heterogeneous concept.* For concepts which are cross-culturally homogeneous, those high in average *H* rank may be termed *cross-culturally amorphous concepts,* while those which are low in average *H* rank may be termed *cross-culturally stereotyped concepts.*

Variation of concepts along a homogeneous-heterogeneous continuum is conveniently indexed by the standard deviation of their *H* ranks across the cultures. Homogeneity is indicative of the fact that, regardless of community sampled, subjects tend to produce about the same diversity of qualifiers — i.e., such concepts are similar in this aspect of usage. Heterogeneity indicates that, depending upon the particular community sampled, subjects will vary markedly in the diversity of qualifiers produced — i.e., such concepts are stereotyped notions in some places and amorphous notions in others.

We can compare concepts which are the most stereotyped cross-culturally with those which are the most amorphous cross-culturally. Table 5:4 gives the *H*-rank data for the ten most stereotyped concepts (upper half) and ten most amorphous concepts (lower half) cross-culturally.[5] Here we can immediately note a difference, although it is not in terms of concrete/abstract as might have been expected. With the exception of DANGER, all of the cross-culturally stereotyped concepts refer to inanimate physical objects or events (CLOUD, ROPE, FRUIT, SMOKE, WIND, LAKE, MEAT, SUN, and MOON); with the exception of FISH, FREEDOM, and possibly LAUGHTER, all of the cross-culturally amorphous concepts refer to animate human individuals or organs (POLICEMAN, HAND, MAN, THIEF, WOMAN, HEART, and DOCTOR). It appears that concepts referring to humans, their activities and processes, are the most productive in the sense of being diversely qualified — they can "mean many things" or have many conditions or aspects.[6]

CROSS-CULTURAL CORRELATIONS IN THE *H* RANKS OF CONCEPTS

Correlations among the *qualifiers* ranked for frequency and diversity ranged between .50 to .70 across these language/culture communities, indicating that there was general agreement in the salience of different modes of qualifying. When the same statistic is applied to the *H* ranks of *substantives* (concepts) across communities, there is much less agreement. Table 5:5 gives the intercommunity correlations for the *H* ranks of substantives, and it can be seen that they are not in the same range — the few high correlations are about .60 and most of them fall in the .20 to .30 range.

---

[5] Note that this table uses only the two-letter symbols for 23 communities.

[6] It is perhaps worth reporting in this connection that in a small study on the permissibility of usage of 10 nouns with a very random sample of 100 verbs (the first verbs on the second 100 pages of Michener's *Hawaii!*), the human nouns WOMAN and DOCTOR could be used with the most verbs, animate but nonhuman nouns like DOG next, and either inanimate-concrete nouns like ROPE or abstract nouns like BELIEF and FREEDOM last. Human languages seem to have been designed for people to talk about people!

TABLE 5:4

H Ranks of 20 Cross-Culturally Homogeneous Concepts

	AE	AD	AP	BF	CB	DH	FF	FR	GK	HC	IF	IT	JP	LA	MK	MS	ND	PO	SW	TH	TK	TZ	YS	MEAN	SD
Culturally Stereotyped																									
CLOUD	76	100	93	89	100	95	27	88	94	56	100	80	46	88	96	99	74	94	34	64	91	94	86	81.0	21.0
ROPE	54	88	91	95	94	97	2	98	95	91	74	97	65	98	53	74	84	99	88	83	100	49	79	80.3	22.6
FRUIT	68	89	71	66	96	83	38	78	66	70	55	91	100	92	31	86	78	76	97	53	32	21	88	70.7	22.3
SMOKE	82	91	42	26	52	100	63	87	60	29	88	64	77	65	94	96	41	83	52	74	68	53	96	68.8	21.5
WIND	72	63	53	30	66	63	46	73	93	68	63	96	78	81	23	94	90	87	25	98	83	34	97	68.5	23.3
LAKE	31	52	33	78	58	88	59	50	47	59	89	86	88	90	57	78	58	93	60	95	95	57	73	68.4	19.4
DANGER	100	53	37	97	51	60	8	80	73	31	82	78	71	61	84	48	100	95	64	73	59	66	87	67.7	22.6
MEAT	46	43	29	87	80	35	34	89	45	67	56	81	93	77	72	89	85	80	83	22	72	74	71	65.7	21.4
SUN	95	96	51	33	37	59	82	57	92	34	79	73	60	42	70	55	55	86	63	84	84	13	76	64.2	21.8
MOON	35	51	85	55	46	37	45	54	48	59	36	54	86	59	75	82	99	60	76	70	97	56	57	62.8	18.7
Culturally Amorphous																									
DOCTOR	49	32	45	2	92	81	77	3	17	30	17	51	3	6	37	19	15	17	30	11	20	12	24	29.6	25.1
FISH	27	7	8	5	33	28	91	30	25	14	22	66	31	47	13	68	14	14	6	12	7	59	28	28.5	22.6
LAUGHTER	56	36	20	1	53	4	37	5	26	19	8	13	57	14	35	31	32	24	13	82	22	47	18	28.4	19.7
FREEDOM	64	57	44	3	15	24	31	35	5	37	38	8	36	28	36	2	4	7	33	5	49	62	17	27.8	19.8
HEART	33	2	4	24	65	7	88	40	3	24	7	21	33	15	19	23	60	27	32	29	2	52	5	26.7	21.9
WOMAN	3	10	5	12	7	34	96	8	22	4	11	14	84	2	29	50	29	6	20	75	16	36	1	25.0	26.5
THIEF	1	26	6	15	64	8	40	13	14	42	6	61	35	10	42	13	13	45	1	23	3	43	11	23.3	18.8
MAN	19	3	12	10	1	6	83	4	18	32	1	5	38	11	1	26	5	1	22	61	1	15	6	16.1	20.4
HAND	17	25	1	4	29	39	6	10	11	11	10	3	20	11	44	3	6	9	12	10	5	16	23	14.1	11.1
POLICEMAN	12	1	2	28	2	1	5	6	2	8	4	2	32	53	15	9	21	4	7	4	6	3	27	11.0	12.7

Rank Order Correlations of Communities on H Ranks of 100 Substantives

	AE	FR	BF	ND	PO	SW	FF	MS	IT	YS	GK	TK	LA	IF	AD	AP	DH	CB	MK	TH	HC	JP	TZ
AE	100	24	14	25	19	24	-05	19	21	27	30	12	17	21	28	26	25	16	09	37	04	10	09
FR		100	40	25	59	15	-15	60	55	52	41	18	37	30	31	-07	24	35	01	19	40	34	11
BF			100	57	50	45	-11	35	35	48	30	27	31	50	30	15	25	31	-11	19	26	13	11
ND				100	39	49	-06	27	26	36	41	36	27	49	19	25	22	25	16	24	06	-01	02
PO					100	20	-12	53	52	54	36	28	20	32	30	14	27	29	13	19	24	25	-07
SW						100	-06	16	11	27	31	31	21	38	42	33	06	05	09	21	10	03	10
FF							100	-01	-13	-04	-14	03	-07	-10	00	-01	08	05	-15	18	-16	00	01
MS								100	60	58	32	16	38	34	21	01	24	33	-06	27	28	42	-14
IT									100	60	41	31	38	30	31	05	28	31	-10	25	36	32	-13
YS										100	48	38	39	53	40	05	26	24	05	30	11	32	-25
GK											100	25	24	53	36	23	06	10	24	33	14	-01	-05
TK												100	35	39	44	48	30	18	29	27	23	10	15
LA													100	46	35	17	45	26	08	-30	20	39	06
IF														100	47	33	33	21	19	-29	11	-01	19
AD															100	46	26	28	17	29	29	17	07
AP																100	22	00	17	28	22	-06	42
DH																	100	51	08	35	27	28	-06
CB																		100	03	15	31	26	-22
MK																			100	05	-05	-09	25
TH																				100	10	25	01
HC																					100	26	00
JP																						100	07
TZ																							100

In other words, our language/culture communities do not agree generally on the salience (degree of amorphousness or stereotypy) of concepts. Nevertheless, there are a few clusters of correlations that suggest ethnolinguistic relatedness — French, Italian, Polish, Serbo-Croatian, and Mexican Spanish all intercorrelate at least .50 or more, the two Afghan samples and Turkish intercorrelate at least .44, and Flemish, Dutch, and Swedish also intercorrelate .45 or better.[7] It might also be noted that whereas Delhi Hindi and Calcutta Bengali correlate .51 on this measure, Mysorean Kannada-speakers from southern India correlate approximately zero with both of these other Indian groups. There is at least the suggestion of linguistic determinism here, and thus support for the Sapir-Whorf hypothesis of psycholinguistic relativity.

ATLAS TABLES 2

INFORMATION INDICES FOR QUALIFIERS

Tables 2 in the *Atlas* give the first 200 *H*-ranked qualifiers from the qualifier-elicitation task, i.e., those modes of qualifying most frequently and diversely used in each community. In Chapter 3 the reasonably high correlations in *H* ranks for qualifiers were noted, as well as the fact that synonyms for English *good* or *big* occurred at the top of the lists in nearly all other language/culture communities. Appendix B presents *Atlas* Table 2 for American English (AE). We assume that qualifiers ranked in this fashion will be useful in both intracultural and cross-cultural research. Table 5:6 gives the 10 highest *H*-ranked qualifiers and the 10 lowest from *Atlas* Tables 2 for 22 communities. Comparison of the first 10 ranked qualifiers for AE (*good, big, great, small, large, bad, little, long, hard, strong*) with the last 10 (*growing, exciting, simple, silver, orange, neat, lots, living, hurting, hairy*) is certainly convincing as to the relative generalities of the qualifiers involved. Presumably, native speakers of the other languages in our sample would feel the same distinction about their own ranked qualifiers, here translated into English.

As an example of the potential use of such information, we offer the Pollyanna hypothesis — that evaluatively positive qualifiers of experience have more frequent usage and are more frequently given the negating affix than the negatively evaluative qualifiers matched as opposites. Boucher and Osgood (1969) made use of the data already available in the *Atlas* to check

---

[7] For this and the following tables we adopt a semi-geographic ordering of communities, beginning with AE (American English) and moving eastward to FR (France) and so on. The Mexican samples are inserted in the convenient gap between Finland (FF) and Italy (IT). This allows the placement of the Mexico City Spanish data near its nearest linguistic relative.

TABLE 5:6

Ten Highest and Ten Lowest H-*Ranked Qualifiers from* Atlas *Tables 2*

	AE	FR	BF	ND
1	good	tall	big	large
2	big	good	good	good
3	great	deep	beautiful	beautiful
4	small	white	little	small
5	large	hard	hard	much
6	bad	black	long	hard
7	little	fine	strong	heavy
8	long	violent	thick	long
9	hard	pleasant	intense	bad
10	strong	soft	bad	thick
191	hairy	sparkling	open	crazy
192	hurting	obvious	golden	clean
193	living	young	dense	narrow
194	lots	beating	tough	excellent
195	neat	knowing	complicated	furious
196	orange	childish	fierce	cruel
197	silver	right	complete	obscure
198	simple	stupid	picturesque	mad
199	exciting	true	burning	well-founded
200	growing	thin	unsuccessful	deformed
	PO	SW	FF	HM
1	big	big	good	big
2	great	good	big	good
3	small	good	firm	beautiful
4	good	small	small	bad
5	long	hard	beautiful	long
6	heavy	beautiful	long	strong
7	terrible	long	bad	quick
8	enormous	strong	pleasant	small
9	black	bad	bad, spoilt	hard
10	curious	amusing	difficult	warm
191	technical	angry	lazy	un-nice
192	lean	even	crooked	particular
193	common	twisted	sharp	uncomfortable
194	shallow	lag	sensitive	changing
195	thin	trustworthy	admirable	mean
196	edible	sour	hairy	saint
197	may	droll	timid	four-legged
198	unfaithful	silent	messy	snappish
199	rational	warming	rotten	careful
200	ugly	transparent	threatening	beloved

TABLE 5:6 (Continued)

MS	IT	YS	GK
1 big	big	big	big
2 good	beautiful	little	good
3 strong	good	nice	beautiful
4 bad	strong	good	small
5 pretty	long	strong	much
6 small	small	hard	strong
7 pleasant	immense	terrible	bad
8 beautiful	hard	necessary	beautiful
9 hard	much	beautiful	deep
10 white	big, thick	fast	clean
191 raw	intimate	plenty	successful
192 cunning	sick-ill	disgusting	unexpected
193 gentle	insistent	unjustified	blind
194 dreadful	frightful	miserable	unrestrained
195 silver-plated	loving	honest	good
196 brave	empty	ideal	fat
197 wicked-accursed	lasting	crazy	boiled
198 voracious	picturesque	insufficient	joyful
199 adorable	red	irresistible	sensible
200 speedy	brown	wanted	the least

TK	LA	IF	AD
1 good	large	many	good
2 big	beautiful	good	large
3 beautiful	great	big	many
4 much	severe	bad	bad
5 wicked	small	small	much
6 bad	long	little	ruined
7 long	strong	beautiful	black
8 small	plentiful	pretty	white
9 sweet	white	black	big
10 yellow	red	kind	little
191 cracked	sparkling	noisy	grey
192 raw	intense	savagely	nervous
193 cunning	surprising	sure	trouble
194 cooked	homely	closed	living
195 unshakeable	joyful	cut	absolute
196 distinguished	free	successful	past
197 famous	dark	golden	manliness
198 moneyed	circular	angry	world
199 tight	fascinating	frightening	notorious
200 working	pedigreed	correct	experience

TABLE 5:6 (Continued)

	DH	CB	MK	TH
1	good	good	good	good
2	beautiful	beautiful	big	much
3	many	big	slight	big
4	big	awful	much	pretty
5	more	profuse	dark	little
6	bad	bad	fair	small
7	black	black	severe	not good
8	long	little	bad	die
9	sharp, swift	extreme	dreadful	black
10	small	tall	small	long
191	easy	salty	pricking	young
192	half, incomplete	pitiless	sharp	monk
193	endless	ill	iron	afraid
194	incomplete	dense	fat	durable
195	unbreakable	exact	unselfish	readable
196	thin	seven	saltless	sports
197	wicked	awkward	brisk	uncertain
198	flat	ample	wooden	artificial
199	of good character	incomplete	all	interesting
200	worth seeing	valuable	invisible	good deeds

	MM	HC	JP[a]
1	big	big	big
2	small	great	pretty
3	pretty	beautiful	beautiful
4	good	frightening	reliable
5	strong	very big	fearful
6	long	small	small
7	tall	lovable	glad
8	white	huge	strong
9	black	long	splendid
10	red	good	good
191	splendid	very deep	important
192	permanent	faithful	green (fresh)
193	fighting	very big	brave
194	pretty (fine)	tight	conceited
195	resplendent	easy	manly
196	thick	holy	continuous
197	empty (idle)	fierce	beautiful
198	overcast	hard	unfeeling
199	godly	fortunate	shallow
200	sick	well-known	poor

[a] For Japan (JP) lowest ranks are 175 to 184.

some of the subhypotheses involved here. (1) Across some 15 communities (available at the time), the positively evaluative members of pairs of accepted opposites were shown to have significantly higher H ranks than their negatively evaluative contrasts. (2) When the application of any negative affix (e.g., in English, *un-, non-, in-,* etc.) was tested against positively and negatively evaluated qualifiers, there was a highly significant tendency to attach the negative affix so as to make a positively evaluative member of any pair of opposites negative (e.g., *un*happy but not *un*sad in English).[8] The Pollyanna hypothesis implies that these differences — apparently universal — are due to the social psychological pressure to "say nice things." Of course, it may be that "nice" qualifiers occur earlier in language experience and hence the negative affixes must be applied to them — but this is itself consistent with a Pollyanna hypothesis.

ATLAS TABLES 3

The data entering into the factor analyses described in Chapter 4 were ratings of the standard 100 substantives against the final refined set of 50 scales, with 20 subjects rating each concept. The emphasis in Chapter 4, however, was on cross-cultural similarities. In this section we will emphasize *differences* in the affective factor structures. We shall also consider factorizations based on one type of oblique rotation (Oblimax) — and a new type of analysis which minimizes weights of the dominant affective dimensions — in an effort to amplify cultural differences.

The American English data drawn from *Atlas* Table 3 are given in Appendix C as an illustration. In these tables the scales for each solution are ordered so that the five scales loading highest on each of the identified factors appear first as clusters; these scales, from one of the orthogonal solutions, become the indigenous SD for each community, it will be recalled. The remaining scales are then ordered by factor according to their maximum loading. Both polar terms are given in the orthogonal solution (always in English), but the sign of a loading should always be attributed to the left-hand term (e.g., it is *nice,* not *awful,* that has a positive E loading in Appendix C). All scales having their maximum loading on a given factor have been rotated so that their loading on it is always positive (e.g., *momentary* goes along with *fresh, full, funny,* etc., as part of Factor V in the American English orthogonal solution).

---

[8] It may also be noted that in DiVesta's data on the development of meaning in children, the evaluatively positive members of pairs typically appear earlier in age level and maintain a higher frequency-diversity of usage than their evaluatively negative opposite numbers.

DIFFERENCES IN SCALE MEANINGS

The orthogonal solution for the indigenous factor analyses is a starting place for the search for differences in modes of qualifying. To any reader looking at Table 4:3 with a discerning eye, there are ·some very interesting differences in the scales that make up particular dimensions.

Metaphors of affect. Fine inspection of the composition of the E factor reveals subtle differences in terms of the metaphorical use of qualifiers for Evaluation. Some of the scales seem to reflect a preoccupation with social interaction (e.g., *likable, sympathetic, merciful, loyal, honest,* etc.), some seem to reflect emotional reactions (e.g., *happy, gay, calm,* etc.), some refer to aesthetic-sensory experiences (e.g., *sweet, beautiful, soft, gentle, mild,* etc.), and some seem to deal with abstract qualities (e.g., *good, beneficial, helpful*). If we total up these four types of scales, as in Table 5:7 for each language/culture community, certain intriguing similarities and differences emerge. For the Malaysian language (MM) Evaluation is dominantly "abstract" in character; for Flemish (BF) "emotional"; for Arabic (LA),

TABLE 5:7

Metaphors for Evaluation

	LANGUAGE COMMUNITY	AESTHETIC-SENSORY	SOCIAL	EMOTIONAL	ABSTRACT
AE	American English	2	0	3	1
FR	French	0	2	3	1
BF	Flemish	1	0	4	1
ND	Dutch	2	0	3	1
SW	Swedish	0	4	1	1
FF	Finnish	2	0	3	1
MS	Mexican Spanish	1	3	1	1
IT	Italian	2	2	1	1
YS	Serbo-Croatian	3	1	0	2
GK	Greek	0	4	1	1
TK	Turkish	5	0	0	1
LA	Arabic	0	4	0	2
IF	Iranian Farsi	0	2	1	3
AD	Afghan Dari	1	2	0	3
AP	Afghan Pashtu	2	1	0	3
DH	Hindi	0	1	2	3
CB	Bengali	2	0	1	3
MK	Kannada	3	1	1	1
TH	Thai	2	1	1	2
MM	Malaysian	1	1	0	5
HC	Hong Kong Cantonese	0	3	0	3
JP	Japanese	2	2	1	1
	Total	31	34	27	41

Greek (GK), Swedish (SW), and, to a lesser extent, Mexican Spanish (MS) it is clearly "social"; for Turkish (TK) it is "aesthetic-sensory" (Kannada (MK) also tends toward the "aesthetic-sensory"). The other communities extend Evaluation to combinations of two metaphorical types: American (AE), Dutch (ND), and Finnish (FF) to the "emotional-sensory" combination and Italian (IT) and Japanese (JP) to the "social-sensory" combination; the two Persian languages, Afghan Dari (AD) and Iranian Farsi (IF) display a "social-abstract" combination, as does the Cantonese (HC) language community; French (FR) is "social-emotional"; Pashtu (AP) is "sensory-abstract"; Hindi (DH) is "emotional-abstract"; and finally Bengali (CB), Thai (TH), and Serbo-Croatian (YS) have the interesting combination of "abstract-sensory." A similar analysis was performed for Potency and Activity, but the classifications were either uninformative (for Potency) or too diverse (for Activity).

Factor loadings of translation-equivalent scales. There have been many common scales — in translation, of course — represented in the preceding materials. These were usually scales among the top six high-loading scales on the indigenous factors. In Table 5:8 we list 12 scales that have very near complete representation among our sample of languages. For each, the loadings for the factors designated as Evaluation, Potency, or Activity in the indigenous analyses are given. The scales have been ordered from those most clearly homogeneous cross-culturally on E, P, and A to those most heterogeneous. Thus *good–bad, evil* and *beautiful, pretty, attractive–ugly, unattractive* are commonly Evaluative, but *young–old* varies across communities in its factor dominance on E, P, or A. The loadings have been oriented so that a positive value indicates that the left-hand term is positively correlated with the Good, Strong, or Active pole of the E, P, and A dimensions.

Looking first at Evaluation scales, *good-bad* is always a stable and pure Evaluator, with the possible exception of Finnish (FF), where it has some negative Potency (or should we say some positive weakness); where *good-bad* has any Activity loading, it is negative. *Beautiful-ugly* for Afghan Dari (AD) and Hindi (DH) is not so strongly Evaluative; however, it should be recalled that Afghan Dari had a second-order Evaluation factor that split the E scales, lowering all loadings (but *beautiful* loads only .32 on this second E factor). *Clean-dirty* is highly and purely Evaluative for most groups, but there are some exceptions: Belgium (BF), Finland, Greece (GK), Iran (IF), and Delhi. For Iranians *clean* loads somewhat on the positive end of Potency while for Delhi it has a slightly Passive loading. *Rich* (vs. *poor*) is highly Evaluative for both Americans (AE) and Thai (TH); it is more Potent for Greeks and more Active for the Afghan Dari group. Iranian Farsi has a relatively high P loading for *light, bright* vs. *dark,* but the scale is generally Evaluative for all groups except perhaps Malaysia (MM).

TABLE 5:8

E, P, and A Loadings for Some Key Common Scales[a]

		good-bad			beautiful-ugly / pretty-ugly			clean-dirty			rich-poor			light-dark / bright-dark			big-little / large-small		
		E	P	A	E	P	A	E	P	A	E	P	A	E	P	A	E	P	A
AE	American English	93	03	-05	91	00	-07	90	-06	-04	80	21	-09	78	05	-07	-05	81	24
FR	French	93	-06	-10	90	07	07	:	:	:	:	:	:	79	-12	07	34	80	-17
BF	Flemish	84	00	-16	88	09	12	73	-09	-08	:	:	:	83	00	-17	01	77	07
ND	Dutch	91	10	06	83	07	25	:	:	:	:	:	:	:	:	:	-07	70	39
SW	Swedish	94	02	03	:	:	:	:	:	:	59	02	21	64	01	07	-06	66	-04
FF	Finnish	80	-33	-17	94	-05	-12	78	-10	-10	61	-17	16	57	-16	-11	-19	49	-43
MS	Mexican Spanish	95	-12	-01	91	00	-20	:	:	:	:	:	:	76	01	12	27	76	-31
IT	Italian	93	05	-19	91	11	-05	:	:	:	63	11	-03	:	:	:	00	73	17
YS	Serbo-Croatian	93	14	06	:	:	:	:	:	:	:	:	:	81	27	03	12	84	14
GK	Greek	88	05	-17	:	:	:	70	-21	-04	38	46	14	73	23	01	09	81	10
TK	Turkish	92	-13	-12	94	-07	-04	89	-04	-06	:	:	:	:	:	:	01 / 09	54 / 64	-44 / -42 [c]
LA	Arabic	95	-12	-06	92	-20	-06	93	-09	01	63	-02	-06	:	:	:	56	59	-30
IF	Iranian Farsi	91	17	06	:	:	:	78	29	09	:	:	:	59	42	27	36	77	26
AD	Afghan Dari	81	18	20	75	07	26	:	:	:	12	07	46	:	:	:	17	62	21
AP	Afghan Pashtu	92	15	00	91	11	06	:	:	:	:	:	:	:	:	:	:	44	14
DH	Hindi	88	02	-16	61	-01	-35	77	11	-30	:	:	:	:	:	:	12	44	14
CB	Bengali	93	-11	-16	94	08	-13	:	:	:	:	:	:	:	:	:	27	65	-07
MK	Kannada	86	01	03	83	01	12	:	:	:	85	01	04	:	:	:	04	68	-03
TH	Thai	94	-04	-02	92	06	-01	91	01	00	:	:	:	76	22	-03	52	61	-10
MM	Malaysian	94	06	-02	:	:	:	93	00	-08	:	:	:	35	23	-13	18	81	14
HC	Hong Kong Cantonese	96	06	00	91	05	03	89	01	06	:	:	:	:	:	:	13	85	-01
JP	Japanese	94	08	-16	91[b]	02	-13	91[b]	02	-13	:	:	:	:	:	:	36	58	00

[a] From solutions shown in Table 4:4.
[b] Kitanai-kireina (ugly, dirty=beautiful, clean).
[c] Big-little, large-small.

TABLE 5:8 (Continued)

		strong-weak			heavy-light			fast-slow quick-slow			hot-cold warm-cold			high-low			young-old		
		E	P	A	E	P	A	E	P	A	E	P	A	E	P	A	E	P	A
AE	American English	04	67	13	-45	57	-18	-14	22	64	06	45	36	29	64	-23	39	-42	56
FR	French	20	77	08	-45	60	-30	-07	30	74	47	17	43	47	47	-15	66	-13	45
BF	Flemish	-28	64	25	-64	41	25	05	04	68	74	06	18	47	50	15	35	-51	39
ND	Dutch	00	56	34	-47	63	19	-10	13	67	65	19	32	52	23	-42	:	:	:
SW	Swedish	11	77	14	:	:	:	-07	11	77	49	-23	47	-03	60	-01	32	-50	23
FF	Finnish	-13	49	-31	-39	37	-55	18	46	53	55	19	11	-07	32	33	43	09	53
MS	Mexican Spanish	07	65	26	:	:	:	22	19	56	45	04	38				42	-26	45
IT	Italian	-19	79	-06	-56	43	-22	03	12	55	63	05	01	30	43	34	45	-08	25
YS	Serbo-Croatian	-07	72	18	:	:	:	-10	03	71	73	11	12	27	68	-05	61	-33	39
GK	Greek	09	21	65	:	:	:	-01	-34	64	32	-10	-08	:	:	:	19	-26	46
TK	Turkish	27	49	00	-29	54	-37	05	49	51	68	05	22	36	57	23	43	-02	55
LA	Arabic	60	56	21	-49	52	-16	23	48	61	23	22	33	72	24	-13	66	20	-15
IF	Iranian Farsi	17	51	54	04	70	-17	-12	24	70	40	08	56	:	:	:	:	:	:
AD	Afghan Dari	53	24	51	:	:	:	03	36	82	32	-21	-02	38	50	16	:	:	:
AP	Afghan Pashtu																		
DH	Hindi	56	50	08	-10	59	28	11	-10	61	-31	21	15	38	30	02	:	:	:
CB	Bengali							:	:	53									
MK	Kannada	26	44	29	:	:	:	-18	19	:							:	:	:
TH	Thai	:	:	:	06	67	22	29	00	76	-73	07	19				35	-67	05
MM	Malaysian																		
HC	Hong Kong Cantonese	-01	69	36	:	:	:	-18	08	78	-48	09	22	52	59	08	:	:	:
JP	Japanese	46	65	17	18	76	-17	03	03	60	50	20	50	54	37	15	:	:	:

Turning now to Potency scales, *big-little* (or *large-small*) shows four distinct types of loadings. (1) It is a relatively pure Potency scale for English, Flemish, Swedish (SW), Italian (IT), Serbo-Croatian (YS), Greek, Afghan Dari, Kannada (MK), Malay, and Cantonese (HC). (2) It is relatively high on Potency, but is positive on Evaluation as well, for French (FR), Iranian Farsi, Bengali (CB), Thai, and Japanese (JP). (3) *Big* has relatively high Potency and is also positive on Activity in Dutch (ND) and perhaps Iranian Farsi. (4) *Big* has Potency but *little* is positive on Activity for Finnish, Mexican Spanish (MS), Arabic (LA), and both of the Turkish (TK) scales. *Strong-weak* — a defining scale for pancultural factors — shows more variation in the indigenous analyses: for Afghan Dari it is not a Potency scale at all but of equal parts E and A; for Greeks *strong* is mainly Active, but for the Finns *weak* is Active. When *heavy* has any sizable E loading, it is always negative, and for the Finns and the Turks, *heavy* is also negative in Activity.

Turning finally to the Activity factor, *fast, quick–slow* is most stable, always being high on the Activity dimension. For Finnish, Turkish, and Arabic *fast* also has some loading as a positive P scale, but this is contradicted in Greek, where *fast* has some negative Potency loading. The remaining three A scales — *hot, warm–cold, high-low,* and *young-old* — show considerable variation, and some significant groupings of differences do appear. *Hot* is negatively Evaluative for Hindi and Thai (the two most equatorial communities using this scale) and positively Evaluative for Flemish, Dutch, Finnish, Italian, Serbo-Croatian, and Turkish; it is Potent only for the Americans. *High* is relatively +E for Lebanese and Dutch, and only the Finns and Italians show any positive Activity for this scale. *Young* has +E loadings for French, Italian, Serbo-Croatian, and Arabic; for the Flemish and Thai, it is *old* that has positive Potency. *Young* is one of the most Active qualifiers for American, Finnish, Spanish, Greek, and Turkish subjects.

DIFFERENCES IN FACTOR MEANINGS

Orthogonal factorization forces independence among factors — without, of course, requiring that they be identifiable as E, P, and A. Oblique factorization allows one to look for lack of independence among factors, i.e., tendencies to "collapse" the affective space. It might be hypothesized, for example, that more aggressive societies would display greater fusion of E, P, and A — the Potent tending simultaneously to be the Good and the Active — and more pacifistic societies would maintain greater independence. For each of our communities we have selected that Oblimax rotation which best fits the orthogonal solutions given in Chapter 4 (indigenous analyses) and have then determined the intercorrelations among factors.

Oblique factor "types." Table 5:9 presents these data. Except for LA, AD, AP, and JP (four factors rotated) and MS, YS, DH, and CB (five factors rotated), all are based on rotations of three factors. Utilizing an r of $\pm.40$ as a criterion of significant relation, we have "characterized" communities in terms of these intercorrelation patterns. Thus EPA indicates significant positive correlations among all three factors, PA means correla-

TABLE 5:9

*Correlations of Oblique Primary Axes Identified as Evaluation,
Potency, and Activity*

AE	(PA)			Ego	FR	(E-A)			Ego	BF	(E-A)			Ego
E	100			1.4	E	100			0.9	E	100			1.1
P	−05	100		1.2	P	26	100		0.5	P	16	100		0.8
A	26	*59*	100	1.4	A	*−66*	−14	100	1.3	A	*−57*	−06	100	0.5

ND	(0)			Ego	SW	(0)			Ego	FF	(EA)			Ego
E	100			1.4	E	100			1.5	E	100			1.0
P	−04	100		0.6	P	−01	100		0.7	P	−10	100		0.2
A	−14	23	100	0.6	A	07	−22	100	1.3	A	*63*	01	100	1.1

MS[a]	(0)			Ego	IT	(EA)			Ego	YS[a]	(0)			Ego
E	100			0.6	E	100			1.1	E	100			1.7
P	34	100		0.3	P	−07	100		1.0	P	23	100		1.3
A	−36	−10	100	0.8	A	*47*	−06	100	1.7	A	27	30	100	1.4

GK	(E-A)			Ego	TK	(EA)			Ego	LA[b]	(PA-E)			Ego
E	100			1.8	E	100			0.6	E	100			1.7
P	07	100		0.8	P	−11	100		0.1	P	*−53*	100		1.6
A	*−67*	36	100	1.7	A	*49*	24	100	1.6	A	*−45*	*76*	100	−0.6

IF	(EPA)			Ego	AD[b]	(EA)				Ego	AP[b]	(EP)				Ego
E	100			2.2	E₁	100				1.8	E₁	100				2.0
P	*62*	100		1.0	E₂	*77*	100			..	E₂	*43*	100			..
A	*51*	*64*	100	2.4	P	16	15	100		0.2	P	*43*	*47*	100		1.7
					A	*62*	*63*	19	100	1.2	A	−19	10	19	100	1.6

DH[a]	(0)			Ego	CB[a]	(0)			Ego	MK	(E-A)			Ego
E	100			0.7	E	100			1.8	E	100			1.1
P	−06	100		0.6	P	24	100		1.1	P	−12	100		−0.4
A	−03	01	100	−0.5	A	12	39	100	1.7	A	*−46*	06	100	0.3

TH	(0)			Ego	MM	(E-A)			Ego	HC	(EPA)			Ego
E	100			1.3	E	100			1.1	E	100			1.8
P	29	100		0.2	P	−15	100		0.2	P	*63*	100		1.3
A	−19	−24	100	0.6	A	*−54*	39	100	0.8	A	*56*	*40*	100	1.3

JP[b]	(0)			Ego
E	100			0.9
P	−17	100		0.4
A	−12	−31	100	0.3

[a] Based on five factors.
[b] Based on four factors.

tion of Potency and Activity but neither with Evaluation, E-A indicates significant *negative* relation between E and A, and so forth, with a 0 indicating independence among all three oblique factors. Following a hunch that these fusion "types" might bear some relation to the meanings of the ego concept of the teen-age subjects involved, we have added the raw (unstandardized) E-P-A profiles for I, MYSELF from *Atlas* Tables 8 (see below) to the data in Table 5:9. There are rather marked differences among cultures in types of E, P, and A fusions and — since these involve relations among factors across 100 concepts — they probably strike rather deeply into the ways these young people view their worlds. And, although we cannot suggest any statistic here, there seem to be some correlated differences in ego profiles.

The total-fusion *EPA type,* with all factor correlations greater than .40, include IF (ego profile 2.2, 1.0, and 2.4 on E, P, and A respectively) and HC (profile 1.8, 1.3, 1.3). This type (hypothesized as "aggressive") may be contrasted with *0 type* (hypothesized as "pacifistic"), which includes ND (1.4, 0.6, 0.6), SW (1.5, 0.7, 1.3), MS (0.6, 0.3, 0.8), DH (0.7, 0.6, −0.5), TH (1.3, 0.2, 0.6), and JP (0.9, 0.4, 0.3), as well as YS (1.7, 1.3, 1.4), which tends toward the EPA type, and CB (1.8, 1.1, 1.7), which just missed being a PA type by an *r* of .39 rather than .40. Omitting YS and CB, we observe that our two EPAs (IF and HC) have higher Evaluations of themselves and attribute more Potency and Activity to themselves than any 0 types (with the single exception of SW on A = 1.3). The *PA type,* characterizable as having Value and Dynamism dimensions of affect, but not correlation between them, includes AE (1.4, 1.2, 1.4) and nearly CB (1.8, 1.1, 1.7), and the *EP type* has only one member, AP (2.0, 1.7, 1.6) ; it is worth noting that these three communities also have relatively high E, P, and A for the ego. The *EA type* (with the Good going along with the Active) includes FF (1.0, 0.2, 1.1), IT (1.1, 1.0, 1.7), TK (0.6, 0.1, 1.6), and AD (1.8, 0.2, 1.2) — which share high Activity and, with the exception of IT, a low attribution of Potency to the self. There is no *E-P type,* but there are several *E-A type* communities: FR (0.9, 0.5, 1.3), BF (1.1, 0.8, 0.5), GK (1.8, 0.8, 1.7), MK (1.1, −0.4, 0.3), and MM (1.1, 0.2, 0.8) all identify the Good with the Passive, and like the EAs these tend to have low Potency for the self. The only remaining community fits the *PA-E type* (that is, the *negation* of Dynamism goes with Goodness), and this is the Lebanese Arabic (1.7, 1.6, −0.6) ; perhaps appropriately, this is the only group (except DH) to attribute negative Activity to the ego.

But are we to conclude that Iranian, Hong Kong Chinese, American, Afghan Pashtoon, and perhaps Yugoslav and Calcutta Bengali teen-agers (and their cultures) are "aggressive" or "militant," while Dutch, Swedish, Mexican, Hindi, Thai, and Japanese are "meek" and "pacifistic"? Hardly, from these data alone, but yet there are these related fusion and ego data to conjure with. We may also note that *both* EAs and E-As seem to share low attribution of Potency to the ego, while LA, for whom the Good are *simultaneously* Weak and Passive, have the highest Potency along with the lowest Activity egos. Are we to conclude that people who attribute *either* high or low Activity to concepts in general for some reason see themselves as Weak (rather than as either Active or Passive as might have been expected)? And do the Lebanese perceive "the world" (as represented by 100 diversified concepts) as being Good to the extent that it is "insipid" (both Weak and Passive) because they see themselves as Good and Strong, but very Passive — or vice versa? There may well be some deep personal-cultural relations here but, whatever they may be, they are not related in any obvious way to either language spoken or gross aspects of culture. Probably these factor-fusion and ego-feeling characteristics reflect long-term and unique cultural experiences and hence orientations, and it would be interesting to see how stable these characteristics are over long time spans and if they do change with traumatic cultural experiences (e.g., it would have been interesting to compare the Japan of the 1930s with the Japan of today — and tomorrow).

Partialing out effects of E, P, and A. When in the SD technique subjects are required to judge every item, many (in fact, probably a majority) of the items would be semantically anomalous and would violate what Chomsky (1965) has called "selection rules" (*honest-dishonest* TORNADO, *hard-soft* POWER, *true-false* BABY, etc.). In such cases judgments seem to be made on a metaphorical basis, with shared affect apparently being the prime determinant (thus TORNADO *dishonest* since it is ⁻E, POWER *hard* since it is ⁺P, and BABY *true* because it is clearly ⁺E). In Chapter 7 this argument will be elaborated further. In effect, the SD technique as usually employed functions to *amplify* the magnitudes of the gross affective factors at the expense of finer, more denotative features of meaning.

To the best of our knowledge, the partialing procedure — essentially the method of complete multivariate selection as developed by Thomson and Lederman and reported in Thurstone's *Multiple Factor Analysis* (1947) — was first applied to SD-type data by our Finnish colleague Dr. Jorma Kuusinen in his study (1969) on the domain of personality concepts. Refactoring of the scale intercorrelations after the effects of E-P-A had been partialed yielded a set of meaningful factors that were clearly relevant to personality. In the present case we wished to eliminate from the 50-scale correlation matrices (for all of our communities) the contributions to the interscale correlations due to affective E-P-A and then to see if the factors appearing in refactoring (a) were interpretable, (b) tended to be pancultural, and (c) if not, tended to yield sensible "clusters" of communities. The 12 scales representing E, P, and A in the *indigenous* factorizations (see Table 4:3), four for each factor, were partialed from the correlation matrices in each case. These twelfth-order partial correlation matrices were then analyzed by the method of principal components and rotated by the Varimax method. This procedure was carried through to five or more factors, utilizing the constant-ratio-of-variance criterion for determining the cutoff point.

Because the results of this analysis are inherently interesting, Table 5:10 presents the complete results (but with only the highest-loading scales for each factor being given). This table was derived in the following fashion. First, cutoff points for scale loadings were made (the criteria being either an abrupt reduction of magnitude or an (apparent) abrupt shift in semantic flavor, both of which typically occur together). Then the indigenous factors were given what seemed to be appropriate labels — which the reader can judge for himself (question marks are added in the table where we felt particularly uneasy with our labels). At this point it was obvious from inspection of the entire set of partialed factors that although none of the factors was "universal" in the way that E, P, and A are, there was indeed considerable replication of factors having very similar semantic "flavors" (which, again, the reader must judge for himself). Therefore, the similar sets of factors were organized into "types" (I through XX), as shown in Table 5:10. It must be emphasized that the factors listed under a given "type" for specific cultures are simply based upon our intuitions; they are *not* common factors based upon a pancultural factor analysis of the type reported at the end of Chapter 4.

Type I is shared by 8 of our total 22 communities (AE, SW, FF, YS, GK, LA, AD, and HC) and it appears to be a kind of Moral Evaluation (*honest-dishonest, straight-crooked, honorable-despicable, true-false, civilized-barbaric,* and the like). It is noteworthy that none of our Western European, Latin, or Indian communities have a factor like this once E is partialed out, while Americans, Scandinavians, Yugoslavs, and two Middle Eastern communities (GK and LA) do have such a Morality factor. It is also worth noting that "morality" seems to coincide with "politics" for YS, with "religious in-group" for AD, and with "filial piety" for HC. Type II appears to be a different kind of E, which might be called Social Evaluation; five communities share it (SW, MS, IT, DH, and TH), and they have no geographical or other obvious similarities. This type is characterized by personal warmth (*warm-cold, affectionate–ill-tempered*), social conscience (*charitable-cruel, tender-hard*), and social appropriateness of behavior (*well-behaved–naughty, grateful-ungrateful*). Type III was originally coded as two types, Comfort (FR, IT, and LA) and Austerity (YS, MK, and MM), but they seem to be the poles of one dimension of another kind of E. Again, there appears to be no basis for the grouping. Type IV is yet another way of evaluating — in this case, Personal Competence (*industrious-lazy, talented-untalented, skillful-unskillful*); the existence of such a factor

TABLE 5:10

*Indigenous Factors, after Partialing E, P, and A Indigenous
Marker Scales, Organized on Basis of Apparent Semantic Similarities*

I

AE "Morality"
straight-crooked	.81
smart-dumb	.77
sane-mad	.71
honest-dishonest	.62
true-false	.57
faithful-unfaithful	.56

SW "Character" (?)
straight-crooked	.87
insensitive-sensitive	.83
happy-sad	.75
boiled-raw	.65

FF "Honor"
good-bad	.77
honorable-despicable	.74
valuable-worthless	.63
compulsory-voluntary	.59
right-wrong	.49

YS "Humaneness" (?)
humane-inhumane	.77
for the people–against....	.69
justified-unjustified	.68
political-apolitical	.64

GK "Veracity"
right-wrong	.71
true-false	.67
superior-inferior	.63
brilliant-dark	.60
eternal-temporary	.59

LA "Morality"
honest-dishonest	.76
learned-ignorant	.65
civilized-barbaric	.55
brave-cowardly	.53

AD "Religiosity"
humane-inhumane	.90
religious-irreligious	.80
moslem-heathen	.77
learned-ignorant	.76
brotherly-unbrotherly	.73
courageous-timid	.73

HC "Benevolence"
kind-cruel	.70
filially pious–impious	.65
yielding-pushy	.60
righteous-treacherous	.57
clean-dirty	.50

II

SW "Sensuality" (?)
warm-cold	.62
sweet-sour	.54
right-wrong	.53
clear-smoky	.52
red-blue	.52
unstable-stable	.52
soft-hard	.51

MS "Sociality"
grateful-ungrateful	.74
charitable-cruel	.68
relaxed-tense	.56
polite-crude	.53
safe-dangerous	.52

IT "Humanness"
nice-awful	.67
affectionate–ill-tempered	.64
tender-hard	.64
mortal-immortal	.61
sensitive-insensitive	.61

DH "Sociality" (?)
with somebody–alone	.71
two-folded–unfolded	.69
lackluster-radiant	.57

TH "Delicacy"
fragrant-foul	.71
well-behaved–naughty	.71
clean-dirty	.65
human-animal	.64

III

FR "Ease"
easy-difficult	.78
indulgent-severe	.56
abundant-rare	.52

IT "Comfort"
comfortable-uncomfortable	.76
rich-poor	.64
desirable-undesirable	.56

YS "Non-austerity"
unnecessary-necessary	.69
short-long	.55
warm-cold	.49

LA "Comfort" (?)
comfortable-uncomfortable	.61
low-high	.56
narrow-wide	.55
simple-difficult	.51

MK "Satisfaction"
melodious-harsh	.65
plain-colorful	.58
hasty-considered	.50
temporary-permanent	.48

MM "Non-austerity"
noble-mean	.60
excessive-lacking	.57
near-far	.50
cooked-uncooked	.40
internal-external	.40

IV

MS "Competence"
wise-foolish	.67
responsible-irresponsible	.64
industrious-lazy	.62
bold-cautious	.62

MM "Skillfulness"
clever-dumb	.68
skillful-unskillful	.68
industrious-lazy	.58

HC "Success"
succeeding-failing	.70
lucky-unlucky	.64
happy-sad	.61
humane-bestial	.54
talented-untalented	.54

TABLE 5:10 (Continued)

JP "Competence"		MM "Sensory Aesthetic"		VII	
great-worthless	.71	clear-turbid	.67	SW "Superficiality"	
clever-foolish	.67	bright-dark	.60	amusing-boring	.69
decent-indecent	.67	sweet-sour	.58	useless-useful	.69
fine-trifling	.66	wide apart–dense	.56	long-short	.60
true-false	.59	clean-dirty	.49	existing-nonexisting	.54
skillful-unskillful	.57			thin-thick	.53

V

FR "Aesthetic Value"		HC "Abstract Aesthetic"		TK "Superficiality" (?)	
pretty-ugly	.74	refined-common	.68	unemotional-emotional	.59
marvelous-awful	.72	beautiful-ugly	.59	easy-difficult	.58
perfect-imperfect	.57	eternal-transitory	.56	wet-dry	.58
colorful-pale	.43	infinite-finite	.40	cheap-expensive	.57

IT "Abstract Aesthetic" (?)		JP "Sensory Aesthetic"		IF "Gaudiness"	
unbroken-broken	.60	new-old	.76	colorful-colorless	.70
absolute-relative	.60	delicious–not delicious	.68	badly colored–well colored	.68
simple-complicated	.59	sweet-salty	.55	large-tiny	.58
light-heavy	.46	white-black	.44	uninfluential-influential	.49

LA "Sensory Aesthetic"		VI		AP "Superficiality"	
clean-dirty	.70			thin-thick	.57
brilliant-matte	.70	AE "Utility"		useless-useful	.50
beautiful-ugly	.67	useful-useless	.77	unfaithful-faithful	.48
smooth-coarse	.61	needed-unneeded	.73	lean-fat	.48
		helpful-unhelpful	.53	light-heavy	.46
AD "Aesthetic Value"		everlasting-momentary	.50	unlimited-limited[a]	.45
new-old	.73			not excellent–excellent	.44
lovely-ugly	.71	FR "Importance"		ignorant-learned	.40
magnificent-paltry	.66	indispensable-superfluous	.76		
whole-broken	.64	important-insignificant	.70	DH "Extro/Introversion"	
colorful-colorless	.62	useful-useless	.53		
		sad-gay	.45	open-closed	.67
DH "Aesthetic Value"				gay-sober	.63
ambrosial-poisonous	.79	IT "Importance"		current–not current	.53
superior-inferior	.74	important-unimportant	.76	pretentious-heartfelt	.50
sweet-bitter	.72	valuable-worthless	.71		
pure-impure	.67			HC "Superficiality"	
		GK "Necessity"		superficial-deep	.69
MK "Aesthetic Value" (?)		necessary-unnecessary	.72	easy-difficult	.64
attractive-repulsive	.55	important-unimportant	.65	balanced-extreme	.63
wide-narrow	.52	useful-useless	.59	shallow-deep	.59
dangerous-safe[a]	.50			ordinary-wonderful	.58
best-mean	.50	MK "Utility"		cheap-precious	.56
		useful-useless	.67		
TH "Sensory Aesthetic"		piercing–not piercing	.63	VIII	
pretty-ugly	.73	ordinary-wonderful	.59	BF "Commonness"	
plentiful-depleted	.47			much-little	.81
pleasing-hurting	.45	HC "Beneficence"		common-rare	.81
refreshing-withering	.43	useful-useless	.72	cheap-expensive	.60
whole-broken	.42	beneficial-harmful	.68		
		omnipotent-powerless	.65		

[a] Scales we thought might have been reversed but which, on careful checking, apparently were not.

TABLE 5:10 (Continued)

ND "Ordinariness"		SW "Maturity"		TK "Prudence"	
common-special	.78	full-empty	.71	colorless-colorful	.65
stupid-clever	.69	rich-poor	.66	wise-stupid	.62
dull-shiny	.57	old-young	.63	careful-careless	.61
trivial-impressive	.55	fearless-fearful	.60	straight-round	.53
familiar-strange	.53				
		FF "Maturity" (?)		IF "Stability"	
LA "Commonness"		thick-thin	.66	certain-uncertain	.73
plentiful-rare	.77	distant-near	.56	real-unreal	.70
much-little	.68	rounded-angular	.54	correct-wrong	.62
common-uncommon	.68	old-young	.51	interminable-terminable	.62
general-particular	.56				
apparent-hidden	.56	IT "Maturity"		**XI**	
		mature-immature	.76		
DH "Ordinariness" (?)		exact-inexact	.72	BF "Age"	
ordinary-extraordinary	.58	just-injust	.53	old-new	.82
unexpected-expected[a]	.49			old-young	.81
impatient-patient[a]	.45	**X**		old-fashioned–modern	.80
		BF "Predictability"		YS "Age"	
CB "Ordinariness"		known-unknown	.73	old-new	.78
pale-colored	.70	predictable-unpredictable	.65	old-young	.77
ordinary-extraordinary	.59	definite-indefinite	.63	stale-fresh	.61
torn-intact	.56			bitter-sweet	.40
worst-best	.55	ND "Predictability"			
nonviscous-viscous	.54	predictable-unpredictable	.67	AP "Age"	
		expected-unexpected	.65	old-young	.61
MK "Commonness" (?)		old-fashioned–modern	.47	strong-weak	.59
common-uncommon	.61	known-unknown	.47	unsightly-colorful	.46
bearable-unbearable	.57			brave-cowardly	.39
tight-loose	.49	SW "Reliability"		hating-loving	.39
little-plenty[a]	.48	reliable-unreliable	.75		
		shallow-deep	.60	CB "Age Power"	
JP "Commonness"		round-angular	.42	aged-youthful	.73
necessary-unnecessary	.71	easy-difficulty	.42	old-new	.72
common-rare	.70			strong-weak	.47
thankful-troublesome	.61	MS "Familiarity"		famous-obscure	.47
ugly, dirty–beautiful,		known-unknown	.68		
clean	.57	true-false	.56	MM "Age"	
near-far	.55	natural-artificial	.54	old-new	.77
		grand-insignificant	.53	original-imitation	.74
		abundant-scarce	.53	old-young	.61
		pessimistic-optimistic	.53	dangerous-safe	.58
IX				far-near	.53
BF "Societal"		YS "Social Predict-		animal-human	.38
quiet-impetuous	.76	ability"			
calm-violent	.71	constricted-ramified	.66	**XII**	
necessary-accidental	.69	socialistic-capitalistic	.59	ND "Dependability"	
useful-useless	.65	shallow-deep	.58	safe-dangerous	.67
serious-frivolous	.65	calm-agitated	.57	firm-loose	.62
steady-changing	.65	same-different	.52	slow-fast	.59
		happy-unhappy	.50	steady-changing	.41

[a] Scales we thought might have been reversed but which, on careful checking, apparently were not.

TABLE 5:10 (Continued)

FF "Security"
weak-strong	.64
reassuring-frightening	.56
safe-dangerous	.55
happy-unhappy	.49

GK "Security"
good-bad	.77
friendly-hostile	.77
safe-dangerous	.74
superb-awful	.65
easy-uneasy	.61
tame-savage	.60

TH "Security" (?)
wet-dry	.71
found-lost	.60
have–not have	.54
mother-father	.47
hating-loving[a]	.47

JP "Confidence"
easy-trying	.70
relaxed-tense	.67
calm-violent	.60
optimistic-pessimistic	.56
loose-tight	.53

XIII

IF "Intimacy"
auspicious-ominous	.60
short–tall, long	.58
local-nonlocal	.54
best-worst	.52
gentle, mild–severe	.52
warm-cold	.51

AP "Intimacy"
acquainted-stranger	.73
domestic-foreign	.72
expensive-cheap	.62
pashtoon-coward	.54
elder-younger	.53
cooked-uncooked	.41

CB "Intimacy"
alive-dead	.62
indigenous-foreign	.56
pleasing-saddening	.52
white-black	.45
kind-cruel	.40

TH "Intimacy"
mine, ours–his, hers, theirs	.62
short-tall	.60
stay-leave	.52
narrow-wide	.51
near-far	.48

XIV

IT "Openness"
open-closed	.67
near-far	.59
uncolored-colored	.56
sensitive-insensitive	.42

TK "Openness"
wide-narrow	.60
open-closed	.51
shiny-dull	.49
red-yellow	.45

CB "Openness"
open-shut	.70
light-heavy	.63
thin-thick	.63
shiny-dull	.56
free-fettered	.55

XV

FR "Modernity"
modern-old	.73
open-closed	.51
allowed-prohibited	.51
found-lost	.50

GK "Expansiveness"
open-closed	.63
lucky-unlucky	.62
joyful-sad	.60
young-old	.56

TK "Fulfillment"
fresh-stale	.63
clean-dirty	.48
industrious-lazy	.47
new-old	.46
wet-dry	.45

LA "Fullness-of-Life"
orderly-scattered	.61
full-empty	.59
industrious-indolent	.59
generous-stingy	.58

TH "Fulfillment"
beginning-ending	.76
long-short	.67
occur-disappear	.51
rich-poor	.41
harmful-useful[a]	.41

HC "Self-Actualization"
hollow-solid[a]	.72
free-restricted	.63
new-old	.56
infinite-finite	.46

XVI

FF "Dynamism"
wise-stupid	.67
lively-subdued	.62
ripe-raw	.45
hot-cold	.44
getting bigger–getting smaller	.44
brave-timid	.40

GK "Alertness"
cunning–simple-minded	.67
ripe (mature)–unripe (immature)	.66
curious-indifferent	.61

LA "Vitalness"
alive-dead	.70
compassionate-cruel	.68
vivifying-fatal	.56
safe-dangerous	.56

AP "Alertness"
alive-dead	.82
awake-asleep	.81
fast-slowly	.74
brave-cowardly	.68

MM "Vitality"
healthy-sick	.80
energetic-weak	.70
happy-sad	.69
fat-thin	.55

JP "Vitality" (?)
hot-cold	.73
red-blue	.70
pliable-rigid	.65
thick-thin	.62

[a] Scales we thought might have been reversed but which, on careful checking, apparently were not.

TABLE 5:10 (Continued)

XVII		
AE "Toughness"		
hard-soft		.86
tough-tender		.82
rough-smooth		.70
loud-soft		.66
harsh-mild		.57
BF "Toughness"		
heavy-light		.78
tough-tender		.76
hard-soft		.76
dark-light		.60
ND "Sharpness"		
hard-soft		.70
loud-soft		.62
angular-rounded		.62
FF "Difficulty"		
difficult-easy		.64
rough-smooth		.57
hard-soft		.47
MS "Toughness"		
hard-soft		.74
strong-weak		.52
dry-wet		.49
YS "Toughness"		
heavy, difficult–light, easy		.66
cunning-guileless		.59
hard-soft		.54
TK "Toughness"		
strong-weak		.55
unlovable-lovable		.54
hard–soft (flexible)		.52
AD "Durability"		
firm-loose		.64
hard-soft		.61
strong-weak		.50
CB "Rigidity"		
unyielding-yielding		.75
hard-soft		.74
difficult-easy		.62

MK "Cruelty"	
encroaching-protecting	.65
rough-soft	.59
poisonous–not poisonous	.59
pitiless-piteous	.56
hard-soft	.55

XVIII	
IT "Magnitude"	
long-short	.61
dense-sparse	.60
high, tall–short	.58
abundant-scarce	.56
GK "Abundance"	
abundant-scarce	.68
full-empty	.62
TK "Magnitude"	
deep-shallow	.63
infinite-finite	.55
many-few	.52
IF "Quantity"	
more-less	.86
much, many–little, few	.75
detailed-brief	.68
AD "Quantity"	
very much–little	.80
many-few	.80
powerful-powerless	.56
AP "Magnitude"	
long-short	.67
much, more–less	.59
cold-hot	.51
thick-scattered	.46
full-empty	.46
DH "Magnitude"	
wide-narrow	.63
dense-scattered	.63
big-little	.58
much, many–little, few	.57
CB "Quantity"	
numerous-scarce	.89
many-one	.88
many-few	.86
much-little	.82

JP "Magnitude"	
wide-narrow	.77
long-short	.76
big-little	.75
high-low	.45
deep-shallow	.44

XIX	
AE "Brightness"	
shiny-dull	.77
light-dark	.72
sharp-dull	.63
beautiful-ugly	.59
dangerous-safe	.56
FR "Brightness"	
light-dark	.79
white-black	.75
blonde-brunette	.63
shiny–not shiny	.49
BF "Brightness" (?)	
yellow-blue	.56
active-passive	.54
high-low	.52
white-black	.51
SW "Brightness"	
shiny-dull	.77
light-dark	.62
distinct-indistinct	.43
FF "Brightness"	
light-dark	.83
white-black	.75
lively-tired	.59
MS "Brightness"	
light-dark	.78
white-black	.71
bright-dull	.61
YS "Brightness"	
bright-dark	.77
white-black	.72
IF "Brightness"	
white-black	.79
fresh-old	.67
light-dark	.53

TABLE 5:10 (Continued)

XX		MM "Thermal-Hell"		AD "Status"	
AE "Thermal-Dermal"		fiery-watery	.67	astride-afoot	.78
hot-cold	.87	hot-cold	.62	rich-poor	.69
burning-freezing	.87	poisonous-nonpoisonous	.59	military-civil	.69
dry-wet	.63	round-oval	.56		
		cruel-gentle	.53	**AP "Unique" (?)**	
				complete-incomplete	.65
FR "Thermal"		**HC "Intensity" (?)**		bitter-sweet	.60
hot-cold	.69	scorching hot–cool	.70	colorful-unsightly	.53
red-green	.57	strong-weak	.65	overt-covert	.51
unhealthy-healthy	.55	red-green	.61		
		strong-willed–weak-		**DH "Femininity" (?)**	
ND "Thermal-Dermal"		willed	.61	white-black	.64
yellow-blue	.64	**JP "Thermal" (?)**[b]		rounded-pointed	.64
warm-cold	.60	hot-cold	.73	clean-dirty	.54
dry-wet	.59	red-blue	.70	short-tall	.54
red-green	.56	pliable-rigid	.65	beautiful-ugly	.52
		thick-thin	.62		
MS "Thermal-Dermal"				**MK (??)**	
suffocating-fresh	.76	Unassigned		plenty-sufficient	.58
hot-cold	.60			quiet-noisy	.54
dry-wet	.58	**FR "Tangibility" (?)**		public-secret	.44
boring-amusing	.55	clear-sighted–blind	.53		
		superficial-deep	.51	**JP "promptness" (?)**	
AD "Thermal"		mortal-immortal	.49	early-late	.74
burning-frozen	.79	hard-soft	.48	fast-slow	.72
warm-cold	.76	solid-fragile	.47	solid-fragile	.51
		heavy-light	.46	unpredictable-predictable	.47

[b] Same as "Vitality" for JP but under XVI.

for MS, MM, HC, and JP seems reasonable enough, but one wonders why no more communities yield such a factor.[9]

Type V has been dubbed Aesthetic Value, but it clearly includes at least two subtypes — what might be called Abstract Aesthetic Value (*perfect-imperfect, whole-broken, eternal-transitory,* etc.) and Sensory Aesthetic Value (*smooth-coarse, refreshing-withering, delicious–not delicious,* etc.). IT and HC clearly are the Abstract type and TH, MM, and JP clearly are the Sensory type, with FR, LA, AD, DH, and MK combining both types of scales. What is really notable here is the absence of any factor identifiable as Aesthetic for AE, MS, all Western Europeans except FR, both Scandinavian communities (SW and FF), and all Mediterranean communities

[9] It is, of course, true that a partialed factor of a given type can only appear if in the original qualifier-elicitation phase the teen-agers in a given community happened to use qualifiers of the semantic type productively. However, the fact that, e.g., the Japanese boys do use qualifiers like *clever, skillful,* and *worthless* productively is itself evidence of the importance of this dimension of judgment for them.

except IT (that is, YS, GK, and TK); on the other hand, the only Asian communities which do *not* have an Aesthetic factor are IF, AP, and CB. Six communities share Type VI, a Utility factor (AE, FR, IT, GK, MK, and HC (*useful-useless, valuable-worthless, important-unimportant,* etc.); there is no geographical basis for this grouping, but intuitively they share a "businesslike" orientation. Again, one wonders at the absences, e.g., of LA and JP.

Type VII, which we usually called Superficiality, is a kind of E factor in reverse (*amusing, thin, easy, cheap, badly colored, gay, pretentious, shallow,* etc.). It is shared by six of our communities (SW, TK, IF, AP, DH, and HC), but it is hard to perceive any common ground among them, except that all but SW are Asians. Type VIII appears in seven communities (BF, ND, LA, DH, CB, MK, and JP), the presence of all three Indian cultures along with both BF and ND being notable; it is characterized by scales like *common-rare, trivial-impressive, ordinary-extraordinary,* and *near-far* and might be dubbed Common Ordinariness. It might be noted that this factor type tends to be in complementary distribution with Type VII (Superficiality); with the exception of DH which appears on both, and hence VII and VIII may be reflections of a single underlying factor.

Turning now to less obviously evaluating factors, Types IX, X, XI, and XII all seem to reflect an underlying Predictability dimension of judgment. AE, FR, LA, AD, DH, and HC are the only communities which do not appear on one or another of these factor types. Type IX seems best characterized as a Maturity factor (*quiet-impetuous, full-empty, distant-near,* and *mature-immature* itself), and it is shared by BF, SW, FF, and IT; the appearance of both Scandinavian communities is notable. Type X may be termed a Predictability factor (but it shades into "reliability," "familiarity," "prudence," and "stability" in various loci); characteristic scales are *predictable-unpredictable, known-unknown, expected-unexpected,* and *certain-uncertain.* Both BF and ND display such a factor, along with SW, MS, YS, TK, and IF; the political "coloration" of this factor for YS is most interesting — *constricted, socialistic, shallow, calm, same,* and *happy* being the positive poles. A factor clearly identifiable as Age (see the pancultural minor factors, Chapter 4, p. 186) appears in five of our communities BF, YS, AP, CB, and MM), all widely separated geographically and culturally. The characteristic scales for Type XI, of course, are *old-young* and *old-new,* but the added scales in each case give a special semantic flavor to Age suggestive of underlying teen-age attitudes (e.g., *old-fashioned* for BF and *stale* and *bitter* for YS, implying negative attitudes; *strong* and *famous* for CB, implying respectful attitudes; and the *strong* and *brave* vs. the *unsightly* and *hating* of AP and the *original, dangerous,* and *animal* for MM, certainly suggesting ambivalence in feeling toward the elderly in their societies). Type XII was most often dubbed Security, and we find it for ND, FF, GK, TH, and JP; the most typical scales are *safe-dangerous, reassuring-frightening, happy-unhappy,* and their quasi synonyms. The shifts in orientation from characteristics of the situation which is secure (*steady* and *firm* for ND and *relaxed, calm,* and *optimistic* for JP) to the external conditions for security (the *reassuring* of FF, the *friendly,* and *tame* of GK, and perhaps the *found, have,* and *mother* of TH) are worth noting.

Factor Type XIII presents an interesting pattern which we have called Intimacy because it always includes one or more in-group vs. out-group scales (e.g., the *local-nonlocal* of IF, the *acquainted-stranger* of AP, the *indigenous-foreign* of CB, and the *mine, ours–his, hers, theirs* of TH) along with one or more scales suggesting warmth and tenderness (*gentle* for IF, *kind* for CB, and *stay-leave* for TH). The positive scales for AP are particularly interesting — *acquainted, domestic, expensive, pashtoon, elder,* and *cooked* (vs. *uncooked*). It is worth noting that such an Intimacy (or In-group/Out-group) factor is restricted to Central Asia (IF, AP, CB, and TH). Type XIV appears in only three widely separated communities (IT, TK, and CB) and, while seeming to have a shared semantic flavor, it can only be labeled in terms of the common scale as Openness (*open–closed, shut*); other suggestive scales are *shiny-dull, sensitive-insensitive,* and *free-fettered,* and these seem to relate XIV to XV, which we have termed Fulfillment (this being the most encompassing term we could come up with). Type XV appears in six communities (FR, GK, TK, LA, TH, and HC) which pretty much span the world but only include a single Western group (FR); *modern, free, joyful, fresh, industrious, orderly, beginning, open,* and *found* (vs. *lost*) contribute to the semantic flavor of release and fulfillment.

Type XVI moves away from E into a fusion of P and A, which we have always referred to as Dynamism. Looking across the six communities which seem to have such a factor (FF, GK, LA, AP, MM, and JP), we note the frequent presence of both Activity scales (*lively, hot, curious, alive, fast*) and Potency scales (*getting bigger, brave, ripe*(?), *healthy, thick*); the semantic flavor varies from the "alertness" of GK and AP to the "vitality" of LA, MM, and JP. Types XVII and XVIII are two variants of generalized Potency with which we are also familiar: XVII warrants the label Toughness, the most frequent polar terms being *hard, tough, loud, rough, strong,* and *difficult;* it has representation everywhere in our sample except East Asia (TH, HC, and JP). Closer inspection suggests two finer types of Toughness; the first appears to be more person-oriented (i.e., +Human), as witness the *cunning* of YS, the *unlovable* of TK, and the *encroaching* and *pitiless* of MK, and the second appears to be more thing- or task-oriented (i.e.; ⁻Human), as witness the *heavy* of BF, the *angular* of ND, the *difficult* of FF, and the *firm* (vs. *loose*) of AD. Type XVIII, on the other hand, is a clear Magnitude factor, characterized by such terms as *long, dense, abundant, full, deep, more, much, many, wide,* and *high.* It is noteworthy that not a single Western European (including AE), Scandinavian, or Latin

American community comes up with a Magnitude factor, whereas all Mediterraneans (except YS), all West Asians (except LA), and two of the three Indians (excepting MK) do have one — yet only JP of the East Asians (not TH and HC) has such a factor. Is it possible that societal histories of scarcity are operating here?

The last two factor types are well defined, more denotative in nature, and have already been suggested in the pancultural analysis (Chapter 4, pp. 184, 186, 188). Type XIX clearly labels itself as Brightness (*shiny, light, white, yellow, distinct, bright*); it is also limited to cultures in northern (SW, FF) and temperate (AE, FR, BF, YS, IF) climes, with MS marginal. One wonders at the absence of it in AD, AP, and JP, however. Not a single one of our really Mediterranean (IT, GK, TK, LA), Indian (DH, CB, MK) or Southeast Asian communities (TH and HC) has a Brightness factor. Type XX is a factor that has already been dubbed Thermal-Dermal because it often includes both the thermal quality (*hot, burning, warm* vs. *cold, freezing, cool*) and the dermal quality (*dry-wet*), both of which are skin senses, of course. Most interesting from the viewpoint of sensory synesthesia, we typically find the red end of the spectrum (*red, yellow*) associated with hot-dry and the blue end (*green, blue*) with cool-wet. There is no clear climatic selection here, however; temperate AE, FR, ND, AD, and JP as well as much less temperate MS, MM, and HC appear. What is intriguing, though, is that, with the single exception of FR's *unhealthy-healthy*, only the cultures in the more torrid zones include "vitalness" scales with the thermal-dermal (MS, *suffocating-fresh;* MM, *poisonous-nonpoisonous, cruel-gentle;* HC, *scorching hot–cool, strong-weak, strong-willed–weak-willed*).

There were only six indigenous partialed factors which we were unable to assign to semantic groupings as above. There was one each for FR (*clear-sighted, superficial, mortal, solid* — "tangibility"?), for AD (*astride, rich, military* — "status"?), for AP (*complete, bitter, colorful, overt* — ??), for DH (*white, rounded, clean, short, beautiful* — by any chance a "femininity" factor?), for MK (*plenty, quiet, public* — ??), and for JP (*early, fast, solid, unpredictable* — "promptness"?). Several methodological and theoretical issues are raised by the results of factoring these partialed matrices, but we shall reserve consideration of them for Chapter 7 (pp. 401-406).

ATLAS TABLES 4

The results of indigenous factorizations for 22 communities were reported in Chapter 4 (Table 4:3, pp. 124-131). It will be recalled that in nearly all cases it was possible to identify E, P, and A factors — although admittedly via intuitions about the English translations of scale terms. *Atlas* Tables 4 give the E, P, A, X, and Y (where X and Y refer to the fourth and fifth factors other than E-P-A) factor scores for the 100 original concepts used in the concept-on-scale task. The scores (C) are computed from the indigenous scale factor loadings (A), the 50×50 correlation matrix (R), and the concept/scale means (Z), in the matrix equation $C = ZR^{-1}A$ (Harris, 1967; Horn, 1965; Thurstone, 1947; Tucker, 1971). Since the X and Y factors were usually difficult to interpret, our discussion here will be limited to the concept E, P, and A scores.

There are at least two uses of such scores. (1) From the points of view of our colleagues in various locations, these scores reflect variations in meaning along the affective dimensions uniquely defined by their own indigenous rules of using qualifiers (rather than along those modified E-P-A dimensions that are most comparable panculturally). (2) From a more general point of view, it is of major interest to see to what extent the translation-equivalent concepts which score highest and lowest on indigenous Es, Ps, and As tend to be common across cultures. Communality in this case would simultaneously suggest that there are certain universal tendencies in the attribution of affect and provide indirect validation of our assignments of indigenous factors to E, P, and A categories. Lack of communality here could indicate either gross cultural differences in the attribution of affect to concepts or incomparability of the indigenous factors labeled E, P, and A (or both).

CONCEPT ALLOCATION IN THE E-P-A SPACE

Before asking about communalities in affect attribution, however, there is a prior question: are the 100 concepts distributed in the indigenous E-P-A spaces more or less homogeneously? The answer to this question is an emphatic *no.* As can be seen by inspecting Table 5:11, the "positive" regions of the space (+E, +P, +A) are more densely populated than their "negative" counterparts, this being most marked for E and least for A. Since these original 100 concepts were selected from lists presumed to be culture-common — and certainly without any E-P-A malice aforethought — it seems unlikely that this is due to biased sampling.[10] This uneven distribution of concepts in the space must be kept in mind in interpreting the data which follow.

COMMUNALITY IN THE ATTRIBUTION OF AFFECT

Table 5:12 lists for each pole of each factor (as assigned) in the indigenous matrices those concepts of the original 100 for which half or more of our communities had scores equal to or greater than ± 1.0 — but the factor scores for *all* communities (on their own indigenous factor equivalents) are

---

[10] As will be seen (this chapter, pp. 246-247), the same unevenness of allocation of concepts of the E-P-A space holds for all 620 concepts in the *Atlas.*

TABLE 5:11

Concept Distributions by Octants in 22 Language/Culture Communities

	Octant								Bipolar Ratios +/−		
	1	2	3	4	5	6	7	8			
Language/ Culture Community	+E +P +A	+E +P −A	+E −P +A	+E −P −A	−E +P +A	−E +P −A	−E −P +A	−E −P −A	+E/−E	+P/−P	+A/−A
AE	47	25	8	2	11	7	0	0	82/18	90/10	66/34
FR	54	4	19	1	14	3	3	1	78/21	75/24	90/9
BF	38	20	10	11	18	2	1	0	79/21	78/22	67/33
ND	42	18	13	4	16	3	2	1	77/22	79/20	73/26
SW	44	13	16	3	10	3	10	1	76/24	70/30	80/20
FF	47	11	16	2	15	7	1	0	76/23	80/19	79/20
MS	52	19	9	1	10	7	0	2	81/19	88/12	71/29
IT	56	15	8	1	13	5	1	0	80/19	89/10	78/21
YS	59	12	5	3	12	8	1	0	79/21	91/9	77/23
GK	67	9	6	2	13	2	0	1	84/16	91/9	86/14
TK	51	18	11	2	14	3	0	1	82/18	86/14	76/24
LA	8	73	1	2	1	7	4	4	84/16	89/11	14/86
IF	46	3	30	5	9	3	3	1	84/16	61/39	88/12
AD	76	6	4	2	5	1	3	3	88/12	88/12	88/12
AP	57	9	10	5	6	1	9	3	81/19	73/27	82/18
DH	42	18	13	4	16	3	2	1	77/22	79/20	73/26
CB	64	11	4	1	16	1	2	1	80/20	92/8	86/14
MK	39	12	24	8	11	3	2	0	83/16	65/34	76/23
TH	44	23	8	8	9	5	3	0	83/17	81/19	64/36
MM	65	4	11	3	6	4	5	2	83/17	79/21	87/13
HC	55	11	10	6	11	4	1	2	82/18	81/19	77/23
JP	32	28	12	7	8	9	2	2	79/21	77/23	54/46
Total[a]	1,085	362	248	83	244	91	55	26	1,778/416	1,782/412	1,632/562

[a] Total adds up to 2,194 rather than 2,200 because six concepts fell precisely at the midpoints of a factor.

listed in each case. The first thing to note in this table is that the number of "positive" concepts (+E, +P, +A) reaching this criterion is consistently *smaller* than the number of "negatives" (−E, −P, −A). Now, given the fact that the bias in concept allocations generally is precisely in the opposite direction, as we have just seen, this is rather paradoxical. Apparently, although there is a general "Pollyanna" tendency toward greater *numbers* of affectively positive concepts, those concepts that are negative in E, in P, or in A are more intensely and universally so (as can be seen from the column means in this table, the degrees of polarization as well as the numbers of communities reaching the criterion are greater for the negative poles).[11] At this point we see no obvious explanation of this, but it is certainly something to conjure with (see Chapter 7, pp. 362-364).

[11] Exactly the same phenomenon appears for the *standardized* scores for the 620 *Atlas* concepts, negatives on all factors being more intensely so than positives.

On Evaluation. Only five concepts — FREEDOM, GIRL, LOVE, MARRIAGE, and MOTHER — have factor scores greater than 1.0 for half or more of the communities. As indicated by asterisks within rows, AE, FF, and AP have highest and equal E for both FREEDOM and MARRIAGE (surely a conflictual state!), and other attributions of highest E can be seen by inspecting the asterisked values in Table 5:12. Either alone or in combination, MOTHER is generally the most highly valued concept for the teen-age boys in our samples (the exceptions being AE, BF, FF, IT, AD and AP, MK, and TH). The contrast between AD and AP is interesting: AD is high on LOVE but low on FREEDOM, MARRIAGE, and MOTHER, whereas AP is high on FREEDOM and MARRIAGE but low on LOVE. As indicated by italics within columns, the Finns and Mysoreans are highest on FREEDOM and the Swedes and Afghan Dari lowest; for both GIRL and LOVE we may observe a West (high) vs. East (low) split, the consistently low E for GIRL in DH, CB, and MK being notable (but not surprising in terms of what we know about these cultures).

TABLE 5:12

Concepts Having Scores on Indigenous Factors $\geq \pm 1.0$ for Half or More of Communities Involved[a]

	+E					
	FREEDOM	GIRL	LOVE	MARRIAGE	MOTHER	Means
AE	1.4*	1.3	1.3	1.4*	1.3	1.3
FR	1.0	1.0	1.4	1.1	1.7*	1.2
BF	1.3	*1.6**	1.5	0.9	1.1	1.3
ND	1.1	1.4	1.5	1.6	1.9*	1.5
SW	*0.4*[b]	1.0	1.1	*0.4*	1.5*	0.9
FF	*1.8**	1.7	1.4	*1.8**	1.0	1.5
MS	1.3	*0.5*	1.5*	1.4	1.5*	1.2
IT	1.1	1.3	*1.6**	1.2	1.5	1.3
YS	1.1	1.3*	0.9	0.9	1.3*	1.1
GK	0.8	0.8	0.6	*0.3*	2.5*	1.0
TK	1.5	1.2	1.0	0.7	1.6*	1.2
LA	0.7	1.0	0.8	1.1	1.2*	1.0
IF	1.0	0.6	0.6	0.9	1.4*	0.9
AD	*0.1*	0.9	1.1*	*0.6*	*0.5*	0.6
AP	*1.6**	1.3	0.6	*1.6**	*0.8*	1.2
DH	1.1	*0.0*	1.3	0.7	1.4*	0.9
CB	1.0	*0.4*	0.6	0.8	1.2*	0.8
MK	*1.5**	*0.4*	*0.4*	0.8	1.4	0.9
TH	0.9	0.8	1.2*	1.2*	*0.8*	1.0
MM	*0.5*	1.0	*0.3*	1.0	1.1*	0.8
HC	1.0	*0.0*	0.8	*0.5*	1.5*	0.8
JP	1.3*	*0.3*	0.9	1.0	1.3*	1.0
Means	1.1	0.9	1.0	1.0	1.3	

[a] AD and AP are not included for P and A because indigenous factor assignments were not clear.
[b] Italics highlight deviant communities for each concept (columns).
* Most extreme values for each community (rows).

TABLE 5:12 (Continued)

	ANGER	BATTLE	CRIME	DANGER	DEATH	DEFEAT	FEAR	GUILT	HUNGER	PAIN	POISON	PUNISH-MENT	SMOKE	SNAKE	THIEF	Means
AE	-2.2	-2.3*	-2.7	-2.0	-1.4	-2.3	-2.0	-1.8	-1.9	-1.8	-1.6	-1.7	-1.6	-0.7	-3.0*	-1.9
FR	-1.9	-2.3*	-2.5*	-1.5	-1.5	-2.1	-2.2	-2.0	-0.8	-1.3	-2.1	-1.8	-1.6	-2.2	-2.3	-1.9
BF	-1.6	-1.6	-2.4*	-1.8	-2.3*	-1.4	-1.4	-2.3*	-1.7	-1.6	-1.2	-2.3*	-0.6	-1.2	-2.0	-1.7
ND	-1.5	-1.9	-2.4	-2.4*	-2.0	-1.8	-2.0	-1.9	-1.3	-1.9	-1.8	-1.9	-0.6	-1.7	-2.5*	-1.8
SW	-2.4	-1.2	-2.5	-2.1	-1.4	-1.6	-1.6	-1.6	-2.7*	-2.0	-2.3	-1.4	-0.8	-1.0	-2.4	-1.8
FF	-1.8	-2.2*	-2.4*	-1.6	-1.8	-2.1	-1.9	-2.1	-1.4	-1.5	-1.6	-2.0	-1.2	-0.8	-2.4*	-1.8
MS	-1.7	-2.0*	-2.9	-1.9	-1.7	-1.6	-1.6	-1.6	-1.6	-1.3	-2.3	-1.7	-1.7	-1.9	-3.1*	-1.9
IT	-1.9	-2.2*	-2.4*	-1.9	-1.8	-1.8	-2.0	-1.7	-2.1	-1.8	-1.9	-2.2*	-0.6	-1.6	-1.9	-1.9
YS	-2.0	-2.1	-3.1*	-1.6	-2.1	-2.1	-1.5	-1.9	-2.1	-2.1	-2.1	-1.1	-1.0	-2.1	-1.9	-1.9
GK	-1.3	-1.2	-3.3	-1.7	-0.7	-1.5	-1.2	-1.8*	-1.4	-1.0	-1.0	-0.6	-1.5	-1.3	-3.9*	-1.6
TK	-2.1	-1.9	-2.2	-1.3	-1.7	-1.7	-1.8	-2.2	-2.4*	-2.4*	-2.2	-2.0	-1.7	-1.3	-2.3	-1.9
LA	-2.3	-0.2	-2.5	-2.0	-1.2	-1.2	-2.1	-1.7	-2.2	-1.7	-2.8*	-1.9	-1.3	-1.7	-2.8*	-1.8
IF	-3.2*	-1.1	-2.7	-2.3	-0.9	-1.0	-1.6	-1.9	-2.1	-1.7	-3.2*	-1.6	-1.5	-0.9	-1.4	-1.8
AD	-1.0	-1.9	-2.2	-2.9*	-0.9	-1.6	-1.9	-2.2	-1.4	-1.9	-1.5	-0.8	-1.1	-1.7	-2.8	-1.7
AP	-2.1	-1.7	-2.1	-2.3	-0.8	-1.6	-1.5	-2.7*	-1.7	-1.8	-2.1	-1.3	-1.3	-2.3	-2.6	-1.9
DH	-2.2	-1.5	-2.6*	-1.4	-1.2	-1.2	-1.9	-1.5	0.1	-1.6	-2.2	-1.1	-1.8	-2.4*	-2.3	-1.7
CB	-1.9	-1.4	-2.8*	-2.3	-1.6	-2.4	-2.2	-2.6*	-1.0	-1.9	-2.1	-1.0	-2.1	-1.6	-2.1	-1.9
MK	-2.6*	-2.0	-1.5	-2.2	-2.0	-1.6	-1.1	-1.5	-0.4	-1.6	-1.9	-2.7*	-2.0	-1.3	-2.4	-1.8
TH	-1.8	-2.2	-2.8*	-2.6*	-2.1	-1.7	-2.4	-2.4	-1.6	-1.9	-2.5	-1.8	-1.7	-1.4	-1.3	-2.0
MM	-2.1	-2.9*	-2.4	-2.6*	-0.8	-1.8	-1.6	-2.3	-2.3	-2.3	-2.6	-1.0	-0.9	-1.2	-2.6	-2.0
HC	-2.2	-2.3	-2.6*	-2.1	-1.2	-1.5	-2.3	-2.5*	-2.0	-1.7	-1.8	-0.6	-1.4	-2.1	-2.6*	-1.9
JP	-1.8	-2.3	-2.8	-2.0	-1.2	-1.8	-1.9	-2.7*	-1.8	-1.5	-2.6	-1.7	-1.0	-1.8	-3.0*	-2.0
Means	-2.0	-1.8	-2.5	-2.0	-1.5	-1.7	-1.8	-2.0	-1.6	-1.7	-2.0	-1.6	-1.3	-1.6	-2.4	

* Most extreme values for each community (rows).

TABLE 5:12 (Continued)

+P

	BATTLE	COURAGE	KNOWLEDGE	PROGRESS	SUN	THUNDER	Means
AE	1.0	1.3	*2.4*	1.4	2.7*	0.9	1.6
FR	2.4*	1.2	1.2	*2.1*	1.8	*2.1*	1.8
BF	1.3*	1.0	*0.0*	0.1	−0.6	*0.0*	0.3
ND	0.2	0.3	*−0.3*	0.8	1.0*	0.9	0.5
SW	−0.2	0.3	0.8	*−0.2*	2.2*	1.2	0.7
FF	*2.7**	1.1	1.2	0.7	1.7	*2.2*	1.6
MS	*3.1*	*0.1*	1.3	1.2	3.2*	1.9	1.8
IT	1.3	2.1*	*0.1*	1.7	1.1	0.3	1.1
YS	1.5	1.4	1.3	1.4	1.6*	0.6	1.3
GK	1.3	1.4	*−0.3*	1.5	2.8*	0.6	1.2
TK	1.5	1.4	2.4*	1.0	2.0	1.7	1.7
LA	2.0*	1.3	0.3	1.1	0.7	1.6	1.2
IF	−1.4	*0.2*	2.0	2.4*	1.6	*−1.0*	0.6
DH	1.2	*0.3*	0.5	1.0	3.6*	1.0	1.3
CB	0.6	0.6	1.6*	1.1	*0.7*	*0.1*	0.8
MK	1.5	2.2*	1.3	*−1.8*	*0.7*	1.0	0.8
TH	2.8*	*2.0*	0.9	1.4	2.1	0.4	1.6
MM	1.0	0.8	1.5	0.9	*4.0**	1.3	1.6
HC	1.1	1.7*	1.2	0.7	1.3	1.1	1.2
JP	1.3	1.8	1.4	1.9*	1.7	1.8	1.7
Means	1.3	1.1	1.0	1.0	1.8	1.0	

−P

	BIRD	CAT	CUP	EAR	EGG	GIRL	HAIR	SEED	WOMAN	Means
AE	−1.8	−1.5	−1.1	−1.9*	−1.9*	−1.6	*−1.8*	−1.8	*−1.8*	−1.7
FR	−1.6	−1.2	−2.5*	−1.5	−2.2	*−1.8*	−1.1	−2.2	*−1.3*	−1.7
BF	*1.3*	*1.6*	−0.8	−1.0	−1.9	2.0*	−1.3	−2.0*	*1.2*	−0.1
ND	−2.4*	−0.9	−1.8	−1.8	−1.8	*−1.9*	−0.9	*−1.9*	*−1.5*	−1.7
SW	−2.1*	−1.1	−1.2	−1.3	−1.6	−1.2	−1.2	−0.7	*−1.9*	−1.4
FF	−0.1	*0.4*	−2.5	−1.1	−2.6*	−0.2	*−2.0*	−1.8	−0.4	−1.1
MS	−2.0	−1.5	−1.5	−1.5	−2.2*	−1.2	−1.1	−1.2	−0.6	−1.4
IT	−1.4	−1.5	−2.4*	−0.9	−2.4*	−0.3	−1.0	−1.7	−1.0	−1.4
YS	−3.0*	−2.2	−1.0	−1.9	−1.9	−1.1	−1.3	−2.2	−1.0	−1.7
GK	−1.1	−2.9	−0.5	−0.7	−3.4*	−0.3	*0.0*	−1.4	−1.1	−1.3
TK	−1.1	−1.8*	−1.3	−1.1	−1.7	*0.0*	−0.9	−1.8*	−0.7	−1.2
LA	−1.8	−1.2	−0.9	*0.8*	−2.5*	−1.4	−1.1	−1.1	−1.0	−1.1
IF	−1.4*	−1.2	−0.3	−1.3	−0.3	−1.1	−1.0	*0.0*	−1.4*	−0.9
DH	−1.5	−0.2	*1.6*	−0.8	*0.5*	−0.8	−0.1	−0.4	−1.8*	−0.4
CB	−1.0	−1.8	−2.1	−0.8	−3.2*	*−1.8*	−0.8	−1.4	−0.9	−1.5
MK	−0.8	−0.9	−1.7	−2.3*	−1.8	*−1.3*	*0.1*	−0.6	−0.3	−1.1
TH	−1.9	−2.1*	−0.5	−1.3	−1.5	*−2.0*	*−1.7*	−1.5	−1.1	−1.5
MM	−1.9	−2.0	−1.8	−1.6	−2.1*	−1.3	−1.4	*−1.9*	−0.2	−1.6
HC	−1.8	−1.5	−1.5	−1.7	−2.1*	*−2.1*	*−1.6*	*−1.9*	*−1.3*	−1.7
JP	−1.7	−1.7	−1.6	−0.7	−1.5	−1.6	−0.9	−1.3	*−1.7*	−1.4
Means	−1.5	−1.3	−1.3	−1.2	−1.9	−1.1	−1.0	−1.4	−1.0	

* Most extreme values for each community (rows).

TABLE 5:12 (Continued)

	BATTLE	BIRD	CAT	DOG	FIRE	GAME	HORSE	THUNDER	Means
					+A				
AE	*0.1*	1.8	1.8	1.9	2.4*	*1.9*	1.3	1.2	1.3
FR	1.4	1.6	*2.4*	1.4	2.8*	*−1.1*	1.6	0.9	1.4
BF	1.1	0.5	0.8	*0.2*	1.9*	1.1	*−0.8*	1.0	0.7
ND	1.2	0.8	−0.6	0.2	2.1	1.0	0.1	2.5*	0.9
SW	*0.1*	*2.3*	1.3	1.3	2.6*	*−0.7*	0.7	1.2	1.1
FF	0.6	2.2*	2.1	1.2	1.8	1.1	*−0.3*	*0.2*	1.1
MS	1.5	2.0	0.8	2.3*	1.8	1.5	2.3*	0.8	1.6
IT	0.2	0.8	−0.1	*0.2*	1.4	−0.2	0.5	1.5*	0.5
YS	1.9*	0.0	1.2	1.8	*0.4*	0.8	0.9	0.8	1.0
GK	3.9*	0.4	0.1	2.0	*−0.2*	0.1	2.0	*2.0*	1.3
TK	1.4	2.3*	1.9	2.3*	1.1	1.1	0.2	1.4	1.5
LA	0.7	1.8	3.7*	*2.4*	1.8	−0.4	2.5	*0.1*	1.6
IF	1.5	−0.1	0.1	0.8	1.8*	−0.2	0.2	*−0.1*	0.5
DH	2.5*	*0.0*	0.5	1.3	0.9	−0.3	1.6	0.8	0.9
CB	2.3	0.4	*−0.3*	1.3	3.2*	0.7	1.0	1.8	1.4
MK	2.5*	*−0.1*	0.6	1.5	1.6	1.6	1.0	1.7	1.3
TH	0.9	1.1	1.2	1.7	0.9	*1.8*	2.4*	1.5	1.4
MM	0.2	0.3	0.8	2.3*	1.5	0.6	1.6	1.6	1.1
HC	0.3	1.8	2.7*	1.7	2.0	1.1	1.8	0.8	1.5
JP	0.8	1.4	1.7	2.0	2.1	1.7	0.7	2.7*	1.6
Means	1.3	1.1	1.1	1.5	1.7	0.7	1.1	1.2	

* Most extreme values for each community (rows).

TABLE 5:12 (Continued)

−A

	CHAIR	CUP	DEATH	HOUSE	LAKE	MOON	ROPE	SLEEP	STAR	STONE	TREE	WINDOW	Means
AE	−1.0	−1.0	−2.8	−1.1	−2.4	−4.5*	−0.7	−0.6	−2.0	−0.9	−0.4	−0.6	−1.5
FR	−0.8	−0.6	−1.2	−1.5	−1.7	−1.7	−1.5	−1.1	−0.1	−1.6	−2.4*	−1.4	−1.3
BF	−1.3	−1.3	−1.2	−1.3	0.4	−0.5	−0.4	−0.1	0.6	−1.7*	−1.0	−1.7*	−0.8
ND	−2.0*	−1.8	−1.3	−0.5	−0.4	−0.9	−1.7	−1.5	0.3	−1.7	−0.5	−1.4	−1.1
SW	−2.4	−1.0	−0.6	−1.6	−0.8	−0.6	−1.5	−1.0	−0.1	−3.4*	−1.8	−1.2	−1.3
FF	−1.1	−0.2	−1.3	−1.8	−0.8	−2.2	−0.1	0.1	−1.4	−3.0*	−1.7	−0.2	−1.1
MS	−1.5	−0.2	−0.5	−0.6	−1.6	−0.9	−0.4	−1.3	−2.0*	−1.3	−1.2	−1.1	−1.1
IT	−1.5	−1.5	0.5	−2.1	−0.1	−0.4	−1.4	0.5	−0.3	−2.5*	−0.6	−0.7	−0.8
YS	−1.9	−2.1	−0.4	−1.1	−1.7	−1.5	−1.0	−0.8	−1.6	−3.3*	−1.3	−0.5	−1.5
GK	−1.4	−1.3	−1.4	−1.5	−1.2	−1.4	−0.6	−2.7*	−0.4	−0.3	−0.3	−1.4	−1.2
TK	−1.3	−0.6	−1.9	−1.6	−0.9	−1.9	−1.2	−0.5	−2.3	−2.6*	−1.8	−2.0	−1.6
LA	−0.3	−0.7	−0.9	−1.0	−1.0	−1.9*	−1.1	−0.8	−0.2	−0.3	−0.2	−0.5	−0.7
IF	−2.3*	−1.0	−1.7	−2.0	−1.6	−0.6	−1.9	−0.9	−1.0	−1.8	−1.3	−1.1	−1.4
DH	−1.3	−2.8*	−0.3	−1.5	−1.1	−1.8	−1.4	−0.7	−1.6	−0.3	0.3	−0.9	−1.1
CB	−0.2	0.3	−0.8	0.0	−1.6	−0.5	−1.0	−2.0*	0.5	−0.4	−1.8	−0.7	−0.7
MK	−1.9	0.8	−1.3	−0.6	−1.0	−1.2	−1.0	−0.1	−1.4	−2.2*	−1.1	−0.6	−1.0
TH	−1.5	0.4	−1.1	−0.5	−1.6	−1.7	−1.4	−1.6	−0.5	−0.9	−1.8*	−0.3	−1.0
MM	−1.9*	−1.6	−1.6	−1.1	−1.4	−1.5	−0.8	−1.1	−1.5	−1.0	−1.2	−1.2	−1.3
HC	−1.9	−1.0	−1.8	−2.1*	−1.6	−1.3	−0.2	−1.9	−1.2	−1.4	−1.2	−1.5	−1.4
JP	−0.7	−1.4	−2.7	−0.5	−3.2*	−1.8	−0.4	−1.0	−1.5	−1.1	−0.8	−0.6	−1.3
Means	−1.4	−1.0	−1.2	−1.2	−1.3	−1.4	−1.0	−0.9	−0.7	−1.6	−1.1	−1.0	

* Most extreme values for each community (rows).

The list of "universally" unfavorable concepts reads like a catalogue of human misery — the emotional states of ANGER, FEAR, and GUILT, the conditions of DANGER, HUNGER, and PAIN, the threats of CRIME, POISON, PUNISHMENT, SNAKE, and THIEF, and then there are BATTLE, DEFEAT, and finally DEATH. Just why SMOKE should be such an intense and shared negative, and what its referent might be, are not clear. Note that here, in contrast to the positives on E, nearly all communities on all concepts have values greater than 1.0. Since most communities were most negative on either CRIME or THIEF, or both, we also asterisk the next concept in abhorrence order for each location; among those *not* stressing CRIME are the Mediterranean and West Asian blocs (GK, TK, LA, IF, AD, AP), and among those *not* stressing THIEF are the West Asian and Indian blocs (IF, AD, AP, DH, CB, MK).

Iranians and Mysoreans most deplore ANGER among the unpleasant emotions, and only the Thai and the Hong Kong Chinese stress FEAR, but GUILT is intensely negative for Belgians, Greeks, Pashtoons, Calcutta Bengali, Hong Kong Chinese, and Japanese. Among the conditions which imperil the human estate, HUNGER seems to be a prime concern for only the Swedes, the Turks, and the Malaysians. Beyond CRIME and THIEF, the specific threat of POISON is strongly felt by the Lebanese and the Iranians on the one hand and by the Thai and Malaysians on the other, but anxiety about SNAKE is not particularly strong for these communities. DEFEAT has its highest negative for Americans (which may be one of the reasons why it is taking so long to get disentangled in East Asia) and for the Calcutta Bengali; DEATH has its highest negative value for the Belgians, but for teen-agers elsewhere it is not much of a concern (relatively remote?).

On Potency. The +P concepts which meet the criterion (more than half of the samples having values greater than 1.0) are BATTLE, COURAGE, KNOWLEDGE, PROGRESS, SUN, and THUNDER — a selection from diverse domains. BATTLE is the most Potent of these concepts for the French, the Belgians, the Finns, the Lebanese, and the Thai; it is COURAGE for the Italians, the Mysoreans, and the Hong Kong Chinese and KNOWLEDGE for the Turks and the Calcutta Bengali; PROGRESS has the highest Potency for Iranians and Japanese (which feels right), and THUNDER is relatively high for the Finns and the French. With the exception of the Swedes, the Dutch, and possibly the Yugoslavs (all of whom have relatively +E also), the locations attributing high P to SUN have quite hot summers (AE in central Illinois, MS, GK, and MM), and the Malaysians actually give a 4.0 E to this concept. Attribution of relatively low Potency to these concepts is also of interest: SW −.2 for BATTLE; ND, SW, MS, IF, and DH all between zero and .3 on COURAGE; BF, ND, IT, GK, and LA all between −.3 and .3 on KNOWLEDGE (with the exception of AE, all high P communities on KNOWLEDGE are from Turkey eastward); BF with a .1, SW with a −.2, and MK with a −1.8 (!)

on PROGRESS; BF with a —.6 on SUN (apparently it rarely gets through the cloud cover); and IF with a —1.0 for THUNDER (a rare occurrence there, we are told).

The ⁻P concepts reaching the criterion seem appropriate enough — BIRD, CAT, CUP, EAR, EGG, GIRL, HAIR, SEED, and WOMAN (with apologies to Woman's Lib!). The BIRD-weak people are the Dutch, the Swedes, and the Yugoslavs and the CAT-weak people are the Greeks, the Turks, and the Thai (the Belgians attribute astonishing +Potency to both, 1.3 and 1.6 respectively); only for the Greeks, the Turks, and the Calcutta Bengali are CATS Weaker than BIRDS, however. The CUP is the Weakest thing imaginable for both the French and the Italians (with the Finns nearly so), but it is amazingly Strong (1.6) for the Delhi Hindi and not very Weak for BF, GK, LA, IF, and TH. The EGG, for rather apparent reasons, is the Weakest of the 100 concepts for nearly half of our communities (AE, FF, MS, IT, GK, LA, CB, MM, and HC), and it is somewhat strong (.5) only for the Delhi Hindi. WOMAN and GIRL tend to have reciprocal patterns, at least at the extremes, only AE and JP attributing quite intense Weakness to both. GIRL is Weaker than WOMAN for FR, ND, MS, LA, CB, MK, TH, MM, and HC; WOMAN is Weaker than GIRL for SW, IT, GK, TK, IF, and DH (and there seem to be no clear regional patterns here); only for BF are both GIRL and WOMAN plus in Potency (2.0 and 1.2 respectively). Somewhat surprisingly (to the authors), SEED is a universally Weak notion — most so for the French, the Belgians, the Dutch, the Yugoslavs, and the Chinese and least so for the Iranians and the Hindi speakers in Delhi.

On Activity. BATTLE, BIRD, CAT, DOG, FIRE, GAME, HORSE, and THUNDER are the most universally Active concepts — the presence of four animals being notable. BATTLE has highest A for two sets of communities, the Yugoslavs and Greeks and the Delhi Hindi and Mysoreans — and both were involved in conflicts in quite recent history (in fact, the data in the Indian groups were collected near the time of the conflict with Pakistan). CATS are very Active for the French, the Chinese, and particularly the Lebanese but somewhat Passive for the Dutch, the Italians, and the Bengali; DOGS are most Active for the Mexicans, the Mediterranean Greeks, Turks, and Lebanese, and the Malaysians (not usually pets?). FIRE is to a considerable degree Active everywhere except in Greece. Both GAME and HORSE display wide variations: GAME is most Active for Americans, Thai, and Japanese but actually somewhat Passive for the French and the Swedes — and one wonders if the "games" implied vary in terms of being matters of sheer "play" or relaxation, or of skill, of strategy. The HORSE is very Active for Mexicans, Lebanese, and Thai but actually Passive for Belgians and Finns — and one wonders if "beasts of pride and display" vs. "beasts of burden and toil" is a variable operating here.

With the exceptions of DEATH and SLEEP, all of the ⁻A concepts refer to physical objects which in one way or another are Passive with respect to the ordinary human observer or user (MOON, STAR, LAKE, and HOUSE; CHAIR, CUP, WINDOW, STONE, and TREE — with ROPE a puzzler). Most Passive of all is STONE, with 7 of the 20 communities having their most extreme values on it (and there are no positive values). Both DEATH and SLEEP show interesting variations: for AE and the Western Europeans (except SW) and also for those in East Asia (from MK through JP), DEATH is a Passive notion, but for MS, IT, YS, and two Indian groups, DH and CB, it is neutral or even somewhat Active (IT); SLEEP is definitely Passive for the Greeks, the Calcutta Bengali, and the Hong Kong Chinese, but it is neutral on Activity for the Belgians, the Finns, and the Mysoreans and even quite Active for the Italians. Exceptions to Passivity trends on these concepts (other than already noted) are CB, MK, and TH (for whom CUP is somewhat Active), CB (for whom HOUSE is neutral), BF (for whom LAKE is a bit Active), BF, ND, and CB (for whom STAR is on the Active side), and DH (for whom TREE is a bit Active).[12] ROPE is consistently, but not very intensely (except for FR, ND, SW, and IF), Passive, somewhat to the surprise of our Center staff.

What are we to conclude about the issue of *communality* in the attribution of affect? Certainly there is high agreement across our world in what things are Bad, Weak, and Passive — and this suggests both validity in our assignment of indigenous factors to E, P, and A and human universals in these aspects of meaning. Presumably, just being humans, CRIME is Bad, EGG is Weak (small, fragile, etc.), and CHAIR is Passive (it just sits there) — and, being teen-age boys, GIRL and WOMAN (with the notable exception of the Belgians) are also Weak. Since, given this evidence for communality in what things are extreme on the negative poles, we cannot attribute the relative lack of universals on the positive poles to failures in factor assignment, we must conclude that the attribution of "positiveness" in value, in strength, and in activity is much more susceptible to cultural influences. Thus FREEDOM is highly Valued by the Finns (for not surprising reasons) but not for the Swedes (because it is taken for granted or because the teenagers there were early in expressing their rebellion against Establishment norms?); PROGRESS is very Potent for the Iranians (because Teheran is the center of a rush toward modernization) but not for the Swedes or the Mysoreans (the former for anti-Establishment reasons and the latter because of unfulfilled expectations); GAME is very Active for AE (for obvious reasons) but definitely not for the French (for unobvious reasons at the moment).

---

[12] Although we do have interpretative material on many of these deviances, it will be reported in subsequent volume(s) in connection with analyses of the categories in which the concepts appear.

The SD as a Measure of Attitude

Despite the plethora of definitions of "attitude," there seems to be a general consensus that (a) it is learned and implicit, (b) it may be evoked by either perceptual or linguistic signs, (c) it is a predisposition to respond evaluatively to such signs, and (d) this predisposition may rate anywhere along a scale from "extremely favorable" to "extremely unfavorable." Without a single exception, the first indigenous factor in our analyses turns out to be Evaluation — and, being both bipolar and graded in intensity in both directions from a neutral point, our E meets the criteria for a measure of "attitude" expressed above.[13] Although the factor itself is presumably innate and universal, *what* things in the human environment acquire + or − values on E is a function (in representational mediation theory) of learning the meanings of signs and hence is highly susceptible to cultural influences. We therefore define "attitude" as the projection of a concept onto the E factor, indigenous or pancultural as the case may be. It is important to note that use of the demonstrably universal E factor makes it possible to measure "attitudes" comparably across cultures — which is manifestly impossible with scales that include items like "I go to church every Sunday" or "I would not admit a Negro to my social club."

In Table 5:13 we give the "attitude" (E-factor) scores for a number of concepts used in the "tool-making" phase which could fairly be called "attitude objects" — CRIME, DOCTOR, FREEDOM, FUTURE, GIRL, LIFE, LUCK, MARRIAGE, MUSIC, PEACE, POLICEMAN, PUNISHMENT, WEALTH, and WORK. The scores are on the *indigenous* E factors, and in interpretation it should again be kept in mind that the subjects in all locations were teen-age males. The "universal goods" are FREEDOM, MARRIAGE, and MUSIC (but only weakly so for the last); the "universal bads" are CRIME and PUNISHMENT. What is perhaps surprising is that LIFE, LUCK, PEACE, WEALTH, and WORK are *not* "universally" positive for our teen-agers. Particularly interesting, because they are unique, are the following: the Greeks have the most favorable attitude for POLICEMAN among these attitude objects (which surely has political implications); the Lebanese favor DOCTOR the most (apparently for occupational aspiration reasons); the Afghan Dari are the only group who are most positive toward WEALTH (as opposed to the Pashtoons in Afghanistan, the Dari speakers tend to be the merchant class); the Hindi speakers in Delhi are the only ones who give WORK their highest valuation (we have

---

[13] For example, Tannenbaum (Osgood, Suci, and Tannenbaum, 1957, pp. 193-195) compared the E-factor scores of subjects judging THE NEGRO, THE CHURCH, and CAPITAL PUNISHMENT with their scores on special Thurstone-type attitude scales devised to tap each of these attitudes separately. Reliabilities of the E-factor scores proved to be higher, actually, than those of the special scales; more important, the E-factor scores correlated with the corresponding Thurstone-type scales as highly as the reliability of the latter would allow.

TABLE 5:13

Indigenous E-Factor Scores for Some "Attitude Objects" in 22 Communities

	CRIME	DOCTOR	FREE-DOM	FUTURE	GIRL	LIFE	LUCK	MAR-RIAGE	MUSIC	PEACE	POLICE-MAN	PUNISH-MENT	WEALTH	WORK	Means
AE	−2.7	1.1	1.4*	0.4	1.3	0.4	0.2	1.4*	0.5	0.9	0.0	−1.7	0.2	−0.4	0.2
FR	−2.5	0.0ᵃ	1.0	0.5	1.0	0.0	0.3	1.1	0.5	1.3*	−1.6	−1.8	−0.1	0.4	0.0
BF	−2.4	−0.5	1.3	0.0	1.6*	1.0	0.8	0.9	1.0	1.1	−1.1	−2.3	−0.1	−0.8	0.0
ND	−2.4	0.5	1.1	−0.2	1.4	0.7	0.1	1.6*	0.9	0.4	−0.9	−1.9	−0.3	0.1	0.1
SW	−2.5	0.6	0.4	−0.1	1.0*	0.1	0.6	0.4	0.5	0.9	0.9	−1.4	0.5	0.0	0.1
FF	−2.4	0.5	1.8*	0.0	1.7	0.3	0.6	1.8*	1.1	0.9	−1.1	−2.0	−0.5	0.1	0.2
MS	−2.9	0.3	1.3	0.7	0.5	0.6	0.2	1.4*	1.1	0.8	−0.1	−1.7	0.1	0.3	0.2
IT	−2.4	0.6	1.1	−0.2	1.3*	0.6	0.9	1.2	1.1	1.0	−0.3	−2.2	−0.3	−0.2	0.2
YS	−3.1	0.8	1.1	1.1	1.3*	0.6	1.1	0.9	0.9	1.1	0.4	−1.1	0.0	0.5	0.4
GK	−3.3	1.3	0.8	0.1	0.8	1.2	0.7	0.3	0.2	1.0	1.4*	−0.6	−0.9	0.5	0.3
TK	−2.2	1.1	1.5*	0.9	1.2	0.5	−0.1	0.7	0.9	−0.1	0.3	−2.0	−0.2	0.6	0.2
LA	−2.5	1.2*	0.7	0.6	1.0	0.4	−0.3	1.1	0.6	0.3	0.7	−1.9	−0.3	0.5	0.2
IF	−2.7	1.0	1.0	0.3	0.6	0.8	0.1	0.9	1.0	1.2*	−0.6	−1.6	−0.2	1.1	0.3
AD	−2.2	0.8	0.1	0.1	0.9*	−0.2	0.8	0.6	0.7	0.6	−0.8	−0.8	0.9*	0.9	0.2
AP	−2.1	0.2	1.6	0.0	1.3	0.7	1.0	1.6	0.3	1.7*	−0.3	−1.3	0.6	0.8	0.4
DH	−2.6	1.0	1.1	0.0	0.0	0.7	0.3	0.7	0.6	1.0	0.4	−1.1	0.6	1.2*	0.3
CB	−2.8	0.4	1.0*	0.5	0.4	0.7	0.3	0.8	0.8	0.6	−0.8	−1.0	0.3	0.4	0.1
MK	−1.5	0.6	1.5*	−0.1	0.4	0.0	0.2	0.8	1.4	0.7	0.5	−2.7	−0.8	0.7	0.1
TH	−2.8	0.4	0.9	1.2*	0.8	0.8	0.3	1.2*	0.9	0.5	0.2	−1.8	0.7	0.8	0.3
MM	−2.4	1.0*	0.5	0.7	1.0*	0.5	0.4	1.0*	0.3	0.9	−0.2	−1.0	0.3	0.4	0.2
HC	−2.6	0.9	1.0	0.4	0.0	0.7	0.2	0.5	0.7	1.4*	0.0	−0.6	−0.2	0.7	0.2
JP	−2.8	0.5	1.3	0.6	0.3	0.0	1.4*	1.0	0.8	1.3	−0.7	−1.7	0.0	0.2	0.2
Means	−2.5	0.7	1.1	0.3	0.9	0.5	0.5	1.0	0.8	0.9	−0.2	−1.6	0.0	0.4	

ᵃ Italics highlight deviant communities for each "object" (columns).

* Most positive attitude for each community (rows).

no information on this item) ; and, most intriguingly, the Japanese teen-agers are the only ones who value LUCK the most.

Looking finally at the objects of attitude themselves, we note the following from Table 5:13. DOCTOR has positive values in the Mediterranean region, for GK, TK, and LA (as well as for AE and MM), but is pretty neutral in all of Europe and most of Asia (in fact, negative for the Belgians). The FUTURE is clearly Good for the Yugoslavs and the Thai but rather dim for the Belgian Flemish, the Dutch, and the Swedes, as well as the Italians and the Mysoreans. GIRL is favored in the West (AE, BF, ND, SW, FF, IT, and YS) but in the East (from IF on) only by Pashtoons and Malaysians. LIFE has only two teen-age groups with scores equal to or greater than 1.0 (BF and GK), while many groups are neutral (FR, SW, MK, and JP) and one even negative (AD) — does this reflect a general attitude among the young today that "life is cheap"? LUCK is a positive value for JP (as noted above) and also for YS and AP, but it is actually negative for TK, LA, and nearly so for IF (fatalism?). WORK has its highest values for IF, AD, AP, and DH, all closely clustered in our sample, but it is somewhat Bad for AE, BF, and IT teen-agers.

Attitudes toward POLICEMAN, PUNISHMENT, and WEALTH show extreme variations across our sample of urban teen-agers. The POLICEMAN has an extraordinarily high value for the Greeks and he is quite favorable for Swedish and Lebanese teen-agers; contrariwise, he is an intensely negative attitude object for the French, the Belgians, and the Finns (and only a little less so for the Dutch, the Afghan Dari, the Calcutta Bengali, and the Japanese) — and it should be kept in mind that this testing was in the early-to-mid-1960s in all cases but AP, CB, and MM. Attitudes toward PUNISHMENT vary from the extremely negative (BF, FF, IT, TK, and MK) to the moderately permissive (GK, AD, and HC), and relations to child-rearing practices will be investigated in the category analyses to be reported in later volumes. WEALTH is actually a negative attitude object in nearly half of our teen-age samples (FR, BF, ND, FF, IT, GK, TK, IF, MK, and HC), and this negative feeling is clearly not regional or, in any obvious way, cultural. The only clearly positive cultures on WEALTH (and they are not intensely so) are the Afghan Dari, the Afghan Pashtu, the Delhi Hindi, and the Thai — and this is a phenomenon with potential significance for the future of the globe.

ATLAS TABLES 5

The bicultural factorizations with American English, discussed in detail in Chapter 4 (pp. 143-154) and illustrated in Table 4:9, are presented in their entirety as *Atlas* Tables 5. For each community's *Atlas,* Table 5 will give complete scale loadings for as many as ten common factors for both the AE scales and the community in question. The AE/community X factors are principal components (unities in the diagonal) of a 100 × 100 (50 AE scales plus 50 community X scales) correlation matrix, the original 100 concepts serving as observations upon which the correlations are computed, or an orthogonal rotation of a set of these principal-component factors. Appendix D illustrates the AE/CB (Calcutta Bengali) bicultural factorization drawn from the CB *Atlas*.

ATLAS TABLES 6

As any community reaches the stage of pancultural scale selection, it is added to the data and a new pancultural factor analysis is performed (see Chapter 4, p. 159ff.). It is from this analysis that scales are selected to represent the three dominant factors of affective meaning. *Atlas* Tables 6 will present the scale loadings from the most current pancultural analysis. Tables 4:15 (pancultural E-P-A factors), 4:18 (recommended scales), and 4:19 (pancultural Factors IV through X) presented selected data from a 21-community pancultural factor analysis. The 21-community factor analysis had 1,050 rows (50 scales for each of 21 communities) and 10 columns (factors). We will extract the 50 rows (scales) corresponding to the community *Atlas* being constructed and present these in *Atlas* Tables 6. Appendix E is Table 6 for the American English *Atlas*. The scales are ordered by factor according to their maximum loading. The sign of the scale should be attributed to the left-hand term (e.g., it is *fast,* not *slow,* that has a positive loading on the A factor in Appendix E). All scales having their maximum loading on a given factor have been rotated so that their loading on it is always positive (e.g., *freezing* goes with *cold, wet,* and *low* on Factor VI). Table 6 for any community will note the date, number, and identification of the communities involved in the particular pancultural analysis. The percentage of *total* variance accounted for by each pancultural factor as well as the percentage of variance accounted for by just the 50 scales of the community will also be indicated.

ATLAS TABLES 7

For multi-lingual–multi-cultural studies the pancultural factor analysis makes it possible to construct a short, efficient SD for each community. We selected four scales to represent the three factors E, P, and A for each community as it entered the 620 *Atlas* concepts testing phase of the project. These scales will usually correspond to the scales listed in Table 4:18, but there will be some variation as the number of communities entering the pancultural factorization increases. However, we have found a high degree of stability for the dominant scales on the first three factors. For example, the four highest-loading scales for AE on Activity — *fast-slow, alive-dead, young-old,* and *noisy-quiet* — have always been the highest-loading scales whether the analysis was for 9 language communities or for as many as the 21 reported in Chapter 4.

Atlas Tables 7 will present the 12 scales and a scale representing a familiarity judgment (see below, pp. 248-250) in the original script, in transliteration (where necessary), and with an approximate English translation of the item. It should be kept in mind that the scales have been selected by analytic criteria and that the translation is *into* English *after* selection. Figure 5:1 uses the Table 7 drawn from the HC *Atlas* as an illustration.

ATLAS TABLES 8

The major effort in what we call Phase II ("tool-using") has been the affective scaling of a large number of diverse concepts, using the short-form SDs derived from the pancultural factor analysis described in Chapter 4. Tables 8 constitute the largest sections of the *Atlas of Affective Meanings,* including as they do the basic measures for 620 concepts in each of 23 communities. Of course, this is not in any sense a "world atlas," but nevertheless it has proven to be a complex and time-consuming endeavor. Tables 8 are arranged alphabetically *in English* for all communities;[14] they include raw and standardized E-P-A composite scores, standardized familiarity ratings, distances from the origin (affective intensity), individual and group polarization measures, and both raw and standardized cultural instability indices. These measures will be described and illustrated in this section,[15] and then the processes of selecting *Atlas* concepts and checking their translation fidelity will be described.

BASIC *Atlas* MEASURES

As an immediate illustration of the types of differences between communities these *Atlas* tables display, Table 5:14 pulls out from Tables 8 the basic measures for only the first three concepts (ACCEPTING THINGS AS THEY ARE, ACCIDENT, and ADOLESCENCE) and for only eight communities, one from each of our geographically defined groups (AE, GG, FF, MS, YS, IF, DH, and JP). We shall refer to this table for illustrations of each basic measure,

[14] Only 16 letters appear in the concept listings of Tables 8, but the full concepts in the languages as tested are given in Tables 9.

[15] The means and standard deviations across the 23 communities for these Tables 8 measures are given here as Appendix F, both to illustrate the format and to provide materials for hypothesis testing and research by interested scholars.

FIGURE 5:1

Illustration of Atlas Table 7 Drawn from the Hong Kong Cantonese
Atlas: *Pancultural Scales Used for 620 Atlas Concepts Testing*

Evaluation

好	壞	*xoo-wraai*	good-bad
可愛	可憎	*xor-qoi–xor zhang*	lovable-hateable
良好	惡劣	*lr/eong xoo–ngok lyt*	good-poor
高尚	卑鄙	*ghoosreonq–bheyx pey*	respectable-despicable

Potency

高大	矮小	*ghow drai–qaai sio*	tall, big–short, small
大	小	*draai-sio*	big-little
強烈	微弱	*kr/eong–mr/ei jreok*	strong-weak
重大	輕微	*crung draai–xhengmr/ei*	significant-insignificant

Activity

靈敏	遲鈍	*lr/eng mann–cr/i dreon*	agile-clumsy
迅速	緩慢	*seonchuk–wruunn mraannx*	fast-slow
紅	綠	*xr/ung–lruk*	red-green
自由	束縛	*zrir jr/ao–chuk brokx*	free-restrained

Familiarity

熟悉	生疏	*shuk sek–shan saoo*	well-known–not well acquainted

TABLE 5:14

Illustrative Basic Measures of First Three Concepts (Atlas Tables 8)
for Sample of Eight Communities

| | Composite Factor Scores | | | Standardized Composite Scores | | | | | | | | |
	E	P	A	E-Z	P-Z	A-Z	F-Z	D-O	P-I	P-G	CI	CI-Z
American English												
ACCEPT THINGS	0.6	0.5	-0.1	-0.2	-0.5	-0.4	-0.4	0.9	1.4	0.6	0.8	1.4
ACCIDENT	-1.8	0.7	0.3	-2.5	-0.2	0.3	-0.4	1.9	1.6	1.2	0.4	-0.7
ADOLESCENCE	0.4	0.4	0.8	-0.5	-0.8	1.2	-0.2	1.0	1.5	0.5	1.0	2.4
Germany, German												
ACCEPT THINGS	-0.3	0.5	-0.3	-0.8	-0.1	-0.5	-0.9	0.6	1.4	0.4	1.0	2.2
ACCIDENT	-2.8	1.7	2.3	-2.9	1.3	1.9	0.1	4.0	2.4	2.3	0.2	-2.1
ADOLESCENCE	2.1	0.9	2.3	1.1	0.3	2.0	0.5	3.3	2.2	1.8	0.5	-0.5
Finland, Finnish												
ACCEPT THINGS	-0.2	0.1	0.1	-0.6	-0.5	-0.2	-0.9	0.3	1.5	0.3	1.1	1.8
ACCIDENT	-2.4	1.2	-0.5	-2.3	0.8	-0.9	-0.5	2.7	1.9	1.5	0.4	-1.4
ADOLESCENCE	1.8	-0.1	1.6	1.1	-0.7	1.5	1.1	2.5	1.9	1.3	0.6	-0.4
Mexico, Spanish												
ACCEPT THINGS	0.8	0.5	0.2	0.0	-0.1	-0.2	0.2	1.0	1.0	0.5	0.4	-0.5
ACCIDENT	-1.8	0.1	0.3	-2.7	-0.7	0.0	-0.6	1.9	1.7	0.9	0.7	1.1
ADOLESCENCE	1.3	0.8	0.9	0.5	0.4	1.3	1.3	1.8	1.4	1.0	0.4	-0.8
Yugoslavia, Serbo-Croatian												
ACCEPT THINGS	1.0	0.7	0.2	0.2	-0.1	0.4	0.4	1.2	1.6	0.7	0.9	1.2
ACCIDENT	-2.2	0.4	0.5	-2.5	-0.5	0.9	-0.8	2.3	1.8	1.1	0.7	0.4
ADOLESCENCE	1.9	0.7	1.2	1.0	0.1	2.1	1.2	2.4	1.6	1.3	0.3	-1.1

TABLE 5:14 (Continued)

	COMPOSITE FACTOR SCORES			STANDARDIZED COMPOSITE SCORES								
	E	P	A	E-Z	P-Z	A-Z	F-Z	D-O	P-I	P-G	CI	CI-Z
IRAN, FARSI												
ACCEPT THINGS	0.6	0.2	0.3	−0.5	−0.3	−0.7	−0.6	0.7	1.3	0.4	0.9	0.7
ACCIDENT	−1.8	0.6	0.6	−2.4	0.5	−0.3	−1.4	2.0	2.0	1.0	1.0	1.3
ADOLESCENCE	1.5	0.8	2.3	0.2	0.9	1.6	0.4	2.8	2.2	1.5	0.6	−0.2
DELHI, HINDI												
ACCEPT THINGS	0.2	0.4	−0.2	−0.8	−0.4	0.0	−4.4	0.5	0.5	0.3	0.2	−1.0
ACCIDENT	−1.5	−0.1	−0.1	−3.0	−1.4	0.3	−1.9	1.5	1.3	0.6	0.7	0.8
ADOLESCENCE	1.1	−0.1	0.0	0.3	−1.4	0.6	0.9	1.1	1.1	0.6	0.6	0.2
JAPAN, JAPANESE												
ACCEPT THINGS	−0.6	0.0	−0.2	−1.0	−0.7	−0.5	−1.1	0.6	1.5	0.4	1.1	2.5
ACCIDENT	−2.0	0.8	0.9	−2.5	0.7	1.3	1.0	2.3	1.8	1.4	0.4	−1.4
ADOLESCENCE	1.7	1.1	1.3	1.4	1.2	2.0	0.4	2.4	1.9	1.4	0.5	−0.7

the mathematical nature of which will be described below; some special information on the measures will also be given.

Raw E-P-A composite scores. The first 3 columns in Tables 8 give the mean E, P, and A scores across 40 subjects for the 4 scales assigned to each of these factors. These constitute the actual "affective profile" for each concept, and it typically reflects the "Pollyanna" bias toward +E and +P (but less so +A) ratings. We call such averages "composite factor scores" to distinguish them from the usual factor scores of concepts, which are the projections of concept points onto factor planes in the E-P-A space.[16] This composite is expressed as a deviation (+ or − to a maximum of 3.0) from the origin of the space, the + being arbitrarily assigned to the Good (E), Strong (P), and Active (A) poles of the factors. We may note in Table 5:14 that ACCIDENT is intensely −E in absolute terms for all communities, although it varies markedly in both P and A.

Standardized E-P-A composite scores. One of the problems in cross-cultural research is guaranteeing the comparability of scales of measurement — here, E, P, and A composite factor scores. Despite the care which we have taken to ensure that these dimensions of qualifying will be commensurate (see the pancultural factor analysis and its logic), it could still be true that a raw composite score of 1.0 on a factor in one culture does not indicate exactly the same intensity as a score of 1.0 in another. This could be true for at least two reasons. (1) Human cultures may display generalized biases toward one or the other poles of common dimensions of qualifying; these are "constant errors" (for example, it seems to be the case that for DH all concepts tend to be viewed as relatively Passive). (2) The particular scales entering into a short-form SD via our criteria may happen to have a shared "denotative contamination" and hence dilute the pure measurement of affect (for example, our TH informants feel that their A scales — *thin-thick* and *soft-hard* — share a denotative "weakness" that can influence the profiles of certain concepts).[17] To provide an alternative way of comparing cultures, we have standardized the composite scores on E, P, and A (E-Z, P-Z, and A-Z in Table 5:14) by using the mean and standard deviation of all 620 concepts for each dimension. The means and standard deviations for E, P, and A for each of the 23 communities are shown in Table 5:15 (labeled "Mean" and "S"). This standardization has the effect of transforming the origin of the space for each culture to the centroid of its own concept points and establishes directly comparable standard units of measurement along the axes. The third columns of Table 5:15 (labeled "Z for +1.00")

---

[16] Of course, "composite factor scores" would be very highly correlated with actual factor scores.

[17] On the other hand, of course, the fact that such scales do load on the pancultural factor indicates that they are used functionally like the A scales of other communities.

TABLE 5:15

Mean and Standard Deviation of Atlas *Concepts for E, P, and A Used to Compute E-Z, P-Z, A-Z, and Standard Score for* +1.00 *Raw Score*

	E			P			A		
	Mean	S	Z for +1.00	Mean	S	Z for +1.00	Mean	S	Z for +1.00
AE	.88	1.07	.11	.92	.76	.11	.08	.62	1.48
FR	.54	.98	.47	.43	.62	.92	.40	.69	.87
BF	.54	1.09	.42	.39	.52	1.17	.18	.57	1.44
ND	.51	.98	.50	.40	.75	.80	.35	.78	.83
GG	.78	1.25	.18	.59	.84	.49	.26	1.04	.71
SW	.56	.79	.56	.30	.37	1.89	.31	.51	1.35
FF	.51	1.25	.39	.49	.84	.61	.30	.90	.78
YC	1.06	.98	−.06	.59	.57	.72	.12	.42	2.10
CS	1.08	1.19	−.07	.78	.65	.34	.69	.72	.43
MS	.84	1.00	.16	.57	.58	.74	.29	.47	1.51
IT	.83	1.23	.14	.56	.64	.69	.26	.52	1.42
YS	.78	1.20	.18	.69	.66	.47	−.10	.62	1.77
GK	1.01	1.18	−.01	.54	.50	.92	.46	.46	1.17
TK	.53	.69	.68	.32	.72	.94	.34	.68	.97
LA	.93	1.16	−.06	.70	.66	.45	−.31	.53	2.47
IF	1.27	1.28	−.21	.31	.52	1.33	.89	.87	.13
AD	.84	1.22	.13	.35	.35	1.86	.37	.49	1.29
DH	.85	.80	.19	.58	.50	.84	−.25	.44	2.84
CB	.82	1.13	.16	.58	.73	.58	.58	.60	.70
MK	.50	.67	.75	.17	.50	1.66	.15	.31	2.74
TH	.73	.99	.27	.46	.58	.93	.04	.46	2.09
HC	.77	1.04	.22	.56	.57	.77	.38	.62	1.00
JP	.37	.96	.66	.39	.57	1.07	.10	.59	1.52
Mean	.76	1.05	.26	.51	.61	.88	.26	.63	1.37

indicate the transformations of a +1.0 concept in raw composite E, P, and A to its value in E-Z, P-Z, and A-Z for each of our communities.[18] As can be seen, in every community the shift on E is negative, being most so for YC, CS, and IF and least so for FR, BF, ND, SW, FF, TK, MK, and JP. Most cultures also display a moderate negative shift on P, but on A there is more variety in the effects of standardization (clearly negative for CS, IF, and CB, actually positive (i.e., negative mean) for YS, LA, and DH, positive for YC, MK, and TH, and nearly neutral for FR, TK, AD, and HC). Another way to demonstrate the unevenness with which the E-P-A space is filled is to assign the 620 *Atlas* concepts (means of raw composites for all communities, data from Appendix F) to the 27 regions of the space gener-

---

[18] It should be noted that the sign of the standardized composite no longer necessarily represents actual positive or negative affect as rated but, rather, whether a concept is on the positive or negative side of the mean for all concepts.

ated by cutting each dimension into three segments: > 0.5 scale unit, between ± 0.5, and < -0.5 (0.5 scale unit being the estimate of a significant deviation from the neutral point). These assignments are shown in Table 5:16. The most densely populated regions are $+E+P\,^0A$ and $+E\,^0P\,^0A$ (150 concepts in each); the most sparsely populated regions are those for which either or both P and A are minus. With decreasing E there is a regular decrease in concept density (from 448 through 97 to 75); that P and A are used less differentially across our cultures is shown by the fact that the majority of all concepts fall within the single scale unit around neutrality ($+298$, ^{0313}, $^-9$ for P and $+156$, ^{0444}, $^-20$ for A). It is also evident from the summary data in Table 5:16 that the positive bias is greatest for E and least for A.

Inspecting the E-Z, P-Z, and A-Z scores for the three concepts given in Table 5:14, we may now note a few interesting differences across the eight communities. ACCEPTING THINGS AS THEY ARE, with the exception of YS, proves to be a rather negative notion (^-E, ^-P, and ^-A) in most sampled locations. ACCIDENT is extremely Bad everywhere, but it varies in interesting ways in P and A — Strong and Active for Germans and Japanese (which in the latter case makes sense to those who have ridden in kamikaze taxis!), Weak but Active for Yugoslavs, Delhi Hindi, and possibly Mexicans, Strong but

TABLE 5:16

Distribution of 620 Atlas *Concepts in the E-P-A Space Defined by Raw Composite Scores (Means for All Communities)*

	$+E$		
	$+P$	^0P	^-P
$+A$	79	54	6
^0A	150	150	1
^-A	5	3	0
	^0E		
$+A$	5	2	1
^0A	25	58	1
^-A	4	1	0
	^-E		
$+A$	8	1	0
^0A	20	39	0
^-A	2	5	0

	+	0	−
E:	448	97	75
P:	298	313	9
A:	156	444	20

Passive for Iranians (where the game of "chicken" at the city intersections is standard) and possibly Finns, and essentially neutral on P and A for the others. ADOLESCENCE is extremely variable across these eight communities — Good, Strong, and Active for the Japanese and somewhat so for the Mexicans, Good and Active for the Germans, Yugoslavs, and Finns, only Strong and Active for the Iranians, Bad and Weak but very Active for Americans, and simply very Weak for the Hindi speakers in Delhi.

Table 5:17 lists the highest- and lowest-scoring concepts from the *Atlas* 620 for each of the primary basic measures used, E-Z, P-Z, A-Z, F-Z, D-O, and CI-Z. These are based on the means for all 23 communities, as given in Appendix F. For urban teen-agers around the world, MOTHER, PEACE, SPRING, HEALTH, and so forth are Good things, and CANCER, CRIME, MURDER, WAR, and the like are Bad things; ELEPHANT, SUN, SEA, TRAIN, and the others listed are Strong things everywhere, while BABY, INSECT, RABBIT, and A POINT are Weak things; BOY, RABBIT, CHAMPION, and MINISKIRT are Active things for teen-age boys, and OLD PEOPLE, PYRAMID, FUNERAL, and, of course, FLOOR are Passive things for them. None of these results are startling, but they do indicate some things young males agree about no matter what their locale or language — and they also testify to the overall validity of the data.

Standardized familiarity scores. To the 12 scales representing E, P, and A in the pancultural SD form for each community, a *familiar-unfamiliar* scale was added. The purpose, of course, was to get a reading on the familiarity of concepts to the teen-age subjects. What we failed to realize until too late, however, was that such a scale is liable to confusion between "familiar as a term" and "familiar as a referent." We should have used two such scales, one to tap familiarity *as a word* and the other to tap familiarity *as a concept.* The first would pick up rare words, loan words, and the like, and the second would pick up concepts that are remote from the subject's experience — DEATH, for example, may be entirely familiar as a word and yet be remote from the average teen-ager's experience. Inspection of the total data and discussions with our colleagues at each group meeting leave us with the impression that if the term was itself unusual (technical like SENSE OF HEARING or a loan word), then "familiar" was interpreted in the first sense, whereas if this was not the case, then "familiar" was interpreted in the second sense, in terms of the subject's familiarity with the concept (referent) itself.

Inspection of the highest- and lowest-scoring concepts on F-Z given in Table 5:17 suggests that this was the case. The universally high FAM concepts (MOTHER, FATHER, BED, WATER, BREAD, HOUSE, SCHOOL, etc.) are certainly things near the focus of personal experience for teen-age school boys; the universally low FAM concepts (REINCARNATION, YEAR 2000, E.S.P.,

TABLE 5:17

*Highest and Lowest Concepts on Some Basic Measures
for the Means of All Communities*

E-Z

Highest: MOTHER (1.4), FRIENDSHIP (1.3), HAPPINESS (1.3), PEACE (1.3), KINDNESS (1.2), SPRING (1.2), BEAUTY (1.1), FREEDOM (1.1), HEALTH (1.1), SUCCESS (1.1)

Lowest: CANCER (−2.7), AIR POLLUTION (−2.6), CRIME (−2.6), EARTHQUAKE (−2.6), MURDER (−2.6), WAR (−2.6), FILTH (−2.5), HELL (−2.5), POISON (−2.5), SUICIDE (−2.5)

P-Z

Highest: ELEPHANT (2.3), SUN (2.2), ATOM BOMB (1.9), MOUNTAIN (1.9), DAM (1.8), SEA (1.8), SUBMARINE (1.8), LION (1.6), SHIP (1.6), TRAIN (1.6)

Lowest: BABY (−3.1), INSECT (−2.4), CHILD (−2.3), RABBIT (−2.3), A SECOND (−2.0), BIRD (−1.9), CHICKEN (−1.9), FLOWER (−1.8), A POINT (−1.8), LIPSTICK (−1.7)

A-Z

Highest: BOY (1.6), RABBIT (1.6), YOUTH (1.6), BIRD (1.5), ADOLESCENCE (1.4), CHAMPION (1.4), CHILD (1.4), DOG (1.4), HEART (1.4), MINISKIRT (1.4)

Lowest: ROCK (−2.1), OLD PEOPLE (−2.0), PYRAMID (−1.9), STONE (−1.9), FUNERAL (−1.8), OLD AGE (−1.8), PRISON (−1.7), WALL (−1.7), DESERTS (−1.6), FLOOR (−1.5)

F-Z

Highest: MOTHER (1.5), FATHER (1.4), BED (1.3), WATER (1.3), BREAD (1.2), FOOD (1.2), HOUSE (1.2), LIGHT (1.2), RIGHT HAND (1.2), SCHOOL (1.2)

Lowest: REINCARNATION (−2.1), STRANGER (−1.9), NEUROTIC PERSON (−1.8), GHOSTS (−1.7), YEAR 2000 (−1.7), E.S.P. (−1.6), HELL (−1.6), MURDER (−1.5), PRISON (−1.5), FATALISM (−1.4)

D-O

Highest: SUN (2.8), ATOM BOMB (2.7), AIRPLANE (2.6), FRIENDSHIP (2.6), LOVE (2.6), MOTHER (2.6), WAR (2.6), EARTHQUAKE (2.5), FREEDOM (2.5), GOD (2.5)

Lowest: DOWN (0.5), BEARD (0.6), MUSTACHE (0.6), TWENTY-EIGHT (0.6), WIDOW (0.6), WIDOWER (0.6), JEWS (0.7), KNOT (0.7), NONBELIEVER (0.7), STRANGER (0.7), YESTERDAY (0.7)

CI-Z

Highest: MOTHER-IN-LAW (1.7), PROSTITUTE (1.5), BEARD (1.3), RICH PEOPLE (1.3), INSECT (1.2), WHISKEY (1.2), ACCEPTING THINGS AS THEY ARE (1.1), FINGERNAILS (1.1), MUSTACHE (1.1), YESTERDAY (1.1)

Lowest: AIRPLANE (−1.2), CHAMPION (−1.1), FRIEND (−1.1), MASCULINITY (−1.1), ARM (−1.0), FATHER (−1.0), FRIENDSHIP (−1.0), LIGHT (−1.0), RIGHT HAND (−1.0), SUN (−1.0)

HELL, etc., and, more or less by definition, STRANGER) are certainly *not* in the everyday experiences of teen-agers. But we can also note that certain concepts rated low in FAM are not really too remote from the experience of most people (for example, NEUROTIC PERSON and MURDER), at least as experienced vicariously in the mass media. This points to another phenomenon associated with familiarity ratings which was noted repeatedly in our group meetings on *Atlas* interpretation — a tendency, apparently somewhat variable across communities, to rate things unpleasant and threatening to ego as relatively unfamiliar ("denial") and to rate things desirable and status-like to ego as relatively familiar ("claiming"). Examples would be ENVY, PLAYING CARDS, and PROSTITUTE ("denial") and CLEANLINESS, LIBRARY, and POCKET RADIOS ("claiming") — when our colleagues often state flatly, but with good humor, that their teen-agers are surely familiar with the former and not particularly with the latter. Referring back to Table 5:14, it can be seen that ACCIDENT has low FAM everywhere but JP and presumably reflects "denial."

Distances from the origin. Distance of a concept from the neutral origin of the E-P-A space is an index of its richness of feeling (i.e., intensity of affect). It is computed from the formula

$$D\text{-}O = (E^2 + P^2 + A^2)^{1/2}$$

as applied to the *raw* composite factor scores (to preserve the actual rating intensities of subjects) and reflects simultaneously the intensities of feeling along all three dimensions. Both ACCIDENT and ADOLESCENCE are intensely affective in all of the communities shown in Table 5:14, but ACCEPTING THINGS AS THEY ARE has fairly high affective intensity only in YS (by virtue of its high ⁺E value). In the mean D-O values tabled in 5:17 for all communities we observe that notions like SUN, ATOM BOMB, AIRPLANE, MOTHER, FREEDOM, and GOD generate the most intense feelings for teen-agers throughout our sample; notions like BEARD, TWENTY-EIGHT, WIDOW, KNOT, STRANGER (perhaps surprisingly), and YESTERDAY, on the other hand, are nearly meaningless affectively.

Individual and group polarization measures. Polarization of concepts in the space defined by SD measurements has been shown to be correlated about .70 with Noble's *m* (Noble, 1952; Jenkins, Russell, and Suci, 1959; Howe, 1965). The latter is essentially a measure of the availability of associations to a word, and it has been shown to have important effects in verbal learning (see Underwood and Schultz, 1960). At least one theory of attitude change (and, more generally, cognitive interaction) has utilized polarization as a variable (Osgood and Tannenbaum, 1955), and numerous studies have been reported in the literature on the relation between polarization and basic psychological processes, including latencies of judgment (Osgood, 1941;

Osgood, Suci, and Tannenbaum, 1957, pp. 155-159), perception (Kjelder-gaard and Masanori, 1962), authoritarianism (Mogar, 1960), semantic satiation (Lambert and Jakobovits, 1960), and other areas. It would therefore seem that availability of polarization norms for a large number of concepts would be useful for researchers in verbal behavior and language generally.

We interpret Noble's m and the SD measure of polarization as being closely related (although independent) indices of the *meaningfulness* of words — the greater the meaningfulness of a word, (a) the more other words will it have strong associations with and (b) the more extreme will be its ratings on SD scales (see Staats and Staats, 1959). Of course, the SD measure is restricted primarily to affective features of meaning. Depending upon one's research interests, there are several methods for indexing meaningfulness from SD data. One, based on composite factor scores, is what we have already discussed as distance from the origin. Another, which also utilizes the generalized distance notion, is computed as the root of the squared and summed deviations from the midpoints of *all* scales. A third — based on the assumption of strict linear departure from neutrality — would be ,the average absolute deviation from the midpoints of scales. Each of these methods yields slightly different values, but they obviously will be highly correlated.

For each *Atlas* concept we have N subjects (replications) rating a concept on n scales (tests), and thus we can deal with either group mean scores or individual subject scores on scales. It is clear that these two different approaches do involve quite different interpretations of the meaningfulness of concepts and can also yield quite different polarization values. In computing the *group measure* (P-G), individual deviations in one direction from the midpoints of scales are scored as positive and deviations in the other are scored as negative. If subjects give intense ratings but disagree among themselves as to direction, there will be cancellation, and the group polarization score will shrink toward zero. In computing the *individual measure* (P-I), the deviations from the midpoint are summed (either as absolute values or as squares) over individuals, and there is no cancellation. Thus, for a concept on which subjects disagree extremely in direction (i.e., in meaning), there will be a large difference between P-I and P-G scores. It should be noted that the maximum value for P-G can only equal, but never exceed, the value for P-I, and this will only occur when all subjects agree on the direction from neutrality of scale ratings. Thus P-G reflects the *cultural meaningfulness* of a concept, taking into account intracultural disagreements on its meaning, and P-I reflects the *individual meaningfulness* of a concept, disregarding intracultural disagreements and thereby reflecting pure intensity of affect.

For the *Atlas* data reported in Tables 8, using the 12-scale pancultural SD instruments, the computation of polarity is based on average absolute deviations from the midpoints of scales. The individual and group polarizations for any concept, *i,* are given by the formulae

$$P\text{-}I = \frac{\sum_i \sum_k |d_{jk}|}{N \cdot n}$$

$$P\text{-}G = \frac{\sum_i |\bar{d_i}|}{n}$$

where

$$d_{jk} = k\text{th subject's deviation from}$$
$$\text{midpoint of } j\text{th scale}$$

$$N = \text{number of subjects}$$

$$n = \text{number of scales}$$

$$\bar{d_j} = \frac{\sum_k d_{jk}}{N}$$

where N equals 40 and n equals 12 scales. Note that ratings on single scales (not composite factor scores) are used here, and the measurements are based on the raw data (not standardized), of course. The mean P-I and P-G values for each of the 620 concepts across our 23 communities are given in Appendix F, and although the highest values are not given in Table 5:17, a few of the extremes may be reported here. AIR POLLUTION, ATOM BOMB, CANCER, EARTHQUAKE, LOVE, MURDER, SUN, and WAR all have P-I values equal to or greater than 2.0 (and it can be noted that there is considerable overlap with the highest D-O concepts above, as would be expected). The highest P-G values are for ATOM BOMB and SUN (both 1.7), EARTHQUAKE, FRIENDSHIP, LOVE, MOTHER, and WAR (all 1.5), and CHAMPION, COURAGE, FATHER, FREEDOM, GOD, HAPPINESS, HEALTH, HERO, HORSE, KNOWLEDGE, MURDER, SEA, SPACE TRAVEL, and YOUTH. All of the concepts which have high P-G are cases where subjects *within* the cultures agree on the directions checked on the scales (i.e., have similar meanings). It should be noted that most of the concepts with high P-I also have high P-G, but this is not necessarily the case with more moderate values. Note in the small sample given earlier in Table 5:14 that ADOLESCENCE for AE and ACCEPTING THINGS AS THEY ARE for FF, YS, and JP have quite high P-I values but relatively low P-Gs. And this leads us to the final basic measure.

Cultural instability index. As already noted, for any concept the value of P-G must be equal to or less than the value for P-I; the value of their *difference* is a direct reflection of what might most generally be termed the "cultural instability" (CI) of the meaning of a given concept. This term is less prejudicial than "conflict index," for example, although this is one of the possibilities. We have taken as our measure of CI the simple difference value obtained by subtracting the group polarization for a concept from its individual polarization: [19]

$$CI = P\text{-}I - P\text{-}G$$

Again, to render these values more comparable across communities, they are standardized across all concepts for each community to a mean of 0.0 and a standard deviation of 1.0; these CI-Z values, given in the last columns of Tables 8 (and in Appendix F), thus vary from high + values (high intra-cultural disagreement) through 0 to high − values (high intracultural agreement).

There are at least three possible interpretations of a large positive CI-Z. (1) The concept may happen to have *two or more different senses,* or even be homonymous, in the language in question; e.g., Americans rating PLAY might be thinking either of a performance on a stage or of the opposite of work. This possibility is purely linguistic, is usually caught in our translation checks (see below), and in any case is always considered the first alternative to be eliminated in our group meetings on interpretation. (2) The concept may simply be *unfamiliar* to most of the subjects, their ratings merely repre-senting random errors about the neutral point which cancel to a near-zero P-G (which may be the case for AE on REINCARNATION where the CI-Z is 2.6). This possibility can be checked against both the standardized FAM ratings (which for AE on REINCARNATION happens to be −1.6, very low) and our colleagues' judgments. (3) The concept may, indeed, be *affectively conflictual* or controversial within the culture, as for example would prob-ably be the case for AE had the concept BLACK POWER been given in racially mixed high schools. This possibility is only considered seriously if both 1 (multiple senses) and 2 (unfamiliarity) have been considered and rejected as unlikely.

When P-I and P-G are nearly equal in magnitude and yield a near-zero CI in subtraction, there are at least two possibilities to be considered. (1) If both have high values, the concept can be said to have *stereotyped meaning-fulness* (i.e., subjects agree on both its semantic direction and its high affec-tive intensity). This will yield a large negative CI-Z (since in the transforma-tion these lowest absolute CI values become negatives), and the CI-Z for GG on ACCIDENT (in Table 5:14) provides a clear example (P-I is 2.4 and P-G is 2.3 and hence there is almost no cancellation). (2) If both P-I and P-G have low values and thus also yield a near-zero CI in subtraction, the concept can be said to have *stereotyped meaninglessness* (i.e., subjects agree on both its lack of semantic direction and its low affective intensity);

---

[19] This measure was first suggested to us by our colleague in Mysore, Dr. A. V. Shanmugam — in his doctoral dissertation (University of Illinois, 1963) — while serving as a research assistant on this project.

this will also yield a large negative CI-Z under transformation. The only way these two types can be distinguished is by careful inspection of the jointly high or jointly low P-I and P-G values — which is why they are included in the *Atlas* Tables 8. The negative CI-Z for DH on ACCEPTING THINGS AS THEY ARE is a case in point — the DH teen-agers all agree in feeling neutral about it.

Referring back to Table 5:14 again, it can be seen that ACCEPTING THINGS AS THEY ARE varies considerably in CI-Z, being very high for Germans, Finns, and Japanese (and apparently representing real cultural conflict in these cases), average for Iranians and Mexicans, and very low for the Hindi in Delhi. ACCIDENT has quite high CI-Z for Iranians and Mexicans and very low CI-Z for Germans and Japanese. ADOLESCENCE has extremely high CI-Z for Americans (which fits, certainly, the situation of real cultural conflict), quite low values for Yugoslavs, but rather average amounts for all other groups. We may look finally at the highest and lowest CI-Z values across all 23 cultures. The highest include MOTHER-IN-LAW, PROSTITUTE, BEARD, RICH PEOPLE, WHISKEY, ACCEPTING THINGS AS THEY ARE, FINGERNAILS, and MUSTACHE — all of which would seem to be likely foci of affective disagreement in teen-age cultures. But also in the highest are INSECT and YESTERDAY, the former perhaps representing the diversity of insect referents (i.e., multiple senses) and the latter probably the diversity in actual individual experiences during "yesterday." The lowest CI-Zs all seem to be cases of stereotyped meaningfulness rather than stereotyped meaninglessness, since both P-I and P-G have high values in all instances — AIRPLANE, CHAMPION, FRIEND, FATHER, SUN, and so forth.

Atlas CONCEPT SAMPLING

In selecting concepts for the *Atlas* (see Chapter 6 for more information), we wished to get as much diversity as possible and yet have adequate representation of as many categories as we could — all within a manageable total number. We wanted concepts that would be intrinsically interesting, that would be potentially differential among cultures, that might tap human universals in symbolism, but that would also sample those everyday aspects of human life — kinship, foods, animals, technologies — which ethnographies usually record. The resulting collection of items of subjective culture runs from A to Z, however, as any good *Atlas* should — from ACCEPTING THINGS AS THEY ARE, ACCIDENT, and ADOLESCENCE through MARRIAGE, MASCULINITY, and MASTER to YESTERDAY, YOUTH, and ZERO — and we shall see in Chapter 6 how this motley assemblage was moulded into meaningful categories. The following were the sources of the concepts.

Original Phase I concepts. It will be recalled (Chapter 3) that the original 100 substantives — used for eliciting qualifiers and then for subsequent concept-on-scale ratings and factorings — were derived mainly from Human Relations Area Files categories and from lists that had been drawn up by ethnolinguists interested in glottochronology as concepts likely to be "culture-common." It seemed reasonable, therefore, to include these 100 concepts (see Table 3:1, p. 72) in the final *Atlas* collection. However, both because an average of five years had intervened and because the original task had involved 50 scales rather than the 13-scale form to be used for the *Atlas* work (and only 20 subjects rather than 40 on each concept), these 100 concepts were intermingled with the others and retested.

Qualifier-elicited concepts. We thought it would be useful to include concepts — not already included in the original 100 culture-common set — that were likely to have high frequencies of usage across our 23-culture sample of communities. For a representative sample of these communities (AE, ND, SW, TK, DH, MK, JP), the 50 qualifier scales surviving the selection procedures described in Chapter 3 (thus, 100 qualifier terms) were used as *stimuli* to elicit substantives as *responses,* an association procedure analogous to that used for eliciting adjectives in the standard Phase I process. Again, 100 high school males served as subjects. In order to restrict association to what in English would be nouns, the converse of the frames used in the qualifier-elicitation task were given (e.g., "The _____ is *pretty*," "The *pretty* _____," for AE). Where the language in question had a gender system — or, more accurately, where adjectives are overtly coded for gender — the task was divided into halves or thirds (depending on the number of genders), with the adjectives on each form in only one of the genders.

The standard Phase I computations were applied to these data to determine the H ranks of the responses. Table 5:18 gives the 15 highest H-ranked substantives (i.e., most productive) for the 7 communities. The responses MAN and HOUSE are in the top 15 for 6 of 7 communities, and WOMAN, GIRL, and PERSON/HUMAN appear for 5 of the 7 communities. The substantives in Table 5:18 marked by an asterisk had already been included in the basic list of 100 used in the "tool-making" stages. Of the 22 high H responses having community overlap, 9 are from this list, testifying to the culture-common assumption made.

Notice that CAR is selected with a high H index for the three Western groups AE, ND, and SW (many of the young males chose to fill in the frames to make "The good CAR," "The big CAR," etc.). DOG was a high-order response for American and Swedish boys, DAY for American and Dutch. For the Delhi Hindi, CLOTH is a high-order response, and SEA and ROAD were common for both Japanese and Turkish. Unique high-rank responses are underlined in Table 5:18: AE — HAIR and FRIEND; JP — FEELING, MOUNTAIN, and BODY; MK — MIND, INTELLECT, FLOWER, COW, SNAKE, and PLACE;

TABLE 5:18

Fifteen Highest H-Ranked Substantive Responses in Order of H

AE	ND	SW	TK	DH	MK	JP
MAN*	MEN	MAN*	CHILD	THING (VASTU)	PERSON	HUMAN (HITO)
PERSON	THING	BOY	MAN*	PERSON	OBJECT	MAN*
GIRL*	BOY	GIRL*	HUMAN BEING	WORK (KAAM)*		BOOK*
BOY	DAY	HOUSE*	ROAD	TALK	ANIMAL	HUMAN (NINGEN)
HOUSE*	GIRL	CHILD	PEN[a]	WORK (KAARY)*	MIND	STORY*
ROOM	WOMAN*	OLD MAN	BOOK*	MAN (MANUSHHY)*	INTELLECT	FEELING
DOG*	MAN*	ANIMAL	DRESS	MAN (AADMII)*	FLOWER	THING (MONO)
CAR	EYE	WOMAN*	GIRL*	CHILD	PLACE	ROAD
PEOPLE	WORD	DOG*	WOMAN*	BOY	WORK*	THING (KOTO)
DAY	HAND*	ROOM	WORK*	GIRL*	HOUSE*	SEA
WATER*	CAR	WORD	ANIMAL	CLOTH	PEOPLE	WOMAN*
HAIR*	CHILD	CAR	TABLE	WATER*	CLOTH	HOUSE*
STORY*	COLOR*	OLD WOMAN	ROOM	THING (CIIJ)	COW	MOUNTAIN
FRIEND*	LEG	TEACHER	SEA	HOUSE*	TALK	BODY
WOMAN*	ANSWER	TREE*	HOUSE*	BOOK*	SNAKE*	WORK*

[a] Underlined items indicate unique high-ranking substantives for given communities.
* Indicates substantives already included in our original Phase I list of 100 substantives.

ND has body parts — EYE, HAND, and LEG, along with COLOR and ANSWER; SW — OLD MAN, OLD WOMAN, TEACHER, and TREE; TK — PEN, DRESS, and TABLE.

To select concepts for *Atlas* testing, the extended lists of substantive responses ranked by the *H* index were merged and ordered by amount of community overlap, determined both by the number of communities responding and by the total frequency. In other words, the list was headed by the responses with overlap in all locations and with highest frequency. The merged list was then reduced by elimination of any of the substantives that had been included in our original list of 100 (71 of these 100 were elicited by more than one qualifier in at least two locations). The 100 remaining substantives were then added to the list of concepts for *Atlas* testing. These 100 concepts are presented in Table 5:19, in their merged-rank order.

Intuited concepts. Three hundred and fifty concepts for *Atlas* testing were selected on an essentially intuitive basis. First we sent requests to all of our colleagues for suggestions of concepts which they, as social scientists, felt would be appropriate, not only for their own cultures but also for comparative purposes across all cultures. The local staff at our Center also worked on this task, consulting the Human Relations Area Files and our social science colleagues at Illinois. These sources were pooled. We then inspected the total sample of nearly 600 concepts for potential categories — obvious ones like color, emotion, kinship, occupation, food, and animal terms but also ones designed to get at more dynamic aspects of culture, like commerce, intergroup relations, and social status. A "finalized" set of 550 (350 intuited plus 200 selected as above) was submitted for testing during the 1965-68 period in most locations. For a variety of reasons (see below), an additional set of 70 concepts was added and tested in the 1968-70 period. The total for the *Atlas* is thus 620 concepts.

TABLE 5:19

One Hundred Concepts for Atlas *Testing Selected from Substantive Elicitation, Ordered by Pancultural Productivity*

1. ROOM	26. THING	51. SENTENCE	76. BED
2. PLACE	27. VOICE	52. GRASS	77. DISH
3. SOUND	28. MILK	53. NEWS	78. HAT
4. WALL	29. WORD	54. FLOOR	79. POT
5. FACE	30. QUESTION	55. WORLD	80. WORKER
6. BABY	31. GLASS	56. MIND	81. BUS
7. BOX	32. LEG	57. SEA	82. COLD
8. LIGHT	33. IDEA	58. ANSWER	83. ROCK
9. PLAY	34. IRON	59. PEN	84. STOVE
10. TRAIN	35. PILLOW	60. WOOD	85. SCENE
11. PERSON	36. ARM	61. KNIFE	86. WALK
12. TALK	37. EXAMINATION	62. WAY	87. YOUTH
13. CAR/AUTOMOBILE	38. LION	63. WRITING	88. SHIP
14. CLOTH	39. BOTTLE	64. LADY	89. SIGHT
15. AIR	40. FOREST	65. LINE	90. SWEATER
16. DRESS	41. JOKE	66. PAINT	91. CROW
17. BALL	42. MONKEY	67. ICE	92. FIELD
18. ELEPHANT	43. THREAD	68. SONG	93. GOOSE
19. APPLE	44. WEIGHT	69. STREET	94. MOMENT
20. PIG	45. STICK	70. PROBLEM	95. SERVANT
21. COUNTRY	46. NAME	71. ROSE	96. PLANK
22. SKIN	47. ROOF	72. SHOP	97. BRIDGE
23. SCHOOL	48. BICYCLE	73. COTTON	98. PATIENT
24. LAMP	49. CAKE	74. LAND	99. CHARACTER
25. MACHINE	50. BEAR	75. STUFF	100. CHEESE

Atlas TESTING PROCEDURES

The subjects were teen-age males, equivalent to those on whom the measuring instruments had been developed.[20] Approximately 600 subjects were involved in each community for the entire task in its several testing phases. A minimum of 40 subjects rated each subset of about 50 concepts on the 12-scale pancultural SDs plus a *familiar-unfamiliar* scale. The usual instructions for the concept-on-scale task were used.

Explicit encouragement was given to our colleagues in each site to exercise their own judgment and eliminate any concepts which, in their own communities, might be inappropriate for reasons of (a) unfamiliarity to their subjects, (b) unavailability of satisfactory translation equivalents, or (c) political, moral, or social sensitivity. We felt that this was a necessary relaxation of standardization, even though it might mean some unevenness of representation of concepts in the *Atlas*. Due to misconstrual of the instructions for the original (550-concept) testing, concepts were arbitrarily reduced to 500 in many locations; these were reinstated in a 1968-69 "*Atlas* Completion" task. Many of the concepts omitted initially on the basis of unavailability of satisfactory translation equivalents were reinstated as a result of our subsequent translation checks, discussed below. And some concepts were added for a really "final" *Atlas* testing to round out certain categories (e.g., we had HUSBAND but no WIFE in the Kinship category, WHITE but no BLACK in the Color category, and so forth).

Table 5:20 presents a list of the concepts omitted by two or more communities in the final 620-concept *Atlas,* along with the symbols of the communities involved. This list is ordered in terms of the number of locations omitting the concepts in question. Recalling the instructions given our colleagues, the typical omissions make good sense — NONBELIEVER IN MY RELIGION, AUTOMATION, CASTE, COMPULSORY MILITARY SERVICE, REINCARNATION, EXTRASENSORY PERCEPTION (presumably unfamiliar to their teen-age subjects), HOMOSEXUAL, PROSTITUTE, ADULTERY, EXCREMENT, URINE, and SEX (unpleasant or tabu), and MY STATE NAME, MY OWN REGION, PRIVACY, CONTEMPLATION (no translation by virtue of apparent lack of the AE concept in the culture). But why IMMIGRANT and BIRTH CONTROL were omitted is not obvious.

[20] We debated trying to obtain representative samples of each culture, but for the reasons given in Chapter 1 (pp. 19-21) we decided against it. However, in order to check at least roughly on what differences might be anticipated as a function of using a sample of homogeneous male teen-agers as against a representative sample, we have obtained a sample stratified on the basis of age, sex, and education in Greece (where the work of our colleague Dr. Vasso Vassiliou on public opinion polling made this feasible) and are now collecting a similar sample in the United States. These data will be presented in our planned subsequent volumes reporting the *Atlas* information.

TABLE 5:20

Thirty-three Atlas *Concepts Omitted by Two or More Communities*

CONCEPT	N	LOCATIONS
HOMOSEXUAL	9	BF, GG, YS, GK, LA, AD, DH, CB, MK
NONBELIEVER IN MY RELIGION	8	BF, FF, TK, LA, CB, MK, TH, HC,
PROSTITUTE	8	BF, GG, FF, GK, TK, LA, IF, CB
ADULTERY	7	BF, GK, TK, LA, IF, AD, JP
AUTOMATION	7	TK, LA, DH, CB, MK, TH, JP
EXCREMENT	7	ND, GG, SW, YS, GK, TK, LA
CASTE	5	AE, GK, TK, IF, AD
COMPULSORY MILITARY SERVICE	5	FF, YS, TK, CB, MK
MY STATE NAME	5	GK, TK, LA, AD, JP
REINCARNATION	5	FF, LA, AD, HC, JP
URINE	5	AE, MS, GK, LA, AD
COMMUNISM	4	GK, LA, IF, AD
EXTRASENSORY PERCEPTION	4	FR, SW, LA, AD
ILLEGITIMATE CHILD	4	BF, TK, AD, MK
IMMIGRANT	4	FF, LA, CB, MK
MY OWN REGION	4	FF, MS, IF, AD
BIRTH CONTROL	3	YS, TK, LA
NEUROTIC PERSON	3	LA, CB, MK
PRIVACY	3	BF, FF, GK
TO QUESTION THINGS AS THEY ARE	3	BF, AD, CB
SEX	3	GG, LA, CB
STUFF	3	BF, GK, LA
TOLERANCE	3	LA, IF, AD
BLACK RACE	2	LA, CB
CHAMPION	2	LA, CB
CONTEMPLATION	2	SW, FF
FINGERNAIL	2	GK, AD
HINDUS	2	TK, LA
PROPHET	2	LA, CB
RACE CONFLICT	2	LA, CB
SODA POP	2	BF, YS
STOVE	2	SW, GK
YELLOW RACE	2	LA, CB

Atlas TRANSLATION CHECKS

It will be recalled that in the early part of Phase I very careful translation checks in our first seven language/culture communities (representing different language families) were made for the original 100 concepts to be used as qualifier elicitors. However, we did not intially exercise the same care in checking the additional 520 concepts to be used in the *Atlas* testings. Our senior colleagues were themselves fluent bilinguals vis-à-vis English, they were by now thoroughly familiar with our general procedures, and most of the concepts were reasonably familiar, single-word concepts like SPHERE, DOWN, PROGRESS, BELIEF, and EDUCATION. It thus seemed to be a relatively straightforward matter to translate these concepts from American English into all other languages. This proved to be a painful — but instructive — error.

The problem. After the first and largest part of the *Atlas* data (between 500 and 550 concepts) had been collected in most locations, it was gradually borne in upon us — by noting anomalous data from many places and checking with our own bilingual colleagues at Illinois — that there had been a considerable but unknown amount of "failure" in translation. For example, we noted that for the Greeks the concept SPHERE was extremely Bad, Strong, and Active (unlike all other communities); our colleague Harry Triandis (himself a native Greek) pointed out with great good humor that the translation into Greek as SFERA ($\sigma\varphi\alpha\tilde{\iota}\rho\alpha$) was quite correct, but unfortunately it was a homonym also meaning BULLET. This is a case of homonymy in the destination language, but American English also has its homonyms, and the Greek translation provides an illustration here as well: Dr. Vasso Vassiliou translated DOWN (which we had intended as "the nether direction") into Greek as CHNOUTHI ($\chi\nu o\tilde{\upsilon}\delta\iota$), which again is entirely correct but would come back into AE as "the soft underfeathers of a duck" — a reasonable "error," since most of our concepts were nouns. One can imagine the lusty guffaws that would arise in Academia if we attempted an interpretation of the low E, high P, and extraordinarily high A of SPHERE in GK in terms of their culture and history!

Homonyms in either source or destination language are only the most lurid examples of translation problems. There are also differences in the relative dominance of different *senses* of words, even though the senses may be shared. One example is the concept FEMALE (or MALE), which is dominantly "gender regardless of species" in most of our translations, but clearly coded +Human for American (teen-age) English. Another is BELIEF, which has dominantly religious connotations (i.e., AE "faith") in many European communities, as well as our small-city Midwest AE sample, but purely cognitive connotations in most other locations. Yet another example is EDUCATION, which was translated in many of our sites in a way that would back-translate into AE as UPBRINGING. And it appears that the only place in the world where EVOLUTION means dominantly the Darwinian notion of man's descent from the apes is in the United States, perhaps particularly in the Bible Belt, and for good historical reasons. Occasionally what was intended as a common noun, and translated correctly as such, turns out either to be a familiar proper name or to have teen-age slang uses in a particular community. For one example, PROGRESS was translated correctly into Spanish for our Mayan subjects as *progreso* — which in Yucatan (YC), but not

Mexico City (MS), happens to be the name of their main pleasure city on the ocean where, if they can save up a few pesos, they go to relax (and, appropriately, PROGRESS had very low A for YC). For another, the number FIVE, correctly translated as *cinco* into Mexican Spanish, happens to be used by teen-agers in Mexico City (accompanied by a flashing of fingers) to signal the passing of a sexy girl.

Checking procedures. Clearly, if our *Atlas* data were to have any dependable value (particularly their interpretation in terms of linguistic and cultural variables), a complete check on all translations was required — to substitute adequate translations of the AE terms (the source language for all others) where failures had occurred and good translations were available, to identify large translation differences (usually in dominant sense) where no better translations were available, and to eliminate from the *Atlas* translation failures which could not be corrected (usually because the AE concept did not exist in culture X). The steps taken constitute a novel approach to translation — forced upon us by the (single-concept) nature of our materials and the large number of destination languages involved, but interesting in its own right.

(1) *Listing of all senses for each AE term, in order given, from a reasonably large and recent dictionary of American English.* The college edition (1960) of *Webster's New World Dictionary of the English Language* was used. To illustrate the steps in the translation check, we select three concepts — COLOR, MAGIC, and STORY — which had different "fates" in the process. The original dictionary senses listed for these concepts are given below.

COLOR
1. the sensation resulting from stimulation of the retina of the eye by light waves of certain lengths
2. the property of reflecting light waves of a particular length
3. any coloring matter
4. any color other than black, white, and grey
5. the color of the face, especially healthy rosiness
6. the color of a person's skin
7. the color of the skin of a Negro or other person not classified as Caucasian
8-10. *plurals*
11. outward appearance; semblance; aspect
12. appearance of truth, likelihood, validity: as, the circumstances gave *color* to his contention
13. kind; sort
14. vivid and picturesque quality or character: as, there is *color* in his writing
15. in *art,* the way of using color
16. in *mining,* a bit of gold

17. in *music,* timbre; also tone color
18. in *phonetics,* the degree of openness of a vowel

MAGIC

1. the pretended art of producing effects or controlling events by charms, spells, and rituals supposed to govern certain natural or supernatural forces; sorcery; witchcraft
2. any mysterious, seemingly inexplicable, or extraordinary power or influence: as, the *magic* of love
3. the art of producing baffling effects or illusions by sleight of hand, concealed apparatus, etc.

STORY

1. the telling of a happening or connected series of happenings, whether true or fictitious; account; narration
2. a fictitious literary composition in prose or poetry, shorter than a novel; narrative; tale
3. such tales, collectively, as a form of literature
4. the plot of a novel, play, etc.
5. a report or rumor
6. (colloq.) a falsehood; fib
7. (archaic) history
8. in *journalism,* (a) a news article, (b) a person or event considered newsworthy

Our original "intentions" in each case had been COLOR in the sense of "object color," MAGIC in sense 1 above, and STORY in the sense of a true or fictitious oral or written account.

(2) *Construction of an AE "dictionary" for our own concepts, comprising a listing of those senses (a) reasonably close to our intended dominant or (b) thought particularly liable to confusion cross-culturally.* Also, the senses were often reworded, both to reduce length of the translation booklet and to increase clarity for nonnative English speakers. To construct this "dictionary" required someone with particular skills and interests in matters semantic, and we asked Dr. John Limber (then on our project staff) to undertake a careful analysis of the senses of each of our AE terms. In some cases there seemed to be no ambiguity — e.g., GIRL in AE has one highly dominant sense as "young human female" (although people in missile research do refer to successful ones as "boys" and to duds as "girls"!). But in other cases there was obvious ambiguity in AE — e.g., HEART as "body organ," "center of anything," "essence," "innermost feelings," "mood," or "energy." The senses listed for our illustrative concepts were:

COLOR

1. sensation resulting from stimulation of the eye
2. property of reflecting waves of certain frequency
3. any coloring matter, e.g., pigment

    4. any color other than black, white, grey
    5. outward appearance

Magic
    1. the pretended art of producing effects or controlling events by charms,
       spells, etc.; sorcery
    2. any mysterious, seemingly inexplicable, or extraordinary power
    3. the art of producing baffling effects or illusions by sleight of hand, con-
       cealed apparatus, etc.

Story
    1. the telling of a happening; narration
    2. a literary composition, e.g., short story
    3. the plot of a novel, play, etc.
    4. a section or horizontal division of a building

As can be seen for COLOR, senses referring to skin color (senses 5-7) were
eliminated, while senses 1-3 were slightly modified for simplicity and/or
clarity. Sense 4 was added for STORY (even though the dictionary clearly
indicated its homonymous status by separate listing) on the ground that
there might have been confusion about our "intention" by our translators.

(3) *Submission of mimeographed "dictionaries" to fluent bilinguals with
respect to each of our languages for careful description of their translations.*
These bilinguals were usually our senior colleagues who had made the original translations, but in the few cases where they were not available, bilinguals
on our campus were used (also given the original translations, of course).
The instructions were: (a) to indicate with an arrow the dominant senses
of the translation used in their language, (b) to mark with Xs all other AE
senses shared by their translation, and (c) to write in on lines provided any
additional, nonshared senses of their translation term (adding arrows if also
dominants). The following were the markings for our three illustrative
concepts given by our Delhi Hindi translator:

Color
    1. sensation resulting from stimulation of the eye
    2. property of reflecting waves of certain frequency
→ 3. any coloring matter, e.g., pigment
    4. any color other than black, white, grey
    5. outward appearance
       joyful intoxication (mood)

Magic
→ 1. the pretended art of producing effects or controlling events by charms,
       spells, etc.; sorcery
    2. any mysterious, seemingly inexplicable, or extraordinary power
X 3. the art of producing baffling effects or illusions by sleight of hand, con-
       cealed apparatus, etc.
X   witchcraft

STORY

   1. the telling of a happening; narration

   2. a literary composition, e.g., short story

→ 3. the plot of a novel, play, etc.

   4. a section or horizontal division of a building

Note that the translation of COLOR was dominant as "pigment" and that for MAGIC was dominantly in the sense of "sorcery" — both very common phenomena across our samples.

(4) *Coding of the AE "dictionary" for dominant senses (and occasionally double-dominant), close-to-dominant senses, remote sense extensions (but still judged polysemous), and homonymous senses (with respect to the dominant) and reordering sense listings accordingly.*[21] This is something that is not indicated in ordinary dictionaries — where listings may, in fact, begin with archaic senses — since at least consensus judgments and, ideally, quantitative data from ordinary native speakers are required (i.e., social science rather than lexicography per se). But we felt that such an ordering of senses for AE was essential if we were to evaluate the adequacies of translations. In this process the fact that our subjects were teen-age males was constantly kept in mind. The following lists give the results of these deliberations for the three exemplar concepts.

COLOR

→ 2. property of reflecting waves of certain frequencies[22]

   1. sensation resulting from stimulation of the eye

   3. any coloring matter, e.g., pigment

   4. any color other than black, white, grey

L 5. outward appearance

L 6. property of being lively

MAGIC

→ 3. the art of producing baffling effects or illusions by sleight of hand, concealed apparatus, etc.

   1. the pretended art of producing effects or controlling events by charms, spells, etc.; sorcery

L 2. any mysterious, seemingly inexplicable, or extraordinary power

STORY

┌→ 2. a literary composition, e.g., short story

└→ 1. the telling of a happening; narration

   3. the plot of a novel, play, etc.

L 4. a falsehood

---

[21] Most of the project staff participated from time to time in a series of weekly afternoon meetings on this task, and discussion was often not unanimous but always animated. The senior staff, 1968-69 (Brukman, Jakobovits, May, and Osgood), participated regularly.

[22] The numbering of the senses given in the translation booklets originally sent to our colleagues was retained in the new booklets to facilitate comparison.

L 5. a newspaper report

H 6. a section or horizontal division of a building

Note that the dominant sense for MAGIC (for teen-age AE boys) was assumed to be 3 (what one sees magicians doing on the stage) and is marked with an arrow, that "outward appearance" and the "property of being lively" (added) were considered large sense differences with respect to the dominant sense of COLOR and are marked with the symbol "L," and that "section of a building" is marked with the symbol "H" to indicate its homonymous status with respect to the now double-dominants for STORY. At this stage some dictionary definitions were modified and some senses which the dictionary had not included were added (e.g., BLIND in the sense of being intentionally, or unintentionally, unaware of something). The coded and reordered sense listings for all concepts were mimeographed for use at the next (field) stage of the translation check. All additional senses that had been reported in the returns from stage 3 above (e.g., DH "joyful intoxication (mood)" for COLOR) were added to the listing along with their community labels (BF, IT, TH, etc.).

(5) *Final check of all translations in the field, leading to the generation of a list of translation failures and large translation differences.* This final translation check required from three to five rather intensive days, the amount of time increasing, as might be expected, with the deviation from AE in both language and culture. The field group in each location for this task always included our senior colleague there (usually the original translator) and at least two additional fluent bilinguals (one of whom, if possible, with training in linguistics or related fields); in nearly all locations one or two young males (who had been teen-agers at the time of the original *Atlas* testing) also participated.

The procedures involved the following: (a) explanation of the AE senses of terms, as required — which was often;[23] (b) coding of each translation term (always using the original script where transliteration had been required for computer data analysis) in much the same manner as had been done by our Center staff for AE itself (arrows for dominant senses; Xs for others shared; adding additional, particularly teen-age slang, senses); (c) a final judgment for each translation as to its closeness of match to AE; (d) a listing of clear translation failures (TFs — misreadings of the AE concept in the original translation task, terms having homonymous senses dominant, like GK SPHERE = BULLET, etc.) and large translation differences (TDs —

---

[23] It soon became evident that dictionary sense statements are by no means transparent to native speakers of other languages (e.g., the fact that SICKNESS and DISEASE are not synonymous in AE, the former being more general and including "ordinary" departures from health (like colds and stomachaches) and the latter being both more serious and usually infectious). Only when such subtleties are explicated can a close match in translation be obtained.

usually inclusion of the AE dominant sense but not as the dominant sense of the translation term); and (e) elicitation of another term, if available, that more closely matched the AE. Particular attention was given to items where the original translation coding (stage 3 above) differed in dominant sense from the final translation coding at this time. A copy of the final translation booklet for each community was sent to the Center, where a master project "dictionary" is presently being compiled; this includes all additional senses of terms as well as some modifications in the AE senses (and occasionally dominants) generated by the field experience.

The following listings for our three exemplar concepts illustrate this final stage of our *Atlas* "dictionary":

COLOR
→ 7. object color; visual attribute of objects based on their differential reflection of wavelengths of light
   1. property of reflecting waves of light
   2. sensation resulting from stimulation of the eye
   3. any coloring matter, e.g., pigment
   4. any color other than black, white, grey
  5L outward appearance
  6L property of being lively
  ND blush
  ND the truth: like telling it as it really is
  ND political *color*
  SW political *color*
  IT colored pencils
  GK painting (nonartistic)
  IF deception, making someone the butt of something
  DH joyful intoxication (mood)
  MK inward feelings: as, one's *colors*
  TH healthy facial color
  HC counter-aggressive: as, to show some *color*
  JP love, kind

MAGIC becomes SORCERY (retested in AE)
→ 4. the supposed use of supernatural powers, black magic, witchcraft
   1. the pretended art of producing effects or controlling events by charms, spells, etc.
   3. the art of producing baffling effects or illusions by sleight of hand, concealed apparatus, etc.; magic
  2L any mysterious, seemingly inexplicable, or extraordinary power

(Note: No additional senses for other communities when changed to SORCERY; *Webster's New World* only gives sense 4 for SORCERY)

STORY
⌐→ 2. a literary composition, e.g., short story
└→ 1. the telling of a happening; narration

3. the plot of a novel, play, etc.
4L a falsehood
5L a newspaper report
7L account of personal experience: as, the *story* of my life
6H a section or horizontal division of a building
FR a confused and boring situation
ND remedy, redress
YC history
MS history
GK history
DH legend, fable
CB legend, fable
MK legend, fable
JP legend, fable

Note that a new dominant, not given in *Webster's New World Dictionary*, has been given for COLOR; in the course of the field work it became obvious that this is the dominant sense of the term in AE (e.g., in "What *color* is your dress," "What *color* are you going to paint the house," "Apples are red [*color*]," etc.), *and* it turned out that it was precisely this sense of COLOR that our translators in most locations had intuitively used, despite the wide variations in their codings without this sense being listed. Note also that the dominant sense for MAGIC has been shifted to that most commonly used in translation around the world, and the AE concept has been retested as SORCERY in this case.

Atlas *retesting*. The lists of TFs (translation failures) and TDs (large translation differences) generated in the field translation check were the basis for decisions as to what concepts needed retesting and where. The Swedish list — which was exceptionally short — is included here as Table 5:21 by way of illustration. These tables also record the reasons, if any could be elicited, for the TFs and TDs, along with the suggested substitute translations. Fourteen concepts were retested in AE, all being cases where a clear majority of the other languages had a different and agreed-upon dominant. Many of these reflect a characteristic of English determiners — the sense shift that often occurs between *a* and *the* and *null* (e.g., (*null*) CHOICE is dominantly "the abstract power or right to choose," whereas *a* CHOICE is dominantly "the act of choosing, a selection"; *a* COUNTRY is a territory or nation, but *the* COUNTRY is dominantly "a rural region" as opposed to the city). Another reason for changing AE concepts was what might best be called "localism" (e.g., DIRT was dominantly "unclean matter" in most places but was "soil" for our Midwest AE subjects and hence was changed to FILTH; PEASANTS meant simply "rural people" in most places but was clearly a term of derogation for AE and hence was changed to COUNTRY PEOPLE).

TABLE 5:21

Swedish TF/TD Concepts

Type	Base Concept	First Translation	Failure or Difficulty	Correction
TD	ADOLESCENCE	UPPVÄXTTID	means "years of growth"	UNGDOMSÅR
TD	BROTHER	BRODER	double-dominant { "fellow member" and "older friend"	BROR
TD	CINEMA	BIO	means "place"	FILM
TF	DISH	MATRÄTT	means "food"	KAROTT
TF	EDUCATION	UPPFOSTRAN	means "upbringing"	UTBILDNING
TF	FAT	FETT	——	FETMA
TF	GROUP	GÄNGET	means "peer group of young people"	GRUPP
TD	ILLITERATE	EJ LÄSKUNNIG	——	ANALFABET
TF	LEG	BEN (STOLS+LÅR)	means "leg" (chair or thigh)	BEN
TF	MARRIAGE	GIFTERMÅL	means "wedding ceremony"	ÄKTENSKAP
TF	MIND	SJÄLSTILLSTÅND	means "state of mind"	MEDVETANDE
TD	PEASANTS	BÖNDER	——	LANTARBETARE
TF	POISON	FÖRGIFTNING	means "poisoning"	GIFT (ÄMNE)
TD	PROGRESS	FRAMSTEG	means "improvement" also	FRAMÅTSKRIDANDE
TD	SENTENCE	DOM (I BROTTMÅL)	means "court sentence"	MENING (GRAMM. BEGREPP)
TF	SEX	KÖN	means "biological division" and "organs"	SEX
TF	THE SOUTH	SÖDERN	means "southern region"	SÖDER
TD	THOUGHT	TANKE	means "a thought"	TÄNKANDE
TD	WEALTH	VÄLSTÅND	means "prosperity"	RIKEDOM

Although this careful checking of the translations of 620 concepts into some 25 languages has been a very time-consuming task, both at our Center and in the field, it has proved to be a very enlightening and scientifically rewarding exercise in its own right. As far as we are aware, there does not exist detailed translation data for single concepts — on ranges of senses and their overlaps in translation equivalents — for as many concepts in as many languages. All of this information is being transferred to IBM cards for final (computerized) lexicographic analysis — of sense overlaps between communities as functions of cultural and linguistic relationships, of the identification of homonyms vs. special vs. near-universal sense extensions, of the apparent psycholinguistic determinants of sense extensions, and so forth. There are also some interesting implications, we think, for the art of dictionary-making. A separate monograph is planned as a report on our translation materials.

On the other hand, of course, our travails in the business of translation could also be viewed as an apposite demonstration of the old refrain "If I had only known *then* what I know *now,* I would have. . . ." Obviously, for all new *Atlas* samples we will now simply have our bilingual translators use the coded and ordered lists of senses in our AE "dictionary" as the basis for selecting the closest-matching translations. However that may be, we feel reasonably confident that now most of the translations of the 620 *Atlas* concepts are as closely equivalent across our sample of communities as can be achieved using AE as the common basis for correspondence. There are some exceptions that we know about — cases where the translations used, even though judged TD, could not be improved upon without using too elaborate and cumbersome phrases — but at least we can flag these with appropriate footnotes. What still worries us, of course, are the instances of ambiguous translation which we *failed* to catch. These will certainly be brought forcefully to our attention by scholars in the languages in question.

ATLAS TABLES 9

Atlas Tables 9 will document the translations of the *Atlas* concepts as well as the 50 scales recorded in *Atlas* Tables 3, 5, and 6 (factor analyses involving the 50 indigenous scales). For languages not using the Roman alphabet (currently 12: GK, LA, IF, AD, AP, DH, CB, MK, TH, MM, HC, JP) a transliteration key to Romanization will be reproduced. This will exclude Cantonese, where the Barnett-Chao phonetic transcription was used (see Barnett, 1950).

In the qualifier elicitation, on the average for each community 1,000 qualifier types have been elicited. From these usually 70 were selected on the basis of H and *phi* as potential bipolar scales (see Chapter 3). Although we asked for and received translations of all $\pm 1,000$ items in the elicitation, no detailed analysis of the adequacy of these translations was made. Often the translations varied from context to context (for example, in HM, *fig-yelő* was translated as *watching* when used to qualify EAR (*fül*) and then was translated as *listening* when qualifying HEAD (*fej*)), and where this was the case we assigned the most frequent translation as the unique English type to "stand for" the unique other-language type. All multiple translations of a unique type were thus changed to a single English qualifier.

After opposites have been assigned in the original script and concept-scale ratings collected, 60 scales are submitted for factor analysis. From these 60 a final set of 50 indigenous SD scales are used for all the analyses reported in a community's *Atlas* Tables 3, 5, and 6. However, the rather loose translations employed have been carefully corrected to render in English the senses appropriate to the 100 concepts against which ratings were obtained (this was done at the time of *Atlas* concept translation-failure checking).

The final section of Tables 9 is a glossary for the *Atlas* concepts in English (but only the shortened 16-character form that appears in Tables 8), listing in alphabetic order the *complete* indigenous form as presented to the subjects in their own script. Although most concepts are single words, there are a few concepts in the original list that are phrases. In some cases single-word concepts have been rendered into phrases in an attempt to secure overlap (or restriction) in meaning for cross-cultural comparability (e.g., TO QUESTION THINGS AS THEY ARE in CS was *dudar de las cosas en su estado actual* and HABIT was *hábito (manera de actuar)*). Translation differences (TDs) are noted by a single asterisk, and what we still consider translation failures (TFs) are marked by double asterisks.

6

Probing Subjective Culture

The *Atlas of Affective Meanings,* described in the previous chapter, is a potential gold mine of information about subjective culture. But the problem, as in mining for precious metals, is to extract the valuable ore in a form as free as possible from contamination with baser materials. In this chapter we can do no more than sample this information, offering some illustrations of how the *Atlas* data can be used to shed light on similarities and differences among cultures. Since the Color category is small in size and yet illustrates well most of our methods of analysis, it will serve as our main exemplar, although evidence from other concept categories will be adduced from time to time. Detailed reporting of the cross-cultural data from all categories must be reserved for further volumes (*The Affective Dimension of Subjective Culture*). In this chapter, as in the last, our emphasis shifts from universals toward uniquenesses, from what seems to be common to the human species toward what seem to be real cultural differences among its various manifestations. However, this is only a shift in emphasis, since we shall find many universals as well as uniquenesses in the attribution of affect.

Imagine 620 "probes" inserted into the bared "brains" of 23 cultures — a vivid, even if perhaps disturbing, image. To the extent that our careful checks (see Chapter 5, pp. 259-269) have yielded close translation equivalents of the 620 concepts, our corresponding "probes" should have roughly equivalent loci in the subjective cultures of the 23 communities. However, the probes are

First draft prepared by Charles E. Osgood.

designed to give only three types of signals — Evaluation "whistles," Potency "rumbles," and Activity "tweetles" — although these measures are quantitatively variable in both direction and intensity.

We shall be looking for patterning in the signals arising from various sets of probes (concept categories). If all or nearly all of the communities give forth the same types of signals from corresponding probes (for example, +E −P −A for Domesticated as compared with Wild Animals), then we shall infer potential *Universals* in the attribution of affect within this region of subjective culture. If certain definable groups of our cultures give forth signals that are distinctively different from those coming from others (e.g., THURSDAY and FRIDAY being more +E and +P than SATURDAY and SUNDAY for LA (Lebanon), IF (Iran), and AD (Afghanistan), all Moslem communities), we shall infer *Sub-universals* in attribution of affect and look for the reason — which, in this example, is entirely obvious (Thursday and Friday being the Moslem weekend and Friday the "day of worship," equivalent to our Sunday). If a particular language/culture community yields clearly deviant signals for a certain set of probes (e.g., Mayan Indian subjects in Yucatan giving forth unusually intense +P and +A for all In-law concepts, WIFE, MOTHER-IN-LAW, and FATHER-IN-LAW), then we shall infer *Uniquenesses* in the attribution of affect and again look for the reasons — in this case, the fact that marriage into an economically viable family is the *sine qua non* of success in this near-subsistence-level culture (many of our YC subjects were actually young married men).

Ideally, any global study of human culture should entail representativeness, in terms of including both diverse societies and diverse aspects of culture within each society. That is, one would like to maximize breadth and depth simultaneously. But, in practice, this ideal can hardly even be approached; funds and time, to say nothing of researcher energies, simply do not permit simultaneous, in-depth study of 20 or more language/culture communities. The anthropological approach is typically "vertical," emphasizing depth at the necessary expense of breadth: the ethnographic field worker investigates one very limited community of humans intensively, striving to come out with an integrated picture that illuminates the interrelations among the various layers of its culture — a kind of cultural cameo. The psychological approach is more likely to be "horizontal," emphasizing breadth at the necessary expense of depth: using measuring instruments assumed to be comparable cross-culturally and cross-linguistically, the investigator obtains a thin slice of information about one layer of culture across as large a number of societies as he can manage — at least, this holds in our case.

But, being well aware of the ideal, both those who slice vertically and those who slice horizontally then try to relate their own findings to other parts of the cultural pie. Anthropologists try to integrate the vertical studies of many investigators into a general cross-cultural picture, using ethnographies or such compilations of data as Murdock's *Ethnographic Atlas* (1967), Textor's *Cross-Cultural Summary* (1967), or the Human Relations Area Files — and they run into troubles, mainly owing to incomparability of methods. Similarly, the terminal goal of our *Atlas* interpretation work is to relate extensive quantitative data on affective meaning to other facets of culture. Using comparable measuring instruments (the pancultural SDs), we have obtained only a thin, horizontal slice of information about the affective dimension of the subjective cultures of 23 human societies, and we are now trying to relate this information to other layers of culture — and we are running into troubles, mainly owing to the intricacies of cultures and questionable validities of native informants, even very highly motivated ones like our own colleagues.

The *Atlas* project has generated a tremendous amount of information. With some 40 subjects in each of some 25 cultures judging each of some 600 concepts against 13 SD scales, we have about 7,800,000 "bits" of raw data. Even when these raw "bits" are statistically compressed into summary measures — the three factor composite scores (means of 40 subjects $\times$ 4 scales for each factor) and the mean score of the familiarity scale — we still have about 60,000 items of information to deal with. But this basic information is then amplified by computations which yield the 10 or so derived measures included in the *Atlases* (see *Atlas* Tables 8, Appendix F). The total number of information units which must be dealt with by ourselves and our colleagues in interpretation thus comes to about 200,000. Obviously, this mass of numbers must be organized into chunks and formats that can be encompassed and comprehended by the human mind.

Chunking was accomplished primarily by assigning the total 620 concepts to about 50 categories of manageable size and assigning these in turn to 12 "super categories" (see Table 6:1 below and accompanying text). Thus Super Category I, Time, includes as categories the Age Continuum (from BIRTH to DEATH with stops in between at concepts like BABY, YOUTH, BRIDEGROOM, MATURITY, PARENTHOOD, MIDDLE AGE, and OLD AGE), Months and Seasons, Time Units (from MOMENT to ETERNITY, including HOUR, DAY, MONTH, YEAR, and CENTURY as well as the concept TIME itself), and the trichotomous category Future/Present/Past (contrasting sets of concepts like TOMORROW/TODAY/YESTERDAY and PROGRESS/WORK/TRADITION).

The data within each category were (computer) analyzed into a standard set of *formats,* designed to highlight potential similarities and differences in the attribution of affect. These formats are (a) basic *Atlas* measures (for each concept in the category, data for all communities and their means), (b) correlations on basic measures (among communities), (c) concept rankings on basic measures (for all communities, plus the mean ranks), (d) componential analyses (in terms of intuited features, with tests based on comparative ranks of concepts), (e) interconcept distance measures (both between communities for the same concepts and within communities for all of the concepts in the category),[1] and (f) intercommunity correlations of distance matrices (designed to get at similarities in conceptual structures). The data within particular categories also lend themselves to various special demonstrations — many of which have been suggested by our colleagues during interpretation sessions. The standard formats will be illustrated with data from the Color category at a later point in this chapter, as will a few of the special analyses drawn from other categories.

CATEGORIES, COMMUNITIES, AND CAUTIONS

Before illustrating how we are using the *Atlas* data to make probes into subjective culture, it will be useful to put the process into perspective. Given the large mass of information available, extraction is always of necessity *selective* in terms of the particular categories of concepts utilized by an investigator. Given our relatively small sample of the world's languages and cultures, interpretation of the information extracted is always of necessity *tentative,* particularly when we refer to potential Universals or Sub-universals. Given problems of translation, questions of statistical significance, and our limited familiarity with the cultures involved, explanations of differences in affect attribution in terms of other cultural data are *liable to error* — despite the efforts made by ourselves and our colleagues in other countries to check translations and to evaluate interpretations. Let us therefore inquire into how our concept categories were determined, into the representativeness of our sample of communities (in terms of both languages and cultures), and into cautions that must be heeded in interpreting the data.

CATEGORIES

As already noted, it would be infeasible to impose a comparative analysis on the entire sample of 620 concepts simultaneously. Some form of chunking by categories is necessary. But, on the other hand, any kind of concept categorization is bound to be somewhat arbitrary, in terms of both the number and the types of categories. We tried to achieve a compromise between sufficiency and feasibility — on the one hand, to compose categories which seemed intuitively consistent with the ways humans structure their experience (e.g., the way a Roget organizes his *Thesaurus*) and, on the other, to allow

---

[1] It might be noted in passing that if such distance measures were computed for all 620 concepts simultaneously, the output would paper the inside and outside walls of the entire eight-story Psychology Building at the University of Illinois (rough estimation!) and, of course, be completely incomprehensible to human minds.

for as much extension as possible so as to minimize the total number of categories.[2] However, it should be emphasized that the underlying *Atlas* data are stored in such a way that we can enter the system via teletype and pull out a complete analysis (our standardized formats) of any set of concepts. Another constraint on the adequacy of our categories is in terms of the number of relevant concepts included in each. Given the deliberately diverse nature of our *Atlas* sampling, the number of concepts appropriate to most categories that are actually included is usually small with respect to the number available in languages (e.g., only eight color terms); some concept categories, of course, are exhaustive (e.g., Days of the Week).

Table 6:1 lists the 47 finalized category titles, as organized into 12 super categories. The actual concepts included in all categories are given in Appendix G. Inspection of Table 6:1 provides some idea of the diversity of areas of human concern that have been sampled. It will be noted that there are two general types of categories: those which we call *continuous* (e.g., Emotions and Occupations) and those which we call, for lack of a better term, *chotomous* (e.g., dichotomous categories like Male/Female and Private/Public and trichotomous categories like Means/Expressives/Ends and Modern/Transitional/Traditional Values).

COMMUNITIES

At the time of this writing we have *Atlas* data available for 23 of our communities.[3] This is a very small sample of human societies, of course. However, given our original sampling restriction — to work mainly with "high cultures," communities having education and literature in their own language, where written tests in the native language could be used — these 23 groups seem to provide a fairly representative sample. Table 5:2 in the last chapter presented thumbnail descriptions of our communities, indicating specific locus of sampling (e.g., Uppsala, Sweden), general geographic region (e.g., northern European), and language family (e.g., Indo-European, Germanic). Figure 6:1 here is a crude outline map of the world, with the locations of our communities superimposed.[4]

[2] Actually, the structure of the categories we have used began in 1964 in connection with a special project on have vs. transitional vs. have-not countries, being designed by Professor Rogelio Diaz-Guerrero, our colleague in Mexico City. In the course of selecting concepts from our *Atlas* which seemed suitable for testing some of his hypotheses, we realized that we were also making a start on a general categorization.

[3] Depending on the date of final drafting, the data to be used in our subsequent volume(s), *The Affective Dimension of Subjective Culture,* will include Afghan Pashtu (AP), American Black English (BE), Brazilian Portuguese (BP), Hungarian Magyar (HM), Malaysian (MM), Rumanian (RR), and possibly a few others.

[4] From this point on in this chapter we will usually refer to our communities by their two-letter codes (see Table 5:1 and Chapter 5, p. 204, n. 7), on the assumption that by now the reader is reasonably familiar with the code and because it saves space.

TABLE 6:1

Forty-seven Categories of Atlas Concepts as Organized into Twelve Super Categories

I. TIME	VII. HUMAN ACTIVITIES

I. TIME
  A. Age Continuum
  B. Months and Seasons
  C. Time Units
  D. Future/Present/Past

II. EGO IDENTIFICATIONS
  A. Kinship
  B. Races/Religions/Continents/Directions/-Isms
  C. Male/Female
  D. In-group/Alters/Out-group
  E. Intimacy-Remoteness Continuum

III. ABSTRACT SYMBOLISMS
  A. Emotions
  B. Numbers
  C. Colors
  D. Geometricals
  E. Days of the Week

IV. CONCRETE SYMBOLISMS
  A. Naturally and Potentially Aesthetic
  B. See-/Hear-/Touch-/Smell-/Tasteables
  C. Means/Expressives/Ends

V. ENVIRONMENTALS
  A. Food Objects
  B. Animals
  C. Habitations

VI. CARNALITIES
  A. Body Parts
  B. Body Characteristics and Processes
  C. Sex and Sensuality
  D. Health and Sickness

VII. HUMAN ACTIVITIES
  A. Occupations
  B. Commercial, Economic
  C. Work/Play
  D. Success/Failure

VIII. INTERPERSONAL RELATIONS
  A. Private/Public
  B. Social Status: Supraordinate/Subordinate
  C. Moral/Immoral
  D. Intergroup Relations: Associative/Neutral/Disassociative
  E. Affiliative/Achievement

IX. SOCIETY
  A. Institutions: Educational/Political, Legal/Marital, Religious/Military/Economic
  B. Modern/Transitional/Traditional Technology
  C. Modern/Transitional/Traditional Values

X. COMMUNICATIONS
  A. Literacy
  B. Language and Literature
  C. Communications Media

XI. PHILOSOPHY
  A. Philosophicals
  B. Supernaturals
  C. Spiritual/Material
  D. Concrete/Abstract
  E. Cognitive/Gut

XII. THINGS AND STUFFS
  A. Static/Dynamic Nature
  B. Static/Dynamic Artifacts
  C. Stuffs

CAUTIONS

The *Atlas* data are liable to many potential sources of bias in interpretation, and it is prudent to acknowledge these at the outset. Here we will merely indicate our awareness of the major problems and describe what steps

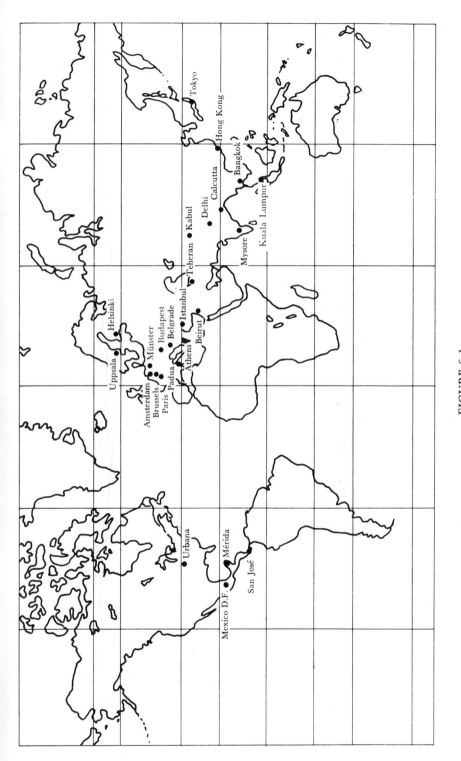

FIGURE 6:1

Distribution of Participating Communities

have been (and will be) taken to minimize them. Nevertheless, since none of these sources of bias can be completely eliminated, let the reader beware — and keep these matters in mind.

Translation fidelity. In the preceding chapter (pp. 259-269) we detailed the steps taken to minimize errors in translation. Using a specially constructed American English "dictionary" that lists the dominant, close, remote, and homonymous senses for all 620 *Atlas* words, we checked the sense correspondence of all translations in all languages involved and retested all translation failures and large translation differences where better terms could be elicited. We now feel confident that nearly all instances of clear translation failure have been eliminated, or the nature of the translation problem can at least be annotated where no improvement was possible (e.g., the fact that BLUE for GG also is frequently used for "drunk").

Statistical significance. Another potential source of bias in interpretation of the *Atlas* data lies in over- (or under-) attribution of significance to similarities or differences. It is clearly infeasible to compute the significances of all possible differences *between* each community and every other on all measures for all 620 concepts, to say nothing of differences *within* each community for all pairs of concepts. From earlier research leading to the present project (see *The Measurement of Meaning,* Ch. 4), we have reason to believe that differences between groups or between concepts on a given composite factor score as large as .5 scale unit would be significant at the 5% level on the average (i.e., would occur by chance only 5 times in 100). However, these background data were all based on AE subjects (and usually college students), and it seemed quite possible that high school subjects might be less reliable and/or cultures might differ markedly in the reliability with which concept-scale judgments are made. If we want to interpret a difference of .5 or more between AE and DH evaluations of COW (to take a crude and obvious example) as representing a "real" affective distinction, then we must be able to justify this interpretation.

To test the applicability of a gross .5 scale-unit difference in factor composite scores within cultures (and, by inference, between cultures), we have taken random samples of concepts and factors from 6 widely separated communities (ND, IT, GK, MK, TH, and HC) and run significance tests between the subgroups of 40 subjects reacting to different pairs of concepts. Three sets of 33 pairs of concepts were randomly selected such that no pair had been rated by the same subgroup during *Atlas* testing (see Chapter 5, p. 258, for more detail on the design of the *Atlas* testing work). Each of these 3 sets of 33 concept pairs was randomly assigned to one of the 3 factors E, P, and A. The *t* tests were run for the significance of the difference between the means for each concept pair on its assigned factor.

Table 6:2 presents, for each community and for each factor composite,

TABLE 6:2

Minimum Significant and Maximum Insignificant Mean Absolute Difference between Randomly Paired Concepts, p = .05

	E		P		A	
	Min. Signif.	Max. Insignif.	Min. Signif.	Max. Insignif.	Min. Signif.	Max. Insignif.
GK	.39	.38	.29	.40	.28	.34
HC	.58	.54	.44	.39	.39	.44
IT	.30	.61	.51	.54	.33	.36
MK	.43	.39	.56	.53	.51	.39
ND	.58	.54	.44	.37	.49	.53
TH	.55	.41	.52	.43	.43	.59
Median	.50	.48	.48	.42	.41	.42

both the minimum absolute mean difference required for a significant t (with $p = .05$) and the maximum absolute mean difference which failed to reach this level of significance. The former shows how *small* a difference between means on a given factor can actually be significant at the .05 level; the latter shows how *large* a difference between means can be and yet not reach significance at this criterion. It can be seen that, as a matter of fact, although there are differences in the reliability of concept meanings across cultures, they are neither very large nor consistent across the three factors. The median differences (given at the bottom of Table 6:2) — all being .5 scale unit or less — clearly suggest that use of a difference of .5 in a composite score as indicative of significance at the .05 level is a relatively conservative criterion.

Before leaving questions of statistical significance, it should be pointed out that there are many cases where we will be concerned not with the reliability of specific composite scores per se but, rather, with the probable significance of universal trends and deviations from these. Here N will be not 40 subjects contributing to the mean scores of particular concepts but, rather, the number of communities contributing to the dominant trend, or the number of concepts in a category (over which correlations are taken), for examples. The statistical considerations and the "rules of thumb" devised for such cases will be discussed later in this chapter in relation to particular data formats.

Culturological interpretations. As this chapter will illustrate in a small way, the subsequent volumes on the *Atlas* materials *in toto* will represent an attempt to integrate into a coherent picture three major sources of information about the affective dimension of subjective culture: (a) our own quantitative data on the affective meanings of the 620 concepts; (b) the interpretative commentary of our colleagues and others in our 23 communities, elicited in a series of group meetings;[5] and (c) information from the published literature in the various social sciences relating both to our language/culture communities and to our concept categories. The sheer amount of quantitative data on affect available in the *Atlas* has already been noted. Since our 50 or so categories of concepts were designed to sample subjective culture widely, the amount of social science documentation that is at least potentially relevant is immense,[6] and both the staff at the Center and the more than 100 colleagues in foreign countries have limited sophistication — about cultures other than their own, of course, but about their own as well.

Although many regularities and unique deviations in attribution of affect seem to be transparent as to cultural interpretation, there are many more that remain rather opaque, to say the least, and our intepretations must — to use that apposite phrase again — be taken *cum grano salis*. We do not believe that our "horizontal" approach will supplant the "vertical" approach to culture, nor even that it is sufficient within itself. To contribute significantly to our understanding of human culture, the data on affect must be meshed with the richness of "cameo" multilayer studies.

The Universals (with less than 6 of 23 communities being exceptions) are our "hardest" data — in the sense of being most independent of informant interpretations. Many of these, as already noted, are simply instances of face validity (e.g., ANIMAL being more Active than TREE, +Moral concepts being more positively evaluated than ⁻Moral concepts, and Supraordinate concepts like LEADER and HERO being more Potent than Subordinate concepts like FOLLOWER and BEGGAR), but many are not obvious and therefore quite informative. All of the Uniquenesses cry out for interpretation — like the affective closeness of EGO and FRIEND (vs. RELATIVES) for AE and HC and the affective distance of EGO and FAMILY, FRIEND, RELATIVES, and MOST PEOPLE for YS as compared with the closeness for them of EGO to STRANGER — but we often get DKs ("don't knows") on such matters from our informants. Given the limited sampling and somewhat arbitrary geographical groupings of our language/culture communities,[7] the apparent Sub-universals in our data are difficult to justify statistically and (usually) to interpret cul-

---

[5] Dates, locations, and participants of the *Atlas* interpretation group meetings are given in Appendix H.

[6] The authors wish to express their very deeply felt gratitude to Frances McAleavey Adams on our local staff, who has been mainly responsible for searching and organizing this literature in preparation for the *Atlas* interpretation volume as well as this chapter. For the Color category alone, being used as illustration here, she has uncovered and brought to bear some 150 references.

[7] We have designed a computer program which will assess similarities in the attribution of affect for all pairs of cultures regardless of their geographical or other surface relationships, as well as classify the concept categories for which there are significantly higher or lower contingencies than would be expected by chance. Using such data, we will try to test certain "global" hypotheses that have been proposed about cultural diffusion (e.g., Morris Swadesh, *The origin and diversification of language,* 1971).

turally. Some, of course, would be obvious (but not trivial) to students of comparative culture, but others are by no means obvious — e.g., school-related concepts like TEACHER, EDUCATION, and EXAMINATION have low E throughout the West (up to and including YS) but very high E through Asia (from Turkey through Hong Kong, but *not* including Japan), and in the Indian subcontinent Future-oriented concepts have low E and very low P and A, particularly PROGRESS.

THE FORMATS: COLOR CATEGORY AS ILLUSTRATION

It will be recalled that the *Atlas* data for (presently) 23 language/culture communities and 620 concepts are ordered alphabetically by concepts. This makes our information on affect available in flexible form for researchers having diverse concerns. The problem that faced our Center staff, however, was just how to extract from, and then manipulate, this mass of *Atlas* information so as to highlight critical similarities and differences in' subjective culture. Since programs had to be written for both data extraction and subsequent analysis over a large number of concept categories, it was essential that they be as efficient and standardized as possible.[8] We took as "given" the concept categorizations already worked out (Table 6:1) and the basic measures available in the *Atlas* (see Appendix F). We then asked ourselves what kinds of comparative statements we would like to be able to make. Although the questions differed somewhat from category to category — and special tests were often devised to answer these — it seemed that a standardized extraction and manipulation program (really, a linked chain of computer programs) could be devised to answer a large set of generally significant questions about cultural similarities and differences. These "questions" are implicit in the following formats; the "answers," of course, come from the evidence highlighted in the formats.

BASIC MEASURES

The first format is a simple transfer of the basic data for the concepts in a given category (here, Color) from the individual *Atlases* for our 23 communities. However, for convenience in within-category analyses, the data strips are now arranged under each concept according to cultures, AE through JP. Table 6:3 illustrates this format for the first two concepts, COLOR and BLACK; the means and standard deviations for all measures across the 23 communities are also computed, as shown. From the means ("Mn")

---

[8] We wish to express our thanks to Dr. Rhea Das, then on leave from the Indian Statistical Institute in Calcutta, for her help in solving these problems during the long, hot summer of 1966.

TABLE 6:3

Basic Measures for Color Category

	E	P	A	E-Z	P-Z	A-Z	F-Z	D-O	P-I	P-G	CI	CI-Z
					COLOR							
AE	1.5	0.9	−0.2	0.6	−0.1	−0.5	1.1	1.7	1.4	1.0	0.4	−0.6
FR	1.3	−0.1	1.0	0.8	−0.8	0.9	0.7	1.7	1.2	0.9	0.3	−0.9
BF	1.3	0.3	−0.1	0.7	−0.2	−0.5	1.0	1.4	1.2	0.7	0.5	−0.7
ND	1.0	−0.1	0.5	0.5	−0.7	0.2	0.5	1.2	1.2	0.6	0.6	−0.5
GG	2.0	0.2	−0.3	1.0	−0.5	−0.5	0.3	2.1	1.6	1.1	0.6	0.1
.												.
.												.
.												.
JP	0.6	0.3	0.4	0.2	−0.2	0.6	0.3	0.8	1.1	0.4	0.7	0.2
Mn	1.4	0.2	0.3	0.6	−0.5	0.1	0.8	1.5	1.3	0.8	0.5	−0.5
S	0.4	0.4	0.4	0.3	0.4	0.7	0.9	0.4	0.3	0.2	0.2	0.6
					BLACK							
AE	−0.5	0.4	−0.1	−1.3	−0.7	−0.2	−0.5	0.6	1.5	0.5	1.1	2.7
FR	−1.1	1.3	−1.1	−1.6	1.5	−2.2	−0.8	2.0	2.3	1.2	1.1	1.5
BF	−0.1	1.1	−0.7	−0.6	1.4	−1.4	−2.0	1.3	1.6	0.7	0.9	1.7
ND	−0.7	1.3	−0.6	−1.2	1.2	−1.3	0.4	1.6	1.8	0.9	0.9	0.7
GG	−0.9	0.5	−1.3	−1.4	−0.1	−1.5	0.6	1.7	1.4	0.9	0.5	−0.5
.												.
.												.
.												.
JP	−0.7	1.1	−1.2	−1.1	1.3	−2.2	0.0	1.8	1.7	1.0	0.7	0.4
Mn	−0.4	0.7	−0.5	−1.1	0.2	−1.2	−0.2	1.2	1.5	0.7	0.8	0.8
S	0.7	0.6	0.6	0.6	1.0	1.0	0.8	0.7	0.4	0.4	0.3	1.2

it can be seen that COLOR is both more E and more A than BLACK for cultures generally, but BLACK is more P and has higher CI-Z (intracultural disagreement) than COLOR. It can also be seen that COLOR is more Active for the French than it is for the Americans, Belgians, and Germans, while BLACK is much less Potent for Americans and Germans than it is for the others — all of these differences being greater than a full scale unit.

Cultural uniquenesses. To note and record clearly significant deviations of individual cultures from the means on certain basic measures (E-Z, P-Z, and A-Z, F-Z and CI-Z), all cases of deviation equal to or greater than two sigma in either direction are marked by the staff as Uniquenesses. AE has only one significant deviation, WHITE having very high CI. There were no significant deviations on *any* color concepts for FR, ND, GG, CS, IT, YS, TK, AD, and CB. Belgians are unique for their low Familiarity and Finns for their low CI on BLACK; Hindi speakers in Delhi see BLACK as unusually Active. Mysoreans are unique in their significantly high (rated) Familiarity of all color concepts *except* BLACK.[9] The Thai display more Uniquenesses in the meaning of colors than any other community, including a high P and low CI-Z for BLACK and a low P and high A for COLOR. For some of these Uniquenesses we have relevant commentary from our informants, but for many we do not.

Correlations on basic measures. A second format is the matrix of inter-cultural correlations, each culture with every other, for the most independent basic measures — E, P, and A, Familiarity and CI. Here we look for several things: average overall level of correlation (potential Universals), clusters of cultures having higher than average intercorrelation (potential Sub-universals), and cultural "isolates" having low correlations with all other groups (apparent Uniquenesses in the attribution of feeling to concepts in the category). Since these Pearson product-moment correlations are taken over the concepts in a given category, the magnitude of the r (or mean r) neces-sary for significance at any particular level will vary inversely with the number of concepts in the category — the smaller the category, the larger must be the correlation.

With only eight concepts in the Color category, the correlation needed for significance at the .01 level is .83. Although none of the basic measures yields a mean r at this level, the average overall r across cultures on E is .72, so we can conclude that our communities agree reasonably well on the Evalu-ation of color concepts — thus a near-Universal. Two clusters of communities appear in the E matrix: one (with r's $\geq$ .80) includes AE, all Western European locations (but not SW and FF), IT, YS, TK, and JP; the other (with r's $\geq$ .85) includes TK again, along with LA, AD, and CB. It is in-teresting that Turkey, given its geographic location, does relate to both European and Asian groups, between which otherwise correlations are much lower. There is only one clear isolate on the Evaluation of colors, and that is Yucatan (Mayan) Spanish; the highest r for YC is a .33 with JP, and there are many small minus r's. From later formats we will see in what ways YC differs from others in its attribution of affect to colors.

INTRACULTURAL RANKS OF CONCEPTS WITHIN COMMUNITIES

In this simplifying data format the concepts in each category are ranked on each primary basic measure for each community, and mean ranks for each category are computed. Although ranks are a rather gross measure, reflecting order but neither absolute locations on dimensions nor magnitudes of differences between concepts, they do yield an overall picture and permit certain data treatments which could be cumbersome with finer measures —

---

[9] That this is not simply due to a constant bias in the MK *familiar-unfamiliar* scale is evident from the fact that these are standardized (F-Z) scores.

for example, the componential analyses, to be discussed in the next section, which we believe to be a particularly powerful probe into subjective culture.

Table 6:4 gives the ranks of the concepts in the Color category for 23 communities for Evaluation, Potency, Activity, Familiarity, and Cultural Instability, along with the mean ranks. It will be noted that the communities are ordered in our standard geographical subgroupings, running roughly from west to east. The order of concepts in this category is entirely arbitrary. Small numbers represent high ranks (1 being highest) and large numbers low ranks (8 being the lowest rank here). Thus AE's rank 1 on E for COLOR means that this concept is the most highly evaluated of all color concepts for the American sample. The plus and minus signs next to some ranks are computerized aids to the staff in noting Sub-universal patterns and Unique-nesses, a + representing a relatively high rank with respect to the mean for all communities and a — a relatively low rank. These are only "flags" for staff judgment, not absolute criteria; for example, the concept BLUE meets the criterion for coding as a potential E Universal, and therefore the several +s along that strip are not marked as unique deviations. In this table we show the coding system employed: the Us, signed + or — for high or low means, indicate apparent Universals; the heavy black underlinings indicate apparent Sub-universals (𝒰s); and the circles indicate Uniquenesses. This coded information is transferred to the appropriate listings used in group meetings on *Atlas* interpretation.

Universals. The general criterion for assigning a U is that the mean rank across all communities be in the upper or lower third of ranks (which means at least one full rank above or below the average rank of 4.5 here, with 8 concepts) and that no more than 5 of the 23 communities deviate with ranks on the other side of the average (i.e., greater than 4.5 if the mean rank is toward 1 and less than 4.5 if the mean rank is toward 8). The 5/23 criterion is based on the binomial expansion (sign test); since we are not predicting direction (high or low mean rank) in any strict sense, we use the two-tail probability, which for an N of 23 and 5 exceptions is $p \leq$ .01 — i.e., this many exceptions would be expected to occur by chance only 1% of the time if the "true" division were 50/50.

Let us look now at some of the data. The concepts COLOR and BLUE are "universally" (within the limits of our sample and our criterion) positive in Evaluation, whereas BLACK and GREY are negative. High Potency is attributed to RED across our sample and also to BLACK — the latter does not quite reach the criterion (there being 6/23 deviants) — whereas GREY, YELLOW, and WHITE, all desaturated colors, have low Potency. RED and the concept COLOR itself have high Activity, but both BLACK and GREY have low. Both BLACK and GREY are rated relatively Unfamiliar,[10] and whereas BLACK

---

[10] Familiarity judgments were not obtained from our Costa Rican subjects.

TABLE 6:4
Ranks — Colors

EVALUATION

	AE	FR	BF	ND	GG	SW	FF	YC	CS	MS	IT	YS	GK	TK	LA	IF	AD	DH	CB	MK	TH	HC	JP	Mean
COLOR	1	1	1	1	1	3	1	(8−)	2	1	2	2	1	(4−)	1	3	4−	4−	1	2	1		(5−)	2.3 U+
BLACK	8	8	7	8	8	8	7	(4+)	7	8	8	8	8	7	8	8	8	8	8	8	7	8	7	7.5 U−
GREY	7	7	8	7	7	7	7	7	8	7	7	7	7	5+	5+	5+	(3+)	7	6	6	7	8		6.8 U−
RED	(2+)	5	(2+6)	5	4	5	5	6	6	6	5	(7−5)	4	5	6	5	6	4	(7−5)			4		4.9
YELLOW	6	6	4	6	1+	2+6	6	(3+4)	5	6	6	6	6	6	8−	7−	1+(5)	3+1+	6			6		4.8
BLUE	3	2	3	2	(5−)	1+4	(5−)1+4	(5−)1+4	1+	1+	4	2	(5−)4	2	3	(6−4)	3	2				3		3.0 U+
GREEN	5	3	3	5	4	(6−2)	4	4	3	3	2	(1+3)	(1+7−)	(1+7−)	5	5	4	3				4		3.5
WHITE	4	5−	5−4	(6−3)	3	(1+5−3)	3	(1+5−3)	(4//)	3	3	2	2	(6−2)	2	3	3	2				(1+)		3.3 *West/East?*

POTENCY

	AE	FR	BF	ND	GG	SW	FF	YC	CS	MS	IT	YS	GK	TK	LA	IF	AD	DH	CB	MK	TH	HC	JP	Mean
COLOR	(2+)	(6−)	5	4	4	4	(6−)	(6−5)	5	5	5	(2+4)	5	(6−3)	(1+4)	7−	6−5	7−	6−5	5	(2+3)	3		4.3
BLACK	(5−)	(1+)	1+	1+3	3	3	(1+1+2)	2	3	4	(5−2)	1+	(5−)1+	7−	8−	1+1+	1+1+	(6−1)	(6−1+)	2.8
GREY	(8−)	(3+7)	7	5	5	7	(2+8−)	8−	7	8−	1+	(3+7)	(3+7)	5	8−	7	(3+8−)	(3+8−)	(4+)	6.1 U−
RED	1	2	2	2	1	2	(2+)	1	2	2	1	2	2	4−	2	3	4−	4−	2	1	2	2.2 U+
YELLOW	6	8	6	8	7	(5+8)	7	6	8	7	7	6	8	8	6	(5+8)	(5+8)	7	7	6.9 U−
BLUE	3	4	3	3	2+	1+4	(2+1+4)	5	4	(1+1+)	3	3	5	(8−3)	3	4	(1+6−5)	(6−4)	5	3.7
GREEN	4	7−(4)	6−	6−(3)	6−6−3	4	3	3	4	4	4	3	4//	(1+5)	2+3	2+3	(3//4)	5	(6−)	4.0 *Climatic?*
WHITE	7	5	8−	7	8−7	8−7	(3+7)	6	6	6	6	8−7	7	(2+6)	8−6	3+2+	8−	(3+8−)	6.0 U−

TABLE 6:4 (Continued)

ACTIVITY

	AE	FR	BF	ND	GG	SW	FF	YC	CS	MS	IT	YS	GK	TK	LA	IF	AD	DH	CB	MK	TH	HC	JP	Mean
COLOR	3	2	3	2	4	3	2	8-	6-	6-	3	1+	5	2	2	2	3	4	4	3	2	3	3	3.3 U+
BLACK	2+	8	8	7	7	8	8	1+	7	8	7	8	8	6	7	8	6	7	1+	5	4+	8	8	6.5 U-
GREY	8	7	7	8	8	6	7	7	8	7	8	5	7	7	8	4+	6	8	2+	7	7	7	7	6.7 U-
RED	1	1	1	1	1	3	4	1	1	2	5-	2	6-	6-	1	1	6-	1	1	1	1	1	1	2.4 U+
YELLOW	7-	5	2	4	2	2	1+	3	2	4	1+	2	4	5	1+	7-	8-	2	7-	8-	3	5	2	3.8
BLUE	4	6	5	3	5	4	4	5	3	2+	6	4	6	3	4	2+	5	6	5	4	4	6	6	4.3
GREEN	6	4	6	5	3+	5	6	6	4	3+	4	7-	3+	4	4	3+	5	8-	3+	7-	5	6	5	4.9
WHITE	5	3	4	6-	6-	7-	5	2+	5	5	3	1+	1+	7-	5	6-	3	2+	6-	1+	2+	4	4	4.1

FAMILIARITY

	AE	FR	BF	ND	GG	SW	FF	YC	CS[a]	MS	IT	YS	GK	TK	LA	IF	AD	DH	CB	MK	TH	HC	JP	Mean
COLOR	1+	4	4	5	8-	2	2	1+		2	1+	7-	5	3	7-	1+	7-	5	6	1+	2	5	6	3.9 *Note uniquenesses*
BLACK	8	8	8	6	6	3+	5			8	8	8	7	8	7	8	4+	6	7	8	6	6	7	6.7 U-
GREY	7	7	7	4	7	6	8			5	7	6	4	2+	6	4	2+	7	5	7	7	7	8	6.0 U-
RED	3	6	3	2	1+	5	4	8-		7-	2	5	1+	6	3	6	1+	8-	2	6	1+	5	5	4.0
YELLOW	6	3	2+	1+	5	4	1+	4		1+	4	6	4	5	6	8-	8-	3	6	4	8-	3	3	4.4
BLUE	2	1+	5	7-	2	1+	3	2		4	5	6	8-	2	1+	2	5	2	1+	5	5	3	4	3.4
GREEN	5	2	6	3	3	7-	7-	6		3	6	3	2	4	4	7-	1+	3	2	3	3	4	2	3.9
WHITE	4	5	1+	8-	4	8-	6-	7-		6-	3	1+	3	1+	3	5	3	4	4	4	1+	2	1+	3.8

[a] No familiar-unfamiliar scale was rated by Costa Ricans.

TABLE 6:4 (Continued)

CULTURAL INSTABILITY

	AE	FR	BF	ND	GG	SW	FF	YC	CS	MS	IT	YS	GK	TK	LA	IF	AD	DH	CB	MK	TH	HC	JP	Mean	
COLOR	7	8	6	8	5	8	4	8	7	(2+)	8	8	7	8	3+	3+	6	6	5	6	6	(3+)	4	5.9	U-
BLACK	1	1	5-	8-	4	8-	3	1	1	(1+)	1	4	1	3	2	1	2	2	1	1	(8-)	2	3	2.8	U+
GREY	5	5	4	6	4	(1+)	5	4	3	5	3	3	2	3	6	4	4	2	3	4	(1+)	3	(8-)	4.0	
RED	6	3	8-	7-	5	3	(1+)	4	3	7-	4	6	6	(1+)	5	7-	3	4	3	5	4	(8-)	5	4.7	
YELLOW	4	2	2	1+	1+	6-	7-	7-	5	6-	2	2	4	(6-)	2	(1+)	1+	3	5	8-	6-	(1+)	2	3.7	High diversity
BLUE	(8-)	4	5	2+	2+	7	2+	5	(8-)	4	5	5	(1+)	7	(8-)	5	7	7	4	7	5	4	7	5.2	
GREEN	3+	6	7	4	3+	1+	6	6	7	6	7	(8-)	4	7	6	8-	8-	7	5	(5)	2+	1+	6	5.2	
WHITE	(2+)	7-	3	3	6	(2+)	6	2+	2+	(8-)	1+	6	5	5	4	(8-)	5	6	8-	8-	7	7-	6	4.6	High diversity

has high CI (Cultural Instability, or possible "conflict"), with only Thai as an exception (rank 8), the concept COLOR has low CI generally (intra-cultural agreement). The exceptions to these Universals automatically become either Sub-universals or Uniquenesses and will be treated as such. Interpretation of apparent Universals, in terms of both our informants' commentary and information from the published literature, will be deferred until we have reviewed the results of the componential analyses, based on these rank data.

Sub-universals. The criterion here is more judgmental than statistical. If two or more geographically neighboring communities display the same direction of extreme deviation, they are marked as a Ⅴ. If such a Sub-universal is "broken" by an exception within itself, it is also underlined in black, but with the exception bracketed (e.g., DH (CB) MK TH on the E of YELLOW). Quite frequently more massive "blocs" are evident in the data: here we note a possible West/East bloc (breaking between YS and GK) on the Evaluation of WHITE, with the former (except CS) having relatively low E and the latter (except DH) having relatively high E. On the potency of GREEN we note another type of blocking, with Western Europe (except BF) having low P, West and South Asian (except IF) having high P, and the Far East having relatively low P again — and a climatic (moist/arid) interpretation suggests itself. Sub-universals are best summarized in terms of the sets of communities with which group meetings were held, since one must look for patterns *across* concepts in the data. A few examples will serve to illustrate Sub-universals in the Color category.

The *Western European* communities (except BF) agree on a low Potency for GREEN and a high CI for YELLOW (no agreed-upon interpretation for the former, but common negative connotations for the latter). The two *Scandinavian* communities agree on a high Evaluation of YELLOW (along with low CI) and low Familiarity for both GREEN ("factual"?) and WHITE ("denial," or less winter light?), and a geographic interpretation seems reasonable.[11] The three *East Asian* communities (TH, HC, and JP) have definite and almost exclusive agreement on the high Familiarity and low CI (high internal agreement) of WHITE.

Uniquenesses. The criterion for marking communities as being uniquely deviant (circles) varies both with the number of concepts in a category and with whether the item has already been scored as a Universal. In the case of Universals, *all* deviants are circled, unless they are already included as Ⅴs (Sub-universals). In the general case the criterion is a deviation from the mean rank equal to approximately one-quarter of the total ranks, and the absolute deviation in ranks thus keeps increasing with the

---

[11] Checking our records, we find that the original *Atlas* data were collected in Sweden in the months of December and January and in Finland in the month of February.

size of the category (i.e., 2 ranks from the mean for an 8-concept category (as here for colors) but 8 ranks from the mean for a 32-concept category). Deviations of this magnitude in the *same* direction as the mean rank of a Universal are usually not marked, since they merely contribute to the universal trend. Even though the computer assigns +s and −s as an aid, judgment is still required, e.g., when the row distributions tend toward bimodality (note, for example, that 2s and 6s are not marked for COLOR on Familiarity, even though they deviate from the mean rank by ±2 ranks).

Interpretation of Uniquenesses — occurring in ranks, componential analyses, and distance matrices, as well as in basic measures and special tests (and often being repetitious)— is most dependent upon their total patterning for each community. The marked deviations in rank of a few communities may be mentioned here by way of illustrating the data. For our Midwest AE subjects the concept BLACK has unusually low Potency but high Activity (and we suspect contamination with Race concepts); the Mayan YC show a pattern of extreme deviancy for all non-hues (COLOR, BLACK, GREY, WHITE), and this will be considered later; the GK are notable for their low E, low FAM, and high CI for BLUE (low E, our informants said, is probably because blue is the color of an unpopular and unusually poor soccer team;[12] the low FAM may be attributable to the fact that the term used, although the most common, is not a Greek word in origin; and the high CI is probably due to multiple senses); the Afghans attach unusually high E, P, and FAM to GREEN along with low CI (according to informants, green is associated with prosperity, the spring, and fertility, as well as having religious significance in Islam).

COMPONENTIAL ANALYSES OF RANKS

The rankings on the various basic measures lend themselves to a powerful semantic analytic procedure known as "componential analysis." This method, developed by ethnolinguists over the past two decades (see, for example, Goodenough, 1956; Lounsbury, 1956), has become a standard ethnographic technique. It has been applied particularly to the domain of kinship terminology (see Wallace and Atkins, 1960, for an excellent interpretative review), but not exclusively. For example, it was applied by Conklin (1955) to the color terms used by the Hanunóo (a Philippine culture). Brightness (white/black) and Hue (red/green) were found to be basic contrasts, creating a four-way classification system; within this basic system finer differentiations are made, often on more connotative bases (e.g., *dryness* vs. *freshness* or *succulence,* but including *deep* vs. *pale* and hence apparently the Saturation dimension).

---

[12] We kept reminding our participants at the group meetings that the subjects were teen-age boys, and *their* probable views of the world should be kept in mind.

As typically used by ethnolinguists, componential analysis is employed to generate an elegant and systematic structural description of the kinship (or any other) lexical domain of a particular society, including definitions of the kin terms as combinations or conjunctions of the semantic components that have been isolated. Many linguists and anthropologists, however, go beyond the purely descriptive or structural use of componential analysis to search for the psychological (or cognitive, as it is often phrased) realities behind the system for a particular society (cf. Goodenough, 1956; Wallace and Atkins, 1960). The reasonable assumption being made is that those features of kinship which are explicitly coded as part of a linguistic system ought to be more salient to its users, ought to make more of a difference psychologically, and hence ought to show up in various measures of perception, cognition, and behavior generally. Romney and D'Andrade (1964) carry this approach a step further, stating that they are "equally interested in the other side of the coin, that is, in those aspects of the individual's psychological or cognitive structure which are not represented in formal analyses" (p. 146). In a study of the subjective aspects of American kinship, these authors tested the general hypothesis that the more semantic components two kin terms have in common, the greater should be the similarity of responses to them. The hypothesis was borne out for free-recall, SD, and triad-judgment data.

Our use of componential analysis has a somewhat different purpose: rather than merely providing a structural description of the semantic relations (usually denotative) among concepts in a given category, or even relating the description to other aspects of culture, *we wish to use the technique as a means of discovering underlying cognitive bases for the differential attribution of affect* (our dependent variable). Thus in the Kinship category we will ask if those kincepts coded Male on a Sex feature have consistently different feeling-tones than those coded Female; the answer in this particular instance is that, although denotative Sex has no consistent effects as far as Evaluation and Activity are concerned, it has massive, universal effects on Potency — Males being more P than their Female counterparts. However, unlike the exhaustiveness characteristics of ethnolinguistic analyses of lexical domains in particular cultures, most of our categories are incomplete to varying degrees (and in different ways); this is because of the limited yet diverse nature of our *Atlas* concept sample. In the Kinship category, for example, we did not include separate terms for older vs. younger siblings, and we certainly could not include the eight or so distinctive terms for types of cousins among the Afghans.[13] Furthermore, in our attempt to discover

---

[13] Where such multiple translations of single AE terms, but no matching summary terms, were found (e.g., *father's brother* and *mother's brother* but no *father's-or-mother's brother,* for AE UNCLE), we have usually tested all finer variants and entered their average values in the *Atlases* with appropriate notes.

universal trends we must use the same components across all of our cultures rather than derive from language usage components that are unique to each culture, as is done in "ethnoscience" (see, e.g., Conklin, 1955; Frake, 1962; Metzger and Williams, 1963).

Selecting components. The first step in componential analysis of any category is to intuit what seem to be its underlying denotative features. In some cases, like Geometricals (from a POINT through various forms to IN-FINITY), the intuitions come quite easily in terms of physical properties — Dimensionality (Many/3-1/None), Concreteness (Real/Hypothetical), Solidity (Solid/Plane Figures), Angularity (Angular/Rounded), and Sidedness (Four- vs. Three-Sided); in others, like Kinship, we can rely on the spadework done by ethnolinguists. But in many categories, like Habitations, Sex and Sensuality, Modern/Transitional/Traditional Values, Institutions, and Communications, the intuitions come much harder, and we have less confidence in the psychological reality of the suggested components. The general procedure is to first try to intuit the "obvious" denotative features which divide the concepts in a category into gross sets and then, by testing pairs of concepts which remain as "synonyms" and yet are obviously not, to add the minimal number of other features necessary to distinguish all nonsynonymous concepts from each other.

Although differential effects upon affect *may* testify to the validity of an intuited component (or at least some correlate of it), failure of a component to differentiate affect attribution is not evidence against its psychological validity for meaning generally — for example, both Concrete/Abstract (ICE/COLD, ROCK/WEIGHT, etc.) and Organic/Inorganic (ROPE/STEEL, CLOTH/GLASS, etc.) are certainly reasonable denotative components for our Stuffs category, yet they display no relation in our data to how people attribute E, P, and A. In the case of the Color category the components used are simply the physical dimensions of light — Brightness, Hue, and Saturation — along with a Color/Non-color component, which we added.

Coding concepts on components. The second step is to code each concept on each of the intuited semantic components. As shown in Table 6:5, on the fourth component (Color/Non-color) the terms COLOR, RED, YELLOW, BLUE, and GREEN are coded + and the terms BLACK, GREY, and WHITE are —. In some cases the signs of features are quite arbitrary, e.g., here calling the red end of the spectrum +Hue. We use the convention of assigning 0 for true neutrality on a feature (thus GREY is 0 on the Brightness component) and 00 for irrelevance of a feature for a concept (thus COLOR is 00 on Hue because it can refer to any hue, and BLACK-GREY-WHITE are 00 because they have no hue). Although codings for concepts in a category like Colors (or Geometricals, or Time Units, or Stuffs) are presumably independent of culture, this is not the case for many categories (e.g., the Age Continuum, the Intimacy-Remoteness Continuum, and Body Characteristics and Processes). In every group meeting there was lively disagreement about the (AE) codings of Emotions: is DEVOTION Activated or Deactivated? Is HOPE Cognitive or Affective? Is ANGER Supraordinate or Subordinate? Is PLEASURE Social or Individual? Our usual "solution" to this problem has been to assign 0s as codings where there is clear cross-cultural disagreement.

Componential tests. The ideal tests for influence of components upon attribution of affect are minimal pairs of concepts — that is, concepts whose feature codings differ on only the component in question and maximally so (+/−). In the Kinship category, for example, there are many minimal pairs for the Sex component (UNCLE/AUNT, BROTHER/SISTER, FATHER/MOTHER, and HUSBAND/WIFE, to mention only part of the roll), but there are few for Nuclearity (BROTHER/UNCLE, SISTER/AUNT and BROTHER-SISTER/COUSIN), and two of these are confounded with Generation. Where insufficient numbers of "pure" tests are available, we often accept "half-step" tests (+/0 or 0/−) and try to balance out confounded features with "double" tests (e.g., the BROTHER-SISTER/COUSIN test above is designed to eliminate confounding with Sex).

The tests for the Color category are given in Table 6:5. For Brightness there is only one minimal pair (WHITE/BLACK), so two "half-step" tests are added (WHITE/GREY and GREY/BLACK — with GREY (0) having a double function); for Hue, RED/BLUE and YELLOW/GREEN provide perfect tests, as can be seen from their code strips; similarly, RED/YELLOW and BLUE/GREEN provide perfect tests for the Saturation component (the ends of the spectrum being more saturated for the human eye naturally than the middle). The tests for Color/Non-color are not very satisfactory because both involve the same left-hand concept (COLOR/GREY and COLOR/WHITE-BLACK, a "double" test to control for Brightness), and any peculiarities of the meaning of this one concept (here, COLOR), whether owing to translation or to cultural differences, can markedly affect the result. In general, the purpose of multiple componential tests is to minimize the effects of affective peculiarities associated with particular concepts.

Componential analysis results. The componential tests are carried out by the computer against the ranks of concepts on each primary measure (E, P, A, FAM, and CI). The results for the Color category are shown in Table 6:6. If the left-hand term (positive coding on component) for a particular test on a particular community has a higher rank than the right-hand term (negative coding), then the computer records a + in the column for the community and if conversely, a −; thus on the first test of the Hue component on E, AE is + (RED more E than BLUE), FR is − (RED less E than BLUE), and so forth. In the case of "double" tests, both of the subtests (here, COLOR/WHITE and COLOR/BLACK) must go the same way if either a + or a − is to be assigned; if they split, a 0 is recorded. The staff again marks

TABLE 6:5

Component Codings for Componential Analysis for Colors

Components:

(1) Brightness (bright⁺/dark⁻)

(2) Hue (red⁺/blue⁻)

(3) Saturation (rich⁺/pale⁻)

(4) Color/Non-color $(+/-)$

CODINGS	BR	HUE	SAT	COLOR
COLOR	00	00	00	+
BLACK	−	00	00	−
GREY	0	00	00	−
RED	00	+	+	+
YELLOW	00	+	−	+
BLUE	00	−	+	+
GREEN	00	−	−	+
WHITE	+	00	00	−

Tests:

(1) Brightness: WHITE⁺/BLACK⁻; WHITE⁺/GREY⁰; GREY⁰/BLACK⁻

(2) Hue: RED⁺/BLUE⁻; YELLOW⁺/GREEN⁻

(3) Saturation: RED⁺/YELLOW⁻; BLUE⁺/GREEN⁻

(4) Color: COLOR⁺/GREY⁻; COLOR⁺/WHITE-BLACK⁻

this output format with Us, ⱴs, and circles, and the same criteria as used for ranks are also applied here. Note that to aid the staff in these codings, the computer prints out the number of communities assigned + and the percentage that this number is of all communities.

Universals. In reporting the universal trends in our color data for ranks and their componential analysis, we shall try to relate them to the very extensive literature on color affects, connotations, and associations.[14]

As a whole component Brightness (WHITE) is universally Good (⁺E), Active (⁺A), and Familiar (⁺FAM) as compared with Darkness (BLACK), but Darkness is more Powerful (⁺P) and more "conflictual" (⁺CI); we have already seen that BLACK and GREY have universally low ranks on Evaluation, Activity, and rated Familiarity, and BLACK has high Cultural Instability as well. Given the fact that humans are primates and depend more on vision

[14] At this point we are interested in support, or lack thereof, of what appear to be Universals in our data; in the last section of this chapter we will reconsider our findings and the literature in terms of theoretical issues. Full integration with the literature must be reserved for the volumes on *The Affective Dimension of Subjective Culture*. See also Adams and Osgood (1973).

TABLE 6:6

Componential Analysis — Colors

EVALUATION

U+ Bright/Dark

	+	TOT	+/TOT	AE	FR	BF	ND	GG	SW	FF	YC	CS	MS	IT	YS	GK	TK	LA	IF	AD	DH	CB	MK	TH	HC	JP
WHITE/BLACK	23	23	1.000	+	+	+	+	+	+	+	+	+	+	+	+	+	+	+	+	+	+	+	+	+	+	+
WHITE/GREY	22	23	0.957	+	+	+	+	+	+	+	+	+	+	+	+	+	+	+	+	(−)	+	+	+	+	+	+
GREY/BLACK	16	23	0.696	+	+	−	+	+	+	+	+	+	−	+	+	+	−	+	−	+	+	+	+	+	+	−

U− Hue: red/blue

	+	TOT	+/TOT	AE	FR	BF	ND	GG	SW	FF	YC	CS	MS	IT	YS	GK	TK	LA	IF	AD	DH	CB	MK	TH	HC	JP
RED/BLUE	6	23	0.261	+	−	+	−	+	−	+	−	(+)	−	−	+	+	−	−	−	+	+	+	+	−	−	−
YELLOW/GREEN	6	23	0.261	−	+	−	−	+	+	+	−	−	−	−	−	−	−	−	−	+	+	(−)	+	−	−	−

Sat: rich/pale

	+	TOT	+/TOT	AE	FR	BF	ND	GG	SW	FF	YC	CS	MS	IT	YS	GK	TK	LA	IF	AD	DH	CB	MK	TH	HC	JP
RED/YELLOW	12	23	0.522	+	+	+	+	+	+	+	−	−	−	−	+	+	−	−	+	−	+	−	+	+	+	+
BLUE/GREEN	16	23	0.696	+	+	+	+	+	+	+	+	○	+	−	(−)	−	+	+	+	(−)	−	+	+	+	+	+

U+ Color/Non-color

	+	TOT	+/TOT	AE	FR	BF	ND	GG	SW	FF	YC	CS	MS	IT	YS	GK	TK	LA	IF	AD	DH	CB	MK	TH	HC	JP
COLOR/GREY	21	23	0.913	+	+	+	+	+	+	+	□	+	+	+	+	+	+	+	+	(−)	+	+	+	+	+	+
COLOR/WHITE	17	23	0.739	+	+	+	+	+	+	+	−	+	+	+	+	+	0	+	+	+	+	+	+	+	+	+
COLOR/BLACK	22	23	0.957	+	+	+	+	+	+	+	−	+	+	+	+	+	0	+	+	+	+	+	+	+	+	0

POTENCY

?U− Bright/Dark

	+	TOT	+/TOT	AE	FR	BF	ND	GG	SW	FF	YC	CS	MS	IT	YS	GK	TK	LA	IF	AD	DH	CB	MK	TH	HC	JP
WHITE/BLACK	3	23	0.130	−	−	−	−	−	−	−	+	−	−	−	−	−	(+)	−	−	+	−	−	−	(+)	−	−
WHITE/GREY	11	23	0.478	+	+	+	−	−	−	−	+	+	+	+	−	−	+	+	+	(+)	−	+	+	+	−	−
GREY/BLACK	2	23	0.087	−	−	−	−	−	(+)	−	−	−	−	−	−	−	−	−	−	−	+	−	−	−	−	−

Hue: red/blue

	+	TOT	+/TOT	AE	FR	BF	ND	GG	SW	FF	YC	CS	MS	IT	YS	GK	TK	LA	IF	AD	DH	CB	MK	TH	HC	JP
RED/BLUE	17	23	0.739	+	+	+	+	+	−	+	+	+	−	+	+	+	(−)	+	+	(−)	+	+	+	−	+	−
YELLOW/GREEN	1	23	0.043	−	−	−	−	−	−	−	−	−	−	−	−	−	−	−	−	−	−	−	−	−	−	−

TABLE 6:6 (Continued)

	+ TOT	+/TOT	AE	FR	BF	ND	GG	SW	FF	YC	CS	MS	IT	YS	GK	TK	LA	IF	AD	DH	CB	MK	TH	HC	JP
?U+ Sat: rich/pale																									
RED/YELLOW	23 23	1.000	+	+	+	+	+	+	+	+	+	+	+	+	+	+	+	+	+	+	+	+	+	+	+
BLUE/GREEN	13 23	0.565	+	+	+	+	+	+	+	−	−//	+//	+	+//−	−	−	−//+	−	−//−	−	−	−	−//+	−//+	+ *(Blocs)*
U+ Color/Non-color																									
COLOR/GREY	19 23	0.826	+	(−)	+	+	+	(−)	(−)	(−)	+	+	+	+	(−)	+	+	+	(−)	+	+	(−)	+	(−)	+
COLOR/WHITE	18 23	0.783	(+)	−	0	0	0	0	0	0	0	0	(−)	0	0	−	0	+|	0	−	−	+	(+)	+	+
COLOR/BLACK	5 23	0.217	(+)	−	0	0	0	0	0	0	0	0	0	(+)	0	0	−	0	+|	−	−	0	0	(+)	0
U+ Bright/Dark																									
WHITE/BLACK	19 23	0.826	(−)	+	+	+	+	+	(−)	(−)	+	+	+	+	+	+	+	+	(−)	+	−	(−)	+	+	+
WHITE/GREY	19 23	0.826	+	+	+	−	+	+	+	+	+	+	+	+	+	+	−	+	−	+	−	−	+	+	+
GREY/BLACK	14 23	0.609	−	+	+	−	+	+	−	−	+	−	−	+	+	+	+	−	−	−	−	+	+	+	+
?U+ Hue: red/blue																									
RED/BLUE	18 23	0.783	+	+	+	+	+	+	+	+	+	+	+	(−)	+	(−)	−	+	(−)	+	+	(−)	+	+	+
YELLOW/GREEN	14 23	0.609	−	−	+	+	+	+	+	+	−	+	+	+	+	−	(+)	−	−|	+	−	+	+	+	+
Sat: rich/pale																									
RED/YELLOW	15 23	0.652	+	+	+	+	+	+	(−)	(−)	+	(−)	−	(+)	−	−	−	+	+	+	−	−	+	+	−
BLUE/GREEN	16 23	0.696	+	−	+	+	+	+	+	+	+	+	+	+	+	+	+	+	+	+	−	+	+	+	−
U+ Color/Non-color																									
COLOR/GREY	21 23	0.913	+	+	+	+	+	+	+	(−)	+	+	+	+	+	+	+	+	(−)	+	+	−	+	+	+
COLOR/WHITE	14 23	0.609	0	+	+	+	+	+	+	(−)	0	0	+	+	0	0	+	+	(−)	+	+	(+)	+	+	+
COLOR/BLACK	20 23	0.870	+	+	+	+	+	+	+	+	+	+	+	+	+	+	+	+	+	0	0	0	+	+	+

Activity

TABLE 6:6 (Continued)

FAMILIARITY

U+ Bright/Dark	+	TOT	+/TOT	AE	FR	BF	ND	GG	SW	FF	YC	CS	MS	IT	YS	GK	TK	LA	IF	AD	DH	CB	MK	TH	HC	JP
WHITE/BLACK	18	22	0.818	+	+	+	(−)	−	−	−	−	(−)	+	+	+	+	+	+	+	+	+	+	+	+	+	+
WHITE/GREY	16	22	0.727	+	+	+	(−)	+	(−)	(−)	(−)	+	+	+	+	+	+	+	−	+	+	+	+	+	+	+
GREY/BLACK	15	22	0.682	+	+	+	+	−	−	+	+	+	+	+	+	+	+	+	+	(−)	+	+	+	+	+	+

(handwritten: U+)
(handwritten bracket near JP; handwritten note: West/East?)

Hue:: red/blue	+	TOT	+/TOT	AE	FR	BF	ND	GG	SW	FF	YC	CS	MS	IT	YS	GK	TK	LA	IF	AD	DH	CB	MK	TH	HC	JP
RED/BLUE	8	22	0.363	−	−	+	+	−	−	−	−	−	+	−	−	−	−	−	(+)	+	+	+	−	+	−	−
YELLOW/GREEN	8	22	0.363	−	−	+	(−)	+	+	+	+	+	+	//	−	−	−	(+)	−	−	−	−	−	−	+	−

Sat: rich/pale	+	TOT	+/TOT	AE	FR	BF	ND	GG	SW	FF	YC	CS	MS	IT	YS	GK	TK	LA	IF	AD	DH	CB	MK	TH	HC	JP
RED/YELLOW	11	22	0.500	+	+	+	+	−	−	−	−	−	+	+	+	+	+	+	+	+	+	+	+	+	+	+
BLUE/GREEN	14	22	0.636	+	+	+	+	+	+	+	−	−	−	+	+	+	+	+	−	+	+	+	−	+	+	−

Color/Non-color	+	TOT	+/TOT	AE	FR	BF	ND	GG	SW	FF	YC	CS	MS	IT	YS	GK	TK	LA	IF	AD	DH	CB	MK	TH	HC	JP
COLOR/GREY	16	22	0.727	+	+	+	−	+	+	+	+	+	+	(−)	+	(−)	+	(−)	+	(−)	(−)	+	+	+	+	+
COLOR/WHITE	10	22	0.455	+	0	0	(−)	+	+	+	+	+	0	0	0	0	0	(+)	(−)	(+)	0	0	0	0	0	0
COLOR/BLACK	20	22	0.909	+	+	+	+	+	+	+	+	+	// 0	+	+	+	+	(+)	(+)	(−)	+	+	+	+	−	+

(handwritten: West/East?)

CULTURAL INSTABILITY

U– Bright/Dark	+	TOT	+/TOT	AE	FR	BF	ND	GG	SW	FF	YC	CS	MS	IT	YS	GK	TK	LA	IF	AD	DH	CB	MK	TH	HC	JP
WHITE/BLACK	7	23	0.304	−	−	−	+	+	+	+	+	(+)	(+)	−	−	−	−	−	−	−	−	−	−	(+)	−	−
WHITE/GREY	10	23	0.435	+	−	+	−	−	−	−	+	+	−	−	−	+	+	−	−	−	+	+	−	−	−	+
GREY/BLACK	6	23	0.261	−	−	−	(+)	(+)	+	+	−	−	−	−	(+)	−	−	−	−	−	−	−	(+)	−	−	−

TABLE 6:6 (Continued)

?U+ Hue: red/blue	+	TOT	+/TOT	AE	FR	BF	ND	GG	SW	FF	YC	CS	MS	IT	YS	GK	TK	LA	IF	AD	DH	CB	MK	TH	HC	JP
RED/BLUE	15	23	0.652	+	+	+	–	–	–	(+)	+	+	+	+	+	–	+	+	–	+	+	+	+	+	+	+
YELLOW/GREEN	15	23	0.652	–	+	+	+	+	–	–	–	+	+	+	+	+	–	+	+	+	+	+	–	–	(+)	–
Sat: rich/pale	+	TOT	+/TOT	AE	FR	BF	ND	GG	SW	FF	YC	CS	MS	IT	YS	GK	TK	LA	IF	AD	DH	CB	MK	TH	HC	JP
RED/YELLOW	9	23	0.391	–	–	–	–	–	+	+	+	+	+	–	–	–	+	–	–	–	+	+	+	–	–	–
BLUE/GREEN	14	23	0.609	–	+	+	+	+	–	–	+	–	+	+	+	+	–	+	+	+	+	–	–	+	+	–
?U– Color/Non-color	+	TOT	+/TOT	AE	FR	BF	ND	GG	SW	FF	YC	CS	MS	IT	YS	GK	TK	LA	IF	AD	DH	CB	MK	TH	HC	JP
COLOR/GREY	6	23	0.261	–	–	–	(+)	–	–	+	–	–	(+)	–	–	–	–	+	–	–	(+)	–	–	–	–	(+)
COLOR/WHITE	9	23	0.391	–	–	–	–	–	+	+	–	–	0	–	–	–	–	+	–	–	–	(+)	–	–	–	–
COLOR/BLACK	3	23	0.130	–	–	–	–	–	–	–	–	–	0	–	–	–	–	0	–	–	0	–	–	0	0	0

than any other sense, this pattern of Universals seems entirely reasonable. It is in the daylight that humans generally feel safer, are more active, and are more "aware" of the environment (hence Brightness more *familiar*); at night, in the Darkness, the environment becomes more threatening, but it is also the time of sleep (hence the +P and high CI, but also low A).

An extensive literature on color preferences and connotations is quite consistent with these data. With color words as stimuli, Williams (1964), using a form of SD and college students (Caucasians from the South and Midwest and Negroes from the South) as subjects, found WHITE most +E and BLACK and GREY most −E. Winick (1963) interviewed or sent questionnaires to people from 57 different countries (UN representatives, members of consulates, students in the U.S., and so forth) and asked them to note the most "disapproved" (tabu) colors; he reports BLACK as the most disapproved (33 of 57 countries) and WHITE as one of the least (only 6 of 57) — but GREY was hardly ever mentioned (lack of salience as a "color"?). Tatibana (1937) had more than 300 Japanese subjects assign "from memory" colors to binary adjective scales; with respect to Brightness, WHITE was *light* and BLACK *heavy* (for JP we find WHITE rank 8 and BLACK rank 1 on Potency).

As far as Hue is concerned, it has commonly been found in color synesthesia studies (see, for example, Hevner, 1935; Odbert, Karwoski, and Eckerson, 1942) that the red end of the spectrum connotes more Activity than the blue end. This is generally supported in our Universals here: the mean ranks on A for RED and YELLOW are 2.4 and 3.8 whereas those for BLUE and GREEN are 4.3 and 4.9 (although only RED has a significantly high rank); in the componential analysis both tests go in the expected direction (red end +A), but only one of them (RED/BLUE) is significant. On the other hand, it is the blue end that tends to be universally more positive in Evaluation; only BLUE reaches significance in mean rank, but both componential tests show only six deviations. The association of reds and yellows with fire and warmth, particularly for primitive men, is clear enough — and it will be recalled that in factor analysis of SD data the *hot-cold* scale typically loads on the Activity factor. It might be noted that RED also has a high Potency rank. On the other hand, the blues and greens are clearly associated with life-giving water (and many pleasures therein) and the fertility of growing things (and the nourishment provided) — apparently not for our most northern Finns, however.

The literature clearly supports the relation of Hue to affective Activity, along with the higher E of the blue end. First, for color words: Williams's (1964) Caucasian and black AE subjects agree on the high E of BLUE; in Winick's (1963) interview study, BLUE yielded the lowest "disapproval" rate (only 4 of 57 countries, and he notes that these were "national" colors, not to be worn, etc.). Tatibana's (1937) JP subjects found the red end of the spectrum *lively, warm,* and *excitant* but the blue end *lonely, cool,* and *calm.*

Aaronson (1964) reports that under posthypnotic suggestion, the world will be seen in tones of various colors; an "activation" series is observed from red the most activating to blue the most calming.

We find that the naturally saturated colors (here, RED and BLUE) have higher ranks on Potency than naturally desaturated colors (YELLOW and GREEN, as well as WHITE and GREY), but the componential test is significant only for the RED/YELLOW contrast. This component produces no other universal trends, but it must be kept in mind that we are dealing with color words, not color experiences. The literature also contains less information about this component. In studies on the use of colors on advertised products and abstract statues (Osgood, Suci, and Tannenbaum, 1957, pp. 299-302), more saturated colors consistently produced high P judgments. Also using color perceptions, Collins (1924) and Ross (1938, with effects of stage lighting) found +Saturation to increase felt Potency. Wright and Rainwater (1962) found +Saturation colors to load on "forcefulness" and also on "showiness" (which may be due more to our Color/Non-color feature than to Saturation per se); Oyama, Tanaka, and Haga (1963) also report positive correlation between Saturation and the Potency factor. The only data on words as stimuli (and this is a "memory"-of-feeling task) were reported by Tatibana (1937), and his subjects recalled yellows and greens (relatively desaturated colors) as *light* (as opposed to *heavy*) more often than reds and blues.

Our Color/Non-color componential tests are suspect because COLOR (vs. GREY and BLACK-WHITE) was the only left-hand term. Within this limitation, we find that +Color is more E, more A, and less CI than ⁻Color, all of which seems intuitively reasonable. There is little relevant information to be found in the literature. If we interpret +Saturation when applied to +Color as representing "colorfulness" rather than mere saturation (e.g., a rich green vs. a pale greyish green), then according to Wright and Rainwater's (1962) summary of the prior literature, +Saturation (+Color) is preferred to ⁻Saturation (⁻Color) in 17 studies, mainly with actual colors, and this is confirmed for AE and JP subjects by Child and Iwao (1969). Guilford (1934) also notes that the "primaries" (our +Color?) are preferred to "in-between hues."[15]

Sub-universals. For the *Western European* group, an interpretation of many of their deviations in ranks in terms of climate was suggested — e.g., the low E and A of WHITE and the high CI for BLUE. The same interpretation may hold for some of their componential deviations, for example, the higher P of BLUE than GREEN and the higher CI of WHITE than BLACK (at

[15] In this connection, when we check the mean cross-cultural ranks for the four +Color concepts other than COLOR itself (RED, YELLOW, BLUE, GREEN) and compare them with those for the three ⁻Color concepts (BLACK, GREY, WHITE), we find that the former are all higher on E, A, and FAM than the latter (except WHITE) but not on P and CI.

least for ND and GG). The higher FAM of RED as compared with BLUE for BF, ND, and GG was interpreted by our colleagues as probably due to the association of RED with love and sanguinity as against the pejorative uses of BLUE, meaning "tipsy" (GG) and "black-eye" (BF) — thus a kind of "denial" rating on FAM by the teen-age subjects ("I'm not familiar with BLUE"!).

The *Scandinavian* group also showed clear effects of their northern climate upon ranks of color terms — the high E and low CI for YELLOW, for example. The same effects appear in the componential tests: YELLOW (sunlight?) more E than both GREEN and RED, Darks more Familiar than Brights (which is factually true in terms of sunlight hours per day through the year), and their agreement (along with GG) among themselves more on the meaning of BLACK (less CI) than on the meaning of WHITE or GREY. Our Finnish and Swedish colleagues supported the above in their comments.

The low Activity rank of COLOR for our *Latin American* communities has already been noted, and in the componential tests we find that COLOR is less A than WHITE or BLACK (double test). Our Mexican colleagues did emphasize the use of brilliant, saturated colors in painting houses and in indigenous art, along with a dislike of pale colors, and this might have something to do with the low Activity of COLOR (desensitization?) and the low FAM of pale YELLOW and WHITE.

In contrast to the Scandinavians and Latin Americans, *West Asians* (TK, LA, IF, AD) have low E ranks and high CI for YELLOW; on componentials, low A is also attributed to YELLOW (except LA) as compared with GREEN. IF and AD colleagues report that yellow is the color of illness, cowardice, and fear. Both LA and IF go against the grain in having high CI rank for COLOR and more CI for COLOR than for GREY: informants pointed out that COLOR refers to many different things, whereas GREY is just lack of color (emptiness, unimportance).[16] The low A rank for WHITE (except TK) might reflect the fact that it symbolizes peace as well as lack of color, according to our Iranian colleagues.

For all *Indian* groups, translations of COLOR also included the sense of "paint," and the term therefore does not arouse any strong emotional feeling, according to our group-meeting participants. WHITE, however, for CB and MK (not DH) has unusually high rank on Potency and CI, and it is associated with purity and cleanliness generally. DH and MK (not CB) agree on a high E rank for YELLOW, while CB and MK (not DH) have a low A rank for this color; yellow was said to be an auspicious color for DH and MK (widows are not entitled to wear it, for example), whereas for CB the auspicious color is red.

---

[16] This may illustrate a point we kept making at the group meetings — that if an "explanation" really would apply equally well to all cultures, then it is not a sufficient explanation for their deviations from the norm.

The three *East Asian* groups (TH, HC, and JP) agree with each other on the high FAM of WHITE and also agree within their cultures (low CI) on this concept. WHITE is associated with purity by the Thai, with funerals and purity by the Hong Kong Chinese, and with virginity and purity, as well as with death, by the Japanese. It was suggested by our informants that WHITE is associated with respectability (white shirts for businessmen and faculty, white shirts and blouses required for school children) by all three groups.

In the ranks and componential tests, there are occasionally more massive, multigroup Sub-universals. In the case of Color there is a West/East split on the Familiarity of YELLOW vs. GREEN, all Western communities (except AE, FR, and GG) finding YELLOW more FAM and all Eastern communities (the break being between IT and YS) finding GREEN more FAM (except IF). Similarly, on the COLOR/WHITE-BLACK "double test" for Familiarity (with a dividing point again between IT and YS) COLOR tends to be more FAM in the West (except BF and GG) and BLACK-WHITE more FAM in the East (except IF and MK). This last result is actually due primarily to a relatively high FAM of WHITE with respect to COLOR in the East, producing zeroes rather than pluses in the double test.

CROSS-CULTURAL DISTANCES IN MEANINGS OF THE SAME CONCEPTS

This data format is a sample from the (never computed) matrix of affective distances of all concepts in a category from all others, both within and between communities. For each concept category the complete interconcept distance matrix would be computed by the formula

$$_{pq}D_{jk} = \left[\sum_{i}^{3} (_{p}X_{ij} - {_{q}}X_{ik})^2 \right]^{1/2}$$

p,q = communities
X_i = dimensions (E-P-A)
j,k = concepts

Even for a small 8-concept category like Colors, the total matrix would include 16,836 D entries. As shown in Figure 6:2, for this format we select from each bicultural matrix (AE/FR, AE/BF ... AE/JP ... HC/JP) the *diagonal* entries which represent the affective distance between them for the same concepts.[17] About these distances we can ask such questions as: People in which pairs of cultures should communicate easily and accurately about their feelings about (here) colors? People in which pairs of cultures should

[17] That is, the affective distances between the concepts COLOR, BLACK, GREY, RED, etc. for AE vs. FR, YS vs. HC, and so forth. We assume that distances between AE-RED and YC-BLACK, BF-BLUE and JP-GREEN, etc. would be impossible to interpret in any case — unless, of course, one wanted to know what *other* color for the Delhi Hindi is affectively most like the color BLUE for the Iranians!

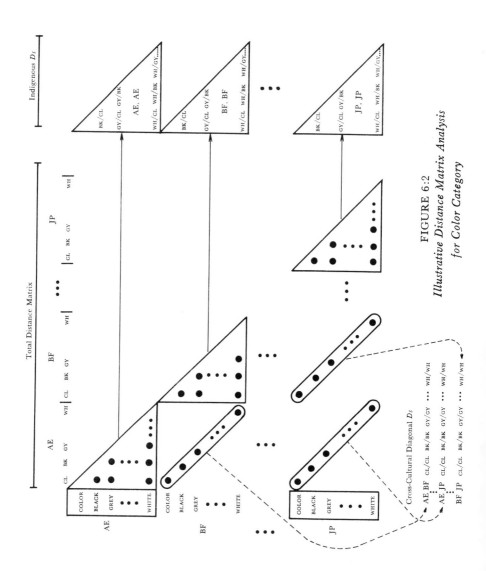

FIGURE 6:2

Illustrative Distance Matrix Analysis
for Color Category

experience difficulty (miscommunicate) in expressing their feelings about colors? Are there certain concepts about which all cultures agree in their feeling-tones? Are there certain cultures whose meanings of particular concepts (colors) are deviant from all others?[18] In the last case we shall also be interested in "why" — that is, on which affective dimensions does the deviancy appear?

Table 6:7 offers just the AE sample of these intercultural distances along with the mean distances over all 253 culture pairs on each concept. The criterion for Universals here was that the mean intercultural D be less than 1.00 and all $D >$ one sigma be accounted for by less than six communities (i.e., the same .01 level as used for ranks and componentials). In the case of Colors GREEN nearly meets this criterion for Universal agreement in meaning, exceptions being only FR, SW, TK, IF, TH, and possibly LA — and it is almost universally E-Z .4 (slightly Good), P-Z —.5 (slightly Weak), and A-Z —.3 (slightly Passive). The criterion for Sub-universals (pairs of cultures having significantly high or low agreement on affect) was that a pair of cultures display distance values less than the mean D (+∅) or more than the mean D (-∅) for *all* concepts (one value on the mean was allowed). The reader will note that, again, the computer aids the staff in making these judgments by marking those Ds which are one sigma above (—) or below (+) the mean D for each concept. The criterion for Uniquenesses ("sore thumbs") was that for a given concept a community have distances greater than the mean D from all other communities (again we allow cases that are equal to the mean) — and we record the reasons in terms of standardized E, P, and A scores.

Sub-universals. As noted in Table 6:7, AE has color feeling-tones much like CS (and nearly meets the criterion with IF), and one would anticipate ease of communication. Elsewhere in the total table (not reproduced) we find that both the Dutch and the Germans relate to the Swedes as far as color meanings are concerned. The Greeks appear as a focus of shared color feelings — with the Turks, the Iranians, the Afghans, the Bengali, and the Mysoreans as well as the Costa Ricans. Looking at the reverse side of this coin — marked differences in feeling-tone for colors and hence predicted difficulties in communication — we find problems for Americans vis-à-vis both Finns and Thai. The Thailand teen-agers also differ significantly from the Swedes, the Costa Ricans, the Italians, the Iranians, and the Hong Kong Chinese. The Finns also differ significantly from the Yugoslavs, the Iranians, and the Bengali.

Uniquenesses. As would be expected from the above, the Thai have many unique color meanings, in fact for all except GREEN and GREY. The concepts

---

[18] We refer to these Uniquenesses as "sore thumbs" — big, purple, swollen appendages that stand out in the mind of the perceiver!

TABLE 6:7

Intercultural Distances for AE on Meanings of Colors

	Color	Black	Grey	Red	Yellow	Blue	U+? Green	White	
AE FR	1.6	2.9−	1.7	1.2	1.5	1.0	1.5−	1.5	
AE BF	0.2+	2.5	1.4	1.7−	1.3	0.5+	0.6	0.6+	
AE ND	1.0	2.1	1.3	1.6	0.8	0.4+	0.8	0.3+	
AE GG	0.6	1.4	1.2	0.8	1.3	0.6	1.2	0.3+	
AE SW	0.2+	1.7	1.2	1.2	1.7	0.5+	1.0	0.9	
AE FF	1.9−	3.2−	2.2−	1.4	2.7−	1.4	1.0	1.6	₩−
AE YC	1.1	2.6	2.7−	0.5+	1.7	1.0	1.3	1.8	
AE CS	0.4+	1.3	0.4+	1.2	1.3	0.4+	0.8	0.6+	₩+
AE MS	0.6	1.8	1.4	0.8	1.1	1.5	1.1	1.0	
AE IT	0.5+	1.1	1.3	1.0	2.1−	0.7	0.9	1.2	
AE YS	2.0−	1.8	1.7	0.5+	1.2	0.6	0.3+	0.9	
AE GK	0.8	1.8	1.5	0.5+	1.1	0.9	1.2	1.2	
AE TK	1.3	2.2	2.1−	0.8	1.5	1.4	1.6−	1.8	
AE LA	1.6	0.5+	3.2−	1.0	2.2−	1.7−	2.1−	2.1	
AE IF	0.4+	1.3	0.7	0.5+	0.6+	0.5+	1.1	0.2+	₩+?
AE AD	0.3+	0.4+	2.4−	0.7	0.9	0.4+	0.9	0.8	
AE DH	1.0	1.3	2.8−	0.4+	2.1−	1.0	0.8	1.7	
AE CB	0.8	1.0	1.4	0.5+	1.0	0.7	1.1	1.3	
AE MK	1.2	0.9	2.6−	1.0	1.1	1.0	0.8	1.3	
AE TH	2.5−	3.8−	2.5−	1.7−	3.0−	2.6−	2.0−	3.3−	₩−
AE HC	1.0	1.3	0.9	1.7−	1.2	0.5	0.6	2.1−	
AE JP	1.2	2.8−	1.6	2.0−	2.6−	0.7	1.1	1.5	
Means	1.14	1.85	1.26	1.16	1.34	1.11	0.95	1.38	
S Dev	0.57	0.92	0.63	0.52	0.66	0.56	0.41	0.73	

COLOR, BLUE, YELLOW, and WHITE are unusually ⁻P and ⁺A, while the concept RED is unusually ⁻E and ⁺P. RED is associated with both communism and blood by the Thai (but, of course, by others also); YELLOW suggests both gold and the robes worn by the monks; BLUE is "a weak color for the Thais — sky-blue, with the properties of light, young, and pale"; and WHITE "is thought to have the properties of being thin, soft, pale, and dilute" — hence, given the pancultural scales, simultaneously Weak but Active. Another example of "sore thumbs" is the Belgians on RED (⁺E, ⁺P, and ⁺A), and there seems to be no particular reason except the association with sanguinity. The Yucatan Mayans are unique in their meaning of BLACK (very high E and quite high A); "in the mythological sense, for the Mayans 'everything happens at night.'" The Mexico City teen-agers have a "sore thumb" for BLUE (⁺E and very ⁺P), and we have our colleagues' comment that this color term is also used to refer to both the police and to 50-peso bills! The Delhi Hindi-speakers seem to have a "thing" about BLACK (unusually ⁻P and ⁺A), and our informants tell us that black is associated with Krishna and hair (hence high A) but also with a felt inferiority of race, black skins being associated with Indians generally, particularly the more southern groups, as contrasted with the (British) white skins.

INTRACULTURAL DISTANCES AMONG THE CONCEPTS IN THE CATEGORY

This data format is a different sampling from the total matrix of inter-concept distances among all communities. Referring back to Figure 6:2, it will be seen that, given the layout of the total matrix in terms of com-munities, the indigenous submatrices from AE to JP (AE-COLOR/AE-BLACK, AE-COLOR/AE-GREY . . . AE-GREEN/AE-WHITE . . . JP-COLOR/JP-BLACK . . . JP-GREEN/JP-WHITE) form triangles along the main diagonal of the total matrix. These submatrices for each community are extracted and printed out; Table 6:8 presents a sample of these indigenous matrices — for the means of all communities, for AE, and for one of each of the subgroups (BF, FF, MS, YS, AD, MK, and TH). The mean interconcept distance for each community, along with the standard deviation of the mean, is also given.

Since these distances are based upon the three factor composite scores, they will necessarily plot in a three-dimensional space, and we sometimes construct models of colored balls and sticks to illustrate similarities or dif-ferences. Figure 6:3 shows such models (in black and white) for (A) Yuca-tan and (B) Hong Kong, which happen to have a near-zero correlation for their distance matrices. These figures also give the E, P, and A reference axes. We may observe, first, the much greater dispersion (mean D) of color concepts for HC as compared with YC. Also notable is the absence of any negative E colors for YC (GREY, BLACK, and YELLOW are all $^-$E for HC). RED is "normally" polarized toward $^+$A for HC but is near "affective mean-inglessness" (origin of the space) for YC; COLOR is close to WHITE and $^+$E and $^+$A for HC, but it is far from WHITE and rather "insipid" (Weak and Passive) for YC; BLACK, on the other hand, is Good and Dynamic for YC, but Bad and rather "insipid" for the Hong Kong Chinese. One can also represent in such models the distances among cultures for the same concept (that is, the intercultural distances discussed in the previous section). If this were done for the concept COLOR, for example, degrees of its meaningfulness (distances from the origin) would appear as concentric rings of increasing diameter. AE, SW, IT, IF, AD, DH, and JP would be tightly clustered about the origin (affectively quite neutral meanings of COLOR), somewhat further out would be FR, GG, YC, TK, LA, CB, and HC, and furthest out (most intensely meaningful) would be FF (COLOR very Strong and Active) and TH (COLOR very Weak and Active).

Even casual inspection of the D matrices in Table 6:8 will reveal many differences. For example, the COLOR/BLACK D is extremely great for both FF and TH (and presumably for different reasons) as compared with other groups, and the values are even greater than one might expect from their

TABLE 6:8

Mean and Indigenous Distance Matrices for Eight Communities

$\overline{CC}$ Means — Mean D = 1.6

	COLOR	BLACK	GREY	RED	YELLOW	BLUE	GREEN	WHITE
COLOR	0.0							
BLACK	2.7	0.0						
GREY	1.9	1.7	0.0					
RED	1.2	2.4	2.2	0.0				
YELLOW	1.1	2.5	1.5	1.6	0.0			
BLUE	0.8	2.4	1.7	1.3	1.2	0.0		
GREEN	0.9	2.3	1.5	1.3	1.2	0.7	0.0	
WHITE	1.1	2.6	1.7	1.7	1.0	1.0	1.0	0.0

AE — D Deviation = 0.72

	COLOR	BLACK	GREY	RED	YELLOW	BLUE	GREEN	WHITE
COLOR	0.0							
BLACK	1.9	0.0						
GREY	2.9	2.4	0.0					
RED	0.4	1.8	3.1	0.0				
YELLOW	1.8	1.6	1.4	2.0	0.0			
BLUE	0.3	1.7	2.6	0.6	1.6	0.0		
GREEN	0.8	1.7	2.2	1.0	1.3	0.5	0.0	
WHITE	1.5	1.9	1.9	1.8	0.6	1.4	1.3	0.0

BF — Mean D = 1.8, D Deviation = 0.83

	COLOR	BLACK	GREY	RED	YELLOW	BLUE	GREEN	WHITE
COLOR	0.0							
BLACK	2.3	0.0						
GREY	2.0	2.4	0.0					
RED	2.0	3.1	3.5	0.0				
YELLOW	1.0	2.5	1.3	2.3	0.0			
BLUE	0.6	2.0	1.8	2.5	1.3	0.0		
GREEN	0.7	2.0	1.8	2.6	1.3	0.1	0.0	
WHITE	1.0	2.9	1.6	2.8	1.0	1.1	1.1	0.0

FF — Mean D = 2.5, D Deviation = 1.62

	COLOR	BLACK	GREY	RED	YELLOW	BLUE	GREEN	WHITE
COLOR	0.0							
BLACK	5.1	0.0						
GREY	3.9	1.6	0.0					
RED	0.4	4.8	3.5	0.0				
YELLOW	1.1	5.8	4.3	1.3	0.0			
BLUE	0.8	4.4	3.1	0.4	1.6	0.0		
GREEN	1.9	3.2	2.0	1.5	2.6	1.2	0.0	
WHITE	1.0	5.1	3.7	1.0	0.8	1.1	2.0	0.0

MS — Mean D = 1.5, D Deviation = 0.63

	COLOR	BLACK	GREY	RED	YELLOW	BLUE	GREEN	WHITE
COLOR	0.0							
BLACK	1.9	0.0						
GREY	1.5	1.2	0.0					
RED	1.5	2.0	2.1	0.0				
YELLOW	0.8	2.2	1.4	1.7	0.0			
BLUE	1.6	2.5	2.8	1.3	2.2	0.0		
GREEN	0.6	1.9	1.4	1.1	0.6	1.7	0.0	
WHITE	0.7	1.9	1.3	1.3	0.4	2.0	0.3	0.0

TABLE 6:8 (Continued)

YS D Deviation = 0.83 Mean D = 1.8

	COLOR	BLACK	GREY	RED	YELLOW	BLUE	GREEN	WHITE
COLOR	0.0							
BLACK	4.2	0.0						
GREY	3.1	1.5	0.0					
RED	2.2	2.2	1.7	0.0				
YELLOW	2.3	2.2	0.8	1.3	0.0			
BLUE	2.0	2.8	2.0	0.9	1.6	0.0		
GREEN	2.7	2.0	1.3	0.9	1.3	0.9	0.0	
WHITE	2.2	2.3	1.1	1.1	0.6	1.1	0.8	0.0

MK D Deviation = 0.35 Mean D = 0.9

	COLOR	BLACK	GREY	RED	YELLOW	BLUE	GREEN	WHITE
COLOR	0.0							
BLACK	1.7	0.0						
GREY	1.1	1.2	0.0					
RED	0.7	1.1	0.7	0.0				
YELLOW	0.8	1.8	1.2	1.1	0.0			
BLUE	0.8	1.0	0.5	0.5	0.9	0.0		
GREEN	0.8	1.0	1.0	0.6	0.9	0.5	0.0	
WHITE	0.6	1.4	1.3	0.7	0.9	0.6	0.3	0.0

AD D Deviation = 0.44 Mean D = 0.9

	COLOR	BLACK	GREY	RED	YELLOW	BLUE	GREEN	WHITE
COLOR	0.0							
BLACK	1.7	0.0						
GREY	0.6	1.1	0.0					
RED	0.5	1.3	0.4	0.0				
YELLOW	1.0	0.7	0.5	0.8	0.0			
BLUE	0.2	1.6	0.5	0.5	0.9	0.0		
GREEN	0.4	2.0	0.9	0.9	1.3	0.4	0.0	
WHITE	0.7	1.6	0.6	0.9	0.9	0.6	0.7	0.0

TH D Deviation = 1.98 Mean D = 2.9

	COLOR	BLACK	GREY	RED	YELLOW	BLUE	GREEN	WHITE
COLOR	0.0							
BLACK	6.2	0.0						
GREY	2.3	4.0	0.0					
RED	3.6	2.9	2.0	0.0				
YELLOW	0.6	6.5	2.6	4.0	0.0			
BLUE	0.5	6.1	2.1	3.7	0.4	0.0		
GREEN	1.1	5.2	1.3	2.8	1.4	1.0	0.0	
WHITE	1.0	7.1	3.2	4.5	0.7	1.1	2.0	0.0

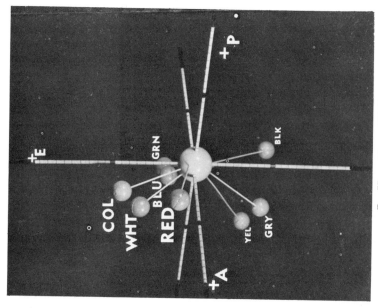

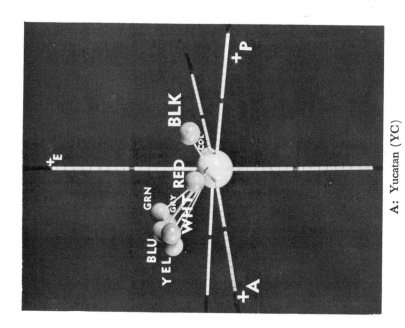

A: Yucatan (YC)	B: Hong Kong (HC)

FIGURE 6:3

Indigenous Inter-Concept Distance (IID) Models of Color Concepts
for (A) Yucatan and (B) Hong Kong

large mean *D*s. BLACK is surprisingly close to YELLOW for AD; indeed, AD is the only place where BLACK is closer to YELLOW than WHITE. For all communities except FF and MS, the RED/YELLOW *D* is much larger than the BLUE/GREEN *D* (which anticipates a universal trend to be considered later, pp. 333-334). BLACK is furthest from WHITE for all communities shown except MS (and YC also, as can be seen from Figure 6:3).

About the indigenous matrices of interconcept distances we ask certain standard questions. (1) How much differentiation is made among the concepts (colors)? (2) Which (color) concepts are closest in feeling-tone and which furthest in feeling-tone for each community? (3) Which (color) concepts appear as "isolates" — that is, have distances from *all* other concepts that are greater than the mean for interconcept distances for that community? (4) In case a generic term is included in the category (here the concept COLOR itself), which of the other, specific concepts is closest to the generic? (5) Which communities display similar structures among the concepts (regardless of absolute magnitudes of distances)?

Returning to Table 6:8 with some of these questions in mind, we may note the following. As to question 1, both the Finns and the Thai show very large differentiations in their feeling-tones for different color concepts (large mean *D*s), whereas the Afghans and the Mysoreans show quite small differentiations. As to question 2, the closest concepts in affect across all 23 communities (means at top of table) are BLUE and GREEN; the furthest in affect are COLOR and BLACK (2.7) and BLACK and WHITE (2.6). The closest and furthest for AE are COLOR/BLUE and GREY/RED, for BF BLUE/GREEN (closest) and again GREY/RED (furthest), for FF COLOR/RED and RED/BLUE (closest) and BLACK/YELLOW (furthest), and the other cases can be noted by the reader. As to question 3, BLACK is an "isolate" (very different feeling-tone than all other colors) for most all of the communities shown, but not for FF, MS, YS (fairly close to GREY), and AD (close to YELLOW, both being ⁻E, ⁻P, ⁻A, and high CI); unusual isolates are RED for the Belgians and COLOR itself for the Yugoslavs. And as to question 4, the closest concept to generic COLOR for the means of all communities is BLUE, followed closely by GREEN; deviants from this norm are FF's RED and MK's WHITE. The "answers" to these standard questions for all 23 communities are presented in concise tabular form in Table 6:9.

(1) *Mean distances.* Using a mean *D* of > 1.90 as a "high" criterion, there are five cultures which differentiate greatly among colors, and these include all three of our East Asian groups, the Thai, the Hong Kong Chinese, and the Japanese; the other two high differentiators are the Dutch and particularly the Finns. Using a mean *D* of < 1.30 as a "low" criterion, there are nine cultures that differentiate relatively little among colors, and all of these with the exception of the Yucatan Mayans cluster geographically, running from the Middle East (Greeks, Turks, and Lebanese) through West Asia

TABLE 6:9

Data Extracted from Indigenous Distance Matrices for Colors

	1	2	3	4	5	6		
					CLOSEST TO	COMPONENTS INFERRED		
	MEAN	IN AFFECT			GENERIC			
	DISTANCE	CLOSEST	FURTHEST	ISOLATES	(COLOR)	FOR 2	FOR 3	FOR 5
AE	1.56	COLOR-BLUE	GREY-RED	BLACK	BLUE RED	⁺Sat. ⁺Col.	Sat. Col.	⁺Sat. ⁺Col.
FR	1.78	GREEN-WHITE	COLOR-BLACK	BLACK	GREEN WHITE	0	Brt. Col.	⁻Sat.
BF	1.81	BLUE-GREEN	GREY-RED	BLACK RED	BLUE GREEN	⁻Hue	Sat. Col.	⁻Hue ⁺Col.
ND	1.90	BLUE-GREEN YELLOW-WHITE	RED-WHITE	BLACK RED	BLUE GREEN	⁻Hue	Brt. Sat. Col.	⁻Hue ⁺Col.
GG	1.72	YELLOW-GREEN	GREY-RED	BLACK ⁺GREY	BLUE GREEN	⁻Sat.	Sat. Col.	⁻Hue ⁺Col.
SW	1.68	COLOR-YELLOW	BLACK-RED RED-WHITE	None	YELLOW BLUE	⁻Sat. ⁺Col.	Col.	⁺Col.
FF	2.47	COLOR-RED RED-BLUE	BLACK-YELLOW	None	RED BLUE	⁺Sat. ⁺Col.	Brt. Sat. Col.	⁺Sat. ⁺Col.
YC	1.14	BLUE-GREEN	COLOR-BLACK	BLACK	GREY GREEN	⁻Hue	Brt. Col.	0
CS	1.47	BLUE-GREEN	GREY-RED	GREY	BLUE GREEN	⁻Hue	Sat. Col.	⁻Hue ⁺Col.
MS	1.50	GREEN-WHITE	GREY-BLUE	None	GREEN WHITE	0	Sat. Col.	⁻Sat.
IT	1.45	COLOR-GREEN	GREY-RED	None	GREEN YELLOW	⁺Col.	Sat. Col.	⁻Sat. ⁺Col.
YS	1.75	YELLOW-WHITE	COLOR-BLACK	COLOR	BLUE tie{WHITE RED}	0	Brt. Col.	0
GK	1.12	COLOR-GREEN	BLACK-WHITE	BLACK	GREEN RED	⁺Col.	Brt.	⁺Col.
TK	1.22	COLOR-WHITE	BLACK-WHITE	BLACK	WHITE GREEN	⁺Brt.	Brt.	⁻Sat.
LA	1.26	BLUE-GREEN	BLACK-BLUE BLACK-GREEN	BLACK	GREY BLUE	⁻Hue	Brt. Col.	0

TABLE 6:9 (Continued)

| | 1 | 2 | 3 | 4 | 5 | 6 | | |
| | Mean Distance | In Affect | | Isolates | Closest to Generic (Color) | Components Inferred | | |
		Closest	Furthest			For 2	For 3	For 5
IF	1.27	COLOR-BLUE GREY-YELLOW	GREY-RED	None	BLUE RED	+Col.	Sat. Col.	+Sat. +Col.
AD	0.87	COLOR-BLUE	BLACK-GREEN	None	BLUE GREEN	+Sat. +Col.	Brt. Sat. Col.	−Hue +Col.
DH	1.11	4 ties, 0.4	3 ties, 2.3 All with BLACK	BLACK	BLUE GREY			0
CB	1.15	YELLOW-BLUE	BLACK-GREEN	BLACK	BLUE YELLOW	+Col.	Brt. Sat. Col.	+Col.
MK	0.95	4 ties, 0.5	BLACK-YELLOW	BLACK	WHITE RED		Brt. Sat. Col.	0
TH	2.85	YELLOW-BLUE	BLACK-WHITE	BLACK	BLUE YELLOW	+Col.	Brt.	+Col.
HC	1.92	COLOR-WHITE	GREY-RED	None	WHITE(0.2) BLUE(1.2)	+Brt.	Sat. Col.	+Brt.
JP	2.42	BLUE-GREEN	BLACK-YELLOW	None	BLUE GREEN	−Hue	Brt. Sat. Col.	−Hue +Col.

(Iranians and Afghans), into India (Hindi, Bengali, and Kannada speakers). The only commentary from either high or low differentiators[19] was, for the Indian groups, that "boys in these regions don't have to deal with colors as much as girls do," and, from one of our West Asian participants, that "by and large, there is no great cultural attention given to color *diversity* in carpets, clothing, homes and etc.; rather, there is more attention given to shades of color and/or color relationships, and thus the low differentiation is in keeping with social practices."[20]

(2) *Closest and furthest in affect.* As can be seen by scanning column 2 of this table, there is great variety in the concepts which are paired as closest

[19] It is our experience that questions of this sort (not related to specific concepts) are the most mind-boggling, despite their often intriguing nature — as here.

[20] See Table 5:10, p. 219, for apparent confirmation where *colorful-colorless* pairs with *badly colored-well colored* for IF.

in their E-P-A profiles. However, looking under 2 in the last set of columns under "Components Inferred," it becomes clear that closeness in feeling is *not* a random matter. There are nine communities where ⁺Color coding is shared by the concepts but none where ⁻Color is shared (that is, no closest pairings among WHITE, GREY, and BLACK. There are six additional communities where shared ⁻Hue seems to be the basis (i.e., BLUE with GREEN) but none where ⁺Hue is shared (no cases of RED with YELLOW). There are a number of other combinations, as well as three marked "0," where *no* components are shared and particular cultural associations may be operating (e.g., the colors combined in national flags). As a kind of Universal, then, we can say that Colors tend to be differentiated from Non-colors and seem more similar among themselves than do Non-colors, and that the blue end of the spectrum is less differentiated than the red. Hogg (1969) reports that combinations of reds with yellows are rated more *usual* and *obvious,* whereas combinations of blues with greens are rated more *unusual* and *subtle.* Further confirmatory evidence (particularly from Berlin and Kay, 1969) will be presented in the last section of this chapter.

The pattern of pairings that are furthest in affect (see column 3) are consistent with this generalization, except that now we look for those components on which the concept pairs have *opposed* signs. For 19 of the 23 communities, contrast on the Color feature (RED/GREY, RED/WHITE, YELLOW/BLACK, COLOR/BLACK, etc.) would account for the affective remoteness; ±Saturation might differentiate in 14 cases, but it is always linked with Color/Non-color; ±Brightness might differentiate 13 times, but 10 of these are linked with Color/Non-color (the other three are all BLACK vs. WHITE); and Hue never appears as the basis — that is, RED, YELLOW, BLUE, and GREEN are never opposed to each other as the most remote in feeling-tone. These facts are also entirely consistent with the Universal suggested above; ⁺Color is sharply differentiated from ⁻Color in affect, and the ⁺Colors are never maximally contrastive in affect.

(3) *Isolates.* Eliminating the eight communities where no color concept could be called an isolate (that is, at least one distance to another concept would be below the mean distance) — and these, incidentally, are interesting doublets (SW+FF, MS+IT, IF+AD, and HC+JP) — all remaining communities have BLACK (12) or GREY (1) or both (1) as isolates by this criterion. The only ⁺Color concept that appears is RED, twice along with BLACK (and, again interestingly, these two communities are BF and ND); the high P, A, and CI of RED for the BF and ND (love, sanguinity, and political leftists) have already been noted. As to the reason for isolation of BLACK and GREY, it will be recalled that both had Universal low ranks on E, on A, and on rated FAM, and no ⁺Color concepts shared such ranks. We have no information from our colleagues on the "doublets" mentioned above. However, looking into the indigenous matrices, it is apparent that in most

of these cases BLACK is close to GREY, but they cannot be treated as joint iso-
lates because GREY in turn is close to other concepts (usually the ⁻Saturation
colors). For IF and AD the reason is different — quite similar feelings about
BLACK and BLUE for the former and about BLACK and YELLOW for the latter.
HC just has a unique color system, with WHITE closest to COLOR and both
BLACK and GREY close to YELLOW.

(4) *Closest to generic* COLOR. It will be seen that in column 5 of Table 6:9
we have listed in order the two concepts closest in affect to COLOR for each
community and then (under 5 in column 6) have looked for their shared
components. But first we record the sheer frequencies of being closest or
next closest to COLOR: BLUE 15, GREEN 12, RED 6, WHITE 6, YELLOW 4, GREY
3, and BLACK 0. Certain pairings of the two closest seldom or never occur —
only three YELLOW-BLUE (SW, colors of national flag, CB, and TH), only
one YELLOW-GREEN (IT), and no cases of YELLOW-RED, YELLOW-WHITE,
RED-GREY, or any combinations of WHITE-GREY-BLACK. Again Color/Non-
color is the main determining component, with the two terms closest to
COLOR sharing ⁺Color for 14 communities and none sharing ⁻Color; when
Hue is shared along with Color (6 communities), it is always ⁻Hue (always
BLUE-GREEN and never RED-YELLOW) ; either ⁺Saturation (RED-BLUE, 3 cases)
or ⁻Saturation (YELLOW-GREEN or WHITE-GREEN, 4 cases) may be shared
along with ⁺Color. There is one case where ⁻Saturation alone seems to be
responsible (GREEN-WHITE for FR) and one case of ⁺Brightness alone (WHITE
for HC, $D = .2$, where the next closest to COLOR is BLUE, but with $D = 1.2$).
The generalization here seems to be that closeness in affect to COLOR is a
function of sharing the semantic-feature codings of COLOR (⁺Color and
±Saturation) — which is certainly reasonable — except that, although Color
is ± on Hue also, relatively undifferentiated BLUE-GREEN again appear together but not more differentiated RED-YELLOW.

(5) *Intercommunity correlations of indigenous distance matrices.* Answers
to this last standard question involve computing the matrix of correlations
among the indigenous matrices of interconcept distances for all pairs of
communities. Correlations are taken over the corresponding cells of these
matrices; e.g., referring to Table 6:8: AE-COLOR/BLACK with YS-COLOR/
BLACK (1.9 vs. 4.2), AE-COLOR/GREY with YS-GREEN/WHITE (1.3 vs. .8),
etc., for the AE/YS correlation. Each r in this matrix indicates how similar the conceptual *structures* are — which concepts are relatively remote,
which form tight clusters, etc. — for given pairs of communities, regardless
of the absolute magnitudes of distances (either large or small mean Ds).

We will not reproduce the entire matrix here, but for some of the communities illustrated in Table 6:8 the correlations are AE/YS .30, AE/BF
.53, BF/TH .64, FF/MK .74, MS/AD .13, and MK/TH .62. Nearly all
intercommunity r's are positive (the only small negatives are between CS
and LA, AD, and DH), but the mean r over all community pairs is not high

(.47) and does not reach the criterion for a potential Universal — i.e., that "all human communities share a similar affective structure for color concepts." As to Uniquenesses (here, isolates, with low *r*'s with all others) no communities meet the usual criterion, but AE and IF (except for their *r* of .79 with each other), SW, YC (except for an *r* of .73 with YS), MS, and HC approach it.

Special Tests

Nearly all categories of concepts either lend themselves to special tests (e.g., plotting of the E ranks of Months and Seasons clearly indicates differences, along with "bumps" and "dips" for school beginnings and holiday periods!) or generate special tests as a consequence of perusing their data (e.g., tabling distances of ego from the various stages of life in the Age Continuum). Many such special tests have been suggested by our colleagues during the group meetings. In the case of the Color category the possible influence upon affect attribution of the colors of national flags was suggested.

The dominant flag colors for each of our communities (e.g., black, yellow, and blue for BF; yellow and blue for SW; green, red, and white for MS; and red and white for TK and JP) were determined from an encyclopedia, and the deviations of the communities having each flag color above or below the means for all communities on E-Z, P-Z, and A-Z were recorded. There were no significant tendencies toward either positive or negative attributions of feeling by our teen-age subjects, although the pattern was for E and A to be somewhat negative for their own flag colors and for P to be somewhat positive. For GREEN and BLUE (where the number of communities having the color in their flags roughly equaled those not having it), we ran *chi*-square tests on each factor for In-flag/Not-in-flag vs. Above-mean/Below-mean, and none even approached significance. The trend for BLUE actually went against the hypothesis that our teen-age subjects were attributing Goodness, Strength, and Activity to colors that happen to be in their flags.[21]

A few illustrations of special tests run in some other concept categories may serve to bemuse — or amuse. Figure 6:4 presents data on the relative distances in affect for BOY/MAN/GIRL/WOMAN concepts in our Male/Female category. The *D* values are those between the pairs of concepts separated (e.g., .8 between GIRL/WOMAN and 2.3 between MAN/WOMAN for the cross-

[21] Of possible culturological interest are the following facts about flag colors per se. Red and white each appear in the flags of 19 of our 23 communities, green and blue for 9 and 10 flags respectively, yellow in only 4, black in only 3, and grey in none. The combination of red, white, and blue is the overwhelming favorite (11/23 communities), and blue and green are in perfect complementary distribution (that is, any flag that has blue never has green and vice versa). It appears that flags are chosen mainly for maximum visual intensity and contrast — thus saturated red and/or blue with white.

FIGURE 6:4

Age vs. Sex as Differentiators of Affect

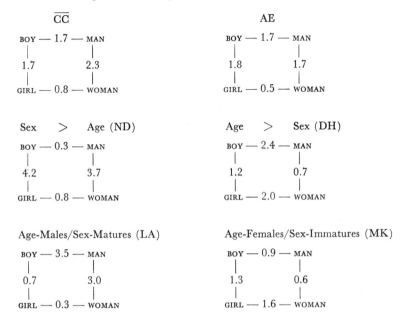

cultural means, $\overline{cc}$). Cultures display very different Sex (BOY/GIRL and MAN/WOMAN) vs. Age (BOY/MAN and GIRL/WOMAN) bases of differentiation. For the means of all cultures in our sample (top left), the Sex of Matures (MAN/WOMAN) and the Age of Males (BOY/MAN) are more significant determiners than, respectively, the Sex of Immatures (BOY/GIRL) and the Age of Females (GIRL/WOMAN)— for our teen-age male samples, of course. Americans, along with nine other communities, come close to this pancultural tendency. The Netherlands Dutch typify the Sex, but not Age, groups — including most Western Europeans (FR, BF, ND, GG, SW, and FF) and also MS, IT, GK, and IF. Age is a more important differentiator of feeling than Sex for both DH and YC but for no others in our sample. The Age of Males and the Sex of Matures as prime determiners are shown in exaggerated form by LA. The only culture in our sample for which the Age of Females and the Sex of Immatures are the most important differentiators of feeling is MK — and it might be noted that our three Indian communities, DH, CB (which is like AE), and MK, all have very different patterns.

Finally, Figure 6:5 shows the distribution of our 23 cultures on three "scales" drawn from the Social Status, Moral/Immoral, and Affiliative/Achievement categories. The "Supraordinateness Scale" shows for each community the algebraic sum of the distances from ego to each of the concepts in

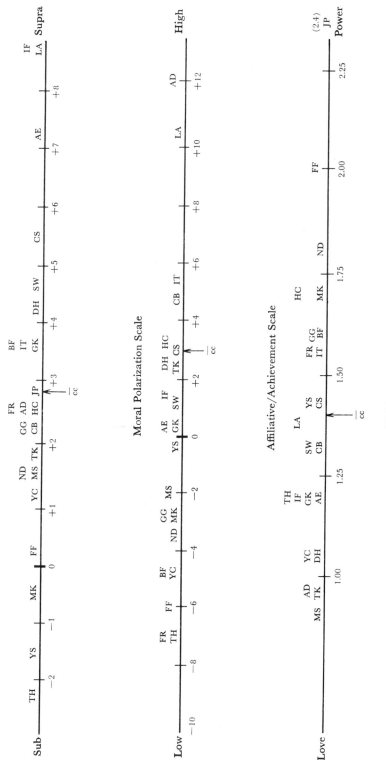

FIGURE 6:5

Three Interpersonal Relations Scales

the pairs LEADER/FOLLOWER, POLICEMAN/BEGGAR, RICH PEOPLE/POOR PEO-
PLE, and MASTER/SERVANT; it will be noted that teen-agers in most of our
groups "identify" more with Supraordinates than with Subordinates, this being most marked for Iranians, Lebanese, and Americans — with only the
Thai, Yugoslavs, and Mysoreans going more toward Subordinates. The
"Moral Polarization Scale" shows for each community the mean distances
(as deviations from the cross-cultural average) between the contrastive concept pairs CHARACTER/SIN, CHARITY/GREED, DEVOTION/ADULTERY, DISCI-
PLINE/CHEATING, DUTY/LYING, FORGIVENESS/GUILT, HONOR/GRAFT, JUSTICE/
CRIME, KINDNESS/MURDER, and MISSIONARY/PROSTITUTE. With a mean D
for all cultures of 3.29, it can be seen that the French, Thai, and Finns make
relatively small differentiations while the Lebanese and Afghans make very
great "Morality" differentiations. The "Affiliative/Achievement (or Love/
Power) Scale" shows simply the average affective distances between RE-
SPECT/POWER, FRIEND/LEADER, COOPERATION/COMPETITION, SYMPATHY/
GREED, ACCEPTING THINGS/TAKING THE INITIATIVE, FAMILY/SUCCESS, GROUP/
CHAMPION, and FRIENDSHIP/WORK. Here one notes that Mexicans, Turks,
Afghans, Mayans (YC), and Delhi Hindi are the highest on the "Love" end
of the spectrum, that Finns, Dutch, Chinese (HC), and Mysoreans are high
on the "Power" end of the spectrum, and that the Japanese are off the ex-
treme high end of the scale. Although commentaries on many of the above
findings are available, we will not consider them in this orientational chapter.

UNIVERSALS IN COLOR PREFERENCE, CONNOTATION, AND ASSOCIATION

There is an unusually rich literature on color — preferences, connotations,
associations (including symbolisms), componential differentiations, evolutionary development, and so forth — and although much of it applies mainly
to the United States, there is enough cross-cultural material to make a search
for Universals feasible. In this final section we shall summarize this literature
and relate it to what we have found to be universal trends in our own data
on affective meanings. But, first, a concise summary of our own Universals
is in order.

Looking first at ranks, the concept COLOR itself is universally positive in
Evaluation and Activity and has low CI. WHITE is characterized only as
having low Potency. BLACK and GREY are alike in having universally low
Evaluation and Activity, but they differ sharply on Potency (BLACK nearly
being ⁺P and GREY clearly being -P), and BLACK has high CI and GREY low
Familiarity. RED is universally Potent and Active, while YELLOW is Impotent
but also nearly ⁺A; BLUE has high Evaluation nearly everywhere in our

sample, but GREEN is distinguished in no way other than having the most agreed-upon affective meaning cross-culturally (near neutral).

Looking now at the results of our componential analyses, Brightness is universally more Evaluated, more Active, and more Familiar than Darkness, but Darkness has more Potency and higher intra-cultural "conflict." The blue end of the spectrum tends to be more positive in Evaluation, but the red end tends to be more Active. Saturated RED is clearly more Potent than Desaturated YELLOW (no exceptions), but Saturated BLUE and relatively Desaturated GREEN form "blocs" across our sample on Potency. +Color is universally more Evaluated, more Active, and more Familiar than −Color, but it must be kept in mind that COLOR itself was the only left-hand term used in the tests against GREY and BLACK-WHITE.

We also found +Color (RED, YELLOW, GREEN, BLUE) vs. −Color (WHITE, GREY, BLACK) to be the strongest determinant of differentiation in feeling, with relatively small differentiation within these two sets; but within the +Color set, the red Hue end (RED vs. YELLOW) is more differentiated than the blue Hue end (GREEN vs. BLUE). Our communities agree quite well on the overall Evaluation of colors (mean *r* of .72), less on their Potency (.50) and Activity (.43), and very little on their Familiarity (.32) or Cultural Instability (.26).

It should be remarked that where — as evidenced in the previous comments on Uniquenesses — we have been able to "account for" exceptions to universal trends in terms of specific cultural factors, the case for the above Universals is strengthened. Here are a few examples: if we account for AE ("cowardice") and IF and AD ("sickness"), then YELLOW being +A reaches the Universal criterion (only 4/23 exceptions); the four exceptions to BLUE being +E include FF ("ice, cold") and GK ("unsuccessful soccer team"); only DH is an exception to GREY being −E, and the term also signifies "ceremonial ashes and light skin color"; YELLOW is more Active than GREEN except where the former is associated with cowardice and sickness (AE, IF, AD) and the latter associated with fertility, youth, Islam, and the like (GK, TK, IF, AD, CB), with only three cultures remaining for whom this was a "DK" (FR, MS, MK) and hence an "unaccounted for" exception.

COLOR PREFERENCES

Our literature search uncovered a large number of studies reporting color preferences. Since the number of AE reports was much greater than that for any other community, and since color preferences have been shown to vary somewhat over time (see Walton, Guilford, and Guilford, 1933), we have omitted AE data prior to 1951. The preference ranks for 31 studies are recorded in Table 6:10, with the language/culture community of the subjects indicated by our symbols and the number of independent studies for each community indicated in parentheses. In order to make this task manageable, we have restricted our literature sample to those reporting on cultures within our *Atlas* sample. As indicated in the footnotes to Table 6:10, we have included experimental preference experiments (usually employing psychophysical methods) and commentary on relative preferences, as well as data from semantic differential studies, and we have not distinguished between the use of color words and color patches as stimuli.[22] The number and type of stimuli were quite variable, there being many more studies involving chromatic than achromatic stimuli, for example; where fewer colors were involved than our seven (omitting the concept COLOR itself) the ranks were adjusted to a scale of seven — which meant, of course, that reported contrasts (e.g., WHITE preferred to BLACK) were assigned ranks 2 and 5 respectively, and single disliked ("tabu") colors, as in Winick's (1963) report, were assigned rank 7.

Casual inspection of Table 6:10 reveals some marked clustering of preference for certain colors — for example, of WHITE in ranks 1 or 2, of GREY and BLACK in ranks 6 and 7, and of GREEN and BLUE *not* in ranks 6 and 7 — whereas others, particularly RED and YELLOW, have wide variation in preference, both within and between cultures. For direct comparison with our own mean ranks in Evaluation across 23 communities, we require some summary rank value for each color. If we take mean ranks over total studies, then consistencies across different communities are discounted; on the other hand, if we take means over number of communities represented, then consistencies across replications within the same communities are discounted. Our solution was to multiply the total number of studies reporting a given rank for a given color (i.e., the sum of the numbers in parentheses) by the number of different communities involved (i.e., the number of community symbols). What this does, in effect, is to weight number of studies by number of communities yielding the same rank — which seems eminently reasonable in a search for Universals. These weighted rank values are the italicized numbers in the cells of Table 6:10.

Table 6:11 compares the mean weighted ranks obtained from the litera-

[22] The sources contributing data to Table 6:10 were: Banerji and Mitra (1942); Basu and Basu (1949); Child, Hansen, and Hornbeck (1968); Child and Iwao (1969); Chou and Chen (1935); Choungourian (1968, 1969); Déribéré (1955); Garth, Ikeda, and Langdon (1931); Garth, Moses, and Anthony (1938); Granger (1955); Harbin and Williams (1966); Helson and Lansford (1970); Hofstätter and Lübbert (1958); Kentler (1959); Norman and Scott (1952); Osgood (1960b); Oyama *et al.* (1965); Oyama, Tanaka, and Chiba (1962); Oyama, Tanaka, and Haga (1963); Shen (1937); Tatibana (1937, 1938); Williams (1964, 1966); Williams and Carter (1967); Williams and Foley (1968); Williams and McMurtry (1970); Williams, Morland, and Underwood (1970); Winick (1963); Yoshikawa, Yagishita, and Matsuda (1970).

TABLE 6:10

Color Preferences[a]

RANK[b]	WHITE	GREY	BLACK	RED	YELLOW	GREEN	BLUE
1	AE(9)[c], GG(2), India[d](1), HC(3), JP(2) — *85[e]*			AE(2), GG(2), CB(1), JP(1) — *24*		AE(2), MS(1), LA(1), IF(1), CB(1), India(1), JP(3) — *70*	AE(5), HC(1), JP(3) — *27*
2	GG(1), MS(1), HC(1) — *3*			AE(1), India(1), HC(2) — *12*	AE(1), JP(1) — *4*	AE(5), GG(1), India(1), JP(1) — *32*	AE(8), GG(1), HC(2), JP(2) — *52*
3				GG(2), LA(1), IF(1), HC(1), JP(1) — *30*	AE(1), MS(1), HC(1), JP(1) — *16*	AE(6), GG(1), CB(1), HC(1), JP(1) — *50*	AE(1), GG(1), India(2), HC(1) — *20*
4	JP(1) — *1*		GG(1) — *1*		AE(5), GG(1), India(1), HC(2), JP(1) — *50*	GG(1), HC(2), JP(1) — *12*	AE(3), JP(1) — *8*
5	GG(1) — *1*		JP(1) — *1*	AE(7), India(1), HC(2), JP(2) — *48*	AE(2), GG(2), India(1), HC(1), JP(1) — *35*	AE(1), HC(1) — *4*	GG(1), MS(1), LA(1), IF(1), CB(1) — *25*
6	JP(1) — *1*	AE(6), India(1), HC(2) — *27*	GG(2), HC(1), JP(2) — *15*	AE(2) — *2*	AE(2), GG(1) — *6*		

TABLE 6:10 (Continued)

7	AE(1), TH(1)	GG(3), India(1), HC(1), JP(3)	AE(8), FR(1), BF(1), GG(2), MS(1), IT(1), YS(1), GK(1), IF(1), AD(1), India(2), TH(1), HC(3), JP(1)	JP(1)	AE(5), LA(1), IF(2), CB(1)	FR(1)
	2	32	350	1	36	1

[a] Includes E-factor ratings from semantic differential studies as well as color preference studies and isolated comments on the "goodness" or "badness" of particular colors. No distinction is made between experimental studies using color words and studies using actual colors, introspection, etc.

[b] When fewer colors are used in a study, ranks are adjusted to our 1 to 7 ranks. For example, a preference order RBGY is treated here as R1, B3, G5, Y7.

[c] Where more than one study yielded the same rank for a color, the number of studies is indicated in parentheses.

[d] This Indian community was not one in our sample (neither DH, CB, nor MK).

[e] The weight on a given rank is obtained by multiplying the total number of studies reporting this rank by the number of different communities in our sample represented (here $17 \times 5 = 85$).

TABLE 6:11

*Comparison of Mean Weighted Ranks of Colors in Preference in the
Literature with Mean* Atlas *Ranks on Evaluation*

	MEAN WEIGHTED RANKS (LITERATURE)[a]	MEAN *Atlas* E RANKS[b]
WHITE	1.3	2.5
GREY	6.5	5.9
BLACK	7.0	6.6
RED	3.4	4.0
YELLOW	4.9	4.0
GREEN	2.1	2.8
BLUE	2.6	2.3

[a] Means of weighted ranks (as given in Table 6:10) for each color.
[b] Mean *Atlas* ranks adjusted after elimination of the concept COLOR.

ture (i.e., Table 6:10) with the mean E ranks obtained in our own study (adjusted after omission of the concept COLOR). There are no rank inversions for achromatic colors (WHITE high, GREY low, and BLACK lowest in preference or Evaluation), and among chromatic colors BLUE and GREEN are clearly more preferred than RED and YELLOW for both sources of data. However, there are certain differences: WHITE has highest preference in the literature but is second (after BLUE) in mean E rank for our data; GREEN is slightly preferred to BLUE in the literature, but BLUE is slightly preferred to GREEN in our data; and whereas RED is definitely preferred over YELLOW in the literature, they have identical mean ranks in our SD data — which may be due to inclusion of studies using actual colors (as well as color words) in the literature sample. Nevertheless, the overall correspondence is gratifyingly high.

COLOR CONNOTATIONS

By "connotations" we mean — operationally — adjectival characterizations (e.g., *adventurous, solemn, cowardly*) and emotion-related nominal characterizations which can be readily transformed into adjectives (e.g., *valor, female, passion, anxiety, disgust*). Concrete and abstract nominals which do not reflect feeling directly will be considered later as Associations (e.g., *ceiling, lemon, sky, night*) or as Symbolisms (e.g., *Monday, The Irish, Mourning, Virginity*). One reason for this distinction was to make possible a reasonably direct comparison between the literature on affects of colors and our own E-P-A profiles — which we have for many qualifying adjectives and emotion-related nouns. Again, the literature provided many studies, but we have restricted the sample reported here to those involving our own communities — plus a few studies claiming universal, regional, or religious connotations on what appeared to be sufficient scholarship. The total number of sources used was 37.[23]

The first step was preparation of a large master-table listing, for each affective adjective or noun reported, the color(s) assigned in various communities and in what number of studies. Then each of the words in the master table was coded (+, 0, −) on E, P, and A, either from the loadings in our pancultural factor analysis (adjectives), or from the E-Z, P-Z, A-Z cross-cultural means of *Atlas* concepts (nouns) where available, or by judgments of our Center staff. Connotations for which we had no SD data and which involved only one study in one community were eliminated (unless they seemed to provide some unusual information). Approximately 175 connotative terms are involved in the final analysis. All terms having identical affective codings (e.g., ^{0}E, $^-$P, $^-$A) were collected together, and the total weighted scores (number of studies times number of different communities) for all terms in each set were computed.[24]

Table 6:12 presents these data. We have ordered the colors in terms of their weighted values within each of the 27 sectors of the affective space (all combinations of three factors with three codings on each); thus RED is rank 1 (value, *296*) on $^+$E, $^+$P, $^+$A, rank 2.5 (value, *4*) on ^{0}E, ^{0}P, ^{0}A, and rank 6, along with GREEN and YELLOW (value, *0*), on $^-$E, $^-$P, $^-$A. Connotations (terms reported in the studies sampled) are also given in the same sectors of the space.[25] The reader can judge the affective similarity of the terms in each sector for himself. Again, studies using either color words or color patches were included.

Immediately apparent from the table is the salience of RED, which has a

---

[23] The 37 sources were: Aaronson (1970, 1971); Birren (1969); Cerbus and Nichols (1963); Déribéré (1955); Harbin and Williams (1966); Hevner (1935); Hofstätter and Lübbert (1958); Hofstätter and Primac (1957); Jacobs and Jacobs (1958); Kimura (1950); Kouwer (1949); Luckiesh (1923); Murray and Deabler (1957); Norman and Scott (1952); Obonai and Matsuoka (1956); Osgood (1960b); Oyama *et al.* (1965); Oyama, Tanaka, and Chiba (1962); Oyama, Tanaka, and Haga (1963); Pečjak (1970); Schaie (1961); Shen (1937); Tanaka, Oyama, and Osgood (1963); Tatibana (1937, 1938); Van der Werff and Seinen (1968); Wexner (1954); Wheeler (1969); Williams (1964, 1966); Williams and Carter (1967); Williams and Foley (1968); Williams and McMurtry (1970); Williams, Morland, and Underwood (1970); Winick (1963); Wright and Rainwater (1962).

[24] A study dealing with two or more communities (e.g., Pečjak, 1970) was treated as if a separate study had been made for each community. When a study associated a group of words (e.g., *happy, gay, cheerful*) with a single color, each word of the group was counted separately. This lack of independence made it impossible to use probability statistics in the following analysis.

[25] All terms are shown in the table for set sizes less than eight. Unlisted terms in the larger categories are as follows: $^+$E, $^+$P, $^+$A, — *stimulating, vigorous, valor;* $^+$E, $^+$P, ^{0}A — *benevolence, brave, full;* $^+$E, ^{0}P, $^+$A — *cheerful, happy, gay, jovial, joyful, laughter, fresh, fun, warm;* $^+$E, ^{0}P, ^{0}A — *affectionate, fidelity, pretty, clear, sweet, sensible, cooperation, altruism;* $^+$E, ^{0}P, $^-$A — *serene, restful;* ^{0}E, $^+$P, $^+$A — *dominant, large;* $^-$E, $^+$P, ^{0}A — *heartless, jealousy;* $^-$E, ^{0}P, ^{0}A — *vulgar, evil, contempt, resentful, sour;* $^-$E, ^{0}P, $^-$A — *dejected, depressed, melancholy, unhappy, sorrow, gloomy, solitude.*

TABLE 6:12

Number of Studies Reporting Connotations Weighted by Number of Communities Involved in Our Sample: Arranged by Affective Profiles of the Words Reported[a]

	+P			0P			−P		
				+E Sectors					
+A	adventurous RED	37(8) *296*[b]		exciting RED	43(7) *301*		female GRN	6(3) *18*	
	bright GRN	11(3) *33*		lively YEL	47(4) *188*		young YEL	2(1) *2*	
	courage YEL	8(3) *24*		merry GRN	15(4) *60*		youthful WHT	2(1) *2*	
	energetic BLU	3(2) *6*		playful WHT	8(7) *56*		RED	1(1) *1*	
	healthy WHT	2(2) *4*		pleasure BLU	10(3) *30*		BLU	1(1) *1*	
	love BLK	1(1) *1*		sociable BLK	0(0) *0*		BLK	0(0) *0*	
	male GRY	0(0) *0*		sprightly GRY	0(0) *0*		GRY	0(0) *0*	
	N=10			N=16[c]			N=3		
0A	defending BLU	8(6) *48*		beauty BLU	16(4) *64*		gentle WHT	10(3) *30*	
	high GRN	9(5) *45*		charity WHT	10(5) *50*		light YEL	3(2) *6*	
	hope RED	7(2) *14*		clean RED	8(3) *24*		smooth BLU	5(1) *5*	
	noble WHT	4(3) *12*		good GRN	5(2) *10*		soft GRN	1(1) *1*	
	protective BLK	2(2) *4*		honest YEL	3(3) *9*		tender BLK	1(1) *1*	
	rich GRY	1(1) *1*		straight GRY	1(1) *1*		GRY	0(0) *0*	
	trustworthy YEL	1(1) *1*		sympathy BLK	0(0) *0*		RED	0(0) *0*	
	N=10			N=15			N=5		
−A	dignified BLU	10(1) *10*		calm BLU	33(4) *132*		leisurely BLU	6(1) *6*	
	regal BLK	4(1) *4*		comfortable WHT	18(4) *72*		mildness GRN	3(1) *3*	
	secure YEL	2(2) *4*		patience GRN	10(2) *20*		relaxed WHT	0(0) *0*	
	stately GRY	1(1) *1*		peaceful GRY	8(2) *16*		repose GRY	0(0) *0*	
	RED	1(0) *1*[d]		quiet BLK	2(2) *4*		BLK	0(0) *0*	
	GRN	0(0) *0*		soothing RED	0(0) *0*		RED	0(0) *0*	
	WHT	0(0) *0*		tranquil YEL	0(0) *0*		YEL	0(0) *0*	
	N=4			N=9			N=4		
				0E Sectors					
+A	contrary RED	21(7) *147*		active RED	20(5) *100*				
	masterful BLK	5(1) *5*		extroverted YEL	4(3) *12*				
	passion GRN	1(1) *1*		fast GRN	0(0) *0*				
	rebellious BLU	1(1) *1*		hot BLU	0(0) *0*				
	GRY	1(1) *1*		impulsive WHT	0(0) *0*				
	YEL	0(0) *0*		GRY	0(0) *0*				
	WHT	0(0) *0*		BLK	0(0) *0*				
	N=4			N=5			N=0		

[a] Studies using either color words or color patches as stimuli are included; AE studies done prior to 1951 are excluded, except for Karwoski and Odbert (1938), Hevner (1935), Luckiesh (1923), and Dorcus (1932); E-P-A profiles were estimated from loadings on pancultural factorizations (adjectives) or from standardized composites in cross-cultural means for *Atlas* concepts (nouns) where available, otherwise from staff judgments.

[b] Values should be read: RED, 37 word-color pairings in the literature, times 8 of our communities involved, equals *296* instances.

[c] Main types of connotations are listed for larger categories; see footnote 25 in text for additional terms.

[d] The 1(0)*1* notation indicates that the study in question dealt with presumed universals (without specifying cultures), regional symbols for areas which include one or more of our sample cultures, or religious symbolism pertaining to part of our sample — but not any of our culture samples per se. In order to make this analysis feasible, we did not include studies which reported only on cultures not in our sample.

TABLE 6:12 (Continued)

⁰E Sectors

		+P			0P				−P	
⁰A	big	BLK	16(2) *32*	cool	BLU	5(2) *10*	naive	WHT	6(3) *18*
	constant	RED	11(2) *22*	distant	WHT	2(2) *4*	obedient	BLU	4(3) *12*
	deep	BLU	6(2) *12*	dry	RED	2(2) *4*	shallow	GRN	4(2) *8*
	defiant	GRY	1(1) *1*	near	GRN	1(1) *1*	small	GRY	4(2) *8*
	mysterious	YEL	1(0) *1*		GRY	1(1) *1*	thin	YEL	3(1) *3*
	powerful	GRN	0(0) *0*		BLK	1(1) *1*	weak	BLK	0(0) *0*
	strong	WHT	0(0) *0*		YEL	1(0) *1*		RED	0(0) *0*
	N=9			N=4			N=6		
⁻A	heavy	BLU	5(2) *10*	aged	BLK	3(2) *6*	bashful	GRY	3(2) *6*
	sedate	BLK	4(2) *8*	conservative	GRY	3(2) *6*	passive	WHT	2(1) *2*
	serious	GRY	1(1) *1*	inactive	BLU	3(1) *3*	shy	GRN	1(1) *1*
	thick	WHT	0(0) *0*	slow	WHT	1(1) *1*	submissive	BLU	1(1) *1*
		RED	0(0) *0*	solemn	RED	0(0) *0*		BLK	0(0) *0*
		YEL	0(0) *0*		YEL	0(0) *0*		RED	0(0) *0*
		GRN	0(0) *0*		GRN	0(0) *0*		YEL	0(0) *0*
	N=4			N=5			N=4		

⁻E Sectors

		+P			0P				−P	
⁺A	anger	RED	19(8) *152*	anxiety	BLK	10(2) *20*	fickle	GRY	1(1) *1*
	hostile	GRY	2(2) *4*	disquietude	RED	3(2) *6*	inconstant	YEL	1(0) *1*
	loud	BLK	3(1) *3*	distressed	YEL	1(0) *1*		GRN	1(0) *1*
	noisy	YEL	1(1) *1*	disturbed	GRN	1(0) *1*		BLU	0(0) *0*
		GRN	1(1) *1*	gaudiness	BLU	0(0) *0*		RED	0(0) *0*
		BLU	0(0) *0*	restless	GRY	0(0) *0*		BLK	0(0) *0*
		WHT	0(0) *0*	upset	WHT	0(0) *0*		WHT	0(0) *0*
	N=4			N=7			N=2		
⁰A	cruelty	RED	19(4) *76*	bad	GRY	12(7) *84*	cowardly	YEL	10(7) *70*
	hard	GRY	6(5) *30*	crooked	BLK	14(3) *42*	doubt	GRY	9(7) *63*
	hatred	YEL	6(3) *18*	dark	RED	3(2) *6*	envy	GRN	4(2) *8*
	lust of power	BLK	3(1) *3*	disgust	YEL	2(1) *2*	guilt	RED	1(1) *1*
	pain	WHT	1(1) *1*	distrust	BLU	2(1) *2*	undignified	BLU	0(0) *0*
	rough	GRN	1(1) *1*	fear	WHT	1(1) *1*		WHT	0(0) *0*
	tragic	BLU	1(1) *1*	ugly	GRN	0(0) *0*		BLK	0(0) *0*
	N=9			N=12			N=5		
⁻A	sullen	GRY	1(1) *1*	dull	BLK	32(4) *128*	defeated	BLK	6(4) *24*
		BLK	1(1) *1*	lonely	GRY	22(5) *110*	despondent	GRY	6(2) *12*
		WHT	0(0) *0*	old	RED	8(6) *48*	dim	WHT	1(1) *1*
		RED	0(0) *0*	sad	BLU	11(2) *22*	down	BLU	1(1) *1*
		YEL	0(0) *0*	shame	GRN	2(2) *4*	empty	RED	0(0) *0*
		GRN	0(0) *0*	sick	WHT	2(2) *4*	regret	YEL	0(0) *0*
		BLU	0(0) *0*	somber	YEL	1(0) *1*	stale	GRN	0(0) *0*
	N=1			N=14			N=8		

total of 1,199 weighted associations with emotion words. Its nearest competitor is BLUE with 377; GREEN has the fewest (217). As we shall see later, the prominence of RED is reflected in color terminology as well as in subjective feelings about color.

It is most informative to trace the connotative appropriateness of each color through each dimension of the "space" shown in Table 6:12, holding the other dimensions constant. With E decreasing ($+$ to 0 to $-$) and P and A held constant at 0: WHITE decreases (values *50* to *4* to *1*); GREY and BLACK increase dramatically between ⁰E and ⁻E (*1-1-84* and *0-1-42*); and RED, YELLOW, GREEN, and BLUE drop abruptly between ⁺E and ⁰E (*24-4-6, 9-1-2, 10-1-0,* and *64-10-2* respectively). Varying P while holding E and A at 0: BLACK and RED drop with decreasing Potency (*32-1-0* and *22-4-0* respectively); YELLOW and GREEN, and GREY and WHITE particularly, tend to increase as Potency decreases (*1-1-3* and *0-1-8* for the chromatic former and *1-1-8* and *0-4-18* for the achromatic latter). Varying A with E and P held constant at 0: RED (*100-4-0*) and YELLOW (*12-1-0*) drop as Activity decreases; GREY and BLACK increase (both *0-1-6*) but BLUE and WHITE tend to increase and then decrease (*0-10-3* and *0-4-1* respectively). These trends in the literature confirm the Universals in our componential analyses rather strikingly: Brights (WHITE) are more positive in Evaluation than Darks (GREY, BLACK) and are also more A, while BLACK is more P than GREY or WHITE; the red end of the spectrum is more Active than the blue, but the blue end is more E; Saturated colors tend to be more Potent than Desaturated colors; Color is more positive in Evaluation than Non-color, with the exception of WHITE, which is highly evaluated.

Looking at ranks, WHITE is first or second in six of eight sectors which are neither ⁺A, ⁺P, nor ⁻E and is generally low in rank elsewhere, thus confirming our data, which characterizes WHITE as having high Evaluation and low Potency (but not very low A). We found GREY and BLACK to be universally low in E and A; in Table 6:12 these colors quite regularly increase in connotative appropriateness as we move from ⁺E to ⁻E with the P and A codings held constant; with E and P held constant, they tend to become higher in rank moving from ⁺A to ⁻A (from tops to bottoms of columns).

We found RED universally Potent but also universally Active; looking at the diagonal sectors (⁺P, ⁺A through ⁰P, ⁰A to ⁻P, ⁻A) for each level of E, we find that in the literature the appropriateness of RED decreases simultaneously with decreasing P and A — *296* to *24* to *0* at ⁺E, *147* to *4* to *0* at ⁰E, and *152* to *6* to *0* at ⁻E. YELLOW was simultaneously ⁻P and ⁺A in our data; we would have expected decreasing weights from upper right (⁻P, ⁺A) to lower left (⁺P, ⁻A) at each level of E, but this expectation cannot be tested because of the small Ns of these sectors. However, YELLOW places in the top three *ranks* in six of the eight ⁺A sectors and in four of the eight ⁻P sectors. The universally high E of BLUE in our *Atlas* data, on the other hand, is clearly borne out in the literature survey; in the +E sectors BLUE has highest rank in five of the six which are ⁰A or ⁻A (that is, not highly Active); in the ⁰E sectors it has highest rank in only two; and in the ⁻E sectors BLUE has no highest rank and is rarely mentioned, except in the ⁻E, ⁰P, ⁻A sector (*lonely, sad, melancholy,* etc.). GREEN was distinguished by no Universals in our data; in the literature, however, it is dominantly +E (*190* as compared with *27* for ⁰E and ⁻E combined), but it is not outstanding with respect to P or A.

The E, P, and A characteristics of the colors may be summarized from Table 6:12 as follows. WHITE, with 88% of its weighted associations in +E sectors, 73% in ⁰P sectors,[26] and 45% in ⁰A sectors, is +E, ⁰P (or ⁻P), and ⁰A. GREY, with 88% of its weighted associations in ⁻E sectors, 63% in ⁰P sectors but a larger percentage than any other color (26%) in ⁻P sectors, and 44% in ⁻A sectors, is ⁻E, ⁻P, and ⁻A. BLACK, similarly, is ⁻E, ⁰P, and ⁻A. RED is higher than other colors in the ⁰E sectors and not outstanding in the +E or ⁻E sectors and hence may be considered neutral on E; but it is far higher than other colors in P and A. YELLOW has a smaller percentage of associations in neutral E sectors than any other color (5%) and seems to be bimodal on E; it is +A like RED but, unlike RED, is not +P. GREEN, along with WHITE, has the highest percentage of associations in +E sectors; its P and A are less well defined. BLUE is also strongly +E and firmly ⁰P and ⁻A.

A few anomalous "bumps" in Table 6:12 are due to very specific associations with particular colors and hence probably should have been treated in the next section. Despite the generally low A of BLACK, it ranks highest (10 (2) 20) in the ⁻E, ⁰P, +A sector, but this is mainly attributable to high AE connotations of *distressed, upset,* and *disturbed.* Despite its universal Potency and Activity, RED has a high loading (*48*) in the ⁻E, ⁰P, ⁻A sector, but this is accounted for by the connotation of *shame* (and for five different communities, presumably related to blushing). Similarly we find both YELLOW and GREEN unexpectedly high (*70* and *8* respectively) in the ⁻E, ⁻P, ⁰A sector, but nearly all of this is due to associations with either *jealousy* or *envy* — ND, GG, IT, YS, TK, and JP get yellow, while AE and BF get green, with envy!

COLOR ASSOCIATIONS AND SYMBOLISMS

Inspection of 22 sources in the literature yielded a total of nearly 300 concrete and abstract nominals that we classified as associations.[27] We have

---

[26] However, WHITE shows a steady increase in percentage of mention among all colors in going from the +P (2%) to the ⁰P (11%) to the ⁻P (17%) sectors, thus suggesting it to be ⁻P rather than ⁰P.

[27] Aaronson (1970, 1971); Bastide (1958); Birren (1969); Chou and Chen (1935); Déribéré (1955); Dorcus (1932); Ferguson (1959); Hofstätter and Lübbert (1958); Hofstätter and Primac (1957); Jacobs and Jacobs (1958); Jones (1967);

categorized the nominals into four sets: (a) concrete color identifications — names of things naturally (or normally) having a given color (e.g., WHITE-*chalk*, BLACK-*night*, RED-*blood*, etc.); (b) concrete color associations — names of things culturally associated with a given color (e.g., BLACK-*necktie*, RED-*sacrifice*, YELLOW-*plague*); (c) abstract color associations — terms for non-"point-at-ables" which can only have color metaphorically (e.g., GREY-*Monday*, BLUE-*eternity*, RED-*patriotism*); (d) abstract color symbolisms — culturally significant concepts which certain colors "stand for" or represent traditionally but not in any obvious way metaphorically (e.g., colors associated with castes in India, with certain deities, religions, etc.). Obviously, the boundaries of these categories are somewhat fuzzy. Since some categories, particularly c, contained many items, most redundant (quasi-synonymous) terms reported by only a single source are deleted here.

Table 6:13A lists the most prominent concrete color identifications reported in these studies. The concrete objects associated with particular colors are obvious natural (GREY-*ashes*, GREEN-*grass*) or contemporary artifactual (BLUE-*ink*, WHITE-*ceiling*) Universals, hence are nonarbitrary, and need no special interpretation. However, it is worth noting that most color terms in most languages can be shown to have their origins in the names of concrete things having the (then abstracted) color in question (e.g., English "orange" from the name of the fruit). Table 6:13B presents the terms we coded as concrete associations. Since these are, in a sense, arbitrary and hence more liable to cultural learning experiences (e.g., BLUE-*dress*, WHITE-*doctor*, RED-*sacrifice*), one might expect more variety across communities. This is suggested by the entries for WHITE and RED, but there were too few items in this category to permit any firm conclusions.

The vast majority of associations reported in the literature were readily codable as abstract associations — that is, concepts which have no color literally and hence whose associations with color must be based upon a metaphorical relation (e.g., *virtue, innocence,* and *chastity* have no inherent color and their frequent association with WHITE suggests a common affective mediation). In this sense we can say that such metaphorically based associations are also nonarbitrary. We should therefore expect the associations in Table 6:13C to be affectively similar to the connotations given in Table 6:12 for the same colors. This is overwhelmingly the case: with three exceptions (*mourning* (HC and TH and the Orient generally), *death* (ditto, but also one AE study), and *sin* (two AE studies — "little white lies"?)), WHITE has +E associations — *virtue, purity, truth, heaven,* and the like. GREY has consistently ⁻E (as well as ⁻P and ⁻A) associations — *pessimism, fatigue,* and *boredom,* for example. BLACK is equally ⁻E but has obviously higher P —

Luckiesh (1923); Murray and Spencer (1952); Obonai and Matsuoka (1956); Oyama, Tanaka, and Haga (1963); Shen (1937); Tatibana (1937, 1938); Wheeler (1969); Williams (1964); Winick (1963).

TABLE 6:13

Color Associations Categorized as (A) Concrete Identifications, (B) Concrete Associations, (C) Abstract Associations, and (D) Abstract Symbolisms[a]

A. Concrete Identifications

WHITE: ceiling, chalk, race, snow, light, egg, paper
GREY: overcast sky, clouds, ashes
BLACK: ink, water (HC)[b], race, night
RED: race, blood, apple, fire, sun, brick, rose, stop sign, flesh
YELLOW: race, wheat, straw, gold, fire, banana, lemon, sun(light)
GREEN: sea, leaves, grass, vegetation
BLUE: ink, sky, sea, water, evening

B. Concrete Associations

WHITE: baby, child, daughter, doctor (uniform), flowers, autumn (HC)
GREY: raincoat (HC), hat (HC)
BLACK: dirt, mud, winter, fountain pen (HC)
RED: flowers, sacrifice, flag, fruits, ceremonies (HC), summer, heat, body
YELLOW: fruits, plague
GREEN: spring, nature
BLUE: dress, spring

C. Abstract Associations

WHITE: eternity, the future, virtue, innocence, holiness, chastity, modesty, virginity, purity, integrity, life, mourning, sin, death, truth, heaven, light, marriage
GREY: mourning, discouragement, pessimism, negation, fatigue, boredom, theory (ND), old age, past
BLACK: sin, mourning, humility, death, murder, falsehood, negation, Satan, devils, hell
RED: freedom, patriotism, victory, truth, marriage, festivity, sun, vitality, force, emotions, heat, south, Satan, danger, murder, war, temperament, success
YELLOW: sin, home, future, friendship, festivity (India), force, science
GREEN: truth, faith, innocence, modesty, home, friendship, regeneration, victory, mind
BLUE: eternity, heaven, faith, virginity, the future, life, freedom, integrity, humility, virtue, truth, wisdom, home, friendship, marriage, mourning (HC), death (TK), science, mind

D. Abstract Symbolisms

WHITE: Brahman (highest) caste (India), flag of truce
GREY: mankind (ND)
BLACK: Siva (India), Sudras (lowest) caste (India)
RED: martyrs, Holy Ghost, Kshattriyas caste (India), communism
YELLOW: Vaisyas caste (India), Hinduism, Buddhism, Confucius, Christ, the earth
GREEN: Ireland, Mohammed (Islam)
BLUE: Virgin Mary

---

[a] Since this table is intended as illustrative rather than as data, we do not give actual frequencies (they are generally much lower than for the connotations in Table 6:12); again, no distinction is made between studies using color words vs. color patches.
[b] In cases where the association is both unusual and unique to a given culture, we add the cultural symbol in parentheses.

sin, death, and *murder,* for example, to say nothing of *Satan.* RED shows exactly the combination of ⁺P and ⁺A with either ⁺E or ⁻E that would be predicted — both *victory, vitality,* and *emotions* and *danger, murder,* and *war.* YELLOW displays a pattern similar to RED but less extreme — *home, friendship,* and *festivity,* but also *force* and *sin.* GREEN is mainly ⁺E, which was also the case for connotations (*faith, home, regeneration, victory*). This is also true for BLUE, but now with more Potency (*eternity, life, the future, freedom*) — the *mourning* and *death* associations are restricted to HC and TK respectively.

There were very few associations coded as abstract symbolisms — that is, colors used symbolically but on some basis (apparently) other than shared affect and hence, in that sense, more arbitrary. Most of those listed in Table 6:13D refer to deities, religions generally, and to Indian castes, the exceptions being WHITE–*flag of truce,* GREY–*mankind* (ND), RED–*communism,* YELLOW–*the earth,* and GREEN–*Ireland.* Of course, the color symbolisms for both particular deities and Indian castes may actually be based on affective connotations (witness the fact that the highest (Brahman) caste is white and the lowest (Sudras) caste is black).

As part of a larger study on the affective relations among Colors, Emotions, and Days of the Week, Pečjak (1970) both analyzed the affective distances between the concepts in these categories of our *Atlas* materials and had subjects in seven of our communities (AE, BF, ND, GG, IT, YS, JP) match the terms in each category with those in each other. The correlation between Colors and Emotions across these communities is quite high (+.63), as would be expected from our total evidence for Universals and emotional connotations of color reported in this chapter. The correlation between Colors and Days of the Week was much lower (+.30, with both AE and JP appearing as isolates). Table 6:14 summarizes Pečjak's matching data for Colors and Days of the Week — which we might have categorized as either abstract associations or abstract symbolisms. There are definite clusters: GREY with *Monday* (six of seven communities) but never with *Saturday,* GREEN and BLUE with *Wednesday* (five of nine entries) but never with *Saturday,* YELLOW and GREEN with Thursday (five of eight) but never with *Saturday,* RED with *Saturday* (six of seven) but never with either *Monday* or *Sunday,* and WHITE with *Sunday* (five of seven) but never with any ordinary days of the week except *Wednesday.* Keeping in mind that all except JP are Western and dominantly in the Christian religious tradition (our Moslem communities undoubtedly would show different matchings), it appears that for teen-age boys RED is appropriate for the excitement of Saturday's end of the school week, WHITE is appropriate to Sunday, the day of worship, GREY goes well with the renewal of the work-and-school week on Monday, and most of the other days — except Wednesday in the middle — fit best with desaturated colors like YELLOW and GREEN, or just plain GREY.

TABLE 6:14

Color Associations to Days of the Week (Pečjak, 1970): Communities (N = 7)
Showing Each Association as Highest[a]

	WHITE	GREY	RED	YELLOW	GREEN	BLUE
Monday		AE, ND, BF, GG, IT, YS				JP
Tuesday		GG, IT, YS	JP	ND, BF	AE	JP[b]
Wednesday	AE, YS	GG		YS	BF, IT	JP, ND, YS
Thursday		JP	AE	IT, YS	ND, BF, GG	ND
Friday		BF, IT, YS	ND	JP	AE	AE, GG
Saturday	JP		AE, ND, BF, GG, IT, YS			
Sunday	ND, BF, GG, IT, JP	YS			AE	

[a] At the time Pečjak collected his data BLACK was not included among our color terms.
[b] Double entries indicate bimodal matching patterns.

ON THE CULTURAL EVOLUTION OF COLOR LEXICONS

In a recent book Berlin and Kay (1969) present a case not only for "semantic universals ... in the domain of color vocabulary" but also for an orderly development of all languages in this respect "that can properly be termed evolutionary." As the authors note, this view is opposed to the notion of psycholinguistic relativity associated particularly with the names of Edward Sapir and Benjamin Lee Whorf — as, for that matter, are our own data on Universals. Berlin and Kay offer experimental data on some 20 languages, although except for 31 Tzeltal speakers they admit that they "often had access to only one informant for a language," and bilingual at that. The data were based on color-term elicitation and determination of the foci and boundaries of term usage with respect to a standardized Munsell chart consisting of 320 chips, varying through 40 equally spaced hues at maximal saturation and in eight degrees of brightness. They supplement these data with inferences drawn linguistically from the color vocabularies of 98 languages reported in the literature (e.g., using abstractness and lack of marking as criteria for "basic" color terms).

From these data Berlin and Kay draw two strong conclusions. First, there exists "a total universal inventory of exactly eleven basic color categories ... from which the eleven or fewer basic color terms of any language are always drawn," these being white, black, red, green, yellow, blue, brown, purple, pink, orange, and grey. The primary evidence for the basicness of these terms comes from the close clustering and minimal overlap of the foci for each term across the 20 languages (i.e., the Munsell chips specified by informants as "the best, most typical examples of X") ; the mean interlanguage distances were approximately one chip-width for Japanese, Korean, and Cantonese compared with each other and with the Tzeltal data, which was smaller than the mean intersubject distances for ten Tzeltal speakers. The agreement on the boundaries of the application of color terms was much less, however — which would be predicted from the results of the study by Brown and Lenneberg (1954) on color codability.

The second and "totally unexpected" finding based on the total 98 languages was that there are strict and ordered constraints upon the colors that will be linguistically differentiated when fewer than the 11 abstract color terms are used. Given the 11 basic terms as the maximum, only 22 "types" of terminologies of the 2,048 combinations possible were in fact found (i.e., about 1%), and these adhered quite rigidly to a set of rules of progressive differentiation — rules remarkably similar to those Jakobson proposed (see Jakobson and Halle, 1956) for the development of phonemic distinctions. Although the Berlin-Kay study deals strictly with referential color terminology, largely utilizes small nonurban societies, and has nothing directly to do with the attribution of affect per se, nevertheless there are some very interesting relationships between their stages and our *Atlas* data.

Stage I: WHITE/BLACK. Since this distinction was usually *light* vs. *dark* as well, we can probably identify this primary differentiation, common to all languages, as being in terms of a Brightness feature. Referring back to our Table 6:6, it is noteworthy that this is the only component which displays Universals on all five basic measures — Bright being $^+$E, $^-$P, $^+$A, $^+$FAM, and $^-$CI in comparison with Dark.

Stage II: WHITE/RED/BLACK. The term "red" covers a wide and varying referential range across languages of this type, but it concentrates on the purple-red-orange-yellow-brown regions and avoids the entire green-blue region (which are still only differentiated in terms of *light-dark*). Since there is only a single "color" term, one cannot claim that a differentiation has been set up in terms of Hue; rather, it would appear that the opposition here is really that between Color and Non-color (our fourth component),[28] and it is worthy of note that our Color component has three universal affective relations, Color being $^+$E, $^+$A, and $^-$CI in comparison with Non-color.

Stage III: WHITE/RED/YELLOW or GREEN/BLACK. This further reduction in the scope of the simple *light-dark* might be attributed to differentiation

[28] Berlin and Kay quote Jakobson and Halle to the effect that "there seems to be a phenomenal affinity between optimal chromaticity (pure red) and vocalic compactness, attenuated chromaticity (yellow-blue) and consonantal diffuseness, attenuated chromaticity (greyed) and consonantal compactness" (p. 107). The suggestion that red is the most "strikingly colorful" color is borne out in our data, RED being universally Potent and Active and having far more associations to emotion words than any other color, according to our literature search.

in terms either of a true Hue feature or of the Saturation feature. The Berlin-Kay data as a whole seem to suggest the latter; the red end of the spectrum is naturally saturated for the human eye, whereas the middle region (including both YELLOW and GREEN) are naturally desaturated, and inspection of the actual referents for this fourth color term (glossed as "green" in eight and as "yellow" in nine languages assigned to Stage III) reveals that many of them include *both* yellow and green.[29] In our *Atlas* data the Saturation component displays only one universal affect, however, ⁺Saturation (RED, BLUE) being more Potent than ⁻Saturation (YELLOW, GREEN) — although the more saturated colors also tend to be more Active.

Stage IV: WHITE/RED/<u>YELLOW</u>/<u>GREEN</u>/BLACK. We would interpret this stage as a definite differentiation of yellow vs. green in terms of the Hue feature, accompanied, of course, by a division of the spectrum into red-yellow and green-blue regions. At this stage, note that green and blue are still undifferentiated, and almost without exception in the Berlin-Kay data the "green" term includes both green and blue referents and hence might better be glossed as "blue-green." In our *Atlas* data the red end is universally ⁻E and ⁺A with respect to the blue end. It is also noteworthy that our data showed the red end of the spectrum (RED vs. YELLOW) to be universally more differentiated in affect (distance measures) than the blue end (BLUE vs. GREEN), and the Berlin-Kay data clearly show the RED/YELLOW terminological distinction to hold for more languages than the BLUE/GREEN distinction, and presumably prior in cultural evolution as well, if their theory is valid.

Stage V: WHITE/RED/YELLOW/GREEN/<u>BLUE</u>/BLACK. At this stage blue is finally differentiated from green and the two color regions have separate abstract terms. This may be considered a further differentiation along the Hue dimension. It is interesting that in the following stages further differentiations are still being made earlier (or at least for more languages) in the red region than in the blue region: *Stage VI* — a term for brown is distinguished from yellow (which, it should be noticed, is a simultaneous Brightness and Saturation separation within the red region of the spectrum); *Stage VII* — typically a yet further differentiation within the red region distinguishes orange from red and yellow, and "simultaneously" purple is distinguished in the blue region (presumably in terms of both Hue and Saturation). Actually, beyond Stage VI there are many types of color terminologies, including variable combinations of brown, pink, purple, orange, and grey, and uniformity in cultural development seems to disappear.

The Berlin-Kay study has been sharply criticized on a variety of methodological grounds — inadequacies of their language sample and particularly

---

[29] This interpretation would eliminate the need to distinguish two subtypes of transitions for Stage III to Stage IV (A, green-to-yellow, and B, yellow-to-green), which the Berlin-Kay data hardly support.

their informant samples (apparently often relying only on a single speaker), the bilingualism of many informants with English (and Lenneberg and Roberts, 1956, have shown that this can modify foci as well as boundaries in color-term usage), the biasing of color-term glossing toward the evolutionary theory being tested, and so forth (see particularly a review by Nancy P. Hickerson, 1971) — but nevertheless we suspect that the overall picture will remain the same under more refined methods of study. The convergence of our own *Atlas* data with those of Berlin and Kay certainly adds credence to their view. Is it possible that *affective* features of meaning have contributed to the rather uniform cultural development of color terminologies (if, indeed, such uniformity will be shown to exist)?

We have been able to demonstrate a number of correspondences between our (contemporary, urban, and all-beyond-Stage-VII) *Atlas* community data and the Berlin-Kay assumptions. We find a universal relation between Brightness and Evaluation, and we suggest that this is a biological basic for survival of any primate. We find Color to be related to both Evaluation and Activity and RED to be the most Dynamic (+P and +A) of the +Colors; we suggest that it is typically in the red regions of the spectrum, broadly speaking, that the perceptual signs of ripe food objects, animals, and even other protecting or threatening humans are to be found. The blues and greens are typically "backgrounds" (sea, sky, fields, foliage) rather than "figures" everywhere except possibly in desert environments. We also find greater affective differentiation within the red region of the spectrum than within the blue, which is consistent with this general notion of human species adaptation — with language reflecting those differences in perceptual signs which make a difference in survival. The affective dimensions, or features, of meaning are not only universal in the human species; they are also intimately related to both emotional and motivational states of members of the species. It thus seems quite likely — given the relationships demonstrated in this section — that the *feelings* associated with the referents of color signs do indeed contribute to the cultural evolution of color lexicons.

CHAPTER

7

Issues in Method and Theory

THIS BOOK has been concerned with the study of subjective culture on a cross-societal basis. Comparative study of *objective* culture entails comparing either artifacts and the technologies that produced them (potsherds, tools, habitations, transports, paintings, and so on) or observable human activities (norms of behavior generally, interpersonal roles, child-rearing practices, institutional structures, etc.). Comparative study of *subjective* culture, on the other hand, entails comparing human cognitive processes, either non-linguistic (perceptual styles, motivational patterns, and skills) or linguistic (meanings, beliefs, and the linguistic structures which express them). This distinction between objective and subjective cultures seems to parallel one made by Ward Goodenough (1961): "We have, therefore, two kinds of culture: culture 1, the recurring patterns which characterize a community as a homeostatic system, and culture 2, people's standards for perceiving, judging, and acting. Culture 1, moreover, is an artifact or product of the human use of culture 2 ... individuals can be said to possess culture 2 but not culture 1, which is the property of a community as a social-ecological system" (p. 522).

The aspect of subjective culture to which our own research has been directed is clearly linguistic in nature — the meanings of concepts and the structure of the semantic space within which they are differentiated — and the entry to this domain has necessarily been through language itself. Within

First draft prepared by Charles E. Osgood.

the linguistic domain of human cognition, we have been particularly concerned with those features of meaning which represent affect — the "feeling-tones" that people attribute to the signs of things and events in their environments. The general purposes of the research have been, first, to test the generality across cultures and languages of the three factors of affective meaning — Evaluation, Potency, and Activity — that had appeared regularly in our earlier indigenous studies with English-speaking Americans; second, if such generality could be demonstrated, to construct on its basis comparable psycholinguistic instruments (semantic differentials) for measuring affective meanings in diverse cultures; and third, given such instruments, to utilize them in the comparative study of the affective aspects of subjective cultures around the world.

It should be emphasized that we are dealing with cultural meanings rather than individual meanings. Even though we begin with individual judgments about what concepts mean, individualities are lost in the averaging process, and all of our measures characterize cultural groups as wholes. In the same article quoted above, Goodenough (1961) goes on to say, "Strictly speaking ... no two persons can be said to have exactly the same cultures 2, because every individual in organizing his experience of phenomena, including the actions and utterances of his fellows, necessarily creates his own. But it is also possible to speak of an aggregation of people (a community's members, collectively) as possessing a culture in the sense of culture 2 as distinct from culture 1" (p. 522). It is the subjective (affective) cultures of people in this aggregate sense with which this book is concerned.

At the time of writing this final chapter we are, so to speak, in mid-flight in our exploration of semantic space across cultures. As the details in Chapters 1-4 of this volume document, we have been able to demonstrate the universality (within the limitations of our sample) of E, P, and A as the dominant dimensions within which the affective meanings of concepts are differentiated. On the basis of a pancultural factor analysis it was possible to select, for each language/culture community, those descriptive scales which were functionally most equivalent in representing these underlying features of meaning — thus generating efficient (12-scale) SD instruments for measuring this aspect of culture. As detailed in Chapters 5 and 6, these comparable instruments have been utilized in the measurement of 620 concepts, representing very diverse areas of human concern, in 23 cultures around the world. We are now in the midst of the complex process of interpreting these *Atlas* data, relating our quantitative information on affect to other aspects of culture as reflected in the commentaries of our colleagues and other informants and in the relevant social science literature; this process is illustrated for one small category of concepts (colors) in Chapter 6. Full reporting of the *Atlas* analyses and their interpretations must be reserved for another volume (or, more likely, volumes).

In this chapter we will first review the chapters of this volume, noting and commenting on some of the issues that arose in each. Then some special projects that have been generated from our research will be sketched briefly (since they are already or will be published in their own right). Some of these are offshoots from the mainstream of our cross-cultural work and others are studies by our colleagues in other countries, stimulated by the central project and often utilizing the tools developed in it. And, finally, we will come to grips with what we think are some of the major methodological and theoretical issues raised by or affecting our research.

SOME ISSUES ENCOUNTERED IN COURSE

ON THE STRATEGY OF CROSS-CULTURAL RESEARCH

Technological developments in the twentieth century have made research possible on an international scale that would have been inconceivable at the turn of the century. It is now possible to test hypotheses about human nature that demand cross-cultural and cross-linguistic designs. But these new capabilities bring along with them new problems and new responsibilities. In Chapter 1, using our own study of human semantic systems and studies by the late Hadley Cantril (1965) on patterns of human concern and by Lambert and Klineberg (1967) on children's views of foreigners as illustrations, we considered some of these matters.

The special kinds of *ethical issues* involved in cross-cultural research have long been the concern of anthropologists; among psychologists this concern has come to the fore more recently. The American Psychological Association has had a detailed Code of Ethics for its members, dealing almost exclusively with indigenous research, teaching, consulting, and so forth. Only within the past few years has its Committee on International Relations of Psychology begun the production of an analogous code for cross-cultural research. The problems of *Western bias* — in selection of problems to be studied, in designing the research, and in interpreting the results — are probably impossible to eliminate entirely at this time in world history, given the economic, technological, and even cultural imbalances that exist. A project such as ours — that originates in the United States, is supported by U.S. federal funds, and must finally be reported in the English language — surely cannot escape this bias. However, Chapter 1 indicates how we have tried to minimize it. In a comprehensive review of cross-cultural psychology Triandis, Malpass, and Davidson (1972, pp. 5-11) point up some of the issues here: not simply transporting Western tests and scales into other cultures (we have developed SDs indigenously "from the ground up"); using techniques of analysis which at least potentially allow "emic" (unique) as well as "etic" (universal) cultural patterns to appear (that our procedures meet this criterion is evident in the data presented throughout the book); not depending entirely on componential analysis (as illustrated in Chapter 6) or facet analysis (see Guttman, 1959; Foa, 1964, 1965, 1966), which have the same potential but are more liable to the ethnocentrism of the investigator who usually intuits the components or facets (we will return to this problem).

On the surface, at least, there seems to be an inherent incompatibility between *standardization* and *naturalness* of procedures cross-culturally. Rigid standardization of tasks, instructions, methods, etc. practically guarantees unnaturalness for other cultures and Western bias in the interpretation of results. On the other hand, lack of standardization (i.e., letting each cultural group "do its own thing in its own way") introduces all kinds of uncontrolled and possibly confounding variables, and equally guarantees uninterpretability of results. At a deeper level of consideration, however, it is clear that compromises are feasible — particularly if one presupposes underlying universals in human cultures and languages. In our own case we have given subjects standardized but basically very simple psycholinguistic tasks (giving qualifier associations to substantives, giving familiar opposites to qualifiers, and rating substantives on seven-step scales defined by qualifiers) which, if not as familiar to Thai school children as to American, at least are common human cognitive processes. These tasks are explained to the subjects with instructions which are adapted to and illustrated in each language/culture community — not just translated literally. The critical thing is that the degree of standardization imposed, in the interest of guaranteeing comparability of results, *not* channel the responses of subjects away from what they would be in completely natural situations and toward those normal for the investigators' culture. We believe our procedures have allowed cultural uniquenesses to appear (they do not predetermine *what* qualifiers will be most productive or *what* scale positions will be checked for concepts being rated). The fact that unique patterns of factors appear in the analysis of indigenous matrices with E-P-A partialed out (see Chapter 5, pp. 216-226) is testimony that such freedom did exist — and, conversely, the fact that shared E, P, and A factors appear in the unpartialed pancultural factor analysis (Chapter 4, pp. 159-190) *despite* this freedom is testimony for their universality as underlying dimensions of affective meaning.

Problems of *translation* arise at all stages in cross-cultural work, from explanation and planning with one's colleagues or informants, through preparation of verbal materials and instructions, to interpretation of the results — which obviously have to be returned to the investigators' language in some way. In a very significant theoretical paper on this problem, Werner and Campbell (1970) emphasized the importance of *back-translation* (having one set of bilinguals translate from source to their own target language and another independent set of bilinguals translate the products of the first set back into the source language) and *decentering* (using successive comparisons of original source with back-translated source and of first-translated target with subsequently translated target, monolinguals in each case being the judges, as a means of reaching a compromise translation to which both languages and cultures contribute). Brislin (1970) has contributed an empirical test of these procedures involving 94 bilinguals (with English) at the University of Guam, representing 10 languages, translating or back-translating 6 essays varying in 3 content areas and 2 levels of difficulty. The most relevant result for present purposes was that the number of errors in original and back-translated versions noted by pairs of independent monolinguals in the source language were both reliable and predictive of errors noted by bilinguals comparing source and target versions, as well as predictive of errors in answering questions about the back-translated passages.

In the "tool-making" phase of the present research, translation is involved at only two points — translating the original 100 culture-common substantives into each language (these to be used in eliciting qualifiers and then as the concepts to be judged against the scales derived) and then translating the scale terms back into English so that the results can be interpreted — and at only the first point could translation influence the quantitative results. The "tool-using" (*Atlas*) stage involves two analogous points of translation — of 620 concepts into each language and of the commentaries of our colleagues (usually given in English, since they were all to some degree bilingual, but nevertheless involving "translation" problems on their part) — and, again, only at the first point could translation infidelity influence the actual *Atlas* data. Between these two points in each case, the data are analyzed for each indigenous language (or its transliterations) by the computer, "untouched by Western minds." We will return to a consideration of the translation problems connected with the "tool-using" *Atlas* work at a later point (pp. 406-408).

However, in none of our translation work have we been able to employ either back-translation or decentering techniques. Two conditions are implicitly presumed in the Werner and Campbell (1970) paper: first, that it is *texts* (from sentences to whole essays or instructions, or at least words that are in multiple relation with other words, as in folk taxonomies) rather than single words that are being translated; second, that the translating is *bilingual* (between pairs of languages) rather than multilingual. Most of our translations involve single word-forms (either substantives or qualifiers — although final scale terms are oppositional pairs) ; there is no sentential or larger context to constrain the possible senses of the terms. We tried back-translation at the very beginning of the project, but it failed repeatedly because of multiple senses (most obvious in the case of homonyms), and very familiar, high-frequency words are precisely those with the largest numbers of senses. We found that using groups of about ten fluent bilinguals working independently, looking for cross-speaker agreements and checking back-translation of the dominant sense informally, worked better (see Chapter 3, p. 70). As far as decentering is concerned, its essence is the modification of *both* source and target languages, ". . . aiming at both loyalty of meaning and colloquialness in each language" (Werner and Campbell, p. 398). Obviously, when some 20 languages and cultures are involved and American English is the common source language, one can't keep modifying AE in all 20 directions at once. Furthermore, it seems that the idea of decentering is more relevant to discourse than to single words.

We consider the nature of our *sampling* — of concepts and scales and of language/culture communities, but particularly of subjects within communities — to be a critically constraining factor. It is least so upon the demonstration of universality of the E-P-A structure of the affective meaning system and most so upon the interpretations of our *Atlas* category analyses. Although 100 concepts and 50-60 descriptive scales are a very small sample of the richness of substantives and qualifier modes in natural languages, it must be kept in mind that the concepts were selected to be as diversified as the criteria of culture-commonness and translatability would allow and that the 50-odd scales were selected in terms of their productivity (frequency and diversity) and relative independence in usage for each community. Our sampling of language/culture communities around the world is very small in terms of the total possible and is biased toward "high" as against "low," toward literate as against nonliterate, toward Indo-European as against other languages, and toward northern and western as against southern and eastern communities geographically. But since the same type of structure appears despite our widest variations along all these dimensions, it seems most unlikely that further sampling of human communities will call into question the universality of E, P, and A as affective features of meaning. In terms of a great deal of work with different subject samples within AE, it also seems highly unlikely that this system is somehow uniquely characteristic of male teen-agers in human societies (see Chapter 2, pp. 58-63).

The situation is quite different, however, when we come to *interpretation* of the *Atlas* data, as analyzed in terms of various categories of concepts. Even with 620 concepts, many categories are grossly undersampled. Even though the four scales representing each factor for each culture were selected as being the most nearly functional-equivalent to those employed by all others, their small number enhances the possibility of "denotative contamination" (shifts from generalized affective to specific denotative senses in interaction with particular concepts). And since at this stage we are interested in Sub-universals and Uniquenesses as well as in cultural Universals, the small size of our sample of human communities as compared with the sum of all human communities, along with the biases already indicated, must obviously constrain our use of the terms "universal," "sub-universal," and even "unique." An implicit phrase — "within the 23 communities sampled" — must be added to each such assertion.

The fact that our subjects through all phases were teen-age males in public high schools (except for the Yucatan Spanish sample) and in very particular local regions applies a maximum constraint on interpretation of our *Atlas* data. Perhaps throughout this book, rather than talking about "communities," we should have used Naroll's (1968) term "cultunits" ("people who are domestic speakers of a common distinct language and who belong either to the same state or the same contact group"), and even then we would have to expand "people" in his definition to "male, teen-age, school-attending, urban-dwelling people." Although we are well aware of the severity of this constraint upon culturological interpretations — and in Chapter 6, it will be recalled, we repeatedly warned that our interpretations must be taken *cum grano salis* for exactly these reasons — it is only too easy to slide into an economical but potentially misleading style of reporting. Strictly speaking, the FF in "FF has the highest E for YELLOW" refers to teen-age schoolboys in Helsinki and not to Finnish culture in general.

At a recent conference on the Social Science Utilization of an Atlas of Affective Meanings (sponsored by our project), many of our participants in economics, education, sociology, and political science (but not anthropology and linguistics) expressed concern over the nonrepresentativeness of our samples of communities. Yet they agreed under discussion that, given practical limitations on time and funding and the unlikelihood of getting samples that are both representative within each community and comparable across communities, our opting for samples which were homogeneous with respect to within-community variables but heterogeneous with respect to overall language and culture was at least the best of two evils. And before leaving the matter of our subject samples, another weakness must be admitted — we had no control over the contextual influences that may have been operating in different communities: closeness in time to an exam, a holiday, or even a traumatic event like a flight to the moon or a student riot; the time of the year (see time of test-taking for SW and FF and their color meanings) or the weather of the day; the general morale of the school or the motivating quality of the instructions; and so on ad infinitum. Perhaps this is an inherent weakness of research that must be carried out by many people across long distances and over long periods of time.

BACKGROUND OF THIS RESEARCH

The cross-cultural research reported in this book was based on some ten years of indigenous research with American English-speaking subjects. Chapter 2 provided an interpretative review of this work. A geometric model of semantic space, using the familiar color space as an analogue, was presented and related to the factor-analytic measurement model; the three earliest AE factorizations, various types of two-mode factorial solutions, and a three-mode analysis of SD data (Levin, 1963) were described and critically evaluated. Finally, the results of various studies were brought to bear on the question of generality of the E-P-A affective meaning structure. Generality across diverse samplings of scales was shown, as well as across diverse samplings of subjects (varying in age, sex, political orientation, and normalcy — and many more variables could be added today), but the evidence clearly suggested that when concepts are selected from restricted classes (e.g., Charles Morris's "Ways to Live," personality concepts, political concepts, and so on), factor structures could vary, both in the relative weights of E, P, and A and in the fusion or diffusion of these factors.

These early AE results were largely summarized in *The Measurement of Meaning* (Osgood, Suci, and Tannenbaum, 1957), and this book and the reviews it received set the stage for a number of methodological and theoretical debates which are still going on. In a review titled "Is a Boulder Sweet or Sour?" psycholinguist Roger Brown (1958) took us to task for inadequately defining the kind of meaning we were trying to measure; "the reason why the meaning measured by the differential seems to be best designated *connotative* can only be because *connotation* is a very ambiguous term." (*Later in this chapter we will return to the question of what is measured with the SD technique, pp. 393-394.*) Linguist Uriel Weinreich (1958) also criticized us for claiming to measure connotative (or denotative) meaning when what we were actually measuring was not meaning at all but rather feeling or affect. (*The term "connotative" has been dropped in favor of "affective," but we will still argue later that E, P, and A display all of the functional characteristics of other semantic features.*) Weinreich really lambasted us for claiming to offer too much to the linguist-lexicographer but in fact offering very little. (*Our claim was really rather minimal, but the failure to deliver even that was indeed maximal — for reasons that we now know.*)

Psychometrician Gulliksen (1958) concentrated on scaling problems, suggesting that our 7-step scales were too coarse and that 20 or even 30 steps would be better (*but very cumbersome for subjects and finer than their ordinary use of linguistic quantifiers*), that the SD technique is highly susceptible to concept-scale interaction (*of which we are acutely aware — see below*), and that nonsignificant differences (e.g., in factor structures) found with small numbers of subjects do not reliably rule out the existence of such differences without the use of parallel tests (*the cross-cultural studies reported here seem to satisfy this criticism*). Finally, psychometrician and psycholinguist John B. Carroll (1959) criticized us for using a too grandiose title, *THE Measurement of Meaning*, when very few aspects of meaning were measured (*true, but one can't put a whole book in a title*) and particularly for using too few concepts in our factor analyses to permit definition, mathematically, of more than four or five factors (*this is entirely valid, but the extension to 100 concepts in our cross-cultural factor analyses at least reduces the force of this criticism*). Carroll does conclude his review by characterizing the book with "it is *good*, it is *active*, it is *potent*"! In a recent and penetrating critique of the SD technique, our Finnish colleague Kaarle Nordenstreng (1969b) adds the point that, by its very nature (constructing a simplified "deep structure" out of a much richer "surface structure" of semantic distinctions), factor analysis has a built-in lack of exhaustiveness, and he notes that the philosopher-linguist critics Wells (1957) and Weinreich (1958) had emphasized the crudeness of the SD technique in this respect. We shall return to Nordenstreng's review in a number of other connections.

The question of subject variance. In Chapter 2 (pp. 49-51) it was pointed out that in any two-mode factorization, variance among subjects in their semantic structures is either lost or confounded. In the *stringing-out* method (each subject × concept score treated as a unique event) subject and concept variances are confounded; in the *summation* method (using the means of subjects on items) subject and concept variance is again confounded; in the *average-correlation* method (the separate correlation matrices of each subject on each concept being averaged over subjects) possible intersubject differences in semantic structure are simply washed out. The summation method has been used consistently in our cross-cultural work. The justification of any of these two-mode solutions (and it will be recalled that they yielded very similar results; see Table 2:2) rests on the validity of the assumption that subject variance is, indeed, minimal.

Some inklings that there might be some interpretable variation in individual semantic spaces were given in a study by Tanaka and Osgood (1965). Thirty individual subjects (5 male and 5 female each for AE, FF, and JP) were selected randomly, and their individual correlational matrices among 10 translation-equivalent scales used in rating 24 color-form combination stimuli were computed; these matrices were intercorrelated (yielding a 30 × 30 subject matrix), and this matrix was factored.[1] The unrotated principal-components factor matrix showed the first subject factor to account for 76% of the total variance, the second only 7%, and the third 5%. When these three factors were rotated by the Varimax method, it was found that all Finnish subjects (male and female) loaded highest on Factor I and nearly

---

[1] This is not a three-mode analysis, of course, but the logic is clear enough. If the individual matrices always correlated with each other near 1.00, then there could be only one subject factor, whereas if the 30/30 intersubject matrix displayed patterns of high and low correlation, then some number of subject factors would be operating.

all Japanese subjects highest on Factor II, but the American subjects varied in loading, five being highest on I, one on II, and four on III — but no Finnish or Japanese subjects had their highest loadings on III. While these data provide evidence for inter*cultural* differences in the use of translation-equivalent scales in judging abstract color-form stimuli (see also a study by Ahmavaara and Nordenstreng, 1969, Ch. 9, on a transformational analysis of the synesthesia data for Anglo and Navajo subjects reported by Osgood, 1960b), with the possible exception of the Americans, they do not indicate sizable inter*subject* (within-culture) variance — which is our present methodological concern. In our cross-cultural work we are dealing entirely with cultural meanings (by virtue of the averaging of subjects within each culture), and the question is whether such averaging over subjects is justifiable.

Although not a three-mode solution either, a method of transformational analysis developed by Ahmavaara (1954) puts factor analyses done in two modes (e.g., scales $\times$ concepts) into the same factor space mathematically and then compares them across the third mode (e.g., individual subjects or classes of subjects). Indices of "normal" transformation (where factorial invariance is preserved, but vector lengths shift — thus differences in the salience or *differentiation* attributable to the scales) and of "abnormal" transformation (unique deviations of scales within' an otherwise invariant factor space — thus *shifts in meaning* of the scales) are both provided by the method. There have been a number of applications of this method to SD data (see Ahmavaara and Nordenstreng, 1969). In the present context Nordenstreng (1969a) compared white-collar workers ($N = 111$) and farmers ($N = 66$) in Finland for their scale structures based on interscale correlations for the single concept WORK (this being part of a larger study). Here the total amount of structure difference was very large (over 40% of the common variance), and most of it was attributable to "abnormal" transformation. Examples: for the *modern–old-fashioned* scale, *modern* WORK means more of Justice and Modernity factors for white-collar workers, but more of Esteem and Colorfulness factors for farmers; for the *valuable-worthless* scale, *valuable* WORK implies more of Pleasantness, Efficiency, and Safety factors to white-collars, but more of Justice, Autonomy, and Modernity factors to farmers. This again is evidence for interaction of (sub-)cultural *classes* of subjects with scale structures, but it does not indicate the relative magnitude of inter-individual subject variance.

The three-mode solution (Tucker, 1963a, 1963b) — which was not available for our original AE studies or in the early stages of the cross-cultural project, of course — makes it possible to assess subject variance directly and determine its factorial complexity. In the first application of three-mode technique to SD data (Levin, 1963), application of the equal-ratio-of-latent-roots criterion yielded a precipitous drop between the first subject factor and the second (see Figure 2:3) and thus justified the assumption of minimal subject variance. There have been a number of three-mode factorizations of SD data in recent years. For example, Litt (1966) reported three subject factors for an SD study on the meanings of abstract paintings; Snyder (1967), in a re-analysis of the *Thesaurus* study data (Osgood, Suci, and Tannenbaum, 1957), suggests the possibility of two subject factors. Most recently, Tzeng (1972) has applied the three-mode method to personality differential data obtained from male and female British English, Finnish, and Japanese subjects; in all six analyses, the first subject factor accounted for the lion's share of the variance, with the second factor accounting for only 6% or less of the total variance. But the question still arises as to what is "minimal" subject variance.

Although neither the usual SD technique nor the three-mode solution per se (there being no concept mode) was employed, a study by Wiggins and Fishbein (1969) focused on the question of subject variance in affective semantic systems. They used a concept-free method in which 97 male and female college sophomores rated all possible pairs of 15 scales (5 each for E, P, and A as determined in early SD work) for global similarity of meaning on a 7-step *similar-dissimilar* scale (e.g., overall similarity of *good-bad/passive-active*); if their rating was other than zero similarity, subjects also indicated the orientation of the relation (e.g., *good* with *active* rather than *passive*). The Tucker-Messick (1963) multidimensional scaling model was applied to these data to obtain both scale and subject factors and, for each subject-factor type ("idealized individuals"), their unique scale-factor structure. Three subject factors (accounting together for 73% of the total variance) could be extracted. Scale factors for the first subject factor ("group average") reproduced standard E, P, and A neatly. Inspection of plots of the three subject factors suggested that actual individual subjects varied in their use of scale factors so as to form a cone around the "group average" (extracted as subject Factor I). This cone distribution was cut into ten subsets of individuals ("idealized individuals") — apparently on a somewhat arbitrary basis — and the data for each subset were factored and rotated. At this fine level of analysis, subject differences do appear to exist: for example, "idealized types" 1 and 2 were both judged to "splinter" A into two subfactors; "type" 5 appears to lose an independent A factor, using such scales evaluatively; conversely, "types" 7 and 8 both display a large A factor (56% of total variance) which absorbs most P scales and thus becomes a Dynamism factor.

What are we to conclude from this information? First, as to the original question — whether the subject variance is sufficiently small to justify its being collapsed into a two-mode solution for the purposes of studying cultural meanings — all studies in which subject factors are reported in terms of percentage variances (Levin, 1963; Tanaka and Osgood, 1965;

Litt, 1966; Snyder, 1967; Tzeng, 1972)[2] agree in finding that the first subject factor ("group average") accounts for a very large proportion of the total variance, with the second and subsequent factors accounting for relatively little. Furthermore, as clearly shown in the Levin study (see Figure 2:3) and presumably in the others, the precipitousness of the drop between first and remaining factors is much greater for the subject mode than for either the scale or concept modes. On the other hand, it is apparent from the Nordenstreng, Tanaka-Osgood, and Wiggins-Fishbein studies that the affective semantic systems of individuals within cultures are by no means perfectly homogeneous. In the Wiggins-Fishbein case — where whole scales were judged on global similarity and no concept anchors at all were given — it is at least possible that concept-scale interaction was largely responsible; that is, the real individuals represented by one "idealized individual" may have been thinking about people concepts, about abstract concepts for another "type," or concrete physical concepts, or yet another "type," and so on. However, there is nothing in our behavioral conception of meaning that would deny the possibility of real individual differences in meaning systems, based upon differences in experiences in the learning of signs or in differences in emotionality, intelligence, and the like.

The problem of concept-scale interaction. The existence of concept-scale interaction was repeatedly noted in *The Measurement of Meaning.* The earliest study explicitly on this matter was a master's thesis by Shaw (1955; see pp. 176-177 in Osgood, Suci, and Tannenbaum, 1957), and it was restricted to variations in relations of other scales to *good-bad* as a function of the concept being judged. The variation was considerable, e.g., for *strong-weak* with *good-bad* from as high as .67 on GOD to as low as .03 on TORNADO. Shaw hypothesized that this variation might be due to the overall "evaluativeness" of the concept, and this was clearly supported: with "evaluativeness" indexed independently by the frequencies of either *good* or *bad* given as associations to 20 concepts, the higher the E of the concept the higher the correlations of other scales with *good-bad* (data from Analysis I in Chapter 2). In a more extensive analysis the data for each of the 20 concepts used in the *Thesaurus* study (Analysis III in Chapter 2) were factor-analyzed separately and then their correlational and factorial matrices compared. Briefly, correlations between the same pairs of scales varied as much as from +.60 to −.60, and E scales proved to be the most susceptible to concept variation (e.g., *pleasurable* goes with *feminine* for the concept MOTHER but with *masculine* for the concept ADLAI STEVENSON, for rather obvious reasons). A factor easily identifiable as E appeared for each concept and a factor identifiable as either P or Dynamism appeared for all but two

---

[2] Although not reported in their article, Nancy Wiggins (personal communication) indicates that subject Factor I accounted for 66.3%, II for 4.0%, and III for 2.5% — again, an abrupt drop from I to II.

concepts — but beyond this there was great variation. It was also noted that factor structures can vary in the number, nature, and variance accounted for of factors when *classes* of concepts (e.g., Personality, Political, etc.) as well as *single* concepts are varied.

Tanaka, Oyama, and Osgood (1963) had college girls in both Japan and the United States rate three classes of concepts — patches of color, line forms, and abstract words — against translation-equivalent, 35-scale SDs. Separate scale-by-scale correlation matrices were computed and then factored for each of the six combinations of concept class and culture. Although E, P, and A characterized the first three factors for all concept classes and for both cultures, Activity had the most weight for colors, Potency the most for line forms for AE (and nearly so for JP), and Evaluation clearly the most weight for abstract words (ETERNITY, VIRGINITY, DREAM, etc.). When scale correlation matrices were intercorrelated, cell by corresponding cell, correlations were consistently higher for the two cultures rating the same classes of concepts than for the same culture rating different classes of concepts — a result shown by the italicized values in Table 7:1. This not only indicates concept-scale interaction but further suggests that such interaction effects may be universal rather than unique within particular cultures, at least for such extreme concept classes as colors, line forms, and abstract words.

Nordenstreng (1969a) has also applied Ahmavaara's transformational analysis method (see discussion above in relation to subject-scale interaction) to the question of concept-scale interaction. In this case principal-component factor analyses of 720 subjects × 35 scales for two concepts, TELEVISION and SCHOOL, were first made and rotated by Varimax independently. Four factors, corresponding quite closely in meaning but varying in the relative proportions of variance accounted for, were obtained for each concept. The two factor analyses were then transformed into the same mathematical space by Ahmavaara's method and their "normal" (differences in degrees

TABLE 7:1

Correlations among Scale Intercorrelation Matrices
(Tanaka, Oyama, and Osgood, 1963)

		JAPANESE			AMERICAN		
		Colors	Forms	Words	Colors	Forms	Words
Japanese	Colors	1.00	.51	.33	*.62*	.43	.21
	Forms		1.00	.41	.32	*.52*	.25
	Words			1.00	.36	.28	*.65*
American	Colors				1.00	.43	.41
	Forms					1.00	.24
	Words						1.00

of scale differentiation) and "abnormal" (differences in scale meanings) transformations were compared, the former accounting for most of the total structural difference. It was clear that the semantic space for SCHOOL is more differentiated (i.e., it is more intensely meaningful) than for TELE-VISION. There were some notable shifts in scale meanings also ("abnormal" transformation) — for example, for the scale *impartial-partial,* we find that *impartial* SCHOOL loads higher on Safety, Discomfort, and Modernity factors in contrast with *impartial* TELEVISION, which is more Dangerous and Old-fashioned yet more Comfortable.

The fact of concept-scale interaction seems inescapable. Two questions are posed: First, what, theoretically, is the basis for such interaction? Second, what implications does it have for our cross-cultural research?

In a significant methodological paper Kahneman (1963) analyzed SD ratings into three orthogonal components: (a) variability among the "true scores" of concepts, (b) variability among the constant deviations of individual raters, and (c) variability in the deviations of individuals in rating specific concepts. He had 60 subjects rate 40 concepts on 12 typical SD scales, the 40 concepts being organized into 4 subsets designed to maximize positive or negative correlations between certain pairs of scales. Across all concepts, variance of (a) "true scores" was considerable, of (b) "constant errors" (i.e., subject variance) very small, and of (c) intermediate in magnitude but low in reliability over a week's interval. When the variance of interscale correlations within the four sets of concepts was computed, it was found to be infinitesimal. However, when the correlations between two pairs of scales (*strong-weak/kind-cruel* and *good-bad/large-small,* these having near-zero *r*'s on the average across all concepts) were computed for single concepts, they were significantly positive when the concept "true scores" were on the same sides of the neutral points and negative when on opposite sides. Kahneman attributes this to "constants of exaggeration" among inferentially related scales (variable c above).

Kahneman interprets (a) as real "ecological" differences among concepts and classes of concepts in terms of the properties of their referents (which we might reinterpret as the semantics of *la langue*) and (c) as the "errors" of judgment of particular concepts by particular individuals attributable to their inferences about the congruence among properties (which we might reinterpret as the semantics of *la parole*) — and (b) appears to be related to real subject variance (as discussed earlier). He concludes as follows: "The different correlations found for different *sets* of concepts, such as colors and words, can be attributed to differences in the organization of true scores ... no inferences can be drawn from them to changes in the meaning of scales. ... The different correlations found for *single* concepts are due to individual differences among raters ... and any inference from such correlations to processes occurring within the individual is again necessarily doubtful" (pp. 562-563). Thus in neither case does Kahneman believe that the meanings of *scales* change (normatively in *la langue* or individually in *la parole*) as functions of the concept being judged.

This denial of semantic shifts in concepts and scales brought into inter-action via the SD procedure seems flatly contradictory to both intuition and fact. Most of the high-frequency lexical items in a language have multiple senses, the number tending to increase with frequency of usage (Zipf, 1949). Witness verbs like *make* (in senses of "construct," "cause to exist," "appoint," etc.), nouns like *play* ("recreation," "stage performance," "loose coupling," etc.), and adjectives like *light* ("bright," "lacking weight," "frivolous," etc.). It is furthermore obvious that when words of different form classes are conjoined syntactically, the senses of each tend to select among the senses of the other, to the extent that each is variable — thus the sense of *green* in the phrase *a green policeman* is quite different than in the phrase *a green apple* and, conversely, the sense of *case* in *a full case* as against *a serious case*. It will be recalled that in the Shaw study above, evaluativeness of the concept was predictive of the correlation of other scales with *good-bad*. One of the certain bases of concept-scale interaction is this shifting of senses of both concepts and scales as they are "syntactically" linked in SD items.

However, both concepts (nouns) and scales (adjectives) vary in their susceptibility to such sense shifts. Whereas POLICEMAN is relatively con-strained, COUNTRY is more flexible, and whereas *angular* and *rational* are quite constrained, *hard* and *fine* are much more flexible. And of all dimen-sions of qualification it is probably *good* and *bad* (and evaluators generally) that are most indefinite as to sense — what is *good* for a KNIFE (sharpness) is different from what is *good* for a JUDGE (fairness) which in turn is dif-ferent from what is *good* for a TOOTH (soundness). In interaction with con-cepts, it is probably the less rigidly sensed E scales which tend to shift most as a function of the concept being judged; thus we find that *valuable* corre-lates with *fast* for ATHLETE but with *slow* for SLEEP, and *worthless* correlates with *hard* for PILLOW but with *soft* for KNIFE. This is what has been termed "denotative contamination" (Osgood, 1962), and from the point of view of measuring pure affective meaning it *is* contamination. On the other hand, such concept-scale interaction can be viewed as evidence that the SD tech-nique is *sensitive* to denotative as well as affective features of meaning.

Now, when an entire class of concepts shares certain sets of denotative features (e.g., Occupations all ⁻Concrete, ⁺Human, ⁺Mature, etc.; Stuffs all ⁺Concrete, ⁻Living, ⁻Countable, etc.), those scales which are denotatively common to all instances but nondifferential among them (i.e., which tap the defining features of the class) should tend to drop out of factors be-cause of low variance, or perhaps show up as E, P, or A on a metaphorical basis (e.g., *alive-dead* on A for Occupations). On the other hand, scales which differentiate among the concepts in the class, and in similar ways, should cluster to form a more denotative factor (e.g., *skillful-unskillful, smart-dumb, difficult-easy, high-low,* etc. for Occupations), which may or may not be "contaminated" with affect. And scales which are denotatively irrelevant to the concept class in question (e.g., *hard-soft, wet-dry, sweet-sour* for Occupations) must be used metaphorically and can only contribute to the affective tone of various factors.

In his 1959 review of *The Measurement of Meaning* Carroll pointed out that the standard instructions on SD forms fail to tell the subject whether he is to judge the abstract concept (FATHERS-in-general, DOGS-in-general, GAMES-in-general) or some personally relevant instance of it (my FATHER, that vicious DOG next door, a baseball GAME I saw today). This is quite true, and it undoubtedly contributes to subject variance. Extending this line of argument, Nordenstreng (1969b, pp. 25-29) has suggested that concepts as rated may fall at different levels along a concrete-abstract continuum — from direct, uncoded-in-the-language perceptual experience (e.g., the non-sense figures of Elliott and Tannenbaum, 1963), to singular-referent instances of concepts (MY BEST FRIEND, PARIS, THE GOLDEN GATE BRIDGE), to low-level class concepts (DOG, TREE, FEAR), to higher-level category names (ANIMAL, EMOTION, TIME). In principle, it would seem that a semantic feature theory would incorporate these differences in level of abstraction. Each subordinate in a hierarchy must have added features to distinguish its meaning from other concepts at its own level (e.g., DOG vs. CAT vs. COW, etc.) while entailing all features of its superordinate (ANIMAL), and similarly for still more specific subordinates (POODLE vs. COLLIE vs. DACHSHUND with respect to DOG). Such a feature theory could also incorporate shifts in sense as a function of concept-scale interaction.

Although concepts as given in an SD study (for example, in our *Atlas* work) may vary in their inherent level of abstraction and subjects may vary in their levels of interpretation of the concept along the concrete-abstract continuum, as Nordenstreng (1969b) points out, SD methodology projects all concepts into the same (affective) space and thus loses hierarchical distinctions. In one sense this is justifiable, since the affective features of meaning clearly do not fall within such taxonomic hierarchies but rather seem to parallel denotative systems — witness the fact that POODLE may be $^{+}$E, $^{-}$P, $^{+}$A while ANIMAL may be $^{-}$E, ^{0}P, $^{+}$A. In another sense, however, this means that a great deal of information about the meaning of concepts escapes the SD net (see pp. 393-394 in this chapter for further elaboration of this matter).

What bearing does the fact of concept-scale interaction have upon the cross-cultural research reported here? As far as demonstration of the universality of E, P, and A is concerned, it should have little or no effect; this is because in the "tool-making" phase we dealt with a standard, large, and diversified set of translation-equivalent concepts rather than with classes of concepts varying across our N cultures. However, as far as interpretation of the *Atlas* data (and those of other subprojects in the "tool-using" phase) is concerned — where we *are* concerned with similarities and differences in the meanings of specific concepts across cultures — concept-scale interaction raises problems. With only four scales representing each factor for each community and with the senses of both scales and concepts undoubtedly varying somewhat across communities, the possibility of interaction is very real — even though we tried in our translation checks to maximize congruence of concept senses and in our interpretative sessions with colleagues to identify probable instances of such interaction. So, again, the data on particular concepts for particular cultures must be interpreted *cum grano salis*.[3] It is also likely that individual subjects in all communities will vary in the level of abstractness at which they interpret the concepts, and it is possible that cultures as wholes may vary in abstraction level as well. However, individual variation in this respect can only contribute to subject variance, and cultural variation is itself a valid reflection of cultural differences.

MODES OF QUALIFYING HUMAN EXPERIENCE

The rationale for and technique of eliciting qualifiers as the first step in the cross-cultural project have been described in Chapter 3. A modified word-association procedure, with culture-common substantives (nouns) as stimuli and, per instructions, qualifiers (adjectives) as responses, generated 10,000 qualifier tokens from each community. The distribution characteristics of these language samples proved to fit the lognormal function anticipated very closely, although there were some differences between communities. These samples were computer-analyzed so as to order the qualifier types within each community in terms of productivity in usage over the 100 substantives (frequency and diversity simultaneously indexed by the H statistic), and these ordered lists were then pruned by eliminating qualifiers which displayed correlated patterns of usage with qualifiers higher in the lists. The 60-70 highest-ranked qualifiers in the pruned lists were returned to the field for elicitation of opposites. Factor analyses in which the polar terms of scales served as "concepts" rated against all other scales (scale-on-scale analyses) were done in several communities; although they provided some rather interesting incidental data (see below), the factors obtained replicated those obtained in later concept-on-scale analyses, and hence this procedure was dropped in favor of the much less laborious concept-on-scale method.

Adequacy of qualifier sampling. We feel reasonably satisfied with the

[3] The fact that "translation-equivalent" concepts in the sense of referential agreement may still vary across cultures in their overall patterns of senses probably sets a translation-fidelity "ceiling" on cross-cultural comparability.

adequacy of our qualifier-sampling procedures. The fact that the numbers of translation failures (TFs) and large sense differences (TDs) for the 100 concepts used for qualifier elicitation (included in the *Atlas* 620) were very small in comparison with the other *Atlas* concepts indicates that their translations were generally adequate. The fact that these 100 concepts, which survived careful translation checks on our first seven communities, have with only one or two exceptions in each case proven easily translatable into all subsequent languages suggests that they are, indeed, "culture-common." The fact that the usage distributions of qualifier types and tokens (see pp. 78-83) yield close fits to a lognormal function indicates that our qualifier samples from various communities are statistically representative of qualifiers in the languages as wholes. What variations there were (e.g., AD, AE, HC, and ND showing relatively low stereotypy and JP, MK, LA, and FR relatively high stereotypy) had no obvious cultural bases. The fact that *good* and *big* (or very close synonyms) appear as the most productive qualifiers for 23 of our 25 communities (and the two exceptions — *many* for IF and *beautiful* for TZ (Tzeltal) — certainly do not miss the mark by much) is mute testimony to the dominance of the E and P modes of qualifying, which were to appear later in the concept-on-scale factor analyses.

Evidence for bipolarity in qualifying. Our colleagues have never experienced any difficulty in the opposite-elicitation task used to transform the most productive qualifiers into bipolar scales. This in itself suggests that bipolar organization of modes of qualifying experience is a human universal. In connection with a study on cross-cultural visual-verbal synesthetic tendencies (Osgood, 1960b), it was shown that when 16 pairs of adjectives representing the poles of 8 scales tapping the usual E-P-A factors were rated singly (in random, dispersed orders) against binary "scales" defined by visual alternatives (e.g., *white* vs. *black* circle, *thick* vs. *thin* vertical line, *angular* vs. *rounded* horizontal line, and so on), all of the antonym pairs proved to have reciprocally antagonist profiles for Americans, and all but one pair (*fast-slow*, which had a *positive* correlation for Navajos) had such profiles for Navajos, Mexican Spanish, and Japanese subjects as well. Deese (1964) concludes that his research on adjectival associations largely "confirms the advisability of using the polar-opposite scheme in the semantic differential technique" (p. 355).

In Chapter 3 (pp. 102-110) we presented data from the scale-on-scale judgmental tasks which, using single polar terms as concepts to be rated on all other scales, show that the scale locations of one polar term predicted from the locations of its opposite (the predicted location, of course, being that equidistant from the neutral origin and in the opposite direction) are well within the estimated reliabilities of such judgments for American English (median $d = .24$ scale unit). The median deviations between obtained and predicted scale positions for other communities on the scale-on-scale task were .44 for Cantonese, .47 for French, .32 for Lebanese Arabic, and .20 for Swedish.

Our conclusions about the bipolarity of the semantic space and the scales defining it are flatly contrary to those reached in a monograph by Green and Goldfried (1965). These investigators created unipolar scales for each of the polar terms of 30 scales (drawn from our first factor analysis; see Chapter 2, pp. 45-46), half of which they judged to be obviously bipolar and the other half less obviously so. It turns out that this distinction is really based on the multi-sense or even homonymous nature of the qualifiers in question. Ten concepts (drawn from our earlier *Thesaurus* study; see Chapter 2, pp. 46-48) were judged against "unipolar" 7-step scales running from *very negatively related* through zero to *very positively related,* one for each of the 60 qualifiers (e.g., STATUE *fragrant*).

There are several flaws in this study. (1) The major one was the failure to take into account the multiple senses of single qualifiers. In bipolar scales each qualifier serves to "anchor" the sense of the other (this has also been noted by Nordenstreng, 1969a). This can be demonstrated easily by the existence of two (or more) opposites for a term which are *not* synonymous — for example, from the Green-Goldfried materials: *green*–red (ripe),[4] *short*– long (tall), *tasty*–distasteful (tasteless), *dull*–sharp (bright), *light*–heavy (dark), *thin*–thick (fat), *bright*–dark (dumb), *foul*–fragrant (fresh), *delicate*–rugged (indelicate), *calm*–excitable (rough). These examples account for nearly half of their scales. Although Green and Goldfried recognized this problem, and in fact used multi-senses as a basis for selecting "less obviously bipolar scales," they failed to see that this renders the method inadequate as a test of bipolarity — judgments of *dull* (not bright) can hardly be used to test the bipolarity of a *dull-sharp* scale. (2) Concepts can be ambiguous with respect to certain scales, irrelevant in relation to others, and ubiquitous with respect to still others. A SPONGE, in different states, can be either *wet* or *dry;* a TORNADO is irrelevant with respect to *honest* or *dishonest,* but being marked zero (equidistant between positively and negatively *related* on the Green-Goldfried scale) will contribute to a positive correlation between these opposed terms; and certainly LADIES and COPS are ubiquitous with respect to being *pleasant* or *unpleasant* (and hence could be judged positively *related* to both, but with quite different LADIES or COPS in mind!).

These two sources of ambiguity combine to produce a massive amount of concept-scale interaction — which, in a test of bipolarity, is likely to wash out any evidence, pro or con. Each concept tends to select some sense of

---

[4] The first opposite given is that assumed by the investigators (i.e., listed among our scales and used in this experiment as the other unipolar); the other (in parentheses) is another acceptable opposite that taps a quite different sense of the italicized qualifier.

the qualifier (SYMPHONY, *dull,* meaning not exciting; KNIFE, *dull,* meaning not sharp), and each qualifier tends to select some sense of the concept (*sacred,* MOTHER-role; *cold,* MOTHER-individual). From the materials of their study, compare BABY, ME, and COP with SIN, TORNADO, and STATUE when being rated on *bright;* compare SYMPHONY with MOTHER on *calm* or COP with STATUE on *green.* It is rather remarkable that, under these conditions, the results were as positive with respect to bipolarity as they were, contrary to the Green-Goldfried conclusions: 10 of the 15 "obviously bipolar" and 8 of the 15 "less obviously bipolar" scales yielded quite consistently (> 8 of 10 concepts) negative correlations of their polar terms across the 10 concepts.

Evidence for universal semantic features. The finding that the *H* ranks for translation-equivalent qualifier types across 16 languages (available at the time) were all significantly correlated with English (with *r*'s ranging from the .50s up into the .80s), but were not in any obvious way dependent upon linguistic or cultural factors (Chapter 3, pp. 92-94), implies that human beings, regardless of locus or culture, not only tend to utilize the same kinds of semantic features in characterizing their environments but also tend to order them similarly in salience. Careful semantic analysis of these modes of qualifying (by semantic interaction or other techniques which, unlike the SD, do not amplify affective features) should be a rewarding enterprise.[5] The differentiation of Kannada *andda* and *ssunddara,* both translating into AE as *beautiful,* into generally −Human and +Human codings in terms of the nouns which elicited them as associations is also suggestive of a semantic feature discovery procedure that might be applied more generally and systematically — particularly with languages which are not native to the investigator.

CROSS-CULTURAL GENERALITY OF AFFECTIVE MEANING SYSTEMS

After some preliminary checks on the effects of scale refinement (designed to further reduce the proportions of evaluative scales and allow people in the field to add indigenous scales they considered important), on possible effects of concept ordering in the concept-on-scale task (which proved to be nil), and on the similarity between scale-on-scale and concept-on-scale tasks in terms of factor composition for AE (which proved to be high),

---

[5] See Osgood (1970a) for the rationale and some applications of this interaction technique (with verbs and modifying adverbs). We have done some exploration with our *Atlas* materials also, categorizing concepts (nouns) in terms of the multi-sense verbs (e.g., *move, have, believe*) with which they can be combined; a full and quite successful application of this method has been made by Noordman and Levelt (1970) to the Dutch *Atlas* materials. Levelt (1967, 1969) has utilized the output of this technique as applied to emotion nouns and modifying adjectives (unpublished material by Osgood and Wilkins) for testing certain multivariate methods.

Chapter 4 presents the results of various types of concept-on-scale factorizations — indigenous and cross-cultural (bilingual, bicultural, trilingual, tricultural, and pancultural) — all designed to test the stability of the E-P-A structure despite variations in either language or culture. Evidence for generality of Evaluation, Potency, and Activity as the underlying dimensions of the affective meaning system was, we feel, impressive — but there were a number of intriguing matters raised in the various analyses.

Indigenous analyses. Interpretation of the factorial results for each indigenous "cube" of data (for SW, GK, AP, CB, TH, etc.) actually should be done entirely in each native language by our colleagues and their associates — just as was the case with the early studies on AE reported in *The Measurement of Meaning.* Although this was not done formally, there have been few questions from our colleagues about the E-P-A properties of their own indigenous factors — and these usually concerned the existence of a clear A factor or its fusion with P into Dynamism. An indigenous Activity factor (but never E or P) is also sometimes displaced to fourth in order of magnitude by a unique factor (usually some varient of E, like the In-group–Moslem factor of both AD and AP or a Uniqueness factor of LA). Of course, in doing indigenous research with SD instruments, it is these factors (not the pancultural) which should be used.

Evaluation of the generality hypothesis for these indigenous factorizations by the Center staff necessarily involved translation of all scales into English (with the potential bias that this introduces), and even if the translations were completely faithful, judging whether two sets of scales, one from community X and the other from community Y, really have the same "semantic flavor" is inevitably an intuitive business. Of course, the frequent occurrence of translation-equivalent scales (i.e., *fast-slow,* as translated, appearing in both X and Y sets) supports one's intuitions — except that we realize our bilingual, bicultural, and usually SD-sophisticated colleagues could have bent over a bit to make *xssamdrudi-soofuli*[6] come out as *strong-weak.* And it must be noted that in this intuitive process the AE investigator is necessarily using his *own* semantic system in judging the similarities among the *translated* terms from other languages — which might well have their own, quite different bases for categorizing. Therefore, despite the evident similarities of the (translated) scales assigned to E, P, and A for different communities, we felt this evidence for universality to be somewhat superficial and searched for more justifiable methods.

The logic of cross-cultural factorizations. The only way to make judgments of factorial similarity that are independent of both translation fidelity and semantic intuition is to put the analyses of different community data cubes into the same mathematical space. Then if a scale for community X and

---

[6] A purely hypothetical transliterated scale!

a scale for community Y both have high loading on the same common factor, we can say that they are functionally equivalent — and this without even translating the scales into English or any other language. Of course, in order to *communicate* the flavor of the common factor or semantic feature, one does have to translate eventually, *but the isolation of the factor and the assignment of community scales to it are independent of the translation operation*. However, if two or more three-mode data cubes are to be put into the same mathematical space, at least one of the modes must be common; in our case, since subjects are obviously not the same and scales are only occasionally translation-equivalent, the only candidate for transformation is the concept mode. Our finalized 100 concepts were as translation-equivalent as we could make them, yet there is no guarantee, of course, that they really "mean the same thing" (hopefully they do referentially, but not necessarily affectively). However, the fact that they are translation equivalents of each other means that they provide a basis for common ordering of the data for our various communities and, hence, transformation into the same mathematical space. Lack of semantic equivalence can only throw "noise" into the analysis — the ultimate of which would be like assigning concepts randomly across cultures "as if" they were equivalents — *and decrease the possibility of obtaining interpretable common factors.*

A pancultural factor analysis. As a matter of fact, the pancultural factor analysis to which 21 cultures contributed their scales produced (when finally translated) the clearest evidence for universality of E, P, and A — as if the presence of cross-community clusters served to "pull out" and identify in the indigenous data those scales which are functionally most equivalent in usage (see Table 4:15 and related text). Evaluation is clearly common to all communities and largest in magnitude; Potency (with some variation between Strength and Magnitude) is common to all and next in magnitude; and Activity is common to all (except perhaps LA) but with considerably greater variety of qualifiers involved. What does "loading on the same factor" panculturally *mean* psycholinguistically? If the scale of community X identified as *xssamdrudi-soofuli* and the scale of community Y identified as *strong-weak* both load high on pancultural Potency, this means that the people in X use their *xssamdrudi-soofuli* to differentiate among the 100 translation-equivalent concepts in a way that is functionally equivalent to the way people in community Y use their *strong-weak* — presumably with COURAGE, HORSE, POWER, etc. rated high and BIRD, GIRL, EGG, etc. rated low. And note again, this conclusion is entirely independent of translating *xssamdrudi-soofuli* into Y or translating *strong-weak* into X. It is on the basis of these pancultural functional equivalences that we were able to select subsets of scales to represent E, P, and A in each community which would be maximally comparable with those across all other communities (that is, the pancultural SDs used in the subsequent *Atlas* work).

It will be recalled that in the single-community factorizations reported in Chapter 2 (for AE) and here for the indigenous analyses of all communities, it was rarely the case that factors beyond the massive E, P, and A were interpretable. That this was at least partly due to the limited number of scale variables (usually 50 to 70 or so) is suggested by the fact that in both bicultural and tricultural analyses involving 100 to 150 or more scales, additional factors appeared that were often clearly interpretable (see below). In the pancultural analysis of data from 21 communities, however, approximately 1,050 scale variables were involved, and one might therefore expect to find even more interpretable factors. Of the seven factors extracted beyond E, P, and A, five of them (all but IX and X) proved to be fairly interpretable, although they varied in the number of communities contributing to them in any identifiable way. Since the nature of these minor factors is clearly related to those found in other analyses (e.g., the partialed factorizations reported in Chapter 5) and give rise to some major methodological and theoretical issues, we shall reserve further consideration to the end of this chapter.

Bilingual and bicultural analyses. Two analyses using bilingual subjects, performing the same concept-on-scale task (but with only 20 concepts) in their native language and in English (in counterbalanced orders), were run — in Finland and in Mysore. Whereas in the "indigenous" analyses (i.e., Finns in Finnish and Finns in English factored independently) the orders of magnitudes and semantic flavors of the factors varied considerably as a function of code being used, in the "bilingual" analysis of both samples (i.e., the data for native and English versions transformed into the same space) both the ordering and the semantic flavors clearly were the same.[7] The orders of magnitude of the factors in the "bilingual" analyses for both FF and MK correspond to that in their "indigenous" native rather than their "indigenous" foreign language — as if the intensities of meaningful reactions to signs in the native language are greater than in a second language.

A small variety of bicultural analyses are reported in Chapter 4, and in all of them the E-P-A system appears more clearly than in either the indigenous or the bilingual analyses. In a bicultural analysis of Dutch and Flemish (our two most closely related languages and cultures) the overlaps were nearly perfect, even through a fourth Modernity factor. A bicultural for HC and JP — different language families but possibly similar cultures — yields less agreement, particularly on the Potency factor. But a bicultural for two widely separated groups in both language and culture, Flemish

---

[7] It is noteworthy that the uniquely Evaluative scale *light-gloomy*, for our most northern Finns, appears as the highest-loading E scale when the bilinguals perform in their native Finnish in both "indigenous" and "bilingual" analyses, but it does not appear at all in the top seven E scales in either of the analyses when they perform in English.

and Japanese, yields high similarities through four factors. If we view JP as highly "westernized" — and many of our *Atlas* data do suggest this — then it may be that such bicultural analyses can provide overall indices of cultural similarities and differences, but more evidence is certainly required.

Two tri-community analyses. Two "triplets" of communities immediately suggested themselves for this type of cross-cultural analysis — and for rather different reasons.[8] Our three samples in the Indian subcontinent presumably represent generally similar cultures, yet three different languages. Hindi and Bengali are variants of Indo-European, but Kannada belongs to an entirely different language family, Dravidian. One might, on this basis, have expected CB and DH to be more similar to each other than either to MK, but this is not borne out in any obvious way. Like most of our data, this suggests that cultural variables have more influence on affective meaning systems and attributions than purely linguistic variables do. In fact, what is most notable about this trilingual analysis is that two special types of "magnitude" factors, beyond identifiable E, P, and A, appear as Factors IV (Size) and V (Numerosity or Bountifulness) for all three Indian communities.[9] This finding strongly suggests that carefully selected cross-cultural factor analyses of this sort can be used to draw out special modes of qualifying experience which are shared by certain human communities (related by geography, religion, level of development, historical ties, and so on) and perhaps unique to these subgroups.

The other "triplet" provides a most interesting simultaneous contrast between both language and culture. Whereas Afghan Dari and Iranian Farsi are both close variants of Persian, Afghan Pashtu belongs to a different subfamily of the Indo-European language family (Dari and Pashtu are mutually unintelligible, although there are many loan words). And whereas Dari and Pashtu speakers in Afghanistan share a very similar culture (although the former was sampled in Kabul and the latter in a smaller urban center, Kandahar), it is relatively "underdeveloped" in comparison with the humming metropolis of Teheran where the IF data were collected. Which two of these three language/culture communities will tend most to relate — the two with common language or the two with common culture?

The evidence again clearly favors culture over language, as the data in Table 4:14 demonstrated. Although an Evaluation factor was shared, it was clearly dominated by IF; a factor second in magnitude, In-group–Moslem, in the tri-community analysis was shared by AD and AP, but IF had only remotely related scales, the highest IF loading being only .33; a Potency

[8] Although YC, CS, and MS might also suggest themselves, this cannot be done since for both YC and CS Spanish the "tool-making" stage was omitted and the MS pancultural scales were adapted for *Atlas* work.

[9] Both of the factors appear in additional communities in analyses where dominant E-P-A are partialed out (see pp. 216-226 in Chapter 5).

(Magnitude) factor was shared, but again clearly dominated by IF, whereas a shared Activity factor was dominated jointly by AD and AP; a Toughness factor was shared by AP and AD, but again the IF loadings were low and the scales unrelated in semantic flavor. In every case, then, affective structure similarity seems to be a function of cultural rather than linguistic relatedness. Thus both the Indian tri-community analysis (by virtue of the factorial *similarity* of its three culturally similar but linguistically different groups) and the West Asian tri-community analysis (by virtue of the factorial *dissimilarity* along cultural rather than linguistic lines) suggest that culture has more weight than language in detemining affective meaning structures.

An *Atlas of Affective Meanings*

Chapter 5 was intended both as a guide to the use of our *Atlas* materials (which will be available for single language/culture communities or for sets of communities of any size, including all we have available) and as a source of analyses that serve to illustrate its use, as well as to shed further light on some of the issues which concern us in this volume. To suit the first purpose, the chapter was organized in terms of the ordering of the types of tables to be found in each community's *Atlas* (see Table 5:1). This ordering follows the "tool-making" procedures but includes the basic measures for the full 620 *Atlas* concepts as well. Here we shall follow this organization, picking up matters of interest to method and theory as we go.

Modes of qualifying. *Atlas* Tables 1 present all qualifiers given to each of the 100 concepts with a frequency greater than one, along with the H values and diversity indices for each concept. These are quite massive tables, of course, as are many of the other *Atlas* tables, but it is felt that only such detailed materials can be of use to anthropologists, linguists, psychologists, and others interested in, for example, testing notions about language universals, selecting materials for their own cross-cultural research, and so on.[10] As one illustration of the use of Tables 1 data, we ordered the 100 translation-equivalent concepts in terms of their H values (i.e., H ranks) and then correlated these ranks across communities.

Looking first at concepts which are cross-culturally most stereotyped (i.e., low H ranks — subjects agreeing on a small number of ways of qualifying) and comparing them with concepts which are cross-culturally most amorphous (i.e., high H ranks — subjects varying and yielding a large number of different ways of qualifying), we find that CLOUD, ROPE, FRUIT, SMOKE, and

[10] To facilitate use of the *Atlas* materials by scholars in various fields, Table 9 in each community's *Atlas* gives the transliteration rules (where other than Roman scripts are used) from which native-language forms for concepts and scale terms can be derived.

WIND are the most stereotyped and POLICEMAN, HAND, MAN, THIEF, and WOMAN are the least stereotyped nearly everywhere. A few exceptions, e.g., CLOUD being quite amorphous for FF and POLICEMAN being quite stereotyped for LA, can be noted in Table 5:4. It is obvious that +Human concepts tend to be the most variably qualified (see Chapter 5, p. 201, n. 6).

It will be recalled that correlations between cultures in the *H* ranks of *qualifiers* were generally quite high (in the .50-.70 range) — i.e., humans agree pretty well on the relative salience of various modes of qualifying things. What about *substantives?* As Table 5:5 demonstrated, correlations in the *H* ranks of the 100 nouns were quite low across our communities — few *r*'s rose above .50 and many were in the .20-.30 range (the AD/AP *r* is only .46, for example). It would appear that substantives (forms that refer to people, objects, events, abstractions) are much more susceptible to cultural influences, and hence more variable across human communities in their stereotypy-amorphousness, than are qualifiers (forms that highlight the attributes or properties of diverse kinds of things). This certainly has implications for universals in linguistic structure, and it also suggests that the numbers and diversities of concept factors should be greater than descriptive scale factors.

Information indices for qualifiers. Tables 2 in the *Atlas* give the *H* values, *H* ranks, and total frequency and diversity scores for the 200 highest *H*-ranked qualifiers in each sample. Table 5:6 gave the 10 highest *H*-ranked (most productive) and 10 lowest *H*-ranked (least productive) qualifiers for the 22 communities on which such data were available — as translated into English, of course. The familiarity and E-P flavor of the high *H* qualifiers, as compared with the relative unusualness and semantic diversity of the low *H* qualifiers, is intuitively obvious for AE (*good, big, great, small,* etc. vs. *growing, exciting, simple, silver,* etc.). At least in translation, the same is suggested in the highs and lows for other cultures (the commonness of *good* and *big* in the highs and the commonness of "unusuals" in the lows, e.g., ND's *obscure,* SW's *droll,* MS's *silver-plated,* MK's *invisible,* and HC's *well-known*). However, only native speakers of the other languages really can make this judgment. Working with the native scripts for these 22 samples of high and low *H*-ranked qualifiers, one could make a rather neat test of the cross-cultural generality of G. Kingsley Zipf's (1949, pp. 60-66) "Law of Abbreviation of Words" — that the more frequently used (productive) word-tools will tend, for the sake of overall behavioral economy, to become shorter in length. Computing the mean length in number of letters *of the English translations* of high and low *H*-ranked qualifiers, we obtain a grand mean of 5.1 letters for highs as compared with a grand mean of 6.8 letters for lows. But, of course, this is not the way to do it.

Indigenous factorizations. Atlas Tables 3 give the loadings of all scales on the factors derived in the indigenous factor analyses, and in Chapter 5 we were interested more in evidence for uniqueness than in evidence for universality. We found, first, that our communities do differ in what types of scales become *metaphors of generalized Evaluation* (Table 5:7): YS, TK, and MK include mainly Aesthetic-Sensory modes in their highest-loading E scales (*sweet, beautiful, soft,* etc.); SW, MS, GK, and LA use mainly Social modes of evaluating (*likable, sympathetic, merciful,* etc.); AE, FR, BF, ND, and FF employ mainly Emotional modes of evaluating (*happy, gay, calm,* etc.); and IF, AD, AP, DH, CB, and MM use dominantly Abstract modes of evaluating (*good, beneficial, helpful,* etc.). HC splits between Social and Abstract, and IT, TH, and JP have no dominants. Although the Aesthetic-Sensory and Social modes display no obvious cultural or regional bases, the Emotional mode is restricted to European groups and the Abstract mode to Asian groups. In either case it seems that these differences in which modes of evaluating tend to become most productive and hence generalized must tap rather deep cultural orientations.

We also made *oblique factor analyses* of the indigenous data cubes to see if our cultures varied in the degree and type of fusion of E, P, and A, and the "types" thus determined were related to the affective profiles of the ego concept (I, MYSELF). Total-fusion EPA (all three factors correlated positively greater than .40), PA (Value and Dynamism), and EP (Benevolent Potency and Activity) types included IF + HC, AE + CB, and AP respectively, and all have very +E, +P, and +A self-concepts. EA (the Good going with the Active) and E-A (the Good going with the Passive) types, including FF, IT, TK, AD, FR, BF, GK, MK, and MM respectively, *both* are characterized by attributing rather low P to the self. And the 0 type (essential independence among all three affective factors), which includes ND, SW, MS, DH, TH, and JP, usually has low P and low A values for ego, as well as quite consistently lower E for ego than the EPA, PA, and EP types.[11]

It is perhaps not just a matter of chance that, comparing modes of evaluating (above) with types of factor fusions, we find that with the exception of AE and possibly HC (which is split between Social and Abstract) *all* communities using Aesthetic-Sensory, Social, and Emotional scales as generalized evaluators (TK, MK, GK, SW, MS, FF, FR, BF, and ND) are in EA, E-A, or 0 fusion types and *consistently attribute low Potency to the self* (relatively). On the other hand, of the four clear EPA, PA, and EP types (AE, IF, CB, and AP) all except AE (Emotional) use dominantly Abstract modes of evaluating, *and all* (including AE and HC) *attribute higher Potency to the self than any of the communities in the EA, E-A, and 0 fusion types* (including AD and DH, which are also Abstract evaluators).

[11] YS was intermediate between the 0 and EPA types, having moderate *r*'s among all factors (and quite high E, P, and A scores for the self). LA was a type unto itself, PA-E (that is, Dynamism being negative E), and ego was Good and Strong, but Passive.

Table 5:10 in Chapter 5 presented 20 *"types"* of *partialed factors* which appear across subsets of communities after effects of dominant E, P, and A have been removed. Although we shall reserve for later a consideration of the methodological and theoretical issues raised by such factorizations, at this point is it of interest to inquire into possible relations between these partialed factor "types" and the "types" of Evaluation modes and oblique factor fusions just discussed. Partialed Factors I (Morality), V (Aesthetic Value), VI (Utility), VIII (Ordinariness), XIV (Openness), XV (Fulfillment), XVI (Dynamism), XVII (Toughness), XVIII (Magnitude), XIX (Brightness), and XX (Thermal-Dermal) have no apparent relations to either Evaluation modes or E-P-A fusion — even though one might have expected at least I, V, and XVI to have some relations. Three of the five communities defining II (Social Evaluation) do generalize the Social mode of evaluating (SW, MS, and IT), but the two others (DH and TH) do not; all of the communities defining III (Comfort-Austerity), that is, FR, IT, LA, YS, MK, and MM, fall in the EA, E-A, 0, and PA-E (LA) fusion types; three of the four communities defining IV (Personal Competence) emphasize the Social mode of evaluating (MS, HC, and JP, but not MM) ; four of the six definers of VII (Superficiality) emphasize the Abstract mode of evaluating (IF, AP, DH, and HC, but not SW and TK) ; all of the definers of XIII (Intimacy or In-group) emphasize the Abstract mode of evaluating (IF, AP, CB, and TH), and all but one of them (TH) fall in the EPA, PA, and EP types of fusion. Partialed Factors IX (Maturity), X (Predictability), XI (Age), and XII (Security) are all defined by communities falling in the EA, E-A, and 0 fusion types and characteristically displaying low ego Potency (BF, ND, SW, FF, IT, MS, YS, GK, TK, MM, TH, and JP) — the only exceptions being IF on X and CB on XI.

Although it is impossible to estimate the statistical significance of these patterns of relations among modes of evaluating, fusions of E-P-A in oblique factorizations, and loadings on factors appearing after elimination of the effects of E-P-A, there do seem to be nonchance and potentially informative cultural phenomena operating here. What will be most important is to see if the patternings of Sub-universals and Uniquenesses in the total *Atlas* data, with over 600 concepts organized into some 50 categories, correspond in relevant cases to the groupings noted here — but this must await full analysis and interpretation of the *Atlas* categories.

Concept allocations and polarizations on E-P-A factors. It will be recalled that in Chapter 5 the allocations of concepts to the E-P-A space (in terms of their raw factor scores) were given both for the original 100 concepts on indigenous factors (pp. 226-239, data from *Atlas* Tables 4) and for all 620 concepts on the pancultural factors (pp. 246-247, data from *Atlas* Tables 8). In both cases the bias toward the positive poles of factors was marked, most so for E and least so for A, with concept population densities being much greater in the ⁺E, ⁺P, and ⁺A regions than in the opposite regions (see Tables 5:16 and 5:17). This bias is consistent with the "Pollyanna hypothesis" proposed by Boucher and Osgood (1969) to account for the facts that for 13 of our communities (a) ⁺E qualifiers are significantly more frequent in usage than their ⁻E opposites and (b) "positive" qualifiers are explicitly marked to form "negatives" (e.g., happy → *un*happy but not sad → *un*sad) significantly more frequently than the reverse, implying priority of "positive" forms in language time (see Greenberg, 1966a, and Hamilton and Deese, 1971, for further evidence). The fact that this bias also applies to P and A (even if not as extremely as E) is also consistent with the findings reported by Osgood and Richards (1973) in a paper titled "From Yang and Yin to *And* or *But*": the insertion of *and* or *but* in sentences like *X is sweet ____ kind* or *X is sweet ____ dumb* can be predicted with high accuracy not only from congruence in polarity of the adjective pairs when dominant on the *same* factors but also from their congruence in polarity across *different* affective factors, as in *X is sweet ____ brave* (⁺E and ⁺P) or *X is sweet ____ cowardly* (⁺E and ⁻P) — i.e., there appears to be a general "positive-ness" (yang) vs. "negativeness" (yin) operating here.

However, data on the polarization of concept meanings — both for the raw factor scores of the original 100 concepts on the indigenous factors (see Table 5:12) and for the standardized composite factor scores for the total 620 concepts in the *Atlas* (see Table 5:17) — indicated that affectively negative concepts (on E, on P, and on A) are both more intense affectively and more universally so. On the face of things, at least, this seems para-doxical. Why should the density of concepts be greater in the positive direc-tions of the space and yet those that *are* in the negative directions be more intense and agreed upon? After giving some thought to the matter, it appears that there may be a rather straightforward explanation. Let us assume that for our teen-age populations generally there is a rather strong tendency toward conformity with what is conceived as socially desirable[12] and avoid-ance of giving negative ratings when in doubt (i.e., the Pollyanna tendency). This should result in a general "push" away from the neutral region toward positive directions. But, on the other hand, concepts which are perceived as clearly *non*desirable socially (e.g., CHEATING, ADULTERY, ATOM BOMB, SUI-CIDE, and the like) should not be subject to this pressure and hence should yield quite consistently negative ratings.

This "explanation" has several implications. For one thing, one would expect the distributions of standardized scores to be skewed in the negative direction and even to have a bimodal tendency, with a "bump" toward the negative poles (most so for the E factor). Inspection of our total data indi-cates that this is the case for most communities. The distributions for the

---

[12] Ford and Meisels (1965) have shown that there is a high correlation between the E-factor loadings of scales and their rated social desirability.

means (see Appendix F) of standardized E, P, and A composite scores across all 23 communities for the *Atlas* 620 concepts are displayed in Figure 7:1. The skewness toward the negative poles is clear for all three factors; the bimodal "bump" is only apparent for the E factor. For another thing, one might expect there to be some relations between the degrees of "positive" bias (Pollyannaism) in different communities, as indexed by the deviations of the means of the raw scores on the factors, and other aspects of the total data. One such might be the ego profiles of the teen-age subjects: when degrees of bias are correlated with the E, P, and A values for I, MYSELF, across the 23 communities, all three reach significance ($r_E = .59$, $r_P = .67$, $r_A = .81$). Apparently, the more subjects value and attribute dynamism to themselves, the more they attribute these qualities generally to their environments. Another possibility would be the profiles of certain concepts representing Modern vs. Traditional Values (our Category IX-C): correlating degrees of bias with the differences on E, P, and A between TAKING THE INITIATIVE and ACCEPTING THINGS AS THEY ARE across the communities ($r_E = -.03$, $r_P = -.12$, and $r_A = .28$). Obviously, there is no relationship in this case.

Bicultural factorizations with AE. Although any sets of bicultural analyses against any community as a base can easily be obtained from our data, *Atlas* Tables 5 present only those against AE as a base — on the undoubtedly ethnocentric (but contemporarily realistic) ground that more investigators utilizing SD technique will be working between AE and X than between any cultures X and Y. Table 4:9 presented a sample of these AE/X factorizations. In them it was clear that (a) an E factor with high and shared loadings appears in every bicultural analysis, (b) a shared Potency factor is always second in magnitude (except with ND), and (c) Activity is less likely to be overlapping, more likely to be displaced in order of magnitude, and more likely to have scales of different "flavors" for AE and X. Although AE was often "dominant" on these bicultural factors (simply by having somewhat higher scale loadings, either because of clarity of E, P, and A in the AE data or because of higher reliabilities in some cases), this was not always the case.

One question that arises is to what extent a given community's indigenous or pancultural factors (here, AE) are "modulated' in semantic tone as a function of combined factoring with the scales of other individual communities. In Table 7:2 the loadings of all AE scales that appear among the top five (for E) or top four (for P and A) in the ten bicultural factor analyses reported in Table 4:9 are given; the loadings on these AE scales in the indigenous and pancultural analyses are listed in the first two columns. It can be seen that what is dominantly E for AE shifts very little as the community X it is factored with changes: MS and MK cause no shifts; ND, FF, TK, LA, IF, AD, and TH occasion only a single scale shift (and it

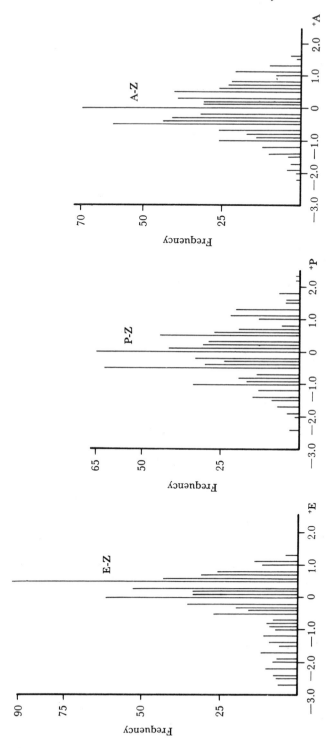

FIGURE 7:1

*Distribution of Mean Standardized E, P, and A Composite Scores
For 620 Atlas Concepts*

TABLE 7:2

AE Indigenous, Pancultural, and Other E, P, and A Scales Selected in Bicultural Factorizations

	AE→with		ND	FF	MS	GK	TK	LA	IF	AD		MK	TH
E	In-dig.	P-C	I[b]	I	I	I	I	I	I	I		I	I
nice-awful[a]	.96	.94	.94	.94	.96	.93	.96	.94	.91	.91		.95	.95
sweet-sour	.94	.90	.93	.93	.92	.90	.93	.90	.90	.88		.92	.93
good-bad	.93	.92	.89	.91	.93	.93	.93	.92	.90	.90		.92	.92
helpful-unhelpful (P-C)	.90	.89	.86	.88	.90	.91	.90	.90	.87	.88		.89	.88
heavenly-hellish (Indig.)	.93	.87	.93	.91	.91	.87	.90	.88	.89	.86		.90	.91
beautiful-ugly	.91	.85	.90										
happy-sad	.91	.87		.91				.91					.91
faithful-faithless	.89	.88				.91				.88			
useful-useless	.89	.87				.90							
needed-unneeded	.89	.89						.89					
mild-harsh	.92	.85										.90	
P			III	II	II	II	II	II	III	II	III	II	II
powerful-powerless	.75	.68	.68	.70	.68	.70	.68	.62	.52	.56	.32	.74	.64
strong-weak	.68	.57	.71	.66	.64	.62	.59	.57	.50	.52	.39	.69	.60
big-little	.81	.67	.81	.83	.80	.61	.74	.66	.80	.47	.70	.80	.81
deep-shallow	.69	.57	.54	.67	.66	.53	.67	.62	.72	.45	.50	.64	.63
long-short	.64	.50	.63						.64		.61		
heavy-light	.57	.55					.60	.60		.58			.64
high-low	.64	.51					.61		.66		.56		
rough-smooth	.43	.49								.58			
hard-soft	.45	.48								.58			
A			II	III	III	III	III	III	IV	IV	IV	IV	III
young-old	.56	.45	.20	.34	.39	.53	.54	.40	.48	.20		.49	.45
fast-slow	.64	.60	.51	.65	.68	.41	.60	.64	.63	.35		.65	.72
noisy-quiet	.56	.40	.58	.51	.44	.41	.58	.44	.42	.31		.64	.63
alive-dead	.55	.56	.38	.48	.53	.45	.52	.52	.57	.27		.55	.48
sharp-dull	.29	.23	.40			.40							
burning-freezing	.37	.17		.36							.44		
known-unknown	.48	.16			.47			.45					
fresh-stale	.10	.20				.39							
burning-freezing	.37	.22							.50				
hot-cold	.36	.21							.53		.45		
powerful-powerless	.18	.08									.34		

[a] Italicized scales are those selected as the highest on the AE indigenous and AE pancultural (15 communities, 1964) — see Tables 4:3 and 4:15. All are identical on both except *helpful-unhelpful* (only P-C) and *heavenly-hellish* (only Indig.).
[b] Factor numbers are as given in Table 4:9.

is always some other scale for either *helpful* or *heavenly*) ; and the only two-scale shift occurs for GK, where *faithful* and *useful* replace *sweet* and *heavenly*. A similar picture holds for P, except that the same scale is nearly always replaced (and the AE/AD factorization produces two distinct P factors — see below) : combinations of AE with FF, MS, and MK cause no shifts in AE scales; combinations with ND, GK, TK, LA, and TH produce a single shift (either *long, heavy,* or *high* for *deep* or *strong*) ; and IF causes two shifts (*high* and *long* for *powerful* and *strong*). The A factor is shifted not at all when in combination with TK, MK, and TH; it shifts by only one scale when with ND, FF, MS, and LA (and *young* is always replaced by *sharp, burning,* or *known*) ; combination with GK or IF produces a double shift (*sharp* and *fresh* for *fast* and *noisy* for GK and *burning* and *hot* for *young* and *noisy* for IF) ; and the AE/AD combination yields the only case of a triple-scale shift (*hot, burning,* and *powerful* replace *fast, noisy,* and *alive*). As can be seen in Table 4:9, AD has no identifiable A factor in the bicultural analysis with AE, although it does have one in its indigenous analyses (see Table 4:3).

The American English/Afghan Dari analysis provides the clearest case in which a bicultural factorization serves to differentiate what is usually a single generalized factor into two readily identifiable and meaningful independent factors. Since two Potency factors were identified (see Table 4:9 and text), we have two quite different sets of displacements from the usual AE P scales. On bicultural II, *heavy, high,* and *rough* take the places of *strong, big,* and *long* (but not *powerful*), leaving what we may call a Toughness factor; on bicultural III, *high* and *deep* replace *powerful* and *strong* (but *big* and *long* remain), leaving what we may readily identify as a Magnitude factor.[13] This suggests that finer semantic features are operating within the "cones" of indigenous E, P, and A factors to further differentiate the meanings of qualifiers. Apparently one can use bicultural factorization as a means of probing into the finer structure of gross, higher-order factors. In general, however, the data from these AE/X bicultural analyses indicate that (at least for AE) the semantic "flavors" of its affective factors remain reasonably constant across combinations with other cultures. There were only 2 instances of 3 AE scales being shifted (and both involved AD), there were 5 instances of 2 scales being changed, there were 14 cases of single-scale shifts, and there were 10 instances of no shift.

Atlas Tables 6 and 7 simply record for each community the loadings of all scales on the pancultural factor analysis (Tables 6) and the scales in the 12-scale SDs utilized in collecting the *Atlas* data on 620 concepts (Tables 7). There are no matters of particular methodological or theoretical signifi-

---

[13] Both **Toughness** and **Magnitude** appear in quite a number of the partialed factor analyses (see Chapter 5, pp. 216-226 and Table 5:10).

cance involved here. Similarly, *Atlas* Tables 8 present the basic measures for all 620 concepts for each community, obtained from application of the pancultural SDs; these measures have already been described in Chapter 5 (pp. 241-254).

PROBING SUBJECTIVE CULTURE

Chapter 6 provides a transition from this volume, primarily on the "tool-making" and hypothesis-testing phases of our work, to the volumes that will report detailed analyses and interpretation of the categories of concepts (see Table 6:1) included in the *Atlas of Affective Meanings,* our major "tool-using" project. After emphasizing the constraints upon our data in terms of sampling and the cautions that must be observed in interpretation, the small Color category was used to illustrate the standard data formats (Basic Measures, Intracultural Ranks of Concepts, Componential Analyses of Ranks, Cross-cultural and Intracultural Distances among Concepts), obtained with linked computer programs, that are designed to highlight potential Universals, Sub-universals, and Uniquenesses in the data. Illustrative commentaries from the group meetings on *Atlas* interpretation with our colleagues and some particularly relevant information from the extensive literature on color were given, but in keeping with the purpose of the present volume detailed interpretation of the patterns of Sub-universals and Uniquenesses was omitted. However, because of their inherent interest, the Universals we found in color preferences, connotations, and associations were related to the literature (mutually supporting relations being demonstrated) and to Berlin and Kay's (1969) theory of the cultural evolution of color lexicons (and our data do tend to support the essentials of their theory).

On the notion "universal." Something needs to be said about our usage of the term "universal" in interpreting the *Atlas* data. In the first place, we are using it in a *statistical sense* (nonchance tendencies within a sample of world communities), not in the absolute sense (there are no exceptions known) often used by linguists, anthropologists, and philosophers. There are, of course, some absolute universals in natural human languages (usually their defining characteristics) — such as the use of the vocal-auditory channel, the interchangeability of speaker/hearer roles, the hierarchical levels of units within units, and the componential differentiation of items within levels of units — but one would not expect such culturally sensitive aspects of language as the attributions of affect to display many universals of this absolute type. Furthermore, when some dependent variable is a function of several antecedent conditions (i.e., there are several interactive principles operating), it is to be expected that certain combinations of conditions will generate exceptions to universal trends, thereby rendering them merely statistical (but nonetheless interesting). To draw an analogy from general behavior theory,[14] although the combination of practice and reinforcement leads to increased habit strength (higher probability of response, or learning), practice *without* reinforcement leads to decreased habit strength (lower probability of response, or extinction) — thus superficially an exception to a behavioral universal.

We have employed what we consider to be a fairly conservative criterion of significance for what we call "universals" — basically, one which excludes from this classification any data items (ranks, componential tests, distance measures) with more than 5 of our 23 communities going in the contrary direction. The probability of a 5/18 ratio falls at a $p < .01$ probability of chance determination by the binomial expansion sign test (two-tail test, since we are not predicting the direction of universals from any theory). Of course, this criterion is based on the assumption that our 23 communities are independent of each other, and to the extent that Sub-universal "blocs" exist (as they certainly do for certain aspects of the data), this assumption is not met. However, (a) if the *deviants* are dispersed, there is no problem; (b) if deviants are clustered and counted as single communities, then the significance of the "universal" is actually enhanced; (c) if the *dominants* (reflecting the presumed universal trend) form "blocs" as well as the deviants, then presumably we should deal statistically with N equal to "blocs" rather than equal to communities. But things are not this simple, since the geographical "blocs" (which were the basis for our groups on interpretation meetings) rarely hold together throughout any item of data.

We have picked a number of "universals" and "near-universals" at random from our rank and componential-test data and compared our standard procedure (each community contributing independently to an N of 23) with one in which "blocs" (when they go the same way, either among deviants or dominants) are counted as if they were single communities. In most cases, with reduced Ns for *both* deviants and dominants, the significant results remain about the same. It is true that non-independent "blocs" may be based on other than geographic grounds — but since we have no *a priori* way of making such assignments, this must remain a moot question. Finally, as noted earlier in this chapter, the limited size and biased sampling of our communities (more literate than nonliterate, more urban than rural, more northern hemisphere than southern, more Indo-European than any other language, more Christian than any other religion — and only teen-age male) place even more stringent limits on our use of "universal."

On componential analysis. We consider componential analysis to be a powerful way of probing into subjective culture for Universals, Sub-universals, and Uniquenesses — particularly because, in principle, *it is relatively*

[14] The expression of such a theory here is not elegant but is sufficient for present purposes!

independent of the meanings of specific concepts and looks for consistencies among sets of concepts that are minimally contrastive on only a single feature or property. But, in practice (at least as we have employed it), the situation is not so clear. For one thing, the limited size of our concept categories usually means that the number of contrastive tests of a given component is small (sometimes two, often three or four, and rarely five or more). For another, one or two concepts may dominate in the test of a given component (e.g., COLOR being always the + member in the three tests made on the Brightness component). And for yet another, the tests are sometimes "confounded" (concepts contrasting on more than the component in question). There are a number of other issues which we will consider.

Since it often happens that the same component has been applied to several categories, *cross-category analyses* (which we call "crosscatans" for short) can be made for all revelant concept pairs, including pairs in the total *Atlas* which did not happen to fall together in any of our somewhat arbitrary categories. This makes it possible to minimize the problems raised above for single categories. For example, a Human Age component appears in the Age Continuum category (OLD PEOPLE/BABY, OLD AGE/YOUTH, MATURITY/ADOLESCENCE) as well as the Kinship category (RELATIVES/COUSINS, GRANDFATHER/BRIDEGROOM, GRANDMOTHER/BRIDE, with the last two being confounded with Consanguinity), and from the *Atlas* at large we can add MAN/BOY and WOMAN/GIRL, thus accruing eight tests. This crosscatan componential test clearly demonstrated that Young is universally +A with respect to Old, whereas Old universally has higher CI (within-culture instability or conflict) — for our teen-age male subjects, of course. Crosscatan tests of this sort are being made for a large number of semantic components that are replicated across our categories and will be reported separately.

There is one general point that needs to be made regarding all between-concept comparisons (in relative ranks, in componential tests, and in intra-cultural distances). It is often assumed by those only casually exposed to this research that our teen-age subjects in each community were directly asked to rank the concepts on E, P, and A, to compare concepts X and Y and say which is more E, more FAM, more conflictual (CI), and so forth, or to judge how similar (close) or dissimilar (far) two concepts are. This, of course, was not the case. All concepts were presented independently and in deliberately randomized orders having nothing to do with any of our categories or components. *All between-concept comparisons were made by the computer and not by the subjects at the time of data collection.* On the one hand, this means that we are only inferring what subjects *might* have said if, for example, asked "Which is more active, red or blue?"; on the other hand, this greatly increases the flexibility of the data for providing "answers" to a wide diversity of questions.

As was noted in Chapter 6, our use of componential analysis has a different purpose than in ethnoscience generally. Rather than simply providing an elegant structural description of a given lexical domain, we wished to use the method as a means of discovering the underlying cognitive bases for the attribution of affect. Semantic components intuited (usually denotative) become for us the independent variables, and quantitative data on affective meaning are the dependent variables. This raises a number of issues. Is our method of componential analysis and its application cross-culturally legitimate? Is it susceptible to ethnocentric bias? Can the validity and relevance (for attribution of affect) of our intuited components be tested?

In a thoroughly delightful little article titled "The First (and Perhaps Only) Non-linguistic Distinctive Feature Analysis," Joseph Greenberg (1967) first gives the essential characteristics of purely linguistic componential analysis (as applied to phonemic systems) — units (phonemes) are specified by choices from a finite number of (usually binary) values over a finite set of dimensions (voicing, nasality, etc.). He then demonstrates that Aristotle's doctrine, in which the four elements of his physics (earth, air, water, and fire) are resolvable into the combinations of two binary oppositions (hot-cold and moist-dry), fulfills all of the logical requirements of the linguistic model. And Greenberg then, in a review of superficially analogous componential models in other fields, demonstrates that Aristotle's physics is the *only* other "pure" distinctive feature theory. Atomic theory in chemistry fails because (a) its elements (features) do not fall into mutually exclusive subsets (i.e., are not oppositions), (b) they enter compounds in quantitative form (i.e., are continuously variable), and (c) the compounds (phonemes) may have different internal ordering arrangements such that the same pattern of elements in the same proportions may yield quite different compounds (e.g., butane and isobutane). Gene theory fails for yet another reason, (d) that opposed values on a feature (e.g., brown vs. blue eyes) can be compatible and fuse (i.e., a unit may have a 0 coding on a feature as well as the feature being simply irrelevant, 00).

Finally, according to Greenberg, the componential analyses applied to kinship and other domains by the "ethnosemantic" school of anthropology fail to satisfy the "pure" case on grounds (b) continuousness and (c) internal ordering arrangements. Now, there is no *a priori* reason to expect that semantics should follow the same principles of (b) discreteness of coding, (c) unorderedness of features, and (d) lack of fusion within features, as phonemics. [15] In our own thinking about the matter, while accepting the notion of (a) polar opposition within semantic features, we have assumed that (b) continuous coding on semantic features is the general case (with

---

[15] And, indeed, there is still debate over whether phonemic systems actually follow these principles, except by artful (and arbitrary) translations of continuousness, for example, into finer sets of binary discreteness.

discrete binary coding being the psychological result of special conditions, e.g., frequency of usage), (c) features are hierarchically ordered, again generally in terms of their frequency of usage (with taxonomic hierarchies being automatic special cases resulting from entailment), and (d) "fusions" within features do indeed occur (and, in fact, are responsible for the emergent dynamics of cognitive interaction — see Osgood, 1970a, and Osgood and Richards, 1973). Incidentally, at no point does Greenberg claim that *only* the "pure" linguistic model is legitimate, either in the physical sciences (obviously) or in language.

Our method of employing componential analysis is basically similar to those of ethnoscience — the notion of bipolar features, the use of minimal contrasts, the attempt to eliminate all cases of identical codings where synonymy is not intuitively the case, and even the use of discrete (three-way, $+$, 0, $-$) coding for convenience (the symbol 00 being used for irrelevance). But there are some significant differences too. First, by the nature of our problem, the components intuited are presumed to be generally applicable across all human communities (rather than unique for each culture). Second, we (the investigators) have "dreamed up" the components ourselves (rather than deriving them from the discriminative use of language by ordinary native speakers — of American English, to say nothing of other language communities). The first difference is inevitable if semantic universals are to be sought, and it is probably defensible on just this ground. The second, however, means that our componential analyses (in terms of both the nature of the components and the coding of concepts on them) are highly susceptible to Western ethnocentric bias — and, worse, liable to what can best be termed scholarly schizophrenia.

There are, however, safeguards against both ethnocentric bias and scholarly schizophrenia on our part. In the first place, note that *there is no way in which our selection of and coding on features can influence the patterning of the quantitative data on affect.* To take on outrageous example, if we were to intuit an Advertised/Nonadvertised component and apply it to the Modern/Transitional/Traditional Technology category (e.g., TELEPHONE$+$, AUTOMOBILE$+$, AUTOMATION$-$, BUS$-$, etc.) and if such a feature only existed in our own minds or only in American culture, there is no way other than chance that such a component could yield evidence for Universals in E, P, or A. In other words, only if the components used do in fact tap "universal" differences-that-make-a-difference in meaning can they yield other than chance results across our sample. Of course, this does not protect us from failures to intuit viable features or from bias in coding concepts on valid features.

In the second place, *it is possible to test the validity of intuited denotative components as bases for attributing affect.* The problem of validity has been raised in ethnoscience more generally. Robbins Burling (1964), for example, has argued that the criteria for evaluating componential analyses (e.g., of kinship and other lexical systems) have usually been subjective — in terms of the elegance, simplicity, or efficiency of an analysis, or its intuitive validity if one happens to be a member of the culture in question — while what is needed are objective, *external* (behavioral or other) criteria. In our own case, since the denotative components of concepts are independent variables and their affective meanings are dependent variables, we can use the componential codings of the concepts in each category (i.e., the differences along their paired $+/0/-$ code strips) to generate a *predictive* distance matrix and then test the overall validity of the componential predictions against the *obtained* distance matrices, either for the concept means across all communities or for each indigenous community. If the correlations between predictive and obtained matrices are uniformly high, then the components are not only valid (in the general ethnosemantic sense) but are also relevant to the attribution of affect. If they are high for some communities but low for others, then we have evidence for deep cultural differences in cognitive organization. However, if the correlations are uniformly low, then either the components are ill conceived[16] *or* they are irrelevant as far as the attribution of affect is concerned. In other words, it is entirely possible for a denotative feature to be universally valid in semantics and yet have nothing to do with how people *feel* about things; the Concrete (Physical) vs. Abstract feature (which discriminates, e.g., STONE/WEIGHT, ICE/COLD, FIRE/HEAT, etc.) is obviously valid and basic, but our data show that it in no way predicts E, P, and A. Such validity analyses will be made for all categories and reported in later volumes.

On measuring distances. The distance measures we obtain are based on the generalized distance formula (see Chapter 6, pp. 301-314) as applied to the standardized (E-Z, P-Z, A-Z) factor composite scores. From the total matrix of such distances we extract (a) *inter*cultural distances for the same concepts and (b) the *intra*cultural distances between all concepts within each category. There are, of course, many metric and nonmetric multidimensional scaling techniques (e.g., Torgerson, 1958, and Green and Carmone, 1970), and distance matrices can be obtained from all of them. However, most of these methods use not scaled data on each attribute (which we have via the SD technique) but rather some variant of paired comparison technique; as the N of concepts increases, the N of judgments required of the subjects increases geometrically — and prohibitively as far as our *Atlas* data are concerned. However, our multidimensional scaling (SD)

---

[16] It is also possible with a somewhat more complicated program to determine which combinations of features optimize prediction and which features fail to contribute to, or even lower, predictiveness. Dr. Oliver Tzeng of our Center staff has already devised such validity checks and has applied them to our Time Units and Emotions categories successfully.

and distance-determining methods can be compared with other methods now available on small concept categories (like Colors) to see how comparable the methods are. It has been suggested[17] that our present methods may tend to overweigh the E factor, since concepts are more differentiated on this than the other factors, and the Carroll-Chang (1970) method (INSCAL) might provide a better way of pinpointing cultures in the space and identifying their clustering. In connection with later volumes we are planning a context-free community/category contingency analysis, designed to reveal clustering of communities that is independent of geographical, religious, or other *a priori* considerations and clustering of categories that is independent of our rather arbitrary assignments to "super categories" (see Table 6:1).

The intercultural distance matrices serve to highlight cultures which deviate markedly from all (or very nearly all) others in how they attribute affect to a particular concept (what we have called "sore thumbs"). Such items are always checked in group meetings as possible translation failures, and, when not, they usually represent a readily identifiable cultural Uniqueness (e.g., the MS Uniqueness of BLUE and its association with both the police and 50-peso bills, the DH Uniqueness of GREY and its association with the British and favored fairness of skin). They also highlight pairs of communities across which communication in the category should be facilitated by shared affect (small *D*s between them for all concepts) or confounded by incongruent affect (large *D*s between them). It has been suggested[18] that such "predictions" of relative ease or difficulty in cross-culture communicating in certain conceptual domains should be empirically verifiable under controlled experimental conditions, and we would like to try some tests of this sort. It is an interesting case in which one can pretty well guarantee close agreement in referential meaning while deliberately varying agreement in affective meaning.

The intracultural distances can provide answers to a great variety of culturally significant questions — how much affective differentiation in a given domain is made by one culture, or set of cultures, as compared with another (there are gross differences here, the East Asians making very great distinctions among Colors and the West Asians rather little, for example) ; which cultures display similar conceptual structures in a given domain and which very different (again there are gross differences here, and in the case of Colors they were independent for the most part of obvious cultural relationships) ; and so on. It should be noted that similarities in what we term "conceptual structures" are based upon correlations across corresponding cells

[17] By Dr. Roy D'Andrade at our recent conference on Social Science Utilization of an Atlas of Affective Meanings.

[18] By Drs. Rita Simon, Albert Hirschman, and others at the same conference mentioned in n. 17.

of the indigenous distance matrices (i.e., relative distances) and, hence, represent similarity of patterning which is independent of absolute concept localizations in the common E-P-A space.

SOME SPECIAL PROJECTS

During the past decade, more or less in parallel with our "tool-making" and *Atlas* work, a number of special research projects have been initiated and carried along. These have involved many of our colleagues in other countries, both in design and execution, as well as members of the Center staff. These include both methodological and substantive studies on the SD technique, rather extensive work on a "personality differential" (PD) and a "graphic differential" (GD), and a special study of "changing cultural mores" in some half-dozen of our communities. Since most of these studies have been, or soon will be, published in their own right, only brief summaries will be given here.

THE PERSONALITY DIFFERENTIAL AND CULTURAL "THEORIES OF PERSONALITY"

In the middle 1960s colleagues in three of our communities (Drs. Jorma Kuusinen in Finland, Mathilda Jansen in the Netherlands, and Yasumasa Tanaka in Japan) agreed on a general design for investigating semantic structures in the personality domain with the SD technique. In essence, the design involved having both male and female (mature) subjects rate some 40 concepts in the personality domain (e.g., MY IDEAL SELF, THE TEACHER I ADMIRED MOST, A BRIDE, MY BROTHER) against 50 to 60 scales, the scales being derived from (a) the pancultural SDs of each community, (b) the "personality factors" obtained in an earlier pilot study in AE by Dr. Edward Ware (see Osgood, 1962), and (c) the application of our qualifier-elicitation procedures with the personality nouns (or noun phrases) as eliciting stimuli. More than half of the scales were derived in the latter fashion (c) to guarantee "personality-relevant" dimensions in the total set. With some variations in materials and procedures, this study was run in FF, ND, and JP (by the investigators listed above) and later was extended to BF (Dr. Robert Hogenraad), BrE (British English, Dr. Peter Warr and Ms. Valerie Haycock), and TH (Dr. Weerayudh Wichiarajote).

As has been evident in the data throughout this book, application of the SD technique to diverse types of concepts, including personality ones, amplifies three massive affective factors (E, P, and A) and tends to damp finer, more denotative factors (see p. 392ff. for the "why" of this). Is there any way in which the influence of the dominant affective features can themselves be "damped" so as to allow other, more denotative features to appear? One cannot minimize the influence of E-P-A simply by eliminating from the PD task those scales which normally load high on these factors, since these affective features are "in the heads" of native speakers and contribute to the judgments on all scales. However, one can determine the partial correlations of all scales with E, P, and A factors (as represented by their marker scales in the pancultural SDs), eliminate the portions of interscale correlations these account for, and then re-factor the residual correlation matrix. What this does, in effect, is to minimize the influence E, P, and A factors presumably had on determining subject judgments of *all* concept-scale items — thereby accomplishing statistically what some mysterious surgery might have accomplished in making the subjects affectively aphasic!

Jorma Kuusinen, while a visiting scholar at our Center in 1967-68, had exactly this insight and applied a partialing technique to his Finnish PD data. As can be seen in Table 7:3, the usual unpartialed (principal-components and Varimax rotation) factor analysis yielded E (Factor I), P (Factor IV), and A (Factor II) loud and clear — along with what might be called a Broad-mindedness (Tolerance) factor — but little else. However, when the partialing procedure was applied, the re-factorization yielded a very different picture, as evident in Table 7:4. Six readily interpretable "personality" factors appeared, and the total variance was spread more evenly

TABLE 7:3

Finnish Personality Differential: Varimax Rotation of Six Factors, Whole Data

Factor I (52.2%)		Factor III (10.9%)	
moral-immoral	.98	broad-minded–narrow-minded	.90
reputable-disreputable	.97	relaxed-tense	.71
obedient-disobedient	.96	sense of humor–no sense of	
trustworthy-untrustworthy	.95	humor	.67
predictable-unpredictable	.94	individualistic-regular	.65
good-bad	.93	tolerant-intolerant	.63
diligent-lazy	.93		
tangible-intangible	.93		
honest-dishonest	.93		
necessary-unnecessary	.92		
clean-dirty	.92		
rational-irrational	.92		
faithful-unfaithful	.90		
Factor II (11.5%)		**Factor IV (8.5%)**	
fast-slow	.91	sturdy-delicate	.95
agile-clumsy	.89	large-small	.92
courageous-timid	.67	heavy-light	.86
inventive-uninventive	.67	strong-weak	.67
attentive-inattentive	.65		
individualistic-regular	.63		

TABLE 7:4

Finnish Personality Differential: Varimax Rotation of Six Factors, Partialed Data

Factor I (19.3%)		Factor IV (11.9%)	
trustworthy-untrustworthy	.96	usual-unusual	.88
honest-dishonest	.93	predictable-unpredictable	.79
faithful-unfaithful	.83	poor-rich	.69
straight-crooked	.78	regular-individualistic	.67
reputable-disreputable	.76	obedient-disobedient	.67
clean-dirty	.70		
Factor II (18.7%)		**Factor V (11.7%)**	
selfish-unselfish	.90	sense of humor–no sense of	
wholesome-unwholesome	.87	humor	.85
impatient-patient	.78	sad-glad	.73
proud-humble	.77	broad-minded–narrow-minded	.72
tough-tender	.76	tolerant-intolerant	.66
excitable-calm	.74	relaxed-tense	.60
self-confident–insecure	.67		
Factor III (15.6%)		**Factor VI (8.3%)**	
logical-intuitive	.89	sociable-solitary	.84
rational-irrational	.83	beautiful-ugly	.81
knowing-unknowing	.82	gregarious–self-contained	.63
attentive-inattentive	.75	polite-impolite	.58
wise-stupid	.69		
inventive-uninventive	.66		
careful-careless	.66		

across them: I, a Trustworthiness factor (19%); II, what might be called a Self-righteousness factor (19%); III, a Rationality factor (16%); IV, a Predictability factor (12%); V, a Tolerance factor (12%)[19]; and VI, a Sociability factor (8%). Although these factor labels are imposed on the data, the included scales seem to justify them quite well. Kuusinen's (1969) findings for the Finnish PD data enlivened the possibility that — with universal E-P-A "damped" — features specific to the personality domain could be obtained. Then one might be in a position to answer this theoretically interesting question: *are the nonaffective dimensions in terms of which personalities are characterized* (i.e., "theories of personality") *also universal or are they culturally unique?*

It is beginning to appear that the answer, as is so often the case, will be a compromise between the two extreme positions of universality and uniqueness. Recently Dr. Oliver Tzeng (1972), while a research assistant on our staff, developed a new approach to the "damping" problem, based on Ledyard Tucker's three-mode factoring techniques. In essence, Tzeng's method

[19] Kuusinen assures us that the Finnish scale translated as *sad-glad* does have this orientation on the Tolerance factor, and appropriately so.

partitions the PD data into what he terms Affective and Denotative spaces and assigns all scales to the four quadrants: Q_{11}, the pancultural marker-scale loadings (from which the purity of these markers when functioning in the homogeneous personality domain can be determined); Q_{21}, the non-marker-scale loadings in the Affective space; Q_{12}, the loadings of E-P-A marker scales on factors in the Denotative space (which should be near zero); and Q_{22}, the loadings of non-marker scales in the Denotative space (from which the semantic "character" of the nonaffective factors can be determined). Tzeng applied his new procedure to the male and female data separately in three communities where PD samples had been collected (Finnish, Japanese, and British English). The results for JP females will have to suffice for illustration. Table 7:5A gives the higher-loading scales in the Affective space, and it can be seen that E, P, and A are clearly defined (this was the case for all six subject groups). Table 7:5B gives equivalent

TABLE 7:5

JP-Female Salient Scales for
(A) Affective Dimensions and (B) Denotative Dimensions

A. AFFECTIVE DIMENSIONS

I		II	
happy-sad	54.40	heavy-light	41.25
good-bad	69.66	big-little	51.07
comfortable-uncomfortable	70.47	brave-cowardly	33.40
pleasant-unpleasant	67.57	hard-soft	38.96
liked-disliked	70.13	strong-weak	39.43
obedient-disobedient	68.15	energetic-inert	33.33
light-dark	67.45	busy–not busy	27.81
reputable-disreputable	66.68	high-low	25.88
kind-unkind	65.02	tense-relaxed	24.67
serious-frivolous	64.20		
wise-foolish	61.79	III	
honest-cunning	59.72	soft-hard	24.43
warm-cold	59.25	noisy-quiet	42.94
moral-immoral	58.43	vivid-subdued	47.24
tender-tough	57.87	excitable-calm	37.37
interesting-uninteresting	57.68	extroverted-introverted	35.64
meaningful-meaningless	57.64	proud-humble	35.17
beautiful-ugly	56.45	violent-calm	34.78
serious-silly	54.98	impudent-modest	34.65
great-inferior	54.66	sociable-solitary	32.24
enthusiastic-indifferent	54.45		
loved-hated	53.82		
diligent-lazy	53.38		
familiar-unfamiliar	52.20		
smiling-grave	52.06		

TABLE 7.5 (Continued)

B. DENOTATIVE DIMENSIONS

I		IV	
logical-intuitive	44.49	tangible-intuitive	42.99
calm-excitable	34.01	familiar-unfamiliar	38.77
sophisticated-naive	27.43	predictable-unpredictable	38.39
rational-irrational	21.52	comprehensible-incomprehensible	35.07
unhappy-happy	20.91	usual-unusual	21.52
cold-warm	20.66	easy-difficult	21.17

II		V	
tense-relaxed	41.14	flexible-stubborn	30.48
sensitive-insensitive	39.57	calm-excitable	29.03
busy–not busy	39.29	clever-stupid	22.07
enthusiastic-indifferent	28.49	calm-violent	19.54
diligent-lazy	20.92		

III	
usual-unusual	38.79
regular-individualistic	35.95
sociable-solitary	25.24
calm-violent	24.42
insensitive-sensitive	23.26
restrained-free	22.55
crooked-candid	20.68

data for the Denotative space, and we may note what could be identified as (I) a "Cold Rationality" factor, (II) an "Energeticness" factor, (III) a "Uniqueness" factor (in terms of the negative pole), (IV) a "Predictability" factor, and (V) a "Calm Flexibility" factor.

In Tzeng's data as a whole it appears that some of the Denotative factors are universal — at least insofar that one can speak of three cultures (both males and females) defining "universality" — and, of course, E, P, and A are found to be Universals (in the Q_{11} spaces). Table 7:6 summarizes the factor identifications (appropriately in quotes) across all six groups of subjects. A factor labelled as "Predictability" appeared in all six samples, all but the Finnish subjects yielded a "Rationality" factor, and three groups (BrE males, FF males, and FF females) show a "Morality" factor. As far as sex is concerned, each of the three cultures displays at least one factor difference: British males (but not females) have "Morality" and "Extro/Introversion" factors, and conversely for "Ambitiousness" and "Dogmatism"; Finnish females differ from Finnish males only in having an additional "Integrity" factor; and Japanese males have a "Sophistication" factor (not shared with the females), while Japanese females have a "Calm Flexibility" factor (not shared with the males). However, the differences between cultures are greater than within, as can be seen from inspection of Table 7:6.

TABLE 7:6

Cross-Cultural Semantic Components of Meaning in Personality Ratings

	BE-M	BE-F	FF-M	FF-F	JP-M	JP-F
Evaluation	E	E	E	E	E	E
Potency	P	P	P	P	P	P
Activity	A	A	A	A	A	A
"Predictability"	IV	IV	II	III	III	IV
"Rationality"	II	I			IV	(I)[a]
"Morality"	I		I	I		
"Extro-Introversion"	III					
"Ambitiousness"		II				
"Dogmatism"		III				
"Humility"			III	IV		
"Sociability"			IV	V		
"Integrity"				II		
"Energeticness"					I	II
"Uniqueness"					II	III
"Sophistication"					V	
"Flexibility"						V

[a] But here "Cold Rationality."

For examples, the Finns have a unique "Humility" factor and the Japanese a unique "Energeticness" factor. This, of course, is a very small sample of human communities[20] (and it must be admitted that labeling personality factors remains a pretty intuitive business), but nevertheless this research suggests that culturally unique "theories of personality" (along with universal E-P-A and some other more denotative dimensions) will be identified. Although neither partialing nor three-mode analyses were made, Warr and Haycock (1970) also suggest that "secondary variants" (within E, P, and A) will be found to depend upon cultural differences.

THE GRAPHIC DIFFERENTIAL AND A LANGUAGE-FREE MEASURE OF AFFECT

Given the universality of E, P, and A as dimensions of affective meaning and the growing evidence that shared affect is the common mediator of metaphorical and synesthetic relations among linguistic and perceptual signs respectively, the prospect for creating a nonlinguistic, graphic differential (GD) seems bright. Working with four language/culture groups (American college students, Mexican Spanish-speaking and Navajo subjects in the American Southwest, and Japanese college students), and using pairs of

[20] Since the writing of Tzeng's doctoral thesis, PD data collections have been nearly completed in Thailand, and the already available Belgian Flemish and Netherlands Dutch are now available — to which we hope to add several additional communities in the near future.

oppositional visual forms on cards (e.g., BLACK vs. WHITE CIRCLES, JAGGED vs. SMOOTHLY-CURVED LINES, SATURATED vs. PALE-COLORED CIRCLES), Osgood (1960b) was able to demonstrate strong universal trends in visual-verbal synesthesia and found evidence for E, P, and A factors in visual polarities — when subjects simply pointed to visual alternatives as "appropriate" to various words (HEAVY, MAN, HONEST, EX-CITEMENT, YELLOW, SAD, and so forth). Running this sort of procedure in reverse, so to speak, Elliott and Tannenbaum (1963) had U.S. Air Force trainees rate 70 abstract visual forms against 20 SD scales representing E-P-A and other potential factors. They found clear evidence for three factors corresponding to E (*ugly-beautiful, pleasant-unpleasant, careful-careless*), P (*large-small, heavy-light*), and A (*fancy-plain, excitable-calm, active-passive, complex-simple*), as well as a factor less clearly defined as "Hardness-Angularity" (*hard-soft, angular-rounded, cool-warm*).

At our Center in 1967, under the direction of Dr. Leon Jakobovits, we initiated an exploratory study directly on the development of a graphic differential. From a large number of contrastive pairs of visual patterns (suggested by our foreign colleagues and augmented by the Center staff), the 64 pairs shown in Figure 7:2 were selected for cross-cultural investigation. Along with AE, data were collected in New Delhi by K. G. Agrawal, in Helsinki by Pertti Oünap, in Munich by Suitbert Ertel, and in Tokyo by Yasumasa Tanaka.[21] Subjects rated subsets of a total of 50 randomly selected concepts from the *Atlas* (e.g., LOVE, TONGUE, SLEEP, POLICEMAN, LAUGHTER, LIFE) against 7-step scales defined by the 64 oppositional pictograms as well as against the 12-scale pancultural SDs for each community.

The results can be summarized quite succinctly here. (1) Using the pancultural SD scales as markers of E, P, and A, a multicultural factor analysis (see Chapter 4, p. 159ff., for the ordinary SD analogue) yielded clear evidence for a universal E factor (defined by shared sets of symmetrical vs. nonsymmetrical forms). There was reasonably good evidence for P and A for FF, GG, and JP but not for AE and DH, and the high-loading pictorial scales varied much more than for E. (2) There was evidence for "denotative contamination" for P (e.g., *angular* vs. *rounded* pictograms correlated highly with concepts like ANGER, CHAIR, and POLICEMAN vs. CLOUD, SMOKE, and SNAKE. (3) When the data for Abstract vs. Concrete verbal concepts were analyzed separately, the correspondence between verbal and visual E-P-A scales proved to be much higher for the low-imagery Abstract concepts — as might be expected from the "contamination" effects above.

These results may indicate an inherent limitation upon the development of a language-free GD; however, there were a number of flaws in the design of this study (as viewed with hindsight, of course). For one thing, many of

---

[21] Data were later collected for ND by Ton Smolenaars.

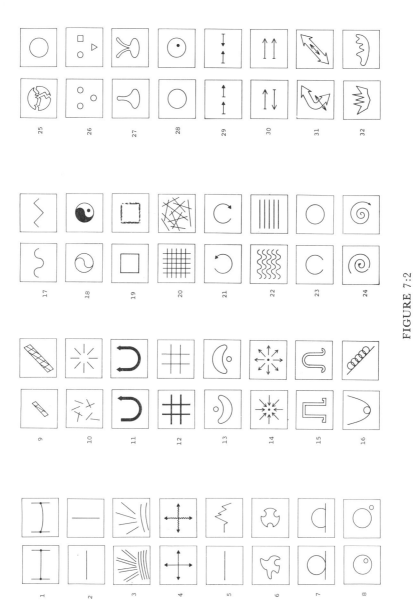

FIGURE 7:2
Pictograph Scales as Used in Graphic Differential

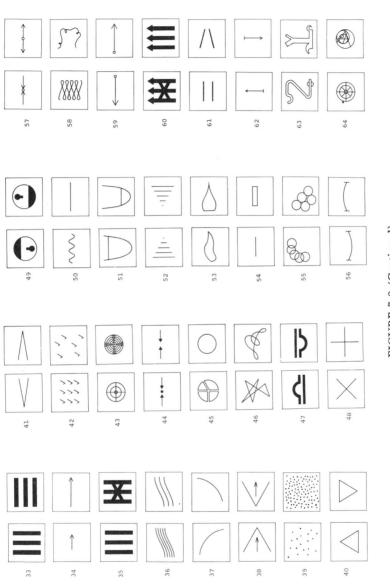

FIGURE 7:2 (Continued)

the pictograms were quite complex, and hence easily perceivable as at least caricatures of real objects, rather than being simple and abstract visual polarities (as used for the most part by Osgood, 1960b). For another, the *random* selection of 50 verbal concepts from the *Atlas* was probably less satisfactory than would have been a sample designed to maximize extremes of E, P, and A (which can be done, of course, from our data; see Chapter 5, p. 248 and Table 5:17). As a matter of fact, checking the 50 concepts used, we find that although E is well represented by polar concepts in both directions, *all* of the concepts happened to be $^+$P and most fairly polar (thus reducing variance on this dimension), and most of them were nonpolar on A (that is, near ^{0}A).[22] Since, as Jakobovits in his published report on this study (1969) has stressed, a reliable, affectively validated, and universally applicable graphic differential would have many values — being applicable to nonliterates and other linguistically deprived populations,[23] potentially providing insights into the nature of synesthesia and metaphor, and contributing to the psychology of aesthetics — we plan to continue research in this direction.

A STUDY OF CHANGING SOCIAL MORES

This project had its origins in discussions at the Teheran conference ("of the whole") in the summer of 1967. The general purpose was to use SD and other techniques to obtain evidence on the rates of cultural change (using progressive differences between grandparental, parental, and teen-age generations, ideally within the same family-household units as controls) in various areas of subjective culture. The overall design included 3 basic dimensions of variation — 3 generations, 2 sexes, and 2 milieus (urban and rural) — and it envisaged 40 family units within each milieu. Between 20 and 30 concepts were carefully selected by the Center staff and local participants to be potentially sensitive to changing attitudes and values in (a) contemporary human societies generally (to be tested in all communities) and (b) each community specifically (to be tested only indigenously). Table 7:7 here provides illustrations. Three types of measures are involved: a short-form SD (actually given in verbal form in the total interview with each subject), including the pancultural scales for each community, several Modernity scales (*modern–old-fashioned, new–old*), and a *familiar–unfamiliar* scale; an open-ended "definition" question (e.g., "What does having LEISURE TIME mean to you?") for each concept; and an application of the antecedent/

22 These facts were brought to our attention by one of our staff, Miss Patrice French, who is piloting in AE another GD study with a more suitable set of concepts.

23 Dr. Sylvia Sheinkopf (1970) has shown that when severely impaired aphasics "describe" their meanings of simple concepts by pointing to the visual alternatives designed by Osgood (1960b), their performance (i.e., affective meanings) proves to be very similar to that of normals.

TABLE 7:7

Study of Changing Cultural Mores in
(A) Culture-Common Concepts and (B) Culture-Specific Concepts

A. CULTURE-COMMON CONCEPTS

MODERNIST

1. BUYING THINGS ON CREDIT
2. TREATING ALL PEOPLE AS EQUALS
3. PLANNING FOR THE FUTURE
4. MARRYING SOMEONE OF A DIFFERENT RACE OR RELIGION
5. LETTING YOUNG WOMEN GO OUT ALONE
6. PROVIDING SEX EDUCATION
7. ALLOWING YOUNG PEOPLE TO MAKE THEIR OWN DECISIONS
8. WOMEN WEARING MINISKIRTS
9. KEEPING UP WITH THE NEWS OF THE WORLD
10. CHANGING ONE'S JOB

TRADITIONALIST

11. WORKING WITH ONE'S HANDS
12. BEING FAITHFUL TO ONE'S RELIGION
13. SAVING MONEY
14. RESPECTING PEOPLE IN POSITIONS OF AUTHORITY
15. HAVING MANY CHILDREN
16. PUNISHING CHILDREN SEVERELY WHEN THEY DISOBEY
17. KNOWING WHAT ONE'S NEIGHBORS ARE DOING AND THINKING
18. RESPECTING THE VIEWS OF ONE'S ELDERS
19. GIVING FIRST LOYALTY TO ONE'S FAMILY
20. RELYING ON "TRIED-AND-TRUE" FAMILY REMEDIES AND MEDICINES

B. CULTURE-SPECIFIC CONCEPTS

UNITED STATES

1. LEGALIZING THE USE OF MARIJUANA
2. SUPPORTING U.S. ACTIONS IN VIET NAM
3. SUPPORTING THE DEMANDS OF NEGROES FOR EQUAL RIGHTS
4. GIVING COLLEGE STUDENTS MORE VOICE IN THEIR OWN EDUCATION
5. HAVING LUXURIES
6. DEMANDING LAW AND ORDER
7. ACCEPTING THINGS AS THEY ARE
8. LANDING A MAN ON THE MOON
9. ACHIEVING PEACE THROUGH MILITARY STRENGTH
10. HAVING LEISURE TIME

MEXICO

1. SUPPORTING YOUNG PEOPLE IN THEIR DEMANDS FOR SOCIAL CHANGE
2. AT HOME THE MOTHER SHOULD HAVE THE SAME AUTHORITY AS THE FATHER
3. ALLOWING MARRIED WOMEN TO WORK OUTSIDE OF THE HOME
4. ALLOWING WOMEN TO GO TO THE UNIVERSITY
5. WISHING THE FIRSTBORN TO HAVE THE SAME OCCUPATION AS THE FATHER
6. SUPPORTING THE IDEA OF WOMEN KEEPING VIRGINITY UNTIL MARRIED
7. ONE SHOULD NEVER QUESTION THE WORD OF THE FATHER
8. SUPPORTING THE IDEA THAT MEN ARE SUPERIOR TO WOMEN

HONG KONG

1. HAVING YEAR-END FAMILY GATHERINGS
2. HAVING A ROOM OF ONE'S OWN
3. GETTING ALONG AT EASE WITH WHATEVER IS HAPPENING
4. BEING SYMPATHETIC WITH MENTALLY DISTURBED PEOPLE
5. HAVING A SON INSTEAD OF A DAUGHTER
6. FILIAL PIETY TOPS ALL OTHER VIRTUES
7. WIDOWS REMARRYING
8. ARRANGED MARRIAGES
9. WIFE BEING EMPLOYED BY SOMEONE TO WORK OUTSIDE HER HOME
10. LEAVING ONE'S HOME LEVEL TO SETTLE PERMANENTLY ABROAD
11. BELIEVING IN WIND AND WATER

subsequent implication technique (e.g., "What leads to having LEISURE TIME?" — and "What does having LEISURE TIME lead to?" — with appropriate modulations of the verb for the various concepts) as developed by Dr. Harry Triandis and his associates (Triandis, Tanaka, and Shanmugam, 1966; Triandis, Vassiliou, and Nassiakou, 1968). The latter two measures are "open-ended" and require some form of content analysis for quantification.

This study of changing cultural mores is presently being conducted in AE (Chicago, Dr. Tulsi Saral), MS (Mexico City, Mr. Nahum Martinez-Reyes), YS (Belgrade, Dr. Tomislav Tomeković), TH (Bangkok, Drs. Weerayudh and Nuanpen Wichiarajote), HC (Dr. Brian Young), and JP (Tokyo, Dr. Yasumasa Tanaka and Miss Yoko Iwamatsu). The collection of U.S. data and computer analysis of all data on this project have been in the hands of Dr. Tulsi Saral.[24] Selection of the conceptual materials, selection of the samples, and collection of the data — which, given the fact that this study is entirely based upon interviewing individual subjects, is a time-consuming and expensive process — have been virtually completed for MS, TH (with a reduced sample of 120 urban and 120 rural subjects), and HC, and the work in YS and JP is nearly completed — but (except for TH as indicated) only for the urban half of the planned sampling. Difficulty was encountered in all locations, but particularly in the East Asian communities (TH, HC, JP), in locating and interviewing grandparent-generation members of the same family units. As a result, we recommended substituting, where necessary, male or female members of the same generation and having the same status (i.e., as having teen-age grandchildren) for unlocatable or uninterviewable in-sample subjects.

Dr. Saral has the analysis of AE (Chicago) data well under way. A factor analysis of concepts across scales was made to determine concept clustering patterns. Four strong factors have emerged, using the overall data (all 240 subjects). The first factor — which contains concepts like RESPECTING PEOPLE IN POSITIONS OF AUTHORITY, RESPECTING THE VIEWS OF ONE'S ELDERS, and SAVING MONEY — could be legitimately called a *Traditional* factor. The second factor — comprising concepts like LETTING YOUNG WOMEN GO OUT ALONE, PROVIDING SEX EDUCATION, and MARRYING SOMEONE OF A DIFFERENT RACE OR RELIGION — could be termed a *Liberal* factor. The third factor — containing concepts like TREATING ALL PEOPLE AS EQUALS and SUPPORTING THE DEMANDS OF NEGROES FOR EQUAL RIGHTS — can be called *Egalitarian;* this factor also has *negative* loadings on the concepts PUNISHING CHILDREN SEVERELY WHEN THEY DISOBEY and HAVING MANY CHILDREN. The fourth factor has positive loadings on SUPPORTING U.S. ACTIONS IN VIET NAM and

[24] Formerly of our Center staff; now university professor of communications science at the new Governors State University near Chicago, but still associated with our staff as an associate.

LANDING A MAN ON THE MOON and negative loadings on concepts like CHANG-ING ONE'S JOB, HAVING LEISURE TIME, and HAVING LUXURIES. For want of a better term, we are calling this a *Nationalistic-Conservative* factor.

An analysis of variance was carried out as well for the AE sample, using generation, sex, and socio-economic status of the respondents as independent variables and SD ratings on five dimensions — Evaluation (E), Potency (P), Activity (A), Modernism/Traditionalism (M), and Familiarity (F) — as dependent variables. There are many significant differences in terms of these variables. As far as generation is concerned, teens (Ts) see WOMEN WEARING MINISKIRTS as most Good, Active, and Familiar and grandparents (GPs) least; GPs see GIVING FIRST LOYALTY TO ONE'S FAMILY and RESPECTING THE VIEWS OF ONE'S ELDERS as most Good and Potent and Ts the least. Less expectedly, we find that it is GPs who most value KEEPING UP WITH THE NEWS OF THE WORLD and Ps (parents) least, while it is Ts who see GIVING COLLEGE STUDENTS MORE VOICE IN THEIR OWN EDUCATION as most Good and Familiar but Ps (*not* GPs) who see this as least Good and Familiar! As far as sex is concerned, it is interesting that females find KEEPING UP WITH THE NEWS OF THE WORLD, GIVING COLLEGE STUDENTS MORE VOICE IN THEIR OWN EDUCATION, and WORKING WITH ONE'S HANDS more Good, more Potent, and more Active than do males (of all generations). On the other hand, it is the males who see SUPPORTING U.S. ACTIONS IN VIET NAM and PUNISHING CHILDREN SEVERELY WHEN THEY DISOBEY more Active and more Modern (strangely). Finally, with regard to socio-economic status, it is "uppers" who see KEEPING UP WITH THE NEWS OF THE WORLD and TREATING ALL PEOPLE AS EQUALS as most Valuable and "lowers" least; the converse (lowers most and uppers least) holds for the Modernness of PUNISHING CHILDREN SE-VERELY WHEN THEY DISOBEY. It is the "middles" who attribute the most Value to PROVIDING SEX EDUCATION and ACHIEVING PEACE THROUGH MILITARY STRENGTH and lowers the least, and middles also perceive the most Potency in SAVING MONEY and lowers least. We anticipate interesting results in the cross-cultural comparisons to be made when all of the data are in.

CONTRIBUTIONS BY COLLEAGUES AND STAFF

Demonstration of the ubiquitousness of E, P, and A and development of indigenous SD instruments in the course of this demonstration have en-gendered a great deal of research by our colleagues in other countries. Fur-thermore, the compilation of *Atlas* data for some 25 communities has provided a source of materials that has been utilized in testing diverse hypotheses, both by the staff of the Center for Comparative Psycholinguistics and by colleagues elsewhere. Only a sampling of this activity can be cited here.

A considerable number of *methodological studies* have been made. Both Tanaka (Tanaka and Osgood, 1965; Tanaka, Oyama, and Osgood, 1963) and Nordenstreng (1969a, 1970) have been concerned with clarifying the nature of subject-scale and concept-scale interactions, and Nordenstreng (1968) has made a comparison of SD judgments with other methods of meaning similarity analysis. Kostić and Das (1971), in reporting the YS concept-on-scale data, have shown that the SD technique gets at unrestricted, nonlexical aspects of meaning common to all speakers, and the same authors are presently investigating adjective-noun semantic compatibility and its implications for SD technique. Noordman and Levelt (1970) have made the only full-scale (to date) application of semantic interaction technique to a Dutch-*Atlas*-nouns/multi-sense-verbs intersection (see Osgood, 1970a). Ertel (1965) demonstrated that the results of a German concept-scale factor analysis could be used to develop an "impression differential" in which the dimensions are defined by nouns (rather than adjectives) loading positively or negatively on E, P, and A factors. He used factor analysis as a method whose results are used as feedback criteria for eliminating successively concepts and scales from the original sample in order to obtain, in the final analysis, a balanced distribution of common variance among uncorrelated factors (principle of "dimensional representativeness").

There have also been *contributions of a substantive nature*. For example, in India, K. G. Agrawal (1970) reports a study on color symbolism, comparing the affective meanings of colors in an object context with abstract color labels, and Kuppuswamy and Agrawal (1967) report a factorial study of the meaning of the concept WORK. L. C. Singh (1967) reports the development of an occupational differential in India, and he has also studied the effects of orthography and pronunciation of concepts upon their affective meanings. In Finland, Nordenstreng (1968) contributes an SD study on the perception of complex sounds, comparing the semantic structures for speech and music. In Yugoslavia, Pečjak, Musek, and Tatjana (1970) have demonstrated the influence of group affiliations upon the evaluative meanings of critical political concepts. And in Japan, Tanaka has contributed several studies on political concepts, including concepts related to nuclear arms proliferation and testing, using the SD technique (Tanaka and Iwamatsu, 1968; Tanaka, 1970, 1971). In Germany, Ertel (1973) studied the effects of E, P, and A and "balance" of visual art displays on preference choice trying to link affective meaning considerations with Berlyne's theory on curiosity.

Increasingly over the past several years there has been *utilization of the Atlas data* for testing various hypotheses. Among our colleagues, we have studies by Ertel (1972 — draft of a book titled *Words, Sentences and the Ego*) on the effects of the Evaluation and the Dynamism (P + A) of words upon various sentence-understanding and -creating phenomena; by Pečjak (1970) on the metaphorical relations among Colors, Emotions, and Days of the Week (utilizing our *Atlas* data for these categories); by Tanaka (1972) in a paper titled "Values in the Subjective Culture: A Social Psychological View"; and by Triandis (1973) in a paper titled "Intercultural Conceptions of Work and Non-work." Among our own Center staff, we have studies by Boucher and Osgood (1969), utilizing the productivities of qualifier pairs defining scales in relation to their E loadings; by Osgood and Richards (1973), utilizing the affective loadings of AE scales in predicting the discriminative usage of *and* vs. *but* in conjoined predications; and by Patrice French (on-going research), utilizing affective intensity measures (distances from the origin) and factorial purity measures (ratios of dominant to nondominant factor loadings) and showing that the latter predict latencies of concept/scale-pole forced judgments better than the former. Both Nordenstreng in Finland (Ch. 9 in Ahmavaara and Nordenstreng, 1969) and Young (1970) in Hong Kong have utilized Osgood's (1960b) data or method demonstrating cross-cultural generalities in visual-verbal synesthesia.

SOME MAJOR METHODOLOGICAL AND THEORETICAL ISSUES

The object of concern in this book is *Homo loquens*. Although many higher organisms communicate, man is the only talking animal.[25] In a historical regress that extends back in time to our earliest inferences about man as a social animal, he has been "taught" to talk by other talking humans. Being a characteristic of the human species, and only the human species, one would expect to find massive similarities transcending language boundaries. Yet the obvious differences between languages have often obscured the more subtle, but probably more fundamental, similarities from the view of language scholars and scientists. In the history of language study (by linguists, anthropologists, psychologists, and philosophers) one discerns a kind of pendulum-swinging from concern about uniquenesses to concern about universals, and back again to uniquenesses, and back yet again to universals — and, interestingly enough, the various disciplines involved seem to swing more or less in unison. As one of three "summarizers" of a conference on Language Universals in April, 1961 (the others were Roman Jakobson for linguistics

---

[25] True, the chimpanzee has recently been shown capable of acquiring many of the characteristics of human languages, including syntactic "rules" and novel "rule-bound" combinations, under special training conditions (e.g., using natural sign language of the deaf (Gardner and Gardner, 1969) or a manipulative language in which objects are signs (Premack, 1971)). But to date there is no evidence that any nonhuman, earth-bound species has developed a language naturally and transmitted it from generation to generation.

and Joseph Casagrande for anthropology), the first author of this book began his remarks as follows (in Greenberg, 1966b) :

> At this conference we have been witness to a bloodless revolution. Quietly and without polemics we have seen linguistics taking a giant step from being merely a method for describing language to being a full-fledged science of language. Of course, as is true of any revolution, the step is only "in progress" and the participants do not see themselves as revolutionary; but in the eyes of a sufficiently remote observer, the change can be noted and its significance recorded. . . . All of the papers prepared for this conference, and the discussion that completed it, take this revolution for granted. Twenty, even five, years ago, this could not have happened — without bloody eyes and heads. [P. 299]

In this final section we shall consider some of the issues that people run into when they try to make a case for *either* universality or uniqueness in human language or culture.

Psycholinguistic Relativity or Universality?

As was pointed out at the very beginning of this book (Chapter 1, p. 4), if the psycholinguistic relativity hypothesis — that how we perceive, how we think, and even how we philosophize are determined by the structure of the language we speak — were accepted literally in its extreme form, then cross-linguistic comparisons of subjective cultures would be impossible in principle. But comparative studies in linguistics (e.g., in the on-going Ferguson, Greenberg, *et al.* project on language universals at Stanford) as well as in psycholinguistics (e.g., the on-going Slobin, Ervin-Tripp, *et al.* project on language development at Berkeley, and our own on-going project on meaning systems here at Illinois) are gradually making it clear that, along with uniquenesses which render human languages mutually unintelligible, there are indeed massive universals which render them mutually translatable. Again, the reader is reminded that we use the term "universal" in a statistical rather than an absolute sense (see pp. 368-369 in this chapter). If one demanded only absolute universals (without any exceptions), then very few would be found, and they would be essentially uninteresting *descriptive* facts about language. With a complex phenomenon like language, where many interacting laws are operating, only a statistical notion of universals is defensible, and it can yield universal regularities of general *theoretical* interest.

One form of the psycholinguistic universality hypothesis — that all languages are arbitrarily and superficially different ways of expressing events in a common, underlying human cognitive system (including both syntactic and semantic aspects or components) — actually does not rule out linguistic or cultural differences. Just as we may have paraphrases within a single language — both structural (*The boy kissed the girl/The girl was kissed by the boy*) and lexical (*He walked slowly and casually along the path/He me-*

andered along the path) — so can we have "paraphrases" across languages, both expressing the same underlying cognitive preconditions. Similarly, in subjective culture, two groups of humans may share the same underlying semantic *system* (i.e., the same types of features or components) and yet *allocate* concepts within the system differently (thus BEGGAR may be more highly valued in culture A than culture B because of his religious significance) or apply the features differently (thus in culture X the sex feature may not be used as a distinguisher among preadolescent individuals — hence a CHILD but no BOY or GIRL). As we read them, both Chomsky (1965, 1968) and the generative semanticists (like Lakoff, McCawley, and Ross) seem to share this sort of universality hypothesis with psycholinguists like Slobin (1971) and Osgood (1971), although they clearly differ in whether *what* is universal is specifically linguistic (former) or generally cognitive (latter).

One thing that has rarely been explicitly acknowledged is the fact that linguistic or cultural *differences* could not be identified and studied in any rigorous way if there were not underlying *samenesses* in terms of which comparisons could be made. Donald Campbell (1964), however, has made this point most forcefully:

> In essence, we could only observe differences in perception because these differences were small. Had any of our groups perceived in a radically different way from ourselves, we could not have determined that fact.... The total context of agreement provides the firm platform from which we can note a particular, localized discrepancy.... Within the area of applied epistemology, our methods illustrate one important general principle: Discrepancy can be noted and interpreted only against the background of an overwhelming proportion of nondiscrepant fit, agreement or pattern repetition.... It was the recurrent "fixedness" of 99.9 per cent of the stars which made the wanderings of the few planets interpretable as such. [Pp. 325-327]

In the present case (as we believe has been amply demonstrated), it is the existence of a common affective meaning system, with its E, P, and A dimensions, that makes it possible to compare human communities in terms of their attributions of affect to various aspects of subjective culture.

When we do find differences — what we have called either Sub-universals or Uniquenesses — the question arises as to whether they are attributable to language or culture.[26] What is impressive in our data as a whole is the lack of evidence for linguistic determinism of differences in affect attribution. Here we need merely refer to the main types of evidence. (1) *Productivity of qualifiers* (Chapter 3, pp. 89, 95, Tables 3:6 and 3:8): The two most productive qualifiers across 25 communities are always close synonyms of *good* or *big,* and correlations between AE and 16 other communities (available at the time of the analysis) in both the frequencies and diversities of

---

[26] Assuming, of course, that they are not attributable to simple translation failures.

usage of translation-equivalent qualifiers were all significant and ranged from the mid .40s to low .80s — yet the magnitudes of the correlations showed no relation to language families. (2) *Indigenous and pancultural factor analyses* (Chapter 4, pp. 124-131, 160-162, Tables 4:3 and 4:15) : In the indigenous analyses there were certain differences (e.g., in the weight of the E factor, in the relative weights of P vs. A) as there were in the pancultural analysis (e.g., in overlap with dominant cultures on the factors), but in neither case was there evidence for linguistic determinism.

The most critical evidence comes from bilingual and from bicultural and tri-community factor analyses. (3) *Bilingual analyses* (Chapter 2, pp. 65-66; Chapter 4, pp. 137-143) : In an early study Kumata and Schramm (1956), using translation-equivalent AE and JP scales, found that indices of factorial similarity were as high for bilinguals taking the SD test first in one language and then in the other as they were for AE controls taking the test twice over the same time intervals. In this volume we describe two studies, one with Finnish/English and the other with Kannada/English bilinguals, and although there were minor shifts in the salience of factors for the Finnish subjects (not for the Kannadese), there was no strong evidence for variation as a function of language family. (4) *Bicultural analyses* (Chapter 4, pp. 143-154) : In ten AE/X bicultural factorizations (see Table 4:9), although there are variations in overlaps on factors, they correspond in no obvious way to language grouping (e.g., on A it is ND which has the least overlap, not LA or TH). In bicultural factorizations other than with AE (see Tables 4:10 through 4:12) we find that although BF and ND (similar in both language and culture) show very high similarities, the BF/JP bicultural analysis yields higher similarities than the HC/JP one (and this is presumably attributable to the westernization of Japan, since one would assume — certainly in written language — greater linguistic similarities between JP and HC, even though they represent different language families). (5) *Tri-community analyses* (Chapter 4, pp. 154-159, Tables 4:13 and 4:14) : In one tri-community analysis (Delhi Hindi, Calcutta Bengali, and Mysore Kannada) one might have expected the similarity pattern to be DH + CB (both Indo-European) vs. MK (Dravidian), but nothing of this sort appears. In the other tri-community analysis (Iranian Farsi, Afghan Dari, and Afghan Pashtu) one might have expected the two variants of Persian (IF and AD) to be more similar than either with the more remote Pashtu (AP) if linguistic determinism were operating, but it was clearly AD + AP vs. IF (the much more urban site) in the data.

On the Whys and Wherefores of E, P, and A

It must be confessed that when research on semantic differentiation began over two decades ago, the first author (see Osgood, 1952) rather confidently expected that the dimensions of the semantic space would correspond quite closely to the ways the sensory nervous system differentiates the universe — i.e., in terms of the various sensory modalities and their qualities and quantities. The fact that such a result would have been flatly contrary to the implications of a representational mediation theory of meaning — in which meanings are assumed to derive from the behaviors we make to things signified — was not self-evident at that time. The repeated appearance of gross affective factors (E-P-A), with their more response-like than stimulus-like character, was thus consistent with the theory, even if unexpected. At a much later point in time, stimulated by Kuusinen's paper on the partialing technique (1969; see pp. 376-377 in this chapter), one of the authors of this book (Miron, 1969) raised this issue again in a paper titled "What Is It That Is Being Differentiated by the Semantic Differential?" and another author (Osgood, 1969) tried to answer with a paper bearing the same title as the heading above. It is an issue that ramifies into philosophy (the denotation/connotation distinction), into human physiology and development (the nature of affective meaning), into the misty regions of metaphor and synesthesia (where affective meaning appears to be the common medium), and finally into the question of the powers and limitations of the SD technique itself.

In defense of the SD as a measure of connotative meaning. In reviews of *The Measurement of Meaning* (Osgood, Suci, and Tannenbaum, 1957) our claim that the SD measured "connotative" rather than "denotative" meaning was frequently criticized (particularly by Brown, 1958; Carroll, 1959; and Weinreich, 1958), and in subsequent writings we have shifted to the use of "affective" meaning. This shift was partly on the grounds of the fuzziness of the term "connotation" in philosophical and semantics discussions. This seems an appropriate time to return to the issue. In a comprehensive review of the connotative/denotative distinction as it has been debated in relation to the SD technique, Nordenstreng (1969b, pp. 19-23) makes the point that an operational definition of "connotative meaning" as being that which the semantic differential measures is unsatisfactory, and what is needed is nonoperational definition of the two types of meaning. We agree, and in this section we will suggest a nonoperational definition that may, perhaps, clarify the nature of connotative meaning and justify our early usage of the term.

If one is asked "Is a BABY *large* or *small?*" he is likely to reply "small." And if he is asked "Is a TARANTULA *large* or *small?*" he is likely to reply "large." Yet if he is asked "Is a BABY *larger* or *smaller* than a TARANTULA?" he will certainly say "larger." If BABY can be *small* and TARANTULA *large* in the former "absolute" context, yet BABY can be *larger* than TARANTULA in the latter "relative" context, then clearly there must be different reference points for the judgments in each case. Within the hierarchical tree of nominals, BABY falls below the node of human organism and TARANTULA below the node of spider; a BABY *is* small (for a human being) and a TARANTULA *is* large (for a spider). We could also say that BABY connotes "a small one" whereas TARANTULA *connotes* "a large one," each in reference to its own superordinate class. It is precisely this "kind" of meaning that is properly called "connotative" and which the semantic differential taps.[27] The SD is thus an unusual kind of psychophysical method in which a series of different questions of the former type are asked about a single "stimulus" and judgments *relative to its superordinate* are given as replies. Thus a GALE is *strong* for a wind, RHODE ISLAND is *small* for a state, a GAZELLE is *fast* for an animal, and so forth.

In all other psychophysical methods with which we are familiar (even the so-called "absolute judgment" methods) a single question of the latter (comparative) type is asked about a series of stimuli arrayed along some dimension (e.g., scaling the loudness of tones), and judgments *relative to some standard at the same hierarchical level* are given as replies. Thus this tone is *louder* than that tone, this odor is *pungent* with respect to that odor, and this baby is *small* in comparison with babies in general. Note that when one says "Nina is a small baby," he is expressing the judgment that Nina is small *for a baby;* he is not saying that Nina is small *for a human being*.[28] We suggest that it is this "kind" of meaning that is properly called "denotative." Note that whereas one can say BABY *connotes* "a small one," one cannot say that BABY *denotes* "a small one." It may well be that this characteristic of the SD technique prevents familiar denotative features from appearing, regardless of the analytic method applied.

The primordiality of the affective meaning system. Even if it were agreed that the SD technique gets primarily at connotative meaning in the sense described above, this still would not explain the dominance and universality of E, P, and A. It was M. Brewster Smith who first pointed out the remarkable similarity of our Evaluation, Potency, and Activity factors to Wilhelm Wundt's three dimensions of feeling — Pleasantness/Unpleasantness, Strain/Relaxation, and Excitement/Quiescence. More recent experimental studies of the meanings of facial expressions of the emotions have also typically yielded three-dimensional systems which are very E-P-A-like — Schlosberg's (1954) Pleasantness/Unpleasantness, Rejection/Attention, and Tension/

[27] In at least some philosophical discussions of meaning, "connotation" has been used to refer to a concept's analytic entailments (see Ryle, 1957), and this is close to what is meant here — i.e., the concept BABY *entails* human organism, which in turn entails animal, and so on.

[28] In this connection Kostić and Das (1971, p. 68) have suggested that whereas adjectives are normally applied to nouns to restrict or constrain the meaning of the noun (e.g., *a sharp knife* means *sharp for a knife*), "in the semantic differential, meaning is being described without being reduced or restricted" (e.g., when KNIFE is judged *sharp* on the SD, it is not *sharp for a knife* but rather *sharp for an implement*).

Sleep and Osgood's (1966a) Pleasantness, Control, and Activation are examples. It was also this close resemblance of the dimensions of feelings and meanings of facial signs to the E-P-A system that led us to use the term "affective meaning system."

Consistent with a behavioral theory of meaning, it is these pervasive affective features that dominate much of human behavior. Contrary to Chomsky (see his *Language and Mind,* 1968) and the rationalists, we humans are still animals at base. What is important to us now, as it was back in the age of Neanderthal man, about the sign of a thing is, first, does it refer to something *good* for me or *bad* for me (is it an antelope or a saber-toothed tiger)? Second, does it refer to something which is *strong* or *weak* with respect to me (is it a bad saber-toothed tiger or a bad mosquito)? And third, does it refer to something that is *active* or *passive* with respect to me (is it a bad, strong saber-toothed tiger or a bad, strong pool of quicksand which I can simply walk around)? Survival, then and now, depends upon the answers.

We can also note the primordiality of the neurophysiological correlates of affective reactions. We know that the autonomic nervous system, with its organizational centers in the midbrain, is primitive neurologically and physiologically. It seems possible that affective meaning is intimately related to the functioning of the nonspecific projection system as it mediates autonomic reactions from hypothalamic, reticular, or limbic systems to the frontal lobes. Both are gross and nondiscriminative, but highly generalized, systems and both are associated with the emotional, purposive, and motivational dynamics of the organism. But there is more to it than this, we think. It is precisely because this affective reaction system is so generalized — can participate equally with all of the sensory modalities and yet is independent of any of them — that its gross but pervasive structure overshadows the more discriminative semantic systems.

If the E-P-A meaning system is primitive phylogenetically, it might also be expected to appear early in the course of ontogeny. In Chapter 2 (pp. 58-60) we reviewed some of the studies on SD-determined semantic factor structures as functions of age (Small, 1958; Donahoe, 1961; DiVesta, 1964a, etc.), intelligence (Ware, 1958), and sex (Lazowick, 1955; Ware, 1958; Small, 1959; Hallworth and Waite, 1963). We note first that there are no differences in factor structure or weight of E as functions of either intelligence or sex. As far as factor structure as a function of age is concerned, all studies report stable E, P, and A systems down to the youngest ages (third-graders for Small, second-graders for DiVesta, and first-graders for Donahoe). However, when concept profiles are considered, Donahoe reports that profiles stabilize at adult levels for E and P at ages 9 (third-graders) and 12 (sixth-graders) respectively, but those for A did not vary across age levels.[29]

---

[29] Whether this means that A stabilizes earlier than E and P (which seems unlikely) or that the concepts were relatively undifferentiated on A for all groups is not clear.

That young children (6 years old) as compared with older children (12 years old) do show confusions within factors (e.g., confusing *good, pretty, clean,* and *happy* as well as *big, heavy, long,* and *thick*) has been demonstrated by Ervin and Foster (1960). These authors observe both (a) that such properties are often correlated in experience (e.g., the bigger the heavier and vice versa) and (b), most insightfully, that the descriptive terms whose denotative meanings are not yet distinguished by the small child are identical with those descriptive terms which are linked connotatively in metaphors (i.e., in the SD data) even in adults. If there is a gradual "unfolding" of P and A from a gross fusion with E (the yang and yin of things) in the course of development, then it must occur earlier than six years of age and will require much more refined techniques for demonstration.[30]

Synesthesia, metaphor, and E-P-A. Early studies by the late Professor Theodore Karwoski of Dartmouth College and his associates (Karwoski and Odbert, 1938; Odbert, Karwoski, and Eckerson, 1942; Karwoski, Odbert, and Osgood, 1942) made it clear that auditory-visual synesthesia is not a phenomenon displayed by freak individuals whose sensory "wires are crossed." It is rather, a fundamental characteristic of human thinking, involving lawful translations from one modality to another along dimensions made parallel in cognizing. When sensory dimensions were represented by words — thus a shift from synesthesia to metaphor — the lawfulness of the process became even more apparent and stable across individuals (e.g., *loud* going with *near* rather than *far, treble* being *up* and *bass* being down, *major* being *light* and *minor* being *dark,* and so forth). It was in these studies with Karwoski on synesthesia and metaphor that the basic logic of the semantic differential technique had its origins.

Somewhat later very similar notions were expressed by two gestalt psychologists, Heinz Werner and Bernard Kaplan (see *On Expressive Language,* 1955, edited by Werner), under the general notion of "physiognomic language" — by which was meant pervasive affective dynamics in the perception of objects, lack of distinction between person and object qualities in these respects (personification), total organismic involvement in the process, and the resulting "embeddedness of the perceived object in an atmospheric context of feeling and action" (p. 12). These notions are illustrated in a delightful experiment by Kaden, Wapner, and Werner (1955): subjects were to adjust luminant words in front of them in otherwise total darkness "to eye level" by raising or lowering the projection of the words with a hand dial. The striking finding was that words like RISING and CLIMBING had to be *lowered* relative to the pre-experiment determination of "at eye level,"

---

[30] However, using the "release from proactive inhibition" technique, unpublished research by Pender has indicated significant disinhibition for E but not for P and A for second-graders, with sixth-graders showing some effect for A but still not P (see Wickens, 1972, pp. 200-201).

while words like PLUNGING and FALLING had to be *raised* — i.e., the upward-meaning words seemed higher and the downward-meaning words lower phenomenally.

The same kind of relation between word meanings and perceptual signs was explored cross-culturally by Osgood (1960b). Navajo, Mexican Spanish, Japanese, and American subjects related translation-equivalent words (HAPPY, STRONG, MAN, WOMAN, BLUE, SAD, etc.) to visual alternatives displayed on cards (e.g., a *white* circle vs. a *black* circle, a *large* circle vs. a *small* circle, a *curved* line vs. a *jagged* line) by simply pointing to that alternative which seemed "to go best with" the word in question. Thus, given HAPPY, the typical subject would point to the *colorful* (not colorless), the *clear* (not hazy), the *up* (not down), and the *white* (not black) sides of the appropriate cards. Not only were E-P-A factors evident in these visual polarities for all cultures, but words opposed in meaning (both nouns and adjectives) typically displayed reciprocal profiles against the visual polarities, and cultures agreed significantly on what aspects of meaning were related to what dimensions of visual experience.

On a different but related problem — phonetic symbolism — Miron (1961) was able to demonstrate lawful connotations of speech sounds within as well as between language (American English/Japanese) when CVC syllables which were nonsense in *both* languages were rated on appropriate SD scales. On the Potency factor, for example, AE and JP showed correlations of .57 and .91 for vowels and consonants respectively, the former also being correlated with the frequency of the second vowel formant — low frequencies being associated with felt power and magnitude affectively. On Evaluation front consonants were judged more pleasant than back, again for both groups.

In his book on phonetic symbolism, *Psychophonetik*, Ertel (1969) reports on a study in which German and Czech subjects rated translation-equivalent concepts of their own language on scales defined by "meaningless" phonetic qualifiers. Relying on adjectival marker scales which were also used, the results of separate factor analyses of the data in both groups showed great similarity of E and P loading of the phonetic scales. Thus, for example, the scale *fango-mnuhf* (German), *fango-mnûf* (Czech) is evaluative in both language groups, *karno-leli* (German and Czech, identical script) has a high loading on the Potency factor in both groups, etc. The similarities of factorial loadings were more impressive than the language-specific differences. In another study, eight pairs of words with positive/negative E, positive/negative P, and positive/negative A respectively were translated into 25 foreign languages. The pairs of words were presented visually (transcription) or orally (taped native speakers). For all three groups of word-pairs, although not for every word-pair, the subjects were able to guess above chance which word of a pair of foreign words had positive Evaluation, or positive Potency, or positive Activity respectively, under both presentation conditions.

Testimony to the primitiveness of the affective meaning system is the fact that visual-verbal synesthesia does not appear to be lost even in severely impaired anomic (naming difficulty) aphasics. Roman Jakobson (in Werner, 1955, and Jakobson and Halle, 1956, Part II) first suggested two basic types of aphasia on linguistic grounds — those with *similarity* disfunctioning (difficulty making paradigmatic lexical substitutions) and those with *contiguity* disfunctioning (difficulty with syntagmatic, syntactic sequencing). Working with a few patients of the former type (anomic), Osgood and Miron (1963, pp. 133-135) obtained evidence suggestive of minimal impairment of affective meaning, using the visual-verbal synesthesia task described above (Osgood, 1960b). However, it remained for Sylvia Sheinkopf (1970) to clearly demonstrate that anomic aphasics perform very much like normals on this same task — pointing appropriately to the visual alternatives for words — despite their manifest difficulties in naming and word finding.

Yet further testimony to the primitiveness of the affective meaning system and its cross-modality pervasiveness is to be found in studies of nonverbal (gestural, postural, facial) communication among humans. In one study of hand gesturing, for example, Gitin (1970) had subjects rate 36 photographs of just hands in various posturings against 40 SD scales; her first three factors were clearly A (*active, interesting, exciting,* etc.), E (*pleasant, good, friendly,* etc.), and P (*dominant, strong, certain,* etc.), and in this order of magnitude. In summarizing many studies reported in a recent book on nonverbal communication, Mehrabian (1972) proposes three primary referential dimensions — positiveness of interpersonal relationship (our E), relative status (our P), and responsiveness interpersonally (our A). Why? "Our answer is based on the premise that non-verbal behavior is a developmentally earlier and more primitive form of communication which man shares with animals" (p. 14).

What about purely verbal metaphor? It will be recalled that for five cultures Pečjak was able to predict from their *Atlas* profiles which Colors, Emotions, and Days of the Week would be judged as most "belonging together" (see Chapter 6, pp. 330-331) ; correlations between Emotions and both Colors and Days were highly significant, those between Colors and Days less so. In the future we plan to make more "metaphor" predictions and tests of this sort on our total *Atlas* data on about 25 language/culture communities. Some details from the Tanaka, Oyama, and Osgood study already described (1963; see this chapter, p. 347) seem particularly relevant here. Apart from the overall similarities between Japanese and American factors, it was interesting to see how the particular scales connoting Evaluation, Potency, and Activity shifted as the concept class changed from Colors, to Forms, to Abstract Words — and generally in the same ways for both culture groups. Take the

Potency factor, for example. Potency is connoted by qualities like *strong* and *deep* when Colors are being rated; when Forms are being rated, properties like *hard, angular,* and *sharp* carry the Potency connotation; and when Abstract Words like LOVE, WAR, ART, and PEACE are being rated, we find that qualities like *real, distinct,* and *near* acquire Potency implications. We have here the stuff from which metaphors are made. When we say of an abstract notion like LOVE that it is *near* and *real,* or of a color like RED that it is *strong* and *deep,* or of a form that it is *hard* and *sharp,* we are conferring the feeling of power equivalently. Note that the scales keep varying with the concepts being cognized, yet beneath this apparent uniqueness is the common affect or feeling.

What, in theory, is the underlying nature of synesthesia and metaphor? Miron (1969) has emphasized "the presence of already shared, non-contradictory features between the two words" if metaphorical extensions are to occur, and he goes on to state that "precisely those words marked by features which are more general in their application will tend to be used more (often in metaphors) ..." (pp. 191-192). The general principles operating here seem to be these: (1) Synesthetic translations and metaphors tend to occur when the number (or weight) of shared semantic features are sufficient to override differentiating opposed-sign features; thus the shared features of *thunder* and *shout* can override the $+/-$ opposition on a Human feature, in effect personifying the thunder in *the thunder shouted down the mountainside.* (2) The pervasiveness of affective E-P-A features — their independence of hierarchically organized denotative features and their weight in the meaning system generally — suggests that shared affective features will be the primary basis for synesthetic and metaphorical translations; thus it is primarily the shared +Potency of *thunder* and *shout* that carries the metaphor (note that *the thunder whispered down the mountainside* is strange, indeed). Put quite simply, shared affective meaning is the common coin of metaphor and synesthesia.

It is because such diverse sensory experiences as a *white* circle, a *straight* line, a *rising* melodic progression, a *sweet* taste, and a *caressing* touch all share a common positive E that synesthetic translations easily occur among them. It is because such diverse verbal concepts as *black, traitor, filth, vicious,* and *misery* share a common negative E that metaphorical substitutions among them easily occur and oppositions become anomalous (e.g., *black hope, white filth, vicious joy,* and *sweet misery*), even if, like the last, the very anomalousness may reflect insights into the complexities of human nature. In an early cross-cultural demonstration of this phenomenon, Solomon Asch (1955) found that for six widely separated languages (Old Testament Hebrew, Homeric Greek, Chinese, Thai, Malayalam, and Hausa) the morphemes for *straight* vs. *crooked* "universally" meant as well *honest, righteous,* and *comprehendible* vs. *dishonest* and *wily* in the personality domain. He also reported that although the metaphors of *hot* vs. *cold* varied somewhat across his sample (e.g., rage for Hebrew, enthusiasm for Chinese, and sexual arousal for Thai for *hot* vs. self-control for Hebrew, indifference for Chinese, and loneliness for Thai for *cold*), the $+$A vs. $^{-}$A distinction was clearly shared.

On the powers and limitations of the SD technique. The "why" of E-P-A is simultaneously the reason the SD technique is insufficient as a general procedure for discovering or validating semantic features. Since in the SD technique every concept must be rated on every scale, this means that TORNADO must be judged *fair* or *unfair,* MOTHER must be judged *hot* or *cold,* and SPONGE must be judged *friendly* or *unfriendly.* Among the 100 concepts used in the concept-on-scale task cross-culturally, only very few will be denotatively relevant for making non-anomalous "sentences" with *hot-cold* (*A fire is very hot/*Sympathy is ? hot-cold*) or *hard-soft* (*A tooth is quite hard/*Thunder is ? hard-soft*), yet our subjects must somehow deal with items like *hot defeat* vs. *cold defeat* and *hard power* vs. *cold power.* That they do deal with such items — and in very consistent ways — is evidence for the ubiquitousness of metaphorical determinism.

In other words, the SD technique literally *forces* metaphorical usage of most scales with most concepts. Owing to the dominance of affect in determining such usage, scales that could be used denotatively rotate toward those affective dimensions on which they have their dominant loadings — *sweet-sour* toward E, *hard-soft* toward P, *hot-cold* toward A. Since, in factor analysis, the major dimensions are mathematically inserted through the largest clusters of correlated variables, this means that the shared affective features — E, P, and A — will be amplified and the many, finer features of meaning will be damped. This, along with the connotative nature of the meaning tapped, is why the SD is insufficient as a measure of meaning — which is not to say that it is invalid or unreliable for measuring *affective* meaning and demonstrating the universality of its E-P-A features.

The *power* of the SD technique lies, first, in its natural adaptability to the very powerful procedures of multivariate statistics, in which factor analysis is a means of discovering semantic features and distance analysis is a means of rigorously specifying semantic similarities and differences. It lies, second, in the fact that it is a componential model and has all of the efficiency of such models — describing the meanings of a large number of concepts and qualifiers in terms of a relatively small number of distinguishing features. But unlike most componential systems in linguistics and anthropology, its features are continuous rather than hierarchial in organization (i.e., there is no logical priority or entailment of certain features with respect to others).[31]

---

[31] Note that E, P, and A are not "nested" within each other or under any particular node in the familiar taxonomic tree for substantives. Rather, they are independently applicable at all levels, for both Concretes and Abstracts and from top to bottom in degrees of feature specificity (e.g., to MIND as well as to ANT).

It lies, third, in the fact that it provides a systematic sampling of the distributions of usage of terms rather than the haphazard "compelling examples" characteristic of most philosophical and linguistic semantics.

The *limitation* of the SD technique lies, first (as elaborated above), in the fact that by forcing metaphorical usage of terms, it enhances affective features at the expense of other features of meaning. Since equally ubiquitous features like Concrete/Abstract, Animate/Inanimate, and Human/Nonhuman apparently are *not* the major bases for metaphor, they are ineffective in determining SD judgments and do not appear as factors. It lies, second, in the fact that the SD does not provide a sufficient characterization of the meaning of concepts. Both the pair NURSE/SINCERITY and the pair HERO/SUCCESS have near identical E-P-A scores (i.e., occupy nearly the same point in the three-dimensional space), yet they obviously do not have the same meaning (one can say *She's a cute nurse* but certainly not *She's a cute sincerity*, and *Our hero challenged them to fight* but not *Our success challenged them to fight*.[32] It lies, finally, in the fact that the SD technique uses only one type of "sentence" (Noun (Be) Quantifier Qualifier — e.g., *Tornados are very unfair*) and does not take full advantage of the semantic constraints of word-upon-word in phrases and sentences for identifying and validating semantic features. It is because of these limitations that, in recent years, we have been developing and applying what we call a semantic interaction technique (see Osgood, 1970a), in which what can and cannot be said easily in ordinary language (e.g., *sudden surprise* but not **sudden melancholy*; *plead with humbly* but not **plead with tolerantly*) by native speakers is the basis for inferring the features necessary to account for such judgments. This technique does appear to have wider applicability and does not amplify affective as against nonaffective features — but this is another story for another book.

ORTHOGONALS, OBLIQUES, PARTIALS, AND/OR THREE-MODES?

Is it possible that, quite apart from the connotative and metaphor-based meanings that the SD technique seems to generate, there are also purely methodological reasons for failure to "discover" the types of semantic features with which linguists and philosophers are familiar? We have tried a variety of multivariate methods in an attempt to answer this question, and here we will briefly review the results in relation to the question of just what the SD does (or might) measure. This review will lead us back to the most

---

[32] But it must be pointed out that *any* subset of semantic features must be equally insufficient. If one uses only Concrete/Abstract, Animate/Inanimate, and Human/Nonhuman, then all of the interesting ways in which humans differentiate humans — male vs. female kincepts, skilled vs. unskilled occupation-cepts, and old vs. young organism-cepts, for example — disappear, and WIFE has the same meaning as HUSBAND, LAWYER the same as BEGGAR, and MAN the same as BOY.

basic issue of all: is it *meaning* that is being measured by the SD or something else entirely?

Orthogonal vs. oblique solutions. Throughout our research with the SD technique we have relied primarily on orthogonal (principal-components) factorizations of the qualifier (scale) space. This type of solution extracts factors progressively in terms of proportions of total variance accounted for and aligns each successive factor at right angles to all those preceding (i.e., factors necessarily have zero correlation with each other). This method thus makes a very fundamental assumption about the nature of the semantic system (for qualifiers) : that the distinguishing features are independent of each other. In other words, although the adjectives defining particular factors may not fall at right angles to each other in the space, the factors (features) do. An oblique solution, on the other hand, places factors successively through the tightest clusters of variables, regardless of the angles between them (i.e., allowing correlations of any magnitude among factors). Note that this method does not rule out the theoretical possibility that features are independent, even though the factors may be to some degree correlated; languages may just happen to have more qualifiers which represent multiple features than "pure" qualifiers with codings on only a single feature.

In Chapter 5 (pp. 214-216) we reported the results of oblique (Oblimax-rotated) solutions for the indigenous data cubes for all communities. Since E, P, and A were still identifiable as salient factors in all cases (although occasionally displaced by double variants of E), we could identify "types" of communities in terms of the nature of the correlations among factors. Using a criterion of $\geq$.40 as a criterion of factor fusions, of 22 communities, 8 showed no fusions (i.e., essentially orthogonal relations), 8 showed "positive" fusions (the Good, the Strong, and/or the Active poles going together), and 6 showed "negative" fusions (the Good typically going with the Passive but never with the Weak). Highly suggestive was the fact that the "positive" fusion communities like AE, IF, and HC generally had much higher factor scores for the ego concept (I, MYSELF), particularly on P, seeing themselves as better, *stronger,* and more active than generally did either the "negative" fusion communities like FR, BF, and MK or the no-fusion communities like MS, DH, and JP. However, these oblique solutions neither provide evidence for factors beyond E-P-A nor resolve the issue of feature independence.

The massive pancultural factorization, by virtue of the very large number of scales included (1,050), did provide evidence for factors beyond E-P-A (I, II, and III) — although they were not necessarily identifiable for all communities. However, these additional factors (see Chapter 4, pp. 178-189, Tables 4:19 and 4:20) seem only vaguely related, if at all, to the features linguists and lexicographers emphasize. While Factor V does appear to combine both Humanness and Abstractness and Factor VIII appears to be a generalized Age dimension (both human age and traditional values), the others — like Thermal-Dermal or Climatic VI, Work-and-Play or Seriousness IV, and Immediacy or Usualness VII — surely are not familiar denotative features of meaning.

Orthogonal vs. partialed solutions. Given the dominance of E-P-A in our cross-cultural results, attempts to eliminate or control these affective factors, so that others might be identified, were obviously in order. Following Kuusinen's lead in the personality domain, we applied the partialing technique to the indigenous data cubes (100 concepts by 50 scales) for all of our communities, looking for factors which were interpretable and possibly "universal" across our sample (see Chapter 5, pp. 216-226, Table 5:10). Twenty "types" of factors shared by three or more communities were identified: eight of these "types" were special modes of evaluating (Moral E, Social E, Comfort (vs. Austerity), Competence, Aesthetic E, Utility, Superficiality (-E), and Ordinariness (also -E)). Less obviously but still mainly evaluative were a set of factors suggesting an underlying "predictability" dimension (Maturity, Reliability or Stability, Age (characterized by both *old-young* and *old-new*) and Security) and an Intimacy, an Openness, and a Fulfillment factor. Three "types" representing variants of P and/or A were Dynamism (a familiar fusion of P and A), Toughness, and Magnitude. Only two "types" of a more denotative nature were identified — a Brightness factor (*shiny, distinct, light,* etc.) and a Thermal-Dermal factor (*hot, dry,* etc.) already noted in the pancultural analysis. Although the patterning of these partialed factors across our communities was interesting culturologically, only a few of them could be called "denotative" in the usual sense (e.g., Competence, Utility, Age, Magnitude, and Brightness).

Orthogonal vs. three-mode solutions. Although the three-mode type of multivariate analysis is clearly appropriate to SD data, since it involves three sources of variance (subjects, concepts, and scales), this method was not available at the time we began our studies. Rather, we collapsed the subject variance into cultural means for concept-on-scale items and then used two-mode analyses. Our justification for this *now* is the fact that SD data typically yield one very large subject factor, with the remaining factors accounting for (usually) 6% or less of the total variance (see this chapter, pp. 343-346). However, if one thinks of our communities as analogous to "individuals," then a number of interesting applications of three-mode-type analyses to SD data suggest themselves. Under the impetus of Dr. Oliver Tzeng of our Center staff, two of these have been piloted.

One application is an improvement upon the partialing technique. For any concept domain (Tzeng worked with personality concepts for three communities, BrE, FF, and JP; see pp. 378-380 in this chapter), the data are assigned to two spaces, Affective (marker scales) and Denotative (non-marker scales), and then factorizations of the "subject" (culture groups) mode and the concept mode can be done for each space, the Denotative space being the most interesting at this point. As illustrated in Tzeng's thesis (1972), one can determine both scale and concept factors for each "culture type" and compare them. The other application is a refinement of our *Atlas* category analyses (see Chapter 6). Using cross-products between communities in their interconcept distance matrices, communities are assigned to "idealized culture types"; the coordinates of the centroids of each community cluster (their "point of view") are used to create an "ideal" interconcept distance matrix; finally, each of these "ideal" matrices is factored separately in the concept mode, yielding concept dimensions and projections of concepts on them. Tzeng has applied this procedure successfully to the data of 17 communities on the Kinship category. Five "idealized culture types" were found, and they differed in culturally interpretable and significant ways (see Tzeng, Osgood, and May, 1974).

The methodological explorations summarized here raise a number of theoretical issues. For one thing, in just what sense do the partial and three-mode procedures "eliminate" affect? In the partialed cross-cultural factor "types," most were ways of attributing feeling (Morality, Aesthetic E, Predictability, Toughness, etc.) and similarly for the three-mode analyses of personality-concept data (Morality, Rationality, Dogmatism, Sophistication, etc.). Given the mathematical nature of these techniques, it would appear that these factors are "gutless E-P-As" — that is, modes of attributing affect that are distinguishable (e.g., moral, social, aesthetic, and so on) once the common affect per se has been statistically taken out. But these modes are still more "connotative" in nature than "denotative." Since partialing and three-mode procedures do control for the amplification of affect forced by metaphorical usage of terms in the SD technique, this strongly implies that it is the "absolute" nature of SD judgments (e.g., BABY is *small* — for a human being, the superordinate node; see pp. 393-394) which is responsible for the regular appearance of "connotative" rather than "denotative" features of meaning. And as was noted earlier in connection with the Tanaka-Oyama-Osgood (1963) study, when the superordinate category shifts (in this case, from Colors to Forms to Abstractions), the qualifier dimensions which connote Evaluation, Potency, and Activity shift as well.

And this brings us to a very fundamental question: are affective E, P, and A *semantic* features in any sense at all? The late Uriel Weinreich raised this issue in his review of *The Measurement of Meaning:* "The 'psychological states' whose projections the semantic differential is out to capture occur, no doubt, in speech behavior, too, but such emotive influence is an aspect of all experience and behavior, and is not restricted to language or even to communication in general, in which meaning (signification and reference) are distinctive components" (p. 360).[33] The two alternatives here are these: (1)

---

[33] We might note in passing that meaning itself is not restricted to language either, being clearly conveyed by perceptual signs (see Osgood, 1971).

E-P-A are basic dimensions of emotion or feeling which parallel and interact with semantic features, but are not themselves affective in nature. (2) E-P-A are very pervasive and primitive affective features, and they have all of the functional properties of other semantic features. We hold the second position, of course, but to resolve this issue it must be demonstrated that E, P, and A satisfy the criteria that characterize generally accepted features, such as ±Human and ±Sex. While no claim for exhaustiveness can be made, at least the following criteria seem to be met.

(1) *Componential nature of (usually bipolar) features* (see Greenberg, 1967). E, P, and A are obviously not a unidimensional system but a multi-dimensional one, and the features combine freely to yield compound affective meanings just as the components of kinship systems (e.g., Sex, Generation, Consanguinity, and so on) combine to yield the compound denotative meanings *father, aunt, brother, grandmother, wife,* and so on.[34]

(2) *The intuitive sharing of semantic commonness across diverse forms.* Just as one intuitively "feels" the common $+/-$ Sex distinction between *man, boy, son, uncle, husband* vs. *woman, girl, daughter, aunt, wife,* so also, we claim, does one intuitively "feel" the shared $+/-$ Evaluation distinction between *love, agree, help, sweet, friend* vs. *hate, disagree, hinder, sour, enemy,* and similarly for P and A.

(3) *Clustering of affective and nonaffective features in word combinations.* This is what Weinreich (1966, pp. 419-429) has referred to as "linking"; to use his example, "a construction such as *white + wall* may be said to have the semantic effect of construing an entity which possesses just the semantic features of *white* and *wall.*" Similarly, one may construe semantically *a good husband* as an entity which has just the features of *good* (+E) and of *husband* (+Human, +Male, +Marital). Now, if affective components can cluster with nonaffective components just as freely as nonaffectives with each other, how can one claim that the former are not semantic in nature?

(4) *Determination of semantic congruence and incongruence.* This is what Chomsky (1965) referred to as "selection rules," although at that time he was apparently conceiving it as a syntactic rather than a semantic process. Just as *John admires sincerity* is acceptable because of the congruence of the +Human codings of *John* and *admire* (whereas *Sincerity admires John* is unacceptable because of the opposed codings of *sincerity* and *admires* on the same feature), so we would argue that *Saints admire virtue* is acceptable because of the congruence of the three terms on +E (whereas *Saints admire duplicity* is unacceptable in ordinary language because of the opposed −E coding of *duplicity* — unless one assumes that the speaker has a negative

---

[34] The fact that E, P, and A are continuous rather than discrete features is not a criterion. For any features along which comparisons can be made (e.g., relative height, width, speed, intelligence, etc.), continuousness of coding must be assumed (e.g., as in *John is taller than Paul but shorter than Sam.*)

evaluation of *saints!*). Osgood and Richards (1973) have shown that very fine degrees of congruence or incongruence among adjectives in terms of measured E, P, and A effectively determine the selection of *and* vs. *but* in conjunctive sentences of the type *X is sweet* _____ *kind, X is weak* _____ *brave,* and so on.

(5) *Production of anomalies via opposed codings on features.* This is merely the extreme case of 4 above. Just as *She will make someone a nice husband* is anomalous because of the incongruence of *she* and *husband* on the Sex feature, so is *That bitch will make someone a nice wife* anomalous because of incongruence on E. Just as *a pensive boulder* is anomalous owing to $+/-$ codings on Animate and Human, so is *a husky jellyfish* anomalous owing to $+/-$ codings on Potency. In sum, in terms of at least these criteria of semanticity, E, P, and A appear to satisfy the necessary conditions.

SOURCES OF FALLIBILITY IN CULTUROLOGICAL INTERPRETATIONS

Cross-cultural studies of this magnitude and duration are beset on all sides by potential biases in interpretation — of omission as well as commission. This is most clearly the case for the "tool-using" phases (particularly for the *Atlas* data), but certain biases can also affect our interpretations of data collected in the "tool-making" phases. In this final section we will review some of the major sources of potential bias in our data, including problems of translation, of sampling, of Western influence, of assuming "sameness" when "difference" is in fact the case, and vice versa. We will indicate what we have done to minimize bias, as well as what we think should be done to check the validity of interpretations.

On the limitations of translation equivalence. Before making any attempt at culturological interpretation of data, one should eliminate the possibility of translation bias as the reason for apparent cultural differences. Werner and Campbell (1970) put it very succinctly: "The strategy of cultural comparison has to be one of competitive interpretation of obtained differences, in which difference in culture ... is only *one* of the possible explanations. Imperfections of translation will ubiquitously appear among the plausible rival hypotheses" (p. 415). We have utilized to varying extents all three strategies for circumventing the language barrier (see Chapter 1, pp. 15-16) : *language-invariant instruments* — demonstration of the universality of the E-P-A structure and development of comparable cross-linguistic SDs for measuring affective dimensions of subjective culture; *language-free instruments* — our work on the development of a graphic differential (see this chapter, pp. 380-384) represents movement in this direction, but we have much further to go; and *translation-equivalent instruments* — we have had to take this path in the translation of concepts, both for the 100 substantives used in the "tool-making" phases and for the 620 concepts used in the *Atlas* work.

Werner and Campbell and others have emphasized the importance of both back-translation and decentering as means of minimizing translation failure and monocultural bias. But, as we pointed out earlier in this chapter (pp. 338-340), the two conditions presumed implicitly by Werner and Campbell — that words to be translated are in context (phrases, sentences, texts, situations) and that the translating is bilingual (between a single pair of source and destination languages) — could not be met in our research. The concepts to be translated were typically single word-forms, without any delimiting context, and we were aiming for equivalence across some 25 languages (with AE as the common source) rather than just a single pair (AE/X).

So we had to devise other procedures. (1) In translating the original substantives to be used in "tool-making," we simply had small sets of bilinguals (as balanced as possible and often bicultural as well) translate from AE into X and rate their confidence in the two alternative translations for each AE term. For seven different language families (see Chapter 3, p. 70), if after discussion a concept failed to have an agreed-upon translation, it was dropped for all languages. The ease of subsequent translation of the surviving 100 concepts into some 20 additional languages is testimony to the culture-commonness and translatability of these terms. (2) Translating the 620 *Atlas* concepts into some 25 languages and checking the translation fidelity proved to be a very laborious, albeit educational, task (which is detailed in Chapter 5, pp. 259-269). We found that we had to construct a "project dictionary" which, unlike most dictionaries, ordered the senses of each AE concept from dominants, through polysemes of decreasing closeness, to homonyms liable to confusion with the intended sense (where "intended" was the assumed dominant for AE teen-age males). Using this "dictionary," and carefully explaining and illustrating the various senses to our foreign colleagues, greatly reduced the difficulty and error in translation — although there undoubtedly remain some translation failures and many translation differences (in sense dominance). It should be emphasized again that at only these two points in the "tool-making" and "tool-using" (*Atlas*) phases respectively could translation infidelity influence the data per se, although the potential influence upon interpretation remains.

There is a paradox here: *if perfect translations could be obtained* (with no differences in the meanings of translation-equivalent terms), *then there would be no culture differences.* In other words, if members of two cultures agree right down the line on the denotation (external reference), the connotation (internal reference, in terms of hierarchical superordination and subordination), the affect (attribution of E, P, and A), the associations with other terms, etc. of concepts like UNCLE or SYMPATHY, then there is perfect cultural equivalence as well as linguistic equivalence of the terms — and, presumably, of the behaviors predictable in relation to the concepts. Now, this state of affairs is likely to be very rare — even for individuals within a given language/culture community. This is the ultimate limitation on translation fidelity. The ideal solution to the apparent dilemma posed here is this: to guarantee as far as possible that the denotations (external references) and connotations (internal hierarchical references to other concepts in the taxonomies of terms) [35] of concepts are the same, and then interpret differences (in affect, in association, in behavior) in terms of cultural variables. Differences between AE and DH in the meaning of cow provide an obvious example.

Although this ideal is easy to state in principle, it is very hard to achieve in practice — and as Werner and Campbell (1970) point out, "*An interpreter is not an adjunct to a cross-cultural–cross-language project, he is central to its success.* . . . Such a person is more important than any of the 'rules' we are here proposing." Amen! The entire success of our project (but not its failures) has been dependent upon the care and the skill with which our senior colleagues and their associates have handled the translating and interpreting tasks. The fact that most of them have been bicultural as well as bilingual with respect to English has, we believe, been more a source of correction than of bias. However, there still remains some limit on the degree of translation fidelity that can be assumed. This was evident in our attempts to demonstrate correspondences across communities in the productivity of their modes of qualifying (Chapter 3, pp. 92-94) and to interpret the evidence for additional pancultural factors beyond E-P-A (Chapter 4, pp. 178-189), as well as the results of oblique and partialed factor analyses already discussed. And, of course, the translation bugaboo comes back to haunt us in the complex process of interpreting results of the *Atlas* category analyses, as illustrated in Chapter 6 on the Color category. In the last analysis, given the variable ways lexicons of different languages carve up the world, the semantic spheres of translation-equivalent terms can only approach perfect coincidence, never reach it.

Limitations due to sampling. If there is one malady shared by scientists of all types, it is the tendency to generalize beyond the constraints of their data bases — whether it be from the spectral shifts of light from certain distant galaxies, from the effects of drugs upon one species to the effects upon another, or from the characteristics of one set of human cultures to culture in general. Although our samples in this project were nearly all teen-age, school-attending males in particular (usually urban) regions of

---

[35] To include connotative agreement, in the sense used here, assumes that the cognitive structuring of concepts in terms, e.g., of Concrete/Abstract, Living/Nonliving, Animate/Inanimate, etc. is universal — which may well not be the case, at least at the lower levels of such tree-like structures.

their countries, we have been aware of our own tendency to overgeneralize to communities as wholes and even to countries or regions as wholes. On the basis of our varied subject samplings in AE (see Osgood, Suci, and Tannenbaum, 1957) and our cross-cultural results for the "tool-making" phase, we do not believe that our restricted subject samples could have any great influence upon the E-P-A structure of the affective meaning system. But they could have marked influence upon the *Atlas* data and its interpretation. Although the analysis is not yet complete, we are checking on the influence of "teen-age maleness" by collecting representative samples (age-, sex-, and education-wise) in both Athens, Greece, and Chicago, Illinois; we hope to be able to identify those concepts (and concept classes) which are peculiarly sensitive to the teen-age, male nature of our *Atlas* samples.

With regard to interpretation of the *Atlas* data, the problem of sampling goes beyond the "teen-age maleness" of our subjects — to limited sampling of human communities (most "high" and literate rather than "low" and nonliterate, more Indo-European than otherwise in language types, more northern and western than southern and eastern). Nevertheless, the sample of 23 language/culture communities seems large and diverse enough to at least support the notion of "potential human universals" *as hypotheses* when as many as 18 of the 23 all go the same way on any of our cross-cultural tests (of ranks, of components, of distances, and so on). In a sense, these universal tendencies are immune to the foibles of culture-bound human interpreters — not as far as their interpretations of the Universals are concerned (e.g., in terms of biological, cultural, or "states of the world/states of human cognition" types of explanation), but as being dependable facts.[36] It is the Sub-universals and Uniquenesses that are most susceptible to interpretative bias — and yet are the most in need of interpretation. As we at the Center with respect to some of the Uniquenesses of AE and as our colleagues for their own cultures soon discovered in *Atlas* interpretation sessions, we often don't even feel too confident "culturologizing" about our *own* communities. Although consistent patterns in the data increase confidence in their interpretation, we must again give warning that such interpretations should be taken *cum grano salis*.

Deep vs. superficial similarities and differences. At the end of the first, orientational chapter of this book, we raised the issue of interpretation in terms of four deceptively simple questions: when is the "same" really the same? when is the "same" really different? when is the "different" really the same? and when is the "different" really different? In concluding this final chapter — with the benefit of hindsight over much data — we return

---

[36] It is true, of course, that with a criterion which holds generally for the $p \leq .01$ level, some 1% of the apparent "universals" will still be due to chance — but it is here that the patterning of the data becomes important.

to the same questions. Given the surface variations across both languages and cultures, clear-cut answers are rarely attainable, and ideally one must first eliminate at least three prior reasons for either samenesses or differences.

(1) *That they are attributable to translation failures.* Although this applies mainly to apparent differences, it can also create apparent samenesses — e.g., bicultural colleagues select unusual translations which they think will produce the same feeling-tones as the AE term.

(2) *That they are attributable to unreliability.* Superficial samenesses can be due to insensitivity of the data to fine, but significant, variations in meaning. Superficial differences can often be shown to be based on purely chance, nonsignificant differences in measures.

(3) *That they are attributable to chance.* Here by "chance" we mean something other than statistical unreliability — namely, same or different reasons for the superficial sameness. A set of cultures may reliably display the same E, P, and/or A for a given concept or a given componential test, and yet members of the set may have different cultural reasons (e.g., AE, BF, IT, YS, TK, and HC may all display a ⁻E⁻P⁻A pattern for their translations of KING and yet have quite different reasons).

In what follows we shall assume that these preconditions for interpretation have been met. We have checked translations carefully, statistical criteria were applied consistently in the determination of sameness and difference, and samenesses owing to different reasons were checked in our group meetings on *Atlas* interpretation. However, we can never *really* know how many little fish have slipped through our nets.

The "same" really *is* the same. In the search for human universals this is the answer one desires. At the very beginnings of the "tool-making" phase of this research we were able to demonstrate significant correlations across communities in the productivity orderings of qualifiers (i.e., humans agree pretty well on relative saliencies of diverse modes of differentiating their experiences); even the two most productive qualifiers were regularly identifiable as close variants of *good* (E) and *big* (P). At the termination of "tool-making" (the pancultural factor analysis, which is free from translation bias or dependence) we were able to demonstrate the sameness of E, P, and A across cultures, even though the specific scales varied from place to place. In the "tool-using" *Atlas* phase (as illustrated for the Color category in Chapter 6) we have found many facts that meet our criteria for Universals — no more than 5 "deviants" in our sample of 23 communities. Although many of these are obvious (like DOCTOR being more E than BEGGAR and LEADER being more P than FOLLOWER) — but not trivial because they attest to the overall validity of the data — others are certainly not obvious (like the red end of the spectrum being more A than the blue end and future-oriented concepts being more E than past-oriented concepts) and point to certain characteristics of humanness, no matter where it is found. As noted earlier, such Universals are our hardest data, being the most independent of culturological interpretation by ourselves and our colleagues. In this connection, Triandis, Malpass, and Davidson (1972) point out that studies designed to prove cross-cultural generalities are not as dependent upon methodological details as those designed to reveal cultural differences, "since if the same finding is obtained in spite of differences in the stimuli, responses and people, it must be a strong finding" (p. 14).

The "same" is really *different*. This, of course, is what relativists would like to demonstrate for any claims made by universalists, and, given the ultimate limits on both translation and interpretation, this philosophical position is hard to refute. In our own indigenous factorizations, for example, it was shown that even the common E factors had different "flavors" — some communities generalizing sensory modes of evaluating, some social modes, some aesthetic modes, and so forth — and what remains as "common" is the underlying feeling-tone itself. Furthermore, with E-P-A partialed out, the "types" of residual factors are seldom universal across communities. Even in the pancultural factor analysis certain communities tended to have relatively low loadings, particularly on P and A. However, when the *indigenous* loadings of pancultural scales for these communities (notably LA, AD, and IF on P and GK, TK, DH, CB, and MK on A) are compared with their loadings on the pancultural factors, we find that *both* are low, clearly implying relatively low reliabilities rather than substantive factorial differences (see Chapter 4, pp. 165-167, Table 4:16). As far as the *Atlas* results are concerned, although the Universals probably stand up because of the large N involved (it is difficult to conceive of 18/23 communities displaying the same phenomenon for as many different reasons), what we have termed Subuniversals are clearly more suspect, and indeed in the "*Ψ*-ing" interpretative work at our group meetings Sub-universals often do disintegrate into Uniquenesses.

The "different" is really the *same*. This, of course, is what universalists would like to show is the case for what superficially appear as cultural differences. The critical issues involved in arriving at a decision between "different" really same or really different are (a) translation fidelity and (b) interpretability by informants. If translation is accurate (within the limits indicated on pp. 407-408) and Sub-universal or Uniqueness is interpretable with confidence, then the "different" probably *is* different. If either the translation is a failure or informants find an accurately translated item culturologically uninterpretable ("don't know"), then we just don't know whether the "different" is really the same or really different. The above applies particularly to interpretation of the *Atlas* data, of course. In the case of our pancultural factor analysis, on the other hand, since functional similarities in scale usage across concepts are independent of translation, we can make a strong claim that the superficially different (the *sweet-sour* of

AE, the *friendly-unfriendly* of MS, the *merciful-cruel* of MK, and the *ambrosial-poisonous* of DH) are really the same (reflect the underlying Evaluation factor) at some deeper level — and this conclusion, it should be noted, is independent of informant judgments.

The "different" really *is* different. As has been emphasized in this chapter (p. 391), one can only note differences within an overall context of sameness. The whole purpose of our "tool-making" phase was to first demonstrate the universality of the E-P-A structure of affective meaning and then use demonstrably comparable pancultural SDs to measure samenesses and differences in subjective culture. We can feel reasonably confident, therefore, that when both the conditions of translation fidelity and informant interpretability are met, statistically reliable "differences" across cultures in the attribution of feeling *are* real differences. Thus, if we find that in one set of communities OLD PEOPLE and OLD AGE have relatively high E and *high* P, whereas in another set the same concepts have high E but *low* P — and our informants can give explanations with reasonable confidence — we are justified in interpreting such differences in culturological terms. And if a consistent pattern for an Age feature emerges across concepts (in within-category and across-category componential analyses), then we have even stronger justification. Given the often admitted fallibility of our colleagues and ourselves as sensors of our own cultures, even reliable differences that are uninterpretable are worth reporting — since interpretations may be forthcoming from readers of our reports. In the last analysis, however, differences that are most likely to "make a difference" in cross-cultural social science will be those which are predicted as hypotheses deriving from the theories of social scientists — and for such purposes our data are always available.

What about the "why" of samenesses or differences? Here we may briefly note three common bases for attributing cause, while admitting that our data per se provide little reason for choice among them. (1) *Common vs. different cultural origins:* Samenesses can be due to a common cultural "ancestor" or a common cultural "source" which, through diffusion (conquest, migration, trade, travel, etc.), spreads across human communities. We find certain universals of kinship affect, and these might have origins in very ancient human groups. On the other hand, it is clear in our data that contemporary influence of Western (particularly American) culture, through travel, movies, and the like, is having a homogenizing impact throughout much of the world. Differences, of course, would be attributed to different "ancestors" (e.g., East Asian vs. Western European) or different "sources" (e.g., Moslem vs. Christian religio-social diffusions). (2) *Innate commonness vs. difference:* Here one must distinguish between *specific* attributions of affect to particular aspects of subjective culture and *general* attributional tendencies; the former seem most unlikely to be innately determined (e.g., unique low E of GREEN for DH — which, it will be recalled, was interpreted as signifying Pakistan and the Moslem religion). Samenesses might be attributed to the innateness of deep cognitive structures in the human species; differences might reflect variations in innate cognitive structures and processes within the human species (but this assumption is liable to circularity and probably untestable). (3) *Common vs. different physical environments:* This assumes, in effect, an interaction between common human cognitive structures (innately determined) and common or variable environmental influences. Thus communities in similar environments (e.g., the northern temperate zones vs. the tropical zones, regardless of race) will share certain cultural characteristics. No doubt all of these causal factors are operating.

Finally, we have the problem of how one can test the validity of our findings and of our interpretations of them. Ideally, we should do specialized (in relations to our *Atlas* concepts and categories) ethnographies for each of our 25 or so human communities — in fact, following Campbell's ideal model (1964, pp. 330-333), with at least two independent ethnographers, one external and one internal to each culture — but this is obviously infeasible. Actually, the ultimate criterion for the validity of culturological inferences from the linguistic domain (whether ethnographies, folk taxonomies, or our *Atlas* data) is the accuracy of predictions *from* such indices of subjective culture *to* indices of objective culture — cultural behavior in the widest sense. This was illustrated nicely for kinship terminology by Floyd Lounsbury (1956). The Pawnee have the same word for mother's brother's wife, ego's wife, and the sisters of ego's wife. According to Pawnee social norms, an adolescent should have his first sexual experience with his mother's brother's wife, and after marriage sexual intercourse with his wife's sisters is permitted. The common term for own wife, wife's sisters, and mother's brothers' wives accurately reflects this behavioral generalization.

Up to the date of this writing, we have done relatively little to get outside of the verbal trellis, but a variety of behavioral checks are planned for the near future. A few examples must suffice. We plan to correlate the inter-concept distances within categories with analogous distance matrices generated by native speakers making judgments about the global similarity of the meanings of the same terms. We plan to check predictions as to relative ease or difficulty in communicating cross-culturally within a given conceptual domain (e.g., Occupations, Colors, and Emotions) — as made from between-culture correlations among D matrices for these categories — against actual communicative performances by pairs of individuals or groups in jointly solving problems in these categories. The *Atlas* data generate predictions about metaphors across conceptual categories (e.g., that Colors having the highest E-P-A profile similarities with certain Emotions will be better metaphors) and, extending the pioneering work of Pečjak (1970) on this problem, we plan to check such predictions against actual acceptance or rejection of potential metaphors by native speakers in our communities. Although we will not be able to check all of the behavioral implications of our data in these ways, evidence for validity in such varied samples will imply validity of the whole.

APPENDIXES

APPENDIX A

Qualifier Elicitation for Selected Concepts Drawn from American English (AE) and Calcutta Bengali (CB) Atlas Tables 1.

A: AMERICAN ENGLISH

Substantive Stimuli	H	DIV	Qualifier Responses
BATTLE	.044	39	BLOODY(24),NA(15),FIERCE(5),WON(5),FIGHT(4),HARD(4),BIG(3),FIGHTING(3),BAD(2),GREAT(2),LONG(2), TERRIFIC(2),TOUGH(2),DANGEROUS(2).
BIRD	.044	35	NA(17),RED(14),BLACK(7),BLUE(7),SMALL(7),DEAD(5),LARGE(5),PRETTY(5),BEAUTIFUL(2),BIG(2),BROWN(2), CHIRPING(2),GRACEFUL(2),YELLOW(2).
BOOK	.045	36	GOOD(15),INTERESTING(11),NA(10),BLUE(9),READ(7),BLACK(7),SMALL(3),STORY(3),ALGEBRA(2),ENGLISH(2), HISTORY(2),MYSTERY(2),NEW(2),OLD(2),THICK(2).
BREAD	.039	25	NA(24),STALE(14),WHITE(10),BROWN(6),DRY(5),FRESH(5),GOOD(4),HARD(4),TASTY(4),DAILY(3),MOLDED(3), MOLDY(3),EATEN(2),SOFT(2).
COURAGE	.048	50	NA(19),GREAT(15),BRAVE(6),LITTLE(4),STRONG(4),MUCH(3),XX(3),ENOUGH(2),GOOD(2),REAL(2).
CUP	.040	30	NA(23),BROKEN(13),SMALL(9),FULL(7),WHITE(6),LARGE(5),ROUND(5),CRACKED(4),CLEAN(3),BLACK(2),CHINA(2), DIRTY(2),PETITE(2).
DANGER	.019	17	NA(73),LITTLE(4),XX(4),BAD(3),LURKING(2),TERRIBLE(2),UNSEEN(2).
DEFEAT	.043	40	NA(3),XX(7),BAD(5),TERRIBLE(5),UTTER(5),BEATEN(3),HONORABLE(3),SAD(3),COMPLETE(2),EASY(2),GREAT(2), LAST(2),SHAMEFUL(2),UNBEARABLE(2).
EAR	.041	34	NA(29),BIG(8),DIRTY(7),LARGE(7),SMALL(6),LITTLE(6),LEFT(4),CLEAN(3),LITTLE(3),SORE(3),GOOD(2),HUGE(2),INFECTED(2), SHARP(2),XX(2),RED(2).
FRUIT	.038	33	NA(36),RIPE(10),GOOD(7),JUICY(5),SWEET(5),DELICIOUS(4),FRESH(3),ROTTEN(3),ASSORTED(2),TASTY(2).
GIRL	.036	31	PRETTY(40),BEAUTIFUL(11),SMALL(7),NA(6),BIG(3),CUTE(3),FAT(2),NICE(2),SHAPELY(2),SHARP(2),UGLY(2).
HEAT	.039	33	HOT(27),NA(18),INTENSE(8),WARM(8),UNBEARABLE(3),COLD(2),DRY(2),LITTLE(2),RADIANT(2),RED(2),STEAM(2), SULTRY(2),TREMENDOUS(2).
HOUSE	.038	27	BIG(22),LARGE(18),WHITE(12),NA(8),OLD(6),RED(4),BEAUTIFUL(3),NEW(3),BRICK(2),CLEAN(2),HUGE(2),SMALL(2), WELL-BUILT(2).
HUSBAND	.045	41	NA(27),GOOD(8),XX(7),FAITHFUL(3),MAD(3),MEAN(3),NICE(3),STRONG(3),UNDERSTANDING(3),BIG(2),JEALOUS(2), LOVING(2),OLD(2),POOR(2),UNHAPPY(2),WONDERFUL(2),YOUNG(2).
LAKE	.042	32	NA(18),BLUE(11),CLEAR(10),DEEP(9),LARGE(7),SMALL(6),BIG(5),CALM(3),WAVY(3),PRETTY(2),QUIET(2),ROUND(2), WIDE(2),SHALLOW(2).
LOVE	.046	47	NA(26),TRUE(8),MUCH(6),GREAT(5),WONDERFUL(5),BEAUTIFUL(3),REAL(3),DEEP(2),LAST(2),PASSIONATE(2), EVERLASTING(2).

APPENDIX A (continued)

B: CALCUTTA BENGALI

BATTLE	.034	27	AWFUL(35),NA(20),HORRIBLE(11),BIG(4),DOMESTIC(4),VIOLENT(2),GREAT(2),DEADLY(2),LONG(2).
BIRD	.033	24	BEAUTIFUL(37),FLYING(18),RED(7),BLACK(5),BRISK(5),LITTLE(3),WHITE(3),BIG(2),YELLOW(2),BAD(3),BLUE(2),NA(2).
BOOK	.039	31	GOOD(25),BEAUTIFUL(20),NA(6),BIG(5),TORN(5),NEW(5),LITTLE(3),RED(3),COUNTLESS(2),HUGE(2),RIGID(2),BAD(2),WELL-KNOWN(2).
BREAD	.045	30	HARD(11),WARM(9),SOFT(9),GOOD(8),NA(7),SWEET(6),STALE(5),BAD(5),ROTTEN(4),BAKED(4),NOT STALE(3),VERY TASTY(3),FRIED(2),ROUND(2),UNRIPE(2),EATEN(2),FAT(2),BURNT(2),DRY(2),EVIL(2).
COURAGE	.043	30	PROFUSE(14),LIMITLESS(10),EXTREME(10),AWFUL(9),HONEST(8),EXTRAORDINARY(5),DARING(5),UNPRECEDENTED(4),HORRIBLE(4),UNRULY(4),IMPOSSIBLE(2),BIG(2),GOOD(2),TREMENDOUS(2),INVINCIBLE(2),TERRIBLE(2),NA(2).
CUP	.041	32	BEAUTIFUL(22),ONE(11),CRACKED(9),NA(8),LITTLE(7),WARM(7),GOOD(3),MAGNIFICENT(3),WHITE(3),BIG(2),FOUR(2),FILTHY(2),FULL TO THE BRIM(2).
DANGER	.040	29	HORRIBLE(18),AWFUL(16),PROFUSE(12),BIG(8),GREAT(7),APPROACHING(5),NA(5),COUNTLESS(2),HEAVY(2),TREMENDOUS(2),RIGID(2),DEADLY(2),TRIVIAL(2),GRAVE(2).
DEFEAT	.041	32	AWFUL(20),NA(19),REGRETTABLE(10),UNTHINKABLE(6),BAD(4),RIGID(3),FALSE(3),EXTREME(2),GRAND(2),TREMENDOUS(2),SERIOUS(2),PROFUSE(2),TRAGIC(2),CRUEL(2),GRAVE(2),BEAUTIFUL(2),XX(2).
EAR	.041	26	CUT(17),BIG(11),TALL(11),LITTLE(8),DEAF(7),THIN(6),UPRIGHT(4),FAN LIKE(4),PIERCING(4),BAD(3),SHORT(3),ROTTEN(3),CLEAN(3),BEAUTIFUL(3),BENT(2).
FRUIT	.028	20	RIPE(40),SWEET(27),BEAUTIFUL(7),UNRIPE(6),GOOD(3),NOT STALE(2),SOUR(2).
GIRL	.033	22	BEAUTIFUL(28),GOOD(20),BRISK(16),LITTLE(8),NAUGHTY(5),CALM(5),SHY(2),WELL-KNOWN(2).
HEAT	.041	30	INTOLERABLE(17),AWFUL(14),ACUTE(12),TERRIBLE(10),WARM(7),PROFUSE(5),IMPOSSIBLE(3),HORRIBLE(3),NA(3),EXTREME(2),QUITE(2),TERRIFIC(2),ABUNDANT(2),HEATED(2).
HOUSE	.027	17	BEAUTIFUL(45),BIG(22),GOOD(8),RIPE(5),CRACKED(4),HIGH(3),GRAND(2),TWO-STORIED(2).
HUSBAND	.048	39	GOOD(14),NA(10),BEAUTIFUL(7),DEAD(6),TRUSTED(5),KIND(5),REAL(4),DEAR(3),HONEST(3),XX(3),RICH(2),TREMENDOUS(2),GODLY(2),POOR(2),NOBLE(2),WELL-KNOWN(2),FAITHFUL(2),PROPER(2),COURTEOUS(2),AFFECTIONATE(2),FIT(2).
LAKE	.039	26	LITTLE(18),BIG(14),DEEP(13),SALTY(8),LARGE(7),DRY(7),GRAND(4),TALL(4),BEAUTIFUL(4),FAMOUS(3),ROUND(2),STUPENDOUS(2).
LOVE	.047	39	DEEP(14),PROFUSE(10),ENDLESS(8),GENUINE(6),BEAUTIFUL(5),CORDIAL(4),MAGNIFICENT(4),NA(4),EXTRA-ORDINARY(3),EXTREME(3),SEVERE(3),REAL(3),INSEPARABLE(2),UNPRECEDENTED(2),EXCEEDING(2),BIG(2),MENTAL(2),HONEYED(2).

APPENDIX B

TABLE 2 AMERICAN ENGLISH

H-INDICES, H-RANKS, FREQUENCY, AND DIVERSITY SCORES FOR THE 200 HIGHEST H-RANKED QUALIFIERS IN THE QUALIFIER ELICITATION TASK

RNK	QUALIFIER	H	FRQ	DV
1	GOOD	.2281	436	63
2	BIG	.1401	264	60
3	GREAT	.0905	191	41
4	SMALL	.0817	156	54
5	LARGE	.0758	153	45
6	BAD	.0724	150	43
7	LITTLE	.0675	129	52
8	LONG	.0632	162	27
9	HARD	.0526	154	24
10	STRONG	.0429	122	22
11	BLACK	.0385	112	18
12	RED	.0362	97	21
13	LOUD	.0360	172	12
14	WONDERFUL	.0327	72	33
15	WHITE	.0313	85	21
16	NICE	.0306	69	30
17	BRIGHT	.0299	127	10
18	BEAUTIFUL	.0272	69	23
19	OLD	.0265	62	24
20	PRETTY	.0246	83	19
21	BLUE	.0218	61	16
22	HOT	.0206	94	14
23	TERRIBLE	.0176	46	18
24	SOFT	.0163	51	15
25	BROWN	.0159	54	15
26	AWFUL	.0145	39	19
27	DIRTY	.0145	46	14
28	DEEP	.0139	47	12
29	TALL	.0132	45	13
30	MUCH	.0125	43	10
31	SHARP	.0120	38	12
32	SHORT	.0117	34	16
33	FAST	.0116	34	15
34	COLD	.0114	38	12
35	HAPPY	.0111	47	11
36	YELLOW	.0111	40	14
37	QUICK	.0109	30	16
38	MANY	.0108	46	11
39	DARK	.0108	38	13
40	GREEN	.0099	48	11
41	ROUND	.0098	31	12
42	BROKEN	.0095	43	8
43	CLEAN	.0093	26	14
44	HIGH	.0090	27	13
45	NEW	.0088	23	16
46	HUGE	.0085	24	13
47	HEAVY	.0085	30	10
48	BEST	.0083	28	13
49	YOUNG	.0071	21	12
50	ROUGH	.0070	22	11
51	KIND	.0069	27	8
52	CLEAR	.0067	31	7
53	GRAY	.0067	26	8
54	FULL	.0064	23	10
55	WET	.0064	38	6
56	TRUE	.0062	27	9
57	SWEET	.0061	21	11
58	SMART	.0061	21	9
59	NECESSARY	.0060	16	14
60	MEAN	.0060	19	10
61	SLOW	.0056	23	9
62	LOVING	.0055	24	8
63	REAL	.0052	20	8
64	FRESH	.0051	18	10
65	QUIET	.0050	16	10
66	UGLY	.0050	16	9
67	HELPFUL	.0049	17	8
68	BLOODY	.0048	32	2
69	TASTY	.0047	28	4
70	ROTTEN	.0045	22	5
71	THICK	.0043	25	5
72	MAD	.0043	23	3
73	POOR	.0042	23	10
74	TREMENDOUS	.0041	12	11
75	FINE	.0041	12	11
76	STRANGE	.0041	14	7
77	WARM	.0041	19	8
78	DEAD	.0040	15	8
79	HORRIBLE	.0040	16	8
80	EASY	.0038	14	6
81	LASTING	.0037	15	8
82	FUNNY	.0034	15	8
83	EXTREME	.0034	14	5
84	DELICIOUS	.0033	10	10
85	UNUSUAL	.0032	14	7
86	DANGEROUS	.0031	29	4
87	TIGHT	.0031	14	6
88	FAITHFUL	.0031	14	6
89	SAD	.0031	14	7
90	LIGHT	.0030	13	7
91	SUDDEN	.0029	12	7
92	WIDE	.0029	17	7
93	FAT	.0028	10	8
94	IMPORTANT	.0028	14	6
95	SORE	.0028	14	5
96	LOVELY	.0027	11	7
97	WORKING	.0027	11	7
98	LAST	.0026	11	6
99	UNBEARABLE	.0026	11	6
100	TERRIFIC	.0026	9	8
101	RIGHT	.0026	27	8
102	COOL	.0026	31	7
103	EVERLASTING	.0025	26	8
104	SMOOTH	.0025	23	10
105	INTERESTING	.0023	38	6
106	FRIENDLY	.0022	27	9
107	INTENSE	.0022	21	11
108	SILENT	.0021	21	9
109	WRONG	.0021	16	14
110	DEADLY	.0020	19	10
111	BURNING	.0020	23	9
112	ROARING	.0020	24	8
113	UNKNOWN	.0019	20	8
114	WEAK	.0019	18	10
115	STUPID	.0019	16	10
116	WANTED	.0018	16	9
117	PEACEFUL	.0018	17	8
118	FIRST	.0018	32	2
119	SPOILED	.0018	28	4
120	PAINFUL	.0016	22	5
121	TOUGH	.0016	25	5
122	SMELLY	.0016	23	3
123	COMPLETE	.0016	23	10
124	HANDSOME	.0015	12	11
125	HARSH	.0015	12	11
126	LAZY	.0015	14	7
127	UNHAPPY	.0015	19	8
128	PERFECT	.0015	15	8
129	ACHING	.0015	16	8
130	RICH	.0015	14	6
131	RUNNING	.0015	15	8
132	SINCERE	.0014	15	8
133	EVIL	.0014	14	5
134	CRAZY	.0013	10	10
135	GENTLE	.0013	14	7
136	PLEASANT	.0013	29	4
137	POWERFUL	.0013	14	6
138	SKINNY	.0013	14	6
139	USELESS	.0013	14	7
140	DRY	.0013	13	7
141	SHINING	.0013	12	7
142	RAGING	.0013	17	7
143	SEVERE	.0013	10	8
144	SQUARE	.0013	14	6
145	SHINY	.0013	14	5
146	HONEST	.0013	11	7
147	BRILLIANT	.0013	11	7
148	DIFFERENT	.0013	11	6
149	ENORMOUS	.0013	11	6
150	FEW	.0013	9	8
151	LIKE	.0013	10	7
152	COLORED	.0013	13	6
153	CUTE	.0013	12	5
154	HURT	.0012	11	5
155	FIERCE	.0012	17	5
156	WILD	.0012	11	5
157	FLOWING	.0012	13	5
158	COLORFUL	.0012	8	7
159	EXCELLENT	.0012	7	7
160	ONLY	.0012	23	4
161	SERIOUS	.0012	8	6
162	SNEAKY	.0012	5	5
163	STILL	.0012	9	5
164	ENJOYABLE	.0012	9	5
165	FALSE	.0012	7	5
166	LONELY	.0012	7	5
167	REFRESHING	.0011	8	6
168	LOYAL	.0011	12	3
169	BRAVE	.0011	12	4
170	BITTER	.0011	5	6
171	CALM	.0011	8	6
172	HALF	.0011	3	4
173	HONORABLE	.0010	7	6
174	WORTHY	.0010	6	6
175	NOISY	.0010	7	7
176	AMERICAN	.0010	7	5
177	CROOKED	.0010	8	5
178	CRUEL	.0010	5	5
179	HEALTHY	.0010	8	5
180	HEAVENLY	.0010	10	6
181	HUMAN	.0010	7	7
182	KNOWN	.0010	5	6
183	TIRED	.0010	6	5
184	USEFUL	.0010	6	5
185	WICKED	.0009	6	6
186	OPEN	.0009	6	6
187	HOPEFUL	.0009	7	3
188	RESTFUL	.0008	5	7
189	STRICT	.0008	9	4
190	COMMON	.0008	9	4
191	HAIRY	.0008	5	4
192	HURTING	.0008	17	5
193	LIVING	.0008	18	3
194	LOTS	.0008	8	4
195	NEAT	.0008	11	4
196	ORANGE	.0008	6	4
197	SILVER	.0008	6	5
198	SIMPLE	.0008	6	5
199	EXCITING	.0008	5	3
200	GROWING	.0008	6	3

	H	FRQ	DV
NON-ADJECTIVES	1.556	2389	100
NON-RESPONSES	.154	262	77

APPENDIX C

TABLE 3 AMERICAN ENGLISH

SCALE LOADINGS IN THE FACTOR SPACE BASED ON INDIGENOUS FACTORIZATIONS OF THE CONCEPT-IN-SCALE TASK

ORTHOGONAL PRINCIPAL COMPONENT FACTORS

BI-POLAR SCALES		I	II	III	IV	V	VI	VII	VIII	IX	X
NICE	AWFUL	96	-02	-09	-04	06	14	03	05	-01	03
SWEET	SOUR	94	02	-04	07	09	-03	03	10	04	04
HEAVENLY	HELLISH	93	-00	-21	05	08	02	03	06	-01	03
GOOD	BAD	93	03	-05	-17	-11	18	04	06	-01	07
MILD	HARSH	92	-21	-07	03	10	-01	-01	03	02	18
BIG	LITTLE	-05	81	-24	01	17	05	-07	20	10	-18
POWERFUL	POWERLESS	16	75	18	-27	11	21	-04	-32	13	12
DEEP	SHALLOW	04	67	13	-39	06	32	-16	-11	06	-17
STRONG	WEAK	29	64	-23	32	18	07	04	-08	-01	19
HIGH	LOW	-14	22	64	-08	13	-13	-19	-11	-28	06
FAST	SLOW	-39	25	56	-25	31	-06	27	13	02	14
NOISY	QUIET	39	-42	56	02	15	-07	07	21	07	08
YOUNG	OLD	16	10	47	-24	-40	00	-40	02	24	-15
ALIVE	DEAD	53	13	55	-16	-01	-33	00	-06	-25	15
KNOWN	UNKNOWN	16	10	47	04	16	03	13	18	-01	05
HAPPY	SAD	91	-00	13	-03	15	-01	02	18	-01	05
BEAUTIFUL	UGLY	90	-06	04	04	16	05	-02	19	-10	03
CLEAN	DIRTY	90	02	-02	-22	-05	03	-01	-01	04	01
HELPFUL	UNHELPFUL	89	17	04	-12	-22	23	-04	-00	04	03
FAITHFUL	UNFAITHFUL	89	09	01	-17	-09	-16	19	-02	-03	07
USEFUL	USELESS	89	02	04	-19	-16	19	-02	-02	-03	07
NEEDED	UNNEEDED	88	13	08	-06	-20	-12	12	-12	09	16
SANE	MAD	87	-20	00	14	03	-16	03	08	-14	16
FINE	COARSE	86	16	01	-09	-16	03	18	01	12	-14
HONEST	DISHONEST	85	-16	06	-16	-22	13	07	11	09	10
SAFE	DANGEROUS	82	-09	06	-11	13	11	11	07	11	-05
WHITE	BLACK	79	-16	06	-22	13	10	07	-04	-23	19
RICH	POOR	81	21	-09	11	12	04	-09	14	-12	-19
FRESH	STALE	81	10	-00	32	-14	03	12	04	-06	-12
SHINY	DULL	79	24	-04	09	28	-07	00	10	14	-02
SMART	DUMB	72	30	24	04	-18	-20	14	-08	13	-10
SMOOTH	ROUGH	69	-43	07	15	02	-20	21	-03	-03	-21
LIGHT	DARK	66	05	-37	-25	19	09	-16	-23	-20	00
SOFT	LOUD	65	-37	08	19	09	-16	-12	26	00	02
TENDER	TOUGH	77	-36	08	04	-05	-24	-12	-17	02	-09
STRAIGHT	CROOKED	77	30	11	-05	-21	-21	-03	-00	01	39
TRUE	FALSE	72	36	04	19	09	-16	17	02	-09	00
FULL	EMPTY	69	32	04	-05	-24	-12	26	00	-10	09
UNBROKEN	BROKEN	66	-06	-08	-08	-27	-17	-23	04	-36	00
SOFT	HARD	65	45	09	24	10	-17	02	24	14	-17
EVERLASTING	MOMENTARY	47	32	-33	-14	-14	02	-36	-28	-35	-04
ROUND	SQUARE	02	64	02	-04	12	-11	-23	04	-36	24
LONG	SHORT	64	57	-18	12	-03	-25	13	09	25	26
HEAVY	LIGHT	02	64	-23	-04	12	-11	-17	-23	-24	-36
SERIOUS	FUNNY	-45	57	-18	-23	-03	09	-17	20	-15	-28
SHARP	DULL	-31	47	29	65	-12	20	-19	16	-03	03
BURNING	FREEZING	-10	43	35	63	-12	20	-29	-19	-08	06
HOT	COLD	06	45	36	-12	-20	-26	19	03	24	26
DRY	WET	03	13	52	-48	10	13	-11	34	-08	03
MANY	FEW	03	-12	12	-15	-04	67	-54	67	06	-15

OBLIQUE OBLIMAX FACTORS

LEFTHAND TERM	I	II	III
HEAVENLY	94	11	-19
NICE	92	01	-08
SWEET	89	00	-03
GOOD	88	02	-03
BEAUTIFUL	87	02	-07
BIG	07	72	-10
OLD	-14	71	-48
DEEP	04	70	-20
LONG	12	59	-12
HIGH	37	58	-11
FAST	-36	-33	66
NOISY	-56	-24	59
ALIVE	28	-35	57
KNOWN	-03	-30	49
BURNING	-22	01	44
MILD	87	-13	-09
CLEAN	85	-04	-04
HELPFUL	84	-01	-01
NEEDED	84	03	00
USEFUL	82	05	07
WHITE	80	-00	-13
SOFT	80	09	-30
HONEST	80	06	05
FINEST	80	-17	-03
HAPPY	79	02	12
RICH	76	19	04
SANE	75	05	-01
SHINY	75	-07	-11
LIGHT	70	-33	-05
FRESH	69	10	14
SMOOTH	66	18	11
TENDER	65	-02	29
STRAIGHT	63	15	10
TRUE	66	18	11
SMART	57	-38	-00
UNBROKEN	64	18	11
FULL	57	43	-26
EVERLASTING	45	-00	-16
ROUND	-33	53	-08
SERIOUS	10	35	31
HEAVY	01	34	24
POWERFUL	-07	02	44
STRONG	02	17	-10
FEM	27	08	37
HOT	-07	08	37
SHARP	-02	-03	14

E, P, & A PARTIALLED FACTORS

LEFTHAND TERM	I	II	III	IV	V
STRAIGHT	81	03	13	04	13
SMART	77	-05	14	20	00
SANE	71	02	-27	-02	-01
HONEST	62	-14	-15	08	-20
TRUE	57	-03	18	07	03
HARD	13	86	-14	07	03
TOUGH	57	82	20	-06	12
ROUGH	-31	70	-14	17	-12
LOUD	18	66	-08	11	-30
HARSH	04	57	-03	14	05
SHINY	-00	06	77	03	-02
LIGHT	-09	-05	72	21	04
SHARP	28	-21	63	21	-13
BEAUTIFUL	-35	-07	59	-03	-03
DANGEROUS	-04	-01	18	21	27
HOT	01	03	15	87	01
DRY	30	19	-07	63	-07
HIGH	24	03	-13	26	-08
FEW	12	-07	06	08	77
USEFUL	-09	21	-12	08	73
NEEDED	09	02	-06	-10	53
HELPFUL	10	-07	04	-26	50
EVERLASTING	14	-16	03	01	49
UNBROKEN	56	00	07	05	25
FAITHFUL	50	-06	11	14	28
CLEAN	49	10	-16	-04	-12
SQUARE	-29	52	-34	06	-15
COARSE	05	47	-23	-29	17
HEAVY	-12	39	-35	07	17
SAD	08	08	55	14	09
WHITE	-07	-08	39	-25	-16
SHORT	-03	-08	31	-13	-02
FULL	-26	06	26	-11	-25
FRESH	35	21	-01	01	39
UNKNOWN	57	43	-26		
SERIOUS	45	-00	-16		
GOOD	00	00	00	00	00
NICE	00	00	00	00	00
SWEET	00	00	00	00	00
HEAVENLY	00	00	00	00	00
STRONG	00	00	00	00	00
POWERFUL	00	00	00	00	00
BIG	00	00	00	00	00
DEEP	00	00	00	00	00
FAST	00	00	00	00	00
ALIVE	00	00	00	00	00
NOISY	00	00	00	00	00
YOUNG	00	00	00	00	00

APPENDIX D

TABLE 5 CALCUTTA BENGALI
SCALE LOADINGS IN THE SPACE BASED ON BI-CULTURAL FACTORIZATION WITH AMERICAN ENGLISH

(VARIMAX ROTATION OF FIVE PRINCIPAL COMPONENT FACTORS)

PART I: BENGALI BI-POLAR SCALES		I	II	III	IV	V	PART II: AMERICAN ENGLISH BI-POLAR SCALES		I	II	III	IV	V
BEAUTIFUL	UGLY	94	03	05	-02	13	NICE	AWFUL	96	-05	-06	-03	05
LOVELY	REPULSIVE	93	05	02	-06	13	GOOD	BAD	94	01	-04	01	08
PLEASING	SADDENING	92	07	02	-02	13	SWEET	SOUR	93	-07	-02	-05	01
SUPERIOR	INFERIOR	91	11	01	-05	12	HEAVENLY	HELLISH	92	-02	-12	-09	-03
KIND	CRUEL	91	09	-05	-17	-10	HELPFUL	UNHELPFUL	91	-00	-03	-00	10
HUGE	MINUTE	28	78	04	-09	13	BIG	LITTLE	-01	77	02	19	-08
BIG	LITTLE	24	70	01	-06	12	LONG	SHORT	02	65	-01	02	12
POWERFUL	POWERLESS	06	64	48	02	18	POWERFUL	POWERLESS	18	63	37	10	-14
STRONG	WEAK	13	59	36	12	22	STRONG	WEAK	08	63	21	18	05
DEEP	SHALLOW	05	59	06	-23	-21	DEEP	SHALLOW	-09	61	-05	10	-26
SHARP	BLUNT	-11	33	66	-04	-13	FAST	SLOW	-16	-02	70	08	-02
FAST	SLOW	-46	18	61	-11	20	ALIVE	DEAD	49	-05	52	-22	-06
INDUSTRIOUS	LAZY	17	34	61	-19	-09	NOISY	QUIET	-39	15	49	-08	05
ALIVE	DEAD	47	13	55	-12	-13	SHARP	DULL	37	26	40	16	-01
INTENSE	MILD	-32	38	42	28	01	KNOWN	UNKNOWN	14	-07	37	08	06
HOT	COLD	-38	01	45	62	-07	BURNING	FREEZING	-09	09	44	59	-19
VISCOUS	NONVISCOUS	08	19	-19	55	32	DRY	WET	08	-13	-04	53	-14
DIFFICULT	EASY	-41	36	02	53	22	HOT	COLD	07	11	45	48	-25
THICK	THIN	08	12	-16	47	16	MANY	FEW	02	-06	-01	08	68
RED	BLUE	27	-05	40	43	01	NEEDED	UNNEEDED	90	00	-02	01	06
NUMEROUS	SCARCE	05	03	-04	01	87	USEFUL	USELESS	89	04	01	05	07
MANY	FEW	23	02	-02	04	85	BEAUTIFUL	UGLY	89	-04	-02	-03	16
MANY	ONE	-16	-10	-04	-08	82	FAITHFUL	UNFAITHFUL	89	06	11	02	-07
MUCH	LITTLE	09	06	-00	03	74	MILD	HARSH	89	-20	-02	-16	06
GOOD	EVIL	91	12	-06	-01	14	CLEAN	DIRTY	89	-15	-01	08	-04
GOOD	BAD	90	07	-03	-02	16	HAPPY	SAD	88	-06	13	-08	11
FAMOUS	OBSCURE	87	15	05	05	13	SANE	MAD	87	02	07	01	-12
HONEST	DISHONEST	87	21	-00	-08	-04	HONEST	DISHONEST	86	08	06	-07	-09
BEST	WORST	86	09	-00	07	17	SAFE	DANGEROUS	84	-22	-05	-01	06
ELEVATED	DEPRESSED	85	23	14	08	08	FINE	COARSE	82	-23	07	-18	07
GAY	SOBER	84	-00	15	-16	-09	WHITE	BLACK	81	-12	-04	05	-04
SHINY	DULL	76	23	28	03	01	RICH	POOR	80	16	01	-02	05
QUIET	UNRULY	75	-11	-40	-12	-16	LIGHT	DARK	78	02	11	09	02
SOFT	HARD	63	-33	-04	-53	-21	SHINY	DULL	78	16	15	-04	02
WHITE	BLACK	62	01	07	18	14	FRESH	STALE	77	-03	18	-20	-02
YIELDING	UNYIELDING	58	-38	-08	-53	-16	SMART	DUMB	77	08	32	16	-16
CERTAIN	UNCERTAIN	54	02	-01	17	-07	STRAIGHT	CROOKED	76	13	15	09	-13
STRAIGHT	CURLY	54	12	14	05	-11	SOFT	LOUD	73	-31	-18	-20	06
INTACT	TORN	52	-14	-16	29	21	TRUE	FALSE	70	22	18	04	-16
INDIGENOUS	FOREIGN	46	04	05	-16	17	SMOOTH	ROUGH	70	-46	00	-22	06
HIGH	LOW	42	34	10	37	-05	TENDER	TOUGH	70	-40	04	-31	-06
COLORED	PALE,FADED	36	-17	01	34	30	FULL	EMPTY	67	20	10	05	10
NEW	OLD	28	-19	24	02	-13	UNBROKEN	BROKEN	63	-08	-02	-04	03
OPEN	SHUT	22	50	21	-35	-03	SOFT	HARD	56	-47	10	-34	-00
FREE	FETTERED	33	48	32	-27	-01	EVERLASTING	MOMENTARY	50	31	-17	06	-09
TALL	SHORT	05	48	05	-38	25	ROUND	SQUARE	41	-10	-02	-02	06
HEAVY	LIGHT	-21	36	-24	34	11	OLD	YOUNG	-32	56	-34	14	-20
EXTRAORDINAR	ORDINARY	-29	31	08	18	07	HIGH	LOW	32	55	08	16	-18
AGED	YOUTHFUL	-15	26	-25	-01	-21	HEAVY	LIGHT	-38	53	-17	18	-18
RIPE	RAW	-01	31	22	38	-06	SERIOUS	FUNNY	-29	41	-08	19	-36

APPENDIX E

TABLE 6 AMERICAN ENGLISH
SCALE LOADINGS IN THE SPACE BASED ON A 21 LANGJAGE/CULTURE PAN-CULTURAL FACTOR ANALYSIS*

(PRINCIPAL COMPONENTS FACTORS, RUN JUNE 1970, TOTAL VARIANCE = 1050)

FACTOR % TOTAL VARIANCE	BI-POLAR SCALES	I (31.4%)	II (6.9%)	III (4.8%)	IV (3.5%)	V (2.8%)	VI (2.6%)	VII (2.0%)	VIII (2.0%)	IX (1.7%)	X (1.5%)
NICE	AWFUL	94	-15	-08	-09	00	-01	-04	02	-00	-03
GOOD	BAD	92	-09	-12	03	-01	-08	02	-05	-04	-05
SWEET	SOUR	90	-14	-00	-15	08	04	01	02	07	00
HELPFUL	UNHELPFUL	89	-09	-09	08	-01	-13	03	-02	-08	-05
NEEDED	UNNEEDED	89	-06	-10	08	00	-12	-05	00	-12	01
BIG	LITTLE	-01	68	-29	-32	-07	08	14	-17	15	-05
POWERFUL	POWERLESS	22	68	08	02	-12	-06	11	-08	-23	-01
STRONG	WEAK	11	57	-13	08	-24	-11	26	-13	-11	-07
DEEP	SHALLOW	-09	57	-11	-23	16	11	-18	-06	27	08
HEAVY	LIGHT	-34	55	-23	12	-00	-12	01	-02	18	11
FAST	SLOW	-14	22	61	15	-38	-00	08	-06	-06	-15
ALIVE	DEAD	52	12	55	15	03	-22	10	-04	09	07
YOUNG	OLD	32	-39	45	06	04	-03	24	21	-13	27
FAITHFUL	UNFAITHFUL	88	05	05	11	04	-07	-01	-09	08	-08
HEAVENLY	HELLISH	88	-14	-10	-22	10	02	-12	-03	03	-03
USEFUL	USELESS	87	-04	-09	04	-05	-06	-00	-05	-10	-01
HAPPY	SAD	87	-09	13	-14	01	-01	13	06	14	-03
SANE	MAD	87	05	07	09	21	-05	08	-07	12	03
HONEST	DISHONEST	86	05	01	-02	19	-07	08	-11	02	-03
BEAUTIFUL	UGLY	85	-15	-02	-21	-09	04	00	03	20	-10
MILD	HARSH	85	-29	04	-15	05	-04	-11	-03	05	01
CLEAN	DIRTY	84	-18	-02	03	08	07	-04	-05	0	-10
SAFE	DANGEROUS	84	-28	-07	11	07	-08	10	-04	-07	01
WHITE	BLACK	77	-14	-02	-02	01	07	-23	01	-00	-20
SMART	DUMB	77	20	28	08	18	01	01	-00	10	-07
FINE	COARSE	77	-27	15	-17	14	02	-07	10	15	-05
RICH	POOR	77	06	-09	-29	03	05	-03	18	-09	03
SHINY	DULL	75	08	07	-28	-09	08	-11	06	11	-21
LIGHT	DARK	74	-03	03	-16	-14	21	-19	03	-04	-23
STRAIGHT	CROOKED	74	19	05	12	19	05	08	03	07	-12
FRESH	STALE	73	-05	20	-28	04	-02	-05	05	-10	04
TRUE	FALSE	67	23	07	04	07	01	-03	-12	03	-06
FULL	EMPTY	66	14	01	-23	-14	-02	-06	13	-05	09
SOFT	LOUD	66	-42	02	-16	05	-07	-32	-14	10	08
TENDER	TOUGH	64	-43	27	-26	22	02	-15	-09	04	13
SMOOTH	ROUGH	63	-49	20	-12	14	01	-13	05	11	-02
UNBROKEN	BROKEN	58	-13	03	14	04	-13	-17	01	08	-08
SOFT	HARD	52	-48	36	-25	08	-01	-18	-17	12	17
EVERLASTING	MOMENTARY	47	19	-17	08	04	-14	-17	-17	16	-11
SHARP	DULL	38	38	23	-15	-02	28	15	17	09	-07
HIGH	LOW	30	51	-15	-33	01	31	-03	-17	11	-11
LONG	SHORT	02	50	-18	-33	-10	-06	13	-02	22	14
SERIOUS	FUNNY	-31	47	-17	05	28	13	-26	-01	-06	11
FEW	MANY	-03	12	11	05	37	24	-19	-22	-15	-17
BURNING	FREEZING	-08	29	19	05	-14	69	05	-10	05	21
HOT	COLD	10	33	21	01	-06	65	04	-15	03	23
DRY	WET	08	00	-17	28	07	54	31	-13	16	06
NOISY	QUIET	-30	34	40	03	-11	-06	44	17	-05	-06
SQUARE	ROUND	-36	20	-02	12	33	07	39	25	15	-13
KNOWN	UNKNOWN	16	05	16	18	-08	-07	32	-13	-24	21
COMMUNITY FACTOR % TOTAL VARIANCE		(1.9%)	(0.5%)	(0.2%)	(0.1%)	(0.1%)	(0.2%)	(0.1%)	(0.1%)	(0.1%)	(0.1%)

* 50 SCALES EACH FROM: AE, FR, BF, ND, SW, FF, MS, IT, YS, GK, TK, LA, IF, AD, AP, DH, CB, MK, TH, HC, JP.

APPENDIX F

Means, Standard Deviations, and N of 12 Basic Measures across 23 Communities
for 620 Concepts from <u>Atlas</u> Tables 8.

CONCEPT	E	P	A	E-Z	P-Z	A-Z	F-Z	D-O	P-I	P-G	C-I	CI-Z	N
ACCEPT THINGS AS	0.4	0.2	0.1	-0.3	-0.5	-0.3	-0.7	0.8	1.3	0.5	0.8	1.1	
	0.5	0.3	0.3	0.5	0.4	0.5	1.1	0.3	0.3	0.2	0.3	1.1	22
ACCIDENT	-1.9	0.6	0.5	-2.5	0.1	0.3	-0.2	2.1	1.7	1.2	0.5	-0.5	
	0.5	0.5	0.6	0.3	0.8	0.9	0.9	0.6	0.3	0.4	0.3	1.0	23
ADOLESCENCE	1.3	0.5	1.1	0.5	0.0	1.4	0.4	1.9	1.6	1.0	0.6	-0.1	
	0.6	0.4	0.6	0.6	0.7	0.7	0.7	0.7	0.3	0.4	0.2	0.9	23
ADULTERY	-1.0	0.5	0.2	-1.7	-0.1	-0.1	-1.2	1.4	1.6	0.7	0.8	0.7	
	0.7	0.5	0.5	0.6	0.8	0.7	0.7	0.7	0.3	0.3	0.3	1.3	16
AFRICA	0.5	1.1	0.1	-0.2	1.0	-0.4	-0.4	1.4	1.5	0.9	0.6	0.0	
	0.5	0.4	0.6	0.4	0.5	0.8	1.1	0.5	0.3	0.3	0.2	0.6	23
AGGRESSIVE,BEING	-1.0	0.9	0.8	-1.7	0.6	0.8	-1.0	1.8	1.7	1.1	0.6	0.0	
	0.7	0.5	0.6	0.7	0.7	0.8	0.9	0.6	0.3	0.3	0.2	1.0	22
AIR POLLUTION	-2.0	1.2	0.2	-2.6	1.1	-0.0	-0.2	2.4	2.0	1.3	0.6	0.1	
	0.6	0.5	0.5	0.5	0.9	0.9	1.0	0.8	0.3	0.4	0.2	1.0	21
AIR	1.5	0.6	0.5	0.7	0.2	0.5	0.6	1.9	1.6	1.2	0.5	-0.6	
	0.5	0.6	0.6	0.4	0.9	1.0	0.8	0.6	0.3	0.3	0.2	0.8	23
AIRPLANE	1.6	1.6	0.9	0.8	1.8	1.1	0.6	2.6	1.9	1.6	0.3	-1.2	
	0.5	0.4	0.8	0.3	0.6	1.0	0.8	0.6	0.3	0.3	0.1	0.6	23
ALLIANCES	1.0	1.0	0.2	0.3	0.8	0.0	-0.5	1.7	1.6	1.0	0.6	0.1	
	0.8	0.4	0.7	0.6	0.5	0.9	0.9	0.7	0.3	0.4	0.2	1.0	21
ANGER	-1.5	0.5	0.5	-2.2	-0.0	0.5	0.1	1.8	1.7	1.0	0.6	0.0	
	0.4	0.5	0.5	0.3	0.9	0.8	0.8	0.6	0.3	0.3	0.2	1.2	23
ANIMAL	1.0	0.5	0.9	0.2	-0.0	0.9	0.6	1.5	1.4	0.9	0.5	-0.4	
	0.6	0.4	0.6	0.6	0.5	0.7	0.8	0.6	0.3	0.3	0.2	0.7	23
ANSWER	0.9	0.4	0.4	0.1	-0.2	0.2	0.3	1.1	1.2	0.7	0.6	-0.2	
	0.4	0.3	0.4	0.3	0.4	0.4	0.6	0.4	0.2	0.2	0.3	0.8	23
APPLE	1.7	-0.0	0.1	0.9	-0.9	-0.2	1.0	1.8	1.4	0.9	0.6	-0.3	
	0.3	0.4	0.4	0.2	0.6	0.6	0.8	0.3	0.3	0.2	0.2	0.8	23
APRIL	1.1	0.2	0.4	0.4	-0.5	0.3	0.7	1.4	1.4	0.7	0.6	0.0	
	0.7	0.3	0.5	0.5	0.5	0.5	0.8	0.7	0.4	0.4	0.3	0.9	23
ARGUMENT	-0.2	0.6	0.5	-0.8	0.1	0.3	-0.1	1.2	1.5	0.8	0.7	0.5	
	0.8	0.4	0.5	0.8	0.7	0.7	0.9	0.4	0.3	0.2	0.3	1.0	23
ARM	1.5	0.7	0.8	0.6	0.3	0.8	0.9	1.9	1.5	1.1	0.4	-1.0	
	0.4	0.5	0.7	0.2	0.7	0.8	0.8	0.7	0.3	0.4	0.2	0.6	23
ARMY	0.6	1.4	0.6	-0.1	1.5	0.6	0.1	2.1	1.9	1.3	0.6	-0.1	
	1.1	0.5	0.9	0.8	0.9	1.1	1.1	0.6	0.2	0.4	0.3	1.1	23

ARTIST	1.4	0.6	0.6	0.6	0.2	0.6	0.1	1.8	1.6	1.0	0.6	-0.1	
	0.6	0.4	0.7	0.4	0.7	0.9	0.8	0.7	0.3	0.4	0.3	1.0	23
ASIA	0.6	1.4	0.0	-0.2	1.4	-0.5	0.2	1.8	1.5	1.0	0.5	-0.4	
	0.8	0.4	0.7	0.7	0.5	0.8	1.1	0.5	0.3	0.3	0.2	0.6	23
ASTROLOGY	0.8	0.6	-0.0	-0.0	0.1	-0.4	-0.9	1.2	1.4	0.7	0.7	0.3	
	0.6	0.5	0.5	0.5	0.6	0.8	1.0	0.6	0.3	0.4	0.2	0.8	23
ATHEISTS	-0.6	0.0	-0.1	-1.3	-0.9	-0.6	-1.3	0.9	1.3	0.5	0.8	0.6	
	0.7	0.3	0.4	0.7	0.6	0.6	1.0	0.6	0.4	0.3	0.3	1.1	23
ATOMIC BOMB	-1.7	1.7	0.9	-2.4	1.9	0.9	-0.9	2.7	2.2	1.7	0.5	-0.5	
	0.6	0.5	0.9	0.6	0.6	1.3	1.1	0.7	0.3	0.3	0.2	1.1	23
AUGUST	1.3	0.3	0.4	0.5	-0.2	0.3	0.9	1.5	1.4	0.8	0.6	-0.0	
	0.3	0.4	0.5	0.3	0.6	0.6	0.7	0.4	0.3	0.3	0.2	0.8	23
AUNT	1.2	0.3	0.2	0.4	-0.4	0.0	0.5	1.3	1.4	0.7	0.7	0.2	
	0.5	0.3	0.4	0.4	0.4	0.7	0.7	0.6	0.3	0.3	0.3	1.3	23
AUTHOR	1.2	0.6	0.3	0.4	0.2	0.1	0.1	1.5	1.4	0.9	0.5	-0.5	
	0.5	0.3	0.7	0.4	0.5	0.7	0.9	0.6	0.3	0.3	0.2	0.8	23
AUTHORITY	0.6	1.0	0.1	-0.2	0.8	-0.1	-0.2	1.4	1.5	0.8	0.7	0.4	
	0.8	0.4	0.6	0.6	0.5	0.7	0.9	0.5	0.3	0.3	0.3	1.0	23
AUTOMATION	1.2	0.9	1.1	0.3	0.6	1.2	-0.2	1.9	1.6	1.1	0.5	-0.4	
	0.5	0.4	0.4	0.4	0.4	0.5	0.9	0.6	0.4	0.4	0.2	0.8	16
AUTOMOBILE	1.5	0.9	0.9	0.7	0.7	0.9	1.0	2.1	1.8	1.3	0.5	-0.6	
	0.5	0.5	0.8	0.3	0.7	1.0	1.2	0.7	0.3	0.3	0.2	0.9	23
BABY	1.7	-1.4	0.7	0.9	-3.1	0.7	0.4	2.4	1.9	1.4	0.5	-0.4	
	0.4	0.5	0.5	0.3	0.6	0.9	1.0	0.5	0.3	0.4	0.2	0.6	23
BALDNESS	-0.9	0.0	-0.5	-1.6	-0.8	-1.2	-0.7	1.2	1.5	0.7	0.8	0.6	
	0.8	0.3	0.3	0.6	0.6	0.7	0.7	0.6	0.3	0.3	0.3	1.4	23
BALL	1.2	0.2	0.7	0.4	-0.6	0.6	0.8	1.5	1.5	0.9	0.6	0.0	
	0.5	0.4	0.6	0.4	0.5	0.6	1.0	0.6	0.3	0.3	0.2	0.8	23
BANKER	0.7	0.6	0.2	-0.1	0.2	-0.1	-0.5	1.2	1.6	0.7	0.8	0.8	
	0.6	0.4	0.6	0.5	0.6	0.7	0.9	0.6	0.3	0.3	0.3	1.0	23
BARBER	0.7	0.1	0.5	-0.1	-0.6	0.3	0.4	1.2	1.5	0.7	0.8	0.7	
	0.8	0.4	0.6	0.6	0.5	0.6	0.9	0.6	0.3	0.3	0.3	1.1	23
BATH	1.8	0.3	0.4	1.0	-0.3	0.3	1.1	2.0	1.6	1.1	0.5	-0.4	
	0.3	0.5	0.5	0.3	0.7	0.8	1.0	0.4	0.3	0.2	0.2	0.8	23
BATTLE	-1.2	1.2	0.7	-1.9	1.2	0.6	-0.6	2.0	1.8	1.2	0.6	-0.2	
	0.5	0.4	0.8	0.5	0.6	0.9	1.0	0.6	0.2	0.3	0.2	1.0	23
BEARD	0.2	0.1	-0.2	-0.5	-0.8	-0.7	-0.2	0.6	1.3	0.4	0.9	1.3	
	0.4	0.3	0.3	0.4	0.5	0.6	1.0	0.3	0.3	0.2	0.3	1.0	23
BEAR	-0.2	1.4	0.1	-0.9	1.4	-0.3	-0.3	1.6	1.6	0.9	0.7	0.3	
	0.6	0.6	0.5	0.7	0.8	0.7	0.7	0.5	0.3	0.2	0.2	0.9	23

BEAUTY	1.9	0.5	0.8	1.1	0.0	1.0	0.4	2.3	1.8	1.3	0.5	-0.4	
	0.5	0.7	0.5	0.4	1.0	0.9	1.0	0.6	0.3	0.3	0.2	1.0	22
BED	1.7	0.5	-0.2	0.9	-0.1	-0.7	1.3	1.9	1.6	1.0	0.6	-0.2	
	0.3	0.4	0.5	0.3	0.5	0.8	0.9	0.4	0.3	0.2	0.2	0.7	23
BEER	0.4	0.3	0.3	-0.4	-0.4	0.2	-0.2	1.2	1.6	0.7	0.8	1.0	
	1.0	0.4	0.4	1.1	0.6	0.7	1.3	0.6	0.4	0.3	0.3	1.1	23
BEGGAR	-0.8	-0.5	-0.5	-1.5	-1.7	-1.2	-0.5	1.3	1.5	0.8	0.6	0.0	
	0.7	0.5	0.4	0.6	0.8	1.0	1.4	0.5	0.3	0.3	0.2	0.7	23
BELIEF	1.2	0.8	-0.0	0.4	0.5	-0.4	0.0	1.5	1.5	0.9	0.6	0.0	
	0.6	0.5	0.6	0.4	0.6	0.7	0.8	0.7	0.3	0.4	0.3	0.9	23
BICYCLE	1.3	0.5	0.5	0.5	-0.1	0.5	1.0	1.6	1.5	1.0	0.6	-0.3	
	0.4	0.4	0.5	0.4	0.6	0.6	0.9	0.5	0.3	0.3	0.2	0.7	23
BIRD	1.6	-0.7	1.2	0.8	-1.9	1.5	0.7	2.2	1.7	1.3	0.4	-0.9	
	0.4	0.6	0.7	0.3	0.8	0.8	1.2	0.7	0.4	0.4	0.2	0.9	23
BIRTH	1.3	0.0	0.6	0.5	-0.8	0.5	0.3	1.6	1.6	0.9	0.7	0.4	
	0.5	0.4	0.4	0.5	0.8	0.6	0.9	0.5	0.3	0.2	0.3	1.2	23
BIRTH CONTROL	0.7	0.5	0.3	-0.1	-0.0	-0.0	-0.8	1.0	1.4	0.6	0.8	0.7	
	0.6	0.3	0.4	0.5	0.4	0.5	0.9	0.5	0.3	0.3	0.3	1.1	20
BLACK	-0.4	0.7	-0.5	-1.1	0.2	-1.2	-0.2	1.2	1.5	0.7	0.8	0.8	
	0.7	0.6	0.6	0.6	1.0	1.0	0.8	0.7	0.4	0.4	0.3	1.2	23
BLACK RACE	0.7	0.9	0.6	-0.1	0.7	0.4	-0.4	1.4	1.5	0.9	0.6	0.0	
	0.6	0.4	0.7	0.6	0.6	0.8	0.9	0.7	0.3	0.4	0.3	0.9	21
BLANKET	1.5	0.4	-0.2	0.7	-0.1	-0.6	1.0	1.7	1.5	1.0	0.5	-0.5	
	0.4	0.4	0.6	0.3	0.6	1.0	0.9	0.5	0.3	0.3	0.2	0.8	23
BLIND	-0.6	-0.0	-0.6	-1.3	-0.9	-1.4	-1.0	1.2	1.5	0.8	0.7	0.5	
	0.9	0.4	0.3	0.9	0.8	0.7	1.2	0.6	0.3	0.3	0.3	1.0	22
BLOOD	0.8	0.5	0.8	-0.0	-0.1	1.0	0.8	1.5	1.6	0.9	0.7	0.3	
	0.8	0.4	0.6	0.5	0.5	0.7	1.0	0.7	0.4	0.4	0.3	0.9	23
BLUE	1.3	0.3	0.1	0.5	-0.4	-0.2	0.8	1.4	1.3	0.8	0.6	-0.2	
	0.4	0.4	0.4	0.3	0.5	0.6	0.9	0.4	0.3	0.2	0.2	0.8	23
BODY	1.5	0.8	0.8	0.7	0.5	0.9	1.1	2.0	1.6	1.2	0.4	-0.7	
	0.4	0.4	0.7	0.2	0.6	0.9	0.9	0.6	0.3	0.4	0.2	0.6	22
BOOK	1.7	0.6	0.0	0.9	0.2	-0.4	1.1	2.0	1.6	1.1	0.5	-0.5	
	0.5	0.4	0.7	0.2	0.5	0.7	0.9	0.6	0.3	0.3	0.2	0.7	23
BORROWING MONEY	-0.8	0.0	-0.2	-1.5	-0.8	-0.7	-0.6	1.2	1.4	0.7	0.7	0.5	
	0.8	0.4	0.4	0.7	0.6	0.8	0.9	0.6	0.3	0.3	0.3	0.9	23
BOTTLE	0.6	0.2	-0.3	-0.2	-0.6	-0.9	0.4	0.8	1.1	0.5	0.7	0.2	
	0.3	0.4	0.3	0.3	0.6	0.7	1.0	0.3	0.3	0.1	0.3	0.8	23
BOX	0.7	0.2	-0.3	-0.1	-0.5	-0.9	0.4	1.0	1.2	0.6	0.6	-0.1	
	0.4	0.4	0.5	0.4	0.6	0.7	0.8	0.3	0.3	0.2	0.2	0.6	23

```
BOY             1.4   0.5   1.2   0.6  -0.1   1.6   0.9   2.0   1.6   1.1   0.5  -0.6
                0.4   0.5   0.5   0.3   0.8   0.6   1.0   0.6   0.3   0.3   0.2   0.7   23

BRAIN           1.6   0.7   0.9   0.8   0.3   1.1   0.7   2.1   1.8   1.2   0.5  -0.3
                0.5   0.5   0.8   0.3   0.7   1.0   0.7   0.7   0.3   0.3   0.2   0.6   23

BREAD           1.6   0.1   0.0   0.8  -0.7  -0.3   1.2   1.8   1.5   1.0   0.5  -0.4
                0.5   0.5   0.6   0.3   0.7   1.0   0.7   0.6   0.3   0.3   0.2   0.7   23

BRIDE           1.8  -0.1   0.8   1.0  -0.9   0.9   0.3   2.2   1.7   1.2   0.5  -0.5
                0.4   0.7   0.6   0.4   0.9   0.7   0.7   0.5   0.3   0.3   0.2   0.9   23

BRIDEGROOM      1.5   0.7   0.7   0.7   0.2   0.8   0.1   1.8   1.6   1.0   0.6  -0.3
                0.4   0.3   0.5   0.4   0.4   0.6   0.8   0.5   0.4   0.3   0.2   0.7   23

BRIDGE          1.2   1.3  -0.3   0.4   1.2  -1.0   0.6   1.9   1.5   1.1   0.5  -0.6
                0.5   0.4   0.4   0.3   0.6   0.5   0.9   0.5   0.3   0.3   0.2   0.5   23

BROTHER         1.6   0.7   0.8   0.8   0.2   0.9   1.1   2.1   1.6   1.2   0.5  -0.7
                0.5   0.6   0.7   0.4   0.7   0.7   1.1   0.6   0.3   0.4   0.3   0.8   23

BUDDHISTS       0.4   0.4  -0.1  -0.3  -0.2  -0.5  -0.9   0.9   1.3   0.6   0.7   0.6
                0.7   0.3   0.5   0.7   0.6   0.7   1.2   0.5   0.3   0.3   0.3   0.9   23

BUS             0.7   1.1   0.3  -0.0   1.0  -0.0   0.9   1.6   1.6   0.9   0.6   0.1
                0.6   0.5   0.7   0.4   0.7   0.8   0.9   0.5   0.3   0.3   0.2   0.8   23

BUSINESS        1.2   1.0   0.5   0.4   0.8   0.3   0.1   1.8   1.6   1.1   0.6  -0.2
                0.4   0.4   0.7   0.3   0.5   0.8   1.3   0.5   0.2   0.3   0.2   0.7   23

BUTTER          1.4  -0.1   0.1   0.6  -1.0  -0.2   0.9   1.5   1.3   0.8   0.5  -0.4
                0.3   0.4   0.4   0.2   0.5   0.8   0.9   0.4   0.3   0.2   0.2   0.6   23

CAKE            1.5   0.1   0.2   0.7  -0.7  -0.1   0.6   1.6   1.5   0.9   0.6  -0.0
                0.5   0.4   0.4   0.4   0.6   0.8   1.1   0.5   0.2   0.3   0.2   0.6   23

CANCER         -2.1   1.0  -0.2  -2.7   0.7  -0.8  -1.0   2.4   2.0   1.3   0.7   0.2
                0.7   0.5   0.5   0.6   0.9   0.8   0.9   0.8   0.3   0.4   0.2   0.9   23

CANDY           1.2  -0.3   0.2   0.4  -1.3  -0.1   0.8   1.4   1.5   0.8   0.7   0.3
                0.4   0.4   0.4   0.4   0.5   0.9   0.9   0.4   0.3   0.2   0.3   1.0   23

CANNED FOODS    0.8   0.0  -0.1   0.1  -0.8  -0.5   0.3   1.0   1.3   0.6   0.7   0.5
                0.6   0.2   0.3   0.5   0.4   0.7   0.8   0.4   0.3   0.2   0.3   0.9   23

CAPITALISM      0.1   0.7   0.2  -0.5   0.3  -0.2  -0.7   1.2   1.5   0.7   0.8   0.8
                0.8   0.5   0.5   0.7   0.7   0.6   1.7   0.6   0.4   0.3   0.2   0.8   23

CART            0.7   0.5  -0.1  -0.0  -0.1  -0.7  -0.2   1.2   1.5   0.7   0.8   0.7
                0.5   0.5   0.6   0.5   0.8   0.9   1.1   0.5   0.3   0.2   0.2   0.6   23

CASTE          -0.3   0.5  -0.2  -0.9  -0.1  -0.6  -0.8   1.1   1.3   0.7   0.7   0.0
                1.0   0.4   0.5   0.8   0.7   0.9   2.0   0.6   0.4   0.4   0.3   1.0   18

CAT             0.6  -0.5   1.0  -0.1  -1.5   1.3   0.8   1.4   1.5   0.8   0.7   0.4
                0.4   0.4   0.6   0.4   0.5   0.7   1.0   0.6   0.3   0.4   0.2   0.9   23

CENSORSHIP     -0.3   0.5  -0.0  -1.0  -0.1  -0.4  -0.6   1.0   1.4   0.6   0.7   0.6
                0.8   0.4   0.5   0.6   0.6   0.8   0.8   0.5   0.3   0.3   0.3   1.2   23
```

CENTURY
```
0.6  0.9 -0.1 -0.1  0.6 -0.7 -0.1  1.2  1.3  0.7  0.6 -0.2
0.3  0.4  0.5  0.2  0.4  0.7  0.8  0.4  0.4  0.3  0.3  0.8   23
```

CHAIR
```
1.1  0.2 -0.6  0.4 -0.5 -1.4  1.1  1.4  1.3  0.8  0.5 -0.4
0.5  0.3  0.5  0.3  0.4  0.8  1.0  0.5  0.3  0.2  0.2  0.8   23
```

CHAMPION
```
1.6  1.3  1.2  0.8  1.3  1.4  0.6  2.4  1.8  1.4  0.4 -1.1
0.6  0.5  0.7  0.4  0.6  0.8  0.8  0.8  0.4  0.5  0.3  0.8   21
```

CHARACTER
```
1.1  0.7  0.2  0.3  0.4 -0.1  0.0  1.5  1.4  0.9  0.5 -0.4
0.6  0.4  0.5  0.5  0.6  0.5  0.7  0.6  0.4  0.3  0.2  0.7   23
```

CHARITY
```
1.7  0.7  0.1  0.9  0.4 -0.2  0.1  1.9  1.6  1.1  0.5 -0.4
0.6  0.5  0.5  0.5  0.7  0.4  0.9  0.7  0.3  0.4  0.3  1.1   23
```

CHEATING
```
-1.7  0.1  0.1 -2.4 -0.8 -0.2 -1.0  1.8  1.7  1.0  0.8  0.6
0.5  0.5  0.5  0.4  0.9  0.9  1.0  0.5  0.2  0.2  0.3  1.0   23
```

CHEESE
```
1.1  0.1 -0.1  0.4 -0.7 -0.5  0.6  1.3  1.3  0.7  0.6 -0.1
0.4  0.3  0.4  0.3  0.4  0.8  0.9  0.4  0.3  0.2  0.2  0.6   23
```

CHESS
```
1.2  0.4 -0.3  0.4 -0.2 -0.9 -0.1  1.5  1.6  0.9  0.7  0.5
0.6  0.4  0.7  0.5  0.6  0.9  0.6  0.7  0.3  0.3  0.3  0.8   23
```

CHICKEN
```
1.0 -0.7  0.7  0.2 -1.9  0.7 -0.0  1.6  1.6  0.9  0.7  0.4
0.7  0.6  0.4  0.6  0.8  0.7  1.1  0.8  0.3  0.4  0.3  1.2   21
```

CHILD
```
1.6 -0.9  1.1  0.8 -2.3  1.4  0.9  2.3  1.9  1.3  0.6 -0.3
0.4  0.6  0.6  0.3  0.8  0.8  1.1  0.5  0.3  0.3  0.2  1.0   23
```

CHILD, ILLEGIT.
```
-0.4 -0.2  0.2 -1.1 -1.2  0.0 -1.4  0.8  1.3  0.5  0.8  0.9
0.6  0.3  0.4  0.5  0.5  0.8  1.2  0.4  0.4  0.2  0.3  0.8   19
```

CHOICE, A
```
1.0  0.6  0.2  0.2  0.2 -0.1  0.4  1.4  1.3  0.8  0.5 -0.2
0.7  0.3  0.5  0.7  0.4  0.5  0.8  0.6  0.3  0.3  0.2  0.7   23
```

CHRISTIANS
```
0.9  0.6  0.1  0.1  0.1 -0.3  0.3  1.2  1.3  0.7  0.6  0.2
0.7  0.5  0.4  0.6  0.6  0.5  0.8  0.8  0.4  0.4  0.3  1.1   21
```

CINEMA
```
1.3  0.6  0.8  0.5  0.2  0.8  0.6  1.8  1.6  1.0  0.6 -0.1
0.6  0.3  0.6  0.5  0.4  0.6  0.5  0.6  0.3  0.3  0.2  0.9   23
```

CIRCLE
```
0.7  0.1 -0.1 -0.0 -0.6 -0.5  0.2  0.9  1.1  0.5  0.6 -0.0
0.4  0.3  0.4  0.3  0.3  0.5  0.7  0.4  0.3  0.2  0.2  0.7   23
```

CITY
```
1.1  1.2  0.6  0.3  1.2  0.5  0.6  2.0  1.7  1.1  0.5 -0.3
0.7  0.4  0.8  0.4  0.6  0.9  0.8  0.5  0.3  0.3  0.2  0.6   23
```

CIVILIZATION
```
1.4  1.1  0.3  0.7  1.0  0.1  0.4  2.0  1.7  1.2  0.5 -0.4
0.7  0.4  0.7  0.5  0.6  0.8  0.9  0.7  0.3  0.4  0.3  1.0   23
```

CLEANLINESS
```
1.9  0.7  0.3  1.0  0.3  0.1  0.9  2.2  1.6  1.2  0.5 -0.6
0.7  0.6  0.7  0.5  0.9  1.0  0.6  0.6  0.3  0.3  0.3  0.7   23
```

CLERGYMAN
```
0.9  0.4 -0.1  0.2 -0.1 -0.5 -0.1  1.3  1.4  0.8  0.7  0.2
0.6  0.5  0.5  0.5  0.7  0.7  1.3  0.5  0.2  0.3  0.2  1.1   23
```

CLERK, FEMALE
```
1.3 -0.1  0.9  0.5 -0.9  1.1 -0.3  1.7  1.6  1.0  0.6  0.0
0.5  0.5  0.4  0.4  0.7  0.8  0.8  0.6  0.3  0.3  0.2  0.9   23
```

```
CLOTH             1.4  0.2 -0.0  0.6 -0.5 -0.4  0.7  1.5  1.4  0.8  0.5 -0.5
                  0.4  0.5  0.5  0.3  0.7  1.0  1.1  0.5  0.3  0.3  0.2  0.6   23

CLOTHES           1.5  0.1  0.2  0.7 -0.7  0.0  1.0  1.7  1.4  0.9  0.6 -0.3
                  0.4  0.4  0.5  0.4  0.5  1.0  1.0  0.5  0.3  0.3  0.2  0.6   23

CLOUD             0.7  0.5  0.1 -0.1  0.1 -0.1  0.5  1.0  1.4  0.7  0.7  0.5
                  0.4  0.5  0.4  0.3  0.7  0.7  0.9  0.5  0.3  0.3  0.2  0.8   23

COFFEE            1.0  0.1  0.2  0.2 -0.6 -0.0  0.9  1.2  1.4  0.7  0.7  0.5
                  0.5  0.4  0.5  0.4  0.4  0.7  0.9  0.5  0.3  0.3  0.3  1.1   23

COLD             -0.6  0.6 -0.2 -1.3  0.2 -0.6  0.5  1.1  1.5  0.7  0.8  0.7
                  0.7  0.3  0.5  0.5  0.5  0.9  0.8  0.6  0.3  0.3  0.2  1.1   23

COLONIALISM      -0.6  0.6  0.0 -1.3  0.2 -0.4 -1.3  1.4  1.6  0.8  0.8  0.6
                  1.0  0.5  0.6  0.9  0.8  0.9  1.0  0.5  0.4  0.3  0.2  1.0   23

COLOR             1.4  0.2  0.3  0.6 -0.5  0.1  0.8  1.5  1.3  0.8  0.5 -0.5
                  0.4  0.4  0.4  0.3  0.4  0.7  0.9  0.4  0.3  0.2  0.2  0.6   23

COMMUNISM        -0.4  0.9  0.2 -1.1  0.6  0.0 -1.1  1.4  1.7  0.9  0.8  0.8
                  1.0  0.5  0.6  0.9  0.7  0.8  0.9  0.8  0.3  0.4  0.3  1.5   18

COMPETITION       0.9  1.0  0.7  0.1  0.8  0.8  0.2  1.8  1.6  1.1  0.5 -0.3
                  0.9  0.4  0.7  0.8  0.6  0.8  1.2  0.8  0.3  0.4  0.3  0.8   23

COMPULSORY SERV.  0.2  0.9  0.4 -0.6  0.8  0.1 -0.4  1.6  1.7  1.0  0.7  0.5
                  1.2  0.4  0.7  1.0  0.8  0.9  0.8  0.7  0.3  0.3  0.3  1.0   18

CONFLICT         -1.1  0.7  0.4 -1.7  0.3  0.3 -0.5  1.5  1.6  0.9  0.7  0.3
                  0.6  0.3  0.6  0.5  0.6  0.8  0.7  0.6  0.3  0.3  0.2  0.9   23

CONTEMPLATION     1.2  0.7 -0.1  0.4  0.4 -0.5 -0.3  1.5  1.5  0.9  0.6 -0.1
                  0.6  0.3  0.5  0.4  0.5  0.6  1.0  0.6  0.3  0.3  0.2  0.8   21

CONTEMPT         -1.4  0.3 -0.1 -2.1 -0.4 -0.5 -1.1  1.6  1.6  0.9  0.8  0.6
                  0.7  0.5  0.3  0.5  0.9  0.7  0.9  0.5  0.3  0.2  0.3  1.0   23

COOPERATION       1.7  0.9  0.5  0.9  0.7  0.4  0.5  2.1  1.6  1.2  0.4 -0.8
                  0.5  0.3  0.6  0.3  0.3  0.6  0.6  0.5  0.2  0.2  0.2  0.6   23

COTTON            1.3 -0.3 -0.1  0.5 -1.3 -0.6  0.5  1.5  1.4  0.8  0.6 -0.1
                  0.5  0.4  0.6  0.4  0.7  1.0  0.7  0.4  0.3  0.2  0.2  0.9   23

COUNTRY           1.4  1.1  0.3  0.6  1.0 -0.0  0.7  2.0  1.6  1.1  0.5 -0.6
                  0.6  0.4  0.7  0.5  0.7  0.8  0.9  0.7  0.3  0.4  0.2  0.9   23

COURAGE           1.7  1.4  0.6  0.8  1.4  0.5  0.4  2.4  1.8  1.4  0.4 -0.9
                  0.5  0.4  0.7  0.3  0.5  0.8  0.9  0.6  0.2  0.3  0.2  0.7   23

COUSIN            1.1  0.3  0.6  0.3 -0.4  0.7  0.3  1.4  1.5  0.8  0.7  0.3
                  0.6  0.3  0.5  0.4  0.5  0.8  1.0  0.7  0.3  0.4  0.3  1.1   22

COW               1.3  0.9 -0.2  0.5  0.6 -0.7  0.7  1.7  1.6  1.0  0.6 -0.2
                  0.5  0.5  0.6  0.4  0.8  0.9  1.0  0.5  0.3  0.3  0.2  0.6   23

CREATURE          1.1  0.3  0.7  0.2 -0.4  0.7  0.3  1.7  1.5  1.0  0.5 -0.4
                  0.9  0.6  0.6  0.9  1.0  0.7  1.0  0.6  0.3  0.3  0.2  0.7   22
```

CREDIT	0.4	0.3	0.0	-0.3	-0.2	-0.4	-0.3	0.9	1.3	0.5	0.8	0.7
	0.7	0.5	0.3	0.6	0.7	0.5	1.0	0.6	0.3	0.3	0.2	1.1	22
CRIME	-1.9	0.6	0.3	-2.6	0.1	-0.0	-0.9	2.2	1.9	1.2	0.7	0.2
	0.5	0.7	0.6	0.4	1.1	1.0	1.1	0.5	0.2	0.3	0.2	1.3	23
CROW	-0.7	-0.3	0.5	-1.4	-1.3	0.4	0.0	1.1	1.4	0.7	0.7	0.4
	0.5	0.4	0.6	0.5	0.7	0.9	1.1	0.5	0.2	0.2	0.2	0.7	23
CUBE, A	0.5	0.2	-0.3	-0.2	-0.5	-0.9	0.1	0.8	1.1	0.5	0.6	0.1
	0.5	0.3	0.3	0.4	0.5	0.6	0.7	0.4	0.4	0.2	0.3	0.8	23
CUP	1.1	-0.5	-0.4	0.3	-1.6	-1.0	0.8	1.4	1.4	0.8	0.6	-0.2
	0.4	0.4	0.4	0.3	0.6	0.8	1.0	0.4	0.3	0.3	0.3	0.8	23
DAM	1.3	1.6	-0.1	0.5	1.8	-0.6	0.2	2.2	1.8	1.2	0.6	-0.3
	0.6	0.6	0.6	0.4	0.8	0.9	1.0	0.6	0.3	0.3	0.2	0.7	23
DANCING	1.4	0.3	0.8	0.6	-0.3	0.9	0.3	1.8	1.6	1.0	0.6	0.1
	0.4	0.5	0.5	0.5	0.7	0.7	0.8	0.5	0.4	0.3	0.2	0.6	23
DANGER	-1.4	0.9	0.4	-2.0	0.5	0.1	-0.2	1.8	1.6	1.0	0.6	-0.3
	0.6	0.4	0.5	0.6	0.6	0.6	1.0	0.5	0.3	0.3	0.2	0.8	23
DAUGHTER	1.5	-0.1	0.9	0.8	-1.0	1.1	0.2	2.0	1.7	1.2	0.5	-0.5
	0.7	0.6	0.5	0.6	0.8	0.8	1.0	0.6	0.3	0.3	0.2	0.7	23
DAY	1.4	0.4	0.6	0.6	-0.1	0.5	0.8	1.6	1.4	0.9	0.5	-0.5
	0.5	0.3	0.4	0.3	0.5	0.4	0.6	0.5	0.3	0.2	0.2	0.6	23
DEAF	-0.8	-0.1	-0.6	-1.5	-0.9	-1.4	-1.1	1.2	1.5	0.8	0.8	0.7
	0.7	0.3	0.5	0.7	0.6	0.8	0.8	0.7	0.3	0.3	0.3	1.0	23
DEATH	-1.4	0.6	-0.5	-2.1	0.1	-1.2	-0.6	1.7	1.7	1.0	0.7	0.5
	0.4	0.4	0.5	0.3	0.6	0.7	1.0	0.4	0.2	0.3	0.2	0.9	23
DEBT	-1.3	0.4	-0.2	-2.0	-0.3	-0.8	-0.7	1.5	1.5	0.7	0.8	0.7
	0.7	0.3	0.4	0.5	0.6	0.6	0.7	0.6	0.3	0.3	0.4	1.3	23
DECEMBER	1.0	0.5	0.1	0.2	0.1	-0.3	1.0	1.3	1.5	0.7	0.8	0.7
	0.6	0.3	0.5	0.6	0.4	0.8	0.8	0.6	0.3	0.3	0.3	1.1	23
DEFEAT	-1.3	0.3	-0.2	-2.0	-0.3	-0.7	-0.4	1.5	1.6	0.8	0.8	0.6
	0.7	0.5	0.4	0.4	0.8	0.8	1.1	0.7	0.3	0.4	0.2	0.9	23
DEFENSE	1.1	1.1	0.6	0.3	1.0	0.4	0.2	1.9	1.7	1.1	0.6	-0.2
	0.7	0.4	0.8	0.5	0.5	0.9	0.7	0.6	0.3	0.3	0.3	0.7	23
DEMOCRACY	1.5	1.0	0.3	0.7	0.8	0.1	0.4	1.9	1.6	1.1	0.5	-0.5
	0.5	0.4	0.5	0.4	0.4	0.6	0.8	0.6	0.3	0.3	0.3	0.9	23
DESERTS	-0.9	0.9	-0.7	-1.5	0.7	-1.6	-1.0	1.6	1.7	1.0	0.7	0.3
	0.7	0.4	0.5	0.6	0.7	0.7	1.2	0.7	0.3	0.4	0.3	1.2	22
DETERMINATION	1.1	1.0	0.4	0.4	0.9	0.3	-0.2	1.8	1.6	1.1	0.5	-0.4
	0.6	0.5	0.6	0.6	0.7	0.8	0.9	0.6	0.4	0.4	0.3	0.9	23
DEVELOPMENT	1.3	0.9	0.3	0.5	0.7	-0.0	-0.1	1.8	1.6	1.0	0.6	-0.2
	0.6	0.5	0.7	0.5	0.6	0.9	0.8	0.7	0.3	0.4	0.3	0.9	23

Word													N
DEVIL	-1.8	0.6	0.4	-2.5	0.1	0.1	-1.2	2.1	1.8	1.2	0.7	0.2	
	0.5	0.5	0.7	0.5	0.9	1.1	1.1	0.6	0.3	0.3	0.2	0.9	23
DEVOTION	1.4	0.8	0.1	0.6	0.5	-0.2	-0.1	1.7	1.5	1.0	0.6	-0.2	
	0.6	0.4	0.4	0.5	0.6	0.5	0.8	0.6	0.3	0.3	0.3	1.1	23
DIALECT	0.7	0.4	0.2	-0.1	-0.1	-0.1	-0.0	1.1	1.2	0.6	0.6	-0.0	
	0.6	0.3	0.5	0.4	0.5	0.6	0.8	0.5	0.3	0.2	0.2	0.6	22
DICTIONARY	1.4	0.9	-0.1	0.6	0.7	-0.6	0.4	1.8	1.7	1.1	0.6	0.0	
	0.7	0.4	0.7	0.4	0.6	1.1	0.9	0.7	0.3	0.4	0.2	0.8	22
DISCIPLINE	1.0	1.0	0.1	0.3	0.7	-0.2	0.4	1.7	1.6	1.0	0.6	-0.1	
	1.0	0.4	0.6	0.8	0.6	0.6	1.2	0.7	0.3	0.4	0.3	1.0	23
DISCUSSION	1.0	0.7	0.6	0.2	0.3	0.5	0.4	1.5	1.5	0.9	0.6	-0.2	
	0.7	0.3	0.6	0.7	0.5	0.6	0.8	0.6	0.2	0.3	0.3	1.0	23
DISEASE	-1.9	0.5	-0.3	-2.5	-0.0	-0.8	-0.2	2.1	1.8	1.1	0.7	0.3	
	0.6	0.4	0.5	0.3	0.7	0.8	0.8	0.6	0.3	0.3	0.3	1.0	23
DISH	1.0	-0.0	-0.3	0.2	-0.9	-0.9	0.5	1.2	1.3	0.6	0.6	0.0	
	0.4	0.4	0.4	0.4	0.6	0.7	0.9	0.4	0.3	0.2	0.3	0.8	23
DIVORCE	-1.2	0.3	0.0	-1.9	-0.4	-0.4	-1.0	1.4	1.5	0.8	0.7	0.4	
	0.6	0.4	0.4	0.6	0.6	0.7	0.9	0.5	0.3	0.2	0.3	1.1	23
DOCTOR	1.5	0.9	0.6	0.7	0.7	0.5	0.6	2.0	1.6	1.2	0.5	-0.5	
	0.6	0.2	0.7	0.5	0.4	0.8	0.7	0.6	0.2	0.3	0.3	1.0	23
DOG	1.1	0.6	1.1	0.3	0.1	1.4	0.9	1.9	1.5	1.1	0.5	-0.7	
	0.7	0.5	0.7	0.6	0.6	0.8	0.9	0.7	0.3	0.4	0.2	1.0	23
DOWN	-0.0	-0.0	-0.1	-0.7	-1.0	-0.5	-0.5	0.5	1.1	0.3	0.8	0.7	
	0.4	0.3	0.3	0.4	0.6	0.7	1.2	0.3	0.4	0.2	0.3	1.2	22
DREAM	1.0	0.2	0.4	0.2	-0.5	0.3	0.4	1.2	1.4	0.7	0.7	0.3	
	0.5	0.3	0.4	0.5	0.4	0.6	0.5	0.4	0.3	0.2	0.2	0.8	23
DRESS	1.3	-0.2	0.4	0.5	-1.1	0.2	0.5	1.5	1.4	0.8	0.6	-0.1	
	0.4	0.5	0.5	0.4	0.8	0.9	0.8	0.4	0.3	0.3	0.3	0.9	23
DRUNKENNESS	-1.7	0.2	-0.0	-2.3	-0.5	-0.5	-1.0	1.8	1.8	1.0	0.8	0.7	
	0.5	0.5	0.6	0.5	0.9	1.0	1.0	0.6	0.3	0.3	0.3	1.0	23
DUTY	1.0	1.0	0.2	0.3	0.8	-0.1	0.4	1.6	1.5	0.9	0.6	-0.0	
	0.8	0.4	0.6	0.6	0.7	0.7	0.9	0.7	0.3	0.4	0.3	1.0	23
E.S.P.	0.8	0.6	0.4	0.0	0.1	0.1	-1.6	1.2	1.5	0.7	0.7	0.6	
	0.6	0.4	0.5	0.5	0.5	0.6	1.4	0.5	0.2	0.3	0.2	0.9	18
EAR	1.4	-0.1	0.5	0.6	-1.0	0.6	1.0	1.7	1.5	1.0	0.5	-0.5	
	0.5	0.5	0.7	0.4	0.6	0.9	1.0	0.6	0.4	0.3	0.2	0.6	23
EARTHQUAKE	-1.9	1.4	0.6	-2.6	1.4	0.5	-0.9	2.5	2.0	1.5	0.5	-0.6	
	0.5	0.6	0.7	0.4	0.7	0.9	1.0	0.8	0.3	0.4	0.3	1.1	23
EAST	0.6	0.7	0.1	-0.1	0.3	-0.3	0.0	1.2	1.3	0.7	0.6	-0.0	
	0.7	0.4	0.5	0.6	0.5	0.5	1.1	0.5	0.3	0.3	0.3	0.9	23

EATING	1.6	0.4	0.4	0.8	-0.2	0.2	1.0	1.8	1.6	1.0	0.5	-0.3	
	0.3	0.4	0.4	0.3	0.5	0.6	1.0	0.4	0.3	0.2	0.2	0.6	23
EDUCATION	1.5	1.0	0.2	0.7	0.7	-0.0	0.8	2.0	1.7	1.2	0.5	-0.3	
	0.7	0.5	0.7	0.5	0.6	1.0	1.1	0.8	0.2	0.4	0.3	1.2	23
EGG	1.2	-0.4	0.0	0.4	-1.5	-0.3	0.8	1.4	1.4	0.8	0.6	0.0	
	0.4	0.4	0.4	0.3	0.5	0.6	0.9	0.4	0.3	0.2	0.3	0.8	23
ELECTRICITY	1.2	1.1	0.9	0.4	1.0	1.0	0.8	2.0	1.8	1.3	0.5	-0.7	
	0.6	0.5	0.8	0.5	0.5	1.0	1.0	0.7	0.3	0.3	0.3	0.9	23
ELEPHANT	0.8	1.9	-0.3	0.0	2.3	-1.1	0.3	2.2	1.8	1.3	0.5	-0.5	
	0.5	0.4	0.6	0.6	0.5	0.9	1.1	0.4	0.3	0.3	0.2	0.7	23
EMPTY SPACE	-0.1	0.2	-0.5	-0.8	-0.5	-1.1	-1.1	0.9	1.4	0.6	0.8	0.7	
	0.6	0.3	0.5	0.6	0.6	0.9	1.0	0.5	0.4	0.3	0.3	1.0	23
ENEMY	-1.5	0.5	0.4	-2.2	0.0	0.3	-1.0	1.9	1.7	1.1	0.7	0.2	
	0.8	0.5	0.6	0.8	0.9	0.8	0.9	0.6	0.3	0.3	0.3	1.3	23
ENVY	-1.6	0.2	-0.0	-2.2	-0.6	-0.4	-0.7	1.8	1.7	0.9	0.8	0.7	
	0.8	0.5	0.4	0.7	0.9	0.8	0.7	0.6	0.2	0.3	0.3	1.0	23
ETERNITY	0.8	0.9	-0.4	0.1	0.7	-1.0	-1.2	1.5	1.6	0.9	0.7	0.4	
	0.6	0.5	0.5	0.5	0.6	0.7	1.0	0.5	0.3	0.3	0.2	0.9	23
EUROPE	1.2	0.9	0.2	0.4	0.6	-0.1	0.2	1.7	1.5	1.0	0.5	-0.5	
	0.4	0.4	0.6	0.3	0.6	0.7	0.8	0.5	0.3	0.3	0.2	0.6	23
EXAMINATION	0.3	0.8	0.1	-0.4	0.4	-0.3	0.6	1.4	1.5	0.8	0.7	0.4	
	1.1	0.4	0.5	0.9	0.6	0.7	1.1	0.5	0.3	0.3	0.2	0.6	23
EXCREMENT	-0.5	0.1	-0.0	-1.2	-0.7	-0.4	-0.0	0.8	1.3	0.5	0.8	0.7	
	0.7	0.4	0.3	0.6	0.6	0.7	0.9	0.5	0.4	0.2	0.4	1.0	16
EYES	1.8	0.2	0.9	0.9	-0.5	1.1	1.1	2.2	1.7	1.3	0.5	-0.6	
	0.6	0.6	0.8	0.4	0.8	1.0	0.9	0.6	0.3	0.3	0.2	0.7	23
FACE	1.4	0.1	0.4	0.6	-0.7	0.2	0.9	1.6	1.4	0.9	0.5	-0.3	
	0.4	0.4	0.6	0.3	0.5	0.8	0.9	0.4	0.3	0.2	0.3	0.9	23
FACTORY WORKER	0.9	0.8	0.5	0.1	0.5	0.4	0.2	1.5	1.4	0.9	0.5	-0.3	
	0.7	0.4	0.7	0.5	0.5	0.8	0.8	0.8	0.3	0.4	0.3	0.8	23
FAILURE	-1.4	0.2	-0.1	-2.1	-0.5	-0.6	-0.6	1.6	1.6	0.9	0.8	0.7	
	0.5	0.4	0.4	0.4	0.8	0.9	0.6	0.5	0.3	0.3	0.3	1.3	23
FALL	0.7	0.3	0.0	-0.0	-0.3	-0.4	0.6	1.1	1.4	0.6	0.7	0.6	
	0.7	0.2	0.5	0.6	0.4	0.7	0.6	0.5	0.3	0.2	0.2	0.8	22
FAMILY	1.7	0.8	0.6	0.9	0.5	0.5	1.1	2.1	1.6	1.2	0.5	-0.7	
	0.4	0.4	0.7	0.3	0.5	0.8	0.7	0.5	0.3	0.3	0.2	0.7	23
FAMILY, BIG	0.8	1.1	0.6	0.0	0.9	0.4	0.1	1.7	1.6	0.9	0.6	0.1	
	0.6	0.3	0.7	0.6	0.5	0.8	0.9	0.5	0.3	0.3	0.3	0.9	23
FARMER	1.3	0.9	0.3	0.5	0.6	0.2	0.3	1.8	1.6	1.1	0.5	-0.2	
	0.6	0.4	0.8	0.4	0.5	1.0	1.0	0.7	0.3	0.3	0.3	0.9	23

FAT	-0.5	0.6	-0.5	-1.2	0.1	-1.3	-0.4	1.2	1.5	0.8	0.7	0.4	
	0.7	0.5	0.5	0.5	0.9	0.8	0.8	0.6	0.3	0.3	0.3	1.0	23
FATALISM	-0.6	0.4	-0.1	-1.2	-0.3	-0.6	-1.4	1.1	1.4	0.6	0.8	0.8	
	0.8	0.4	0.4	0.7	0.7	0.6	1.5	0.5	0.3	0.2	0.3	1.0	23
FATHER	1.9	1.2	0.5	1.1	1.2	0.3	1.4	2.4	1.8	1.4	0.4	-1.0	
	0.4	0.4	0.8	0.3	0.5	0.8	1.0	0.6	0.2	0.3	0.2	0.5	23
FATHER-IN-LAW	0.5	0.5	-0.0	-0.2	0.0	-0.4	-0.5	1.0	1.5	0.7	0.8	1.0	
	0.7	0.4	0.4	0.6	0.6	0.7	1.3	0.5	0.3	0.3	0.2	1.0	23
FEAR	-1.4	0.4	0.1	-2.0	-0.3	-0.3	-0.5	1.5	1.6	0.9	0.7	0.3	
	0.5	0.5	0.5	0.3	0.9	1.0	0.7	0.5	0.2	0.3	0.2	0.9	23
FEBRUARY	0.6	0.0	0.2	-0.2	-0.7	-0.1	0.7	0.9	1.3	0.6	0.8	0.6	
	0.6	0.3	0.5	0.5	0.7	0.9	0.9	0.5	0.3	0.2	0.2	1.1	23
FEET	1.2	0.5	0.7	0.4	-0.0	0.7	0.8	1.6	1.5	1.0	0.5	-0.3	
	0.6	0.4	0.6	0.4	0.6	0.7	1.2	0.7	0.4	0.3	0.3	0.8	23
FEMALE(GENDER)	1.5	-0.0	0.8	0.7	-0.8	0.9	0.5	1.8	1.7	1.0	0.7	0.3	
	0.6	0.6	0.5	0.6	0.8	0.7	1.1	0.7	0.4	0.4	0.3	0.9	22
FEMININITY	1.5	0.0	0.6	0.7	-0.7	0.6	0.3	1.8	1.6	1.0	0.6	0.0	
	0.4	0.6	0.6	0.4	0.8	0.8	0.7	0.6	0.4	0.3	0.2	0.9	23
FESTIVALS	1.6	0.7	0.8	0.8	0.4	0.7	0.7	2.0	1.7	1.1	0.5	-0.5	
	0.6	0.4	0.7	0.5	0.5	0.7	0.8	0.7	0.3	0.4	0.3	0.9	23
FIELD	1.5	0.8	-0.1	0.7	0.4	-0.6	0.6	1.8	1.5	1.0	0.5	-0.3	
	0.5	0.4	0.5	0.4	0.5	0.5	0.9	0.6	0.3	0.3	0.2	0.7	23
FIGHTING	-1.1	1.0	0.8	-1.8	0.7	0.8	-0.3	1.9	1.7	1.2	0.6	-0.2	
	0.6	0.6	0.8	0.5	1.0	0.9	0.8	0.6	0.3	0.4	0.3	1.0	23
FILTH	-1.9	0.0	-0.3	-2.5	-0.8	-0.9	-0.3	2.0	1.6	0.9	0.6	0.1	
	0.6	0.4	0.3	0.4	0.7	0.8	1.1	0.6	0.3	0.3	0.3	1.0	23
FINGERNAIL	0.4	-0.3	-0.0	-0.4	-1.3	-0.3	0.4	0.8	1.5	0.6	0.9	1.1	
	0.6	0.3	0.4	0.5	0.5	0.8	0.8	0.4	0.4	0.3	0.3	1.2	21
FINGERS	1.4	0.2	1.0	0.6	-0.5	1.2	0.8	1.9	1.6	1.1	0.5	-0.4	
	0.7	0.4	0.6	0.6	0.6	0.8	0.8	0.6	0.4	0.3	0.2	0.8	23
FIRE	0.1	0.9	0.9	-0.7	0.6	1.2	0.7	1.6	1.7	1.0	0.7	0.4	
	0.8	0.4	0.7	0.8	0.6	0.8	0.9	0.6	0.2	0.3	0.2	0.9	23
FISH	1.1	-0.0	0.8	0.3	-0.8	1.0	0.8	1.5	1.4	0.9	0.6	-0.2	
	0.4	0.4	0.5	0.3	0.5	0.6	0.7	0.5	0.3	0.3	0.2	0.7	23
FIVE	0.4	-0.2	0.0	-0.3	-1.2	-0.3	0.4	0.8	1.1	0.5	0.7	0.1	
	0.6	0.4	0.3	0.5	0.7	0.5	1.0	0.4	0.4	0.2	0.3	1.0	23
FLAG	1.5	0.9	0.4	0.7	0.6	0.2	0.9	1.9	1.7	1.1	0.6	-0.3	
	0.8	0.6	0.5	0.6	0.9	0.7	0.9	0.7	0.4	0.4	0.2	0.6	23
FLOOR	0.9	0.7	-0.6	0.2	0.3	-1.5	0.8	1.4	1.3	0.8	0.5	-0.4	
	0.4	0.4	0.4	0.3	0.7	0.6	0.9	0.5	0.3	0.3	0.2	0.8	23

```
FLOWER        1.9 -0.6  0.4  1.1 -1.8  0.4  0.9  2.2  1.7  1.2  0.5 -0.5
              0.4  0.6  0.6  0.4  0.8  1.0  0.9  0.5  0.3  0.3  0.2  0.7   23

FOG          -0.7  0.3 -0.3 -1.4 -0.3 -0.8  0.1  1.1  1.5  0.7  0.8  0.8
              0.8  0.3  0.5  0.6  0.6  1.1  0.9  0.6  0.3  0.3  0.3  0.9   23

FOLLOWER      0.3  0.4  0.5 -0.5 -0.2  0.3 -0.8  1.0  1.4  0.6  0.8  0.7
              0.8  0.3  0.5  0.7  0.6  0.7  0.8  0.6  0.4  0.3  0.3  1.0   23

FOOD          1.8  0.5  0.3  1.0 -0.0  0.2  1.2  2.0  1.5  1.0  0.5 -0.7
              0.4  0.5  0.5  0.1  0.5  0.7  0.9  0.4  0.3  0.2  0.2  0.5   23

FOREIGNER     0.6  0.4  0.5 -0.1 -0.2  0.4 -1.0  1.0  1.3  0.6  0.6  0.1
              0.4  0.4  0.4  0.4  0.6  0.6  1.4  0.4  0.3  0.2  0.3  0.9   23

FOREST        1.3  1.3 -0.3  0.5  1.3 -1.0  0.4  2.0  1.7  1.1  0.5 -0.3
              0.7  0.4  0.5  0.6  0.6  0.6  0.8  0.6  0.3  0.4  0.3  0.8   23

FORGIVENESS   1.5  0.6  0.1  0.7  0.2 -0.2  0.0  1.8  1.5  1.0  0.5 -0.3
              0.6  0.4  0.4  0.4  0.6  0.5  0.9  0.6  0.2  0.3  0.3  0.7   23

FOUR          0.3 -0.3 -0.1 -0.4 -1.3 -0.5  0.4  1.0  1.2  0.6  0.7  0.2
              0.8  0.5  0.4  0.6  0.7  0.7  1.0  0.5  0.4  0.3  0.3  0.7   23

FREEDOM       1.9  1.2  0.5  1.1  1.2  0.3  0.7  2.5  1.9  1.4  0.5 -0.6
              0.8  0.6  0.8  0.7  0.9  0.9  0.9  0.3  0.5  0.2  0.8        23

FREE WILL     1.5  0.9  0.5  0.7  0.7  0.3  0.2  1.9  1.6  1.1  0.5 -0.5
              0.5  0.4  0.6  0.3  0.5  0.8  0.6  0.6  0.3  0.3  0.3  0.8   22

FRIDAY        0.7  0.3  0.1 -0.1 -0.3 -0.2  0.8  1.0  1.2  0.6  0.7  0.3
              0.7  0.3  0.5  0.5  0.6  0.6  0.9  0.6  0.4  0.3  0.3  1.0   23

FRIEND        1.9  0.8  0.7  1.1  0.4  0.8  1.1  2.3  1.6  1.3  0.4 -1.1
              0.3  0.3  0.7  0.3  0.4  0.8  0.9  0.4  0.2  0.2  0.2  0.5   23

FRIENDSHIP    2.1  1.2  0.6  1.3  1.1  0.6  1.0  2.6  1.9  1.5  0.4 -1.0
              0.4  0.5  0.7  0.3  0.6  0.7  0.9  0.5  0.3  0.3  0.2  0.5   23

FRUIT         1.8  0.1  0.1  1.0 -0.7 -0.2  1.1  1.9  1.5  1.0  0.5 -0.5
              0.3  0.4  0.5  0.2  0.5  0.7  1.0  0.4  0.3  0.2  0.2  0.6   23

FUNERAL      -1.1  0.4 -0.9 -1.7 -0.3 -1.8 -0.4  1.6  1.7  1.0  0.7  0.3
              0.6  0.4  0.7  0.5  0.8  1.2  0.7  0.8  0.3  0.4  0.3  1.2   23

FUTURE        1.3  0.9  0.4  0.5  0.6  0.2 -0.6  1.7  1.5  1.0  0.5 -0.6
              0.5  0.4  0.6  0.4  0.5  0.7  0.9  0.7  0.4  0.4  0.2  0.7   23

GAME          1.5  0.6  1.0  0.7  0.2  1.1  0.7  2.0  1.7  1.2  0.5 -0.5
              0.5  0.4  0.6  0.4  0.6  0.7  0.5  0.7  0.3  0.4  0.2  0.8   23

GHOSTS       -0.9  0.1  0.1 -1.6 -0.6 -0.3 -1.7  1.2  1.5  0.7  0.8  0.7
              0.6  0.5  0.5  0.7  0.9  0.9  1.1  0.4  0.4  0.2  0.3  0.9   23

GIRL          1.8 -0.3  1.0  1.0 -1.2  1.2  0.7  2.2  1.7  1.2  0.6 -0.3
              0.5  0.6  0.5  0.4  0.7  0.7  0.8  0.6  0.3  0.4  0.2  0.9   23

GLASS         1.0 -0.0 -0.3  0.2 -0.9 -0.8  0.7  1.2  1.4  0.7  0.7  0.2
              0.4  0.3  0.4  0.4  0.6  0.7  1.1  0.4  0.3  0.2  0.2  0.6   23
```

GOD	1.7	1.4	0.4	0.9	1.5	0.2	0.2	2.5	1.9	1.4	0.5	-0.6	
	0.9	0.7	0.9	0.7	1.1	1.1	1.3	1.0	0.4	0.5	0.3	1.1	23
GOOSE	0.9	-0.0	0.4	0.1	-0.9	0.2	0.4	1.1	1.4	0.7	0.8	0.6	
	0.5	0.3	0.5	0.5	0.6	0.7	1.0	0.5	0.3	0.2	0.2	0.7	23
GOVERN CLERK	0.4	0.2	-0.1	-0.4	-0.5	-0.4	-0.4	0.9	1.4	0.6	0.8	0.8	
	0.7	0.4	0.5	0.5	0.6	0.7	0.9	0.5	0.3	0.3	0.3	1.0	23
GOVERNMENT	0.3	0.8	-0.0	-0.4	0.5	-0.5	-0.2	1.3	1.7	0.8	0.8	0.9	
	0.9	0.6	0.6	0.7	0.9	0.7	0.8	0.6	0.3	0.4	0.4	1.4	23
GRAFT	-0.7	0.3	0.1	-1.5	-0.3	-0.2	-1.1	1.3	1.6	0.7	0.8	0.9	
	1.1	0.5	0.4	1.0	0.9	0.5	1.2	0.8	0.3	0.4	0.3	1.4	22
GRAMOPHONE	1.6	0.3	0.7	0.8	-0.4	0.6	0.6	1.8	1.5	1.0	0.5	-0.4	
	0.4	0.3	0.6	0.4	0.5	0.7	0.8	0.5	0.3	0.3	0.2	0.9	23
GRANDFATHER	1.6	0.4	-0.5	0.8	-0.2	-1.2	0.7	1.8	1.7	1.1	0.6	0.0	
	0.5	0.5	0.6	0.3	0.8	1.1	1.0	0.5	0.3	0.3	0.2	0.6	23
GRANDMOTHER	1.4	-0.1	-0.4	0.6	-0.9	-1.0	0.8	1.7	1.7	1.1	0.7	0.1	
	0.6	0.6	0.6	0.5	0.9	1.0	1.0	0.5	0.2	0.2	0.2	0.7	23
GRASS	1.3	-0.4	0.3	0.5	-1.5	0.1	0.7	1.5	1.5	0.9	0.7	0.2	
	0.5	0.5	0.5	0.4	0.8	0.9	1.0	0.5	0.3	0.3	0.2	0.7	23
GREED	-1.4	0.3	0.1	-2.1	-0.4	-0.3	-0.9	1.6	1.6	0.9	0.8	0.6	
	0.7	0.4	0.4	0.6	0.7	0.7	0.9	0.5	0.3	0.2	0.3	0.9	23
GREEN	1.1	0.2	0.1	0.4	-0.5	-0.3	0.7	1.3	1.3	0.7	0.6	-0.2	
	0.4	0.4	0.4	0.3	0.4	0.5	0.8	0.4	0.3	0.2	0.3	0.8	23
GREY	0.1	-0.0	-0.5	-0.6	-0.9	-1.1	0.2	0.9	1.1	0.5	0.6	0.1	
	0.6	0.3	0.5	0.5	0.5	0.7	0.5	0.4	0.3	0.2	0.2	0.7	23
GROUP	1.2	0.9	0.7	0.4	0.6	0.7	0.4	1.7	1.6	1.0	0.6	-0.2	
	0.5	0.4	0.7	0.4	0.6	0.7	1.0	0.7	0.2	0.4	0.3	1.0	23
GROWING	1.2	0.8	0.4	0.5	0.5	0.3	0.2	1.7	1.6	1.0	0.6	-0.2	
	0.7	0.3	0.6	0.6	0.5	0.7	0.8	0.5	0.3	0.3	0.2	1.0	23
GUILT	-1.3	0.5	-0.0	-1.9	-0.1	-0.4	-0.5	1.5	1.4	0.8	0.6	0.0	
	0.7	0.5	0.3	0.6	0.8	0.6	1.1	0.6	0.3	0.3	0.2	0.8	23
GYPSY	0.0	0.3	0.6	-0.7	-0.3	0.4	-0.7	0.9	1.3	0.6	0.8	0.7	
	0.6	0.2	0.6	0.5	0.5	0.7	0.8	0.6	0.3	0.2	0.3	1.0	22
HABIT	0.4	0.4	0.0	-0.3	-0.1	-0.4	0.1	0.9	1.4	0.6	0.8	0.8	
	0.6	0.3	0.4	0.5	0.4	0.7	1.1	0.4	0.2	0.2	0.2	0.9	21
HAIR	1.3	-0.0	0.2	0.5	-0.9	-0.0	0.9	1.4	1.4	0.8	0.6	-0.0	
	0.4	0.5	0.5	0.3	0.6	0.9	0.9	0.4	0.3	0.3	0.2	0.8	23
HAND	1.5	0.5	0.8	0.7	-0.0	0.9	1.1	2.0	1.6	1.1	0.5	-0.6	
	0.4	0.5	0.7	0.3	0.6	0.9	1.1	0.6	0.3	0.3	0.2	0.7	23
HAPPINESS	2.1	0.7	0.8	1.3	0.4	0.9	0.7	2.5	1.8	1.4	0.4	-0.7	
	0.5	0.5	0.6	0.4	0.6	0.6	1.0	0.6	0.4	0.4	0.3	0.8	23

```
HAT                  0.9 -0.3 -0.1  0.1 -1.3 -0.6  0.3  1.1  1.3  0.6  0.7  0.2
                     0.5  0.3  0.5  0.4  0.4  0.9  1.0  0.5  0.3  0.3  0.2  1.0   23

HATE                -1.6  0.5  0.2 -2.2  0.0 -0.2 -1.0  2.0  1.8  1.1  0.7  0.3
                     0.8  0.7  0.6  0.7  1.2  1.0  0.8  0.7  0.4  0.4  0.3  1.2   23

HEAD                 1.5  0.6  0.5  0.7  0.2  0.3  0.8  1.8  1.5  1.0  0.5 -0.5
                     0.4  0.3  0.8  0.3  0.4  0.9  0.7  0.5  0.3  0.2  0.2  0.8   23

HEALTH               1.9  0.9  0.7  1.1  0.7  0.8  0.5  2.4  1.8  1.4  0.4 -0.8
                     0.8  0.5  0.5  0.7  0.6  0.6  0.8  0.6  0.3  0.3  0.2  0.8   23

HEARING,SENSE OF     1.6  0.6  0.8  0.8  0.1  0.9  0.6  2.0  1.7  1.2  0.5 -0.4
                     0.7  0.5  0.5  0.6  0.7  0.7  0.7  0.7  0.3  0.3  0.3  0.9   23

HEART                1.6  0.3  1.1  0.8 -0.2  1.4  0.8  2.1  1.7  1.2  0.5 -0.4
                     0.5  0.6  0.7  0.3  0.7  0.7  0.8  0.6  0.3  0.3  0.2  0.7   23

HEAT                 0.3  0.6  0.2 -0.5  0.1 -0.0  0.3  1.1  1.4  0.6  0.7  0.6
                     0.6  0.5  0.5  0.6  0.8  0.7  1.0  0.5  0.4  0.3  0.3  1.0   23

HEAVEN               1.8  1.2 -0.0  1.0  1.1 -0.5 -0.6  2.3  1.8  1.3  0.5 -0.5
                     0.5  0.7  0.6  0.4  0.9  0.8  1.1  0.7  0.4  0.4  0.3  0.8   23

HELL                -1.8  1.0 -0.2 -2.5  0.7 -0.9 -1.6  2.2  1.8  1.3  0.6 -0.3
                     0.4  0.6  0.7  0.3  0.8  1.0  1.1  0.6  0.3  0.4  0.2  0.7   23

HERBS                0.8 -0.0 -0.0 -0.0 -0.8 -0.4 -0.1  1.0  1.4  0.6  0.8  0.7
                     0.5  0.5  0.4  0.4  0.8  0.6  1.2  0.4  0.3  0.2  0.3  0.9   23

HERO                 1.6  1.3  0.9  0.8  1.4  1.0  0.2  2.4  1.8  1.4  0.4 -0.8
                     0.5  0.4  0.8  0.4  0.6  1.0  0.8  0.7  0.2  0.4  0.2  1.0   23

HINDUS               0.4  0.2 -0.0 -0.3 -0.4 -0.5 -0.9  0.9  1.3  0.6  0.7  0.3
                     0.7  0.4  0.5  0.8  0.7  0.9  1.9  0.6  0.4  0.3  0.3  1.1   21

HISTORY              1.1  1.1 -0.1  0.3  1.0 -0.5  0.5  1.7  1.6  1.0  0.6  0.1
                     0.6  0.3  0.6  0.4  0.5  0.7  0.8  0.6  0.3  0.4  0.3  0.9   23

HOMOSEXUAL          -1.0 -0.3  0.1 -1.7 -1.2 -0.2 -1.7  1.5  1.6  0.8  0.7  0.4
                     1.0  0.5  0.5  0.9  0.9  0.7  1.1  0.6  0.3  0.3  0.3  0.9   14

HONOR                1.6  1.2  0.4  0.8  1.1  0.3  0.2  2.1  1.7  1.2  0.5 -0.4
                     0.5  0.5  0.5  0.3  0.5  0.6  0.7  0.6  0.3  0.4  0.3  1.0   23

HOPE                 1.4  0.8  0.3  0.6  0.5  0.1  0.6  1.8  1.6  1.0  0.6 -0.2
                     0.5  0.4  0.6  0.4  0.5  0.7  0.6  0.6  0.3  0.4  0.3  1.0   23

HORSE                1.6  1.3  1.0  0.7  1.3  1.2  0.7  2.4  1.8  1.4  0.4 -0.9
                     0.6  0.5  0.7  0.4  0.6  0.9  0.8  0.8  0.3  0.4  0.2  0.7   23

HOSPITAL             0.8  1.0  0.1  0.0  0.8 -0.2  0.3  1.6  1.6  1.0  0.7  0.2
                     0.9  0.4  0.6  0.7  0.5  0.7  1.0  0.6  0.3  0.3  0.3  0.9   23

HOTEL                1.1  0.8  0.2  0.4  0.5 -0.2  0.1  1.5  1.4  0.9  0.5 -0.4
                     0.6  0.4  0.5  0.5  0.6  0.6  0.7  0.5  0.3  0.3  0.3  0.8   23

HOUR                 0.9  0.2  0.2  0.1 -0.4 -0.0  0.7  1.1  1.3  0.6  0.7  0.3
                     0.5  0.3  0.5  0.3  0.5  0.6  0.8  0.5  0.3  0.3  0.3  0.9   23
```

```
HOUSE            1.7  1.1 -0.3  0.9  1.0 -0.9  1.2  2.2  1.7  1.2  0.5 -0.6
                 0.4  0.4  0.6  0.2  0.6  0.9  1.0  0.5  0.2  0.2  0.2  0.8   23

HUNGER          -1.4  0.6 -0.1 -2.0  0.1 -0.5 -0.3  1.7  1.6  0.9  0.7  0.2
                 0.7  0.5  0.4  0.6  0.7  0.7  1.4  0.6  0.3  0.3  0.3  0.9   23

HUSBAND          1.4  0.9  0.6  0.6  0.6  0.5  0.4  1.9  1.6  1.1  0.5 -0.5
                 0.6  0.4  0.7  0.6  0.5  0.8  0.8  0.6 ·0.3  0.4  0.3  0.9   23

I(MYSELF)        1.3  0.7  1.0  0.5  0.3  1.3  0.9  1.9  1.7  1.1  0.5 -0.4
                 0.4  0.5  0.7  0.4  0.7  0.9  1.0  0.7  0.3  0.4  0.2  0.7   23

ICE              0.6  0.7 -0.2 -0.1  0.2 -0.8  0.5  1.1  1.4  0.7  0.7  0.6
                 0.5  0.4  0.4  0.5  0.5  0.8  0.6  0.4  0.3  0.2  0.3  1.0   23

IDEALISM         1.1  0.9  0.5  0.3  0.6  0.4 -0.8  1.6  1.6  1.0  0.7  0.2
                 0.7  0.4  0.5  0.6  0.7  0.6  1.4  0.7  0.3  0.4  0.3  1.3   22

IDEA             1.3  0.7  0.5  0.5  0.3  0.4  0.2  1.6  1.4  0.9  0.5 -0.5
                 0.4  0.4  0.6  0.4  0.5  0.6  0.6  0.4  0.3  0.3  0.2  0.6   22

ILLITERATE      -0.9 -0.3 -0.5 -1.6 -1.4 -1.3 -1.2  1.2  1.4  0.7  0.7  0.3
                 0.6  0.2  0.5  0.5  0.5  1.0  1.3  0.5  0.3  0.3  0.3  1.0   23

IMMIGRANT        0.4  0.4  0.5 -0.3 -0.2  0.3 -0.9  0.9  1.2  0.6  0.7  0.3
                 0.5  0.3  0.4  0.4  0.6  0.5  0.9  0.5  0.3  0.2  0.3  0.9   19

IMMORTALITY      0.9  0.8 -0.2  0.2  0.5 -0.7 -1.4  1.3  1.5  0.8  0.8  0.6
                 0.6  0.4  0.4  0.6  0.6  0.5  1.1  0.6  0.3  0.3  0.3  1.0   23

INDEPENDENT      1.4  0.7  0.4  0.6  0.4  0.2  0.2  1.7  1.5  1.0  0.6 -0.3
                 0.5  0.4  0.5  0.5  0.5  0.5  0.9  0.5  0.3  0.3  0.3  0.8   23

INFINITY         0.4  1.0 -0.3 -0.3  0.8 -0.9 -1.1  1.3  1.4  0.8  0.6  0.1
                 0.5  0.5  0.5  0.4  0.6  0.6  1.0  0.6  0.4  0.3  0.3  0.9   23

INITIATIVE,TAKE  1.2  0.7  0.7  0.4  0.3  0.6 -0.2  1.6  1.5  0.9  0.5 -0.4
                 0.4  0.4  0.5  0.4  0.7  0.6  0.9  0.7  0.2  0.4  0.4  1.2   23

INSANE          -1.4  0.2  0.1 -2.0 -0.5 -0.3 -1.2  1.5  1.6  0.8  0.7  0.4
                 0.5  0.4  0.6  0.4  0.9  1.0  0.9  0.6  0.4  0.3  0.3  1.0   23

INSECT          -0.4 -1.0  0.8 -1.1 -2.4  0.8  0.1  1.5  1.8  0.9  0.9  1.2
                 0.6  0.6  0.5  0.6  0.9  0.9  1.0  0.7  0.3  0.4  0.3  1.3   22

INSURANCE        1.3  0.7  0.0  0.5  0.3 -0.3  0.2  1.5  1.3  0.8  0.5 -0.5
                 0.6  0.4  0.5  0.3  0.4  0.6  0.8  0.6  0.3  0.3  0.2  0.6   23

INTESTINES       0.6  0.3  0.4 -0.2 -0.3  0.3 -0.1  1.0  1.3  0.7  0.7  0.3
                 0.6  0.4  0.4  0.5  0.5  0.5  0.7  0.5  0.3  0.2  0.2  0.7   22

IRON             0.7  1.3 -0.6 -0.1  1.3 -1.4  0.7  1.8  1.5  1.0  0.5 -0.4
                 0.6  0.5  0.6  0.4  0.6  0.7  1.0  0.6  0.3  0.3  0.2  0.5   23

JANUARY          0.7  0.5  0.0  0.0 -0.0 -0.3  0.7  1.1  1.4  0.6  0.8  0.8
                 0.5  0.3  0.5  0.5  0.6  0.8  0.9  0.5  0.3  0.2  0.3  1.2   23

JAZZ MUSIC       1.1  0.5  0.8  0.3  0.0  0.9 -0.0  1.6  1.6  0.9  0.7  0.5
                 0.5  0.3  0.6  0.4  0.4  0.8  0.7  0.6  0.3  0.3  0.3  1.0   22
```

JEWELRY	1.3	0.2	-0.2	0.5	-0.5	-0.7	0.1	1.4	1.5	0.8	0.7	0.4	
	0.6	0.4	0.4	0.5	0.6	0.6	0.9	0.5	0.3	0.2	0.2	0.8	23
JEWS	0.2	0.2	0.2	-0.5	-0.5	-0.2	-0.7	0.7	1.3	0.5	0.8	0.7	
	0.6	0.3	0.5	0.6	0.6	0.6	0.9	0.4	0.3	0.2	0.2	0.9	22
JOKE	1.0	0.1	0.7	0.2	-0.7	0.7	0.6	1.4	1.4	0.8	0.6	-0.1	
	0.8	0.3	0.5	0.8	0.4	0.7	0.9	0.6	0.3	0.3	0.2	0.7	23
JULY	1.4	0.2	0.5	0.6	-0.4	0.4	0.9	1.6	1.5	0.9	0.6	-0.3	
	0.6	0.3	0.5	0.6	0.4	0.7	0.8	0.7	0.4	0.4	0.2	0.8	23
JUNE	1.3	0.3	0.5	0.5	-0.4	0.4	0.9	1.5	1.5	0.9	0.6	-0.1	
	0.6	0.4	0.5	0.6	0.5	0.7	0.9	0.7	0.4	0.4	0.3	1.0	23
JUNGLE	0.1	1.4	-0.0	-0.6	1.4	-0.6	-0.8	1.6	1.6	0.9	0.7	0.4	
	0.5	0.5	0.7	0.5	0.7	1.0	1.1	0.5	0.3	0.2	0.3	0.8	22
JUSTICE	1.5	1.2	0.1	0.7	1.1	-0.3	0.5	2.1	1.7	1.2	0.5	-0.4	
	0.9	0.5	0.7	0.7	0.6	0.8	0.9	0.8	0.3	0.4	0.3	0.8	23
KINDNESS	2.0	0.7	0.5	1.2	0.3	0.4	0.6	2.2	1.7	1.2	0.5	-0.6	
	0.5	0.5	0.5	0.4	0.6	0.6	0.8	0.6	0.3	0.3	0.3	0.9	23
KING	0.7	0.8	0.1	-0.0	0.5	-0.3	-0.1	1.4	1.6	0.9	0.7	0.6	
	0.8	0.4	0.6	0.8	0.7	0.8	1.1	0.6	0.3	0.3	0.3	1.4	23
KISSING	1.9	0.6	0.7	1.1	0.2	0.7	0.5	2.2	1.9	1.3	0.6	-0.2	
	0.6	0.7	0.5	0.6	1.0	0.6	0.9	0.7	0.4	0.4	0.2	0.6	23
KNIFE	-0.2	0.5	0.2	-0.9	-0.0	-0.0	0.7	0.9	1.5	0.7	0.8	0.6	
	0.5	0.4	0.5	0.5	0.5	0.8	0.7	0.4	0.3	0.2	0.2	0.9	23
KNOT	0.1	0.2	-0.3	-0.6	-0.6	-0.9	0.2	0.7	1.2	0.5	0.7	0.7	
	0.4	0.4	0.3	0.4	0.6	0.5	0.8	0.3	0.3	0.2	0.2	0.8	23
KNOWLEDGE	1.9	1.2	0.4	1.1	1.2	0.1	0.6	2.4	1.8	1.4	0.4	-0.8	
	0.4	0.5	0.8	0.2	0.0	0.9	1.0	0.6	0.3	0.3	0.2	0.5	23
LABOR UNIONS	1.0	1.0	0.4	0.2	0.8	0.2	-0.3	1.6	1.5	1.0	0.6	-0.1	
	0.7	0.5	0.7	0.5	0.6	0.8	0.9	0.7	0.3	0.4	0.3	1.1	23
LABORATORY	1.2	0.9	0.2	0.5	0.6	-0.2	0.2	1.6	1.5	0.9	0.5	-0.4	
	0.5	0.4	0.6	0.3	0.5	0.7	1.1	0.7	0.4	0.3	0.3	0.8	23
LADY	1.3	-0.2	0.5	0.5	-1.0	0.4	0.4	1.6	1.6	0.9	0.7	0.5	
	0.6	0.5	0.5	0.5	0.5	0.7	0.9	0.8	0.6	0.3	0.2	0.8	23
LAKE	1.4	0.7	-0.0	0.6	0.3	-0.5	0.4	1.7	1.5	1.0	0.6	-0.2	
	0.5	0.4	0.5	0.4	0.6	0.8	0.8	0.5	0.4	0.3	0.2	0.6	23
LAMP	1.3	0.0	0.1	0.5	-0.7	-0.3	1.0	1.5	1.4	0.8	0.6	-0.0	
	0.5	0.4	0.6	0.4	0.5	0.9	1.2	0.5	0.3	0.3	0.2	0.7	23
LAND	1.3	1.2	-0.4	0.4	1.2	-1.1	0.7	1.9	1.6	1.1	0.5	-0.6	
	0.5	0.5	0.6	0.4	0.7	0.7	0.6	0.6	0.4	0.4	0.2	0.9	22
LANGUAGE	1.4	0.8	0.6	0.6	0.4	0.4	1.0	1.9	1.5	1.1	0.5	-0.6	
	0.4	0.5	0.7	0.3	0.5	0.8	0.8	0.6	0.3	0.3	0.2	0.8	23

LAUGHTER	1.5	0.3	0.9	0.7	-0.4	1.0	0.9	1.9	1.5	1.1	0.4	-0.9	
	0.4	0.5	0.6	0.4	0.6	0.8	0.9	0.5	0.3	0.3	0.2	0.7	23
LAW	0.9	1.2	-0.1	0.1	1.1	-0.6	0.0	1.7	1.6	1.0	0.6	-0.1	
	0.8	0.5	0.7	0.5	0.5	0.8	0.8	0.8	0.4	0.4	0.3	0.7	23
LAWYER	0.8	0.8	0.5	0.0	0.5	0.4	-0.2	1.4	1.5	0.9	0.6	-0.1	
	0.7	0.4	0.6	0.5	0.5	0.8	1.0	0.6	0.2	0.3	0.3	0.9	23
LEADER	1.2	1.2	0.7	0.4	1.2	0.6	0.3	2.0	1.7	1.2	0.5	-0.6	
	0.6	0.4	0.8	0.5	0.5	0.9	0.7	0.7	0.3	0.4	0.3	0.9	23
LEFT HAND	0.9	0.1	0.1	0.1	-0.7	-0.2	0.7	1.0	1.3	0.6	0.7	0.5	
	0.4	0.4	0.4	0.2	0.5	0.6	0.7	0.4	0.2	0.2	0.2	0.7	23
LEG	1.4	0.6	0.8	0.6	0.2	0.9	1.0	1.9	1.5	1.1	0.4	-0.8	
	0.5	0.5	0.7	0.3	0.5	0.7	⁻1.0	0.6	0.3	0.3	0.2	0.6	23
LEISURE	1.2	0.0	0.4	0.4	-0.7	0.3	0.1	1.6	1.6	0.9	0.7	0.4	
	1.0	0.3	0.8	1.0	0.4	1.2	1.2	0.8	0.3	0.4	0.3	1.2	23
LIBRARY	1.7	1.0	-0.2	0.9	0.7	-0.7	0.8	2.1	1.6	1.2	0.5	-0.6	
	0.5	0.4	0.7	0.3	0.5	0.8	0.9	0.6	0.3	0.3	0.2	0.6	23
LIFE	1.5	0.9	0.7	0.7	0.6	0.7	0.6	2.0	1.7	1.1	0.6	-0.3	
	0.5	0.4	0.7	0.3	0.4	0.7	0.6	0.6	0.3	0.3	0.2	0.7	23
LIGHT	1.8	0.6	0.8	1.0	0.2	0.9	1.2	2.2	1.7	1.3	0.4	-1.0	
	0.4	0.6	0.8	0.3	0.8	1.0	0.9	0.6	0.4	0.4	0.2	0.8	23
LINE	0.8	0.1	-0.0	-0.0	-0.6	-0.4	0.4	1.0	1.2	0.6	0.6	-0.0	
	0.4	0.5	0.4	0.3	0.7	0.6	0.8	0.4	0.3	0.2	0.2	0.8	23
LION	0.0	1.5	0.8	-0.8	1.6	0.8	-0.2	2.0	1.8	1.2	0.6	-0.0	
	0.6	0.4	0.8	0.7	0.6	1.0	1.0	0.4	0.2	0.2	0.1	0.7	23
LIPSTICK	0.7	-0.5	0.3	-0.1	-1.7	0.2	-0.3	1.1	1.4	0.6	0.8	0.8	
	0.5	0.4	0.4	0.5	0.5	1.0	0.7	0.4	0.3	0.2	0.3	0.9	23
LIPS	1.7	-0.2	0.9	0.9	-1.2	1.2	0.8	2.0	1.6	1.1	0.5	-0.5	
	0.4	0.5	0.5	0.3	0.7	0.8	0.9	0.5	0.3	0.2	0.2	0.7	23
LOTTERIES	0.5	0.3	0.3	-0.2	-0.3	0.1	0.2	0.9	1.3	0.6	0.7	0.6	
	0.5	0.3	0.4	0.4	0.6	0.6	0.8	0.5	0.3	0.3	0.3	0.9	23
LOVE	2.0	1.2	0.8	1.1	1.1	0.8	0.7	2.6	2.0	1.5	0.5	-0.7	
	0.5	0.6	0.7	0.4	0.8	0.7	0.6	0.7	0.4	0.4	0.2	0.7	23
LUCK	1.6	0.5	0.5	0.7	0.0	0.4	-0.1	1.8	1.5	1.0	0.5	-0.3	
	0.5	0.4	0.4	0.5	0.5	0.6	1.0	0.6	0.3	0.3	0.2	0.6	23
LYING	-1.7	-0.0	0.1	-2.3	-0.9	-0.2	-0.4	1.8	1.7	0.9	0.8	0.6	
	0.5	0.4	0.4	0.4	0.8	0.9	1.1	0.5	0.3	0.3	0.3	1.0	23
MACHINE	1.2	1.3	0.7	0.4	1.3	0.7	0.7	2.1	1.7	1.3	0.5	-0.6	
	0.5	0.5	0.8	0.3	0.7	0.9	0.8	0.6	0.3	0.3	0.2	0.6	23
MALE(GENDER)	1.2	1.2	0.8	0.4	1.2	0.8	0.8	2.0	1.6	1.2	0.4	-0.8	
	0.5	0.5	0.7	0.4	0.6	0.8	1.0	0.7	0.4	0.4	0.2	0.8	22

MAN	1.3	1.1	0.8	0.5	1.0	0.8	0.9	2.0	1.6	1.2	0.4	-0.8	
	0.4	0.5	0.7	0.3	0.7	0.8	1.1	0.7	0.3	0.3	0.2	0.7	23
MAP	1.3	0.3	-0.1	0.5	-0.2	-0.6	0.8	1.4	1.3	0.8	0.6	-0.2	
	0.4	0.3	0.4	0.3	0.4	0.5	0.8	0.5	0.3	0.2	0.2	0.7	23
MARCH	0.9	0.3	0.2	0.2	-0.3	-0.0	0.7	1.1	1.3	0.6	0.7	0.3	
	0.3	0.3	0.3	0.3	0.5	0.6	1.0	0.3	0.4	0.2	0.3	1.1	23
MARRIAGE	1.6	0.8	0.5	0.8	0.4	0.4	-0.3	1.9	1.6	1.1	0.5	-0.4	
	0.5	0.4	0.5	0.4	0.4	0.5	1.2	0.5	0.2	0.3	0.2	0.7	23
MASCULINITY	1.6	1.3	0.8	0.7	1.2	0.8	0.3	2.3	1.7	1.3	0.4	-1.1	
	0.5	0.5	0.8	0.4	0.6	0.8	1.3	0.7	0.3	0.4	0.2	0.7	23
MASTER	0.2	0.7	0.2	-0.5	0.3	-0.1	-0.5	1.2	1.5	0.7	0.8	0.9	
	0.8	0.4	0.4	0.7	0.6	0.8	0.9	0.5	0.4	0.3	0.3	1.1	22
MATURITY	1.2	0.8	0.3	0.4	0.4	-0.0	-0.2	1.6	1.5	0.9	0.6	-0.1	
	0.6	0.5	0.5	0.5	0.6	0.6	0.7	0.7	0.3	0.4	0.3	1.0	23
MAY	1.5	0.2	0.6	0.7	-0.4	0.5	0.8	1.7	1.5	0.9	0.6	-0.2	
	0.5	0.4	0.6	0.4	0.6	0.8	0.8	0.6	0.4	0.4	0.2	0.8	23
MEAT	1.2	0.4	0.1	0.4	-0.1	-0.2	0.7	1.4	1.4	0.8	0.6	0.0	
	0.5	0.4	0.5	0.4	0.5	0.8	0.7	0.5	0.3	0.2	0.3	1.0	23
MEDICINE	1.1	0.5	0.2	0.3	-0.1	0.0	0.3	1.5	1.5	0.9	0.7	0.2	
	0.7	0.6	0.5	0.5	0.8	0.7	1.1	0.7	0.3	0.4	0.2	0.9	23
MEMORY	1.5	0.8	0.5	0.7	0.4	0.5	0.5	1.9	1.6	1.1	0.5	-0.5	
	0.6	0.5	0.7	0.4	0.6	0.8	0.9	0.7	0.3	0.4	0.3	1.1	23
MIDDLE AGE	0.7	0.5	0.1	-0.0	0.0	-0.3	-0.5	1.0	1.3	0.6	0.6	0.2	
	0.4	0.3	0.4	0.3	0.5	0.7	1.4	0.4	0.3	0.2	0.2	0.8	23
MIDDLE CLASS	0.8	0.5	0.2	-0.0	-0.1	-0.1	0.1	1.0	1.2	0.6	0.6	-0.1	
	0.5	0.4	0.3	0.4	0.5	0.3	0.9	0.5	0.3	0.3	0.2	0.9	23
MILK	1.7	0.2	0.3	0.9	-0.4	0.1	1.1	1.9	1.4	1.0	0.5	-0.6	
	0.4	0.5	0.5	0.2	0.6	0.8	0.9	0.4	0.3	0.2	0.2	0.8	23
MIND	1.4	0.8	0.7	0.6	0.5	0.8	0.3	2.0	1.7	1.2	0.5	-0.4	
	0.6	0.6	0.8	0.4	0.8	1.2	1.0	0.8	0.3	0.5	0.3	0.9	23
MINISKIRT	1.4	-0.4	1.1	0.6	-1.5	1.4	0.3	2.0	1.9	1.2	0.7	0.2	
	0.8	0.6	0.5	0.7	0.8	1.1	1.0	0.9	0.3	0.5	0.4	1.5	22
MISSIONARY	1.4	0.7	0.3	0.6	0.3	0.1	-0.1	1.7	1.6	1.0	0.6	0.1	
	0.6	0.5	0.6	0.5	0.7	0.6	1.0	0.7	0.3	0.4	0.3	0.9	23
MOMENT	0.7	-0.3	0.7	-0.1	-1.3	0.7	0.2	1.1	1.3	0.7	0.6	0.1	
	0.3	0.4	0.5	0.2	0.6	0.8	0.7	0.4	0.4	0.2	0.3	0.8	23
MONDAY	0.0	0.2	-0.1	-0.7	-0.4	-0.5	0.8	1.0	1.3	0.6	0.7	0.5	
	0.9	0.3	0.5	0.7	0.5	0.8	0.8	0.5	0.4	0.2	0.3	1.1	23
MONEY	1.2	0.7	0.4	0.4	0.2	0.2	0.9	1.5	1.6	0.9	0.7	0.3	
	0.5	0.3	0.4	0.4	0.5	0.6	0.7	0.5	0.3	0.2	0.2	0.9	23

MONKEY	0.3	-0.1	1.0	-0.4	-1.0	1.1	0.2	1.3	1.5	0.8	0.7	0.5	
	0.6	0.4	0.8	0.6	0.6	0.9	0.9	0.7	0.3	0.3	0.2	0.9	23
MONTH	0.7	0.4	0.2	-0.1	-0.2	-0.0	0.3	0.9	1.3	0.6	0.7	0.4	
	0.6	0.3	0.3	0.5	0.4	0.5	0.9	0.5	0.3	0.2	0.3	0.8	23
MOON	1.5	0.7	-0.3	0.7	0.3	-0.9	0.5	1.8	1.6	1.0	0.6	0.1	
	0.4	0.3	0.7	0.3	0.4	0.9	0.9	0.5	0.3	0.3	0.3	0.9	23
MOSLEMS	0.1	0.4	0.2	-0.6	-0.1	-0.1	-0.6	1.0	1.3	0.6	0.7	0.4	
	0.8	0.4	0.6	0.8	0.8	0.9	1.2	0.7	0.4	0.4	0.3	0.9	22
MOTHER	2.2	0.7	0.7	1.4	0.5	0.7	1.5	2.6	1.9	1.5	0.4	-0.9	
	0.4	0.7	0.8	0.3	0.9	0.9	0.9	0.6	0.3	0.3	0.2	0.5	23
MOTHER-IN-LAW	0.0	0.3	-0.0	-0.7	-0.3	-0.5	-0.3	0.8	1.6	0.6	1.0	1.7	
	0.7	0.4	0.4	0.6	0.6	0.7	1.1	0.5	0.3	0.3	0.2	1.0	23
MOUNTAINS	1.1	1.7	-0.6	0.3	1.9	-1.5	0.2	2.2	1.8	1.2	0.5	-0.4	
	0.5	0.4	0.5	0.5	0.6	0.7	0.8	0.6	0.3	0.3	0.3	0.9	23
MURDER	-2.0	0.8	0.4	-2.6	0.4	0.1	-1.5	2.4	2.1	1.4	0.6	0.1	
	0.9	0.7	0.7	0.8	1.1	1.0	1.0	0.5	0.3	0.3	0.3	1.1	23
MUSIC	1.9	0.6	0.7	1.1	0.2	0.6	0.9	2.2	1.7	1.2	0.5	-0.7	
	0.4	0.4	0.7	0.3	0.5	0.8	0.7	0.5	0.3	0.3	0.2	0.5	23
MUSTACHE	0.3	-0.1	-0.1	-0.5	-1.0	-0.6	-0.0	0.6	1.3	0.4	0.9	1.1	
	0.4	0.3	0.3	0.3	0.5	0.5	0.9	0.3	0.3	0.1	0.3	0.8	23
MY CITY NAME	1.2	0.9	0.5	0.4	0.7	0.4	0.9	1.8	1.8	1.1	0.7	0.1	
	0.8	0.7	0.7	0.7	1.2	1.0	0.7	0.9	0.3	0.5	0.3	1.4	21
MY NAME	1.3	0.5	0.5	0.5	0.0	0.4	0.8	1.6	1.5	0.9	0.6	-0.2	
	0.7	0.4	0.4	0.6	0.5	0.7	1.0	0.7	0.3	0.3	0.2	0.8	23
MY NATION NAME	1.5	0.9	0.5	0.7	0.8	0.4	0.8	2.1	1.8	1.2	0.6	-0.0	
	0.8	0.8	0.7	0.6	1.4	1.1	1.0	0.9	0.3	0.5	0.3	1.1	21
MY OWN REGION	1.4	0.8	0.2	0.6	0.4	0.0	0.6	1.7	1.7	1.0	0.7	0.1	
	0.7	0.5	0.4	0.6	0.7	0.8	0.8	0.6	0.3	0.3	0.2	0.9	18
MY OWN TONGUE	1.6	1.0	0.4	0.9	0.7	0.2	1.2	2.1	1.7	1.2	0.5	-0.4	
	0.6	0.6	0.8	0.5	0.7	1.0	0.9	0.8	0.3	0.5	0.4	1.2	23
MY STATE NAME	1.2	0.8	0.4	0.4	0.5	0.2	0.5	1.7	1.7	1.0	0.7	0.1	
	0.7	0.5	0.7	0.6	0.7	0.9	0.9	0.8	0.3	0.5	0.3	1.3	17
NAIL	0.3	0.3	-0.3	-0.4	-0.4	-0.9	0.4	0.9	1.5	0.7	0.8	0.7	
	0.5	0.5	0.5	0.4	0.7	0.8	0.7	0.5	0.3	0.2	0.2	0.8	23
NAKEDNESS	0.4	0.1	0.5	-0.4	-0.7	0.4	-0.5	1.1	1.4	0.7	0.8	0.8	
	0.9	0.4	0.5	0.9	0.6	0.8	1.0	0.6	0.3	0.3	0.3	1.0	22
NAME	1.3	0.2	0.0	0.5	-0.4	-0.4	1.0	1.4	1.3	0.8	0.5	-0.3	
	0.4	0.4	0.4	0.3	0.6	0.5	1.0	0.4	0.3	0.2	0.2	0.7	23
NATIONALISM	0.9	1.0	0.4	0.1	0.9	0.2	-0.1	1.7	1.6	1.0	0.7	0.2	
	0.9	0.5	0.7	0.7	0.8	0.9	1.2	0.7	0.4	0.4	0.3	1.2	23

NECKTIE	1.0	-0.2	0.0	0.3	-1.1	-0.3	0.6	1.2	1.3	0.7	0.6	-0.1	
	0.5	0.4	0.4	0.4	0.5	0.9	0.7	0.4	0.3	0.3	0.2	0.7	23
NEED	-0.0	0.5	0.2	-0.7	0.0	-0.2	0.2	1.1	1.3	0.6	0.7	0.3	
	0.9	0.4	0.5	0.8	0.6	0.7	1.0	0.5	0.3	0.3	0.3	1.1	23
NEGRO	0.7	0.9	0.5	-0.1	0.7	0.4	-0.5	1.5	1.6	0.9	0.6	0.0	
	0.7	0.4	0.7	0.6	0.6	0.7	0.7	0.7	0.4	0.4	0.3	1.3	23
NEUROTICPERSON	-1.0	0.2	0.0	-1.6	-0.5	-0.4	-1.8	1.2	1.4	0.7	0.8	0.7	
	0.6	0.5	0.4	0.5	0.8	0.6	1.6	0.5	0.4	0.2	0.3	0.9	20
NEUTRALITY	0.8	0.3	-0.1	0.1	-0.3	-0.6	-0.4	1.0	1.2	0.5	0.7	0.3	
	0.4	0.2	0.3	0.4	0.4	0.5	0.8	0.4	0.3	0.2	0.3	1.0	23
NEWSPAPERS	1.4	0.4	0.6	0.6	-0.1	0.6	1.1	1.7	1.6	1.0	0.6	-0.1	
	0.4	0.4	0.5	0.3	0.5	0.6	0.8	0.5	0.3	0.3	0.2	0.7	23
NEWS	1.0	0.7	0.7	0.3	0.2	0.7	0.6	1.6	1.4	0.9	0.5	-0.7	
	0.5	0.4	0.6	0.4	0.5	0.6	1.0	0.6	0.3	0.3	0.2	0.7	23
NIGHT	1.1	0.5	-0.1	0.3	-0.1	-0.6	0.9	1.4	1.5	0.8	0.7	0.5	
	0.5	0.4	0.4	0.4	0.5	0.6	0.8	0.5	0.3	0.3	0.3	0.7	23
NOISE	-1.1	0.7	0.6	-1.8	0.3	0.4	0.3	1.6	1.6	0.9	0.6	0.1	
	0.6	0.5	0.6	0.5	0.8	0.9	0.8	0.7	0.4	0.4	0.3	1.1	23
NON-BELIEVER	-0.4	-0.0	-0.1	-1.1	-1.0	-0.6	-1.2	0.7	1.3	0.4	0.8	1.0	
	0.6	0.3	0.5	0.6	0.6	0.9	0.9	0.5	0.4	0.3	0.3	1.0	15
NORTH	0.5	0.8	-0.1	-0.2	0.6	-0.5	-0.1	1.3	1.4	0.7	0.6	-0.0	
	0.6	0.4	0.6	0.5	0.5	0.8	1.2	0.4	0.4	0.2	0.3	0.9	23
NORTH AMERICA	1.0	1.3	0.5	0.3	1.3	0.3	0.1	1.9	1.6	1.1	0.5	-0.4	
	0.5	0.5	0.7	0.4	0.6	0.8	0.7	0.7	0.3	0.4	0.2	0.5	23
NOSE	1.1	-0.2	0.3	0.3	-1.1	0.2	0.9	1.3	1.3	0.7	0.6	-0.2	
	0.5	0.4	0.5	0.4	0.5	0.8	0.9	0.5	0.4	0.3	0.2	0.6	23
NOVEMBER	0.5	0.4	-0.1	-0.3	-0.1	-0.6	0.7	1.0	1.3	0.6	0.7	0.3	
	0.7	0.3	0.5	0.5	0.5	0.8	0.8	0.4	0.4	0.2	0.3	1.2	23
NUMBER	0.7	0.4	0.0	-0.0	-0.3	-0.3	0.5	1.1	1.3	0.6	0.6	0.0	
	0.6	0.3	0.5	0.4	0.4	0.5	1.0	0.4	0.3	0.2	0.3	0.7	23
NURSE	1.7	0.4	1.0	0.9	-0.1	1.2	0.2	2.2	1.8	1.3	0.5	-0.5	
	0.8	0.6	0.6	0.7	0.8	0.9	0.6	0.7	0.2	0.4	0.2	1.0	23
NYLON	1.2	-0.1	0.4	0.5	-1.0	0.4	0.4	1.5	1.4	0.8	0.6	-0.3	
	0.4	0.6	0.5	0.4	0.7	0.9	0.9	0.5	0.3	0.3	0.2	0.7	23
OCTOBER	0.6	0.4	0.0	-0.1	-0.1	-0.4	0.7	1.0	1.3	0.6	0.7	0.3	
	0.7	0.3	0.5	0.5	0.6	0.7	0.9	0.6	0.4	0.3	0.2	0.9	23
OLD AGE	-0.4	-0.1	-0.9	-1.1	-1.1	-1.8	-0.3	1.2	1.6	0.8	0.8	0.8	
	0.6	0.4	0.6	0.4	0.8	1.1	1.0	0.5	0.3	0.2	0.3	1.1	23
OLD PEOPLE	0.7	-0.3	-1.0	-0.0	-1.3	-2.0	0.5	1.4	1.6	1.0	0.6	0.0	
	0.5	0.6	0.6	0.4	0.9	1.0	1.1	0.5	0.3	0.2	0.2	0.8	22

ONE HUNDRED	0.8	0.5	0.2	0.1	-0.0	-0.1	0.2	1.1	1.3	0.6	0.7	0.2	
	0.4	0.3	0.3	0.4	0.4	0.6	0.7	0.4	0.4	0.2	0.2	0.8	21
ONE MILLION	1.3	1.3	0.3	0.5	1.3	0.1	-0.7	2.0	1.7	1.1	0.6	-0.2	
	0.6	0.5	0.5	0.6	0.6	0.7	1.0	0.7	0.4	0.3	0.2	1.0	23
ONE	0.3	-0.5	0.0	-0.4	-1.7	-0.3	0.5	1.0	1.3	0.6	0.7	0.4	
	0.7	0.5	0.3	0.6	0.7	0.7	1.0	0.4	0.3	0.2	0.2	1.0	23
ORPHAN	-0.0	-0.3	0.1	-0.7	-1.3	-0.1	-0.9	0.8	1.4	0.6	0.8	0.7	
	0.7	0.3	0.5	0.6	0.6	0.9	0.8	0.5	0.3	0.3	0.3	1.0	23
PAINT	1.3	0.3	0.2	0.5	-0.4	-0.1	0.6	1.5	1.4	0.8	0.6	-0.2	
	0.6	0.4	0.5	0.5	0.5	0.7	0.9	0.5	0.3	0.3	0.2	0.7	23
PAIN	-1.6	0.7	0.2	-2.3	0.3	-0.1	0.4	1.8	1.6	1.0	0.6	-0.1	
	0.5	0.4	0.5	0.4	0.7	0.9	0.9	0.6	0.3	0.3	0.3	1.2	23
PAPER	1.2	-0.2	0.1	0.4	-1.2	-0.2	0.9	1.4	1.3	0.8	0.6	-0.1	
	0.5	0.5	0.4	0.3	0.8	0.9	0.9	0.5	0.3	0.2	0.2	0.8	23
PARENTHOOD	1.5	1.0	0.4	0.7	0.9	0.2	-0.2	1.9	1.7	1.1	0.6	-0.1	
	0.5	0.4	0.6	0.3	0.6	0.7	1.1	0.6	0.2	0.3	0.2	0.7	23
PASSION	0.6	0.8	0.6	-0.2	0.5	0.6	-0.1	1.4	1.6	0.8	0.7	0.4	
	0.7	0.5	0.5	0.7	0.6	0.6	0.9	0.5	0.3	0.3	0.3	1.3	23
PAST, THE	0.6	0.5	0.0	-0.2	-0.0	-0.4	-0.0	0.9	1.4	0.5	0.8	0.9	
	0.3	0.3	0.4	0.2	0.4	0.6	0.7	0.3	0.3	0.1	0.3	0.9	23
PATIENT	-0.5	-0.3	-0.5	-1.2	-1.3	-1.1	-0.3	1.1	1.4	0.7	0.7	0.3	
	0.7	0.4	0.5	0.7	0.8	1.0	0.8	0.5	0.3	0.3	0.3	1.1	23
PATRIOT	1.3	1.2	0.8	0.5	1.1	0.8	-0.2	2.1	1.8	1.3	0.5	-0.5	
	0.9	0.5	0.6	0.8	0.7	0.7	1.2	0.9	0.4	0.5	0.3	1.0	23
PEACE	2.1	0.9	0.1	1.3	0.6	-0.3	0.5	2.4	1.8	1.3	0.5	-0.3	
	0.5	0.5	0.6	0.4	0.6	0.7	0.8	0.6	0.3	0.3	0.2	0.6	23
PEASANTS	1.1	0.9	0.2	0.3	0.6	-0.0	0.2	1.7	1.6	1.0	0.6	-0.2	
	0.8	0.3	0.7	0.7	0.4	0.9	0.8	0.6	0.3	0.3	0.2	0.9	22
PEN	1.2	-0.3	0.3	0.4	-1.3	0.0	0.6	1.4	1.5	0.8	0.7	0.1	
	0.5	0.5	0.4	0.4	0.7	0.5	0.9	0.5	0.3	0.3	0.2	0.9	23
PENCIL	1.1	-0.3	0.1	0.4	-1.3	-0.3	1.0	1.4	1.4	0.8	0.6	0.1	
	0.5	0.5	0.4	0.4	0.6	0.7	0.9	0.5	0.4	0.2	0.3	1.0	23
PEOPLE, MOST	0.6	0.5	0.4	-0.1	-0.0	0.2	-0.0	1.0	1.3	0.6	0.7	0.5	
	0.5	0.4	0.4	0.4	0.6	0.5	1.0	0.6	0.3	0.3	0.3	1.0	23
PERFUME	1.3	-0.1	0.5	0.5	-1.0	0.4	0.3	1.6	1.6	0.9	0.7	0.2	
	0.7	0.5	0.5	0.6	0.7	1.0	0.8	0.6	0.3	0.3	0.3	0.8	23
PERSON	1.1	0.6	0.6	0.3	0.2	0.5	0.7	1.4	1.3	0.8	0.5	-0.5	
	0.4	0.3	0.6	0.3	0.5	0.6	1.1	0.6	0.3	0.3	0.3	1.0	23
PERSPIRATION	-0.4	0.0	0.4	-1.1	-0.8	0.2	0.4	0.9	1.4	0.6	0.8	0.9	
	0.7	0.3	0.3	0.6	0.4	0.7	1.0	0.4	0.3	0.2	0.2	0.8	23

PHILOSOPHY	1.1	1.0	-0.2	0.4	0.7	-0.6	-0.5	1.7	1.5	1.0	0.6	-0.2
	0.6	0.3	0.7	0.4	0.4	0.8	1.0	0.5	0.3	0.3	0.3	0.7	23
PICTURE	1.4	0.2	-0.0	0.6	-0.5	-0.4	0.7	1.5	1.4	0.8	0.5	-0.3
	0.3	0.4	0.5	0.3	0.5	0.7	0.9	0.4	0.3	0.2	0.2	0.7	23
PIG	-0.2	0.6	-0.2	-0.9	0.2	-0.8	0.2	1.2	1.6	0.8	0.7	0.5
	0.8	0.5	0.6	0.8	0.8	1.0	1.1	0.5	0.3	0.3	0.2	0.8	23
PILLOW	1.5	-0.3	-0.1	0.7	-1.2	-0.6	0.9	1.7	1.5	1.0	0.5	-0.5
	0.3	0.5	0.5	0.3	0.7	0.8	1.0	0.4	0.3	0.3	0.2	0.6	23
PLACE	1.0	0.4	-0.2	0.2	-0.2	-0.8	0.2	1.1	1.1	0.6	0.5	-0.4
	0.4	0.3	0.3	0.3	0.5	0.4	0.7	0.4	0.3	0.2	0.2	0.6	23
PLANK	0.5	0.8	-0.6	-0.3	0.4	-1.4	0.2	1.3	1.3	0.7	0.6	-0.1
	0.5	0.5	0.5	0.4	0.8	0.7	1.1	0.5	0.3	0.2	0.2	0.8	23
PLAYING CARDS	-0.0	0.3	0.3	-0.8	-0.8	0.0	-0.1	1.0	1.4	0.6	0.8	0.9
	0.9	0.3	0.5	1.0	0.6	0.7	0.8	0.5	0.3	0.2	0.3	0.8	23
PLAYING TENNIS	1.6	0.5	1.0	0.8	-0.0	1.1	0.1	2.1	1.6	1.2	0.5	-0.6
	0.4	0.5	0.8	0.3	0.6	0.8	1.1	0.7	0.4	0.4	0.3	0.9	23
PLAY	1.7	0.6	1.1	0.9	0.2	1.3	0.8	2.2	1.7	1.3	0.4	-0.8
	0.5	0.5	0.7	0.4	0.7	0.6	1.0	0.8	0.4	0.4	0.2	0.8	22
PLEASURE	1.8	0.6	0.9	1.0	0.1	1.1	0.8	2.2	1.7	1.3	0.5	-0.6
	0.4	0.5	0.5	0.4	0.7	0.7	0.9	0.6	0.3	0.3	0.2	0.8	23
POETRY	1.4	0.5	0.1	0.6	-0.0	-0.3	0.4	1.6	1.6	0.9	0.6	0.1
	0.6	0.5	0.6	0.5	0.7	0.8	1.2	0.6	0.3	0.3	0.3	0.8	23
POINT, A	0.4	-0.6	-0.1	-0.3	-1.8	-0.4	0.1	1.0	1.3	0.6	0.7	0.5
	0.5	0.5	0.5	0.4	0.8	0.9	0.9	0.5	0.4	0.3	0.3	1.0	23
POISON	-1.8	0.6	0.2	-2.5	0.1	-0.1	-1.1	2.0	1.8	1.2	0.7	0.2
	0.5	0.5	0.5	0.5	0.7	0.8	1.1	0.5	0.3	0.3	0.2	1.0	23
POLICEMAN	0.5	0.9	0.4	-0.3	0.7	0.2	0.4	1.5	1.6	0.9	0.7	0.5
	0.9	0.3	0.7	0.7	0.6	0.9	0.9	0.6	0.3	0.3	0.3	1.0	23
POLITICS	0.3	1.0	0.4	-0.5	0.8	0.1	0.0	1.4	1.5	0.9	0.6	0.1
	0.8	0.4	0.7	0.6	0.7	0.8	0.9	0.6	0.3	0.3	0.3	1.1	23
POOR PEOPLE	-0.1	-0.2	-0.1	-0.8	-1.2	-0.5	-0.1	0.9	1.4	0.6	0.8	0.7
	0.7	0.4	0.4	0.6	0.8	0.8	1.3	0.3	0.2	0.2	0.2	0.8	23
POT	0.9	0.3	-0.4	0.1	-0.4	-1.0	0.5	1.2	1.3	0.6	0.6	-0.0
	0.4	0.5	0.4	0.3	0.7	0.5	0.9	0.4	0.3	0.2	0.2	0.8	23
POWER	0.8	1.3	0.5	0.0	1.2	0.4	0.1	1.8	1.7	1.1	0.6	-0.1
	0.8	0.4	0.7	0.6	0.4	0.8	0.9	0.6	0.3	0.3	0.2	0.9	23
PRAYER	1.4	0.5	-0.1	0.6	0.1	-0.5	0.5	1.7	1.6	1.0	0.6	0.0
	0.9	0.6	0.6	0.7	1.0	0.5	1.1	0.9	0.4	0.5	0.3	0.9	23
PREGNANCY	0.8	0.6	0.2	0.0	0.1	-0.2	-0.4	1.2	1.5	0.8	0.7	0.5
	0.5	0.4	0.4	0.5	0.6	0.7	1.0	0.5	0.3	0.3	0.2	0.9	22

```
PRESENT, THE      0.9   0.5   0.8   0.1   0.0   0.8   0.5   1.4   1.4   0.8   0.6  -0.1
                  0.4   0.3   0.5   0.3   0.4   0.6   0.8   0.5   0.4   0.3   0.3   0.9   23

PRIDE            -0.1   0.7   0.2  -0.8   0.2  -0.0  -0.3   1.4   1.6   0.8   0.8   0.9
                  1.1   0.7   0.4   1.0   1.1   0.6   0.8   0.6   0.4   0.4   0.3   1.0   23

PRISON           -1.6   0.8  -0.8  -2.3   0.4  -1.7  -1.5   2.1   1.8   1.2   0.6   0.1
                  0.5   0.5   0.4   0.4   0.7   0.7   1.3   0.5   0.3   0.3   0.2   0.9   23

PRIVACY           0.9   0.2   0.0   0.1  -0.5  -0.2  -0.1   1.2   1.4   0.7   0.8   0.6
                  0.7   0.4   0.7   0.6   0.6   0.9   0.9   0.7   0.3   0.3   0.3   1.1   20

PROBLEM          -0.3   0.6   0.1  -1.0   0.1  -0.3   0.1   1.1   1.4   0.7   0.7   0.5
                  0.8   0.4   0.5   0.7   0.6   0.6   1.0   0.5   0.2   0.2   0.2   0.8   23

PROFESSOR         1.2   0.7   0.2   0.5   0.4   0.1   0.1   1.7   1.7   1.0   0.6   0.1
                  0.7   0.5   0.8   0.6   0.7   1.1   1.2   0.8   0.3   0.4   0.2   0.8   23

PROGRESS          1.8   1.1   0.6   0.9   1.0   0.5   0.6   2.3   1.8   1.3   0.4  -0.7
                  0.5   0.5   0.7   0.3   0.6   1.0   0.9   0.6   0.2   0.3   0.2   0.5   23

PROPHET           0.9   0.7   0.2   0.2   0.3  -0.1  -0.5   1.5   1.5   0.9   0.5  -0.2
                  1.0   0.6   0.7   0.8   1.0   0.8   1.2   0.9   0.4   0.5   0.2   0.9   21

PROSTITUTE       -0.8  -0.0   0.4  -1.5  -0.9   0.4  -1.2   1.1   1.6   0.6   1.0   1.5
                  0.7   0.4   0.4   0.6   0.7   0.8   0.9   0.5   0.3   0.2   0.3   1.0   15

PSYCHOLOGY        1.1   0.7   0.1   0.3   0.3  -0.2  -0.4   1.5   1.4   0.9   0.5  -0.4
                  0.7   0.4   0.6   0.5   0.4   0.7   0.9   0.6   0.3   0.3   0.3   0.7   23

PUBLICITY         0.8   0.7   0.7   0.0   0.4   0.7  -0.2   1.5   1.5   0.9   0.6  -0.1
                  0.7   0.5   0.5   0.5   0.5   0.6   1.0   0.6   0.3   0.3   0.3   1.0   23

PUNISHMENT       -1.0   0.6  -0.0  -1.7   0.1  -0.5  -0.2   1.3   1.5   0.8   0.7   0.5
                  0.6   0.4   0.3   0.5   0.6   0.5   0.8   0.5   0.2   0.3   0.2   0.9   23

PURPOSE           1.1   0.7   0.3   0.4   0.4   0.1   0.1   1.5   1.3   0.9   0.5  -0.6
                  0.5   0.4   0.5   0.4   0.6   0.5   0.9   0.6   0.3   0.4   0.2   0.7   23

PYRAMID, A        0.9   1.4  -0.9   0.1   1.5  -1.9  -0.5   2.0   1.5   1.1   0.4  -0.8
                  0.5   0.6   0.5   0.4   0.9   0.7   1.2   0.7   0.4   0.4   0.3   0.8   23

QUESTIONTHINGS    0.2   0.4   0.0  -0.6  -0.2  -0.4  -0.6   0.9   1.4   0.6   0.8   0.7
                  0.7   0.4   0.4   0.6   0.7   0.6   1.3   0.4   0.4   0.2   0.3   1.0   20

QUESTION          0.6   0.4   0.3  -0.1  -0.2   0.0   0.3   1.0   1.2   0.6   0.6   0.1
                  0.5   0.3   0.4   0.4   0.4   0.4   0.8   0.5   0.3   0.2   0.2   0.7   23

RABBIT            1.5  -0.9   1.2   0.7  -2.3   1.6   0.6   2.2   1.7   1.3   0.5  -0.7
                  0.4   0.5   0.6   0.4   0.6   0.6   0.8   0.9   0.6   0.3   0.2   0.8   23

RACE CONFLICT    -1.6   0.9   0.4  -2.2   0.7   0.1  -0.4   2.0   1.8   1.2   0.6  -0.1
                  0.7   0.5   0.8   0.4   0.7   1.1   0.8   0.8   0.3   0.4   0.3   1.2   21

RADIOS,POCKET     1.5  -0.5   0.7   0.8  -1.6   0.7   1.0   1.9   1.7   1.1   0.6  -0.3
                  0.6   0.5   0.5   0.5   0.7   0.6   0.8   0.5   0.3   0.3   0.2   0.8   22

RAILROADS         1.1   1.3   0.3   0.3   1.3  -0.0   0.6   1.9   1.6   1.2   0.5  -0.6
                  0.5   0.5   0.7   0.4   0.6   0.9   0.7   0.6   0.3   0.3   0.2   0.8   23
```

RAIN	0.7 0.8	0.5 0.4	0.6 0.4	-0.1 0.6	-0.0 0.5	0.5 0.8	0.9 0.7	1.3 0.6	1.5 0.3	0.8 0.3	0.7 0.2	0.3 0.8	23
REALISM	0.9 0.7	0.7 0.4	0.3 0.4	0.1 0.6	0.3 0.4	0.1 0.4	-0.7 1.3	1.3 0.7	1.5 0.3	0.8 0.4	0.7 0.3	0.3 1.0	23
REALITY	0.9 0.6	0.8 0.4	0.4 0.5	0.2 0.5	0.5 0.6	0.2 0.6	0.2 0.9	1.5 0.6	1.4 0.4	0.8 0.3	0.6 0.2	-0.2 0.7	23
RED RACE	0.5 0.4	0.7 0.3	0.7 0.6	-0.3 0.5	0.3 0.5	0.7 0.6	-0.7 1.2	1.2 0.5	1.4 0.3	0.8 0.3	0.7 0.2	0.3 0.9	22
RED	0.9 0.5	0.6 0.4	0.5 0.5	0.1 0.4	0.1 0.5	0.4 0.6	0.7 0.9	1.4 0.4	1.4 0.3	0.8 0.2	0.6 0.2	-0.1 0.5	23
REFUGEE	0.0 0.6	0.2 0.3	0.4 0.5	-0.7 0.5	-0.5 0.5	0.2 0.9	-0.7 0.9	0.8 0.5	1.3 0.3	0.5 0.2	0.8 0.3	0.6 1.2	23
REINCARNATION	0.6 0.5	0.4 0.3	0.1 0.3	-0.1 0.5	-0.2 0.5	-0.3 0.5	-2.1 1.4	0.9 0.4	1.3 0.3	0.5 0.2	0.8 0.3	0.7 0.9	18
RELATIVES	1.2 0.5	0.5 0.4	0.3 0.5	0.4 0.4	-0.0 0.5	0.0 0.5	1.1 0.6	1.4 0.6	1.4 0.3	0.8 0.3	0.6 0.2	-0.2 0.7	23
RELIGION	0.8 1.0	0.9 0.4	-0.2 0.7	0.1 0.8	0.6 0.5	-0.7 0.8	0.1 0.9	1.6 0.7	1.7 0.3	0.9 0.4	0.7 0.4	0.5 1.5	23
RESPECT	1.7 0.6	0.9 0.5	0.1 0.6	0.9 0.4	0.7 0.6	-0.3 0.6	0.8 0.9	2.1 0.7	1.7 0.3	1.1 0.4	0.5 0.2	-0.4 0.7	23
RESTAURANT	1.4 0.3	0.4 0.3	0.4 0.5	0.6 0.3	-0.1 0.5	0.1 0.6	0.5 1.1	1.6 0.4	1.4 0.3	0.9 0.2	0.5 0.3	-0.5 0.8	23
RESURRECTION	0.9 0.8	0.7 0.5	0.2 0.6	0.1 0.7	0.4 0.7	-0.2 0.7	-1.4 1.0	1.4 0.8	1.5 0.4	0.9 0.4	0.6 0.3	-0.0 1.2	20
REVOLUTION	-0.2 0.8	1.3 0.5	0.8 0.8	-1.0 0.7	1.3 0.7	0.8 1.0	-0.7 1.0	1.8 0.6	1.7 0.3	1.1 0.3	0.6 0.2	0.1 1.0	23
REWARD	1.6 0.7	0.7 0.4	0.4 0.4	0.8 0.6	0.4 0.6	0.3 0.6	-0.1 0.8	1.9 0.6	1.6 0.3	1.0 0.3	0.6 0.2	-0.2 0.8	23
RICE	1.4 0.5	-0.4 0.4	-0.0 0.3	0.6 0.4	-1.5 0.7	-0.5 0.6	0.9 0.7	1.6 0.4	1.5 0.3	0.8 0.2	0.6 0.3	0.1 0.9	23
RICH PEOPLE	0.2 0.7	0.6 0.5	0.0 0.3	-0.5 0.6	0.1 0.8	-0.4 0.5	-0.1 1.1	1.0 0.5	1.5 0.3	0.6 0.2	0.9 0.2	1.3 0.9	23
RIGHT HAND	1.5 0.4	0.8 0.5	0.9 0.7	0.7 0.2	0.5 0.7	1.1 0.8	1.2 0.9	2.1 0.6	1.6 0.3	1.2 0.3	0.4 0.3	-1.0 0.6	23
RIVER	1.3 0.4	1.0 0.4	0.6 0.6	0.5 0.3	0.8 0.6	0.6 0.8	0.7 0.9	1.9 0.4	1.7 0.3	1.2 0.3	0.5 0.2	-0.5 0.6	23
ROADS	1.0 0.6	0.8 0.4	0.2 0.5	0.2 0.4	0.5 0.6	-0.2 0.6	0.9 0.8	1.4 0.6	1.5 0.3	0.8 0.3	0.6 0.3	0.2 1.1	23
ROCK	0.3 0.4	1.4 0.5	-1.0 0.5	-0.5 0.5	1.4 0.7	-2.1 0.9	0.2 1.1	1.8 0.6	1.5 0.3	1.0 0.3	0.5 0.2	-0.3 0.8	23

```
ROMANCE          1.5  0.5  0.5  0.7  0.0  0.4 -0.1  1.9  1.7  1.1  0.6 -0.2
                 0.7  0.7  0.7  0.6  0.9  0.8  1.0  0.8  0.4  0.5  0.3  0.9   22

ROOF             1.1  1.0 -0.5  0.4  0.8 -1.2  0.5  1.7  1.4  0.9  0.5 -0.5
                 0.4  0.5  0.5  0.4  0.6  0.6  0.8  0.6  0.3  0.3  0.2  0.8   23

ROOM             1.4  0.5 -0.2  0.6 -0.0 -0.8  0.8  1.6  1.4  0.8  0.5 -0.4
                 0.3  0.4  0.4  0.3  0.6  0.6  0.8  0.4  0.3  0.2  0.2  0.6   23

ROOT             0.7  0.5 -0.1 -0.1 -0.0 -0.6  0.2  1.1  1.4  0.7  0.6  0.2
                 0.5  0.4  0.5  0.3  0.6  0.5  0.8  0.5  0.3  0.3  0.2  0.8   23

ROPE             0.5  0.7 -0.2 -0.2  0.3 -0.8  0.3  1.1  1.3  0.7  0.6 -0.1
                 0.5  0.5  0.4  0.4  0.7  0.6  0.7  0.4  0.3  0.2  0.2  0.9   23

ROSE             1.8 -0.5  0.5  1.0 -1.6  0.5  1.0  2.1  1.7  1.1  0.5 -0.3
                 0.4  0.5  0.7  0.3  0.7  1.0  0.8  0.5  0.3  0.3  0.2  0.8   23

RUG              1.3  0.5 -0.3  0.5 -0.0 -0.9  0.6  1.6  1.4  0.9  0.5 -0.4
                 0.4  0.3  0.5  0.3  0.6  0.7  0.6  0.4  0.4  0.2  0.3  0.9   23

RURAL HOUSING    1.2  0.6  0.1  0.4  0.2 -0.2 -0.1  1.6  1.6  0.9  0.6  0.1
                 0.6  0.7  0.5  0.6  1.1  0.8  1.0  0.6  0.4  0.3  0.2  0.9   23

SADNESS         -1.3  0.3 -0.4 -2.0 -0.3 -1.1 -0.8  1.6  1.6  0.9  0.8  0.6
                 0.6  0.4  0.5  0.5  0.8  0.9  0.7  0.6  0.3  0.3  0.3  1.0   23

SALARY           1.8  0.6  0.2  1.0  0.2 -0.1  0.5  1.9  1.5  1.0  0.5 -0.4
                 0.4  0.3  0.4  0.3  0.5  0.5  0.9  0.5  0.3  0.2  0.3  0.8   23

SALT             0.8 -0.0 -0.2  0.1 -0.9 -0.7  0.9  1.0  1.3  0.6  0.6  0.1
                 0.5  0.4  0.3  0.3  0.6  0.5  0.8  0.4  0.4  0.2  0.3  1.1   23

SATURDAY         1.4  0.3  0.6  0.6 -0.4  0.5  1.0  1.6  1.4  0.9  0.5 -0.4
                 0.6  0.3  0.5  0.6  0.4  0.8  0.8  0.7  0.4  0.4  0.2  0.8   23

SAVING MONEY     1.4  0.6 -0.0  0.7  0.2 -0.4  0.5  1.7  1.6  1.0  0.7  0.1
                 0.6  0.4  0.6  0.4  0.5  0.8  0.7  0.6  0.3  0.3  0.3  1.0   23

SCENE            1.3  0.6  0.4  0.5  0.2  0.2  0.2  1.6  1.4  0.9  0.5 -0.2
                 0.7  0.4  0.4  0.5  0.6  0.5  1.1  0.7  0.3  0.4  0.2  0.8   22

SCHOOL           1.3  1.1  0.3  0.5  0.9 -0.0  1.2  2.0  1.7  1.1  0.6 -0.2
                 1.0  0.4  0.8  0.8  0.6  1.0  1.0  0.8  0.3  0.4  0.3  1.2   23

SCIENTIST        1.4  1.0  0.3  0.6  0.9  0.2 -0.1  2.0  1.7  1.2  0.5 -0.3
                 0.4  0.5  0.8  0.3  0.5  1.1  1.1  0.6  0.3  0.3  0.3  0.8   23

SEA              1.3  1.6  0.6  0.5  1.8  0.5  0.7  2.3  1.9  1.4  0.5 -0.4
                 0.6  0.6  0.6  0.5  0.6  0.7  0.7  0.6  0.3  0.3  0.2  0.6   23

SECOND, A        0.7 -0.7  0.8 -0.1 -2.0  0.9  0.6  1.4  1.4  0.8  0.6 -0.0
                 0.4  0.4  0.4  0.3  0.7  0.6  0.7  0.5  0.3  0.2  0.3  1.1   23

SEED             1.3 -0.3  0.4  0.5 -1.3  0.2  0.4  1.6  1.5  0.9  0.6 -0.1
                 0.4  0.6  0.5  0.3  0.7  0.6  1.0  0.5  0.4  0.3  0.2  0.7   23

SENTENCE         0.9  0.3  0.1  0.1 -0.4 -0.2  0.6  1.1  1.2  0.6  0.6 -0.2
                 0.4  0.3  0.4  0.4  0.4  0.5  1.0  0.5  0.3  0.2  0.2  0.7   23
```

SEPTEMBER	0.7	0.3	0.1	-0.1	-0.3	-0.2	0.8	1.0	1.4	0.6	0.8	0.6	
	0.6	0.3	0.5	0.4	0.5	0.7	0.9	0.4	0.4	0.2	0.3	1.1	23
SERVANT	0.9	0.3	0.4	0.1	-0.3	0.2	-0.0	1.2	1.4	0.7	0.6	0.1	
	0.5	0.4	0.5	0.5	0.6	0.6	0.9	0.6	0.3	0.3	0.2	0.7	23
SEX	1.4	0.7	0.9	0.6	0.4	1.0	0.3	1.9	1.6	1.1	0.6	-0.3	
	0.6	0.5	0.6	0.5	0.7	0.7	0.9	0.8	0.3	0.4	0.3	1.2	20
SHAME	-1.1	0.3	-0.1	-1.8	-0.4	-0.6	-0.5	1.3	1.5	0.7	0.8	0.7	
	0.6	0.4	0.3	0.5	0.7	0.6	0.8	0.6	0.3	0.3	0.3	1.1	23
SHIP	1.4	1.5	0.2	0.6	1.6	-0.1	0.6	2.2	1.7	1.3	0.4	-0.8	
	0.4	0.5	0.7	0.3	0.7	0.9	0.9	0.5	0.3	0.3	0.2	0.6	23
SHOES	1.3	0.1	0.1	0.5	-0.7	-0.2	0.9	1.4	1.5	0.8	0.7	0.2	
	0.5	0.4	0.4	0.3	0.5	0.6	0.6	0.5	0.3	0.2	0.3	0.7	23
SHOP	1.0	0.5	0.2	0.2	-0.1	-0.2	0.6	1.3	1.3	0.7	0.5	-0.3	
	0.4	0.3	0.5	0.3	0.5	0.7	1.0	0.5	0.2	0.2	0.2	0.7	23
SICKNESS	-1.7	0.4	-0.3	-2.3	-0.2	-0.8	-0.5	2.0	1.8	1.0	0.7	0.4	
	0.9	0.4	0.6	0.7	0.8	1.0	0.7	0.6	0.3	0.3	0.3	0.9	22
SIGHT	1.7	0.6	0.6	0.9	0.2	0.7	0.9	2.1	1.7	1.2	0.5	-0.4	
	0.5	0.5	0.8	0.4	0.6	1.0	1.0	0.6	0.2	0.4	0.3	0.9	23
SIGHT, SENSE OF	1.7	0.6	1.0	0.9	0.2	1.2	0.8	2.3	1.8	1.3	0.5	-0.8	
	0.8	0.6	0.7	0.7	0.8	0.9	1.0	0.8	0.4	0.4	0.2	0.7	23
SILENCE	0.9	0.2	-0.6	0.1	-0.5	-1.3	0.1	1.3	1.5	0.8	0.7	0.5	
	0.6	0.4	0.6	0.5	0.6	0.9	1.0	0.5	0.3	0.2	0.2	0.8	23
SIN	-1.3	0.4	-0.1	-2.0	-0.2	-0.5	-0.4	1.6	1.7	0.9	0.8	0.7	
	0.8	0.4	0.4	0.6	0.8	0.7	0.9	0.6	0.3	0.3	0.3	1.1	22
SINGING	1.6	0.3	0.7	0.8	-0.3	0.7	0.7	1.9	1.5	1.0	0.5	-0.4	
	0.4	0.4	0.5	0.4	0.4	0.7	1.0	0.5	0.2	0.3	0.3	0.8	22
SISTERS	1.4	0.0	0.8	0.6	-0.8	0.8	0.7	1.7	1.5	0.9	0.6	-0.0	
	0.5	0.5	0.5	0.4	0.6	0.6	1.0	0.5	0.3	0.3	0.3	0.7	23
SKIN	1.2	0.3	0.2	0.4	-0.7	-0.1	0.8	1.4	1.4	0.8	0.6	-0.2	
	0.4	0.5	0.5	0.3	0.6	0.8	0.8	0.5	0.3	0.2	0.2	0.5	23
SLEEP	1.6	0.3	-0.2	0.8	-0.3	-0.7	0.9	1.8	1.6	1.0	0.6	-0.0	
	0.5	0.5	0.6	0.5	0.7	0.9	0.9	0.5	0.3	0.3	0.3	0.5	23
SMELL, SENSE OF	1.2	0.5	0.7	0.4	-0.1	0.7	0.2	1.6	1.6	1.0	0.6	-0.1	
	0.6	0.5	0.6	0.4	0.6	0.8	1.0	0.8	0.3	0.4	0.3	1.1	22
SMOKE	-1.0	0.1	0.0	-1.7	-0.6	-0.3	0.4	1.1	1.5	0.7	0.8	0.8	
	0.4	0.4	0.3	0.4	0.6	0.7	1.0	0.4	0.3	0.2	0.2	1.0	23
SNAKE	-1.4	0.6	0.7	-2.1	0.1	0.7	-0.4	1.8	1.8	1.1	0.7	0.3	
	0.5	0.4	0.6	0.5	0.7	0.7	1.2	0.4	0.2	0.2	0.2	0.8	23
SNOW	1.0	0.2	0.1	0.2	-0.5	-0.1	0.3	1.3	1.5	0.8	0.8	0.7	
	0.5	0.7	0.4	0.6	0.9	0.8	1.1	0.4	0.3	0.3	0.3	1.0	23

SOCIALISM	0.4	0.7	0.1	-0.4	0.3	-0.2	-0.6	1.2	1.4	0.7	0.7	0.4	
	0.8	0.4	0.7	0.6	0.5	0.8	1.3	0.6	0.3	0.3	0.2	1.1	23
SODA POP	1.3	0.0	0.6	0.5	-0.8	0.5	0.7	1.6	1.5	0.9	0.5	-0.4	
	0.6	0.5	0.6	0.6	0.7	1.0	0.8	0.7	0.4	0.3	0.2	1.0	21
SOIL, THE	1.1	1.0	-0.3	0.3	0.7	-1.0	0.7	1.6	1.5	0.9	0.6	-0.2	
	0.5	0.7	0.5	0.3	0.8	0.7	1.0	0.7	0.4	0.4	0.3	0.9	22
SOLDIER	0.8	1.1	0.8	0.1	1.0	0.8	0.3	1.9	1.7	1.1	0.6	-0.2	
	0.8	0.4	0.9	0.6	0.7	1.1	0.9	0.7	0.3	0.4	0.3	1.1	23
SOLITUDE	-0.6	0.3	-0.7	-1.3	-0.4	-1.5	-0.5	1.2	1.5	0.7	0.8	1.0	
	0.7	0.4	0.6	0.6	0.6	0.9	1.0	0.7	0.4	0.4	0.3	1.1	23
SON	1.6	0.6	1.0	0.8	0.1	1.3	0.4	2.1	1.7	1.2	0.5	-0.5	
	0.7	0.5	0.6	0.6	0.8	0.8	0.9	0.7	0.3	0.4	0.2	0.7	22
SONG	1.7	0.4	0.8	0.9	-0.2	0.9	0.8	2.0	1.7	1.1	0.5	-0.4	
	0.4	0.5	0.6	0.2	0.6	0.7	0.9	0.5	0.3	0.3	0.2	0.8	23
SORCERY	-0.0	0.4	0.2	-0.7	-0.2	-0.2	-1.2	1.1	1.4	0.6	0.8	0.7	
	0.8	0.4	0.6	0.8	0.8	0.9	1.0	0.5	0.3	0.2	0.3	1.0	23
SOUL	1.0	0.5	0.4	0.3	0.1	0.3	-0.8	1.4	1.6	0.9	0.7	0.5	
	0.6	0.6	0.5	0.5	0.8	0.9	1.1	0.6	0.3	0.4	0.2	0.9	22
SOUND	0.9	0.5	0.8	0.2	-0.1	0.7	0.7	1.4	1.4	0.8	0.6	-0.1	
	0.6	0.4	0.5	0.4	0.5	0.5	0.9	0.6	0.3	0.3	0.2	0.8	21
SOUTH	1.0	0.5	0.1	0.2	-0.1	-0.3	0.1	1.2	1.3	0.7	0.6	-0.2	
	0.5	0.4	0.5	0.5	0.5	0.6	1.0	0.6	0.4	0.3	0.3	0.7	23
SOUTH AMERICA	0.9	1.0	0.3	0.1	0.8	0.0	-0.1	1.6	1.5	0.9	0.6	-0.2	
	0.5	0.3	0.7	0.4	0.4	0.8	0.7	0.5	0.3	0.3	0.2	0.7	23
SPACE TRAVEL	1.5	1.3	1.0	0.7	1.3	1.1	-0.3	2.3	1.8	1.4	0.4	-0.8	
	0.4	0.5	0.7	0.3	0.7	0.8	1.3	0.7	0.3	0.4	0.3	0.7	23
SPHERE, A	0.7	0.4	-0.0	-0.1	-0.1	-0.5	-0.0	1.0	1.3	0.6	0.7	0.3	
	0.4	0.4	0.4	0.4	0.6	0.6	0.8	0.4	0.3	0.2	0.2	0.9	22
SPICE	0.7	0.1	0.2	-0.0	-0.6	-0.0	0.1	1.0	1.4	0.6	0.8	0.6	
	0.6	0.3	0.4	0.6	0.5	0.7	1.0	0.6	0.4	0.3	0.2	0.9	23
SPIT	-1.0	-0.5	0.2	-1.7	-1.7	-0.1	-0.3	1.3	1.5	0.7	0.7	0.4	
	0.6	0.3	0.4	0.5	0.7	1.0	1.0	0.5	0.4	0.3	0.3	0.9	23
SPRING	2.0	0.3	0.8	1.2	-0.4	0.9	1.0	2.3	1.7	1.2	0.5	-0.7	
	0.4	0.5	0.5	0.3	0.6	0.7	0.8	0.5	0.3	0.3	0.3	0.8	23
SQUARE, A	0.5	0.0	-0.3	-0.2	-0.8	-1.0	0.3	0.8	1.0	0.5	0.5	-0.3	
	0.4	0.2	0.3	0.4	0.4	0.5	0.9	0.3	0.4	0.2	0.3	0.9	23
STAR	1.5	0.8	-0.1	0.7	0.5	-0.7	0.5	1.8	1.7	1.1	0.6	0.1	
	0.4	0.5	0.7	0.3	0.8	0.8	0.7	0.5	0.3	0.3	0.2	0.7	23
STEEL	0.9	1.3	-0.4	0.2	1.3	-1.0	0.3	1.8	1.5	1.0	0.5	-0.5	
	0.5	0.5	0.5	0.3	0.6	0.7	1.0	0.6	0.3	0.3	0.2	0.5	23

STICK	-0.1	0.4	-0.1	-0.8	-0.2	-0.6	-0.0	0.8	1.4	0.6	0.8	0.8
	0.5	0.4	0.4	0.4	0.7	0.7	0.8	0.3	0.3	0.2	0.3	1.0	23
STOMACH	0.9	0.3	0.5	0.2	-0.4	0.4	0.8	1.2	1.3	0.7	0.6	-0.1
	0.5	0.4	0.4	0.4	0.5	0.5	0.9	0.5	0.3	0.3	0.2	0.7	23
STONE	0.1	0.9	-0.9	-0.6	0.5	-1.9	0.5	1.4	1.5	0.8	0.7	0.3
	0.4	0.7	0.5	0.3	1.1	0.6	1.0	0.7	0.3	0.3	0.3	0.9	23
STOREKEEPER	0.8	0.4	0.5	0.0	-0.3	0.3	0.5	1.2	1.4	0.7	0.7	0.2
	0.6	0.4	0.5	0.5	0.6	0.5	0.9	0.5	0.3	0.2	0.3	0.8	22
STORY	1.3	0.4	0.2	0.5	-0.1	-0.1	0.6	1.5	1.4	0.8	0.6	-0.2
	0.4	0.4	0.5	0.3	0.6	0.6	1.1	0.5	0.3	0.3	0.3	0.7	23
STOVE	1.0	0.6	0.0	0.2	0.0	-0.3	0.8	1.4	1.5	0.9	0.7	0.2
	0.6	0.5	0.6	0.4	0.7	0.7	0.7	0.6	0.3	0.3	0.2	0.9	21
STRANGER	0.3	0.3	0.2	-0.5	-0.3	-0.1	-1.9	0.7	1.2	0.4	0.7	0.6
	0.5	0.4	0.3	0.5	0.7	0.8	1.4	0.6	0.4	0.3	0.2	0.6	23
STREET	0.9	0.7	0.1	0.1	0.3	-0.3	0.9	1.3	1.4	0.8	0.6	0.0
	0.5	0.5	0.7	0.4	0.6	0.9	0.8	0.6	0.4	0.3	0.2	0.8	23
STREET CLEANER	0.4	0.3	-0.0	-0.3	-0.4	-0.4	-0.3	0.9	1.5	0.6	0.9	1.0
	0.7	0.4	0.5	0.5	0.5	0.7	1.1	0.4	0.3	0.2	0.3	0.7	23
STUDENT	1.4	0.6	1.0	0.7	0.2	1.2	1.0	1.9	1.6	1.1	0.5	-0.6
	0.6	0.4	0.7	0.4	0.5	0.9	1.1	0.8	0.3	0.4	0.3	0.9	23
STUFF	0.7	0.5	-0.2	-0.1	-0.0	-0.8	0.1	1.0	1.3	0.6	0.7	0.2
	0.5	0.4	0.3	0.5	0.7	0.4	0.7	0.4	0.4	0.2	0.3	0.8	20
SUBMARINE,NUCL.	0.6	1.5	0.8	-0.2	1.8	0.8	-1.0	2.1	1.9	1.3	0.6	-0.1
	0.8	0.5	0.8	0.6	0.6	1.0	0.8	0.6	0.3	0.3	0.2	0.7	22
SUCCESS	1.9	1.1	0.6	1.1	1.0	0.4	0.5	2.4	1.8	1.3	0.4	-0.7
	0.5	0.4	0.7	0.3	0.5	0.7	1.1	0.6	0.2	0.3	0.2	0.7	23
SUICIDE	-1.9	0.2	0.0	-2.5	-0.5	-0.3	-1.4	2.0	1.8	1.1	0.7	0.3
	0.4	0.5	0.5	0.3	0.9	1.0	1.0	0.4	0.3	0.2	0.2	0.8	23
SUMMER	1.5	0.5	0.7	0.7	0.0	0.6	1.1	2.0	1.6	1.1	0.5	-0.4
	0.9	0.5	0.6	0.8	0.6	0.8	0.7	0.8	0.4	0.4	0.3	0.7	23
SUN	1.9	1.8	0.3	1.1	2.2	-0.0	1.2	2.8	2.0	1.7	0.4	-1.0
	0.5	0.4	0.8	0.5	0.6	1.1	0.9	0.5	0.3	0.3	0.2	0.4	23
SUNDAY	1.6	0.2	0.3	0.8	-0.5	0.1	1.1	1.7	1.4	0.9	0.5	-0.3
	0.4	0.4	0.5	0.5	0.5	0.8	1.0	0.5	0.4	0.3	0.3	0.7	23
SURPRISE	0.9	0.6	0.7	0.1	0.2	0.6	-0.4	1.4	1.4	0.9	0.5	-0.4
	0.7	0.4	0.5	0.7	0.5	0.7	1.1	0.7	0.4	0.4	0.3	0.8	23
SWEATER	1.6	0.3	0.0	0.8	-0.3	-0.3	0.9	1.7	1.5	0.9	0.6	-0.3
	0.3	0.3	0.5	0.3	0.3	0.7	0.7	0.4	0.2	0.2	0.2	0.8	23
SYMPATHY	1.6	0.6	0.3	0.8	0.2	0.0	0.5	1.8	1.5	1.0	0.5	-0.3
	0.6	0.4	0.6	0.5	0.6	0.7	0.8	0.7	0.3	0.4	0.3	1.0	23

Word													n
TABLE	1.2	0.6	-0.7	0.4	0.1	-1.5	0.9	1.6	1.4	0.9	0.5	-0.6	
	0.4	0.4	0.5	0.2	0.6	0.6	0.9	0.5	0.3	0.2	0.2	0.7	23
TALK	1.1	0.4	0.5	0.3	-0.2	0.4	0.7	1.5	1.3	0.8	0.5	-0.5	
	0.5	0.3	0.6	0.5	0.4	0.6	0.9	0.4	0.3	0.2	0.3	0.7	23
TASTE, SENSE OF	1.5	0.5	0.8	0.7	-0.1	0.9	0.4	1.9	1.6	1.1	0.5	-0.5	
	0.6	0.5	0.5	0.5	0.7	0.8	0.8	0.7	0.3	0.3	0.2	0.8	23
TEA	1.1	-0.1	0.2	0.3	-0.9	-0.0	0.6	1.3	1.4	0.7	0.6	0.1	
	0.5	0.3	0.5	0.5	0.4	0.9	1.1	0.4	0.3	0.2	0.3	0.8	23
TEACHER	1.0	0.6	0.3	0.2	0.2	0.1	0.7	1.5	1.6	0.9	0.7	0.5	
	0.9	0.4	0.7	0.8	0.7	0.8	1.0	0.9	0.3	0.4	0.4	1.4	23
TELEPHONE	1.5	0.1	0.7	0.7	-0.7	0.7	0.9	1.8	1.5	1.0	0.5	-0.5	
	0.4	0.3	0.6	0.3	0.4	0.7	0.8	0.5	0.3	0.2	0.2	0.5	23
TELEVISION	1.4	0.6	0.6	0.6	0.2	0.5	0.6	1.8	1.6	1.0	0.6	-0.1	
	0.5	0.4	0.6	0.4	0.7	0.8	0.9	0.6	0.3	0.4	0.3	0.8	23
TEN	0.8	0.0	0.2	0.0	-0.8	-0.0	0.0	1.0	1.3	0.6	0.7	0.2	
	0.5	0.4	0.3	0.5	0.7	0.4	0.8	0.5	0.4	0.3	0.3	1.0	23
THIEF	-1.8	0.3	0.7	-2.4	-0.3	0.8	-0.8	2.1	1.8	1.2	0.6	0.1	
	0.3	0.5	0.6	0.5	0.9	0.8	1.1	0.4	0.3	0.2	0.2	1.1	23
THING	0.7	0.2	-0.0	-0.1	-0.5	-0.4	0.1	0.8	1.0	0.5	0.5	-0.3	
	0.4	0.3	0.3	0.3	0.4	0.5	0.9	0.4	0.3	0.2	0.2	0.8	23
THOUGHT	1.3	0.8	0.5	0.5	0.5	0.4	0.3	1.8	1.6	1.0	0.6	-0.1	
	0.6	0.6	0.7	0.4	0.8	0.8	0.9	0.8	0.3	0.5	0.3	0.9	23
THREAD	0.8	-0.4	0.1	0.0	-1.4	-0.2	0.4	1.1	1.2	0.6	0.6	-0.1	
	0.4	0.6	0.5	0.3	0.7	0.9	1.1	0.5	0.3	0.2	0.2	0.8	23
THREE	0.4	-0.4	0.0	-0.3	-1.5	-0.4	0.4	0.8	1.2	0.5	0.7	0.5	
	0.5	0.4	0.3	0.4	0.6	0.6	0.8	0.4	0.4	0.2	0.3	1.0	23
THUNDER	-0.7	1.3	0.8	-1.4	1.2	0.9	0.3	1.8	1.7	1.1	0.6	-0.2	
	0.4	0.5	0.7	0.4	0.7	0.8	0.8	0.7	0.3	0.3	0.2	0.7	23
THURSDAY	0.7	0.3	0.1	-0.0	-0.3	-0.3	0.6	1.0	1.2	0.6	0.7	0.2	
	0.7	0.3	0.5	0.6	0.6	0.6	1.0	0.6	0.4	0.3	0.3	1.0	23
TIME	0.9	0.7	0.4	0.1	0.3	0.2	0.4	1.4	1.5	0.8	0.6	0.2	
	0.5	0.3	0.6	0.3	0.4	0.7	0.7	0.5	0.3	0.3	0.2	0.6	23
TODAY	0.9	0.4	0.4	0.1	-0.3	0.3	0.1	1.1	1.4	0.7	0.7	0.6	
	0.5	0.2	0.4	0.4	0.3	0.6	0.8	0.5	0.3	0.2	0.3	0.9	23
TOLERANCE	0.9	0.5	0.0	0.2	0.2	-0.3	-0.4	1.2	1.5	0.7	0.8	0.8	
	0.6	0.2	0.3	0.6	0.4	0.5	0.9	0.5	0.2	0.2	0.2	0.9	19
TOMORROW	1.0	0.4	0.5	0.3	-0.1	0.4	-0.6	1.3	1.4	0.8	0.7	0.2	
	0.5	0.3	0.4	0.4	0.3	0.5	1.2	0.5	0.4	0.3	0.3	0.9	23
TONGUE	1.2	-0.1	0.8	0.4	-0.9	0.9	0.8	1.5	1.6	0.9	0.6	0.1	
	0.4	0.4	0.6	0.3	0.5	0.9	1.0	0.5	0.2	0.3	0.2	0.8	23

Concept													N
TOOTH	1.1	0.1	0.2	0.4	-0.6	-0.1	0.9	1.4	1.5	0.9	0.6	-0.2	
	0.6	0.5	0.6	0.5	0.7	0.7	0.9	0.6	0.3	0.3	0.2	0.8	23
TOUCH, SENSE OF	1.4	0.5	0.8	0.6	0.1	0.9	0.2	1.9	1.7	1.1	0.5	-0.4	
	0.7	0.5	0.5	0.6	0.6	0.6	0.7	0.7	0.3	0.3	0.3	0.9	23
TRADITION	0.9	0.7	-0.2	0.2	0.3	-0.7	0.3	1.3	1.4	0.7	0.7	0.3	
	0.5	0.3	0.5	0.4	0.5	0.6	0.7	0.5	0.3	0.3	0.3	1.0	23
TRAGEDY	-1.3	0.7	-0.1	-1.9	0.2	-0.6	-0.7	1.6	1.6	0.9	0.7	0.2	
	0.6	0.4	0.6	0.5	0.7	0.8	0.9	0.6	0.3	0.4	0.2	0.9	23
TRAIN	1.2	1.5	0.5	0.5	1.6	0.4	0.9	2.1	1.8	1.3	0.4	-0.8	
	0.5	0.5	0.8	0.4	0.6	1.0	0.9	0.7	0.3	0.4	0.2	0.5	23
TRAVEL	1.7	0.7	0.7	0.9	0.4	0.7	0.7	2.1	1.6	1.2	0.4	-0.7	
	0.6	0.4	0.6	0.5	0.5	0.6	1.0	0.7	0.3	0.4	0.2	0.7	23
TREE	1.5	1.2	-0.5	0.6	1.2	-1.3	0.8	2.1	1.6	1.2	0.5	-0.6	
	0.5	0.5	0.5	0.3	0.6	0.7	0.9	0.5	0.3	0.3	0.2	0.7	23
TRIANGLE, A	0.6	-0.0	-0.2	-0.2	-0.9	-0.7	0.3	0.8	1.1	0.4	0.6	-0.0	
	0.4	0.2	0.3	0.3	0.3	0.5	0.8	0.4	0.4	0.2	0.3	0.8	23
TRUST	1.6	0.9	0.1	0.8	0.7	-0.3	0.4	2.0	1.6	1.1	0.5	-0.7	
	0.5	0.5	0.6	0.4	0.6	0.5	0.7	0.6	0.3	0.3	0.2	0.6	23
TRUTH	1.6	1.0	0.1	0.8	0.8	-0.3	0.5	2.0	1.6	1.1	0.5	-0.5	
	0.6	0.5	0.6	0.5	0.6	0.6	1.0	0.6	0.2	0.3	0.2	0.8	23
TUESDAY	0.5	0.2	0.0	-0.2	-0.5	-0.3	0.8	0.8	1.1	0.5	0.6	0.0	
	0.6	0.3	0.4	0.5	0.5	0.5	1.0	0.3	0.3	0.2	0.3	0.9	23
TWENTY-EIGHT	0.5	0.1	0.1	-0.2	-0.7	-0.2	-0.1	0.6	1.1	0.4	0.7	0.4	
	0.4	0.3	0.2	0.4	0.4	0.5	0.6	0.4	0.4	0.2	0.3	1.1	23
TWENTY-NINE	0.3	0.0	0.0	-0.4	-0.8	-0.4	-0.2	0.6	1.1	0.4	0.7	0.5	
	0.5	0.2	0.3	0.4	0.4	0.5	0.8	0.3	0.4	0.2	0.3	1.1	23
TWO	0.5	-0.4	0.1	-0.2	-1.5	-0.2	0.5	1.0	1.3	0.6	0.7	0.4	
	0.6	0.4	0.3	0.4	0.6	0.7	0.6	0.8	0.3	0.3	0.2	1.0	23
UNCLE	1.4	0.7	0.3	0.6	0.4	0.1	1.0	1.7	1.5	1.0	0.5	-0.4	
	0.5	0.3	0.6	0.3	0.4	0.6	0.7	0.6	0.3	0.3	0.2	0.7	23
UNITED NATIONS	1.2	1.2	0.4	0.4	1.1	0.3	-0.3	1.9	1.8	1.1	0.7	0.3	
	0.6	0.5	0.6	0.4	0.8	0.8	1.0	0.6	0.3	0.4	0.3	1.3	22
UNIVERSE, THE	1.2	1.5	0.0	0.5	1.7	-0.4	-0.9	2.1	1.9	1.3	0.6	-0.1	
	0.6	0.7	0.7	0.4	0.8	1.1	1.2	0.8	0.3	0.5	0.2	1.0	22
UNIVERSITY	1.7	1.4	0.4	0.9	1.4	0.2	0.2	2.4	1.8	1.3	0.4	-0.9	
	0.5	0.4	0.9	0.4	0.5	1.1	0.7	0.6	0.3	0.4	0.3	0.8	23
UP	0.6	0.5	0.2	-0.1	0.2	-0.2	-0.3	1.0	1.2	0.6	0.6	-0.1	
	0.4	0.4	0.3	0.4	0.5	0.4	0.8	0.4	0.4	0.2	0.3	0.8	22
URBAN HOUSING	0.7	0.8	-0.0	-0.1	0.4	-0.5	-0.0	1.4	1.6	0.8	0.7	0.5	
	0.9	0.6	0.5	0.7	0.9	0.6	0.9	0.7	0.4	0.4	0.3	1.2	23

URINE	-0.1	-0.1	0.4	-0.8	-0.9	0.4	0.8	0.9	1.4	0.6	0.8	0.6	
	0.7	0.3	0.3	0.6	0.5	0.7	0.7	0.4	0.3	0.2	0.3	0.8	17
VALLEYS	1.2	0.7	-0.2	0.4	0.4	-0.9	-0.0	1.6	1.5	0.9	0.6	-0.1	
	0.5	0.4	0.5	0.5	0.7	0.8	0.8	0.5	0.3	0.3	0.3	0.9	23
VEGETABLES	1.3	-0.0	0.2	0.5	-0.9	-0.1	0.9	1.4	1.3	0.8	0.6	-0.2	
	0.3	0.4	0.4	0.2	0.5	0.6	0.9	0.3	0.3	0.2	0.2	0.6	23
VILLAGE	1.2	-0.1	-0.1	0.4	-0.9	-0.5	0.1	1.4	1.4	0.8	0.6	0.2	
	0.5	0.5	0.5	0.3	0.7	0.5	1.1	0.5	0.3	0.2	0.3	0.7	23
VOICE	1.3	0.4	0.7	0.4	-0.1	0.7	0.9	1.6	1.4	0.9	0.5	-0.4	
	0.5	0.4	0.5	0.3	0.4	0.6	0.8	0.6	0.2	0.3	0.3	0.9	22
VOTING	1.0	0.7	0.3	0.2	0.3	0.1	-0.4	1.4	1.6	0.8	0.7	0.6	
	0.5	0.4	0.5	0.3	0.6	0.7	0.8	0.6	0.3	0.3	0.3	1.1	22
WALK	1.5	0.3	0.3	0.7	-0.3	0.1	0.7	1.7	1.6	1.0	0.6	-0.2	
	0.4	0.3	0.7	0.3	0.4	0.8	0.9	0.5	0.2	0.3	0.2	0.8	23
WALL	0.5	1.0	-0.8	-0.2	0.8	-1.7	0.4	1.5	1.4	0.9	0.5	-0.5	
	0.6	0.4	0.5	0.5	0.5	0.8	1.0	0.5	0.3	0.3	0.2	0.6	23
WAR	-1.9	1.4	0.5	-2.6	1.4	0.3	-0.9	2.6	2.1	1.5	0.5	-0.5	
	0.5	0.6	0.8	0.2	0.9	1.1	0.9	0.7	0.3	0.4	0.2	1.1	22
WARMTH	1.2	0.5	0.3	0.4	-0.0	0.1	0.6	1.6	1.5	0.9	0.6	-0.0	
	0.8	0.5	0.5	0.8	0.7	0.7	0.8	0.7	0.4	0.3	0.3	0.7	23
WATER	1.7	0.7	0.6	0.8	0.3	0.6	1.3	2.1	1.6	1.2	0.4	-0.8	
	0.5	0.5	0.7	0.3	0.6	1.0	0.9	0.6	0.4	0.3	0.2	0.5	23
WAY	1.1	0.6	-0.1	0.3	0.1	-0.6	0.5	1.4	1.4	0.8	0.6	0.0	
	0.5	0.4	0.5	0.4	0.6	0.6	1.0	0.5	0.3	0.3	0.2	0.8	23
WEALTH	1.2	1.0	0.2	0.4	0.8	-0.1	-0.1	1.6	1.6	0.9	0.7	0.2	
	0.5	0.4	0.4	0.4	0.5	0.7	1.0	0.6	0.3	0.3	0.3	1.0	23
WEDDING	1.7	0.7	0.7	0.9	0.4	0.8	0.0	2.1	1.7	1.2	0.5	-0.3	
	0.4	0.4	0.5	0.5	0.6	0.6	1.0	0.5	0.3	0.3	0.2	0.9	23
WEDNESDAY	0.6	0.2	0.1	-0.1	-0.5	-0.3	0.8	0.9	1.1	0.5	0.6	0.1	
	0.5	0.3	0.4	0.4	0.4	0.5	1.0	0.4	0.3	0.2	0.3	1.1	23
WEEK	0.8	0.3	0.3	0.0	-0.4	0.1	0.5	1.1	1.3	0.6	0.7	0.4	
	0.6	0.3	0.4	0.5	0.5	0.5	0.8	0.5	0.4	0.2	0.3	1.1	23
WEIGHT	0.2	0.7	-0.3	-0.5	0.2	-0.9	0.2	1.0	1.1	0.6	0.6	-0.2	
	0.4	0.5	0.4	0.4	0.7	0.6	0.9	0.5	0.3	0.2	0.2	0.6	23
WEST	0.7	0.6	0.2	-0.1	0.2	-0.3	0.1	1.1	1.3	0.7	0.6	0.1	
	0.6	0.4	0.5	0.5	0.6	0.6	1.1	0.6	0.4	0.3	0.3	1.0	23
WHISKEY	0.1	0.7	0.5	-0.6	0.3	0.3	-0.7	1.3	1.7	0.8	0.9	1.2	
	0.9	0.5	0.5	0.9	0.7	0.7	1.2	0.6	0.3	0.3	0.3	1.0	23
WHITE	1.2	-0.1	0.1	0.4	-1.0	-0.2	0.7	1.4	1.3	0.8	0.6	-0.2	
	0.4	0.4	0.5	0.4	0.6	0.8	0.9	0.4	0.4	0.3	0.2	0.7	23

```
WHITE RACE       0.9   0.8   0.6   0.1   0.5   0.5   0.5   1.5   1.5   0.9   0.6  -0.2
                 0.6   0.5   0.5   0.4   0.6   0.5   0.7   0.6   0.4   0.4   0.3   0.9   22

WIDOW            0.0  -0.1  -0.2  -0.7  -0.9  -0.7  -0.6   0.6   1.3   0.5   0.9   1.0
                 0.4   0.4   0.4   0.3   0.7   0.6   0.9   0.3   0.3   0.2   0.2   0.8   23

WIDOWER         -0.1   0.1  -0.2  -0.8  -0.6  -0.8  -1.0   0.6   1.2   0.4   0.8   0.7
                 0.5   0.3   0.3   0.5   0.5   0.7   0.9   0.2   0.4   0.1   0.3   0.9   23

WIFE             1.7   0.1   1.0   0.9  -0.6   1.1   0.2   2.1   1.7   1.2   0.5  -0.3
                 0.7   0.6   0.6   0.6   0.7   0.9   0.9   0.7   0.3   0.4   0.2   1.0   23

WINDOW           1.3   0.2  -0.3   0.5  -0.5  -0.9   0.9   1.4   1.3   0.8   0.6  -0.2
                 0.4   0.4   0.4   0.3   0.5   0.5   0.9   0.4   0.3   0.2   0.2   0.7   23

WIND             0.4   0.8   0.8  -0.3   0.5   0.9   0.6   1.4   1.5   0.9   0.6   0.1
                 0.6   0.4   0.5   0.6   0.6   0.8   0.8   0.5   0.3   0.3   0.2   0.9   23

WINE             0.2   0.3   0.1  -0.5  -0.4  -0.2  -0.2   1.1   1.5   0.7   0.8   0.9
                 1.1   0.4   0.4   1.1   0.5   0.9   1.0   0.6   0.3   0.2   0.3   0.9   23

WINTER           0.2   0.8  -0.2  -0.5   0.4  -0.8   0.6   1.1   1.4   0.6   0.8   0.8
                 0.5   0.4   0.4   0.6   0.6   0.7   0.7   0.3   0.3   0.2   0.2   0.7   23

WOMAN            1.7  -0.1   0.9   0.9  -0.9   1.0   0.8   2.0   1.7   1.1   0.6  -0.2
                 0.5   0.6   0.6   0.4   0.8   0.8   0.9   0.5   0.3   0.3   0.2   0.9   23

WOOD             1.1   0.8  -0.5   0.3   0.6  -1.3   0.5   1.5   1.4   0.9   0.5  -0.4
                 0.5   0.3   0.4   0.4   0.5   0.6   0.8   0.5   0.3   0.3   0.2   0.9   23

WORD             1.1   0.3   0.2   0.3  -0.4  -0.0   0.8   1.3   1.3   0.7   0.6  -0.2
                 0.4   0.4   0.4   0.3   0.6   0.4   1.0   0.5   0.3   0.3   0.2   0.7   23

WORKER           1.1   0.9   0.5   0.3   0.7   0.4   0.6   1.7   1.6   1.0   0.6  -0.1
                 0.6   0.4   0.7   0.4   0.5   0.8   0.9   0.7   0.3   0.3   0.3   0.8   23

WORK             1.2   1.0   0.5   0.4   0.8   0.3   0.8   1.8   1.6   1.1   0.5  -0.4
                 0.7   0.3   0.7   0.5   0.4   0.7   0.8   0.7   0.3   0.3   0.2   0.9   23

WORLD            1.0   1.4   0.4   0.2   1.5   0.1   0.6   2.0   1.7   1.2   0.6  -0.3
                 0.5   0.4   0.8   0.4   0.4   1.0   0.9   0.5   0.3   0.2   0.2   0.8   23

WRITING          1.1   0.4   0.1   0.4  -0.2  -0.3   0.6   1.4   1.4   0.8   0.6   0.1
                 0.6   0.5   0.6   0.4   0.7   0.7   1.1   0.6   0.3   0.3   0.3   0.9   23

YEAR 2000, THE   0.9   1.1   0.7   0.2   1.0   0.7  -1.7   1.8   1.7   1.0   0.7   0.3
                 0.6   0.5   0.7   0.4   0.6   0.9   1.4   0.7   0.3   0.4   0.2   1.0   22

YEAR, A          1.0   0.5   0.4   0.2   0.1   0.1   0.8   1.3   1.4   0.7   0.7   0.2
                 0.4   0.4   0.5   0.2   0.6   0.5   0.7   0.5   0.3   0.3   0.3   0.8   23

YELLOW           0.7  -0.2   0.2   0.0  -1.1  -0.0   0.6   1.0   1.2   0.6   0.7   0.2
                 0.5   0.4   0.4   0.5   0.5   0.8   0.8   0.5   0.3   0.3   0.2   0.9   23

YELLOW RACE      0.3   0.3   0.5  -0.4  -0.4   0.3  -0.5   1.0   1.4   0.6   0.8   0.8
                 0.6   0.5   0.6   0.6   0.9   0.8   1.4   0.6   0.3   0.3   0.3   1.1   21

YESTERDAY        0.6   0.1   0.2  -0.1  -0.7  -0.1   0.2   0.7   1.3   0.4   0.9   1.1
                 0.5   0.1   0.3   0.4   0.3   0.7   0.6   0.4   0.4   0.2   0.3   1.2   23

YOUTH            1.7   0.9   1.3   0.8   0.7   1.6   0.8   2.4   1.9   1.4   0.5  -0.6
                 0.6   0.5   0.8   0.5   0.7   0.9   0.7   0.8   0.3   0.5   0.2   0.8   23

ZERO            -0.7  -0.4  -0.4  -1.4  -1.5  -0.9  -0.1   1.1   1.4   0.6   0.8   0.8
                 0.8   0.3   0.4   0.6   0.7   0.8   1.0   0.6   0.4   0.3   0.3   0.8   23
```

APPENDIX G

Concepts Included in All Categories

I. --- TIME ---

I-A AGE CONTINUUM

46 BIRTH	30 BABY	88 CHILD	619 YOUTH	3 ADOLESCENCE
262 I(MYSELF)	63 BRIDEGROOM	319 MAN	62 BRIDE	386 PARENTHOOD
325 MATURITY	181 FATHER	343 MOTHER	330 MIDDLE AGE	225 GRANDFATHER
226 GRANDMOTHER	378 OLD PEOPLE	377 OLD AGE	130 DEATH	

I-B MONTHS AND SEASONS

277 JANUARY	184 FEBRUARY	321 MARCH	15 APRIL	326 MAY
283 JUNE	282 JULY	24 AUGUST	479 SEPTEMBER	376 OCTOBER
372 NOVEMBER	132 DECEMBER	515 SPRING	533 SUMMER	175 FALL
606 WINTER	615 YEAR, A			

I-C TIME UNITS

336 MOMENT	476 SECOND, A	258 HOUR	366 NIGHT	128 DAY
594 WEEK	340 MONTH	615 YEAR, A	79 CENTURY	167 ETERNITY
554 TIME				

I-D FUTURE/PRESENT/PAST

614 YEAR 2000, T	214 FUTURE	557 TOMORROW	254 HOPE	425 PROGRESS
431 PURPOSE	419 PRESENT, THE	555 TODAY	90 CHOICE, A	611 WORK
360 NEED	388 PAST, THE	618 YESTERDAY	235 HABIT	561 TRADITION
329 MEMORY	531 SUCCESS	174 FAILURE	262 I(MYSELF)	

II. - KINSHIP -

II-A KINSHIP

25 AUNT	62 BRIDE	63 BRIDEGROOM	65 BROTHER	116 COUSIN
127 DAUGHTER	181 FATHER	182 FATHER-IN-LA	225 GRANDFATHER	226 GRANDMOTHER
261 HUSBAND	343 MOTHER	344 MOTHER-IN-LA	446 RELATIVES	492 SISTERS
504 SON	573 UNCLE	602 WIFE	397 PERSON	395 PEOPLE, MOST
210 FRIEND	262 I(MYSELF)			

II-B RACES/RELIGIONS/CONTINENTS/DIRECTIONS/-ISMS

49 BLACK RACE	442 RED RACE	599 WHITE RACE	617 YELLOW RACE	22 ATHEISTS
66 BUDDHISTS	91 CHRISTIANS	250 HINDUS	342 MOSLEMS	5 AFRICA
20 ASIA	168 EUROPE	370 NORTH AMERIC	510 SOUTH AMERIC	158 EAST
369 NORTH	509 SOUTH	596 WEST	74 CAPITALISM	106 COMMUNISM
135 DEMOCRACY	358 NATIONALISM	499 SOCIALISM	262 I(MYSELF)	351 MY NATION NA
361 NEGRO	280 JEWS	368 NON-BELIEVER		

II-C MALE/FEMALE

318 MALE(GENDER)	323 MASCULINITY	319 MAN	59 BOY	181 FATHER
65 BROTHER	601 WIDOWER	262 I(MYSELF)	186 FEMALE(GENDE	187 FEMININITY
607 WOMAN	217 GIRL	343 MOTHER	492 SISTERS	600 WIDOW
294 LADY	395 PEOPLE, MOST			

II-D INGROUP/ALTERS/OUTGROUP

262 I(MYSELF)	350 MY NAME	176 FAMILY	210 FRIEND	446 RELATIVES
397 PERSON	395 PEOPLE, MOST	525 STRANGER	203 FOREIGNER	444 REFUGEE
267 IMMIGRANT	234 GYPSY	165 ENEMY	89 CHILD, ILLEG	382 ORPHAN
538 SYMPATHY	83 CHARITY	126 DANGER		

II-E INTIMACY-REMOTENESS CONTINUUM

262 I(MYSELF)	350 MY NAME	176 FAMILY	446 RELATIVES	349 MY CITY NAME
354 MY STATE NAM	352 MY OWN REGIO	141 DIALECT	353 MY OWN TONGU	351 MY NATION NA
114 COUNTRY	390 PATRIOT	197 FLAG	574 UNITED NATIO	95 CIVILIZATION
612 WORLD	575 UNIVERSE, TH	395 PEOPLE, MOST		

III. - ABSTRACTS SYMBOLISM -

III-A EMOTIONS

6 AGGRESSIVE,B	11 ANGER	111 CONTEMPT	115 COURAGE	137 DETERMINATIO
140 DEVOTION	166 ENVY	183 FEAR	233 GUILT	238 HAPPINESS
240 HATE	254 HOPE	299 LAUGHTER	314 LOVE	384 PAIN
387 PASSION	408 PLEASURE	420 PRIDE	467 SADNESS	482 SHAME
536 SURPRISE	538 SYMPATHY	262 I(MYSELF)		

III-B NUMBERS

620 ZERO	381 ONE	572 TWO	551 THREE	206 FOUR
196 FIVE	546 TEN	570 TWENTY-EIGHT	571 TWENTY-NINE	379 ONE HUNDRED
380 ONE MILLION	373 NUMBER			

III-C   COLORS

| 105 COLOR | 48 BLACK | 230 GREY | 443 RED | 616 YELLOW |
| 53 BLUE | 229 GREEN | 598 WHITE | | |

III-D   GEOMETRICALS

| 410 POINT, A | 309 LINE | 566 TRIANGLE, A | 516 SQUARE, A | 93 CIRCLE |
| 432 PYRAMID, A | 122 CUBE, A | 512 SPHERE, A | 270 INFINITY | |

III-E   DAYS

| 337 MONDAY | 569 TUESDAY | 593 WEDNESDAY | 553 THURSDAY | 209 FRIDAY |
| 470 SATURDAY | 535 SUNDAY | 128 DAY | 594 WEEK | |

IV. – CONCRETE SYMBOLISMS –

IV-A   NATURAL AND POTENTIALLY AESTHETIC

101 CLOUD	136 DESERTS	194 FIRE	199 FLOWER	200 FOG
204 FOREST	227 GRASS	263 ICE	284 JUNGLE	295 LAKE
341 MOON	345 MOUNTAINS	439 RAIN	456 RIVER	464 ROSE
477 SEED	496 SMOKE	498 SNOW	517 STAR	534 SUN
552 THUNDER	565 TREE	580 VALLEYS	604 WIND	

IV-B   SEE-/HEAR-/TOUCH-/SMELL-/TASTE-(ABLES)

488 SIGHT, SENSE	171 EYES	472 SCENE	400 PICTURE	320 MAP
341 MOON	101 CLOUD	243 HEARING,SENS	156 EAR	508 SOUND
347 MUSIC	583 VOICE	299 LAUGHTER	552 THUNDER	560 TOUCH, SENSE
493 SKIN	263 ICE	288 KISSING	35 BATH	439 RAIN
402 PILLOW	495 SMELL, SENSE	371 NOSE	199 FLOWER	396 PERFUME
398 PERSPIRATION	464 ROSE	496 SMOKE	541 TASTE, SENSE	558 TONGUE
513 SPICE	449 RESTAURANT	328 MEDICINE	72 CANDY	469 SALT
262 I(MYSELF)				

IV-C   MEANS/EXPRESSIVES/ENDS

471 SAVING MONEY	611 WORK	112 COOPERATION	451 REVOLUTION	293 LABORATORY
590 WAY	279 JEWELRY	125 DANCING	538 SYMPATHY	584 VOTING
540 TALK	585 WALK	591 WEALTH	425 PROGRESS	408 PLEASURE
391 PEACE	291 KNOWLEDGE	242 HEALTH	262 I(MYSELF)	

V. - ENVIRONMENTALS -

V-A FOOD OBJECTS

14 APPLE	41 BEER	61 BREAD	69 BUTTER	70 CAKE
72 CANDY	73 CANNED FOODS	85 CHEESE	87 CHICKEN	102 COFFEE
161 EGG	195 FISH	202 FOOD	212 FRUIT	248 HERBS
327 MEAT	332 MILK	453 RICE	469 SALT	500 SODA POP
513 SPICE	542 TEA	581 VEGETABLES	589 WATER	597 WHISKEY
605 WINE

V-B ANIMALS

12 ANIMAL	38 BEAR	45 BIRD	77 CAT	87 CHICKEN
117 COW	121 CROW	149 DOG	163 ELEPHANT	195 FISH
220 GOOSE	255 HORSE	273 INSECT	310 LION	339 MONKEY
401 PIG	435 RABBIT	497 SNAKE	118 CREATURE	262 I(MYSELF)

V-C HABITATIONS

7 AIR POLLUTIO	29 AUTOMOBILE	67 BUS	92 CINEMA	94 CITY
136 DESERTS	204 FOREST	227 GRASS	256 HOSPITAL	257 HOTEL
259 HOUSE	284 JUNGLE	293 LABORATORY	306 LIBRARY	345 MOUNTAINS
403 PLACE	421 PRISON	449 RESTAURANT	466 RURAL HOUSIN	473 SCHOOL
483 SHIP	485 SHOP	501 SOIL, THE	526 STREET	563 TRAIN
578 URBAN HOUSIN	580 VALLEYS	582 VILLAGE

VI. - CARNALITIES -

VI-A BODY PARTS

236 HAIR	60 BRAIN	171 EYES	156 EAR	371 NOSE
558 TONGUE	559 TOOTH	312 LIPS	172 FACE	241 HEAD
17 ARM	237 HAND	303 LEFT HAND	455 RIGHT HAND	193 FINGERS
192 FINGERNAIL	244 HEART	520 STOMACH	275 INTESTINES	304 LEG
185 FEET	52 BLOOD	493 SKIN	54 BODY	262 I(MYSELF)

VI-B BODY CHARACTERISTICS AND PROCESSES

31 BALDNESS	37 BEARD	51 BLIND	129 DEAF	130 DEATH
159 EATING	170 EXCREMENT	179 FAT	232 GROWING	243 HEARING,SENS
307 LIFE	348 MUSTACHE	398 PERSPIRATION	418 PREGNANCY	481 SEX
487 SIGHT	488 SIGHT, SENSE	494 SLEEP	495 SMELL, SENSE	514 SPIT
541 TASTE, SENSE	560 TOUCH, SENSE	579 URINE	262 I(MYSELF)

VI-C SEX AND SENSUALITY

4 ADULTERY	47 BIRTH CONTRO	54 BODY	59 BOY	125 DANCING
156 EAR	171 EYES	187 FEMININITY	217 GIRL	236 HAIR
252 HOMOSEXUAL	288 KISSING	312 LIPS	311 LIPSTICK	314 LOVE
323 MASCULINITY	334 MINISKIRT	356 NAKEDNESS	371 NOSE	387 PASSION
396 PERFUME	427 PROSTITUTE	459 ROMANCE	481 SEX	558 TONGUE
262 I(MYSELF)				

VI-D HEALTH AND SICKNESS

2 ACCIDENT	35 BATH	71 CANCER	96 CLEANLINESS	130 DEATH
145 DISEASE	148 DOCTOR	153 DRUNKENNESS	179 FAT	191 FILTH
232 GROWING	242 HEALTH	256 HOSPITAL	260 HUNGER	272 INSANE
307 LIFE	328 MEDICINE	362 NEUROTICPERS	374 NURSE	384 PAIN
389 PATIENT	411 POISON	486 SICKNESS	532 SUICIDE	262 I(MYSELF)

VII. - HUMAN ACTIVITY -

VII-A OCCUPATIONS

19 ARTIST	26 AUTHOR	33 BANKER	34 BARBER	42 BEGGAR
97 CLERGYMAN	98 CLERK, FEMAL	148 DOCTOR	173 FACTORY WORK	178 FARMER
221 GOVERN CLERK	301 LAWYER	335 MISSIONARY	374 NURSE	392 PEASANTS
412 POLICEMAN	424 PROFESSOR	427 PROSTITUTE	474 SCIENTIST	480 SERVANT
502 SOLDIER	522 STOREKEEPER	527 STREET CLEAN	528 STUDENT	543 TEACHER
547 THIEF	610 WORKER	395 PEOPLE, MOST	262 I(MYSELF)	

VII-B COMMERCIAL, ECONOMIC

28 AUTOMATION	33 BANKER	56 BORROWING MO	68 BUSINESS	119 CREDIT
131 DEBT	173 FACTORY WORK	174 FAILURE	274 INSURANCE	292 LABOR UNIONS
338 MONEY	414 POOR PEOPLE	425 PROGRESS	454 RICH PEOPLE	468 SALARY
471 SAVING MONEY	485 SHOP	522 STOREKEEPER	531 SUCCESS	610 WORKER
611 WORK				

VII-C WORK/PLAY

528 STUDENT	473 SCHOOL	423 PROBLEM	611 WORK	468 SALARY
68 BUSINESS	169 EXAMINATION	407 PLAY	313 LOTTERIES	305 LEISURE
215 GAME	86 CHESS	405 PLAYING CARD	406 PLAYING TENN	262 I(MYSELF)

VII-D SUCCESS/FAILURE

531 SUCCESS	454 RICH PEOPLE	577 UP	81 CHAMPION	452 REWARD
315 LUCK	425 PROGRESS	302 LEADER	420 PRIDE	174 FAILURE
414 POOR PEOPLE	150 DOWN	42 BEGGAR	430 PUNISHMENT	562 TRAGEDY

133 DEFEAT	201 FCLLOWER	482 SHAME	214 FUTURE	419 PRESENT, THE
388 PAST, THE	262 I(MYSELF)			

VII-E PROBLEM-SOLVING STYLE

557 TOMORROW	419 PRESENT, THE	301 LAWYER	610 WORKER	68 BUSINESS
365 NEWS	425 PROGRESS	611 WORK	134 DEFENSE	137 DETERMINATIO
468 SALARY	556 TOLERANCE	271 INITIATIVE,T	440 REALISM	549 THOUGHT
441 REALITY	291 KNOWLEDGE	214 FUTURE	614 YEAR 2000, T	424 PROFESSOR
19 ARTIST	399 PHILOSOPHY	409 POETRY	135 DEMOCRACY	110 CONTEMPLATIO
574 UNITED NATIO	254 HOPE	274 INSURANCE	285 JUSTICE	433 QUESTIONTHIN
264 IDEALISM	151 DREAM	568 TRUTH	39 BEAUTY	

VIII. – INTERPERSCNAL RELATIONS –

VIII-A PRIVATE/PUBLIC

262 I(MYSELF)	350 MY NAME	422 PRIVACY	503 SOLITUDE	43 BELIEF
151 DREAM	417 PRAYER	29 AUTOMOBILE	489 SILENCE	395 PEOPLE, MOST
357 NAME	429 PUBLICITY	188 FESTIVALS	540 TALK	92 CINEMA
592 WEDDING	67 BUS	367 NOISE		

VIII-B SOCIAL STATUS: SUPRAORDINATE/SUBORDINATE

302 LEADER	412 POLICEMAN	27 AUTHORITY	416 POWER	454 RICH PEOPLE
324 MASTER	424 PROFESSOR	287 KING	249 HERO	528 STUDENT
262 I(MYSELF)	395 PEOPLE, MOST	331 MIDDLE CLASS	201 FOLLOWER	42 BEGGAR
266 ILLITERATE	56 BORROWING MO	414 POOR PEOPLE	480 SERVANT	

VIII-C MORAL/IMMORAL

82 CHARACTER	83 CHARITY	140 DEVOTION	143 DISCIPLINE	154 DUTY
205 FORGIVENESS	253 HONOR	285 JUSTICE	286 KINDNESS	335 MISSIONARY
556 TOLERANCE	269 INDEPENDENT	89 CHILD, ILLEG	47 BIRTH CONTRO	433 QUESTIONTHIN
420 PRIDE	532 SUICIDE	78 CENSORSHIP	109 CONFLICT	301 LAWYER
490 SIN	228 GREED	4 ADULTERY	84 CHEATING	316 LYING
233 GUILT	223 GRAFT	120 CRIME	346 MURDER	427 PROSTITUTE

VIII-D INTERGROUP RELATICNS: ASSOCIATIVE/NEUTRAL/DISASSOCIA

567 TRUST	314 LOVE	112 COOPERATION	211 FRIENDSHIP	205 FORGIVENESS
391 PEACE	10 ALLIANCES	104 COLONIALISM	134 DEFENSE	556 TOLERANCE
269 INDEPENDENT	144 DISCUSSION	285 JUSTICE	574 UNITED NATIO	363 NEUTRALITY
451 REVOLUTION	183 FEAR	240 HATE	107 COMPETITION	190 FIGHTING
430 PUNISHMENT	587 WAR	36 BATTLE	109 CONFLICT	436 RACE CONFLIC

VIII-E AFFILIATIVE/ACHIEVEMENT

448 RESPECT	210 FRIEND	112 COOPERATION	140 DEVOTION	538 SYMPATHY
1 ACCEPT THING	322 MARRIAGE	176 FAMILY	231 GROUP	211 FRIENDSHIP
416 POWER	302 LEADER	107 COMPETITION	166 ENVY	228 GREED
271 INITIATIVE,T	223 GRAFT	531 SUCCESS	81 CHAMPION	611 WORK
262 I(MYSELF)				

IX. - SOCIETY -

IX-A INSTITUTIONS: EDUCATIONAL/POLITICAL,LEGAL/MARITAL,RELI

160 EDUCATION	306 LIBRARY	473 SCHOOL	576 UNIVERSITY	543 TEACHER
413 POLITICS	222 GOVERNMENT	574 UNITED NATIO	300 LAW	421 PRISON
301 LAWYER	147 DIVORCE	176 FAMILY	322 MARRIAGE	447 RELIGION
97 CLERGYMAN	68 BUSINESS	292 LABOR UNIONS	76 CASTE	611 WORK
33 BANKER	18 ARMY	108 COMPULSORY S	587 WAR	390 PATRIOT
502 SOLDIER	262 I(MYSELF)			

IX-B MODERN/TRANSITIONAL/TRADITIONAL TECHNOLOGY

23 ATOMIC BOMB	73 CANNED FOODS	545 TELEVISION	437 RADIOS,POCKE	9 AIRPLANE
375 NYLON	28 AUTOMATION	334 MINISKIRT	511 SPACE TRAVEL	162 ELECTRICITY
500 SODA POP	92 CINEMA	544 TELEPHONE	67 BUS	518 STEEL
317 MACHINE	152 DRESS	438 RAILROADS	194 FIRE	212 FRUIT
55 BOOK	540 TALK	75 CART	608 WOOD	289 KNIFE
50 BLANKET	255 HORSE			

IX-C MODERN/TRANSITIONAL/TRADITIONAL VALUES

433 QUESTIONTHIN	425 PROGRESS	474 SCIENTIST	47 BIRTH CONTRO	147 DIVORCE
278 JAZZ MUSIC	511 SPACE TRAVEL	271 INITIATIVE,T	138 DEVELOPMENT	173 FACTORY WORK
176 FAMILY	4 ADULTERY	347 MUSIC	564 TRAVEL	1 ACCEPT THING
561 TRADITION	392 PEASANTS	177 FAMILY, BIG	213 FUNERAL	491 SINGING
582 VILLAGE				

X. - COMMUNICATIONS -

X-A LITERACY

142 DICTIONARY	169 EXAMINATION	266 ILLITERATE	291 KNOWLEDGE	293 LABORATORY
298 LANGUAGE	306 LIBRARY	364 NEWSPAPERS	393 PEN	394 PENCIL
395 PEOPLE, MOST	425 PROGRESS	473 SCHOOL	528 STUDENT	543 TEACHER
613 WRITING	262 I(MYSELF)			

X-B   LANGUAGE AND LITERATURE

13 ANSWER	26 AUTHOR	55 BOOK	141 DIALECT	142 DICTIONARY
251 HISTORY	281 JOKE	298 LANGUAGE	306 LIBRARY	353 MY OWN TONGU
357 NAME	409 POETRY	434 QUESTION	478 SENTENCE	523 STORY
540 TALK	583 VOICE	609 WORD	613 WRITING	

X-C   COMMUNICATIONS MEDIA

19 ARTIST	26 AUTHOR	55 BOOK	78 CENSORSHIP	92 CINEMA
224 GRAMOPHONE	316 LYING	320 MAP	364 NEWSPAPERS	365 NEWS
385 PAPER	393 PEN	394 PENCIL	400 PICTURE	417 PRAYER
429 PUBLICITY	437 RADIOS,POCKE	505 SONG	544 TELEPHONE	545 TELEVISION

XI. - PHILOSOPHY -

XI-A   PHILOSOPHICALS

39 BEAUTY	90 CHOICE, A	110 CONTEMPLATIO	167 ETERNITY	180 FATALISM
207 FREEDOM	208 FREE WILL	219 GOD	268 IMMORTALITY	270 INFINITY
285 JUSTICE	291 KNOWLEDGE	307 LIFE	314 LOVE	315 LUCK
333 MIND	384 PAIN	399 PHILOSOPHY	408 PLEASURE	428 PSYCHOLOGY
441 REALITY	447 RELIGION	474 SCIENTIST	490 SIN	507 SOUL
568 TRUTH	575 UNIVERSE, TH			

XI-B   SUPERNATURALS

21 ASTROLOGY	139 DEVIL	155 E.S.P.	216 GHOSTS	219 GOD
246 HEAVEN	247 HELL	268 IMMORTALITY	315 LUCK	426 PROPHET
445 REINCARNATIO	450 RESURRECTION	506 SORCERY	507 SOUL	

XI-C   SPIRITUAL/MATERIAL

219 GOD	507 SOUL	417 PRAYER	264 IDEALISM	409 POETRY
151 DREAM	43 BELIEF	110 CONTEMPLATIO	285 JUSTICE	208 FREE WILL
319 MAN	425 PROGRESS	611 WORK	440 REALISM	365 NEWS
549 THOUGHT	291 KNOWLEDGE	474 SCIENTIST	315 LUCK	180 FATALISM

XI-D   CONCRETE/ABSTRACT

548 THING	54 BODY	317 MACHINE	345 MOUNTAINS	529 STUFF
12 ANIMAL	539 TABLE	404 PLANK	32 BALL	521 STONE
403 PLACE	507 SOUL	314 LOVE	285 JUSTICE	270 INFINITY
39 BEAUTY	441 REALITY	568 TRUTH	554 TIME	333 MIND

XI-E COGNITIVE/GUT

333 MIND	144 DISCUSSION	399 PHILOSOPHY	235 HABIT	291 KNOWLEDGE
549 THOUGHT	90 CHOICE, A	265 IDEA	43 BELIEF	423 PROBLEM
520 STOMACH	16 ARGUMENT	153 DRUNKENNESS	360 NEED	408 PLEASURE
387 PASSION	260 HUNGER	314 LOVE	115 COURAGE	384 PAIN
262 I(MYSELF)				

XII. - THINGS AND STUFFS -

XII-A STATIC/DYNAMIC NATURE

164 EMPTY SPACE	565 TREE	297 LAND	458 ROCK	462 ROOT
519 STICK	521 STONE	341 MOON	8 AIR	12 ANIMAL
157 EARTHQUAKE	194 FIRE	456 RIVER	475 SEA	604 WIND
534 SUN	529 STUFF	548 THING		

XII-B STATIC/DYNAMIC ARTIFACTS

40 BED	57 BOTTLE	58 BOX	64 BRIDGE	80 CHAIR
123 CUP	124 DAM	146 DISH	198 FLOOR	290 KNOT
296 LAMP	355 NAIL	402 PILLOW	415 POT	460 ROOF
461 ROOM	465 RUG	586 WALL	603 WINDOW	100 CLOTHES
152 DRESS	239 HAT	359 NECKTIE	484 SHOES	537 SWEATER
9 AIRPLANE	29 AUTOMOBILE	44 BICYCLE	317 MACHINE	437 RADIOS,POCKE
457 ROADS	524 STOVE	530 SUBMARINE,NU	563 TRAIN	548 THING

XII-C STUFFS

8 AIR	99 CLOTH	103 COLD	113 COTTON	194 FIRE
189 FIELD	218 GLASS	245 HEAT	263 ICE	276 IRON
297 LAND	308 LIGHT	383 PAINT	385 PAPER	458 ROCK
463 ROPE	498 SNOW	501 SOIL, THE	508 SOUND	518 STEEL
521 STONE	550 THREAD	588 WARMTH	589 WATER	595 WEIGHT
608 WOOD	529 STUFF			

APPENDIX H

Locations, Dates, and Participants of the Atlas *Interpretation Group Meetings*[1]

LATIN AMERICAN
Oaxtepec and Merida (Mexico) (Jan. 29–Feb. 7, 1970, and Feb. 10–18, 1971)

Alberto Berron
University of Yucatan
Victor Castillo-Vales
University of Yucatan
Rogelio Diaz-Guerrero
University of Mexico
Rolando Diaz-Loving
Mexico City
Consuelo Fernandez de Limon
Mexico City
Wigberto Jimenez Moreno
University of Mexico

Evangelina Araña Osnaya
University of Mexico
Marucha Martinez-Reyes
Mexico City
Nahum Martinez-Reyes
University of Mexico
Yolando Lastra de Saurez
University of Mexico
Refugio Vermont-Sales
University of Yucatan
William H. May
University of Illinois

WEST EUROPEAN
Gieten (Netherlands) (April 16–27, 1970)

Francoise Enel
University of Strasbourg
Suitbert Ertel
University of Göttingen
Tamar Grunewald-Schwartz
University of Strasbourg
Robert Hogenraad
Catholic University of Louvain
Mathilda J. Jansen
State Agriculture University,
Wageningen

Perla Korosec-Serfaty
University of Strasbourg
Wilhelm J. M. Levelt
Catholic University, Nigmegen
Pierre Nederlandt
Catholic University of Louvain
Leo Noordman
University of Groningen
A. J. Smolenaars
University of Amsterdam
Dietrich Vormfelde
George-August-University, Münster

[1] Charles E. Osgood, director of the Center for Comparative Psycholinguistics, University of Illinois, attended all group meetings.

SCANDINAVIAN
Helsinki (Finland) (May 8–17, 1970)

Hans Bonnevier
  Swedish Radio, Stockholm
Ulf Himmelstrand
  University of Uppsala
Aarne A. Koskinen
  University of Helsinki
Jorma Kuusinen
  University of Jyväskylä
Marketta Kuusinen
  University of Jyväskylä

Steffan Nilsson
  Swedish Radio, Stockholm
Kaarle Nordenstreng
  Finnish Broadcasting Co., Helsinki
Pertti Öunap
  University of Helsinki
Ritva Rainio
  Aurora, Petas, Finland
Aino Smee
  Helsinki

MEDITERRANEAN
Pugnuchioso (Italy) (June 13–26, 1971)

Dora Capozza
  University of Padua
Francesca Cristante
  University of Padua
Giovanni B. Flores d'Arcais
  University of Leyden
Maria Diamandopoulou
  Athenian Institute of Anthropos
Aleksandar Kostić
  University of Belgrade
Djordje Kostić
  Institute of Experimental
  Phonetics, Belgrade
Corrine Koufacos
  Athenian Institute of Anthropos

Beğlan B. Toğrol
  Istanbul University
Ergun Toğrol
  Istanbul University
Tomislav Tomeković
  University of Belgrade
Smiljka Vasić
  Institute of Experimental
  Phonetics, Belgrade
Forough al-Zaman Minou-Archer
  Illinois-Teheran Research Unit
William Kay Archer
  Illinois-Teheran Research Unit
Gordana Opačić
  University of Illinois

WEST ASIAN
Ramsar (Iran) (July 9–22, 1971)

Doğan Cüceloğlu
  Hacettepe University, Ankara
Bozkurt Güvenç
  Hacettepe University, Ankara
Amir Hassanpour Aghdam
  Teheran University
A. Ahmad Jawid
  Kabul University
Alice Melikian
  American University of Beirut
Levon Melikian
  American University of Beirut

M. A. Asaad Nezami
  Teheran University
Noor Ahmad Shaker
  Kabul University
Batul Shaida
  Illinois-Teheran Research Unit
Forough al-Zaman Minou-Archer
  Illinois-Teheran Research Unit
William Kay Archer
  Illinois-Teheran Research Unit
Gordana Opačić
  University of Illinois

INDIAN SUB-CONTINENT
Hyderabad (India) (August 9–13, 1971)

B. Kuppuswamy
  Institute for Social and Psychological
  Research, Bangalore
Dr. Mahendra
  University of Delhi
Alokananda Mitter
  Indian Statistical Institute,
  Calcutta
V. Muddalinganna
  Bangalore University
K. Sheshagiri Rao
  Institute for Social and Psychological
  Research, Bangalore
Krishna Gopal Rastogi
  National Council of Educational
  Research and Training, Delhi

Raj Rani Rastogi
  Delhi
Prabhu Shankara
  University of Mysore
Ladli C. Singh
  National Council of Educational
  Research and Training, Delhi
Joydeep Sircar
  Indian Statistical Institute,
  Calcutta
Forough al-Zaman Minou-Archer
  Illinois-Teheran Research Unit
William Kay Archer
  Illinois-Teheran Research Unit

EAST ASIAN
Hong Kong (August 3–12, 1970)

John L. M. Dawson
  Hong Kong University
Daniel Han
  Hong Kong University
Rumjahn Hoosain
  Hong Kong University
Yōko Iwamatsu
  Gakushuin University, Tokyo
Peggy Lee
  Hong Kong University
Yoshiki Mine
  Consulate-General of Japan,
  Hong Kong

Jantorn Buranabanpote Rufener
  Chulalongkorn University, Bangkok
Yasumasa Tanaka
  Gakushuin University, Tokyo
Nuanpen Wichiarajote
  College of Education, Bangkok
Weerayudh Wichiarajote
  College of Education, Bangkok
Albany Wong
  Hong Kong University
Brian M. Young
  Hong Kong University

References

Aaronson, B. S. 1964. The hypnotic induction of colored environments. *Perceptual and Motor Skills,* 18: 30.

————. 1970. Some affective stereotypes of color. *International Journal of Symbology,* 2: 15-27.

————. 1971. Color perception and affect. *American Journal of Clinical Hypnosis,* 14 (1): 38-43.

Abelson, R. P. 1960. Scales derived by consideration of variance components in multi-way tables. In H. Gulliksen and S. J. Messick, eds., *Psychological scaling: Theory and applications.* New York: John Wiley and Sons.

Adams, F. M., and Osgood, C. E. 1973. A cross-cultural study of the affective meanings of color. *Journal of Cross-Cultural Psychology,* 4: 135-156.

Agrawal, K. G. 1970. Studies in color symbolism, I: Object context and abstract colour labels. *Indian Journal of Psychology,* 45: 141-157.

Ahmavaara, Y. 1954. Transformation analysis of factorial data. *Annales Academiae Scientiarum Fennicae,* B88: 2.

————, and Nordenstreng, K. 1969. *Transformation analysis of statistical variables: An introduction of group-theoretical ideas into multi-variate analysis.* Helsinki: Transactions of the Westermarck Society, Vol. 17.

Aitchison, J., and Brown, J. A. C. 1957. *The lognormal distribution.* London: Cambridge University Press.

Alexander, S., and Husek, T. R. 1962. The anxiety differential. Initial steps in the development of a measure of situational anxiety. *Educational and Psychological Measurement,* 22: 325-348.

Asch, S. 1955. On the use of metaphor in the description of persons. In H. Werner, ed., *On expressive language.* Worcester, Mass.: Clark University Press.

Banerji, S. and Mitra, S. C. 1942. Studies in aesthetic perception. *Indian Journal of Psychology,* 17: 94-98.

Barnett, K. M. A. 1950. A transcription for Cantonese. *London University School of Oriental and African Studies Bulletin,* 13: 725-745.

Bastide, R. 1958. The language of colours, myths and symbols. *UNESCO Courier,* 11 (6): 24-25.

Basu, R. N., and Basu, M. 1949. Possibility of a racial significance of color preference. *Eastern Anthropologist,* 2 (25): 160-161.

Berlin, E., and Kay, P. 1969. *Basic color terms: Their universality and evolution.* Berkeley: University of California Press.

Birren, F. 1969. *Light, color and environment: A thorough presentation of facts on the biological and psychological effects of color.* New York: Van Nostrand Reinhold.

465

Bopp, J. A. 1955. A quantitative semantic analysis of word association in schizophrenia. Unpublished doctoral dissertation, University of Illinois.

Boucher, J., and Osgood, C. E. 1969. The Pollyanna hypothesis. *Journal of Verbal Learning and Verbal Behavior*, 8: 1-8.

Brislin, R. W. 1970. Back-translation for cross-cultural research. *Journal of Cross-Cultural Psychology*, 1: 185-216.

Brown, R. 1958. Is a boulder sweet or sour? *Contemporary Psychology*, 3: 113-115.

———, and Gilman, A. 1960. The pronouns of power and solidarity. In T. A. Sebeok, ed., *Style in language.* Cambridge, Mass.: M.I.T. Press.

———, and Lenneberg, E. H. 1954. A study in language and cognition. *Journal of Abnormal and Social Psychology*, 49: 454-462.

Burling, R. 1964. Cognition and componential analyses: God's truth or hocus pocus. *American Anthropologist*, 66: 20-28.

Campbell, D. T. 1964. Distinguishing differences of perception from failures of communication in cross-cultural studies. In F. S. C. Northrop and H. H. Livingston, eds., *Cross-cultural understanding: Epistemology in anthropology.* New York: Harper and Row.

Cantril, H. 1965. *The pattern of human concerns.* New Brunswick, N.J.: Rutgers University Press.

Capell, M.D., and Wohl, J. 1959. An approach to the factor structure of clinical judgments. *Journal of Consulting Psychology*, 23: 51-53.

Carroll, J. B. 1959. Review of "The measurement of meaning." *Language*, 35: 38-77.

Carroll, J. D., and Chang, J. J. 1970. Analysis of individual differences in multidimensional scaling via an N-way generalization of "Eckart-Young" decomposition. *Psychometrika*, 35: 283-319.

Cattell, R., ed. 1966. *Handbook of multivariate psychology.* Chicago: Rand McNally.

Cerbus, G., and Nichols, R. 1963. Personality variables and response to color. *Psychological Bulletin*, 60: 566-575.

Child, I. L., Hansen, J. A., and Hornbeck, F. W. 1968. Age and sex differences in children's color preferences. *Child Development*, 39: 237-247.

———, and Iwao, S. 1969. Comparison of color preferences in college students of Japan and the United States. *Proceedings of the 77th Annual Convention of the American Psychological Association*, 4 (pt. 1): 469-470.

Chomsky, N. 1965. *Aspects of the theory of syntax.* Cambridge, Mass.: M.I.T. Press.

———. 1968. *Language and mind.* New York: Harcourt, Brace, and World.

Chou, S. K., and Chen, H. P. 1935. General versus specific color preferences of Chinese students. *Journal of Social Psychology*, 6: 290-314.

Choungourian, A. 1968. Color preferences and cultural variation. *Perceptual and Motor Skills*, 26: 1203-06.

———. 1969. Color preferences: A cross-cultural and cross-sectional study. *Perceptual and Motor Skills*, 28: 801-802.

Cliff, N. 1959. Adverbs as multipliers. *Psychological Review*, 66: 27-44.

Collins, N. 1924. The appropriateness of certain color combinations in advertising. Unpublished master's thesis, Columbia University. Summarized in A. T. Poffenberger, *Psychology in advertising.* New York: McGraw-Hill, 1932.

Conklin, C. 1955. Hanunóo color categories. *Southwestern Journal of Anthropology*, 11: 339-344.

Cook, D. R. 1959. A study of the relationship of the meaning of selected concepts to achievement and ability. Unpublished doctoral dissertation, University of Indiana.

D'Andrade, R. G., and Egan, M. 1971. The color of emotion. Unpublished manuscript, University of California at San Diego.

———, and Romney, A. K. 1964. Summary of participants' discussion. *American Anthropologist,* 66 (3): pt. 2, 230-242.

Deese, J. 1962. On the structure of associative meaning. *Psychological Review,* 69: 161-175.

———. 1964. The associative structure of some common English adjectives. *Journal of Verbal Learning and Verbal Behavior,* 3: 347-357.

Déribéré, M. 1955. *La couleur dans les activités humaines.* Paris: Dunod.

DiVesta, F. 1964a. The distribution of modifiers used by children in a word-association task. *Journal of Verbal Learning and Verbal Behavior,* 3: 421-427.

———. 1964b. A simplex analysis of changes with age in responses to a restricted word-association task. *Journal of Verbal Learning and Verbal Behavior,* 3: 505-510.

———. 1965. Developmental patterns in the use of modifiers as modes of conceptualization. *Child Development,* 36: 186-213.

———. 1966a. A developmental study of the semantic structures of children. *Journal of Verbal Learning and Verbal Behavior,* 5: 249-259.

———. 1966b. A normative study of 220 concepts rated on the semantic differential by children in grades 2 through 7. *Journal of Genetic Psychology,* 109: 205-229.

———. 1966c. Norms for modifiers used by children in a restricted word-association task: Grades 2 through 6. *Psychological Reports,* 18: 65-66.

Dodge, J. 1955. A quantitative investigation of the relation between meaning development and context. Unpublished doctoral dissertation, University of Illinois.

Donahoe, J. W. 1961. Changes in meaning as a function of age. *Journal of Genetic Psychology,* 99: 23-28.

Dorcus, R. M. 1932. Habitual word associations to colors as a possible factor in advertising. *Journal of Applied Psychology,* 16: 277-287.

Eckart, C., and Young, G. 1936. The approximation of one matrix by another of lower rank. *Psychometrika,* 1: 211-218.

Elliott, L. L., and Tannenbaum, P. H. 1963. Factor-structure of semantic differential responses to visual forms and prediction of factor-scores from structural characteristics of the stimulus shapes. *American Journal of Psychology,* 76: 589-597.

Ellis, H. 1900. The psychology of red. *Popular Science Monthly,* 57: 365-375.

———. 1906. The psychology of yellow. *Popular Science Monthly,* 68: 456-468.

Endler, N. S. 1961. Changes in meaning during psychotherapy as measured by the semantic differential. *Journal of Counseling Psychology,* 8: 105-111.

Ertel, S. 1965. Standardisierung eines Eindrucksdifferentials. *Zeitschrift für Experimentelle und Angewandte Psychologie,* 12: 22-58.

———. 1969. *Psychophonetik: Untersuchungen über Lautsymbolik und Motivation.* Göttingen: Verlag für Psychologie Dr. C. J. Hogrefe.

———. 1972. Words, sentences and the ego. Prepublication draft, Institute of Psychology, University of Göttingen.

———. 1973. Exploratory choice and verbal judgment. In D. E. Berlyne and K. B. Madsen, eds., *Pleasure, reward, preference: their nature, determinants, and role in behavior.* New York: Academic Press.

Ervin, S. M., and Foster, G. 1960. The development of meaning in children's descriptive terms. *Journal of Abnormal and Social Psychology,* 61: 271-275.

Ferguson, G. 1959. *Signs and symbols in Christian art.* New York: Oxford University Press.

Foa, U. G. 1964. Cross-cultural similarity and difference in interpersonal behavior. *Journal of Abnormal and Social Psychology,* 68: 517-522.

———. 1965. New developments in facet design and analysis. *Psychological Review,* 72: 262-274.

———. 1966. Perception in behavior in reciprocal roles: The Ringex model. *Psychological Monographs,* 80 (15) (whole no. 623).

Ford, L. H., Jr., and Meisels, M. 1965. Social desirability and the semantic differential. *Educational and Psychological Measurement,* 24: 465-475.

Frake, C. O. 1962. The ethnographic study of cognitive systems. In T. Gladwin and W. C. Sturtevant, eds., *Anthropology and human behavior.* Washington: Anthropological Society of Washington.

Fries, C. C. 1952. *The structure of English.* New York: Harcourt, Brace.

Gardner, B. T., and Gardner, R. A. 1969. Teaching sign language to a chimpanzee. *Science,* 165: 664-672.

Garth, T. R., Ikeda, K., and Langdon, R. M. 1931. The color preferences of Japanese children. *Journal of Social Psychology,* 2:397-402.

———, Moses, M. R., and Anthony, C. N. 1938. The color preferences of East Indians. *American Journal of Psychology,* 51: 709-713.

Gitin, S. R. 1970. A dimensional analysis of manual expression. *Journal of Personality and Social Psychology,* 15: 271-277.

Goodenough, W. H. 1956. Componential analysis and the study of meaning. *Language,* 32: 155-216.

———. 1961. Comments on cultural evolution. *Daedalus,* 90: 521-528.

Granger, G. W. 1955. An experimental study of color preferences. *Journal of General Psychology,* 52: 3-20.

Green, P. E., and Carmone, F. J. 1970. *Multidimensional scaling and related techniques in marketing analysis.* Boston: Allyn and Bacon.

Green, R. F., and Goldfried, M. R. 1965. On the bipolarity of semantic space. *Psychological Monographs,* 79 (6) (whole no. 599).

Greenberg, J. H., ed. 1963. *Universals of language.* Cambridge, Mass.: M.I.T. Press.

———. 1966a. Language universals. In T. A. Sebeok, ed., *Current trends in linguistics,* Vol. 3: *Theoretical foundations.* The Hague: Mouton.

———, ed. 1966b. *Universals of language,* 2nd ed. Cambridge, Mass.: M.I.T. Press.

———. 1967. The first (and perhaps only) non-linguistic distinctive feature analysis. *Word,* 23: 214-220.

Guilford, J. P. 1934. Affective value of color as function of hue, tint, and chroma. *Psychological Bulletin,* 30: 679.

Gulliksen, H. 1958. How to make meaning more meaningful. *Contemporary Psychology,* 3: 115-118.

Guttman, L. 1959. A structural theory of intergroup beliefs in action. *American Sociological Review,* 24: 318-328.

Hackin, R., and Kohzad, A. A. 1953. *Légendes et coutumes Afghans.* Paris: Imprimerie Nationale, Presses Universitaires de France.

Hallworth, H. J., and Waite, G. 1963. A factorial study of value judgments among adolescent girls. *British Journal of Statistical Psychology,* 16: 37-46.

Hamilton, H. W., and Deese, J. 1971. Does linguistic marking have a psychological correlate? *Journal of Verbal Learning and Verbal Behavior,* 10: 707-714.

Harbin, S. P., and Williams, J. E. 1966. Conditioning of color connotations. *Perceptual and Motor Skills,* 22: 217-218.

Harmon, H. H. 1960. *Modern factor analysis.* Chicago: University of Chicago Press.

Harris, C. W. 1967. On factors and factor scores. *Psychometrika,* 32: 363-367.

Harris, Z. S. 1954. Distributional structure. *Word,* 10: 146-162.

Helson, H., and Lansford, T. G. 1970. The role of spectral energy of source and background color in the pleasantness of object colors. *Applied Optics,* 9: 1513-62.

Herdan, G. 1956. *Language as choice and chance.* Groningen: P. Noordhoff N. V.

Hevner, K. 1935. Experimental studies of the affective value of colors and lines. *Journal of Applied Psychology,* 19: 385-398.

Hickerson, N. 1971. Review of basic color terms: Their universality and evolution. *International Journal of American Linguistics,* 37 (4) : 257-270.

Hill, S. 1964. Cultural differences in mathematical concept learning. *American Anthropologist,* 66 (3) : pt. 2, 201-222.

Hofstätter, P. R., and Lübbert, H. 1958. Eindrucksqualitäten von Farben. *Zeitschrift für Diagnostische und Physikalische,* 6: 211-227.

————, and Primac, D. W. 1957. Colors and the color-blind. *Journal of General Psychology,* 57: 229-240.

Hogg, J. 1969. A principal components analysis of semantic differential judgments of single colors and color pairs. *Journal of General Psychology,* 80: 129-140.

Horn, J. L. 1965. An empirical comparison of methods for estimating factor scores. *Educational and Psychological Measurement,* 25: 313-322.

Howe, E. S. 1965. Uncertainty and other correlates of Osgood's D_4. *Journal of Verbal Learning and Verbal Behavior,* 4: 498-509.

Howes, D. H., and Geschwind, N. 1964. Quantitative studies of aphasic language. In D. McK. Rioch and M. O'Connor, eds., *Disorders in communication.* Baltimore: Williams and Wilkins.

Hull, C. L. 1943. *Principles of behavior: An introduction to behavior theory.* New York: Appleton-Century-Crofts.

Jacobs, W., and Jacobs, V. 1958. The color blue: its use as metaphor and symbol. *American Speech,* 33: 29-46.

Jakobovits, L. A. 1969. The affect of symbols: Towards the development of a cross-cultural graphic differential. *International Journal of Symbology,* 1: 28-52.

Jakobson, R. 1955. Aphasia as a linguistic problem. In H. Werner, ed., *On expressive language.* Worcester, Mass.: Clark University Press.

————, and Halle, M. 1956. *Fundamentals of language.* The Hague: Mouton.

Jenkins, J. J., Russell, W. A., and Suci, G. J. 1959. A table of distances for the semantic atlas. *American Journal of Psychology,* 72: 623-625.

Jones, B. 1967. *Design for death.* New York: Bobbs-Merrill.

Kaden, S., Wapner, S., and Werner, H. 1955. Studies in physiognomic perception, II: Effect of directional dynamics of pictured objects and of words on the position of the apparent horizon. *Journal of Psychology,* 39: 61-67.

Kahneman, D. 1963. The semantic differential and the structure of inferences among attributes. *American Journal of Psychology,* 76: 554-567.

Karwoski, T. F., and Odbert, H. S. 1938. Color-music. *Psychological Monographs,* 50 (2) (whole no. 222).

————, Odbert, H. S., and Osgood, C. E. 1942. Studies in synesthetic thinking, II: The roles of form in visual responses to music. *Journal of General Psychology,* 26: 199-222.

Katz, D. 1935. *The world of colour.* London: K. Paul, Trench, Trubner and Co.

Katz, M. 1959. Meaning as a correlate of marital success. Unpublished doctoral dissertation, Columbia University Teachers College.

Kent, G. H., and Rosanoff, A. J. 1910. A study of association in insanity. *American Journal of Insanity,* 67: 37-96, 317-390.

Kentler, H. 1959. Zur Problematic der Profilmethode. *Diagnostica,* 5: 5-18.

Kilby, R. W. 1963. Personal values of Indian and American university students. *Journal of Humanistic Psychology,* 3: 108-146.

Kimura, T. 1950. Apparent warmth and heaviness of colours. *Japanese Journal of Psychology,* 20 (2): 33-36.

Kjeldergaard, P. M., and Masanori, H. 1962. Degree of polarization and the recognition value of words selected from the semantic atlas. *Psychological Reports,* 11: 629-630.

Korman, M. 1960. Implicit personality theories of clinicians as defined by semantic structures. *Journal of Consulting Psychology,* 24: 180-186.

Kostić, Dj., and Das, R. S. 1971. Aspects of meaning revealed by the semantic differential technique. *Zeitschrift für Phonetik, Sprachwissenschaft und Kommunikationsforschung,* 24 (1-2): 55-75.

Kouwer, B. J. 1949. *Colors and their character: A psychological study.* The Hague: Martinus Nijhoff.

Kumata, H. 1957. A factor analytic investigation of the generality of semantic structures across two selected cultures. Unpublished doctoral dissertation, University of Illinois.

————, and Schramm, W. 1956. A pilot study of cross-cultural methodology. *Public Opinion Quarterly,* 20: 229-238.

Kuppuswamy, B., and Agrawal, K. G. 1967. The meaning of work: I. A factorial study. *Journal of Psychological Researches,* 11 (2): 69-74.

Kuusinen, J. 1969. Affective and denotative structures of personality ratings. *Journal of Personality and Social Psychology,* 12 (3): 181-188.

Lakoff, G. 1971. On generative semantics. In D. D. Steinberg and L. A. Jakobovits, eds., *Semantics: An interdisciplinary reader in philosophy, linguistics, and psychology.* London: Cambridge University Press.

Lambert, W. E. 1955. Measurement of the linguistic dominance of bilinguals. *Journal of Abnormal and Social Psychology,* 50: 197-200.

————, and Jakobovits, L. A. 1960. Verbal satiation and changes in the intensity of meaning. *Journal of Experimental Psychology,* 60: 376-383.

————, and Klineberg, O. 1967. *Children's views of foreign peoples: A cross-national study.* New York: Appleton-Century-Crofts.

Lazowick, L. M. 1955. On the nature of identification. *Journal of Abnormal and Social Psychology,* 51: 175-183.

Lees, R. B. 1953. The basis of glottochronology. *Language,* 29: 113-127.

Lenneberg, E. H., and Roberts, J. M. 1956. *The language of experience: A study in methodology.* Indiana University Publications in Anthropology and Linguistics, memoir 13.

Levelt, W. J. M. 1967. Semantic features: A psychological model and its mathematical analysis. Unpublished manuscript, Institute of Communications Research, University of Illinois.

————. 1969. A re-analysis of some adjective/noun intersection data. *Heymans Bulletins.* Psychologische Instituten R. U., Groningen. No. HB-69-35-EX.

Levin, J. 1963. Three-mode factor analysis. Unpublished doctoral dissertation, University of Illinois.

———. 1965. Three-mode factor analysis. *Psychological Bulletin,* 64: 442-452.

Litt, E. N. 1966. A factorial study of responses to abstract paintings. Unpublished master's thesis, University of Illinois.

Lounsbury, F. G. 1956. A semantic analysis of the Pawnee kinship usage. *Language,* 32: 158-194.

Luckiesh, M. 1923. *Light and color in advertising and merchandising.* New York: D. Van Nostrand.

Luria, Z. 1959. A semantic analysis of a normal and neurotic therapy group. *Journal of Abnormal and Social Psychology,* 58: 216-220.

McCawley, J. D. 1968. The role of semantics in a grammar. In E. Bach and R. T. Harms, eds., *Universals in linguistic theory.* New York: Holt, Rinehart & Winston.

McClelland, D. C. 1961. *The achieving society.* Princeton, N.J.: Van Nostrand.

Makal, M. 1954. *A village in Anatolia.* London: Vallentine Mitchell.

Mehrabian, A. 1972. *Non-verbal communication.* Chicago: Aldine-Atherton.

Metzger, D., and Williams, G. E. 1963. A formal ethnographic analysis of Tenejapa Ladino weddings. *American Anthropologist,* 65: 1076-1101.

Miron, M. S. 1961. A cross-linguistic investigation of phonetic symbolism. *Journal of Abnormal and Social Psychology,* 62: 623-630.

———. 1969. What is it that is being differentiated by the semantic differential? *Journal of Personality and Social Psychology,* 12: 189-193.

———, and Osgood, C. E. 1966. Language behavior: The multivariate structure of qualification. In R. Cattell, ed., *Handbook of multivariate psychology.* Chicago: Rand McNally.

———, and Wolfe, S. 1964. A cross-linguistic analysis of the response distribution of restricted word associations. *Journal of Verbal Learning and Verbal Behavior,* 3: 376-384.

Mitsos, S. B. 1961. Personal constructs and the semantic differential. *Journal of Abnormal and Social Psychology,* 62: 433-434.

Mogar, R. E. 1960. Three versions of the F scale and performance on the semantic differential. *Journal of Abnormal and Social Psychology,* 60: 262-265.

Murdock, G. P. 1967. *Ethnographic atlas.* Pittsburgh: University of Pittsburgh Press.

Murray, D. C., and Deabler, H. L. 1957. Colors and mood-tones. *Journal of Applied Psychology,* 41: 277-283.

Murray, H. D., and Spencer, D. A. 1952. *Colour in theory and practice.* London: Chapman and Hall.

Naroll, R. 1968. Some thoughts on comparative method in cultural anthropology. In H. M. Blalock, Jr., and A. B. Black, eds., *Methodology in social research.* New York: McGraw-Hill.

Noble, C. E. 1952. An analysis of meaning. *Psychological Review,* 59: 421-430.

Noordman, L. G. M., and Levelt, W. J. M. 1970. Noun categorization by noun-verb intersection for the Dutch language. *Heymans Bulletins.* Psychologische Instituten R. U., Groningen. No. HB-70-59-EX.

Nordenstreng, K. 1968. A comparison between the semantic differential and similarity analysis in the measurement of musical experience. *Scandinavian Journal of Psychology,* 9: 89-96.

———. 1969a. *Media images of radio, television, and newspaper.* Reports from the Section for Long-Range Planning. Helsinki: Finnish Broadcasting Co.

———. 1969b. Toward quantification of meaning: An evaluation of the semantic differential technique. *Annales Academiae Scientiarum Fennicae,* B161: 2.

————. 1970. Changes in the meaning of semantic differential scales: Measurement of subject-scale interaction effects. *Journal of Cross-Cultural Psychology,* 1: 217-237.

Norman, R. D., and Scott, W. A. 1952. Color and affect: A review and semantic evaluation. *Journal of General Psychology,* 46: 185-223.

Nunnally, J. 1961. *Popular conception of mental health.* New York: Holt, Rinehart & Winston.

Obonai, T., and Matsuoka, T. 1956. The color symbolism personality test. *Journal of General Psychology,* 55: 229-239.

Odbert, H. S., Karwoski, T. F., and Eckerson, A. B. 1942. Studies in synesthetic thinking: I. Musical and verbal association of color and mood. *Journal of General Psychology,* 26: 153-173.

Osgood, C. E. 1941. Ease of individual judgment-processes in relation to polarization of attitudes in the culture. *Journal of Social Psychology,* 49: 403-418.

————. 1952. The nature and measurement of meaning. *Psychological Bulletin,* 49: 197-237.

————. 1953. *Method and theory in experimental psychology.* New York: Oxford University Press.

————. 1960a. Cognitive dynamics in the conduct of human affairs. *Public Opinion Quarterly,* 24: 341-365.

————. 1960b. The cross-cultural generality of visual-verbal synesthetic tendencies. *Behavioral Science,* 5: 146-169.

————. 1962. Studies on the generality of affective meaning systems. *American Psychologist,* 17: 10-28.

————. 1966a. Dimensionality of the semantic space for communication via facial expressions. *Scandinavian Journal of Psychology,* 7: 1-30.

————. 1966b. Meaning cannot be an r_m? *Journal of Verbal Learning and Verbal Behavior,* 5: 402-407.

————. 1969. On the whys and wherefores of E, P, and A. *Journal of Personality and Social Psychology,* 12: 194-199.

————. 1970a. Interpersonal verbs and interpersonal behavior. In J. L. Cowan, ed., *Studies in thought and language.* Tucson: University of Arizona Press.

————. 1970b. Speculation on the structure of interpersonal intentions. *Behavioral Science,* 15: 237-254.

————. 1971. Where do sentences come from? In D. D. Steinberg and L. A. Jakobovits, eds., *Semantics: An interdisciplinary reader in philosophy, linguistics, and psychology.* London: Cambridge University Press.

————, and Luria, Z. 1954. A blind analysis of a case of triple personality using the semantic differential. *Journal of Abnormal and Social Psychology,* 49: 579-591.

————, Luria, Z., and Smith, S. 1972. Blind analysis of another case of multiple personality. *Journal of Abnormal Psychology,* in press.

————, and Miron, M. S. 1963. *Approaches to aphasia.* Urbana: University of Illinois Press.

————, Miron, M. S., and Archer, W. K. 1963. The cross-cultural generality of meaning systems. Unpublished manuscript, University of Illinois.

————, and Richards, M. M. 1973. From Yang and Yin to *and* or *but*. *Language,* 49(2): 380-412.

————, Suci, G. J., and Tannenbaum, P. 1957. *The measurement of meaning.* Urbana: University of Illinois Press.

————, and Tannenbaum, P. 1955. The principle of congruity and the prediction of attitude change. *Psychological Review,* 62: 42-55.

———, Ware, E. E., and Morris, C. 1961. Analysis of the connotative meanings of a variety of human values as expressed by American college students. *Journal of Abnormal and Social Psychology,* 62: 62-73.

Oyama, T., Soma, I., Tomiie, T., and Chijiiwa, H. 1965. A factor analytical study on affective responses to colors. *Acta Chromatica,* 1: 164-173.

———, Tanaka, Y., and Chiba, Y. 1962. Affective dimensions of colours: A cross cultural study. *Japanese Psychological Research,* 4: 78-91.

———, Tanaka, Y., and Haga, J. 1963. Color-affection and color-symbolism in Japanese and American students. *Japanese Journal of Psychology,* 34 (3): 109-121.

Pečjak, V. 1970. Verbal synesthesiae of colors, emotions, and days of the week. *Journal of Verbal Learning and Verbal Behavior,* 9: 623-626.

———, Musek, J., and Tatjana, J. 1970. The influence of group affiliations on the evaluative meanings of critical concepts. *International Journal of Symbology,* 1 (3): 11-16.

Peterson, D. R. 1965. The scope, generality, and meaning of verbally defined "personality" factors. *Psychological Review,* 72: 48-59.

Pierce, J. E. 1964. *Life in a Turkish village.* New York: Holt, Rinehart & Winston.

Premack, D. A. 1971. Language in chimpanzee? *Science,* 172: 808-822.

Ray, V. F. 1953. Human color perception and behavioral response. *Transactions, New York Academy of Sciences,* 16 (ser. 2): 98-104.

Romney, A. K., and D'Andrade, R. G. 1964. Cognitive aspects of English kin terms. *American Anthropologist,* 66 (3): pt. 2, 146-170.

Ross, J. R. 1967. Constraints on variables in syntax. Unpublished doctoral dissertation, Massachusetts Institute of Technology.

Ross, R. T. 1938. Studies in the psychology of the theater. *Psychological Record,* 2: 127-190.

Ryle, G. 1957. The theory of meaning. In C. A. Mace, ed., *British philosophy in mid-century.* London: Allen and Unwin.

Sagara, M., Yamamoto, K., Nishimura, H., and Akuto, H. 1961. A study on the semantic structure of Japanese language by the semantic differential method. *Japanese Psychological Research,* 3: 146-156.

Sapir, E. 1912. Language and environment. *American Anthropologist,* 14: 226-242.

———. 1921. *Language.* New York: Harcourt, Brace.

Schaie, K. W. 1961. A Q-sort study of color-mood association. *Journal of Projective Techniques,* 25: 341-346.

Schlosberg, H. 1954. Three dimensions of emotion. *Psychological Review,* 61: 81-88.

Shanmugam, A. V. 1963. An analysis of semantic effects in mediated transfer. Unpublished doctoral dissertation, University of Illinois.

Shannon, C. E. 1951. Prediction and entropy of printed English. *Bell Systems Technical Journal,* 30: 50-64.

———, and Weaver, W. 1949. *The mathematical theory of communication.* Urbana: University of Illinois Press.

Shaw, D. R. 1955. Variation in inter-scale correlation on the semantic differential as a function of the concept judged. Unpublished master's thesis, University of Illinois.

Sheinkopf, S. 1970. A comparative study of the affective judgments made by anomic aphasics and normals on a nonverbal task. Unpublished doctoral dissertation, Boston University.

Shen, N. C. 1937. The color preference of 1368 Chinese students, with special reference to the most preferred color. *Journal of Social Psychology,* 8: 185-204.

Singh, L. C. 1967. Development of an occupational differential. *Indian Educational Review,* 2: 128-135.

Slobin, D. I. 1971. Developmental psycholinguistics. In W. O. Dingwall, ed., *A survey of linguistic science.* College Park: Linguistics Program, University of Maryland.

Small, E. R. 1958. Age and sex differences in the semantic structure of children. Unpublished doctoral dissertation, University of Michigan.

Snider, J. G., and Osgood, C. E., eds. 1969. *Semantic differential technique: A sourcebook.* Chicago: Aldine.

Snyder, F. 1967. An investigation of the invariance of the semantic differential across the subject mode. Unpublished master's thesis, University of Illinois.

Staats, A. W., and Staats, C. K. 1958. Attitudes established by classical conditioning. *Journal of Abnormal and Social Psychology,* 57: 37-40.

————, and Staats, C. K. 1959. Meaning and *m:* Separate but correlated. *Psychological Review,* 66: 136-144.

Suci, G. J. 1952. A multidimensional analysis of social attitudes with special reference to ethnocentrism. Unpublished doctoral dissertation, University of Illinois.

————. 1960. A comparison of semantic structures in American Southwest culture groups. *Journal of Abnormal and Social Psychology,* 61: 25-30.

Swadesh, M. 1950. Salish internal relationships. *International Journal of American Linguistics,* 16: 157-167.

————. 1971. *The origin and diversification of language.* Chicago: Aldine-Atherton.

Tanaka, Y. 1970. Japanese attitudes toward nuclear arms. *Public Opinion Quarterly,* 34: 25-42.

————. 1971. What Asian youths think about Japan and their ways of life. *Cross-Cultural Social Psychology Newsletter,* 5 (3): 1-5.

————. 1972. Values in the subjective culture: A social psychological view. *Journal of Cross-Cultural Psychology,* 3 (1): 57-69.

————, and Iwamatsu, Y. 1968. An exploratory semantic differential study of the affective and the cognitive components of the attitudes held by Japanese college Ss toward nuclear testings and proliferation. In T. Kawata, ed., *Peace Research in Japan,* Vol. 2. Tokyo: Japan Peace Research Group.

————, and Osgood, C. E. 1965. Cross-culture, cross-concept, and cross-subject generality of affective meaning systems. *Journal of Personality and Social Psychology,* 2: 143-153.

————, Oyama, T., and Osgood, C. E. 1963. A cross-culture and cross-concept study of the generality of semantic spaces. *Journal of Verbal Learning and Verbal Behavior,* 2: 392-405.

Tatibana, Y. 1937. Colour feeling of the Japanese: I. The inherent emotional effects of colours. *Tohoku Psychology Folia,* 5: 21-46.

————. 1938. Colour feeling of the Japanese: II. The expressive emotional effects of colours. *Tohoku Psychology Folia,* 6: 35-80.

Textor, R. B., ed. 1967. *A cross-cultural summary.* New Haven, Conn.: Human Relations Area Files Press.

Thigpen, C. H., and Cleckley, H. 1954. A case of multiple personality. *Journal of Abnormal and Social Psychology,* 65: 135-151.

Thurstone, L. L. 1947. *Multiple factor analysis.* Chicago: University of Chicago Press.

Torgerson, W. S. 1958. *Theory and methods of scaling.* New York: John Wiley and Sons.

Triandis, H. C. 1973. Intercultural conceptions of work and nonwork. In M.

Dunnett, ed., *Work and nonwork in the year 2001.* Monterey, Calif.: Brooks/ Cole Publishing Co.

————, Malpass, R. S., and Davidson, A. R. 1972. Cross-cultural psychology. In B. J. Siegel, ed., *Biennial Review of Anthropology, 1971.* Stanford, Calif.: Stanford University Press.

————, and Osgood, C. E. 1958. A comparative factorial analysis of semantic structures in monolingual Greek and American college students. *Journal of Abnormal and Social Psychology,* 57: 187-196.

————, Tanaka, Y., and Shanmugam, A. V. 1966. Interpersonal attitudes among American, Indian, and Japanese students. *International Journal of Psychology,* 1: 177-206.

————, Vassiliou, V., and Nassiakou, M. 1968. Three cross-cultural studies of subjective culture. *Journal of Personality and Social Psychology Monograph Supplement,* 8 (4): pt. 2, 1-42.

Tucker, L. 1963a. The extension of factor analysis to three dimensional matrices. In N. Friedericksen and H. Gulliksen, eds., *Contributions to mathematical psychology.* New York: Holt, Rinehart & Winston.

————. 1963b. Implications of factor analysis of three way matrices for measurements of change. In C. W. Harris, ed., *Problems in measuring change.* Madison: University of Wisconsin Press.

————. 1971. Relations of factor score estimates to their use. *Psychometrika,* 36: 427-436.

————, and Messick, S. 1963. An individual differences model for multidimensional scaling. *Psychometrika,* 28: 333-367.

Tzeng, O. 1972. Differentiation of affective and denotative meaning systems via three-mode factor analysis. Unpublished doctoral dissertation, University of Illinois.

————, Osgood, C. E., and May, W. H. 1974. Idealized cultural differences in kincept conceptions. *International Journal of Psycholinguistics,* in press.

Underhill, M. M. 1921. *The Hindu religious year.* Calcutta: Association Press.

Underwood, B. J., and Schultz, R. W. 1960. *Meaningfulness and verbal learning.* New York: Lippincott.

Van der Werff, J. J., and Seinen, M. 1968. Persoonbeoordeling door middel van kleuren. *Nederlands Tijdschrift voor de Psychologie en hoar Gresgebieden,* 23 (9): 549-566.

Vendler, Z. 1967. *Linguistics in philosophy.* Ithaca, N.Y.: Cornell University Press.

Wallace, A. F. C., and Atkins, J. 1960. The meaning of kinship terms. *American Anthropologist,* 62: 58-60.

Walton, W. E., Guilford, R. B., and Guilford, J. P. 1933. Color preferences of 1279 university students. *American Journal of Psychology,* 45: 322-328.

Ware, E. E. 1958. Relationships of intelligence and sex to diversity of individual semantic meaning spaces. Unpublished doctoral dissertation, University of Illinois.

Warr, P. B., and Haycock, V. 1970. Scales for a British personality differential. *British Journal of Social and Clinical Psychology,* 9: 328-337.

Weinreich, U. 1958. Travels through semantic space. *Word,* 14: 346-366.

————. 1966. Explorations in semantic theory. In T. A. Sebeok, ed., *Current trends in linguistics,* Vol. 3: *Theoretical foundations.* The Hague: Mouton.

Wells, R. 1957. A mathematical approach to meaning. *Cahiers Ferdinand de Saussure,* 15: 117-136.

Werner, H., ed. 1955. *On expressive language.* Worcester, Mass.: Clark University Press.

——, and Kaplan, E. 1950. Development of word meaning through verbal context: An experimental study. *Journal of Psychology,* 29: 251-257.

Werner, O., and Campbell, D. T. 1970. Translating, working through interpreters, and the problem of decentering. In R. Naroll and R. Cohen, eds., *A handbook of method in cultural anthropology.* New York: American Museum of Natural History.

Wexner, L. B. 1954. The degree to which colors are associated with mood-tones. *Journal of Applied Psychology,* 38: 432-435.

Wheeler, J. 1969. A practical knowledge of color for the congenitally blind. *New Outlook for the Blind,* 63 (8): 225-231.

Whorf, B. L. 1956. *Language, thought and reality.* Cambridge, Mass.: M.I.T. Press.

Wickens, D. D. 1972. Characteristics of word encoding. In A. W. Melton and E. Martin, eds., *Coding processes in human memory.* New York: Winston-Wiley.

Wiggins, N., and Fishbein, M. 1969. Dimensions of semantic space: A problem of individual differences. In J. G. Snider and C. E. Osgood, eds., *Semantic differential technique.* Chicago: Aldine.

Williams, J. E. 1964. Connotations of color names among Negroes and Caucasians. *Perceptual and Motor Skills,* 18: 721-731.

——. 1966. Connotations of racial concepts and color names. *Journal of Personality and Social Psychology,* 3: 531-540.

——. 1969. Individual differences in color name connotations as related to measures of racial attitude. *Perceptual and Motor Skills,* 29: 383-386.

——, and Carter, D. J. 1967. Connotations of racial concepts and color names in Germany. *Journal of Social Psychology,* 72: 19-26.

——, and Foley, J. W., Jr. 1968. Connotative meanings of color names and color hues. *Perceptual and Motor Skills,* 26: 499-502.

——, and McMurtry, C. 1970. Color connotations among Caucasian seventh graders and college students. *Perceptual and Motor Skills,* 30: 707-713.

——, Morland, J. K., and Underwood, W. L. 1970. Connotations of color names in the United States, Europe and Asia. *Journal of Social Psychology,* 82: 3-14.

Wilson, G. 1966. Arousal properties of red versus green. *Perceptual and Motor Skills,* 23: 947-949.

Wilson, K. R. 1941. A study in the associative origins of color preference in young adults. Unpublished master's thesis, Claremont College.

Winick, C. 1963. Taboo and disapproved colors and symbols in various foreign countries. *Journal of Social Psychology,* 59: 361-368.

Wright, B., and Rainwater, L. 1962. The meanings of color. *Journal of General Psychology,* 67: 89-99.

Yoshikawa, T., Yagishita, T., and Matsuda, Y. 1970. Color-mood associations in young children. *Psychologia: An International Journal of Psychology in the Orient,* 13 (1): 57-58.

Young, B. 1970. A cross-cultural replication of visual-verbal synaesthesis in Chinese-English bilinguals. Unpublished manuscript, Department of Psychology, University of Hong Kong.

Zipf, G. K. 1935. *The psycho-biology of language.* Boston: Houghton Mifflin.

——. 1949. *Human behavior and the principle of least effort.* Cambridge, Mass.: Addison-Wesley.

Author Index

Aaronson, B. S., 299
Abelson, R. P., 49
Agrawal, K. G., 388
Ahmavaara, Y., 344, 347, 389
Alexander, S., 64
Asch, S., 399
Atkins, J., 289

Barnett, K. M. A., 269
Berlin, E., 90, 312, 331, 332-334, 368
Bopp, J. A., 61
Boucher, J., 100n, 204, 363, 389
Brislin, R. W., 339
Brown, R., 14, 332, 342, 393
Burling, R., 372

Campbell, D. T., 338-340, 391, 406-408, 413
Cantril, H., 5-36 *passim*, 337
Capell, M. D., 65
Carmone, F. J., 373
Carroll, J. B., 342-343, 350, 393
Carroll, J. D., 374
Chang, J. J., 374
Child, I. L., 299
Chomsky, N., 98, 216, 391, 395, 405
Cleckley, H., 63
Cliff, N., 41
Collins, N., 299
Conklin, C., 289, 291
Cook, D. R., 63

D'Andrade, R. G., 22, 290
Das, R. S., 388, 394n
Davidson, A. R., 337, 411
Deese, J., 94, 352, 363

DiVesta, F., 59, 60, 208n, 395
Dodge, J., 96
Donahoe, J. W., 60, 395

Eckerson, A. B., 298, 396
Elliott, L. L., 350, 381
Endler, N. S., 63
Ertel, S., 388, 397
Ervin, S. M., 60, 396

Fishbein, M., 345-346
Foa, U. G., 338
Ford, L. H., Jr., 363n
Foster, G., 60, 396
Frake, C. O., 291
Fries, C. C., 71

Gardner, B. T., 389n
Gardner, R. A., 389n
Geschwind, N., 79
Gilman, A., 14
Gitin, S. R., 398
Goldfried, M. R., 353-354
Goodenough, W. H., 289, 335-336
Green, P. E., 373
Green, R. F., 353-354
Greenberg, J. H., 363, 371, 390, 405
Guilford, J. P., 299, 318
Guilford, R. B., 318
Gulliksen, H., 342
Guttman, L., 338

Haga, J., 299
Halle, M., 332, 398
Hallworth, H. J., 61, 395
Hamilton, H. W., 363

General Index

Abstract Aesthetic Value factor, 223
Abstractness factor, 187
Activity factor: pancultural, 164; Western influence, 170; concept factor scores, 232-233, 235-236. *See also* Evaluation-Potency-Activity
Aesthetic Evaluation factor, 133
Aesthetic Value factor, 223, 362
Affective Dimension of Subjective Culture, 271, 275n
Affective meaning: and color space, 38-40, 341; and metaphors, 156, 163, 209-210, 216, 396-400; communality in attribution, 227-236; cross-cultural generality, 354-359; and denotative space, 378-380; primordiality, 394-396; neurophysiological correlates, 395. *See also* Evaluation-Potency-Activity
Affiliative/Achievement category, 315-317
Age: factor, 149, 186, 224, 362; component, 314-315, 370
Allerton House conference, 11-13, 69
Ambitiousness factor, 379, 380
American Psychological Association, 337
Antecedent/subsequent technique, 384-386
Aphasics, 61-62, 384n, 398
Arabic bicultural analysis, 148, 149
Associative similarity of words, 94-96
Atlas of Affective Meanings: communities, 18-19, 194, 275, 277; subjects, 20-21, 341; purpose, 33; Tables 1, 193-204, 359-360; Tables 2, 204-208, 360; Tables 3, 208-226, 360-362; Tables 4, 226-239; Tables 5, 239-240; concepts, 241-269, 270; translation senses dic-

tionary, 253, 259, 260, 261-269, 278, 339, 407; concepts intuited, 257; test procedures, 258; concepts eliminated, 258, 259; concepts omitted, 259; concept translation checks, 259-269, 351; retesting, 267; Tables 9, 269-270, 359n; concept categories, 274-275, 276; multiple concept translations, 290n; interpretation, 340; social science utilization, 341; summary, 359-368; Tables 6, 367; Tables 7, 367; Tables 8, 368
Attitude, 62, 237-239, 384
Austerity factor, 217
Average correlation, 49-50, 343

Back-translation, 16, 338-339, 407
Basic measures, 241-254, 273, 368; correlations, 273, 283; uniquenesses, 282
Benevolence factor, 64
Bengali tricommunity analysis, 154-156
Bicultural analysis, 143-154, 157-159, 357-358; non-E-P-A factors, 149-154, 357; with American English, 239-240, 364-367
Bilingual analysis, 137-143, 157-159, 357
Bilinguals, 65-66, 134
Bipolarity in qualifying, 352-354
Blocs, 288
Bountifulness factor, 132, 156, 358. *See also* Numerosity factor
Brightness: factor, 188, 226, 362; component, 289, 292, 298, 312, 318, 326, 332, 333, 334, 370
Broad-mindedness factor, 376